Praise for

BOBBY KENNEDY

"[Tye] has a keen gift for narrative storytelling and an ability to depict his subject with almost novelistic emotional detail. . . . The fair-minded Mr. Tye thoughtfully maps the many contradictions in his subject's life, and his gradual evolution over the years, as he began to clarify his own beliefs (as opposed to those handed down by his father and older brother), shedding his 'Cold Warrior' reflexes and growing increasingly concerned about the poverty and injustice that plagued his country. . . . In these pages, Mr. Tye conscientiously strips away the accretions of myth that have come to surround Robert F. Kennedy, while at the same time creating a sympathetic portrait of this complex, searching man."

—MICHIKO KAKUTANI, *The New York Times*

"Like Alexander Hamilton during our nation's founding, Kennedy was the most dominant figure of his time not to be elected president. . . . Tye has crafted a multilayered, inspiring portrait of RFK. Because the author refuses to avert his eyes from the uglier chapters in Kennedy's life, he provides readers and historians their most in-depth look at an extraordinary figure whose transformational story shaped America at midcentury." —JOE SCARBOROUGH, *The Washington Post*

"A nuanced, balanced, affectionate and mostly favorable portrait . . . [Tye] presents us with a kind of bildungsroman of a young, privileged man who is forced to learn on the job and makes mistakes. . . . We are in Larry Tye's debt for bringing back to life the young presidential candidate who . . . for a brief moment, almost half a century ago, instilled hope for the future in angry, fearful Americans."

—DAVID NASAW, *The New York Times Book Review*

"Very, very good . . . It captures RFK's cold, ruthless side with appropriate relish . . . and it provides fast-paced and very detailed accounts of RFK's early working relationship with soon-to-be-disgraced Wisconsin politician Joe McCarthy."

—*The Christian Science Monitor*

"Captivating . . . [A] state-of-the-art political biography . . . Shedding new light on Kennedy's relationships with Lyndon Johnson and Martin Luther King, Jr., Tye ultimately reveals Kennedy as a work in progress who, by the end of his life, had become a beloved advocate for minorities and the poor."

— *Library Journal* (starred review)

"Tye unflinchingly illustrates the evolution of a statesman who captured the imagination of a generation and whose assassination galvanized a nation. . . . A complete portrait of a complex man whose contributions to history were essential and whose potential will remain forever unknowable."
— *Booklist* (starred review)

"A compelling story of how idealism can be cultivated and liberalism learned . . . Tye's work feels most essential when seen as a mirror of our own times, reflecting back the scant progress our country has made on the issues Kennedy fought hardest for near the end of his life and the cynicism that has so deeply permeated our culture. . . . Tye does an exemplary job of capturing not just the chronology of Bobby's life, but also the sense of him as a person."
—*Los Angeles Review of Books*

"It is difficult to envision anyone getting Robert F. Kennedy more right than biographer Tye does in this superb book. Tye beautifully captures Kennedy's contradictions, his emergence from under the hard-to-like father to whom he remained forever loyal, and his growth into a public figure killed by an assassin's bullet."
—*Publishers Weekly* (starred review)

"Provocative . . . Tye, drawing on fifty-eight boxes of private papers that the Kennedy family had kept under lock for four decades, expertly traces the arc of his subject's metamorphosis 'from cold warrior to liberal icon.' "   —*The New Yorker*

"Mr. Tye's account is nuanced and thorough, and he manages the rare feat of interviewing Kennedy's widow Ethel, now eighty-eight. . . . [RFK's] vision echoes through the decades. 'Only those who dare to fail greatly can ever achieve greatly,' he said in 1966. If only modern-day leaders were so bold."
—*The Economist*

"Tye's vivid journalistic style makes the biography an arresting read. . . . Bobby Kennedy's journey closely mirrors the history of the country, from the Cold War through the civil rights movement, the dissent against the Vietnam War and growing public awareness of poverty in America."   —*San Francisco Chronicle*

"Fascinating . . . The book is most successful in tracing Kennedy's transition from a brash, patrician lawyer to a skilled liberal politician who overwhelmingly identified with those in the greatest need."   —Associated Press

"Tye shows how RFK was not always the progressive hero but a work in progress— after all, Kennedy worked for Joseph McCarthy for a spell. Tye's pages on the assassination are heart-wrenching."   —*New York Post*

BY LARRY TYE

Bobby Kennedy: The Making of a Liberal Icon
Superman: The High-Flying History of America's Most Enduring Hero
Satchel: The Life and Times of an American Legend
The Father of Spin: Edward L. Bernays and the Birth of Public Relations

BOBBY KENNEDY

RANDOM HOUSE
New York

BOBBY KENNEDY

The Making of a Liberal Icon

Larry Tye

LIBRARY OF CONGRESS CATALOGING-IN-PUBLICATION DATA
Names: Tye, Larry.
Title: Bobby Kennedy : the making of a liberal icon / Larry Tye.
Description: New York : Random House, 2016. | Includes bibliographical references and index.
Identifiers: LCCN 2016004991 | ISBN 9780812983500 | ISBN 9780679645207 (ebook)
Subjects: LCSH: Kennedy, Robert F., 1925–1968. | Legislators—United States—Biography. | United States. Congress. Senate—Biography. | United States—Politics and government—1945–1989.
Classification: LCC E840.8.K4 T94 2016 | DDC 973.922092—dc23 LC record available at http://lccn.loc.gov/2016004991

Book design by Simon M. Sullivan

To my mentor, Bill Kovach, and his mentor, John Seigenthaler.

PREFACE

═══

H ISTORY REMEMBERS ROBERT F. KENNEDY as he was in his crusade for president in 1968—a racial healer, a tribune for the poor, and the last progressive knight. His romantic vision for America and the planet made Bobby the uncommon optimist in an age of political distrust and later would inspire both Bill Clinton and Barack Obama in their spirited runs for the White House. "Each time a man stands up for an ideal," RFK reminded us, "he sends forth a tiny ripple of hope, and crossing each other from a million different centers of energy and daring, those ripples build a current which can sweep down the mightiest walls of oppression and resistance." No wonder his audiences swooned.

But there was an earlier Bobby Kennedy whom few recall. Our favorite liberal was nurtured on the rightist orthodoxies of his dynasty-building father and started his public life as counsel to the left-baiting, table-thumping senator Joseph McCarthy. That younger RFK was a bare-knuckled political operative who orchestrated his brother's whatever-it-takes bids for senator and president. As attorney general, Kennedy okayed FBI wiretaps of Martin Luther King, Jr., whom he never trusted or liked. Even guerrilla warfare was in his toolkit: Bobby masterminded cloak-and-dagger operations against Communist Cuba that included blowing up railroad bridges, sabotaging crops, and plotting the elimination of President Fidel Castro. His steely conservatism made him an idol to a young Rudolph Giuliani and younger Bill O'Reilly and Karl Rove. It would ensure him acolytes whose views were so antithetical to his leftist fan base that the two groups could neither talk to nor tolerate each other.

In charting this charismatic man's little-understood transformation from cold warrior to hot-blooded liberal, this book tells the story not just

of Bobby Kennedy but of America at midcentury. The nation was riven
back then. It had lost both its postwar sense of unbounded possibilities
and John F. Kennedy, the youthful president who embodied that enthusiasm and promised new frontiers ahead. In their place were cities in turmoil, whites fleeing to the suburbs as blacks vented their frustrations in
the streets, and a political system unable to respond. Now JFK's messi-
anic younger brother was offering fresh dreams. He imagined a country
split less between right and left, or black and white, than between good
and bad. The Bobby Kennedy of 1968 was a builder of bridges—between
islands of blacks, browns, and blue-collar whites; between terrified parents and estranged youths; and between the establishment he'd grown
up in and the New Politics he heralded. At age forty-two he was on the
way to becoming the tough liberal—or perhaps tender conservative—
who might have stitched back together a divided land and whose vision
seems at least as resonant in today's polarized America.

That healing magic was on graphic display one chilly day in May
1968 when his campaign motorcade rode through the then racially and
ethnically diverse Gary, Indiana. Richard Hatcher, the black mayor,
stood on one side of Bobby in the backseat of the convertible, waving to
the biggest crowds his city had ever seen. Clinging to Bobby from the
other side was Tony Zale, a Polish American steelworker who had boxed
his way out of Gary's ghettos to the middleweight championship of the
world. "The open cars rode through the white part of Gary, and then the
black part, and Kennedy said precisely the same thing to both races: jobs
were better than welfare . . . riots were no solution," remembered a journalist who was there. "The reaction was equally enthusiastic in each
half of the city." It wasn't just that he was the only politician in that
season of strife who was embraced on both sides of the railroad tracks.
Only Bobby was willing to tell each side not merely what it wanted to
hear but what it needed to know.

If the Gary appearance captured his public persona, a less documented car trip that year revealed the man-child who charmed audiences across the country. He'd been visiting a suburban New York
hospital for mentally retarded children and, on his way out, he impul-
sively promised the nine kids he was talking to that he'd take them out
later for his favorite food, ice cream. Knowing his jam-packed schedule,

neither his aides nor the doctors believed him. But ten minutes later he was back, helping the shouting youngsters dress, piling them into his chauffeured car, and letting each of them pick out "one thing" at a nearby store that sold ice cream and candy. Driving away from the hospital afterward he joked, "When those kids tell their parents that Bobby Kennedy took them for a ride and bought them ice cream, they'll never get out of that place."

How hard Americans fell for Bobby is apparent not just in his presidential bid that was catching fire or his accomplishments as attorney general and senator. Equally winning was his boyishness, with the country's collective memory of him framed by that Kennedy smile and an unruly cowlick that flopped onto his forehead. In the history of America, there have been but two non-presidents with whom our relationship was so intimate that we recognize them by their initials—RFK and MLK— and we must reach back to Teddy Roosevelt to find even a president known by an appellation as dear as Bobby. He was, in a way, our little brother, too, which made the loss that much more harrowing when, hours after his most momentous political triumph, an assassin halted his campaign of conciliation.

The dueling aspects of Bobby's political soul were part of his breeding. His father, the speculator and kingmaker Joseph P. Kennedy, saw his third son as the runt of his litter of nine—the lamest athlete, the most tongue-tied speaker, the least likely to matter to the world. Those same traits made Bobby the pet of his mother, Rose, yet even she worried that he was "girlish." Rather than keeping him down, his parents' low expectations drove him to achieve at any cost. To please Rose, Bobby would pray five times a day, while at the same time he embraced too many of his father's less saintly causes and tactics. But this striving shaped Bobby in ways that weren't obvious to his parents and political rivals. While his more assured siblings were confidently charting their own courses, he was listening, learning, and developing a sensitivity that derived from his never being sure he could measure up. The obedient Catholic half of his nature was at war with the rebellious Irish side. All of which left him as vulnerable as he was fierce.

Jack's death plunged Bobby into grief and despair, but it ultimately freed him to find his own path, just as their oldest brother Joe Jr.'s death during World War II had first tormented Jack, then liberated him. Bobby went through nearly a year of undiagnosed and unacknowledged depression, convinced that his meaningful life, along with his career, had died in Dallas. It wasn't only his closest brother that he had lost, but a father whose guiding light had been dimmed two years earlier by a shattering stroke. Decisions that were preordained by his birth order now were his alone and excruciating. Should he run for the Senate or quit public life? Was it okay to challenge his sitting president or must he wait his turn?

Slowly, he saw that people believed in him for himself, not just because of his family and his losses. Bobby Kennedy grew not by reading books, as Jack had, nor by chumming around with the brainy and powerful the way his father did. Experience transformed him. He came to understand poverty the way a novelist might, or a priest, sitting on the dirt floor of a shotgun shack in the Mississippi Delta trying to connect with a starving toddler. It was the same with farmworkers and coal miners. To Bobby, policy was personal and power was its handmaiden. More opportunities were handed to him, and snatched back, than to anyone else in public life, and both sets of experiences stretched him. He turned his back not just on parts of who he had been, but on fundamental aspects of the presidency of the brother he worshipped. He led the charge against the very war in Vietnam for which he and Jack had planted the seeds. He fiercely advocated for a civil rights agenda to which JFK had mainly paid lip service. Within five years of John F. Kennedy's death, Bobby was asserting himself as a politician on the opposite side of the ideological spectrum from where he began—striving, as he put it, "to seek a newer world." The country was in transition politically and culturally, and so was Bobby.

For just that reason, this biography offers a lens into two of the most chaotic and confounding decades of twentieth-century America. Robert Kennedy came of age in the 1950s, with its Cold War and a Greatest Generation that was preoccupied with prosperity. Then he turned up, Zelig-like, at the center of every event that mattered in the 1960s, from the Bay of Pigs and the Cuban missile crisis to race riots and Vietnam. The first half of his career underlines what America was like in the era of Eisenhower, while his last years reflect the Seismic Sixties. His slaying, at almost the same young age as JFK and MLK and so quickly after theirs, signaled to many Americans the end of idealism. "When Robert Kennedy was assassinated, something died within America," says the civil rights leader John Lewis, who dropped to his knees sobbing when he got word of the killing. "Something died within all of us who knew him."

I was among them. I have been captivated by Bobby Kennedy since I was in high school. I taped a poster to my dormitory wall with his inspired (and borrowed) quotation: "Some people see things as they are and say why? I dream things that never were and say, why not?" Kennedy's son David was two years behind me at Middlesex School, his nephew Christopher Lawford a year behind me. Later, when I was a reporter at *The Boston Globe*, I covered the Kennedys repeatedly—especially Ted, whom I interviewed nearly once a month while I was on the environment and health beats. I saw another side of the family, and I came to realize how effectively they could close ranks when, as the *Globe's* roving national writer, I spent two months in Palm Beach covering the rape indictment, trial, and acquittal of William Kennedy Smith, Bobby's nephew. Like anyone growing up in Massachusetts and passionate about politics, I felt the Kennedys were key figures in my world.

Bobby has had more books written partly or wholly about him than all but a handful of figures in recent American history. (There are so many that one is called *An American Drama*, another *An American Melodrama*.) Too many are valentines or diatribes. None pays enough attention to the earliest, hardest-edged part of his career, perhaps because Bobby himself insisted that it mattered less than the facts suggest. So did much of the Kennedy public relations apparatus, which continues to downplay his conservative roots as well as his metamorphosis. I've judged those years by the standard to which the Bobby of 1968 would have held himself. While my focus is on the two decades of Bobby's work life, to give it context I cycle back repeatedly to his beginnings. And while the explosive events of his existence unfolded simultaneously, to ease the reader's burden I tease out a series of defining narratives, from his years as an anticommunist agitator, to his battles with Teamsters and mobsters, to his times as attorney general, senator, and presidential candidate. It is only by examining the nuances of his pilgrimage—it was neither a straight line from conservative to liberal, nor so simple as a frog turning into a prince—that we can peel away the myths and make this unorthodox political figure human and plausible.

I sifted through the mystery of his contradictions with help from people who were closest to him, starting with his wife, Ethel, who has nearly always kept her memories private. When she finally agreed to see me, she talked about Bobby's relationships with such key figures in his life as the two Senators McCarthy, Joe and Gene, along with Jack and Joe Sr. She also helped me understand where he changed and where he did not. Jean Smith, his only surviving sibling, helped, too, as did seven hours of interviews with his aide and closest friend John Seigenthaler. Nicholas Katzenbach and Ramsey Clark explained what it was like working with Bobby and succeeding him as attorney general. Peter Edelman, Adam Walinsky, Frank Mankiewicz, and other staffers told stories of the issues and people Bobby tackled as senator and why their time with him still seems, fifty years on, like the best of their lives. Many cried as we talked. Margaret Marshall, Bobby's guide during the whirlwind Ripple of Hope tour across her native South Africa in 1966, recalled the hope he gave her and sixteen million apartheid-era blacks. I spoke with critics, too, including the *60 Minutes* commentator Nicholas von Hoffman, who saw Bobby as "a trimmer . . . when the wind changed direction, he swung his sails in that direction." I interviewed more than four hundred people over the last four years, too many of whom—including Seigenthaler, Katzenbach, and Mankiewicz—have died since I talked to them. Together they helped me unravel the riddle of why so many of my journalism brethren fell in love with this supposedly ruthless politician. "I'm a sentimental person," explained *The New York Times*'s Anthony Lewis, "and I can be reached by genuine emotion. [Bobby] was a very emotional person, and I felt it was genuine."

The ongoing fascination with Bobby Kennedy's story turns around the grand what-ifs. Could he have won the Democratic nomination and been elected president if he had lived? Would he have carried his raw and untested idealism into the White House and sustained it in ways that defied his brother and could have renewed America? Unlike Jack, Bobby died before he had a chance to deliver or to disappoint. That the path led instead to President Richard Nixon, whose cynicism made him Bobby's polar opposite, adds to the heartache. Bobby Kennedy's history hints at more promise than even his boosters realized at the time of his death, because he drew such a wide range of Americans to his cause. This man, who grew up mingling with queens, popes, and Hollywood idols, forged bonds not just with Negroes, Chicanos, and American Indians, but with the firemen and bricklayers a later generation would call "Reagan Democrats." Who else could claim concurrent friendships with the student radical Tom Hayden and the establishment mainstay Richard Daley?

His era's most nostalgia-wrapped figure, Bobby was also its most avant-garde. He embodied the classic Kennedy blend of godawful disagreeable and transcendent good. But he was more passionate than his brother the president, more provocative, and more accessible. Half Che Guevara, half Niccolò Machiavelli, Bobby was a shaker-upper dedicated to the art of the possible. That he could change so substantially and convincingly over the course of his brief public life helped restore a changing America's faith in redemption. In the end he could become this nation's high priest of reconciliation precisely because he had once been the keeper of our darkest secrets.

CONTENTS

AN RFK CHRONOLOGY

SEPTEMBER 6, 1888   Joseph Patrick Kennedy is born in Boston, eldest child of the businessman and politician Patrick Joseph Kennedy and Mary Augusta Hickey Kennedy, the daughter of a prosperous Irish-born contractor.

OCTOBER 7, 1914   Rose Fitzgerald marries Joe Kennedy in the home chapel of Boston's Cardinal William O'Connell.

NOVEMBER 20, 1925   Robert Francis Kennedy is born in Brookline, Massachusetts, the seventh of Rose and Joe's nine children.

APRIL 11, 1928   Ethel Skakel is born in Chicago, the next-to-youngest of George and Ann Skakel's seven children.

APRIL 30, 1933   Bobby receives his first communion at St. Joseph's Church in Bronxville, New York.

JANUARY 7, 1938   President Franklin Roosevelt names Joe Kennedy the U.S. ambassador to Great Britain.

OCTOBER 5, 1943   Bobby enlists in the U.S. Naval Reserve as a seaman apprentice.

MAY 27, 1944   After attending St. Paul's School and then Portsmouth Priory School, Bobby graduates from Milton Academy (the program lists him as residing in Palm Beach, Florida).

AUGUST 12, 1944   Lieutenant Joseph P. Kennedy, Jr., is killed when his plane explodes during a top secret mission in Europe.

MAY 30, 1946   Bobby is honorably discharged from the Naval Reserve as a seaman second class.

NOVEMBER 5, 1946   John Kennedy is elected to Congress, with some help from his kid brother Bobby.

JUNE 10, 1948   Bobby graduates from Harvard University, earning mediocre grades but winning on the football field the Harvard *H* that eluded his older brothers.

June 17, 1950   Ethel and Bobby marry at St. Mary Roman Catholic Church in Greenwich, Connecticut, with Jack as best man.

JUNE 11, 1951   Bobby graduates from the University of Virginia School of Law, smack in the middle of his class.

JULY 4, 1951   Kathleen Hartington Kennedy—Bobby and Ethel's first child and Rose and Joe's first grandchild—is born.

NOVEMBER 4, 1952   JFK is elected to the U.S. Senate, with Bobby running the campaign.

JANUARY 15, 1953   Bobby goes to work for Senator Joseph McCarthy's Permanent Subcommittee on Investigations, a position he held for seven months.

JANUARY 8, 1955   The Junior Chamber of Commerce selects Bobby as one of its Ten Outstanding Young Men of the year, an honor JFK had received eight years earlier.

NOVEMBER 8, 1960   JFK wins one of the closest presidential elections in history, thanks in part to his crackerjack campaign manager, RFK.

JANUARY 20, 1961   Bobby is sworn in as attorney general, the third-youngest in U.S. history.

MAY 21, 1961   Attorney General Kennedy orders U.S. marshals to Montgomery, Alabama, following attacks on the Freedom Riders.

DECEMBER 19, 1961   Joe Kennedy suffers a stroke from which he never fully recovers.

OCTOBER 1, 1962   Bobby oversees the enrollment of James Meredith as the first black student at the University of Mississippi after federal troops quell riots on campus.

OCTOBER 16–28, 1962   During these fraught thirteen days, Bobby vacillates between hawk and dove but ends up helping his brother end the Cuban missile crisis.

JUNE 19, 1963   At Bobby's urging, President Kennedy submits to Congress the most ambitious civil rights bill ever.

NOVEMBER 22, 1963   JFK is assassinated while riding in a motorcade through Dallas; after rallying the family, Bobby collapses into a severe depression.

NOVEMBER 3, 1964   RFK is elected U.S. senator from New York, outpolling his Republican rival by more than seven hundred thousand votes.

JUNE 6, 1966   Bobby delivers his inspirational "Ripple of Hope" speech at the University of Cape Town in South Africa.

MARCH 2, 1967   Senator Kennedy proposes a three-point plan to end the war in Vietnam, his sharpest break with President Lyndon Johnson.

MARCH 16, 1968   RFK announces his White House bid, in the same hall and with many of the same words that JFK used eight years earlier.

APRIL 4, 1968   On the night that Martin Luther King, Jr., is killed, Bobby delivers a speech in the heart of black Indianapolis so moving that it is one of the few major U.S. cities that doesn't riot.

JUNE 5, 1968   Bobby is gunned down minutes after delivering his victory speech on the night of the California Democratic primary.

JUNE 6, 1968   Bobby dies in Los Angeles's Good Samaritan Hospital at 1:44 A.M., at age forty-two.

DECEMBER 12, 1968   Rory Kennedy, Bobby and Ethel's eleventh child, is born in Washington, D.C.

Author's Note

I USE THE present tense in quoting people I interviewed, the past tense in quoting those whose words come from earlier writings and recordings. I employ terms like *Negro* and *Indian* when writing about the eras when that was how African Americans and Native Americans referred to themselves, and terms like *mentally retarded* and *crippled* when that was accepted usage. I call my subject "Bobby" more often than anything else because that is what those closest to him used and because his widow Ethel said, "I would be uncomfortable if you called him anything else."

BOBBY KENNEDY

Chapter 1

COLD WARRIOR

═══════

ISCIPLES CAME IN flocks that sun-baked May afternoon in 1957, packing the pews at St. Mary's and spilling onto the streets outside the Irish parish in Appleton, Wisconsin, where Joseph Raymond McCarthy had been baptized and now, just forty-eight years later, he was being eulogized. It was the last of three memorials to the fallen senator and the first in the state that had elected him in landslides. Twenty-five thousand admirers from Green Bay, Neenah, and his native Grand Chute had paid their respects at his open casket. Others were keeping vigil outside the church alongside honor guards of military police and Boy Scouts. Flying in to join them were nineteen senators, seven congressmen, and other luminaries, most of whom had supported Joe McCarthy in his relentless assault on Communism. The dignitaries were whisked in a motorcade from the airport in Green Bay to the funeral in Appleton.

But one man faltered on the runway. Robert Francis Kennedy had worked as an aide to McCarthy for seven months before political and personal calculations made him step aside. Now he sat anxiously by himself on the military jet, reluctant to be seen with the conservative lawmakers and conflicted even about being in Wisconsin. His own brother, Jack, had sternly warned him to stay away. When the crowd was gone, Kennedy slipped down the exit ramp unnoticed. Nobody was waiting because no one knew he was coming. He rode into town not with the pack of senators and congressmen but in the front seat of a Cadillac convertible driven by the reporter Edwin Bayley, who was covering McCarthy's funeral for the *Milwaukee Journal*. At the church, Bobby sat in the choir loft, distracted and alone, and at the graveside he stood apart from the rest of the officials from Washington. When the service was over, Kennedy asked Bayley and other journalists not to write about his being there. The reporters, already in the Kennedy thrall, did as he asked.

The relationship between Robert Kennedy and Joseph McCarthy is one of the most implausible in U.S. political history. In the lexicon of American politics, the Kennedy name is shorthand for left-leaning Democratic politics, and it is a tenet of Kennedy scholarship that the first and archetypal family liberal was Bobby. The historical cliché, nourished by his family and friends, posits that Kennedy's going to work for McCarthy was a footnote or an aberration when it was neither. The truth is that the early Bobby Kennedy embraced the overheated anticommunism of the 1950s and openly disdained liberals.* His job with the Republican senator from Wisconsin not only launched Bobby's career but injected into his life passion and direction that had been glaringly absent. McCarthy's zeal, extreme though it was, fired Kennedy's ambition for years to come. He quit McCarthy not because he rejected McCarthyism, but because his advancement was stymied by conflict with fellow staffers. While he did work for the senator for just seven and a half months in 1953, their ties went back a number of years, and they lasted until Bobby made his last visit to McCarthy shortly before the senator died.

His link to McCarthy became a crucible Kennedy couldn't escape, serving for some as a testament to his loyalty and patriotism, for others as a measure of his youthful misdirection and overreaching. Both were right. Bobby was so enamored of the senator that he failed to see the fanaticism that, by the time he signed on, had already made McCarthy's name a synonym for witch hunt and crowned "Low-Blow Joe" the most divisive man in America. Nor did he ever fully sever those bonds or entirely break the bad habits he learned from the senator from Grand Chute. Yet if Bobby was guilty of embracing or tolerating the Red Scare, so, too, was much of the nation in the 1950s. In the end, this McCarthy phase of his life would be a baseline from which to measure Bobby's— and America's—political transformation and growth.

* Americans might have been misled about Bobby's politics, but not the Soviets. "Kennedy is an ultra, an apostle of anti-Communism, who pursues the laurels of McCarthy and Dulles," according to *Za Rubezhom*, a Soviet magazine covering political news (State Department memo, "Soviet Press Criticism of the President's Family," June 19, 1962).

To APPRECIATE HOW he reached that baseline we need to go back to Bobby's beginnings. The story of America's First Family has been recounted so many times that it is part of American mythology. Nearly everyone knows some version of the dogged-upstart-to-fat-cat, East Boston–to–West Wing tale. But Robert Kennedy's pivotal place in that narrative is seldom acknowledged. Overlooked especially is his ongoing and all-important relationship with his father, Joe, and the fact that it was Bobby who was most like him and best suited to take over his leadership of the clan. Even Joe didn't get it at first.

Autocratic, magnetic, and unflinchingly family-focused, Joseph Patrick Kennedy was the model for all nine of his children, but particularly the boys. His upbringing set the pattern for theirs, and his single-minded pursuit of wealth and influence served as a template for what his four sons—and the third most of all—would accomplish in the political realm. Joe's roots ran deep both in his native Massachusetts, where the WASP establishment ruled the landscape into which he was born in 1888, and in his ancestral Ireland, whose call Joe never escaped. Yet the great patriarch's tale is not quite the Horatio Alger version that most of us think it to be. He was a self-starter but was not self-made. His father, Patrick Joseph Kennedy, was one of Boston's most influential and fair-minded political chieftains, serving five one-year terms in the Massachusetts House of Representatives and two two-year stints in the state Senate. He spent still longer as a Democratic ward boss, a post from which he could dole out offices, jobs, and favors in a capital city dominated by Democrats and, increasingly, by Irishmen. While politics was P.J.'s passion, it was his business acumen that gave him the time and resources to indulge it. He started life working with his hands as a brass fitter, then a stevedore. By his early thirties, the teetotaling Kennedy was a partner in three saloons, owner of two retail liquor stores, president of the Sumner Savings Bank, and founder of the Suffolk Coal Company, all of which afforded his wife, Mary Augusta, a life even more comfortable than the one she had grown up with as the daughter of a prosperous Irish-born contractor. She, in turn, pampered her four children—the baby, Margaret Louise, preceded by Mary Loretta, Francis Benedict, and Joseph Patrick.

Patrick charted a purposeful path for his first and favored child, Joe. Attending Catholic schools for his first six years gave Joe a grounding in his culture along with his faith. By grade seven, it was time for him to learn about the Brahmins who really ran things in the Commonwealth of Massachusetts. Theirs was a world of inherited fortunes where it was said that the Lowells talked only to the Cabots, while the Cabots talked only to God.

P.J. had begun to infiltrate that rarefied terrain but, like most hyphenated Americans, he had to defer the dream of true mastery to his son. For now, that meant enrolling Joe at Boston Latin, the country's oldest and the city's most rigorous public school, whose alumni included four Massachusetts governors and five signers of the Declaration of Independence. Young Joseph Kennedy did passably well there, but the faculty recommended he repeat his senior year if he hoped to get into Harvard College, which to Patrick was the point of his son's being at Latin. Following his teachers' advice, Joe stayed on. He was elected class president, reelected captain of the baseball team, and—despite three C's, five D's, and two F's on his entrance exams—admitted to Harvard, with "conditions."

Latin's class of 1908 sent twenty-five students to Harvard, which was half of its graduates and more than any other secondary school anywhere. Few were as self-satisfied as the strapping redhead with freckled cheeks and searing blue eyes. Joe's marks at college were sufficiently high to get him off probation but not nearly enough to get him onto the Dean's List, though that meant less to him than finally making it as a backup on the baseball team. The Hasty Pudding took him in but not the tonier clubs such as the Porcellian, where legend had it that if members didn't earn their first million by age forty, the club would give it to them. Just being at Harvard was a coup for the grandson of a potato farmer from County Wexford and the son of a saloonkeeper—but it wasn't enough for Joe, who could rattle off the stigmata that limited his mobility in Harvard's Protestant temple of traditionalism. He was Irish and Catholic. He had graduated from a public school, not a prep school. He neither came from inherited riches nor had quite enough of the nouveau kind. The only circumstance he could change was the last, and before graduation Joe and a friend launched a sightseeing bus business that netted them $5,000, or $126,000 in today's dollars. Not bad for a summer job.

Joe's school years set the formula for his career in business: Barrel through doors your dad opened; trust your instinct; never fully confide in anybody; use somebody else's money; and snap up bargains others don't, because they are either too shortsighted or too scrupulous. Barely a year after he graduated from Harvard, Boston newspapers were reporting on Joe's takeover of the Columbia Trust Company in East Boston. At age twenty-five, he was the youngest bank president in America. (Less ink was given to how small the bank was, how Patrick had been a minority owner from the start, and how relatives and neighbors lent Joe the money to scoop up a controlling interest.) His next enterprise—helping run Bethlehem Steel's shipyard outside Boston during World War I—netted fewer headlines but made Joe a useful friend in Assistant Secretary of the Navy Franklin D. Roosevelt.

If phase one of his career might be titled "Father Knows Best," the second chapter warrants an even simpler rubric: "Go Where the Money Is." Joe bankrolled movie theaters, then films, in Hollywood when the motion picture business was desperate for cash in the mid-1920s, and he walked away with $5 million in profits and screen siren Gloria Swanson as his mistress. He was an astute speculator during the stock market's most roaring ride ever, and he was one of the few investors canny enough to cash in before it crashed on the infamous Black Tuesday, October 29, 1929. With help from FDR's son James, Joe wangled the rights to import Haig & Haig Scotch and other premium whiskies at the very moment Prohibition was ending in 1933 and a thirsty public was lining up at the bar. So what if he personally abhorred the stereotype of Irish booziness and never drank beyond moderation? This was a matter of money. He even lent William Randolph Hearst a hand in reorganizing his media empire in 1937. As for suspicions that he made his millions working the shady side of the street—raiding companies, short-selling stocks, and bootlegging—they seldom were raised in his presence or substantiated, in part because he was so cagey about his increasingly lucrative investments. Joe's prototype was no longer his affable father, but the frosty Yankees who had blackballed him at Harvard.

Add in all his other deals, as *Fortune* magazine would in 1957, and Joe

had amassed somewhere between $200 million and $400 million—
enough to make him the wealthiest Irish American on earth. That same
year *The Saturday Evening Post* estimated his stock market earnings alone
at between $45 million and $700 million. Managing his estate, the *Post*
added, was a full-time occupation for twenty-odd investment counselors, tax experts, and bookkeepers, all searching for safe havens for the
payouts from Joe's high-risk investments. Whatever the true size of his
fortune, it was almost certainly enough, in today's dollars, to make him
a billionaire. As far back as the 1930s, just twenty years after graduating
from Harvard, he had eclipsed the holdings of most members of the
millionaires-by-forty Porcellian Club. For Joe, the best thing about being
rich was that it freed him to pursue his true passion, public affairs, just as
his father's more modest earnings had liberated him to do so a generation before.*

Joe Kennedy's vision for himself and the world was substantially more
audacious and unfiltered than P.J.'s. Joe meant to serve his country in a
way that would make clear his standing in its highest echelons. His en-
abler was his friend from the shipyard days, now President Franklin Roosevelt, who in 1934 named Joe chairman of the newly minted Securities
and Exchange Commission. Liberals howled, calling Kennedy a conniv-
ing capitalist whose appointment ensured that the agency would fail in
its mission to rein in the out-of-control stock markets that had helped
plunge the country into the Great Depression. FDR, however, grasped
what they didn't: Joe was one of the very few bulls of Wall Street who
realized that the New Deal was the best deal they were going to get and

---

* A case study of Joe's Midas touch was the Merchandise Mart in downtown Chicago. It was
the world's biggest and ugliest commercial building, occupying ninety-three acres of rent-
able space, rising twenty-four stories, and drawing Chicagoans to a block-long speakeasy
that served expensive drinks and free lunches. Joe bought the Mart from a desperate Marshall Field in 1945 for $13.2 million, which was $17 million less than it had cost the department store mogul to build it in 1930 and $18 million less than his accountants said it was
worth. Joe put up just $1 million in cash, and he protected himself from the huge taxes that
had plagued Field by placing his ownership in family trusts. While Field worried that federal
and state lessees, who occupied 40 percent of the space at below-market rates, would move
out when their leases expired, Kennedy wanted them gone. He could and did replace them
with companies able to pay full price. The bottom line: Annual income quickly exceeded
what it had cost to buy the building and helped pay the bills for Kennedy and his heirs until
1998, when the Mart was sold for $625 million, or fifty times what Joe had paid for it. (Nasaw,
The Patriarch, 588–89 and 612, and Whalen, *Founding Father*, 379–80.)

accepted the necessity of its regulations. While Kennedy stayed in the job just fifteen months, that was long enough to prove the president right. An adept executive, Joe managed to sell his fellow denizens of big business on the new rules without watering down those standards. *Time* magazine, in a cover story on Joe shortly before he resigned, called his SEC "the most ably administered New Deal agency in Washington." Joe delighted in that verdict, shared even by reporters who had railed against his appointment, although he had no illusions about why Roosevelt had named him: "He knew that I knew all the angles of trading . . . all the intricacies and trickeries of market manipulation." FDR put it more succinctly: "Set a thief to catch a thief."

Joe returned to his businesses after his stint at the SEC, but his days in the nation's capital reinforced a lesson he had learned from his father and would pass on to his sons: Getting the plum jobs he itched for required scratching backs, New Deal or old. And so as FDR faced another election in 1936, fearing that his White House was perceived as antibusiness, Joe again set aside his doubts about big government and marshaled his clout with the business community on behalf of Roosevelt. "I have no political ambitions for myself or for my children," he wrote disingenuously in a slim self-published book entitled *I'm for Roosevelt* that was widely distributed two months before the election. It derided the "unreasoning malicious ill-will displayed by the rich and powerful against our common leader," and it argued—in this instance genuinely—that "the future happiness of America, which means to me the future happiness of my family, will best be served by the re-election of President Roosevelt."

Roosevelt carried every state but Maine and Vermont. While it is doubtful that that historic landslide owed much to Joe Kennedy's published screed or to his stump speeches, the president felt in his debt. FDR could not give Joe the position he cherished most, treasury secretary, because that would have meant replacing the valued and powerful Henry Morgenthau, Jr. But the president did offer an appointment that Joe knew would ensure his place in history, as the first Irish Catholic American ambassador to Ireland's nemesis, England. It was the kind of backhanded slap at the imperious British that amused Roosevelt, although he saw nothing humorous in the rumors it aroused—fanned, he had no doubt, by Joe himself—that Kennedy would someday replace him in the White House. Joe's ambition was an open secret.

The appointment to London was a sensation when Joe arrived in 1938. The British were enchanted by the Kennedy brood, which by then had its full complement of four boys and five girls, aged five to twenty-two. NINE CHILDREN AND NINE MILLION DOLLARS, the tabloids teased. The official ambassador's residence, which had been the London residence of the banker J. P. Morgan, had eight opulent bedrooms for the family and thirteen more modest ones for servants. Joe brought an informal style the English might have expected of an Irishman, planting his feet on his desk during his first press conference. Queen Elizabeth, the wife of King George VI, was charmed by Kennedy's brash eccentricity in refusing to wear the customary knee breeches when he presented his credentials.* He took over any room he walked into with his soldierlike posture and a smile that brought his face to life. One person who couldn't get enough of him was Prime Minister Neville Chamberlain, whose policy of appeasing the Nazis felt just right to the isolationist Kennedy. But the new ambassador failed to adjust to shifting circumstances as war approached. German troops were storming through Czechoslovakia and Poland, Chamberlain's nemesis Winston Churchill was sounding alarms, and even the neutralists knew it was time to pick sides. By 1940, Great Britain was the last power challenging Hitler and his Axis allies, and Roosevelt was quietly rallying support for the United States to stand behind, if not yet beside, the English.

The conflict between the president's determination to intervene and his ambassador's instinct to keep out reached a climax during Joe's trip back to Boston in November 1940, when he gave an interview to Louis Lyons of *The Boston Globe*. The newspaper's editors saw Kennedy as a local man who meant well, and they envisioned the interview as a breezy feature—but tenacious newsman that he was, Lyons merely moved the bombshells down to paragraph six. "I'm willing to spend all I've got left

---

* He refused in no small measure because his legs curved out so awkwardly, a fact that FDR confirmed at a White House meeting by having the would-be ambassador drop his trousers. "Someone who saw you in a bathing suit once told me something I now know to be true," Roosevelt teased Kennedy. "Joe, just look at your legs. You are just about the most bowlegged man I have ever seen" ("Taft Was the Politest Man in Town," *New York Times*, July 5, 1981).

to keep us out of the war," Kennedy vowed. "There's no sense in our getting in. We'd just be holding the bag." What were Britain's chances against the Nazis? "Democracy," Kennedy told Lyons, "is finished in England. It may be here." What America should do, the diplomat added, is "aid England as far as we can." As for joining the fight, "I say we aren't going in. Only over my dead body."

The story revealed nothing that Joe hadn't been preaching in private, but it was a step too far, not just for the British but for Franklin Roosevelt. Kennedy believed in a laissez-faire foreign policy, even in the current crisis. He was convinced that capitalism, if not democracy, would prevail. In the meantime we should do business with Hitler and his fellow fascists as a way to keep them engaged. For Joe—and later for his next-to-youngest son Bobby—personal realities always trumped policy abstractions. "I have four boys," he had confided to a friend, "and I don't want them to be killed in a foreign war."

The *Globe* story gave Roosevelt the excuse he was waiting for to fire his uncontrollable ambassador, slamming the door on Kennedy's dream of being elected president, or even a ward boss in Boston. Yet Joe was not one to wallow in might-have-beens. His vision all along, as he told a mate, was "that future generations of school children will automatically remember three names together: Washington, Lincoln and Kennedy." If he couldn't be the Kennedy to make that happen, there were always his sons. He had already set up trust funds for all his offspring, ensuring that "financially speaking, [they] could look me in the eye and tell me to go to hell." Now he would zero in on his side of that bargain: His children—he included all of them but had in mind the boys—should give something back to the country that had made the family rich. Self-interested as he was, he was also a patriot.

––––––––––

NAMES WERE CHOSEN with intentionality in the Kennedy family. Patrick Joseph was proud of his son, but calling him Joseph Patrick relieved the boy of the burden of a more ethnic first name and of being a junior. Joe, by contrast, wanted his firstborn to be a chip off his block, and Joe's first choice to carry the Kennedy flag all the way to the top was his namesake, Joseph Patrick Kennedy, Jr. Joe Jr. had all the traits the old man valued.

Standing nearly six feet tall, with chestnut hair, broad shoulders, and sapphire-blue eyes, he radiated a manly magnetism. He could be abrasive or charming, depending on his purpose. But there was no question about his bravery, or where he stood on his father's call for appeasement. He had faced down a Communist firing squad during the Spanish Civil War and had flown so many bombing missions in his second tour with the Naval Air Corps that he was due to come home by the summer of 1944. Instead, the twenty-nine-year-old lieutenant volunteered for his most hazardous mission: piloting a plane loaded with explosives over the English Channel early on the evening of August 12. The plan called for him to turn radio control over to two B-17s that would steer the drone-like weapon to a Belgian launching pad for Germany's dreaded V-2 rockets while he parachuted to safety. But before Joe Jr. and his copilot could eject, their aircraft exploded. The next day a pair of Navy chaplains delivered the horrifying news to the Kennedy family, leaving everybody but Joe Sr. sobbing and wailing. He never would recover, but mourned in private, only later confiding in a letter to a friend that "my plans for my future were all tied up with young Joe, and that has gone smash."

John Fitzgerald Kennedy, the second son, was named after his mother's father, reminding Boston voters of the boy's connection to the impish and affable John F. "Honey Fitz" Fitzgerald, who served two terms as mayor of Boston and three as a congressman. Young John became a war hero like his older brother, although he fought on the water and half a world away. More bookish than Joe Jr. and slowed by a stream of maladies ranging from scarlet fever to whooping cough, John had dreamed of a career out of the limelight. A college professor, maybe, or a journalist. But with his firstborn gone, Joe Sr.'s aspirations shifted to the son he called Jack. It was a simple question of succession, as his grandfather explained on the very day the family learned Joe Jr.'s fate. "At dinner that night Honey Fitz said to Bobby, 'Look, your father and I were counting on Joe Jr. to be the next governor of Massachusetts. Since he's not here . . . it should be Jack,'" recalls Pete MacLellan, a high school friend of Bobby's who was at the dinner. While the office would change, the family's ambitions never did, and just two years after Joe Jr.'s death, John Kennedy ignored the political odds and his precarious health to run for a congressional seat from Massachusetts.

What about Bobby, Joe and Rose's most dutiful and most brittle child? "Robert Francis" was a less calculated selection of names than his brothers'. Robert was as common as appellations came then, whereas Francis could have been a memorial to his paternal uncle, who died before his second birthday; to his maternal grandfather, whose middle name was Francis; or to Saint Francis of Assisi, which is the angelic interpretation the family prefers. Like Saint Francis, Robert F. Kennedy was gentle as well as intense, and he, too, found solace in nature and with animals.

If Rose had had her way, her third son would have entered the priesthood. From the first, she and Joe had informally earmarked who would be each child's primary caretaker, and she was Bobby's. He was her favorite, too, in part because he needed her the most. Rose's mother worried that Bobby would "be a sissy" because he was surrounded by sisters, "but of course," Rose said, "this didn't happen." She was firm with her other eight but referred to Bobby as "my own little pet." He volunteered to sit next to her on the plane when the family was traveling and nobody else offered, and he regularly told her how beautiful she looked.

It was different with Joe. The question of who Robert Francis was and what would become of him didn't even occur to his father in the early years, when his full attention went to the "golden trio" of Joe Jr., Jack, and their second-oldest sister, Kathleen. Just getting a word in at the dinner table was difficult for the younger tier. Bobby felt invisible the way middle children often do, a hazard more pronounced when there are eight siblings. He also was the runt of that impressive litter, standing only five feet nine in a family of six-footers, with little of the Kennedy eloquence, moxie, good looks, or athleticism. What he did have were buck teeth, a slight stammer, and a disposition dark enough for Jack to call him Black Robert. "I was the seventh of nine children," Bobby explained later. "When you come from that far down, you have to struggle to survive." His family got a taste of that tenacity when Bobby was just four. He was so resolved to swim like his big brothers that he jumped into the deep waters of Nantucket Sound prepared to drown if he couldn't float. Luckily Joe Jr. was there to rescue him. "It showed either a lot of guts or no sense at all," Jack said, looking back.

That determination, born of insecurity, was not easily shed. In his teens, Bobby wrote to his father in cramped and barely legible handwriting: "I wish, Dad, that you would write me a letter as you used to Joe & Jack about what you think about the different political events and the war as I'd like to understand what's going on better than I now do." He was pleading less for news than for acknowledgment, and he was thrilled when his father responded with a two-and-a-half-page missive.

Joe had reasons for his low expectations. Like him, Bobby was a second-rate student forced to repeat a year—although the father replayed his last one in high school, whereas the son stayed back in third grade. And unlike his brother Jack, Bobby's most impressive academic achievement was the number of schools he attended—ten in all—rather than his performance at any of them. The changes were a function both of his parents' peripatetic lifestyle and of their changing notions of what was best for Bobby. For high school, Joe arranged for him to attend the prestigious St. Paul's in New Hampshire, but Rose, distressed at the thought of her most devout child steeped in Episcopalianism, transferred him to Portsmouth Priory, a Rhode Island boarding school run by Benedictine monks. He spent three years there, grades eight through ten, but why he left is unclear. Some ex-classmates tie his departure to a cheating scandal in which he at least looked at a pilfered exam. Rose blamed Bobby's disappointment with the Priory's headmaster, food, and accommodations, which became a bit better after Joe's donation to the school building fund. MacLellan, his friend and classmate, offers the likeliest explanation: When Portsmouth couldn't promise that it could get Bobby into Harvard, Joe enrolled him for his junior and senior years at Milton Academy in Massachusetts, where he'd have as clear a shot as Joe had when Patrick sent him to Boston Latin.

In letters home from prep school, Bobby expressed his delight when he avoided failing subjects like English and French, although all he managed in those classes were C's, and in his senior year he got a D in geometry. He also made light of his mediocrity in swimming, football, and romance. Entering Milton as the "new kid," he didn't know his classmates' names and called enough of them "fella" that that quickly became his own nickname. It was one of countless signs that Bobby didn't fit in. "He was neither a natural athlete nor a natural student nor a natural success with girls and had no natural gift for popularity. Nothing came easily for him," remembered his closest schoolmate, Dave Hackett, for whom things did come easily.* "What he had was a set of handicaps and a fantastic determination to overcome them. . . . We were both, in a way, misfits." His friend Piedy Lumet, known in her Milton days as Mary Bailey Gimbel, says Bobby back then was "shy and whimsical and a little bit solitary." And he had a classic pose: "He mostly stood on one foot with the other toe resting on top, his head a little bit down, looking out from underneath his forelock. . . . I thought of him sort of looking like a bat trapped in a pantry, you know? I mean, 'How did I get here?' "

For his part, Bobby told a biographer that "what I remember most vividly about growing up was going to a lot of different schools, always having to make new friends, and that I was very awkward. I dropped things and fell down all the time. I had to go to the hospital a few times for stitches in my head and my leg. And I was pretty quiet most of the time. And I didn't mind being alone." All of that eventually would make him sensitive to children in general, and particularly to the misfits. At the time, it was even more hurtful than he let on.

If bouncing between schools and feeling like a perpetual outlier constituted Bobby's least favorite memories from childhood, his most cherished came from the family's vacation getaways where the only outsiders were ones they had invited. In 1933, when Bobby was barely eight, Joe bought a 15,000-square-foot Mediterranean Revival estate in Palm Beach for the not-so-small fortune of $120,000 (more than $2 million in today's terms). Americans across the continent were devastated by the Great Depression, but not the Kennedys. Their mansion had been built by a Philadelphia department store family who called it La Guerida, or "bounty of war," a name even more appropriate given how Joe made his money. His and Rose's kids flew in from colder climates for Christmas vacations, filling to overflow the six bedrooms. There was half a football field (176 feet) of beachfront to play along, to which Joe added a pool and tennis court. He also indulged himself with an enclosed solarium—his children called it the bull pen—where he spent his days naked but for a hat, with a telephone planted in his ear.

---

* John Knowles got to know Hackett during a summer when both were at Exeter Academy, and he said Hackett was the inspiration for the carefree athlete Phineas in Knowles's coming-of-age novel *A Separate Peace*.

Much as Bobby and his siblings liked Florida in the winter, the house that felt most like home was in Hyannis Port, a little waterfront community on Cape Cod to the southwest of the bustling village of Hyannis. The Cape was not Joe Kennedy's first choice to spend his summers. That would have been Cohasset, which was closer to Boston and in a world of blue bloods who couldn't keep him from renting but made it clear he wasn't welcome. So in 1926 he leased, then four years later bought, the Malcolm cottage in Hyannis Port, where the summering millionaires from Pittsburgh, St. Louis, and Chicago were less hostile. There was one house to start with, a rambling 1904 white clapboard, along with a tennis court, swimming pool, and private beach. Situated at the end of the lane, the sprawling structure's most inviting feature was a long deck with sweeping views of the blue-green Atlantic Ocean. Joe equipped the house with enough amenities to entertain his children, and later his grandchildren, by installing a Swedish bath, private motion picture theater, and wine cellar with sipping room. The two-and-a-half-acre lawn that separated the houses from the water was perfect for touch football. The front porch held a ticker tape machine that let Joe follow the markets, and that also encouraged Rose to retreat to the prefabricated shack in the corner of the yard that was her refuge.

The Cape was where Rose and Joe's children cemented their bonds to one another. The rest of the year they were at boarding school, in the military, or traveling, but whenever they could they headed to Hyannis Port. Ted and Bobby loved visiting on their own when the main house was buttoned up for winter, and they would bundle up in the apartment above the garage to talk about school, girls, and the big dreams of little boys. Joe Jr. taught Bobby to pass and catch a football there. Jack spent endless hours reading in his room and walking on the beach, sometimes letting Bobby tag along beside him. Even his oldest sister, Rose Marie, was there in the early days, before her mental disabilities were deemed unmanageable and she was sent to live at a convent in Rhode Island. That carefree family time was so appealing that a young Bobby would write home asking his parents, "When are you going to open the house in Hyannisport? I will be a constant visitor when you do."

Not all his memories from home and family were sweet ones, however. In the early years Bobby would cower upstairs, with his sisters, while Joe

Jr. and Jack duked it out on the first floor. He lived in fear as well as awe of his dad, too. In summers, when everyone was on hand, Joe expected the children in the dining room five minutes before mealtime. It was a rule so strictly enforced that Kennedys were known to abandon whatever boat they were on and swim for their lives so as not to break it. Rose and Joe drilled into their offspring the importance of knowing what was happening in the world by quizzing them at mealtime, and they fine-tuned everyone's language skills by insisting that only Spanish or French be spoken on specified evenings at the dinner table. Rose oversaw weigh-ins every Saturday to determine who needed calories added or subtracted over the next week. Yet even as their life in Hyannis Port was governed by stricture, what the children remembered more were the parlor games and athletic contests. There were community sailing races on Nantucket Sound and trips to the Cape Cod Creamery on Sea Street. Best of all, for Joe and his kids, was being at home with just the family. They were difficult to tell apart when they smiled, a herd of fiery Irish purebreds. To hell with exclusive Harvard social clubs, and neighbors who didn't like Catholics or Celts. The Cape Cod compound was a place to live out their collective dream of Kennedy self-sufficiency, not just for Joe's children but for the generations to follow. As they aged it would be the only place Kennedy siblings, and Bobby in particular, could always be kids.

Bobby's college career was again reminiscent of his father's—getting into Harvard on the strength of his high school's reputation as much as his own record, and, with grades as mediocre as those at Milton, spending part of his time at college on academic probation. But whereas pursuing and catching women was second nature to Joe, and to his boys Jack and Joe Jr., Bobby had to work at it. "I am now chasing women madly but it looks as if I lack the Kennedy charm as I have yet to find a girl who likes me," he confided to a friend. "But then I don't quit easily so I'm still in there struggling." And while Joe Sr.'s college era was a serene one for America, in Bobby's case World War II intervened. That meant that his first two years after high school were focused less on schoolwork, although he did get academic credit, than on becoming a soldier like his older brothers. He'd enlisted while he was at Milton in 1943, and a year later, with help from his father, he was accepted into the Navy's V-12 College Training Program and the Reserve Officers' Training Corps, at Harvard and then at Bates College in Maine. After two long years of watching the war from ivy-covered campuses, he got the Secretary of the Navy's permission to quit his leadership training and, at the lowly rank of seaman, he was purposely assigned in February 1946 to a destroyer named after the fallen Joe Jr. But the vessel never made it out of the Caribbean, and the only scars Bobby got were the product of a fistfight with a shipmate, a case of infectious hepatitis that showed up the year after his discharge, and the humiliation of once more landing in the shadows of his war-hero brothers.

That fall he headed back to finish his degree at Harvard, where he achieved an athletic honor that had eluded Joe Jr. and Jack during their time at the college. It was more a tribute to Bobby's fortitude than his skill on the football field, since he'd broken his leg in practice early in the season. But the coach was impressed with how he'd continued playing until he literally fell down. So, in the season-ending Harvard-Yale game, Bobby was sent in—cast and all—for just long enough to qualify for the cherished crimson-and-white *H* signaling that he had played for a varsity team.

After college, Bobby knew he "just didn't know anything," he recalled. "I wanted to do graduate work." The only professional schools he considered were business and law, and having "no attraction to business," that left law. His grades in college weren't good enough to get into Harvard or Yale, the law schools he and Joe would have preferred, but the University of Virginia agreed to take him with the understanding that "unless he does better work than he did at Harvard, he is most unlikely to succeed in this Law School." He did, sort of, spending some time studying but at least as much skiing, golfing, and flying off to see his family in Massachusetts and Florida on the weekends. Especially boring to him was a one-hour course on legal research in which he scored a zero. "It's the way he was brought up," explained his law school friend George Tremblay. "He saw how his father operated. . . . He saw how his brothers operated, and, you know, I guess he figured if he ever practiced law that he wasn't going to be spending much time looking up law in some law library, that somebody would be doing this" for him.

Although Bobby's life had been devoted to following the lead of his brothers, there was one domain where he was the trendsetter: marriage.

Bobby was the first of the boys to wed and the first to give Joe and Rose grandchildren, which was a surprise and delight given his early disappointments with girls. It was different with Ethel Skakel, whose honey-blond hair, sparkling eyes, and easy laugh made her appealing if not ravishing. Ethel's ties to the Kennedys were forged years before at Manhattanville College of the Sacred Heart, where she roomed with Bobby's kid sister Jean. The two became best friends, with Jean the straight one of the pair and Ethel her gleeful corrupter. The Manhattanville nuns imposed a rigid code of conduct, which they enforced by handing out demerits and the punishments that went with them. Ethel and Jean had earned enough black marks—for everything from "loud screaming" to putting a sign on a priest's Cadillac saying NICE COLLECTION, FATHER—to jeopardize their coveted off-campus privileges. The girls' solution: toss the demerit book down the incinerator. (Fifty years later, neither will say who did the tossing.) Rose Kennedy came up with a solution of her own: building a temporary wall in their dormitory room to make it harder for the girls to talk and easier for Jean to become again the honor student she had been before meeting Ethel. Some friends, then and later, held Ethel up as a model of quiet sophistication. Others dismissed her as naïve. Both were right, and the blend was disarming. "Her face," her college yearbook said, "is at one moment a picture of utter guilelessness and at the next alive with mischief."

Those idiosyncrasies, Jean was convinced, made Ethel the perfect jaunty tomboy who could bury the blue funks Bobby got from worrying whether he could measure up to the older Kennedy men. Bobby was entering law school when the girls were starting their senior year at Manhattanville in the fall of 1948. Ethel was so star-struck on first meeting him that she now says "it was like looking at George Clooney." As for Bobby, he "was momentarily mad about me," she remembered. "He took me out for two weeks. The only trouble was that for the next two years he took out my older sister" Patricia. Pat finally decided that Bobby was too immature and unlettered; at the same time, Bobby realized that Pat would never care enough about sports or about him. And although Ethel was sufficiently intrigued by Jack Kennedy that she stumped door-to-door in his first campaign for Congress, then based her senior thesis on his book *Why England Slept*, the brother she was truly smitten with had always been Robert Francis. Cheered on by Jean, Ethel kept showing up—on the tennis courts and ski slopes, and at Kennedy family vacations—until Bobby couldn't help but notice. What drew them to each other, however, was more than her persistence and his rebound from Pat. They were each other's second selves. As shy as Bobby could be in social settings, Ethel loved being around people and could keep talking as long as there were listeners. He was complicated; she was easy. "Laughter," Ethel explained, "is better than tears." That uncensored eagerness to jump in made Bobby's siblings feel they had another sister. "If you don't marry Ethel," Jack joked, "I'll marry her." Her devotion to Bobby and to God made Rose forget why, when they were in college, she had walled Ethel off from Jean.

The next challenge was synchronicity. By the time Bobby asked for her hand, Ethel was weighing becoming a nun. "How can I fight God?" Bobby asked Jean as they walked the beach in Hyannis Port. Ethel's spiritual drive wasn't new; she had been attending mass and saying her rosaries every day, and during college she was invited into the Children of Mary, a Catholic lay association that focuses on spiritual development. After months of contemplation, Ethel had an epiphany: The best way to serve her God was by giving her heart to Bobby, the only man she'd ever loved like that, and raising a brood of believers numerous enough to form their own parish.

Ethel was marrying into a family strikingly similar to the one in which she was raised: devoutly Catholic, avidly athletic, and steadfastly anti-communist. George Skakel, her father, was nearly as rich as Joe Kennedy and more self-made. The onetime railway clerk owned the Great Lakes Carbon Corporation, one of America's biggest privately held companies that made energy products such as foundry coke and crude petroleum. Like Rose, Ethel's mother, Ann, was more religious than her husband, although she and George had a modest seven children compared to Rose and Joe's nine and the Skakels were as deep-dyed Republican as the Kennedys were Democrats. The ten-acre Skakel estate in Greenwich, Connecticut, was even larger than the Kennedys' in Hyannis Port or Palm Beach. Ethel and Bobby shared a love of the outdoors and an inability to sit still. She was one of the few people as addicted as he was to victory, in sports and everything else. As for the Kennedys, "I just thought that they were as much fun as our family," Ethel says. She and Bobby even looked like brother and sister, from protruding front teeth to thick mops of hair that made them seem like teenagers.

They were wed on June 17, 1950, at St. Mary Roman Catholic Church in Greenwich, with the reception back at the Skakel home and a honeymoon in Hawaii. Pope Pius XII sent his blessings. George gave away the bride, who was wearing a gown of white satin, and *The New York Times* considered the nuptials newsworthy. Jack Kennedy was Bobby's best man, and younger brother Ted was an usher. Ethel's sister Pat flew in from Ireland to serve as maid of honor. Joe and George settled up afterward for furnishings that Bobby's friends and Ethel's brothers broke during the bachelor party at the Harvard Club. When it was all over—the long flirtations and involved celebrations—the couple headed to Charlottesville for Bobby's last year of law school, and Ethel settled into her lifelong project of being Mrs. Robert F. Kennedy.

———

BOBBY MADE HIS biggest mark at the University of Virginia not in the classroom but at the Student Legal Forum, where he served as president during his third year. He enticed to campus such esteemed speakers as Supreme Court Justice William O. Douglas, *New York Times* columnist Arthur Krock, and former Harvard Law School dean James Landis, all cronies of Joe Kennedy, who delivered a speech of his own to Bobby's schoolmates shortly before Christmas in 1950. Five months later Bobby hosted another of his father's friends, Joseph McCarthy, who was already building his reputation as the most unbridled anticommunist in Washington. It was Bobby's first significant interaction with the senator and an occasion memorable less for McCarthy's fiery talk than for what happened when Bobby and Ethel had him to dinner afterward. McCarthy "asked for a drink right away," recalled E. Barrett Prettyman, Jr., an editor of the law review who was there. "We began to ask him questions. In the beginning, he was very sure-footed in his responses, but as he began to get sloshed, he began to get tangled. . . . He just went to pieces. And he began to *realize* he was embarrassing himself, so he would get more embarrassed, and drink more, and people began to slip out." Before the night was out, McCarthy had pawed a female guest and Bobby had helped him to bed. Prettyman was horrified. But in that early encounter, as in most later ones, Bobby glossed over the senator's flagrant flaws, recalling only that "I liked him almost immediately."

In 1951, Bobby graduated from Virginia smack in the middle of his class, with no idea what to do with his legal degree. He landed his first job later that year—thanks to a phone call from Joe—with the U.S. Justice Department. He spent a couple of months with the Internal Security Division in Washington, investigating Soviet spies, real or imagined, then a few more months in New York at the Criminal Division, helping prepare corruption cases against former officials of the Truman administration. National security and political corruption would be central to his later career, but his officemates from the time remembered only that he was a son of privilege who seldom bothered to cash his paychecks and who often kicked off his shoes and worked in his stocking feet. They also agreed that he was no legal scholar. Barely three months into his work in the Brooklyn U.S. attorney's office, Bobby reluctantly resigned to help his brother Jack, who had won his first race for Congress in 1946 and, in his third term, was readying what looked like a quixotic challenge to Republican senator Henry Cabot Lodge, Jr., of Massachusetts.

While Jack didn't know whether his kid brother was the man for the campaign job, Joe did. The older Bobby got, the more Joe paid attention. And the more the father heard and saw, including Bobby's record as a single-minded prosecutor, the better he realized that this was the one of his children who most clearly mirrored his own wants and needs. Bobby understood Joe's bottom-line message: that family came before anything, and that in a crunch, it was only your siblings and parents you could count on. Bobby felt more deeply and cared more passionately than his brothers and sisters did about matters worldly and personal. He was proudly Celtic like Joe and P.J., and more Catholic than either of them. He saw the world in the same black-and-white terms—good guys and bad—as his father did, in contrast to Jack's more nuanced perspective on international affairs. Communists, for Bobby as for Joe, were the most loathsome of bad guys.

Bobby's performance in that 1952 Senate race convinced Joe just how good this neglected son could be. Nationally, everyone knew the election would be a Republican grand slam. After twenty years of New Deal and

Fair Deal Democrats, the country wanted a change in the White House, and the five-star general who had led the Allied forces to triumph over Hitler was heading the GOP ticket. Henry Cabot Lodge was managing Eisenhower's presidential campaign at the same time that he was running himself for a fourth term in the Senate. The key, Bobby understood, was decoupling Massachusetts from the Eisenhower express and making sure every voter in the Bay State was introduced to another hero in the war against Hitler—his brother Jack. Fearing that anything received in the mail would go out with the garbage, Bobby signed up twenty-eight thousand volunteers who delivered door-to-door nine hundred thousand copies of a tabloid reminding voters not just of JFK's wartime gallantry, but of how JOHN FULFILLS DREAM OF BROTHER JOE WHO MET DEATH IN THE SKY OVER THE ENGLISH CHANNEL. Bobby had his sisters and his mother—wearing skirts embroidered with VOTE FOR JACK KENNEDY—hold parties for every matron and maiden who wanted to sip their tea and shake the hand of their handsome brother John. "Every old woman wants to be his mother," old hands quipped, "and every young woman dreams of being his mistress." It was the 1950s version of social media, and the results were impressive: seventy thousand women of Massachusetts shared the Kennedy kettle, and many stuck around as campaign volunteers.

Even more impressive was the outcome on election day: Eisenhower took Massachusetts by 200,000 votes, a sweep that cost the incumbent Democratic governor Paul Dever his job, but JFK beat Lodge by 71,000 votes thanks to Bobby's unrelenting and nearly flawless campaign to identify his brother's supporters and get them to the polls. If Jack Kennedy was "the first Irish Brahmin," Dever observed after watching Bobby at work, "Bobby is the last Irish Puritan." That wasn't meant as a compliment, but Joe took it as one. Bobby's iron-fisted approach worked. He had split ranks with Dever and other old-school Democrats and looked out only for Jack. Joe had always taught his children that it was not enough to fight hard if you finish second. "For the Kennedys," the patriarch pronounced, "it's the [outhouse] or the castle—nothing in between." Now that Bobby had helped Jack claim the keys to the castle, "Mr. Kennedy found he had another able son," said Lem Billings, Jack's prep school roommate. Joe may or may not have uttered the often repeated line that

Bobby "hates like me," but he did say "Bobby's as hard as nails" and "I'm like Bobby."

Pleased though he was, Joe was not one to look back, even on successes. With the election over and Jack headed to the Senate, Joe demanded of Bobby: "Are you going to sit on your tail end and do nothing now for the rest of your life? You better go out and get a *job*." And Senator Joe McCarthy had one for him, thanks in large measure to the generous donation Joe Kennedy made to the senator's campaign fund.* The elder Kennedy had known the Wisconsin legislator for years and was convinced he would catch on with mainstream America. The Joes had a lot in common: Both were defiant Irishmen, although Kennedy's wealth made him the "lace curtain"† kind whereas McCarthy, who began life as a chicken farmer and grocer, was "shanty" Irish. Each had been an FDR Democrat, then grown disillusioned. Kennedy shared McCarthy's disdain for left-wingers, especially on the home front. Yet as much as a man's politics mattered to Kennedy, that man's temperament mattered more. That is why the Massachusetts magnate could count as friends the ultraconservative Joe McCarthy and the archliberal William O. Douglas, perhaps the only man in America able to make that claim. Kennedy liked that McCarthy "was never a crab. If somebody was against him, he never tried to cut his heart out. He never said that anybody was a stinker. He was a pleasant fellow." Such stilted language was classic Joe Kennedy. Classic, too, was Joe's inability to see or care about McCarthy's victims. When the senator started his anticommunist agitation, "I thought he'd be a sensation," Joe recalled, adding that McCarthy was "the strongest man in the United States next to Eisenhower."

---

* Just how much he gave McCarthy is uncertain, since disclosure of political donations was not required in the 1940s and '50s. The syndicated columnist Drew Pearson put it at $50,000. Secretary of the Senate Bobby Baker said it was ten times that much, which would have made Kennedy McCarthy's most generous benefactor. Kennedy insisted that he gave "only a couple of thousand." Whatever the amount, the money reinforced McCarthy's inclination to stay out of Massachusetts in 1952, when his support could have substantially boosted fellow Republican senator Lodge's standing against Jack Kennedy among Catholic and conservative voters (Pearson and Anderson, "Voters Must Weigh Bobby's 'Know-How,'" *Washington Post*, May 3, 1968; author interview with Bobby Baker; and McCarthy, *Remarkable Kennedys*, 26).

† "Lace curtain" Irish are, according to tradition, a family that can afford the luxury of fruit in the house even when nobody is sick.

Bobby was delighted at the prospect of working for McCarthy, even if his friends and brother Jack were not. Bobby respected McCarthy's ties to the Kennedys. McCarthy had met JFK during World War II in the South Pacific, where Jack would win a medal for rescuing his PT boat crew and McCarthy would pick up the nickname Tail-Gunner Joe along with a reputation for embellishing his combat record and injuries. The senator dated Bobby's sisters Patricia and Eunice in Washington when they visited Jack, and in Hyannis Port, where Eunice thought it fun to push McCarthy out of her father's boat until she learned he couldn't swim. The bachelor also showed interest in younger sister Jean, who was impressed but felt that a twenty-year age gap was too great. McCarthy played shortstop for the Barefoot Boys, the Kennedy softball team, when they staged their annual game against a team of Hyannis Port neighbors they dubbed the Pansies. (McCarthy was benched after making four errors at shortstop.) And he cracked a rib during one of the storied touch football games on the Kennedy lawn. When he was in Palm Beach, McCarthy would stop by the Kennedy mansion for a bourbon and a chat with Joe.

But the connection went beyond the social and familial. Like his father, Bobby was drawn to qualities in McCarthy that echoed his own: his roughneck spirit, his unapologetic embrace of religion, and his willingness to take on and, if need be, shame the political establishment. This third Kennedy son had taken up McCarthy's cause in impassioned debates with friends during his undergraduate years at Harvard in the 1940s. When he was studying law at the University of Virginia, Bobby argued forcefully that President Roosevelt had sold out U.S. interests in his 1945 Yalta agreement with the Soviets on the configuration of postwar Europe. The legislator and his young admirer both had the instincts of alley fighters, which Bobby believed they'd need in a Cold War where the enemy fought dirty. McCarthy had grasped sooner than other politicians just how frightened Americans were of creeping Communism. We had beaten easy-to-see foes in the Nazis and the Empire of Japan, but now our World War II ally of convenience, Soviet Russia, was quietly planting its revolutionary seeds across Europe and in Africa, Asia, and Latin America. China had fallen in 1949 to Mao Tse-tung and the Marxists, with McCarthy and his allies demanding of the Truman administration, "Who lost China?" It was three years since the Wisconsin senator had fueled a Red Scare at home by claiming to have a list of 205 active Communist Party members and Soviet spies who were embedded in the State Department. A year later he went to the Senate floor to denounce former secretary of state George C. Marshall for "always and invariably serving the world policy of the Kremlin." The bloody and inconclusive war in Korea, where China battled on behalf of the North and the United States backed the South, cemented McCarthy's case: His name was now an ism and America was fertile ground for his message about enemies lurking in our midst.

Working for McCarthy's Permanent Subcommittee on Investigations would give Bobby a front row seat at the biggest show in Washington in the early 1950s: the holy war against a Communist conspiracy that the senator called "so immense as to dwarf any previous such venture in the history of man." Bobby, too, was alarmed about what he saw as the "serious internal security threat to the United States," and he thought that "Joe McCarthy seemed to be the only one who was doing anything about it." Bobby had shown where he stood on the issue as early as his first job, at the attorney general's Internal Security Division, when he investigated Bolsheviks. Later, as his brother's campaign manager, he attacked Massachusetts senator Lodge for being soft on Communism. Those views were consistent with his commitment to his faith, since the Catholic Church in the early 1950s was ardently anticommunist and pro–Joe McCarthy. McCarthy, meanwhile, tapped religious imagery in warning his audience that "this is the era of Armageddon—that final all-out battle between light and darkness foretold in the Bible." Bobby suspected then and afterward that the senator's critics were anti-Catholic as well as anti-McCarthy.

There was one last reason why a job with Joe McCarthy was so appealing to Bobby Kennedy. Like so much in Bobby's life, it had to do with Joe Kennedy. Bobby knew his father admired McCarthy, and he saw the senator as a reflection of much that he loved in his dad. By working for a tough-minded jingoist like McCarthy, Bobby hoped he could erase the public's lingering memory of Joe Kennedy as a Nazi apologist and even, as many British had believed him to be, a coward. What RFK failed to see was that his father—an isolationist who argued that Communists, like fascists, could be accommodated until their regimes collapsed from within—was far less of a cold warrior than McCarthy was and than Bobby was becoming. "Joe's *methods* may be a little rough," Bobby would confide about McCarthy to a pair of journalists, "but, after all, his goal is to expose Communists in government, and that's a worthy goal. So why are you reporters so critical of his methods?"

––––––––––

JOE MCCARTHY COULDN'T say no to Joe Kennedy. Of course he would give Kennedy's son a job, it was just a question of what position would be right for Bobby and for the sticky committee politics of 1953. The Wisconsin senator had just been easily reelected and named chairman of the Senate Committee on Government Operations along with its Permanent Subcommittee on Investigations. But McCarthy wanted to hire another ambitious and combative young lawyer, Roy Cohn, to run his staff. Like Bobby, Cohn was a Democrat, had worked in the Justice Department, and boasted family connections, although his were not nearly as powerful as the Kennedys'. Unlike Bobby, Cohn had been a top-notch student at top-drawer schools, and he had a photographic memory along with a record of accomplishment. He'd already helped send America's most notorious spies, Julius and Ethel Rosenberg, to the electric chair, and he had zealously prosecuted a dozen high-level homegrown Communists he said were conspiring to overthrow our government. There was another factor in Cohn's favor: He was Jewish. This gave McCarthy cover at a moment he was being attacked as anti-Semitic by the journalist Drew Pearson and the Anti-Defamation League.* Not giving the top job to Bobby offered McCarthy a different kind of cover, deflecting charges that the appointment was a payoff to his patron Joe Kennedy.

McCarthy's solution was to make Cohn chief counsel. Ex-FBI agent Francis "Frip" Flanagan would stay on as general counsel, and Bobby would start as Flanagan's assistant, with the promise of eventually re-

––––––––––

* McCarthy almost certainly wasn't an anti-Semite, but as always, he gave better than he got, taking to the Senate floor to unfairly brand Pearson a "sugar-coated voice of Russia" (Oshinsky, *A Conspiracy So Immense*, 181).

placing him. The arrangement was confusing even to its architect, who never was one to exercise control over his underlings. When reporters asked who would be doing what, McCarthy sheepishly smiled, spread his hands wide, and confessed, "I don't know." What was obvious was that Bobby was one of six assistant counsels at the committee, earning less than half of what Roy did. With official lines of authority hazy, an informal hierarchy of duties and loyalties took shape. It soon became apparent, Cohn said, that Kennedy "was my enemy," with Flanagan confiding to Cohn that "first of all, he isn't crazy about Jews. Second, you're not exactly a member of the Palm Beach polo set. And thirdly, you've got the job he wanted." For his part, Cohn saw in Bobby the Irish toughs who prowled the streets when he was growing up in the Bronx, and he knew how to bully back. "Roy treats [Kennedy] as a gofer. Literally as a gofer," observed the Washington journalist Murrey Marder. "Not as a lawyer, fellow counselor, or anything like that. As a kid. A rich bitch kid."

McCarthy was as new to the workings of the subcommittee as Kennedy was when they both came aboard in January 1953, but there was no mystery where the chairman stood or where he was heading. The senator said from the start that his subcommittee would be a beachhead in the crusade against Communism, and that he alone would set the agenda and hire and fire staff. To witnesses in his hearings, he seemed like a one-man inquisitor, judge, jury, and executioner. Whichever side one came down on regarding Joe McCarthy—was he an uber-patriot or a bullying demagogue?—anyone aligned with him at that high point in his climb to power knew what they were getting: the scariest man in America.

Kennedy worked on several issues, but the investigation that absorbed nearly all of his time and defined his tenure with the subcommittee was the Greek shipping scandal. It revealed that Greece, West Germany, Norway, and other close U.S. allies were profiting by shipping goods to and from Red China at the very moment that we were at war with China and its North Korean accomplice. Bobby laid out names and numbers for the committee and the public: Western vessels handled 75 percent of the China trade, with the Communist Bloc accounting for just 25 percent. The value of goods shipped by the West added up to $2 billion since the outbreak of war in Korea. More than half the vessels carrying out this trade flew under the flag of our most special overseas partner, Great Britain. And it was not just food and staples that were being traded. British ships carried Communist troops, Kennedy said, along with strategic materials including rubber, fertilizer, and petroleum. Adding to the affront, many of the ships were paid for with loans subsidized by U.S. taxpayers and intended to help our World War II allies rebuild their merchant fleets.

To dig up those figures, Kennedy and his researchers had worked into the nights poring over the Lloyd's of London shipping index, reviewing British parliamentary debates, and rechecking reports from the U.S. Maritime Commission and the Central Intelligence Agency. That kind of doggedness would have confounded anyone who had known Bobby during his lazy law school years, when he still was searching for a calling. The Greek probe catapulted him back into campaign mode, which was double the pace of the typical Capitol Hill staffer then and made him stand out. So did his rumpled bearing. He drove to work in a beat-up station wagon left over from the 1952 Senate race. In the office the sleeves of his J. Press shirts were rolled past the elbows, his collar was open and frayed enough to signal old money to anyone who noticed such clues, his slim necktie was loose, and he continued to wear white woolen athletic socks long after he was advised that they clashed with his narrow-shouldered business suits. What set him apart even more was that rather than pulling strings from behind the scenes, the way anonymous congressional staffers normally did, Bobby was the star witness in the shipping hearings.

McCarthy didn't care how his assistant counsel looked or where he sat as long as he generated blockbuster material like this. "It seems just unbelievable, unheard of, in the history of the world, I believe, that a nation would have ships owned by its nationals transporting the troops to kill its own soldiers," the chairman railed at a hearing in May 1953. Complimenting Bobby on the charts he had prepared that broke down the embarrassing pattern by nation and goods, McCarthy added, "I think it would be an excellent thing if each of the mothers of the 3,700 British casualties could have a copy of that chart." Subcommittee Democrats were equally exasperated, which was a first. "I notice a hundred British ships at a minimum are engaged in this trade and traffic," said Senator

John McClellan of Arkansas. "I wonder how much that offsets, if it does not equal at least, the contribution the British are making in the Korean War on our side as allies. I think it is a pertinent observation. Whose war is it, the United Nations' or the United States' war?"

His senators were delighted by the sparks Kennedy's findings were producing with the media and public, but research findings were not enough. They also wanted to show that Congress could change things even if the State Department couldn't or wouldn't. With Bobby beside him, McCarthy held a press conference to announce that he had personally negotiated a pact under which the Greek owners of 242 cargo vessels agreed to stop trading with Red China, North Korea, and other Communist countries. That, the chairman predicted, would reduce China's seagoing commerce by as much as a third and hasten victory in the Korean War.

The Eisenhower administration was not amused. It was one thing for the Republican senator to hold captive the foreign policy of Democratic president Harry Truman, but now McCarthy was undermining a Republican administration by antagonizing its friends in Britain and stirring up anticommunist critics at home. After months of back-and-forth with the executive branch in the spring of 1953, McCarthy told Kennedy to draft a letter asking the president just what U.S. policy was on our allies trading with our enemies. The senator signed it, and Bobby delivered the letter to the White House. Eisenhower faced a Hobson's choice: embarrassing the British, or defying Congress and the public. Vice President Richard Nixon came to the president's rescue, convincing McCarthy that he had fallen into a partisan trap by writing a letter originally proposed by Democratic senator Stuart Symington. Then Nixon got McCarthy to withdraw the missive before it was officially received by the president. Reporters caught on, but when they asked McCarthy, he lied, saying he had never authorized the letter to be delivered. As for Bobby, he had gotten a lesson in realpolitik. The idealistic young lawyer believed in what the committee was doing and didn't understand why his boss had backed down, since the facts backed him up. When a reporter demanded to know whether he had been to the White House, Kennedy "appeared flustered and asked, 'Did somebody see me go in there?'"

Bobby's role in the shipping investigation earned high marks from most journalists and other commentators, including some who offered their first—and last—words of praise for McCarthy. Drew Pearson, one of McCarthy's earliest and staunchest critics, wrote that the subcommittee "was absolutely right about probing the entire Greek shipping scandal" and should keep pressing. The *New York Times* columnist Arthur Krock said Kennedy had conducted a "Congressional investigation at the highest level, with documentation given for every statement represented as a fact and with conclusions and opinions expressed dispassionately despite the provocations of what is disclosed." What Krock and Pearson didn't say, but was understood, was that Bobby's rigor was the antithesis of his boss's provoke-but-seldom-prove approach. Not bad for a young man who had flunked his law school course on research. McCarthy, meanwhile, bumped Bobby's annual salary from $4,952.20 to $5,334.57— a nice gesture although, even in today's dollars, the total would amount to a modest $47,335.02.

Not everyone was impressed. Winston Churchill's cabinet felt the United States was being predictably isolationist and naïve by not acknowledging how a cutoff in trade with China could harm Hong Kong and England's other Asian outposts and push the Chinese to trade more with the Soviet Bloc. Britain acknowledged that there had been a tenfold jump in exports to China at the start of 1953, but it insisted the rise was temporary, overall shipments were modest, and no goods were weapons-related. America had to understand, the British added, how reliant their island nation was on exports. David Ormsby-Gore, an English diplomat and baron who knew Joe Kennedy and his boys well enough to speculate on patterns in their behavior, was convinced the subcommittee investigation had less to do with Britain's reliability as an ally than with Kennedy clan loyalties: "Deep down Bobby felt that this was a treacherous act by the British and was in line with the history of the way the British had behaved to the Irish people and so on. There was a strong emotional suspicion of Britain and, of course, an anti-colonial attitude which was perfectly natural in America."

Roy Cohn had his own reservations about Bobby's investigation. He said the Allied shipping probe "was so strong and so violently against the President that even McCarthy, who was not one to pull back, thought that this was going a little too far based on the facts in the thing. And he would not back up Bobby insofar as an open break with the White House. . . . [Bobby] was really very militant. I'm not saying I disagreed with his militancy, but he certainly had it."

His eagerness to swipe at Kennedy was not new, but this time Cohn was half right. Bobby was militant—rightfully so—in his pursuit not just of allies who were double-crossing us, but of an Eisenhower administration that had covered it up. Kennedy's official report on the affair, filed in July 1953, argued that "this shocking policy of fighting the enemy on the one hand and trading with him on the other cannot be condoned." In his fealty to McCarthy, however, Bobby failed to appreciate that the State Department and White House were understandably furious that the senator repeatedly questioned their foreign policy, generally on grounds less lofty than with the shipping crisis. Kennedy also bit his tongue when McCarthy caved in to White House pressure to withdraw the letter that Bobby had drafted and the senator had approved. And, as Drew Pearson would point out, when a similar moral quandary came up thirteen years later about America's cutting off aid to countries trading with our battlefield enemy in North Vietnam, a more worldly and, to Pearson at least, a less idealistic Senator Bobby Kennedy voted no.

At the end of July, barely a month after he filed his report on the shipping scandal, Bobby submitted his letter of resignation to the McCarthy subcommittee. It was and wasn't a surprise. He had just started work in mid-January and had not planned to stop that soon. Furthermore, he had nowhere to go. Yet his big investigation was done, and he was unnerved by the office's disarray and his sense that McCarthy might be self-destructing. Frip Flanagan, Bobby's boss and mentor at the subcommittee, had been pushed up to the full committee. J. B. Matthews, an ordained Methodist minister hired to replace Flanagan under the new title of chief of staff, was fired less than three weeks later for publishing an article claiming that Protestant clergy constituted "the largest single group supporting the Communist apparatus in the United States." In early July, all three of the subcommittee's Democrats—Senators John McClellan, Stuart Symington, and Henry Jackson—quit the panel and vowed to stay away until McCarthy gave them a say in how it ran. The chairman's rule by fiat might have been tolerable to Bobby if he had been asked to step into Flanagan's job, something McCarthy had promised him. Kennedy would have been more upset had he known that Jean Kerr, McCarthy's administrative assistant who would soon become the senator's wife, had confided to FBI director J. Edgar Hoover that it would be "unfortunate" if McCarthy tapped Bobby for the post, although she didn't say why and Hoover didn't disagree.

What really scared Bobby was the prospect that with Flanagan gone, there would be nobody to shield him from Roy Cohn. Their relationship had started out sour and quickly turned toxic. The two young lawyers approached the world from opposite poles. Bobby meticulously organized his files, cross-checked depositions, and prepared detailed reports and charts to bolster his findings. By contrast, chaos seemed to follow Roy everywhere. He disdained working out of the subcommittee's crowded suite, preferring a nearby private office building where his desk was stacked high with open folders of scribbled notes. During his reign as chief counsel, phones rang but were not answered, staff filtered in and out without direction, and the confusion was obvious at hearings he staffed. "Most of the investigations were instituted on the basis of some preconceived notion by the chief counsel or his staff members and not on the basis of any information that had been developed," Bobby would say, looking back. "No real spade work that might have destroyed some of their pet theories was ever undertaken." Donald Ritchie, the official historian of the Senate, came to the same conclusion half a century later after reviewing newly opened records of two years of closed-door hearings by Cohn and McCarthy: "After they're finished, after all 500 of these people come in, there's not a single person that McCarthy investigates who goes to jail for perjury or for contempt. . . . Cohn thought he could bully and badger people into confessing and they went off on just wild goose chases in those hearings." Bobby, too, believed in making full use of his investigative powers, but not to the point of bullying and badgering, at least not then.

Two more things got under Kennedy's skin about Cohn. The chief counsel was a homosexual, which was difficult for Bobby to accept. Worse was that Cohn made little effort to hide this fact even as he publicly denied it. In the 1950s, homophobia was ingrained in American culture, and it ran deep in the Kennedy veins. "I think Roy's homosexuality must have bothered Bobby a lot," says Anthony Lewis, a *New York Times* journalist who went to prep school with Cohn and to college with Kennedy and who covered both over the years. "Those were ancient days. . . . Bobby would have been good on gay rights as he was on all such things as soon as somebody told him: 'Hey, these are people.'"

Yet even as Bobby insisted he was quitting the subcommittee simply because of Roy Cohn, nothing about his departure was simple. "When Cohn took complete charge of the staff in June, 1953," he wrote, "I left." In fact, Cohn never took complete charge. Kennedy was slated to report to Matthews when he was named chief of staff on June 22, then to his successor, ex–FBI agent Frank Carr, who was hired after Matthews was fired in early July. And Bobby's letter said his resignation was effective not in June but "as of the close of business July 31," with a story announcing it in the next day's *New York Times*. Although critics would accuse Kennedy of overplaying his conflict with Cohn, understating his time with the controversial McCarthy, and trying to look as if he walked out as a matter of conscience, there was more to his misdirection than that. He likely was doing McCarthy a favor by delaying his official resignation so it would not come at a moment when the subcommittee appeared to be coming unglued. McCarthy had just sacked Matthews, its Democratic members had quit, and maintaining stability—or the appearance of it—was important to the chairman.

When Bobby met with McCarthy to say he was leaving, Kennedy told an interviewer years later, the senator "asked me to stay on for a month. But I said I would have to resign. But he kept me on the payroll for a month." He actually stayed on the payroll for two more months, until August 31, according to Senate records. What work he did in July and August, if any, is unclear, but the "interim" report he finished in late June turned out to be the last one on the Allied shipping situation. He kept secret until after McCarthy died his willingness to delay the timing of his quitting, at which point he began referring to the six months that he worked for the subcommittee instead of the seven that he mentioned in his resignation letter and the seven and a half for which he was paid. To him, the details didn't matter and any obfuscation was a price he willingly paid to stay loyal to his ex-boss.

Bobby's letter of resignation explained that he planned "to enter the private practice of law at an early date," something he never did and never intended to do. "I have enjoyed my work and associations on the

Subcommittee," he wrote to McCarthy. "Please accept my sincere thanks for the many courtesies and kindnesses you have extended to me." The senator's response was even more upbeat, saying "I very much regret seeing you leave" and "I sincerely hope that you will consider coming back later on in the summer."

Letters like these often are window dressing, but in this case they sincerely reflected the bond the senator had formed with his young aide. McCarthy reserved a place for Bobby at his wedding, his dinner table, and his deathbed. Other Kennedy family and friends have downplayed the politically incorrect friendship, but Ethel, who knew it best, neither whitewashes nor sugarcoats. While the public may have thought McCarthy a monster, she says, he actually "was just plain fun. . . . He didn't rant and roar, he was a normal guy." (Cohn, she maintains, truly was monstrous.) Sometimes Bobby would visit the senator at his apartment on Capitol Hill to discuss work. Other times the outings were social, with Ethel and Bobby bringing their toddler daughter Kathleen along. McCarthy "just wanted to hold her. We'd be talking and then he'd say something to her. He was just crazy about her," recalls Ethel. "I have had that kind of bond with somebody else's baby and so I understand that it can happen. It's like falling in love."

That warmth cooled somewhat over the years. As the public perception of McCarthy evolved, so did Bobby's telling of what he said on his way out the door. The *Boston Post* journalist John Kelso was curious, since Kennedy left so soon after the Democratic senators did, so he asked Bobby whether the two were linked. "Although an effort was made in some quarters to bolster the claim that Kennedy, too, had quit in anger," Kelso wrote in 1953, "he himself vehemently denied the allegation." In 1960, three years after McCarthy's death when Bobby was climbing the political ladder, he wrote that "I told McCarthy that I disagreed with the way the Committee was being run, except for the work that Flanagan had done, and that the way they were proceeding I thought it was headed for disaster." Two years later, as he tilted ever more leftward, his explanation grew more colorful: "I told [McCarthy] I thought he was out of his mind and was going to destroy himself. . . . He was on a toboggan. It was so exciting and exhilarating as he went downhill that it didn't matter to him if he hit a tree at the bottom."

No one will ever know just what Kennedy actually told McCarthy in their private exit interview. He may well have warned about Cohn, and he likely let the senator himself off the hook too easily. Casting Cohn as a master manipulator, however true, was also convenient: It let Bobby stay close to McCarthy while distancing himself from the worst of his committee's and subcommittee's excesses. Whatever Bobby's reason for leaving, his timing was just right, since the Wisconsin senator's worst days were just ahead. There are hints that J. Edgar Hoover may have tipped off his friend Joe Kennedy to McCarthy's impending woes, with Joe persuading Bobby it was time to go. That would explain why Bobby quit before lining up another job. Cohn later joked that Bobby owed him a debt of gratitude: "Would Bobby Kennedy have become a liberal icon had he been Joe McCarthy's right hand during his 'witch-hunt.'"

THE NEXT HALF year would be the most tedious in Bobby's twenty-year public life, working for the blandest of ex-presidents. Herbert Hoover is best remembered for two violations of the public good: He ushered in a Great Depression that he seemed incapable of ending, and he rigorously enforced Prohibition at a troubled time when Americans thirsted for a stiff drink. But Presidents Truman and Eisenhower recognized that the mining engineer turned politician knew more than anybody else about efficiency, and they enlisted him to run a blue-ribbon panel aimed at making the government more productive. It was for that noble purpose—in the form of the Commission on Organization of the Executive Branch of the Government—that Bobby signed up in the summer of 1953.

Hoover had been one of Bobby's boyhood heroes, and the former president's portrait would forever occupy a place in Bobby's home, but this job simply didn't engage him.* To compound his misery, Bobby was administrative assistant to one of the commission's most illustrious members: his father. Joe Kennedy was a longtime friend of Hoover, who shared his isolationist views on America's role in the world. It was hard enough for

---

* Bobby admired the "marvelous things" Hoover had accomplished as a mining engineer and in helping Europe after World War I, he told the TV interviewer David Frost in 1968. He also liked that Joe Kennedy had liked Hoover.

Bobby to be indebted to his father for his school admissions and early jobs, but now Joe was Bobby's boss as well. The commission was populated mainly by old men (Hoover had just turned eighty, Joe Kennedy was a spry sixty-four), and Bobby's first assignment was to investigate the Weather Bureau (the only tempests he could forecast were political ones).

Bobby had always had an excess of energy, and while working for Senator McCarthy he had spent it on issues at the heart of the national debate. Now that he was on the sidelines, that steam got bottled up, and the best place to release the pressure was on the athletic field. He did so in nearly heroic style one weekend afternoon just months after he started with Hoover, at a park in Washington, D.C. College students kept hitting baseballs into the middle of a football game Bobby was playing with his brother Ted and their friends. Ted, who was five inches taller than Bobby, faced off against an equally big baseball player, "but Bob broke in and announced that he'd do the fighting. It was like a scene in ancient Rome, with each side putting forth its gladiator," remembered Larry O'Brien, an aide to Senator Jack Kennedy. "It became a bloody brawl, with each man determined to score a knockout. But neither could and finally the fight stopped when they simply couldn't raise their arms any longer."

Bobby had been getting into dustups like that since he was a boy, taking on foes who were beefier than he was but less ferocious. Sometimes it was in the schoolyard, on other occasions in bars. Afterward, no one was ever sure what had set him off, but the fights somehow cleansed him. Now they were happening more often, and it was harder for Bobby to see the risk or to settle down afterward. "That was the period when many people formed their ideas about him—people who didn't know him, who met him in Washington at parties and sometimes found him antagonistic and argumentative; it was because he was frustrated inside," said Lem Billings, Jack's old roommate. "He was filled with so many things he wanted to do, but he felt he wasn't accomplishing anything. . . . He just didn't see his future."

Six and a half months after he started work with the Hoover Commission, he resigned, leaving the weather to take care of itself. Half a year was about the same time Bobby had put in with the McCarthy subcommittee and his other jobs. These short spurts showed a lack of patience— a common failing among his peers, especially those with the financial freedom and political connections to move on quickly. And when the chance opened early in 1954 to return to the action on Capitol Hill and the Subcommittee on Investigations, Bobby jumped. His bosses this time were the Democrats—McClellan, Symington, and Jackson—who a month before had rejoined the panel with a promise from McCarthy that they could hire their own lawyer and play a bigger role in decision making. For McCarthy, the new arrangement ensured that the Senate would give him funds he wanted in order to expand his probes into Communist infiltration of the government. For Bobby, the new job meant a chance to joust again with his bête noire, Roy Cohn, this time from a near-equal position on the other side of the partisan aisle.

The Democrats came back just as McCarthy was raising the stakes in his battle against Communism by challenging the sanctity of the U.S. Army. The senator's special focus was New Jersey's Fort Monmouth, the main research campus for the Army Signal Corps and a linchpin in the command and control of this country's combined armed services. Julius Rosenberg had worked there, and the subcommittee suspected the base was a beehive of spies.* But in mounting this assault on the military, McCarthy made two strategic errors. First, he failed to see that the Cold War was cooling off. The UN Command had signed an armistice in July 1953 with North Korea and China, and many of the same Americans who had backed him in his earlier crusades now were eager for a stand-down with the Soviet Bloc. McCarthy also failed, as he always had, to police the overeager Roy Cohn and his coddled assistant G. David Schine, the scion of a hotel and movie theater magnate who had been working as a committee consultant since the spring of 1953. McCarthy's fealty to Cohn, and Cohn's to Schine, would be the undoing of all three.

Senator McCarthy won the first round on a knockout early in 1954. He made an example of an Army dentist named Irving Peress, who had

---

* McCarthy's probe was spurred in part by reports that material from the Signal Corps labs was turning up in the Soviet Eastern Bloc. That may have been true, but it was also true that the Russians had been U.S. allies during World War II, that they'd openly assigned representatives to the Monmouth labs then, and that as a result—and as a report by the Senate historian concluded years later—"espionage there [was] superfluous" (Executive Sessions, Senate Permanent Subcommittee on Investigations, vol. 1, first session, 1953, xxvii).

invoked the Fifth Amendment in refusing to fill out a loyalty form asking whether he was or had been a member of a subversive organization. Today, that might be seen as a legitimate expression of his rights to free association and privacy, but in the fraught 1950s, loyalty trumped confidentiality, the hint of Communist sympathies could earn one a place on a career-stifling blacklist, and pleading the Fifth was taken as a confession of guilt (McCarthy branded men like Peress "Fifth-Amendment Communists"). Despite that red flag, Peress's bosses had approved his promotion from captain to major and eventually authorized an honorable discharge. It still is unclear whether Peress actually was a Communist (fifty years later he insisted he wasn't "for one minute" while he was in the Army, but he wouldn't say whether he had been before), and the senator was not arguing that a dentist could threaten national security. The point, McCarthy said, was that the military's coddling of Peress—five officers had been involved in his induction, six in his promotion, and thirteen more in his discharge, yet nobody paid proper attention to his unanswered loyalty questions—laid bare the potential for "deliberate Communist infiltration of our Armed Forces." While Bobby returned to the subcommittee too late to weigh in on the Peress probe, in March 1955 he led his own investigation of the dentist, concluding that the Army was guilty of bureaucratic bungling but not of a treasonous breach. In February 1954, however, the question on the lips of every anticommunist American was "Who promoted Peress?"

The Army was not like the Voice of America, the International Information Agency, and other early targets of McCarthy, which lacked the resolve and clout to resist. McCarthy was now slinging his mud at the mighty bastion of the U.S. military. The generals were outraged and their commander in chief was, too. And when McCarthy accused Eisenhower of being a Johnny-come-lately not just to the Peress case, but to the wider "necessity of getting rid of Communists," opinion seemed to turn on the wild and willful senator. The CBS newsman Edward R. Murrow devoted all thirty minutes of his *See It Now* broadcast on March 9, 1954, to exposing McCarthy's overreaching. "The line between investigating and persecuting is a very fine one, and the junior senator from Wisconsin has stepped over it repeatedly," Murrow warned. "This is no time for men who oppose Senator McCarthy's methods to stay silent—or for those who approve." Two days later the Army delivered an even more damaging volley when it leaked to senators and the press a blistering thirty-four-page memo laying out dozens of cases in which Cohn and Schine had applied pressure—including a reported threat to "wreck the Army"—unless it gave a commission to Schine, who was due to report to his draft board. When that effort failed, the McCarthy aides pressed for weekend passes for Schine, clearance for him to serve his time with the subcommittee rather than the armed services, and other privileges never dreamed of for a buck private. The Army had provided a motive for McCarthy's attacks that everyone could understand and even his defenders found offensive: revenge.

Bobby was on the sidelines for those battles, but he was back in the spotlight for another high-profile confrontation the same day the Army unveiled its memo. McCarthy was investigating Annie Lee Moss, a black mother of four and widow who worked as a communications clerk with the Signal Corps. Like Peress, Moss was presented as a case study in the military's cosseting of Communists—but this time it wasn't the witness who came out looking the fool, it was the interrogator, Roy Cohn. In his haste to point fingers, Cohn said Moss had been visited by a white "Communist organizer" named Robert Hall, apparently confusing him with a black union organizer of the same name whom Moss said she did know. A reporter who recognized the slipup tipped off Bobby, who tipped off the Democrats, who charged that Cohn was inept in miscasting Moss, a loyal American, as a subversive. The press recognized that this was more than just normal partisan sniping. A week after his earlier broadside against the Wisconsin senator, Murrow made him the focus of another show, this time proclaiming Moss's innocence and McCarthy's guilt. Bobby had finally succeeded in exposing Cohn's recklessness, although in the process he exposed McCarthy's malfeasance for relying so heavily on Cohn.*

---

* Four years later, evidence would emerge proving McCarthy and Cohn partly right—Moss was listed on the Communist Party rolls as they had charged, although whether she was a security risk continues to be debated—but by that time the senator was dead, Cohn was long gone from the limelight, and Moss had become as much a symbol of Cohn's and McCarthy's callousness as Peress had been of their self-righteous whistle-blowing (Friedman, "Strange Career of Annie Lee Moss," *Journal of American History*, September 2007).

There was one more reverberation for Bobby from the Annie Lee Moss affair. In the wake of her testimony, Senator Jackson asked Bobby to visit FBI headquarters and look at its file on Moss. It was his first encounter with his father's old friend and his future nemesis J. Edgar Hoover, and neither the FBI director nor the Senate aide would forget their strained introduction. Hoover said the file was off-limits to the committee Democrats; Bobby persisted, knowing that the agency had been sharing information with McCarthy and the Republicans. The FBI chief wasn't used to being second-guessed, and he advised his senior staff that "the attitude of Kennedy in this matter clearly shows need for absolute circumspection in any conversation with him." Bobby also took notice, later writing, "They lied to me. . . . They were making information available to the committee, and they were telling me they weren't."

By the end it was Cohn, Schine, and McCarthy who were on trial, not Moss, Peress, or the Army. The Eisenhower administration decided this was the place to take a stand against McCarthy, and it found an unlikely ally in the wily and influential minority leader of the Senate, Lyndon Johnson, who had been advising liberal Democrats not to pounce until the Wisconsin lawmaker did something that offended conservatives, too. Putting the Army in his crosshairs turned the tide. The public might have accepted that individual dentists and teletype operators were fellow travelers or party members, but the notion that the U.S. Army was a nest of Communist moles strained credulity.

The subcommittee held a series of inquiries between April and June 1954 that became known as the Army-McCarthy Hearings. Gavel-to-gavel coverage on two national television networks made these the most widely watched and riveting sessions ever held by Congress. The same cameras that had helped make Joe McCarthy into a national figurehead now helped Americans see the extent to which he had overpromised and underperformed. McCarthy was temporarily relieved of his chairmanship and Cohn of his role as counsel. McCarthy suggested that Bobby run the investigation, but acting chairman Karl Mundt of South Dakota insisted they hire someone new and neutral. Ultimately, the lawyer the public would remember most was Army Special Counsel Joseph Nye Welch, who came from a Brahmin firm in Boston and tangled repeatedly with the senator from Grand Chute. Using his usual method of histrionic accusation, McCarthy called into question the patriotism of a young associate of Welch's who was no longer involved in the case. Welch froze in horror before the cameras. "Until this moment, Senator, I think I never really gauged your cruelty or your recklessness," the Boston barrister exploded in a singular moment that proved McCarthy had met his match. "Let us not assassinate this lad further. . . . Have you no sense of decency sir, at long last? Have you left no sense of decency?"

It was a question much of the country was asking by then. Edward R. Murrow's hard-hitting television exposés had dented McCarthy's armor, as had enterprising newspaper reporters like Philip Potter of the Baltimore *Sun* and columnist Drew Pearson. Over thirty-five days, as many as twenty million Americans watched the 187 hours of televised hearings. The more they heard of Cohn's antics in trying to cushion the Army duties of his sidekick Schine, the less they trusted his charges against the military. The more they saw the senator ignore not just parliamentary procedure but common courtesy, the less they were willing to listen to or believe anything he said.

One thing the cameras could not capture was how the simmering animosities between Cohn and Kennedy were reaching a full boil. Newspaper reporters saw that close-up at the end of a long day of hearings in mid-June, and they couldn't say enough about it. Bobby had been feeding his Democratic senators questions aimed not just at tripping up Cohn and Schine but at exposing them as fools and liars. Schine had already shown his indifference to facts in a monograph he wrote for the subcommittee that put the Russian Revolution in the wrong year and confused Marx with Lenin and Stalin with Trotsky. This time Senator Jackson, at Bobby's coaching, ridiculed Schine's plan for waging psychological warfare against the Communists by enlisting church leaders in a battle for the souls of men and, if that failed, appealing to less noble instincts through the dissemination of Hollywood pinups. When the hearing recessed, Cohn strode up to Kennedy and, according to Bobby, threatened to "get" Jackson by revealing something he had written that was "favorably inclined toward Communists." Kennedy: "Don't you make any warnings to us about Democratic senators." Cohn: "I'll make any warnings to you that I want to—any time, anywhere. Do you want to fight right here?"

Bobby hardly needed more reasons to despise Roy, but Cohn gave him one nonetheless when he tried to smear Kennedy's younger brother Ted with unfounded rumors about Ted's association with "pinkos." For his part, Cohn had his own new gripe: that just before the Army-McCarthy Hearings, Bobby had told Mary Driscoll, McCarthy's longtime secretary, "I couldn't find Joe, but I want you to give him a message. In these hearings, I'm going to do nothing to hurt him. In fact, I'm going to protect him every way I can, and I still feel exactly the same way as I always have about him. But I'm really going to get that little son-of-a-bitch Cohn." Cohn said Driscoll repeated the remarks to McCarthy and then to him, "and any doubts I had as to where Bobby stood were crystal clear." As for his invitation to fisticuffs, Cohn said it was fortunate for him that Senator Mundt had intervened because "I don't think my physical condition, not being a mountain climber or running kayaks up and down the Colorado River or something, I don't think I would have been too much of a match for him."

Bobby threw his punches in ways that Cohn could not see but surely felt as much as if the two had done battle with bare knuckles. He leaked to the press embarrassing material on Cohn and Schine, including a letter Roy had asked subcommittee staff to sign attesting to their loyalty to Senator McCarthy. He tossed lifelines to Annie Lee Moss and other beleaguered witnesses. And when the hearings were done, Bobby was the one who rigorously reviewed every word of testimony. To make sure he got his final report right, he did what the Kennedys would always do, enlisting the help of a more experienced collaborator—in this case James M. Landis, the brilliant former chairman of the Securities and Exchange Commission and a longtime friend of Joe Kennedy's. The two closeted themselves in a rented cottage near the Kennedy home in Hyannis and produced a seventy-eight-page summary of the evidence that was finetuned and evenhanded enough that the subcommittee Republicans accepted everything but the damning conclusions for their own final report, instead of relying on less complete material assembled by their own lawyer. Even McCarthy was impressed by Bobby's fairness.

The full Senate rendered a decisive verdict on its errant colleague. Zeroing in on his failure to cooperate with two panels of senators who had been investigating him—behavior that his fellow lawmakers said was "contrary to senatorial traditions"—they voted sixty-seven to twenty-two to rebuke the Wisconsin Republican. McCarthy scored a semantic victory when "condemn" was substituted for "censure," and a substantive one when no mention was made of his anticommunist jihad. Still, as the condemned senator himself noted, "I wouldn't exactly call it a vote of confidence."* Cohn already was gone, resigning shortly after the hearings concluded rather than waiting to be fired. All the Democrats and half the Republicans present elected to admonish McCarthy, but one name was noticeably missing: Bobby's brother Jack. Recovering from major back surgery, he excused himself from weighing in against a family friend who remained popular in Catholic-heavy Massachusetts. With Bobby's help, JFK had prepared a speech admonishing McCarthy—but only for his abusive language and the misdeeds of his staff.

The roller-coaster ride with Joe McCarthy left its mark on Bobby as it did on America. It got his blood flowing and his mind churning, a welcome change after six months in the slow lane with Herbert Hoover. He made a mortal enemy of Roy Cohn, whom he never forgot or forgave. He had his first brush with legendary personalities who would figure prominently in his life—from Richard Nixon and Lyndon Johnson, who belatedly orchestrated McCarthy's downfall, to J. Edgar Hoover, who was already compiling secret files on this third Kennedy son. Bobby had

---

* History has been even less forgiving, concluding that McCarthy overstated if not fabricated his charges of a Communist conspiracy, a verdict that Stan Evans argues is not merely unjust but the opposite of the truth. Documents he unearthed from American and Soviet archives demonstrate that McCarthy was not a reckless blacklister, says Evans, a journalist and pioneer of the conservative movement. The Russians, Evans maintains, were in fact relentless at infiltrating the U.S. government; high-level American officials covered up those embarrassing breaches, and in the end it was McCarthy himself who was blacklisted by liberal reporters and historians.

Many conservatives, anxious to redeem not just the Wisconsin senator but their own tough stands during the Cold War, have embraced Evans's thesis, which he laid out in meticulous detail in a 672-page book published in 2007. Others, however, say McCarthy did irreparable harm to conservative ideals and deserves the repudiation he got from his contemporaries and those who came after. "McCarthy besmirched the honorable cause of anti-communism. He discredited *legitimate* efforts to counter Soviet subversion of American institutions," William Bennett, secretary of education under President Ronald Reagan and White House drug czar under President George H. W. Bush, wrote in a book published the same year as Evans's. "From this point on, it would only be necessary for disloyal people or groups to yell 'McCarthyism' to distract public attention from real problems." (Evans, *Blacklisted by History*; author interview with Evans; and Bennett, *America: The Last Best Hope*.)

picked up bad habits, like believing the nation was overrun with enemies within, and good ones, like investigating his adversaries with rigor and care. He was back on center stage now, and he would stay there for the rest of his life.

———

HIS TIME WITH Joe McCarthy was the most controversial chapter of Bobby's life precisely because it was so counterintuitive. Neither his detractors nor his defenders could understand how this most revered of progressive Democrats could have jump-started his career as a protégé of the most reviled of reactionary Republicans. Each side settled for answers that reinforced its own simplistic vision of Bobby and conveniently distorted his record.

His enemies have unfairly saddled him with too much of the McCarthy legacy. "Bobby's first investigatory chore for McCarthy had to do with the alleged homosexual influx into the State Department," the conservative columnist Victor Lasky wrote in his RFK biography *The Myth and the Man*. It was a fiction repeated until it was accepted as fact. In truth, McCarthy held a single hearing on the issue and the record makes clear that Bobby was not there. The left was even harsher, with I. F. Stone calling Bobby's investigation of Allied shipping an example of McCarthyism at its worst. In fact, as most of Stone's fellow journalists acknowledged, that probe was just the sort of meticulous research that happened too seldom at McCarthy's subcommittee. Kennedy couldn't win: He was bashed as tone-deaf when he stood by his friend Joe McCarthy, and condemned as backstabbing when he did not.*

It is unclear where the rumor began about McCarthy being godfather to Bobby's firstborn, Kathleen. Authors and journalists echoed it often enough that they stopped footnoting it, but they continued citing it as the clearest sign of how close Kennedy was to McCarthy. Even Kathleen's mother, Ethel, asked recently whether it was true, said, "He was. I think

---

* One unlikely fan was conservative commentator Stan Evans, McCarthy's most passionate defender, who respected Bobby's hard work for the Wisconsin senator as well as his unflinching allegiance. "To the end of McCarthy's life," Evans said in an interview shortly before his own death in 2015, "Bobby Kennedy was devoted to Joe McCarthy" (Author interview with Evans).

he was." Kathleen, who would enter politics herself and know firsthand
the stigma of being associated with Joe McCarthy, has "no idea" where
the rumor came from but double-checked her christening certificate to
confirm that it was false. "It's bizarro," she says, adding that her actual
godfather was Daniel Walsh, a professor at Manhattanville College of
the Sacred Heart, Ethel's alma mater, and a counselor to the Catholic
poet and mystic Thomas Merton.

Bobby's defenders have been equally footloose with the facts about
the Kennedy-McCarthy connection, trying to wash the Wisconsin senator out of Bobby's record. Kenneth O'Donnell, Bobby's Harvard roommate and lifelong friend and colleague, insisted that Bobby "didn't know
Joe McCarthy from a cord of wood" when he went to work for him in
1953, and "even the supposed links between Joe Kennedy senior and
McCarthy are exaggerated." O'Donnell's claim might have been convincing if other friends didn't remember things so differently. The Washington lawyer Barrett Prettyman recalled McCarthy speaking in 1951 at
his and Kennedy's law school, then spending the evening at Kennedy's
home. Years before that, when Bobby was an undergraduate, "he and
Ken O'Donnell would hotly debate about McCarthy. Bobby was all alone
in defending him," said Sam Adams, who played football with Kennedy
and O'Donnell at Harvard.

Others offered more nuanced justifications for why Bobby embraced
McCarthy. To Edwin Guthman, a journalist who became Bobby's press
secretary and crony, it was all about pity—"pity for an acquaintance
who could be a pleasant companion but who had made a ruin of his career; pity for the men and women and their families whom McCarthy
had forced needlessly and unfairly to live under a cloud." He was right
about the former, but it was only belatedly and grudgingly that Bobby
even acknowledged those victimized by McCarthyism and McCarthy. Ted
Kennedy said Bobby went to work for the subcommittee at a time when
"the extent of McCarthy's vile exploitation of anticommunist hysteria
had not yet fully registered with him or indeed the country." The reality
is that it had registered by then with journalists, Presidents Eisenhower
and Truman, and certainly with the targets of McCarthy's inquisitions.
Bobby's daughter Kerry, meanwhile, says her father "vociferously objected to and fought throughout his four months with McCarthy—he

fought against the senator and against Roy Cohn. . . . And after four months, which is not a long time, he left, and he was immediately hired by the Democrats to be their counsel in stopping McCarthy." She is right about Cohn, if not McCarthy, whom Kennedy explicitly vowed to protect as he went after Cohn, and she understates by nearly half the time her father worked for the senator.

Bobby himself felt less inclined to rationalize or explain. His world was divided into friends and fiends, white hats and black, and pariah pal Joe McCarthy would always be one of his righteous ones. "The man is dead," he told one reporter who pushed him to separate himself from McCarthy, "and I'm not going to do it." He preferred not to talk about that part of his past even inside his own family. Yet he had maintained a relationship with the senator from Wisconsin even after a scarlet letter of condemnation had transformed him from the country's most talked-about political figure to its most shunned. Kennedy kept McCarthy in the information loop after the Democrats took over the subcommittee, and he visited the senator about a week before he died.* Most telling, a year after McCarthy's colleagues rebuked him, Bobby could not bring himself to listen to the journalist who had helped expose the flaws in the senator and his movement.

The setting was a Junior Chamber of Commerce celebration in Louisville in January 1955, when Bobby's Allied shipping investigation had won him a cherished place on the chamber's list of ten outstanding young men of the previous year. The keynote speaker was CBS's Murrow. "They had us ten at the top of some bleacher, and when Edward R. Murrow got up to speak, Bobby—I was sitting next to him—started scrambling down the back of the latticework like a monkey, down to the ground," recalls Ernest Hollings, another honoree who would later serve alongside Bobby in the U.S. Senate. "He said, 'I wouldn't be caught dead listening to that son of a bitch.'" At the time, Hollings didn't understand what he meant, but he learned afterward that Kennedy resented Mur-

---

* McCarthy died of acute hepatitis, which was exacerbated by his chronic alcoholism, which may have been exacerbated by manic depression. Bobby watched him slide downhill to the point where he came to hearings drunk and, near the end, couldn't stand up straight and appeared to be "in a trance. His conversation was not intelligible." (Herman, *Joseph McCarthy*, 329–31; Schlesinger, *Robert Kennedy and His Times*, 172–73.)

row for helping topple his friend McCarthy. And it wasn't just Murrow: Bobby kept a list of McCarthy's early enemies, including his brother-in-law Sargent Shriver, and shunned them in ways that made clear he had never quite forgiven them.

Grudges are commonplace in politics, but there was a particular hypocrisy in this one: It ignored Bobby's own rather spectacular role in toppling the senator he had embraced as a mentor and friend. It wasn't only that he had gone to work for McCarthy's Democratic foes. Bobby fed those senators questions on Annie Lee Moss and other controversies that embarrassed not just Roy Cohn and David Schine but their boss, and he meticulously compiled the evidence the full Senate used to call McCarthy to account. Had it been anyone else whose behavior he was critiquing, Bobby would have been quick to pin a name on it: Judas. But he couldn't face his own deep-seated conflicts—between instincts of loyalty and veracity, and between his ideology and his humanity—so he overcompensated by lashing out at others who were more transparent and consistent in opposing the rabble-rouser from Grand Chute.

When he got word that the senator had died in the spring of 1957, Bobby sent his staff home for the day. Kennedy's secretary said that was the first time she ever saw tears in his eyes. "It was all very difficult for me as I feel that I have lost an important part of my life," he explained in his diary. Four days later he joined one hundred priests, two thousand well-wishers, and Vice President Nixon at a pontifical requiem mass for McCarthy at St. Matthew's Roman Catholic Cathedral in Washington. Then he followed the flag-draped mahogany coffin to a rare state funeral in the Senate chamber, listening alongside seventy senators as the chaplain lauded McCarthy's determination "to expose cunning foes who under cowardly cover plot the betrayal of our freedom." The next morning, while Jack stayed home, Bobby honored his former boss and friend by flying to Wisconsin for his burial.

Yet so strong was the new consensus that McCarthy had been a demagogue if not a liar that even Bobby retreated slightly over the years. In Appleton, he preferred to quietly mourn from the choir loft, out of the media spotlight. On a TV news show in 1964, in the midst of his New York Senate campaign in which McCarthy was anathema to most of the electorate, Bobby sought to downplay his role with the Permanent Subcommittee on Investigations: "I saw other investigations taking place in which I had no part, of which I didn't approve. I didn't approve of the procedure. So after working with the committee for approximately five months, I went to Senator McCarthy and said I disagreed with the way the committee was being handled." By the time Bobby ran for president in 1968, he had a convenient new spin on his tenure with McCarthy: "When my complaints to the Senator about the reckless procedures employed in investigations were ignored, I submitted my resignation and, in fact, wrote the minority report which censured the senator." It was true—and it was the first time he had acknowledged, even to himself, his part in his friend's undoing.

In later years Kennedy also would be the one railing against attaching the label of traitor to government workers, or anyone else in a land of free speech, by virtue of their membership in an organization or party. The more mature Bobby would relate not to the rhetoric of a demagogue but to its victims. He would acknowledge rather than justify his earlier errors of judgment and method, be it on Vietnam or on civil rights. But not in this unfledged and boldfaced stage, when his conduct hinted at the worst as well as the best of what would come later. And not with someone who had befriended his family and himself the way Joe McCarthy did.

What Bobby Kennedy couldn't see then, and possibly ever, was that what made Joe McCarthy dangerous was not just the senator's badgering tactics and reckless staffers like Roy Cohn. It was the senator himself. He was a bully and a con man. The state of the nation in the early 1950s was one of dread—of Joseph Stalin, of atomic spies like the Rosenbergs, and of free nations falling like dominoes as Communists took over the planet—and McCarthy masterfully manipulated those fears. He wantonly ruined careers and lives. His line—"McCarthyism is Americanism with its sleeves rolled [up]"—was irresistible, and so, to believers like Bobby, were his coarse charm and bravado.

For Bobby to repudiate McCarthy would have meant parting ways with his father, who was so much like the senator. Both were passionate about their families and their particularized visions of America. Both saw things in Bobby that few did back then, from a willingness to work harder than anyone else to his standing true to unfashionable ideals.

Both were less insightful about their own shortcomings and how they were hurting Bobby even as they were trying to help. Bobby's loyalty to Joe McCarthy ultimately grew out of his devotion to Joe Kennedy—and to the end Bobby defended his friend as he did his father.

The truth is that he had always been of two minds about the controversial senator. "I liked him and yet at times he was terribly heavy-handed," Bobby said. "He was a very complicated character. His whole method of operation was complicated because he would get a guilty feeling and get hurt after he had blasted somebody. He wanted so desperately to be liked. He was so thoughtful and yet so unthoughtful in what he did to others. He was sensitive and yet insensitive. He didn't anticipate the results of what he was doing. He was very thoughtful of his friends, and yet he could be so cruel to others." It was precisely what people would say over the years about Bobby.

Chapter 2

CRUSADING

T HE TWO MEN were like dogs itching for a fight, teeth bared, sniffing one another from head to tail and ready to snap. Each was keenly aware of the other's standing and sway, although neither would admit wanting to be at what was billed as a get-acquainted dinner. They had never even said hello before, and never would again on anything approaching friendly terms. Yet there they were that snowy February evening in 1957, hovering at a long table set for three in a tony suburb of Washington. Both already understood their fates would be linked, which is why they took time afterward to record in telling detail their recollections of the gathering. And when it was finished, the two would disagree over just about everything that was said and done during their two hours together.

On one side of the table sat James Riddle Hoffa, a top lieutenant in the International Brotherhood of Teamsters, who knew his union president, Dave Beck, was about to self-destruct—knew because he almost certainly had leaked the most incriminating evidence of Beck's wrongdoing. On the other side was Robert Francis Kennedy, the Senate investigator to whom Hoffa had fed that dirt, and who just hours before had confirmed that Hoffa had planted a spy on Kennedy's staff. The only other person present was Eddie Cheyfitz, a smooth-tongued Washington lawyer and fixer who had worked for the Teamsters and was hosting the dinner at his home in hopes, he said, that each guest would leave less wary of the other.

"Cheyfitz kept telling me that Hoffa was a good influence. . . . He said Hoffa would answer any questions I had and was anxious to talk to me," Kennedy said later. Hoffa was getting similar advice to give Kennedy a chance: "I said, 'For what?' [Cheyfitz] said, 'He'd like to talk to you.' I said, 'I got nothing to talk to him about.'"

Hoffa greeted Kennedy with a handshake that was strong and firm, but "immediately I was struck by how short he is—only five feet five and a half," remembered Kennedy, who at five nine didn't tower over many men. Cheyfitz had a drink and offered one to his guests; both refused, Hoffa because he never touched alcohol, Kennedy because he drank sparingly and only with friends. The talk at dinner was limited to things that didn't matter and wouldn't make either man feel he had given ground. "I do to others what they do to me, only worse," Hoffa said matter-of-factly. Bobby joked that "maybe I should have worn my bulletproof vest." When they were done eating Cheyfitz's roast beef they moved to the living room, Kennedy standing in front of the fireplace while Hoffa sat on the sofa. Again, the talk was halting and more about the past than what lay ahead. What little information Jimmy volunteered about his union was, according to Bobby, "a complete fabrication." Cheyfitz's détente was not to be.

At 9:30 Ethel telephoned for Bobby. "She probably called to see if you're still alive," Hoffa deadpanned. In a voice meant for everyone to hear, Kennedy said, "I'm still alive, dear. If you hear a big explosion, I probably won't be." Then he made his apologies for leaving early. "As I was going out the door, Hoffa said: 'Tell your wife I'm not as bad as everyone thinks I am,'" Bobby wrote in his memoir. "I laughed. Jimmy Hoffa had a sense of humor. He must have laughed himself as he said it. In view of all I already knew, I felt that he was worse than anybody said he was. . . ."

"On my way home I thought of how often Hoffa had said he was tough; that he destroyed employers, hated policemen and broke those who stood in his way. . . . When a grown man sat for an evening and talked continuously about his toughness, I could only conclude that he was a bully hiding behind a façade."

Hoffa's renderings of the evening were even more florid. He, too, used their handshake to measure "what kind of fellow I got," and Kennedy's fingertip delivery came up wanting: "I said to myself, 'Here's a fella thinks he's doing me a favor by talking to me.'" The rest of the evening reinforced that impression. "The only word that described him is 'condescending,' " Jimmy wrote in his first autobiography. "He asked me numerous personal questions: How much money did I make? How did I happen to get into the union? Why hadn't I tried to go to college? Clearly he was puzzled over the fact that a kid from a poor family, lacking education, could rise to the top of the largest union in the nation."

Five years later, in his second memoir, Hoffa remembered new details: " 'I'd like to talk to Hoffa alone,' Kennedy told Cheyfitz almost as if he was speaking to the butler. 'I came here to get some things straight in my mind,' Kennedy said after Cheyfitz left the room. 'That's okay with me,' I told him." Bobby insisted the Teamsters were infested with racketeers. Jimmy begged to differ: "We don't, absolutely do not and never have had, any underworld connections." Then, out of nowhere, Kennedy laid down a challenge: " 'Hoffa, I'll just bet that I can beat you at Indian hand wrestling.' "

"I leaned back in my chair and looked at him as if he was crazy," Jimmy recalled. "I couldn't believe he was serious but he stood up, loosened his necktie, took off his jacket, and rolled up his sleeve. . . . Like taking candy from a baby, I flipped his arm over and cracked his knuckles on to the top of the table. It was strictly no contest and he knew it. But he had to try again. Same results. . . . He just got up, his face red as fire, rolled down his sleeve, put on his jacket, and walked out of the room. He didn't even stay for dinner. I'm damn certain in my heart that Robert F. Kennedy became my mortal enemy that night."

He was correct about the outcome if not the timing. Their bad blood began even earlier and would stain both men's lives until each died prematurely at the hands of an assassin. Given the influence each wielded, even at that formative point in their careers, the feud would become one of the defining relationships of America in the 1950s and stretching into the '60s. Hoffa was on his way to taking over the Teamsters, and Kennedy was one of the few people capable of slowing his rise. It was Big Labor versus Big Government at a moment when both exercised more power than they ever had or would.

His nearly three years busting racketeers and chasing Hoffa would define Bobby in the public mind even more than the work with Joe McCarthy that he went out of his way to soft-pedal. To fans, this was Bobby finding his path as a missionary. He unraveled layer upon layer of union fraud and battled labor bosses on behalf of a besieged rank and file. To doubters, it was young Kennedy applying the worst lessons of McCarthyism. He ridiculed witnesses who relied on the Fifth Amendment and got branded with a label of ruthless that he would never escape. Both were half right. He was harnessing the conviction as a crusading reformer that would mark his public career, but he was doing it with a single-mindedness and self-righteousness that would earn him legions of enemies as well as admirers. The notion of nuance still eluded him. There remained, at this second critical stage of his career, a fine line between Bobby the white knight and Bobby the zealot.

––––––––

BOBBY HAD REJOINED the Permanent Subcommittee on Investigations in February 1954, three years before his get-to-know-you dinner with Hoffa, taking up the newly created post of counsel to subcommittee Democrats in a Senate still controlled by Republicans. A year later, when the Democrats took back the Senate and the subcommittee, Bobby's life suddenly got better. His side now controlled the hearings and the choice of villains and vices to target. McCarthy remained a member but had been defanged the day the Senate condemned him. The senator who mattered most now was Chairman John McClellan, a crusty, conservative fifty-eight-year-old Arkansan who was as straitlaced as McCarthy was peacockish. Like McCarthy, McClellan let his top lawyer run the show day to day, which suited Bobby so well that he stayed for a total of five and a half years. That was longer than any job he had held, or any he would have later.

McClellan grew close enough to Kennedy during those years that he would liken him to a son, but it was Bobby's actual father who cinched this posting, as he had earlier ones. "I want you to give my son a job. I think it would be good exposure for him—push along his career," the elder Kennedy told McClellan. How much he wanted it was clear in the checks Joe made out to the senator. Senate secretary Bobby Baker says it was $50,000 a year, starting before Bobby graduated from law school and paid as a retainer to McClellan's law firm in Little Rock. McClellan, in a letter to Joe Kennedy seven months after Bobby began his new job, didn't mention an amount but said, "I am grateful for the assistance you gave me in my recent campaign for re-election. You were most kind and generous to do it."

The first order of business for the new subcommittee majority was to clean up old business from when it was under McCarthy's control. In March, Bobby opened a fresh set of hearings into the Army's promotion of the dentist Irving Peress, documenting forty-eight instances of the Army's having mishandled the case but adding that they were not "inspired by subversive interests," as McCarthy had alleged. He also sifted through McCarthy's files on Communist subterfuge in defense installations, again finding the evidence thin. He assured a newspaper reporter that his panel was not "a whit less interested in rooting Communists out of government than it was when Senator McCarthy ran the show." But his actions belied his promise. Mere months after McClellan and Bobby took over, the subcommittee reverted to its pre-McCarthy mission: rooting out government fraud and waste, a task especially appealing to Senate Democrats with a Republican president running that government.

Probes like those seldom cracked the headlines, largely because they were boring. The case of Air Force secretary Harold Talbott broke the mold. He had used his Pentagon stationery and influence to drum up business for a company of efficiency experts in which he had been a partner and his family still owned an interest. Bobby learned about the conflict of interest from Charles Bartlett, a Kennedy friend and Washington correspondent for the *Chattanooga Times*. The committee counsel was deterred neither by his senators' admiration of Talbott nor by the fact that the sixty-seven-year-old secretary was part of Joe Kennedy's social set in Palm Beach. "I talked to Bobby about doing a sort of joint investigation, which we did. He used the committee's facilities, and I used what *I* could," recalled Bartlett. "We finally got to a hearing, which was highly dramatic because there was not a Senator who supported what we were doing. . . . It was only Bobby's persistence that made a success of the hearings, which finally broke in such a way that the President had to request Mr. Talbott's resignation." Bartlett walked away with the 1956 Pulitzer Prize for National Reporting, while Bobby notched a reputation as a bulldog auditor and prosecutor.

Rose Kennedy was surprised by—and proud of—her son's inquiry and its outcome. "I can't imagine Bob investigating some one as old &

matured & as social as Talbott," she wrote her husband in France in July
1955. "You would eat it up." He did, as reflected in his letter to Ethel that
same month: "We have been reading in the papers over here about
Bobby and Talbott and also the foreign radio stations have carried the
Peress summation, so Bobby is gradually earning a place in the sun that
he so well deserves."

Bobby and his team claimed a number of scalps in addition to Talbott's. Their hearings ended the careers of Interstate Commerce Commission chairman Hugh Cross (possible influence peddling) and
Assistant Secretary of Defense Robert Tripp Ross (millions in military
contracts went to his wife). But some witnesses he accused pointed the
finger back at him. Mella Hort, a former government contract administrator, testified that she had confessed to wrongdoing only after Bobby
and an aide "closeted" her in a "hot room" where she was "browbeaten,
badgered and kicked around" to the point where "I'd have sworn I put
the crack in the Liberty Bell." Kennedy, she said, "can be sweet as sugar,
and then the next moment—bam." On its own, Hort's testimony would
seem self-serving, but it reflected a pattern with Bobby, according to
Ralph de Toledano, a conservative syndicated columnist who tallied the
purported misdeeds in his book *RFK: The Man Who Would Be President*.
"Bobby," de Toledano wrote, "had demonstrated once more that he was
dedicated to the Kennedy precept: The important thing is to win."

Bobby never denied wanting to come out on top, although he never
understood how slippery the slope was between fervor and fanaticism.
When he worked late into the night, it went without saying that his staff
would as well. He ran instead of walked up stairs. He pre-interviewed
witnesses to avoid the kinds of embarrassing surprises during public
hearings that had plagued Roy Cohn and Senator McCarthy. That kind
of meticulousness and intensity was built into Bobby's DNA. People increasingly understood what Joe Kennedy meant when he said, admir-
ingly, that "when Bobby hates you, you stay hated." Invited to a
testimonial dinner for his old adversary Cohn, Bobby declined, writing,
"It is my feeling that being anti-Communist does not automatically excuse a lack of integrity in every other facet of life."

Such ferocity made some journalists like de Toledano into lifelong
critics, but it won over many who saw Kennedy and McClellan evolving

into the most effective spotlight team on Capitol Hill. Under Bobby, "the committee has plowed into some remarkable chapters of misdoings— numerous charges of graft and corruption in the handling of Government contracts for military supplies, a charge that public office was used for private gain," Cabell Phillips wrote in a long profile in *The New York Times*. "Kennedy is the meticulous researcher and compiler of evidence; McClellan the shrewd and implacable cross-examiner. Between them they make a great deal of sense and a great deal of progress on whatever chore the Senate assigns to them." Clark Mollenhoff, a journalist who would win a Pulitzer Prize for his coverage of the union rackets, went a step further: "No history of American labor can be written that does not include an account of the dramatic nine-year period in which a stern-faced senator from Arkansas and a boyish-appearing lawyer from Boston rocked the worlds of labor and politics."

Nobody started out more skeptical about Kennedy during those Senate staff years than William O. Douglas, the most impassioned civil libertarian ever to sit on the Supreme Court. He anguished over Bobby's apparent disdain for the Fifth Amendment protection against self-incrimination: "I didn't like to see this committee put a man on the stand just to see how many times they could get him to say, 'I invoke the Fifth Amendment.'" He thought Bobby was "very aggressive," "always overcompensating," and not the kind of person one would choose to spend extended time with. So when Joe Kennedy suggested that Douglas take Bobby along on his trip to the Soviet Union, the justice reacted by looking for a way not to. Douglas found Joe "a crusty reactionary and a difficult man," but he knew the critical role the Kennedy patriarch had played in getting President Roosevelt to appoint him first to the Securities and Exchange Commission, then to the high court. Joe also served as "a kind of father image" for her husband, recalled Mercedes Douglas, his wife at the time. "Bill would do anything for Joe."

And so, hours after Bobby completed his hearings on Air Force Secretary Talbott in the summer of 1955, the young investigator ran to catch a plane to Paris, then another to Tehran, where he met Douglas. From there the two headed off by car, then ship, finally arriving in Baku, the biggest city on the Caspian Sea. Douglas had interrupted a globe-trotting trip with Mercedes, his bride of six months, for the detour with Bobby.

For the next six weeks they toured factories, libraries, and any place they could talk their way into throughout Turkmenistan, Uzbekistan, and other outposts of Soviet rule. The unlikely duo of the fifty-six-year-old justice and his twenty-nine-year-old ward were the first westerners and one of the stranger sights most of the locals had seen.

The interlude itself said a lot about Bobby. It was the kind of break only someone with Kennedy resources and contacts could consider, since it meant taking two months off from his relatively new job, paying out of his own pocket for transportation and other expenses, and having as his only companion one of the most influential men in America. It also was just the sort of excursion Joe Kennedy had hoped for, with Bobby traveling in the rough and seeing for himself the post-Stalin Soviet state. Joe considered adventures like that better training than his boys would get in college or a job, and he foresaw dividends, as he wrote Bobby: "I think that the value of the trip, besides adding stature to your background, is the article and lectures you might give on it. . . . As I have said a thousand times, things don't happen, they are made to happen in the public relations field." To make sure things did happen, Joe also wrote to the Boston public relations maven Eddie Dunn: "When [Bobby] returns from this trip through Russia's provinces he will have a background that will need some building up. . . . I would like you to give some consideration to it and I am enclosing my check for $1000 as a retainer. I hope this will be satisfactory."

Joe got all that he paid for. *The New York Times* printed seven stories on Bobby's travels, starting before he left and ending with a picture of him arriving home with Ethel, who met him in Moscow. The next spring Bobby wrote his own three-page version for the *Times* under the headline THE SOVIET BRAND OF COLONIALISM. In a fourteen-page interview in *U.S. News and World Report,* he talked about what he saw: Russian soldiers doing manual labor, "which is something you don't see in this country"; a museum in Leningrad "devoted completely to ridiculing God"; and, across Central Asia, "the average local person lives in a mud hut, with a mud floor." A month after his return he gave a lecture at Georgetown University. The Russian government had electronic listening devices in his hotel rooms, Bobby said, and the state selected all the books in the libraries. "All I ask," he concluded, "is that before we take any more drastic steps [toward détente] that we receive something from the Soviet Union other than a smile and a promise—a smile that could be as crooked and a promise that could be as empty as they have been in the past."

Justice Douglas, not surprisingly, had a different take on the Soviets and found his mate wearying. "At almost every stop and at every introduction, Bobby would insist on debating with some Russian the merits of Communism," Douglas recalled. "The discussions were long, sometimes heated, but as I told Bobby, they were utterly fruitless because he could no more convince them than they could convince him." Worse still for Douglas, Bobby "carried ostentatiously a copy of the Bible in his left hand. And he spent his time on the planes not going over Russian agricultural or industrial statistics, but reading the Bible." Having refused to eat or drink most of what was offered along the way—even the caviar—Bobby became deathly ill near the end of the trip, with a temperature Douglas estimated at 105. Kennedy wouldn't let any Russian doctors examine him, but by then he was becoming delirious and Douglas summoned one anyway. It took three hours for the physician to get there, and when she did she administered massive doses of penicillin and streptomycin. "That dear lady never left Bobby's room for thirty-six hours," Douglas reported. "When she emerged, her eyes were bright and she said, 'Now he'll be all right.' "

The KGB kept tabs on Bobby in Russia the way Hoover's FBI increasingly was doing back home, and it was equally unimpressed with this young son of a family both organizations would come to know intimately. "Kennedy was rude and unduly familiar with the Soviet people that he met," the Russian spy agency reported to the Kremlin—an observation that reflected cultural differences as much as Bobby's idiosyncrasies. He took pictures of crumbling factories, shabbily dressed children, inebriated officers, and other scenes intended "to expose only the negative facts in the USSR." In meetings with government officials he "posed tendentious questions and attempted to discover secret information." Lastly, the KGB report said, "he has a weakness for women" and asked his Intourist handler to dispatch to his hotel room a "woman of loose morals" (the report didn't say whether the handler obliged).

But that was not the full story of Bobby's travels. His detailed journal entries did focus on Russian vulnerabilities, but he also included a section marked "good things" that described the proliferation of libraries and schools and an amnesty for criminals. His simplistic Cold War take on U.S.-Soviet tensions became more nuanced. Rather than making a scattershot attack on Soviet crimes, he zeroed in on a question few were asking then: Where were the million Kazakhs and other Central Asians who had vanished during the drive to replace individual land and labor with collective farms? (Answer: Some had been killed, others were in gulags.) He also pointed a finger at the West, saying it could not credibly attack Soviet colonization of areas like Central Asia while it had its own colonies in Asia, Africa, and elsewhere. "We are still too often doing too little too late," he said, "to recognize and assist the irresistible movements for independence that are sweeping one dependent territory after another."

This was how Bobby Kennedy learned—by seeing things with his own eyes. Experience enriched and informed his better instincts. He ventured into the most remote of the Soviet republics at the very moment the Warsaw Pact was forming and most Americans were staying as far away as they could. Once there, he filled his journals with engrossing, if not always eloquent, observations. In Iran, he was disturbed by the shah's proliferation of palaces, calling them "a tremendous waste of land and money." In the Soviet republics he agonized that "a defendant in a criminal trial can refuse to answer questions but there is an assumption by the judge of guilt. No jury—the judge sits by himself." His questions drilled deep in a way that could put people off, but they were neither casual nor abstract. He did fight back when new ideas conflicted with ones he had long held, which frustrated Douglas and others who mistook it for bullheadedness. It was, instead, the very way he grew and evolved.

By the end of their adventure, the Supreme Court justice had started to revise his opinion of his young companion. "I began to see a transformation in Bobby," Douglas wrote later. "In spite of his violent religious drive against Communism, he began to see, I think, the basic, important forces in Russia—the people, their daily aspirations, their humanistic traits, and their desire to live at peace with the world." Mercedes Douglas, who along with Ethel had been waiting for the men in Moscow, was even more impressed with Bobby's growth. Experience flushed a lot of ideas out of his system—she likened it to an enema—and his trip to Russia represented the "undoing of McCarthyism."

———————

ETHEL WAS LESS worried about how the trip had transformed Bobby's politics than about how it had sapped his health. "What have you done to my husband?" she demanded of Douglas when he delivered a frail and flushed Bobby to her in Moscow in September 1955. A classic Kennedy welcoming party—Ethel accompanied by two of Bobby's sisters—greeted him like a returning warrior, yet they were eager to get on with a gamesome itinerary that included dinner at the American ambassador's, a performance of the ballet *Swan Lake*, and an excursion to Leningrad. For Ethel, fretting interspersed with fun was becoming the yin and yang of life with Bobby Kennedy.

Ethel had displayed plenty of wifely aptitudes during their five years of marriage, but she conceded from the start that cooking was not among them. She regularly burned the bacon and once had to call her sister for instructions on fixing a collapsed soufflé. On another occasion she managed to whip up four dishes of vegetables for guests, then realized she had not remembered to cook the meat. After one too many nights of dining out, or getting by on Cheese Dreams,* she broke down and hired a cook—an indulgence that became a standard for these Kennedys. Laundry was a challenge, too, which she solved by sending it out for washing and ironing. It helped that Bobby's wardrobe consisted mainly of tattered khaki pants and that his favorite food was chocolate ice cream drenched in chocolate sauce. Ethel did take care of the English bulldog, Toby Belch, that they got back when Bobby was in law school. What she also did was complete her husband and make him blossom.

Since childhood, Bobby had obsessed about whether he could be the equal of his lionized father and big brothers. Ethel made him feel he could be their better. She managed the home front, letting him forget household and child-rearing responsibilities that he knew she'd remem-

———————

* An open-faced sandwich consisting of bread, cheddar cheese, and butter, cooked in a skillet. Bacon can be added, along with eggs and/or tomatoes.

ber. Her lightness relieved his heaviness. Her love was the kind he had craved—without conditions. She so relished having his children that she would stay pregnant for nearly half of their eighteen years of marriage. She even stood by Bobby's defense of Senator Joseph McCarthy, defying anyone who complained to "name one person [McCarthy] has hurt." Seldom did she show jealousy—not of his men friends, of his endless hours at work, or even of rumors of his romantic liaisons. It was not that Ethel was a martyr, but she felt secure that their partnership would remain as solid as steel as long as they lived. He reinforced that message by taking her with him on work trips that wives seldom made; she reciprocated by dazzling diplomats as well as journalists. When she couldn't go, he sent love missives, one a day, in the language of whatever land he was visiting. Bobby, his sober-minded sister Eunice said, "would never have been the man that he became without his wife. I wouldn't say that about my other brothers." When an interviewer asked Bobby his major achievement in a life brimming with them, he shot back: "Marrying Ethel."

Their married life had begun in 1950 in a modest house on leafy Cameron Lane in Charlottesville near the University of Virginia School of Law. After graduation there were months-long stints in Greenwich, Hyannis Port, New York, Washington, and, during Jack's first Senate campaign, Boston. By the time they moved back to Washington in 1953 their family had grown to four, with Kathleen an eighteen-month-old toddler and Joe's namesake, Joseph Patrick II, an infant of four months. Ethel searched street by street in Georgetown until she found a four-bedroom rental that met Bobby's spending cap of $400 a month. They could have afforded more, with his million-dollar trust fund and the cash the Skakels were willing to kick in. But Bobby wanted to make a point: His family would not be overly extravagant. It was the kind of tight-fistedness that Joe Sr. encouraged yet seldom achieved among his offspring, and it was the first and only time that Ethel would live within a budget or that Bobby would insist on it.

Georgetown had just been converted into a historic district, with stately brick townhouses offering a sanctuary in the fast-moving capital to executives, diplomats, lawmakers, and a privileged few congressional staffers. Bobby delighted in the setting but still relaxed in daredevil fashion. The full-speed sledding down Montrose Park slopes brought yelps of joy from Thunder and Lightning, his two German shepherds. He took the children for rides in the black Cadillac convertible with the top—and the gas pedal—all the way down. Pickup games of football seemed never to end, even when his head collided with the metal fence of the adjacent tennis court. Eleanor McPeck, a fifteen-year-old neighbor, was there for much of it, and it was her mother who found a pile of towels to soak up the blood from his head gash. "It was terrible," she said, "and Mommy was not a Kennedy lover." Bobby and Ethel even rode a rented pony cart in the woods at a breakneck pace. "I don't know how to express it, but it is a quality I definitely identify with Bobby . . . an image of speed, which I'm calling recklessness," says McPeck. "I thought, 'If they challenge me to do it, okay, I'll do it.' But I remember being scared." She also remembers her father, the agent for the Kennedys' rental, having to deal with the stack of broken china left in the basement when they moved out. "It's like [they thought] somebody else would pick it up."

If their life was defined partly by privilege, it also would be etched in tragedies and gutsy responses. Before he turned nineteen, Bobby had lost his brother Joe in the wartime explosion over the English Channel. A second plane crash, this one over France on a trip meant for pleasure, took his twenty-eight-year-old sister Kathleen. In the fall of 1955, Ethel's parents, George and Ann Skakel, set off for a work trip to California aboard his company plane, a military surplus World War II bomber. The flight exploded midair over Oklahoma. Ethel, who was just twenty-seven, absorbed her losses the way the Kennedys had theirs, grieving in private and donning not just a brave face but a smile at the funeral. Yet she would never again fly when she could drive or take a train, and when she did get on an airplane it was with butterflies in her stomach and her hand reaching for reassurance from whoever was in the next seat.

Bobby's own calamities made him empathic with other people's, no matter the shape they took. "We were driving back from the airport at night to go to Bobby's house, and we ran into a dog and killed the dog. . . . The dog raced in front of the car and there was no way of stopping," recalled Charles Spalding, a friend of Jack's and later of Bobby's. "We went into every single house for ten miles, I suppose, until we finally found the person who was the owner. And Bobby explained what had happened and said how terribly sorry he was and asked about the dog—could he replace it or was there anything possible that could be done. It was so typical of him."

By early 1957, the time came for the Kennedys, now a family of seven, to escape the skinny row houses and streets of Georgetown and find a more sprawling setting like those Bobby and Ethel had cherished as kids. They didn't have far to look. Jack and his wife, Jackie, were anxious to move back into the city from their Georgian manor house in McLean, a barely populated Virginia suburb thirty minutes west of Washington. Jack charged Bobby the same $125,000 he had paid for the five-and-a-half-acre estate, which had been the home of the former attorney general and Supreme Court justice Robert H. Jackson.* The compound took its name—Hickory Hill—from the centuries-old trees that dotted the rolling pastures. The house itself was luxurious but comfortable, with high ceilings, gold draperies, marble fireplaces, crystal chandeliers, and a candlelit dining room. Its fourteen rooms gave Bobby and Ethel space to expand should they keep making babies, as they knew they would. The kids couldn't contain themselves when they pulled into the arched driveway for the first time. Kathleen, the eldest, tumbled out of the car first, followed by four-year-old Joey, three-year-old Bobby Jr., two-year-old David, and, in the arms of her parents, the baby, Mary Courtney.

In this perfect setting, Bobby could re-create those parts of his youth he cherished and reshape ones he didn't. Bobby and Ethel mimicked Rose and Joe's practice of using mealtimes for current events quizzes, testing the children with questions such as "What did John Paul Jones say and where did he say it?" Family had come first in the homes where Bobby and Ethel grew up, and the same ethic held at Hickory Hill. When Kathleen skinned her knee, or Joey wouldn't share with Bobby Jr., Bobby offered the same stern lesson he had heard at their age: "Kennedys don't cry." This batch of Kennedys, too, refused to come in second if they could help it. Ethel kept a card catalog modeled after Rose's to track each child's

---

* Alan Dabbiere, the current owner of Hickory Hill and a history buff, debunks the standard press account that it had served as headquarters for the Civil War general George B. McClellan, since the mansion wasn't built until five years after the end of the Civil War. And while Jack did turn over the property to Bobby, Dabbiere says the owner of record before and immediately after that transfer was their father, Joe Kennedy.

shoe size, vaccinations received and tonsils removed, and other statistics vital to raising them and telling them apart. She also helped them remember their lineage by displaying everywhere pictures of the Kennedy family, and she gave them a taste of their nation's prized history by hanging on a wall across from the front door a rare copy of the Emancipation Proclamation signed by President Abraham Lincoln.*

But the children at Hickory Hill were less bound by the strict discipline that governed Bobby's boyhood homes. There were no Saturday night weigh-ins and no dress code mandating sports jackets at the dinner table. The kids paid less of a price for being late to meals. They could and did interrupt, whether Bobby was conferring with staff or Ethel was being interviewed by a reporter. "Grandma had a great intellect and she'd say, 'Dear, I think it would be much better if when the children came home from school you gave them an apple and not ice cream with hot fudge and whipped cream,'" Ethel recalls of Rose's visits. "I must have more than fifty letters from her in that vein. She was so thoughtful and she wanted the children brought up correctly. But she was made of sterner stuff and I just wanted them to have a little fun."

That spirit extended to Bobby's workplace. The children's watercolor drawings adorned the walls of every office he inhabited, and from the time they toddled, Ethel brought them to the Senate hearing rooms to watch Daddy at work. As much as he held his brood to high standards, his love was never conditional. And while travel was as much a part of his work as his father's, he never lived away for long intervals the way Joe had. He made a point of getting home to his family for dinner at least three nights a week, and, whenever he could, he brought work and workmates home for lunch.

Bobby needed Hickory Hill as a home base after all the moves he had made as a child, starting in Brookline, Massachusetts, then to Riverdale and Bronxville in New York, and off to London with his father the ambassador. He boarded at high schools in New Hampshire, Rhode Island, and Massachusetts, and at college and graduate school in Cambridge, Lewiston, and Charlottesville. He had spent summers in a seaside man-

---

* Half a century later, Ethel sold Hickory Hill for just over $8 million and the Emancipation Proclamation for $3.8 million.

sion overlooking Nantucket Sound, and winter vacations were in Joe's six-bedroom compound on fashionable North Ocean Boulevard in Palm Beach. Married life had also meant perpetual moves, back and forth to Washington, then to a series of rented houses. Bobby would always be the glue that held together the world of his parents and siblings, a fact his father had acknowledged in 1955 by naming this son executor of his estate. But now, finally, Bobby had a home of his own and the stability he had coveted. His manor near the Potomac River provided a haven and a mooring. The move-in could not have been timed better: The family arrived at Hickory Hill just a month before Bobby's dinner with Jimmy Hoffa, in the midst of a crusade against union graft that would upend his world and let him find himself.

———

U.S. SENATORS DIDN'T like ruffling feathers in that get-along era when everyone loved Lucy and father knew best—but they could and did when the people who elected them got angry enough. That is what happened in 1956 when a mobster tossed sulfuric acid into the eyes of Victor Riesel, a syndicated reporter investigating corruption in New York's garment, construction, and trucking industries. The nation was incensed, and in January 1957, the Senate chartered a Select Committee on Improper Activities in Labor and Management to suggest legislative fixes that would make all labor and business organizations more open and honest. While the special committee promised to make its inquiry broad-based, from the start it focused on scandals brewing within the nation's biggest and richest union—the International Brotherhood of Teamsters, Chauffeurs, Warehousemen and Helpers of America. Senator McClellan and his Permanent Subcommittee on Investigations had already begun probing, but the Teamsters insisted that any look at labor practices be undertaken by the Labor Subcommittee and its more union-friendly chairman, Senator John F. Kennedy. JFK, whose eyes were on the White House, was glad to pass on the political hot potato, and a compromise was reached: McClellan would chair the new eight-member body, with four senators coming from the Labor Committee and the rest from McClellan's Government Operations Committee. There would be equal numbers of Democrats and Republicans.

That sounded even-handed, but McClellan would run what became known as the Rackets Committee with an authority nearly as absolute as Joe McCarthy had exercised in his investigations in the early 1950s, when McClellan and the other Democrats quit in protest. McCarthy was on the new labor-management panel, and his old aide Bobby Kennedy served as its chief lawyer and top researcher. Kennedy was initially skeptical about taking on the mighty Teamsters, whose truckers had the power to keep America moving or stop it in its tracks. He became convinced when Clark Mollenhoff, an intrepid reporter at the *Des Moines Register and Tribune*, brought him ever stronger evidence not just of the need for an investigation of labor vices, but of why the problem-plagued Teamsters was the place to start. "I assumed he was just another young lawyer who didn't want to take on the job of fighting the labor racketeers," recalled Mollenhoff. "I didn't blame him completely, for there were few prosecutors with the interest and the courage."

In August 1956, Bobby signaled to his staff that it was about to launch one of the deepest and broadest congressional inquiries ever. His assistant assumed a four-inch-deep receipt box would be adequate to hold the file cards on sources, targets, and leads. Mollenhoff suggested she get a full drawer. Nobody imagined that the probe would stretch for three years and the index cards alone would fill three cabinets with fifty file drawers. Much of the media back then knew Bobby only as Jack Kennedy's little brother, Joe's socialite son, and McCarthy's bulldog inquisitor. To the Teamsters, he appeared to be just the latest in a line of congressional investigators they had been able to outsmart and outlast. Liberals perceived him as a union buster who, if he kept an open mind, would see that management was the problem, not labor. He was about to defy all those low expectations, just as he had growing up as the forgotten child in a family of overachievers. He wasn't sure what lay ahead but couldn't wait to have at it.

To gear up, he hired accountants, lawyers, and other analysts, then borrowed more from the Internal Revenue Service and General Accounting Office. The staff eventually reached 104, with a hundred applicants for each opening. Most were in their late twenties and early thirties, enterprising, diligent, and certain they were right. Like their boss, they knew nothing about the underworld, and little about union statecraft or human frailties. But they worked harder than anybody except Bobby knew they could, interviewing an average of thirty-five witnesses to find one they wanted to testify publicly, then screening those few for up to five hours for each hour they would spend on the stand. Every field hearing required eight months of spadework by two investigators and six accountants. They tracked, minute by minute, the union officials' hotel check-ins, gasoline purchases, phone calls to business partners and mistresses, and visits to lockboxes. Documents were stacked floor to ceiling, with each indexed and cross-indexed.

Pierre Salinger went to work for the committee following the demise of the magazine he worked for, *Collier's*. One night he threw a party for seventy-five overworked staffers. Bobby and Ethel didn't leave until 2:30 in the morning, yet two and a half hours later, the beefy researcher was jolted awake by a call from Kennedy: "I'll be by to pick you up in twenty-five minutes. We've got a big day coming up." That spirit—part frat boy, part Marine—was infectious, and Salinger became one of a long list of Senate aides who stayed on with the Kennedys, in his case, as White House press secretary. Bobby, who had the only office with a door, captured that camaraderie when he posted on his wall excerpts from a speech by Winston Churchill: "We shall not flag or fail. . . . We shall never surrender."

The Rackets Committee's first target was a sitting duck. Dave Beck had started as a laundry truck driver and eventually clawed his way to the Teamsters presidency. The stocky, baldheaded Beck fancied himself the statesman of big labor, and he brought to his union a businesslike discipline, entree to the Eisenhower White House, and a sprawling headquarters a block from the Capitol that everyone called the Marble Palace (they called Beck "His Majesty the Wheel"). Along the way he dipped into the union treasury to support a lifestyle lavish enough to set off alarms for journalists like Mollenhoff and for Teamsters insiders, who passed on their suspicions to Kennedy and his forensic investigators. Although many of the incriminating files had been shredded, the committee early in 1957 pieced together evidence that Beck had taken $370,000 in membership funds that he did not intend to pay back. Among those whose pockets he picked was the widow of his best friend. Beck, who eventually would be convicted of income tax evasion and embezzlement, insisted it was all a case of bookkeeping errors. By the end of his hearings, Kennedy wrote, "Dave Beck had been shown to be cruel, stingy, avaricious and arrogant. But had he not been so arrogant, his other faults would not have been so pronounced."*

Beck was a warm-up. Bobby had always been able to sniff out where the real power lay, and his target early on was the man who had been building a base in the Midwest that rivaled Beck's on the West Coast. Nobody knew more about trucking than Jimmy Hoffa. In contrast to the hoity-toity Beck, Hoffa relished his image as the "Teamsters' teamster." He even looked like an eighteen-wheeler, built low to the ground and tough to roll over. Everything from his fingers to his disposition was thick and calloused. He lost his father at age seven, helped his mother feed the family by snaring birds and rabbits, and married a girl he'd met on a picket line after arriving for their first date with a bloody bandage on his head. He had been teargassed and billy-clubbed for the sake of the union. He had watched his brother get shot and, between 1937 and 1946, Jimmy was arrested sixteen times, leading to three convictions. He hated lawyers, politicians, and puffed-up union men like Dave Beck. His disdain for the trappings of office that had ensnared Beck, combined with an utter lack of scruples, made Hoffa a tougher adversary and, for Bobby, a more alluring one.

Their radically different backgrounds and outlooks made a Kennedy-Hoffa feud seem inevitable. Bobby grew up with the privileges that come with money and elite education; Jimmy prided himself on rising to the top of his field despite having started life as a strawberry picker and never making it past the ninth grade. Bobby had the leanness and elegant bones of an Irish setter; Jimmy was squat and rough-hewn like a pit bull. Truth telling was Bobby's calling card and he prided himself on the accuracy of his recall. Jimmy loved weaving and reweaving yarns: Did Bobby stick around for dinner that night in 1957 at Eddie Cheyfitz's

---

* What really stuck in Bobby's craw was how "Beck 'mothered' his son. . . . He never allowed Dave, Jr. to go out alone, insisted on ordering all the meals, selected all his friends, even though the younger Beck was a grown man. As a result, Dave, Jr. had become a jellyfish. . . . I knew by this time something about the crimes Dave Beck, Sr. had committed as president of the Teamsters Union, but to me his attitude toward his son was his worst sin" (RFK, *Enemy Within*, 41–42).

house, as Jimmy said in his first book, or did he walk out without eating, which made for a better story in his second?

Yet for all their attempts to accentuate their differences, Jimmy Hoffa and Bobby Kennedy had more in common than either could acknowledge. Both were determined to outwork their colleagues and each other, with Bobby heading back to the office when he saw the lights on in Jimmy's nearby office and Jimmy, once he heard that story, routinely leaving them on when he left for the night. Each had hard eyes that didn't let go. Both compensated for insecurity about being short with outsized bluster. Each had a distinctive tic—Jimmy twirled his ruby ring around his stubby finger, Bobby twirled a lock of hair around his lean finger. Both wore white socks with dress suits and did push-ups in the office. Bobby was one of the few who could outcharm Jimmy, or be even surlier, depending on his audience and mood. Each was self-justifying and unblushingly competitive, qualities that inspired steadfast friends and mortal foes alike. Journalists compared both men to coiled steel traps— and each knew better than anyone else how to set off the other.

Kennedy suspected from the beginning that Hoffa, anxious to replace his nominal boss, was the ultimate source of the juicy morsels he had been fed about Beck's malfeasance. He grew more convinced when Hoffa denied it. What Bobby knew for sure was that a lawyer named John Cye Cheasty had turned up in his office saying that Hoffa paid him to get a job with the committee, then to pass sensitive information back to the ambitious Teamsters leader. Kennedy hired Cheasty and turned him into a double agent. On the afternoon of Kennedy's get-acquainted dinner with Hoffa in February 1957, the FBI was taking pictures of Cheasty handing committee documents to Hoffa, who showed his gratitude by handing back a wad of bills. A month later, on the evening of March 13, agents sprang their trap: Cheasty passed on another stack of records, Hoffa thanked him and put the manila envelope into his pocket, and when he walked back into his hotel the Teamsters official was surrounded by G-men. They arrested him on federal bribery and conspiracy charges and brought him to the federal courthouse just before midnight. On hand to gloat were Bobby and Ethel, who'd been tipped off by J. Edgar Hoover and in turn roused all the reporters they could find.

It was the opening salvo in a clash that would last both of their lifetimes, and that was imprinted—asymmetrically—in each of their minds. "He stared at me for three minutes, with complete hatred in his eyes," Bobby recalled. "Then somehow we got into a discussion about who could do the most push-ups." Jimmy said he could manage thirty-five; Bobby insisted he could do more. It was a childish exchange—who was tougher?—but no more so than their supposed arm wrestling at Cheyfitz's dinner. Hoffa remembered the late-night scene at the courthouse this way: "I said, 'Listen, Bobby, you run your business and I'll run mine. You go on home and go to bed. I'll take care of things. Let's don't have no problems.' He was very unhappy because I called him Bobby. He's a kid, a spoiled kid." They agreed on one thing about the encounter: Bobby was so confident Jimmy would be convicted that he told reporters if it didn't happen, "I'll jump off the Capitol."

Hoffa's trial that summer showed how cocky Bobby had been in underestimating him. The union boss retained as his attorney the storied trial lawyer Edward Bennett Williams, who had represented Joe McCarthy and Dave Beck and, just a year before, had offered Bobby a job at his law firm. Now Williams was ready to do whatever it took for Jimmy. He used his role in jury selection to seat as many blacks as possible—in the end, eight out of the twelve. Williams then portrayed the chief prosecution witness and even the judge as segregationists, and the defense as civil rights pioneers. The boxing champ and black icon Joe Louis made a surprise appearance in the courtroom, courtesy of the Teamsters, and, in full view of the jury, greeted Hoffa like an old friend.* Whether it was Williams's legal arguments or his theatrics that made the difference, the jury quickly pronounced the Teamsters boss not guilty. Hoffa, who could have spent thirteen years in the slammer, reacted even quicker: "I sent [Bobby] a parachute. I also sent along a one-word note. All it said, in great big letters, was: 'JUMP!'" As for Kennedy, he reacted with "utter

---

* Bobby's team said Louis was brought to Washington at the expense of the Teamsters and was eventually given a job through Teamsters contacts. Jimmy said one of his lawyers was Louis's girlfriend and eventually his wife, and that's why the boxer came. He also said prosecutors were equally brazen in appealing to Negro jurors by having a Negro lawyer on their team. Louis and Hoffa weren't old pals, although they were longtime acquaintances. And Hoffa, who referred to blacks as "jigs" and "niggers," was no civil rights hero. (Sheridan, *Fall and Rise of Jimmy Hoffa*, 36; Hoffa and Rogers, *Trials of Jimmy Hoffa*, 152–53; Brandt, *I Heard You Paint Houses*, 109; and Neff, *Vendetta*, 81–83.)

disbelief" when a congressional aide handed him a note saying Hoffa had gotten off. And, as always, he needed someone to blame. It must have been the "unpreparedness and ineffectiveness of the Government attorneys who prosecuted the case," he said, in contrast to Williams's wizardry. Even worse were the jurors, two of whom had multiple convictions for drunkenness while another had been fired from his government job after refusing to answer a lie detector test on whether he was a homosexual. "Such people are not prohibited from jury service," Bobby noted, "but they certainly are persons the Government might find antagonistic to the aims of law enforcement in a criminal court."

The Kennedy-Hoffa battle was joined. In the next venue, the red-carpeted, marble-columned Caucus Room where his Senate panel met, Bobby didn't have to rely on lawyers beyond his control or on proving guilt beyond a reasonable doubt. Now, he sought to demonstrate how Hoffa had enriched himself at the expense of his rank-and-file members, and the case that best defined the alleged self-dealing involved a truck leasing company called Test Fleet. Shortly before the company was formed in 1948, Teamsters drivers in Detroit had gone on strike against a huge new-car hauler called Commercial Carriers, which wanted to replace driver-owned trailers with its own rigs. The walkout seemed to be working until Hoffa ordered the strikers back to work and arranged a settlement that gave Commercial the terms it wanted. Commercial, in turn, handed Test Fleet a lucrative deal that included a loan to buy its hauling equipment, the use of Commercial's accountants, and, over eight years, profits of $155,092 to the company's two owners. Jimmy's wife, Josephine, was one of those proprietors, the wife of his Teamster associate the other—facts not immediately apparent since both were doing business under their maiden names.

What did the unusual arrangement prove? Nothing, maintained Hoffa. There was no tit for tat with Commercial, and launching Test Fleet let him see the trucking business from the inside, the same way he did when he bought part or all of an investment company, wholesale grocery firm, brewery, racetrack, professional prize fighter, or Florida land scheme. Kennedy called that hogwash: "The Teamsters who never got their jobs back after the 1948 strike thought that Hoffa did not have

to own a company to have ample feeling for the problems of employers. . . . The strikers were bitter then. They are still bitter." The Test Fleet
matter wasn't settled then, and it wouldn't be until five years later, when
Jimmy and Bobby faced off in a setting with stricter rules and higher
stakes.

Hoffa's selling out his drivers for self-enrichment violated Kennedy's
precepts of fairness and fealty. Even more unforgivable was that Jimmy
was eroding the integrity of the Teamsters by abetting the actions of
union thugs and betraying reformers like lifelong trucker Floyd Hook of
Pontiac, Michigan. Hook and other rank-and-filers were meeting one
night in a union hall when a fleet of twenty-five black Cadillacs rolled
into town, each full of men with clubs. At their head was Hoffa, who, as
Kennedy pieced together based on evidence presented to his committee,
"had come to instill in these people some understanding of the proper
place of union members in his Teamsters." Hook continued complaining
about two union officers he said were taking payoffs from employers in
return for not enforcing worker protections. The result, Kennedy said,
was that "the Hook family began to be subjected to vicious persecution."
A car followed Floyd. Another car stayed parked across from his home,
and calls warned him to "tell your children to be careful on the way to
school today, it would be unfortunate if a truck ran them down." Floyd's
wife had a "nervous breakdown" and left to live with relatives in Indiana.
He stayed to fight—until he was fired and, with no backing from the
union, had to leave Michigan and join his wife in Indiana. When the
committee probed, it learned that Hoffa was getting a share of the kick-
backs that had angered Floyd.

Again, Kennedy described this as typical for Hoffa—of "the convicted
killers, robbers, extortionists, perjurers, blackmailers, safecrackers, dope
peddlers, white slavers and sodomists who were his chosen associates."
Again, Hoffa insisted the only pattern was that Bobby Kennedy—"a vicious bastard" with "a psychotic mania to 'get' me at any cost"—didn't
understand the trucker's rough-and-tumble world. "I'm not saying that
everyone all down the line was lily-pure," he added. "What I'm saying is
that there wasn't much I could do about isolated instances or wrongful
action when there were no responsible complaints, when the leadership

refused to complain, when the finances were sound. . . . And I had not put those leaders in office."*

Both combatants made their case to the press at the time and in memoirs afterward, although the battle for media attention was not an even one. Jimmy avoided most reporters, assuming they would never give him a square deal. When John Bartlow Martin offered to show him a seven-part series he was writing for the influential *Saturday Evening Post*, Jimmy said he "didn't want to see it, he didn't care what I wrote." By contrast, Bobby habitually leaked documents to reporters, then counted on them letting him inspect a draft of the article. "Bobby and I spent the better part of the day going over [the series], not an easy negotiation—he was as tenacious with me as with the witnesses," Martin recalled. "What bothered him most, I think, was my view that there were similarities between him and Hoffa. He never had thought of it and he simply refused to believe it."

The public could sense their antagonism the very first time Hoffa showed up in person before Kennedy's committee, on August 20, 1957. Newspaper reporters lined one side of the cavernous hearing room, seven television crews filled the other, and, up front, photographers snapped pictures of the lawmakers and their star witness. Bobby, seated next to Chairman McClellan facing the crowd, jumped right in:

> **Kennedy:** Since you have been with the Teamsters union, you have been arrested a number of times, have you?
>
> **Hoffa:** That is correct.

---

* Harold Gibbons, a member of the Teamsters General Executive Board, gave the McClellan Committee an even more rousing defense: "In three years of investigation in connection with our union, reputed to be completely dominated by racketeers and hoodlums, one hundred and six names were mentioned. We searched high and low for sixteen of these names and never found them. . . . Nine of these names we found to be members of the union who had never held any position other than as members. . . . Thirty-four of those mentioned were former officers or employees but who were no longer associated with the Teamsters. . . . There were thirteen, as a total, who could be said to be law-breakers who were at the time we filed this report still members of the Teamsters and holding office. Out of a membership of more than 1,700,000, that's not a bad record. It seems to me that in a three-year investigation as widespread as it was, that to be able to come up with only thirteen violators . . . was a case of the mountain having labored and brought forth a mouse" (*Trials of Jimmy Hoffa*, 168–69).

Kennedy: How many times, approximately, do you think?

Hoffa: Well, I don't know, Bob. I haven't counted them up. I think maybe about 17 times I have been picked up, took into custody of the police, and out of the 17 times, 3 of those times—in many instances these were dismissed—but in 3 of those times I received convictions.

Kennedy: Now, the first one was in 1940, was it?

Hoffa: I believe that was an assault and battery, is that correct?

Kennedy: That is not the one I was thinking of.

Hoffa: I am talking about the ones where I was simply taken off of a picket line because of a disagreement with some so-called policeman of authority without any legal authority. I haven't kept track of those.

Kennedy: But there are about 17 in all and you think you have been convicted on 3?

Hoffa: I think you have the record, and you can count them.

He and Bobby were "like flint and steel," Jimmy conceded. "Every time we came to grips the sparks flew." But while Beck during his testimony had claimed his Fifth Amendment rights at the rate of nearly once a minute, Jimmy never did. That didn't mean he answered the committee's questions. During one back-and-forth with Bobby on alleged Teamsters ties to racketeers, Hoffa began by saying, "I cannot recall that, whether or not it was discussed or not, since you don't want my belief, and I can't answer." Pressed again, he replied, "To the best of my recollection, I must recall on my memory, I cannot remember." His language might have been muddled, but it also was carefully calculated, as he conceded: "I sat down and put on paper everything I could think of they might ask questions about. Then I got with the lawyers and went over every item. We'd rehearse what we thought Kennedy would do and we got it right damned near every time. He's not the brightest fellow in the world, you know." Sometimes words alone would not do: "I used to love to bug the little bastard. Whenever Bobby would get tangled up in one of his involved questions, I would wink at him. That invariably got him. 'Mr. Chairman,' he'd shout, 'would you please instruct the witness to stop making faces at me?' "

A record number of witnesses—343 of 1,525—followed Beck's lead in falling back on the Fifth Amendment. Bobby understood the principle but said, "I can think of very few witnesses who availed themselves of it who in my estimation were free of wrongdoing. I know of several who took the Fifth Amendment out of fear, but aside from them, for whom I felt immensely sorry, I know of none whom I should like to work for or have work for me—or have anything at all to do with." There was one more reason certain attestants might have been tempted to take the Fifth—Hoffa signaled they should by holding up five fingers as they approached the stand.

Bobby couldn't prevent a witness from using this constitutional protection, but he did exact a price. He called to the stand one witness after another who he knew, from pre-interviews, would decline to answer his questions. The point wasn't to see if they'd changed their minds. It was to publicly ridicule them. A typical exchange was one with Joey Glimco, the president of a Teamster local in Chicago who was notorious for shaking down everyone from taxi drivers to poultry dealers. When Glimco cited his Fifth Amendment right fifty-five times in one short exchange, Bobby and Chairman McClellan left no doubt how they felt:

Kennedy: You can have a lot of tough people call up witnesses, poor businessmen, poor members of the union, who can't afford to protect themselves, and have them intimidate these people, but you can't come before this committee and answer any questions, can you, Mr. Glimco?

Glimco: I respectfully decline to answer because I honestly believe my answer might tend to incriminate me.

Kennedy: You haven't got the guts to do that, have you, Mr. Glimco?

Glimco: I respectfully decline to answer because I honestly believe my answer might tend to incriminate me.

McClellan: Morally you are kind of yellow inside, are you not? That is the truth about it?

Glimco: I respectfully decline to answer because I honestly believe my answer might tend to incriminate me.

Kennedy's objective in summoning all those witnesses extended well beyond better union-management relations, Hoffa argued. Bobby wanted "the greatest prize in the modern world: the White House." Hoffa's claim made a lot of sense. The politically savvy Bobby had more in mind than just his brother's company when he suggested that Jack join the newly formed select committee, which Jack agreed to do even as two of his rivals for the Democratic nomination—Senators Henry Jackson and Stuart Symington—refused to sit on the panel. To win the nomination in 1960, JFK would need to secure the support of antiunion Southern Democrats while at the same time appealing to the party's pro-labor Northern wing. As the committee's obvious target, the Teamsters saved him from choosing: They had supported President Eisenhower in 1956, so weren't likely to be with the Democrats in 1960, and the powerful and pro-Democratic AFL-CIO was battling Hoffa's union and welcomed another ally almost as much as union-bashing southerners did. As Hoffa predicted, the evils of the Teamsters became almost as constant a refrain as the dangers of the missile gap in Jack Kennedy's campaign for the White House. Hoffa railed against the Kennedy brothers in speeches and articles, and passed on a quieter message via Pierre Salinger: "You tell Bobby Kennedy for me that he's not going to make his brother President over Hoffa's dead body."

Neither Kennedy could have predicted that, thanks to exhaustive television and newspaper coverage of the hearings, for three years Bobby would get more national attention than Jack. Finally, he had emerged from his father's and brother's shadows. This once shy middle child was now inundated with speaking requests (of two hundred and fifteen in 1957, he accepted only eight) and had three fan clubs (the one in Brooklyn said, "We think you are the living end and a real doll").* Even less

---

* Not everyone was a fan. A Teamsters lawyer called him a "vicious little monster." Bobby's reply: "I'm not so little." (Seigenthaler OH, December 24 and 26, 1974, 121, Southern Oral History Program, and Harwood, "With Bobby Kennedy," June 5, 1988.)

foreseeable was how much Bobby reveled in the spotlight. While JFK
played a supporting role as just one of eight committee members, RFK
starred in a drama that Hoffa referred to as McClellan's *Playhouse 90*.*
Sometimes people confused the hard-nosed prosecutor with the more
patrician senator, which was easy since the brothers sat side by side at
the sessions. Each spoke in a distinctive flat Boston accent, glasses high
on his head and hands in perpetual motion. They conferred constantly,
with Bobby telling Jack precisely when to show up to ensure maximum
TV exposure.† Joe also turned up occasionally to suggest that Bobby back
off a bit, for the sake of Jack's relationship with organized labor and for
fear of dredging up old gossip about Joe's bootlegging.

Asking Bobby to back off on Jimmy was like asking the Hatfields to go
easy on the McCoys. Too much honor was at stake, and each man took
too much joy in the other's misery. But it exacted a toll on them, and on
many others. At least eight witnesses suffered heart attacks, and one
dropped dead on the desk of Kennedy's receptionist. Jimmy gained five
pounds in 1958, when the committee kept him so busy he couldn't get
the exercise he was accustomed to, and his son James remembers that
"he would tell us about the problems he was having, what was going on,
and we would meet around the dinner table." Bobby felt the pressure
even more acutely, although it was harder to pinpoint the source.

Kennedy "received anonymous threats from a telephone caller that
someone would throw acid in the eyes of his six children," *The New York
Times* reported in 1959. As inconceivable as that seemed, Bobby knew
better than anyone else about the blinding three years before of the labor
reporter Victor Riesel. Kathleen, Bobby's oldest, remembers that "I had
to wait after school in the principal's office until my mother arrived to
take me home." Ethel says that "during the worst of the hearings, the
most tendentious, the big semis would get off the main roads and come

---

* *Playhouse 90* was a series of ninety-minute television dramas that aired on CBS from 1956
to 1960.

† While Bobby was focused on Senate business during the day, "they were running for President in our office after five o'clock in the evening," when Bobby and his friends would gather
to plot strategy for Jack's 1960 bid, recalled Ruth Young Watt, chief clerk for the Permanent
Subcommittee on Investigations (Ruth Watt OH, September 21, 1979, 181, U.S. Senate Historical Office).

by Hickory Hill with the horns just blaring." When Bobby tried to back into a parking spot near the Capitol, a burly man slipped in first and seemed to dare him to complain. If it had occurred just once, or even twice, it might have been by chance, but three times meant it was pre-planned, said the Kennedy family friend Paul "Red" Fay, Jr.

Yet Bobby didn't worry about himself or even his family. Kennedys, he would maintain over the years with considerable pride and diminishing evidence, could take care of themselves. He had no illusions about Hoffa and his lieutenants: "They have the look of [Al] Capone's men. . . . They have the smooth faces and cruel eyes of gangsters; they wear the same rich clothes, the diamond ring, the jeweled watch, the strong, sickly-sweet-smelling perfume." What made him anxious, Bobby added, was the power these Teamsters exercised in the lives of every American. They drove us to the hospital at birth, delivered us to our graves, and in be-tween manned the trucks that brought us the necessities of life. They are "the most powerful institution in this country—aside from the United States Government itself." Vesting that kind of control in Jimmy Hoffa's unscrupulous hands, Kennedy told anyone who would listen, made him the most dangerous man in America.

For all their tough-guy talk, Kennedy and Hoffa from time to time in-dulged themselves in ways only the entitled could, although both re-mained sensitive to their everyman image and kept quiet about it. In Jimmy's case, that meant taking his private elevator to his walnut-paneled office in the Marble Palace, then having his French chef prepare a lunch of his favorites—cold crab and lobster. If time allowed he might indulge in a steam bath and rubdown in the fifty-thousand-dollar gym he had installed in the basement. Bobby likewise made an opening in his frenzied schedule to drive once a week to Baltimore for a speed-reading course, with Jack sometimes coming along. Instead of the milk and sandwich he typically gulped down at his desk, his butler occasionally brought from Hickory Hill a wicker basket with grilled lamb chops and ice cream. Battling a foe as intrepid as the Teamsters boss would have left most people sorely depleted, but it gave a competitor and sportsman like Bobby a purpose and contentment he had never known. It was, he said, "like playing Notre Dame every day."

HOFFA AND HIS Teamsters were not the Rackets Committee's only targets. Other cases, as Bobby said, "cried out for an investigation." One centered on a union organizer from Los Angeles who wanted to organize jukebox operators in San Diego but was warned away. He went anyway, was knocked out by assailants, and woke the next morning covered in blood and suffering excruciating stomach pain. He headed to a hospital for emergency surgery. "Doctors removed from his backside a large cucumber," Bobby recounted. "Later he was told that if he ever returned to San Diego it would be a watermelon. He never went back."

The committee investigated charges of corruption in a dozen unions, including the Bakers, Operating Engineers, Carpenters, Sheet Metal Workers, Mail Deliverers, and Hotel and Restaurant Workers. Bobby found one official who was spending thousands of dollars of union funds on gifts for his girlfriend. Another used bullies to stifle dissent. He investigated the United Auto Workers, too, mainly to quiet committee Republicans who charged he didn't have the guts to go after a union that Democrats relied on for votes and money. The probe focused on allegations of violence and vandalism during the union's bitter strike in the mid-'50s against the Kohler plumbing company of Sheboygan, Wisconsin. The upshot, Bobby said, was that "after five long weeks—one of the longest hearings we conducted on any one subject—after eighty witnesses, and more than a million words of testimony, we proved that when a strike is long and violent, it will engender great antagonism. And, of course, everybody knew that before we started." The Republicans, egged on by the Teamsters, pounced anyway, accusing him of being in the tank for the UAW. Senator Barry Goldwater of Arizona, Bobby's most outspoken critic, later explained that it wasn't personal: "You're in politics, Bob, whether you like it or not."

While the committee's title had promised hearings on management as well as labor, that happened only as a sidelight to union probes. The committee did unexpectedly dig into organized crime. It concentrated its attention on mobsters infiltrating labor groups, but in November 1957 news broke of a meeting of fifty-eight Mafia dons from across the country at an estate in upstate New York. The famous Apalachin conclave woke the nation to the existence of a Cosa Nostra syndicate and encouraged future committee probes of gangsters.* It also alerted Bobby to the fact that the haloed FBI "didn't know anything, really, about these people who were the major gangsters in the United States." One of those Bobby called to testify was the notorious New York wiseguy Joseph "Crazy Joe" Gallo, who afterward expressed surprise at how fairly he'd been treated (he especially liked Bobby attesting to how dangerous Joe and his brother Larry were). To show his gratitude, Crazy Joe told the committee counsel, "I'll line up my people for your brother in 1960." A bemused Bobby responded that "the second biggest favor he could do for me was to keep his preference quiet—and the biggest favor would be to announce for my brother's opponent. He laughed and went merrily on his way."

All that activity was intended to prove that the panel wasn't singling out any one union. But it was. It had targeted the Teamsters from the start, and it became more aggressive when the insatiable Jimmy Hoffa replaced the colorless Dave Beck. The battle with Hoffa would define Bobby in much the same way that Richard Nixon's career was kicked into gear when, as a young congressman, he chaired high-profile hearings on the accused Soviet spy Alger Hiss that helped catapult him into the Senate, then the vice presidency, and ultimately the Oval Office.

The final verdict on the Kennedy-Hoffa matchup is more ambiguous. Hoffa was an old-school scrapper who had absorbed beatings all his life, on picket lines and at the bargaining table. Now, after more than two years of pounding by Rackets Committee investigators, he was bloodied but still standing. By his count, that constituted victory. He had survived two criminal trials—in Washington for bribery, in New York for wiretapping—both ending in acquittal. Kennedy's committee held 207 days of hearings on the Teamsters, which added up to a longer, harder look than any legislative body had ever taken at any union. It produced evidence that Hoffa had enriched himself and sullied his union's reputation, but it never offered conclusive proof that he had taken even a dime

---

* Bobby got his wake-up call two years earlier, when he started accompanying narcotics agents in New York on their late-night, bare-knuckled busts of drug dens. The young lawyer never forgot the lessons he learned of the seedy sides of Manhattan and, by extension, America (Thomas, *Robert Kennedy: His Life*, 70–71).

of Teamsters money, and it never uncovered the stash of ill-gotten cash Bobby was convinced was out there.

Ironically, all that probing helped Jimmy Hoffa capture nearly 75 percent of the votes in 1957 when he ran for president of the Teamsters. Bobby and his investigators had brought down the incumbent, Dave Beck, who in the wake of his humiliation by the committee declined to seek reelection and eventually went to jail. Kennedy had undervalued the appeal of Hoffa's simple creed—"the fight for more and better." He also miscalculated the allure of Jimmy himself, who, for all his misdeeds, had generally delivered for his members and convinced them that attacks on him were affronts to them. "The [election] outcome," the leftist *National Guardian* newspaper wrote, "was an almost natural reaction of tough men in a tough industry who objected to being told how to run their affairs by an anti-labor Senate committee and a labor leadership which seemingly endorsed governmental intervention in union affairs." Whatever his intent, in the end Bobby Kennedy made Jimmy Hoffa into such a hero to America's 1.5 million Teamsters that if it had been within their power, they would have crowned him president for life. Asked how he felt about boosting the career of the man he had tried to bring down, Bobby admitted to a reporter that he had let down the public and "I have a debt to society."

The investigations left Bobby with another legacy that he hadn't predicted and thought missed the mark—that he was not just determined but grim, and not merely relentless but ruthless. That perception arose out of his disdain for the Fifth Amendment and the broader arena of civil liberties. Whereas democracy extolled the means, the chief counsel extolled the ends, which in this case meant throwing Hoffa out of his union presidency and into jail. It didn't help that Bobby didn't feel obliged to explain himself and wasn't good at it when he tried. A honey-tongued Teamsters lawyer had no such hesitations, and he kept a running list of ways he believed Bobby used innuendo and proximity to incriminate his clients: "We had guilt by association, guilt by marriage, guilt by eating in the same chophouse, guilt by the general counsel's amazement, guilt by somebody else taking the Fifth Amendment, guilt by somebody else refusing to testify. But we think the 'doozer' was the one that happened when the committee was taking testimony concerning a criminal case in which eight defendants were tried for eleven weeks; the jury was out only eight minutes and came in with a verdict of 'not guilty.' The police detective who helped prepare the case said the prosecution felt it was not a fair trial. The Committee nodded in sympathy and agreement. This is guilt by acquittal."

Liberals over the years were even less forgiving. "Though Bobby helped clean a lot of hoodlums and corrupt dictators out of the labor movement, he acted much as had [Joe] McCarthy, equating invocation of the Fifth Amendment with confession of guilt and treating a Congressional investigation as a pillory in which people he disliked could be held up to public scorn," wrote the muckraking journalist I. F. Stone. Paul Jacobs, of the Center for the Study of Democratic Institutions, conceded that "Jimmy Hoffa and the Teamsters Union are the antithesis of what I believe a union leader and a union ought to be" and that Bobby was right to go after them—but within limits that Bobby never understood. He exceeded his committee's mandate by interfering in union affairs, meddling in the judiciary's oversight of the union, and otherwise making life miserable for Hoffa. "Although I have nothing in common with Hoffa, the union leader, Hoffa, the citizen, is me," added Jacobs. "His rights are the same as mine and require the same protection."

Bobby felt his liberal critics failed to appreciate that it took an unrelenting interrogator to bring down an incorrigible malefactor like Jimmy Hoffa. He also believed, with more justification, that he hadn't gotten credit for the tangible accomplishments of his hearings. They had given AFL-CIO president George Meany the evidence he needed to expel the Teamsters from the federation. A federal court named a three-man board of monitors to police the union and propose reforms.* While

---

* John Cassidy, a young lawyer working for the Board of Monitors, remembers being with Hoffa standing at a window looking down into a crowded street in Washington: "He said, 'Cass, come over here. I want to tell you something. You see all those people out there, what do you think of them?' I said, 'I don't know. They look like average people to me, coming and going about their daily business.' He said, 'Do you think I could buy any of those people?' I said, 'I don't know, Mr. Hoffa.' I always called him Mr. Hoffa. And he said, 'Let me tell you something, you don't understand the law under which we operate. We, the human race.' I said, 'What's your view of those people?' He said, 'Well, I could buy any one of them you can see, it's just a question of how much I have to pay.' I looked at him and said, 'Do you really believe that?' He said, 'In my heart, I believe it.'" "That," adds Cassidy, who later worked for Bobby at the Justice Department, " was Jimmy Hoffa" (Author interview with John Cassidy).

Bobby couldn't get the Eisenhower Justice Department to indict as many Teamsters officials as he wanted or to win convictions in cases it did bring, more than twenty targets of its investigations were sent to prison. And while he never won over his liberal detractors, and eventually gave up trying, he did make a fan out of the conservative Barry Goldwater. At first the senator thought Bobby was "a mean little asshole" and the Rackets Committee "was just a vehicle for Jack's campaign for president." But watching how hard Bobby worked—he "never left the staff offices—I mean, *never*—before midnight, subpoenaing hundreds of witnesses and chasing down thousands of documents"—Goldwater came away impressed: "It turned into a forced march and Bobby was like a Marine platoon leader."

Kennedy's investigations also generated such public outrage at union abuses that in 1959 Congress overwhelmingly passed, and the president signed, a law requiring unions to hold secret elections, submit annual financial reports to regulators, and make other reforms. Although the legislation tilted more to business and against labor than the Kennedy brothers had hoped, it proved a boon to the movement for democratic unions and a model for crime control laws. At his final hearing on the Teamsters, Bobby tipped his hat to Jimmy for inadvertently helping Congress see the need for long-delayed reforms: "You do remain still the best argument for the passage of the bill." To which Jimmy answered, "This is still America."

The exchange provided an apt postscript to the rackets inquiry, which lasted three years, generated four million words of testimony from 1,525 witnesses, and boasted a bigger budget, staff, and visibility than the Teapot Dome scandal, the Army-McCarthy hearings, or any previous Capitol Hill inquiry. But that point and counterpoint would not be the last between Kennedy and Hoffa. Bobby called his bestselling memoir on those years *The Enemy Within: The McClellan Committee's Crusade Against Jimmy Hoffa and Corrupt Labor Unions*.* The title was a twist on Joe McCarthy's notion that America was being subverted by embedded Bolsheviks. For Bobby, the depravity of Communism had been replaced by the venality of

---

* That is the one and only book Hoffa read as an adult, according to the investigative reporter Lester Velie (Velie, *Why Jimmy Hoffa Had to Die*, 131).

crooked unions like the Teamsters, which he called a "conspiracy of evil." He still inhabited a heaven-and-hell world—you were either a child of God or in the grip of Lucifer—but now Jimmy Hoffa had replaced Roy Cohn at the top of his enemies list. And young idealist that he was, he still saw his life's work as a crusade.

Chapter 3

BROTHER'S KEEPER

O UTGOING PRESIDENT DWIGHT Eisenhower pinpointed the precise instant when Richard Nixon lost the closest presidential contest in the twentieth century. It was not when John Kennedy wooed the South by picking Lyndon Johnson as his running mate, or when he outcharmed Nixon in the first-ever presidential debates. The moment, Ike said, came just two weeks before the 1960 election, when the Kennedy brothers made a "couple of phone calls." Jack placed his from a hotel bed near Chicago's O'Hare Airport to Mrs. Martin Luther King, Jr. Bobby dialed a Georgia judge from a pay phone on Long Island. Neither call lasted more than a few minutes and both expressed concern that Rev. King had been sentenced to four months on a road gang for a traffic-related violation. Together they helped spring the civil rights leader. Nixon sensed that he, too, should say he regretted King's imprisonment, but he didn't, and neither did Eisenhower. The Kennedy calls were barely noticed in white America, but millions of leaflets trumpeted the news at black churches on the final Sunday before the election in a pamphlet titled " 'No Comment' Nixon Versus a Candidate with a Heart, Senator Kennedy." Nixon captured less than a third of the black vote, a steep drop from Eisenhower's 1956 total and enough to account for the razor-thin victory by Kennedy, who in black America had been the least popular of the Democrats running for president that year.

The legend of those calls has grown with each telling. JFK's to Coretta Scott King was said to be an instinctive reaction to an injustice he couldn't abide. RFK at first reamed out the campaign aides who had encouraged his brother. Thinking it over, he decided Jack and his advisers had been right and, ignoring his own staff, Bobby spontaneously telephoned the sentencing judge and asked him to change his mind. Over time the calls were said to have altered not just the 1960 balloting but racial politics in America for the rest of the century and beyond, with the Republican Party becoming increasingly anathema to African Americans and attractive to white southerners.

That the telephone conversations shaped the election and the partisan divide was true. What lay behind them, however, is a perfect instance of the Kennedys' skillful political manipulation and mythmaking. Statecraft came naturally to Jack, but Bobby had to work to cultivate such skills. By the campaign's end, however, Bobby not only learned all that Jack could teach, he set a new paradigm for engineering a path to the White House—along both the high road and the low—that would embolden even such hardened politicians as Lyndon Johnson and Richard Nixon. That crucial year of electioneering also gave new resonance to the expression "the Kennedy brothers." Each came to depend on the other in ways that were inconceivable in their younger years, and that would lead to a historic sharing of presidential duties and intimacies.

––––––––––

BOBBY'S SCHOOLING IN running a campaign came on the job, and on the run, starting back in 1946. That was when Jack made his first bid for office, for a congressional seat that included parts of Honey Fitz's old House district along with the neighborhood where P.J. had been a Democratic ward boss. A dashing warrior back home now with his six medals, Jack neither needed nor wanted much help from his kid brother Bobby, who was fresh out of his naval tour in the Caribbean and lacking any obvious expertise or acumen. The candidate was already beset by well-intentioned relatives. Honey Fitz made sure that his namesake met every one of his aging cronies, while Joe stage-managed the campaign from his perch at the Ritz Hotel, enlisting pollsters and public relations mavens and dispensing upwards of $250,000. "We're going to sell Jack like soap flakes," he crowed to a friend. And when another candidate for the Eleventh District seat offered to help Jack with some future bid if he would stay out of the current congressional race, the elder Kennedy patiently explained that "my son will be President in 1960." Jack's sisters, meanwhile, hosted house parties and handed out leaflets, with help from

Jean's college roommate, Ethel. As for Bobby, Jack only half jokingly told
his Navy buddy Red Fay that "it's damn nice of Bobby wanting to help,
but I can't see that sober, silent face breathing new vigor into the
ranks. . . . One picture of the two brothers together will show that we're
all in this for Jack. Then you take Bobby out to [the] movies or whatever
you two want to do."

It was a quintessential case of an older sibling patronizing a younger
one, and Bobby didn't hide his hurt. But wanted or not, he was determined to help and knew exactly where he wanted to apply his efforts. In
a Democratic district like the Eleventh, the real action was in the primary, and the most formidable of Jack's nine opponents was the former
mayor of Cambridge, which accounted for a third of the district. Bobby
marched into his brother's Cambridge headquarters, still in his sailor's
suit, and assigned himself three wards in Italian East Cambridge that
were the city's poorest and Jack's longest of shots. He knocked on doors,
shook hands until his were raw, and ate spaghetti whenever it was offered. Bobby wanted no part of the political hacks who made headquarters their home. His kind of people were the neighborhood half-pints, the
kids he joined in pickup games of softball, basketball, and, his favorite,
football. At least one Cambridge pol took notice: "All that propaganda
that the Kennedys were the high-hat kind was dissipated in my area by
Bobby playing with those kids." Primary day put to rest another myth:
that Bobby couldn't help. While Jack beat his closest opponent by a two-
to-one margin, Bobby showed his mettle in enemy territory that his
brother hadn't wanted to contest. Jack lost Bobby's wards, but he won
twice as many votes there as anyone thought possible.

Bobby sat out that year's general election and the next two congressional races, all of which Jack won with hardly any competition. But he
was enticed back in 1952, when Jack gave up his secure House seat to
take on three-term U.S. senator Henry Cabot Lodge, Jr. The Lodges, Epis-
copalians and Brahmins, treated the post as their birthright—much as
the Kennedys would later. Counting the time served by Henry Jr.'s grandfather and great-great-great-grandfather, the Lodges had represented
Massachusetts in the Senate for nearly fifty of the previous one hundred
fifty years. For most Democrats, challenging a Legion of Merit winner
and entrenched incumbent like Lodge would have seemed pointless, es-

pecially in a year when the Republicans had the recent supreme Allied commander atop their ticket. For the Kennedys, father and sons, it was just the attention-getting gambit that could catapult thirty-five-year-old Jack onto a trajectory toward the White House. "Lodge was the major figure in the state and perhaps in the country," Joe would say, adding that if you could beat him, "you beat the number one person." What he didn't say, but everybody knew, was that the race was also a grudge match: Thirty-six years before, Lodge's grandfather had defeated Kennedy's in a race for the Senate.

This time Bobby played the reluctant brother. He was busy launching his own career at the Justice Department and not eager to sink himself back into the family dynamics that he knew would play out during the campaign. Besides, the campaign already had a manager, Mark Dalton, who had run the 1946 congressional race and recently left a thriving law practice when Jack invited him back. None of that mattered to Joe. In the spring of 1952 he accused Dalton, to his face, of spending funds without producing results and having no clue how to unseat a senator that everyone but Joe thought was invulnerable. Dalton listened, then quit at the very moment when the campaign should have been kicking into gear. Bobby had persuaded his Harvard friend Kenny O'Donnell to sign up the previous December. Now, at Jack's direction, O'Donnell was calling Bobby to say he was the only one who could regain control of the campaign—and of the ex-ambassador. "I don't know anything about Massachusetts politics . . . I just don't want to come," Bobby answered, although he knew that his stepping forward would be the only way to get his father to back off. A week later he telephoned O'Donnell to say, "I'm coming up; I've thought it over, and I suppose I'll have to do it."

His first challenge was to give voters a reason to invest in a new senator. After years of war, America had settled into a self-satisfied prosperity—one in which three of five families owned a car, two of three had a telephone, and the average household earned $3,900 a year, which wasn't bad since the average new home cost just $9,050, gas was twenty cents a gallon, and a postage stamp could be had for three cents. The men and women of Massachusetts were equally content with themselves and with their existing senator. On the main issues of the day, there was little to distinguish the moderate Kennedy from the moderate

Lodge. Both wanted the United States engaged with the world and Russia contained. Both favored unions but thought they needed reforming. Both liked budgets that balanced and smaller government. Each had earned a Harvard degree, bore the chiseled countenance of a statesman, and came wrapped in a compelling story of wartime gallantry. What set his brother apart, Bobby realized earlier than anyone else, was Jack's ineffable magnetism—his quiet persuasiveness, idealism without ideology, and the sense that he represented something better without his having to say specifically what. Those were precisely the qualities that had hypnotized young Bobby when the brothers summered together on Cape Cod, and that Bobby wouldn't realize until years later that he possessed, too. The press called it Kennedy magic. By comparison, Lodge seemed too high-society and too yesterday; he was, after all, fifteen years older and had roots that ran back to the Puritans. Kennedy hadn't just gotten off the boat—his family had been here for two generations. But more recent arrivals like him—Irish and Italian, Jews and Slavs—far outnumbered Mayflower Yankees in the Bay State.

To drive home those contrasts, Bobby put in place a campaign framework more scientific and dynamic than any seen before in Massachusetts. He knew they wouldn't win if he relied on the Democratic regulars, who lined up to support the reelection of Governor Paul Dever but had less sympathy for JFK's audacious bid for the Senate. So Bobby set up a parallel structure—a party of, by, and for his brother Jack. The campaign recruited 286 local secretaries, most new to politics but not to their communities. He also set up committees that made everyone involved feel special: Women for Kennedy, Italians for Kennedy, Dentists for Kennedy. So what if the groups overlapped. "The key," Bobby explained, "was that we got a large number of people to do some work instead of trying to get a few people to do a lot of work." While he excelled at organizing, he knew not a thing about schmoozing, which in Massachusetts meant asking thousands of volunteers, "How's by you?"—then listening as if you cared. "I never heard Bob Kennedy ask anyone 'How's the family?'" said Larry O'Brien, who coordinated the field organizers and diagrammed, in a sixty-four-page black-bound book, the nuts-and-bolts organization to implement Bobby's grand strategy. "The entire hand-shaking, small-talking side of politics was repugnant to him; he often said to me, 'Larry, I don't know how you stand it.' "

With the message and sales force in place, they needed a merchandising plan. State law required only twenty-five hundred nomination signatures, but the Kennedy campaign handed in a record 262,324, with all the names going into campaign files and the milestone noted in newspapers. It signed up a hundred thousand new voters, most in districts that always went Democratic. Whereas Democrats typically focused on Boston and a handful of other cities, Bobby insisted on organizing every town with more than six hundred voters, of which there were nearly three hundred. He got the campaign going full tilt in the summer rather than waiting for the traditional Labor Day kickoff. By then, he reasoned, Lodge would have been uncatchable. Bobby was there at headquarters every morning at eight, making decisions that other managers left hanging, charting the course by which his brother and sisters crisscrossed the state, and leaving at midnight or whenever the last stamp was licked. He even inserted his and Ethel's new baby into the fray. When Joseph II was born that September, the popular Archbishop Richard Cushing baptized him in a highly publicized weekday ceremony that a Lodge aide said "cut our hearts out." Bobby was in constant motion, like a jittery welterweight, and the toll could be measured on his bathroom scale: He lost twelve pounds during the campaign. When he saw no KENNEDY FOR SENATOR sign on a building visible to anyone crossing the bridge from Irish Charlestown to the Italian North End, he commandeered the tallest ladder he could find and hung a banner himself. "While I was holding the ladder," JFK assistant Dave Powers remembered, "I was wondering how I could explain it to the Ambassador and Jack when Bobby fell and broke his neck. I also said to myself, if I had his money I would be sitting at home in a rocking chair instead of being up there on the top of that ladder."

One might have expected to find the aging ambassador sitting home in a rocker. He was a year shy of the traditional retirement age and was more prosperous than the silver-spooned Lodges. But he had built his fortune expressly so he could see his sons in high office. Jack had brought Bobby on board largely to tame Joe, and the younger son handled his dad like a master. Anyone passing Bobby's office was likely to hear this pacify-

ing telephone refrain: "Yes, Dad. Yes, Dad." In truth, Joe backed off willingly; he knew Bobby was hard-boiled like him and as fixated on Jack's
winning. But both brothers recognized there were certain pivotal objectives that nobody but their father would have the brashness or venality
to accomplish as they tried to take down a three-term incumbent.

Newspaper endorsements were key back then, and *The Boston Post*
broke with Lodge days before the election—and a day after Joe agreed to
lend its editor a cool half million dollars. Joe denied any link, but Bobby
conceded, "There was a connection," and Jack told a reporter, "We had
to buy that fucking paper, or I'd have been licked." It was Joe who realized that Lodge's role as campaign manager for Eisenhower created an
opening with Massachusetts supporters of Eisenhower's Republican opponent, Senator Robert Taft. When Taft lost his bid for the nomination,
his followers found a home in Independents for Kennedy, an organization Joe dreamed up in between sending fat checks to the conservative
Taft and the liberal Democratic candidate Adlai Stevenson. Organizations with misleading names like Improvement of Massachusetts Fish
Industry were founded with an equally political purpose: to let Kennedy
family members and others circumvent the thousand-dollar state spending limit. Each of seven Kennedys gave one thousand dollars to each of
five such front groups.

Joe Kennedy's generosity also helped ensure that Senator Joe McCarthy wouldn't use his clout with Catholics and conservatives to help his
fellow Republican Lodge, who was no fan of McCarthy. But just when Joe
thought he had expunged McCarthy and McCarthyism from the campaign, an old New Dealer whom Jack had recruited to bolster his standing with liberals proposed a newspaper advertisement simultaneously
attacking McCarthy and Communism. Gardner "Pat" Jackson believed
his ad, which underlined Jack's support for civil liberties, was just the
split-the-difference solution the candidate and campaign manager
wanted. Joe thought the idea was insane, and when Jackson started to
read the text at a campaign meeting, Joe erupted. "I can't estimate how
long he poured it out on me," Jackson recalled. "It was just a stream of
stuff—always referring to 'you and your sheeny friends.' "* The next

---

* "Sheeny" is an ethnic slur for a Jew.

morning an embarrassed Jack tried to explain his father to Jackson: "I guess there isn't a motive in it which I think you'd respect, except love of family." Moments later he corrected himself: "And more often than not, I think that's just pride." Joe denied the incident ever took place, saying that "Pat Jackson has been living off that story for years."

A similar mix of love and pride drove Bobby to make his own uncompromising declarations during the campaign. A group of Boston pols of the kind his grandfather called Dearos—for "dear old North End," the city's oldest and quaintest neighborhood—wandered into Kennedy campaign headquarters one day and were shocked on two counts by what they encountered. They couldn't believe a twenty-six-year-old was running a serious statewide campaign. Worse, rather than being welcomed as sage advisers, they were barely acknowledged. You have two options, the campaign manager told them: Lick stamps or get lost. They left and never returned, which was just what Bobby had in mind. "Those politicians just wanted to sit around and talk about it and have their pictures taken at the rallies," he said. "That's all they did."

He took the same brick-wall approach with Democratic governor Dever, a favorite of the Dearos, making clear there would be no merging of campaigns and that the Kennedys could look out for themselves. Dever was beside himself, knowing how difficult it would be for him to win on his own, and he telephoned Joe: "I know you're an important man around here and all that, but I'm telling you this and I mean it. Keep that fresh kid of yours out of my sight from here on in." Dever presumed that Joe would side with him and the other slighted old-timers. None of them grasped that Bobby was operating from Joe's playbook and with his backing. It was no accident that one heard the very phrases used over the years to smear the father now visited upon his son: He was vindictive, ambitious, frosty, and ruthless; he behaved like a spoiled brat; he played dirty pool; he was an SOB.

"Ruthless" was the label that stuck. Journalists and political foes would use that adjective throughout Bobby's career, from his years with the Rackets Committee to his work as attorney general and legislator. But it first came up here, in this Senate campaign where he was, finally, in charge. Those who got to know him realized that he was more rude than ruthless. He was too shy and unassimilated to make nice the way

Jack did. And he was too busy. Besides, who cared what people thought of him so long as they liked his older brother, the one asking for their votes? Jack withstood shocks throughout a nasty campaign because Bobby offered himself as the lightning rod. While JFK emerged with his honor intact, Bobby was branded as a consigliere. "You can't make an omelet without breaking the egg," Jack said looking back. "Every politician in Massachusetts was mad at Bobby after 1952 but we had the best organization in history." Joe understood even better: "Ruthless? As a person who has had the term applied to him for 50 years, I know a bit about it. Anybody who is controversial is called ruthless. Any man of action is always called ruthless. It's ridiculous."

The payoff came on election day. It was clear early that evening that Eisenhower would achieve his clean sweep, but the Massachusetts Senate race was a nail-biter. In an era before computers and electronic calculators, when results arrived community by community, Bobby tallied each with his faithful slide rule. By three in the morning the trend confirmed the success of his strategy of going it alone and drumming up support town by town. Jack beat Lodge by 71,000 votes, bucking national as well as state trends that favored the GOP and doomed Governor Dever. Kennedy's margin of victory was almost identical to the number of ladies who attended the receptions hosted by Rose Kennedy and her daughters, and Lodge made the connection: "It was those damned tea parties." Rose had a different take: "At last, the Fitzgeralds have evened the score with the Lodges!" But Joe knew that while his money, his wife, and his girls had done a lot, this triumph was Bobby's at least as much as Jack's.

Bobby was less confident. He attributed Jack's win in large part to the shortcomings of Senator Lodge, whom Bobby described as "a very, very lazy man as a campaigner." The "philosophy of the campaign," the young manager said, was enlisting an army of volunteers and pushing them as hard as they'd allow. What about strategy and judgment? "I don't think politics requires much," he insisted, "except effort." It was classic Bobby: uncomfortable looking back, tongue-tied, and not wanting to ballyhoo his role even when he had pulled off the most improbable of victories and helped write the manual for the modern congressional campaign.

Jack understood those feats whether or not Bobby did, which is why, four years later, he asked his little brother to once again interrupt his career as a Senate sleuth and serve as political point man. By now Jack had shifted his attention to the national stage and set his sights on the second spot on a 1956 Democratic presidential ticket headed once again by former Illinois governor Adlai Stevenson. It was early for a little-accomplished first-term senator to be making a move—too early, felt Joe, who saw the ticket as doomed to the same trouncing by Eisenhower as four years before. But if Jack wanted to try, Bobby would be there at the convention on Chicago's South Side, buttonholing delegates he didn't know and pitching the case for a fresh face from the voter-rich North-east. He'd even do what Jack dreaded most: He'd let Dad know that his sons were ignoring his counsel. Kenny O'Donnell listened as Bobby placed the call to Joe's vacation home on the French Riviera. "The Ambassador's blue language flashed all over the room," recalled O'Donnell. "The connection was broken before he was finished denouncing Jack as an idiot who was ruining his political career. Bobby quickly hung up the telephone and made no effort to get his father back on the line. 'Whew!' Bobby said. 'Is he mad!'"

Stevenson left it to delegates to pick his number two, figuring it would add drama to a convention with hardly any. He was right, with seven senators, two governors, and the mayor of New York all scrambling for votes. It came down to just two—Jack and Senator Estes Kefauver of Tennessee—with Kennedy at one point just fifteen votes shy of victory. Kefauver won out in the end, having earned the reward by making two bids for president and chairing a Senate committee that took on orga-nized crime. Joe, who may have played an unseen role in the reversal, was delighted, but Bobby would call that defeat one of his most disap-pointing moments. He acknowledged that he had been outplanned and outhustled, which were the very skills that had helped him stage Jack's successful run for the Senate. He didn't know, until then, what it felt like to lose. Crushed as he was, by the time he reached Jack's hotel room he had steeled himself to buck up his brother: "This is the luckiest thing that ever happened to you." He was right. Jack's strong run had left him a leading contender for the nomination in 1960, and losing the second spot on the ticket had eliminated the possibility that his Catholicism would be blamed for Stevenson's inevitable drubbing.

Bobby extracted a series of hardheaded lessons from the setback. First, he needed a better grasp of the parliamentary procedures of the convention and ways to keep tabs on delegates. This was Bobby in his familiar role as campaign mechanic. Second, he learned that schmoozing, however unpleasant, counted. Kefauver "had *visited* [delegates] in their home. He had sent them Christmas cards. We couldn't shake them," Bobby recalled. "Believe me, we've sent out lots of Christmas cards since." This was Bobby the backslapper, an uncomfortable task he took on for Jack's sake. His learning continued when he accepted Stevenson's request to help in the general election campaign, although now he focused on what not to do. Bobby had detected one bad habit in Stevenson: reading rather than only referring to the text of speeches. The candidate also spent too much valuable time shaking hands, and he was forever losing his luggage, his speeches, and his way to the next campaign stop. "In 1952, I had been crazy about him. I was excited in 1956, at the start," Bobby said. "Then I spent six weeks with him on the campaign and he destroyed it all." In the end, a more worldly-wise and cynical Bobby quietly marked his own ballot for Eisenhower.

He had never disguised the fact that he saw the Stevenson campaign as a dress rehearsal for the bid everyone knew Jack would make four years hence. But the calculating way he took perpetual notes and kept the campaign at a distance made him seem more like a journalist than a Stevenson partisan. The candidate found that tremendously off-putting—he referred to Bobby as the Black Prince—and so did the real reporters. "Bobby had come along without the slightest intention of helping Stevenson. The Kennedys could hardly wait for Stevenson to lose to begin their campaign for Jack," Harrison Salisbury, a Pulitzer Prize winner and op-ed editor at *The New York Times*, wrote in his memoir. "Still, I thought Bobby might at least go through the motions. He could have appeared at Stevenson's side in the Catholic towns and made a few calls to the Catholic bosses. Not Bobby. Not once did he lift a finger. . . . He was a hard-nerved political operator, I thought, a typical Kennedy."

OUTSIDERS, WHO SAW the family as a tight-knit, like-minded tribe, believed in the idea of a "typical Kennedy." Joe had planned it that way, and he taught his children that siblings and parents come first and last, while journalists and other interlopers should be kept beyond arm's length. That was why he set up worlds-unto-themselves family compounds on Cape Cod and in Palm Beach. A brood of nine children made it even easier, constituting their own social club, baseball team, and campaign clique. Joe saw his kids as interchangeable enough that when Joe Jr. died, the family could transfer its political dreams to Jack, and after him to Bobby.

Inside the clan, the differences in personality were dramatic and defining, most notably Bobby versus Jack. Growing up, the two were separated by a yawning eight and a half years. Bobby wasn't quite eleven when Jack headed to Harvard; by the time Bobby started there, Jack had been to war and back. Bobby cherished memories of Jack taking him for walks and telling him about faraway and fantastic universes. Jack mainly remembered Bobby squealing when the older siblings and their friends raided Joe's liquor cabinet. As they grew, more than years came between them. "All this business about Jack and Bobby being blood brothers has been exaggerated," said their sister Eunice, who was midway between the two agewise. "They had different tastes in men, different tastes in women." Jack had gotten a small sample of his brother's capabilities in the 1946 congressional campaign, but Bobby's work was mainly on the sidelines, and the two seldom socialized in Jack's early years in Washington.

So when Joe insisted he include his younger brother on his trip to the Middle East and the Orient in the fall of 1951, Jack moaned that Bobby would be "a pain in the ass." Yet traveling in close quarters for twenty-five thousand miles, including to trouble spots like Vietnam, let Jack see Bobby as a grown man with his own opinions. The brothers met Pakistan's first prime minister, Liaquat Ali Khan, just before he was murdered, and they saw India's first prime minister, Jawaharlal Nehru, who Bobby said "didn't pay the slightest attention to my brother but was just destroyed by my sister Pat." For Jack, the trip was a quick way to beef up his foreign policy résumé; it went deeper for Bobby, who was struck by the human dimension of scenes he witnessed and people he encountered: "These countries were struggling for independence, or had just gained their independence and were trying to right themselves and create a future." Having Bobby along began as a burden for Jack, but in the end it saved his life. Bobby arranged for his brother to be flown to a U.S. military hospital on Okinawa when an adrenal condition flared up, and he sat at his bedside when Jack's temperature shot up to 107. "They didn't think he could possibly live," Bobby remembered. It was the second time priests had given the congressman last rites.

By the time the brothers got home, they had forged a bond and discovered how much they shared. Both were weaned on beach and ocean, which would draw them back forever. Each had contemplated a career in journalism or academia that would let them explore the world and share their observations. Neither started out as a good speaker but both made up for it with self-effacing humor and irony. Bobby was as intelligent as Jack, although less of an intellectual; Jack had Bobby's toughness, although he was better at disguising it. "They were kind of twin spirits," Ethel says. "One would start a sentence and the other would finish it." Both were ambitious for their own sake, and for their father's, although Jack had less to prove, and he had Bobby as a buffer.

The defining distinctions in temperament and outlook crystallized as the two spent more time together as young adults. Jack would always be the handsome older brother whose silky-smooth polish made begrudging Bostonians tag him as a "Fifth Avenue Catholic" and "Harvard Irishman." Bobby was all Gaelic, bristling with energy and trusting his gut. If the Church had been their calling, Jack would have been pope, Bobby a parish priest. Jack looked past women he met unless they were young and gorgeous. Bobby was interested in nearly everybody, grasping a hand and peering into a face in ways that made a person feel a genuine connection. Each stood as the other's best man when they married, but when Jack wanted to relax, he turned to his even younger brother Ted, not the more prudish Bobby. When Joe offered all his children one thousand dollars for not drinking until age twenty-one and another thousand for not smoking, Bobby collected, Jack indulged. "Jack has always been one to persuade people to do things," his father said. "Bobby tends to tell people what to do."

Their singularities were easy to spot on the football field. Jack hung back, protecting his wounded back and aristocratic bearing, while Bobby charged into anyone, kids included, who was foolish enough to stand between him and the end zone. It was apparent, too, in the swimming pool. Both made the Harvard team, where their acclaimed coach Harold Ulen remembered Bobby as "very heavy in the water," while Jack "could float very well." That, family biographers Peter Collier and David Horowitz wrote, was a metaphor for what separated the two: "Jack's sensibility was buoyantly literary; Bobby's was heavily moral, however inchoate. Bobby sought responsibility as compulsively as Jack tried to evade it."

Those very divergences let them construct a brotherly alliance that would become as celebrated in the political sphere as the one between Wilbur and Orville Wright in aviation. Each brother had trained for his role in their campaigns, Bobby by molding himself into a relentless prosecutor, Jack by reading, traveling, and perfecting his smile. The division of labor was perfect—Jack as statesman, Bobby as hatchet man—and perfectly suited to the Kennedy family business. "It was politics that brought them together," Eunice said. "That's a business full of knives. Jack needed someone he could trust, someone who had loyalty to him. Jack knew he had a person like that with Bobby around." The newspaper columnist Stewart Alsop called it a "sweet-and-sour brother act" in which "Jack uses his charm and waves the carrot, and then Bobby wades in with the stick." Theirs was a reversal of normal sibling roles, with the younger doing extraordinary things for the elder. Bobby was his brother's keeper. Sometimes that role brought out his warmheartedness, but it could also make Bobby defensive and vindictive. When Bobby told someone "No," Jack added "I'm sorry." Jack made friends, Bobby enemies— the appropriate outcomes for a politician and his sideman.

Yet those roles belied their characters in ways that elevated Jack and diminished Bobby. "John Kennedy was a realist brilliantly disguised as a romantic, Robert a romantic stubbornly disguised as a realist," observed Arthur Schlesinger, Jr., biographer to both. Joe realized from the start that the yin-and-yang tandem could be unstoppable, and Jack came to see that over time. The press called Bobby as steely as Joe, and Jack as tender as Rose, but they had it exactly backward. "Jack would cut you off at the knees," said Kenny O'Donnell. "Bobby would say, 'Why are we doing that to this guy?'"

Bobby and Jack were the fulcrum of Kennedy dynamics in those years, but other relationships were forming that would fascinate the public as the Kennedys became America's First Family. None was more beguiling than Jackie's with Bobby. Jacqueline Lee Bouvier had met John Fitzgerald Kennedy in the spring of 1952, just as Bobby was taking over the Senate campaign. She realized from the first that being involved with Jack meant being entangled with his family, particularly the patriarch, and she reached Joe in a way that none of his other daughters-in-law could. She also instinctively understood the Kennedy mix of mind-boggling narcissism and unmatched altruism.

Jackie saw the tender promise of Bobby that neither the public nor Jack appreciated back then. When her second pregnancy went wrong and the daughter she planned to name Arabella was stillborn, Jack was unreachable off the coast of Italy. It was Bobby who rushed to her bedside, consoling her and quietly arranging for the baby's burial. When Jackie sat dumbfounded by the family's fascination with sports, Bobby would explain, then let her know it was okay to cheer from the sidelines. "You knew that, if you were in trouble, he'd always be there," she said of her brother-in-law. He is "the one I would put my hand in the fire for." Reading press reports of his ruthlessness, Jackie added, "I just thought, 'If they could have known the compassion of that boy.'" And hearing everyone else describe Bobby as the son most like Joe, she insisted he was in fact "least like his father."

One arena in which Bobby had always shown his softer side was his faith. All the Kennedys called themselves Catholic, but Bobby practiced his religion in ways that endeared him to his mother and distinguished him from Jack. During his three years at Portsmouth Priory School, he went to church the required four times a week plus the three optional services. Ritual played an even bigger part of life in his and Ethel's home than it had in Rose and Joe's. The young couple outfitted each of the thirteen bedrooms with a Bible, holy water, and a crucifix or statue of Saint Mary. There were prayers every morning, before and after each meal, and at bedtime when the children assembled to recite as one "Now I lay me down to sleep." Benediction was offered for the family, too, and as the list of deceased relatives grew, the children named each one and asked God to vault them straight to heaven. Also named were the saints they prayed to—Anthony to end poverty and find a parking place, Francis for the growing menagerie, and Christopher when they took off in a plane. Bobby's Saint Christopher medal never left his neck, which made sense given his nonstop traveling.

Most observers assumed Ethel was the keeper of the flame of faith, and that she was more wed to liturgy than Bobby. But the reassurance he found in his religion was apparent when, as a young man, he stepped over the railing and volunteered as an altar boy at St. Francis Xavier Church in Hyannis, to the delight of his mother, who attended early mass every morning. He did the same thing in random cities across America during his many investigations and campaigns. "The priests couldn't believe the delicacy with which he did it," recalls advance man James Tolan. "They told me they never saw an individual serve mass in that way other than a seminarian."

His Catholicism was integral to his politics, too. It reinforced the sense of public service drilled into the children by Rose and Joe. It was consistent with his commitment to the sanctity of the family—and to big ones like he was born into and that he and Ethel would more than replicate. Bobby shared the Church's conscientious division of the world into good and evil, along with its judgment that Communists are godless and the poor blessed. His life centered on three totems in those years of early adulthood: the Democratic Party, the Kennedy family, and God.

But he distinguished between the faith's divinity and its hierarchy. While he held the former sacrosanct, he had always challenged Church authorities, from parish priests to the pope. Back in his undergraduate days, he joined other Harvard Catholics at lectures by Father Leonard Feeney, an influential Jesuit priest who warned that the Jews "are trying to take over this city" and preached that only Catholics could be saved. Bobby was embarrassed enough by those diatribes to discuss them with his brother Ted and his father, who arranged for him to meet with Archbishop Cushing to convey his concern. Even a Kennedy found it difficult to confront a prelate in those days, and Bobby's courage likely played a role in Feeney's eventual expulsion from his order and excommunication from the Church. In later years, Bobby lobbied the pope to name a liberal replacement for New York's archconservative Cardinal Francis Joseph Spellman. And when he piled the children into the station wagon for the ride to church—they had to attend starting as toddlers, although they stayed in the back with a nursemaid until they were "church broke"—he "always carried a Bible with him," recalls Bobby Jr. "When the priest started talking about the right-wing stuff he would pointedly read the Bible or he would read the Catholic newspapers at the back of the church." He called it "an awful thing" that the Church taught that babies, his or anyone's, were born in sin. He told his kids that "priests were Republicans and nuns Democrats." He also told them they needn't trust clerics to mediate the word of God when they could read it for themselves in the Old Testament and the New.

That next generation of Kennedys loved the family vacation retreats at least as much as Bobby and his siblings had, in Palm Beach and especially on Cape Cod. Bobby eventually bought the Hyannis Port house next to Joe's, Jack the one next to that, with other siblings moving nearby. The six acres on which the three original houses sat became known as the Kennedy compound. With so many children and later grandchildren on hand, there had to be rules. Each guidepost offered a lens into the Kennedy way of doing things. It had been okay since Bobby and Jack were young to grab a ride to town with the chauffeur, but only if he was heading there on an errand. It was all right to go sailing, if you let the governess know. The tennis courts were open anytime, but siblings had to take turns. As they aged, Joe's offspring and their guests were welcome to join him for a drink before dinner, but just one, and only until the dinner bell rang. One way to know where you ranked in the Kennedy hierarchy, and where the sibling who invited you did, was whether you got a seat on the family plane for the trip back to Washington (Jack's and Bobby's friends generally did, Ted's and the girls' rarely). The one topic that Joe had always banished from the dinner table was money (Bobby's habitual line was "Send the bill to the Park Agency," which managed Joe's millions).

Every rule, including that one, had an exception. It manifested itself one night when Joe was on a tirade. "There is no one in the entire family, except for Joan and Teddy, who is living within their means. No one appears to have the slightest concern for how much they spend," he stormed. Then he turned to Ethel and said, "And you, young lady, you are the worst." It was true, but it was more than Bobby could take. "I think you have made your point," he said, as Ethel ran out of the room and he followed. When they returned minutes later, Jack rescued the evening, the way no one but Jack could. "Well, kid, don't worry," he said to Ethel. "We've come to the conclusion that the only solution is to have Dad work harder." Even Joe laughed.

The Kennedys had a rulebook, too, for playing their favorite game (football) in their favorite spot (the great lawn), although it was not one any professional or college team would recognize. A standard guideline for Bobby, Jack, and the rest was that if you could touch the ball, you should be able to catch it. No need to suggest plays if you were a guest, no matter whether you had quarterbacked in high school or the pros; the Kennedys handled the play calling. Bobby's personal rules depended on the composition of his team. If it was big and slow, he allowed passing only from behind the line of scrimmage, since scrambling wouldn't help. If it was light and fast, it was okay to throw the ball anywhere, anytime, to anyone in front of you or behind.

The rules so confused Dave Hackett, Bobby's friend since high school, that he drafted a training manual. At the dinner table, "prepare yourself by reading The Congressional Record, US News & World Report, Time, Newsweek, Fortune, The Nation, The Democratic Digest, The Ensign, and the manual How to Play Sneaky Tennis. . . . Anticipate that each Kennedy will ask you what you think of another Kennedy's (a) dress, (b) hairdo, (c) backhand, (d) latest achievement. You will find that 'Terrific!' is a satisfactory answer." As for athletic contests like football, "the only way I know of to get out of playing is not to come at all, or to come with a broken leg . . . if you want to become popular, show raw guts. . . . Oh yes! Don't be too good. Let Jack run around you every so often." And "don't, under any circumstances, let Ethel fool you. Never treat her either as pregnant or as a woman. Her husband has spent all of his spare time developing her change of pace, her timing on reverses, her endurance, and so forth, and she will make you look silly."

The singer Andy Williams saw that firsthand when he showed up on the Hickory Hill tennis court with his big toe in a cast. "You're not going to let a thing like a little old broken toe stop you—we need a fourth," Ethel said. Williams inspected the other players—the elite mountaineer Jim Whittaker with a bandage covering a recent vein surgery, Ted Kennedy wearing a back brace, and Ethel seven months pregnant—then grabbed a racket.*

Since these were the Kennedys, there were rules for politics as well, although no friend would dare write them down: Forgive your enemies, but never forget their names. Don't get mad, get even. When you screw up, say so, no excuses. Guests were instructed that what went on in Hyannis Port must not be divulged to anyone outside the family, and above all not to the press. In all matters, Kennedys by birth came first, with in-laws like Sargent Shriver and Peter Lawford distant seconds. There also was a first among the Kennedy equals: the paterfamilias, Joseph Patrick. The last and unifying edict was that everyone be held to the rulebook but the Kennedys themselves.

———

BOBBY WAS THE first and singular choice to quarterback the campaign to which all the others had been building: Jack's 1960 bid for the presidency. No one else could be counted on to execute the tactical details and craft a master strategy. Nobody else could be trusted with the family secrets of paying for and pulling off a venture this bold. No one, with the exception of Joe, had earned it more, by getting Jack to the point where he was not just one of the wannabes but the man to beat for the Democratic nomination.

The Kennedys knew from the first that their biggest obstacle to the nomination would be a candidate who was too wily to show his cards. So in the fall of 1959, nearly a year before the Democratic convention in Los Angeles, Jack dispatched Bobby to the ranch in Stonewall, Texas, that Lyndon Baines Johnson had initialed after himself, the same way he had his wife and daughters. It wasn't an assignment that Bobby relished, and he was determined not to play LBJ's game. So, direct Bostonian that he was, he tried to get to the points fast: Are you running for president? If not, whom will you back? But that was neither the Southern way nor

---

* Joe encouraged the competition within the family by, among other things, offering a thousand-dollar prize to the daughter-in-law who invited the best dining partner for him at a dinner for ten she hosted. "I was [Ethel's] candidate," recalled Nancy Dickerson, CBS's first female correspondent. "She wanted to book me 'before Eunice gets you'" (Dickerson, *Among Those Present*, 69).

Johnson's. First, Bobby had to accompany him on the deer hunt he staged for all his guests, especially ones he knew would be uneasy in that setting. Bobby was handed a powerful shotgun instead of the standard rifle, and when he fired, the recoil sent him reeling backward and to the ground, wounding his brow and his ego. "Son," LBJ said, "you've got to learn to handle a gun like a man." Bobby took away three messages from his trip—that Johnson would neither run himself nor seek to block Jack's candidacy (wrong on both), and that he didn't fight fair (right). LBJ's custom of ambushing his prey from the comfort of an elevated concrete platform "isn't hunting," Bobby concluded, "it's slaughter."

JFK and Bobby mapped out a strategy for the nomination that called for entering ten primaries, of which only two really mattered. The first bellwether would be on April 5 in Wisconsin, an uncomfortable setting for a Massachusetts Democrat. With a political heritage that swung between La Follette progressivism and McCarthy conservatism, there was no natural fit for Kennedy-style moderation. The Wisconsin economy was built on cheese, milk, and other commodities that the Kennedys consumed in substantial quantities without caring how they got to the kitchen table. Add to that an opponent, Hubert Humphrey, who was a popular senator from the bordering state of Minnesota, and most campaign managers would simply have skipped Wisconsin and headed directly to the next week's primary in Illinois. Not Bobby. All those hurdles let him position his brother just where he wanted him: as the underdog. He'd advised Jack not to run in Wisconsin, Bobby told reporters, some of whom believed him. Savvier ones knew that a third of the state was Catholic like the Kennedys and, as *The New York Times* was reporting, that private Kennedy polls showed him with 60 percent support among Wisconsin Democrats. Bobby managed the campaign just as he had orchestrated congressional investigations, learning as much as possible about the outcome before wading into battle, lowering expectations so that a modest victory looked major, and seldom ducking journalists but almost never confiding in them.

Humphrey might have had a shot if the race had been fought on a more level field. The Kennedys opened eight offices to Humphrey's two. Bobby had on his staff one of America's savviest pollsters, Louis Harris, who could measure shifts in public opinion quickly enough for the candidate to adjust. Harris was backed up by an army of Bobby and Jack's siblings, friends, and retainers from Massachusetts and Washington, while Humphrey relied on volunteers from Minnesota able to drive down on the weekends, along with support stitched together at the eleventh hour from unions and the state party. Jack flew in on the *Caroline*, his private twin-engine Convair equipped with a bed, galley, and desk with a swivel chair; Hubert motored down in a rented bus that his staff outfitted with an army cot, blanket, and pillow. "Once, as we started into the darkness of the rural countryside, I heard a plane overhead," Humphrey recalled. "Bundled in layers of uncomfortable clothes, both chilled and sweaty, I yelled, 'Come down here, Jack, and play fair.'"

Always the Happy Warrior, Humphrey said he didn't mind being outgunned or out-glamored, but he couldn't forgive the "ruthlessness and toughness" displayed by the Kennedys, and most of all Bobby. One upsetting instance was "Bob Kennedy's peddling the story that my campaign was being financed by Teamster president Jimmy Hoffa," Humphrey complained later. "Both he and Jack knew the story was untrue and could have stopped it." Equally infuriating were anonymous anti-Catholic mailings sent across the state—mainly to Catholic households—which ensured a turnout of angry Catholic Democrats along with Catholic Republicans who crossed over. The apparent culprit in both cases was Paul Corbin, a Kennedy aide famous for his whimsical and deceitful tactics. "If you have a job and you want to get it done, and you don't care *how* it's done," said campaign aide Helen Keyes, "send Paul Corbin out to do it." Corbin was sufficiently devoted that he eventually converted to Catholicism so that Bobby and Ethel could be his godparents. Bobby loved him back, above all for his outrageousness. Humphrey was right that whether or not Bobby ordered up the dirty tricks, he did nothing to stop them, and their success ensured they were a fixture of U.S. campaign culture from then on.

Jack beat Humphrey by a comfortable 12 percentage points, but it was shy of a knockout blow in the eyes of a skeptical press and an angry opponent. Humphrey had won four of ten congressional districts and insisted he would fight on in West Virginia, the next major battleground. The Mountain State's coal-based economy was as impoverished as the Badger State's was affluent, its politics as ethically challenged as Wisconsin's was righteous. And whereas one in three Wisconsinites was Catholic, in West Virginia it was just one in ten. The Kennedys' private polls this time revealed a challenge steeper than any Bobby had conjured up in the Midwest: While surveys in West Virginia that winter had shown Jack ahead 70 to 30 percent, media reports filtering in from Wisconsin caused such hemorrhaging that Jack suddenly found himself trailing by 20 percent as the May 10 primary approached. Asked why, his advisers explained, "No one in West Virginia knew you were a Catholic in December. Now they know."

It is difficult today to conceive that Catholicism could have been such a stigma as recently as 1960. After all, one in four Americans was Catholic then, making it the biggest religious denomination in the country. John Kennedy was not the first Catholic nominated for president; Al Smith had been the Democrats' standard-bearer thirty-two years earlier. But Smith was crushed by Herbert Hoover, a Quaker, and the anti-Catholic vote was believed to have been the reason. The same questions raised with Smith in 1928 resurfaced in 1960 in Charleston, Huntington, and the sweeping hills and coal-ravaged hollows of West Virginia. Could a Bible Belt state like this, where Protestants were the mainstream and Southern Baptists the biggest denomination, trust a Roman Catholic? And, as Bobby put it, would ministers "start telling people that they can't vote for a Catholic because the Pope is coming over?" Kennedy aides in Washington advised ducking the explosive issue. Those on the ground in West Virginia said that that wasn't an option. The candidate and his brother ended up making the call, the same way Barack Obama would half a century later when race rather than religion was the target of bigots. JFK did not just affirm his faith, he remade the primary campaign and the entire election into a referendum on how tolerant Americans were.

It was a master stroke and the only option. The issue would have festered whether or not he addressed it. Rabid anti-Catholics stood ready to vote against him either way, and this strategy provided a chance to tilt wavering voters his way. His most famous address on the topic would come in September before the Greater Houston Ministerial Association, but he gave a similar talk in a paid telecast in West Virginia, with Franklin Roosevelt, Jr., as his interlocutor. "When any man stands on the steps of the Capitol and takes the oath of office of President, he is swearing to support the separation of church and state," Kennedy said, looking straight into the camera. "If he breaks his oath, he is not only committing a crime against the Constitution . . . he is committing a sin against God." The candidate pushed every button that mattered to West Virginians—allegiance to country over pope, the notion that no sin was greater than one against God, and a reminder that FDR Jr., the son of an icon whose portrait still hung in the homes of many West Virginians, was in Kennedy's corner. The use of symbols like those was a trademark not just of John but of Robert Kennedy, and later in the campaign, Bobby would make a speech of his own in Cincinnati that touched similar chords: "I can't imagine that any country for which my brother Joe died could care about my brother Jack's religion when it came . . ." He stopped there, tears visible to those with him on the podium, unable to get out the last words.

The primary was not fought exclusively on such high ground. This was, after all, a state where buying votes was almost as common as paying election workers. Here, unions, party bosses, and other interest groups customarily handed out printed slates to remind voters who they'd promised to pick among the fifty candidates on the ballot. It was familiar terrain for the Kennedys, reared as they were in Massachusetts's equally crooked system of ward bosses and influence trading. Early in the campaign an anonymous Minnesotan sent the Kennedy camp records suggesting that Humphrey had dodged the draft during World War II. The charge would surely set off sparks in West Virginia, which boasted the highest proportion in the nation of men serving—and dying—in the military. It was true that Humphrey had not served, but even Bobby and Jack knew that labeling him a draft dodger could backfire, since it stretched the facts: He had tried several times to enlist but was rejected first for family reasons (he was married and a father), then because he was an "essential civilian" (teaching Army Air Corps cadets), and finally because of his health (a double hernia, color blindness, and lung troubles). The Kennedys gave the records to a *New York Times* reporter on the condition that he use them only with their clearance. Their self-restraint wore thin as Humphrey attacked JFK's record, his integrity, and, as the Kennedys saw it, his religion. ("Poor Little Jack!" teased Hubert, who was just six years older. "I wish he would grow up and stop acting like a boy.") Finally the Kennedy side hit back, hard and low. "I resent any man who has claimed he was 4-F all the way through the war when he really stayed out at his own request until just before the end of the war," FDR Jr. said as he campaigned for JFK in the coal mining county of Fayette. Roosevelt would later insist that Bobby pushed him to get tough, calling night after night "asking me, 'When will you lower the boom?'" Larry O'Brien, the Kennedy aide who had received the leaked conscription files, said Roosevelt acted not under orders from either Kennedy but out of pique that Humphrey was taking swipes at him. Hubert said he would never forgive Franklin Jr. or Bobby.

Humphrey was equally outraged by the Kennedy money pouring into the state, which in the end affected the voting more than the back-and-forth over his draft record. "I don't have any daddy who can pay the bills for me," the Minnesotan complained. Allegations flew, too, about the Kennedys' paying off local officials, journalists, and voters. "No one would prove it," wrote Harrison Salisbury of *The New York Times*, "but everyone knew that a vote for Kennedy was worth $5 in 1960 money. The district leaders had stacks of cash and spread it around." Larry O'Brien acknowledged that he had "cash at hand" and said that one time, he called his secretary "and whispered, 'Bring me five.' Phyllis kept the money in the suitcase under her bed, and in a moment she appeared in the lobby and slipped me five hundred dollars, not the five thousand I'd agreed to." O'Brien said the money went to pay poll workers and other "legitimate Election Day expenses," that "neither Jack nor Bob Kennedy knew what agreements I made," and that "our total outlay statewide was about $100,000 including radio and television, less than a candidate for Congress in any *one* congressional district would expect to spend."* Bobby was both adamant and elliptical on the role of Kennedy largesse: "There may have been some vote buying for some people with whiskey, money, or both, but they weren't votes for us and it wasn't our whiskey and it wasn't our money."

---

* Judge Marjorie McKenzie Lawson, a Kennedy campaign coordinator in West Virginia, said there was nothing wrong with the kind of modest walking-around money she was given: "It was doled out at about a dollar an hour to people who were willing to ride around and talk to people in the woods somewhere and bring them to meetings" (Lawson OH, October 25, 1965, 15–18, JFKL).

Certainly, the Kennedy money carried weight, but most analysts agree it never was as much as claimed by the candidates Jack clobbered. When the mudslinging was through and the votes were counted that May evening in West Virginia, the balloting turned out just the way Bobby had plotted. JFK won 61 percent of the votes to Humphrey's 39 percent, a margin ten points wider than in Wisconsin and enough to bury the idea that a Catholic couldn't prevail in a Bible Belt Protestant stronghold. Bobby understood that this was the last difficult primary they would face and, while the victory didn't ensure the nomination, it gave them reason to celebrate for the first time in those grueling months. He did so that very night, with a gesture that, while not entirely appreciated, revealed him as something more than a gutter warrior. After midnight, he called Humphrey saying he wanted to come by his headquarters. Humphrey didn't want to see him but said he would. Joseph Rauh, a Humphrey adviser, described the scene:

> The door opened. Bobby walks in. It was like the Red Sea opening for Moses. Everybody walked backwards, and there was a path from the door to the other side of the room where Hubert and Muriel were standing. I'll never forget that walk if I live to be a hundred. Bobby walked slowly, deliberately, over to the Humphreys. He leaned in and kissed Muriel. I've always wondered whether she had on her mind at that moment that she was going to poke him because she was really not very happy about the outcome. Anyway, he was very nice and gracious and it was the right thing for him to have done. But at the moment, it sure was something.

After West Virginia, Humphrey bowed out of the race, leaving JFK to face mainly token opposition from favorite sons in the remaining contests. But only fifteen states and the District of Columbia held primaries in 1960; the stop-Kennedy movement still saw hope in the vast number of unpledged delegates, and in Lyndon Johnson, the powerful Senate majority leader. Johnson was savvier and richer than Humphrey, and more willing and able to slug it out with Kennedy. LBJ had been taking Jack's measure for the eight years they served together in the Senate, and he was convinced the Massachusetts Democrat was too young and green to entrust with the White House. While he waited until a week before the Democratic convention in July to officially announce his candidacy, he had been maneuvering behind the scenes at least since Bobby visited his ranch the previous autumn, and now he put his wiles to work.

Sure that the Kennedys were planting doubts about whether he was healthy enough to serve after a near-fatal heart attack in 1955, LBJ beat them to it. Jack is a "little scrawny fellow with rickets," he whispered to a reporter from the *Chicago Daily News* in a late-night conversation aboard his private plane. Making a tiny circle with his fingers, Johnson asked, "Have you ever seen his ankles? They're about so round." His sleuths in the pharmaceutical and medical communities, meanwhile, confirmed that Kennedy had Addison's disease, a serious condition in which the adrenal glands don't produce enough hormones. "Doctors," a senior LBJ aide announced at a press conference a day before LBJ confirmed he was running, "have told me he would not be alive if it were not for cortisone."

If LBJ thought his adversaries naïve and unready, Bobby's same-day response to the medical charges made him think again. Johnson's attack, he told reporters, was a sign that "there are those within the Democratic party who would prefer that if they cannot win the nomination themselves they want the Democrat who does win to lose in November." Jack, he insisted, "does not now nor has he ever had an ailment described classically as Addison's Disease." Bobby proceeded to release a statement from JFK's doctors proclaiming his health "excellent" and a page from his political biography attesting to the family's openness in acknowledging his "adrenal insufficiency." The hair-splitting denials typified the Kennedy way of doing what it takes to win. Jack did in fact have Addison's. His adrenal glands were not just producing insufficient hormones, they were withering away. He had been getting cortisone injections for a decade, with Joe going so far as to stash emergency supplies of the drug in safety deposit boxes wherever his son traveled. No one learned any of that at the time, however. The counterattack worked, notwithstanding its contravention of Bobby's investigatory zeal for truth telling. LBJ was compelled to disavow his aide's allegations and to eat crow.

Bobby was everywhere now. He put out brush fires ignited by LBJ and other adversaries and rallied his staff of former Rackets Committee aides and longtime Kennedy minions. He campaigned personally at roadside rallies and Rotary Clubs, his least favorite part of the job. Even when he wasn't there, aides half-joked that "little brother is watching." He helped Jack plot strategy when they talked by phone every night and had a free hand with tactics. The image of a well-oiled campaign juggernaut was a myth invented after the fact by journalists. Politics requires thinking on one's feet, and nobody was better at ad-libbing than Bobby, whether it was counterstriking on Jack's health or gambling on the religious tolerance of West Virginia voters. Often he would give overlapping or even identical assignments to two different staffers, infuriating them but guaranteeing that the job got done. Now, more than ever, the team consisted of nice guy Jack and that SOB Bobby.

As the convention neared, he drilled into staffers that they could not make any misstep that would give their opponents an opening. Few knew that Bobby himself had uncharacteristically made just that sort of mistake two weeks before the delegates arrived. It happened at a pool party at Hickory Hill in honor of Clark Mollenhoff, the reporter he had worked with at the Rackets Committee who had broken his neck in a car crash the previous fall. After eight months, his cast finally was off, but he was wearing a neck brace and told Bobby he couldn't swim yet. The beefy Mollenhoff was walking along a gangplank that ran over the pool, on his way to the bar, when "out of nowhere came this form in swimming trunks with the spray all over him, like a young god coming out of the water," remembered Fletcher Knebel, a reporter with the Cowles newspaper chain. Bobby "gives Clark a push. Clark takes one big step trying to get to the side of the pool, misses, catches his foot in the trough, rolls right over on his neck. Boom! . . . First thing that went through my mind was—Clark was a good friend of mine—one, he's dead and two, Kennedy has lost the nomination." Mollenhoff picked himself out of the pool and told Knebel, "No, no, no, I feel fine." Knebel planned to write a story on what he had seen—evidence that Bobby was "not only ruthless, he's idiotic"—but Mollenhoff persuaded him not to. Nor did any other reporter who was there. "It just shows you how people were about the Kennedys," Knebel told a Kennedy Library interviewer years later. "If Nixon's brother had jumped out of the pool like that it would have been headlined everywhere."

Bobby demanded from his staff clear-eyed assessments of where every convention delegate stood, and he did whatever it took to line them up for Jack. The Kennedys had agreed to let Governor Michael DiSalle run uncontested as a favorite son in his state of Ohio if he publicly announced that he really was for JFK. Bobby knew the endorsement would matter most if it came early; DiSalle balked about jumping on an empty bandwagon. Bobby headed to Ohio to meet with the governor, and afterward DiSalle called JFK and Kenny O'Donnell to complain. "He told me that Bobby was the 'most obnoxious kid he'd ever met,' that Bobby practically had called him a liar and said 'We can't trust you. You will do what you're told,'" O'Donnell recalled. "In essence, Bobby'd done exactly what he'd been told to [by Jack], of course." That Kennedy brashness worked, with the Buckeye governor pledging his delegation to JFK; other officeholders got the message. Bobby told Alabama governor John Patterson to cast for JFK just four of his fourteen delegates on the first roll call. If a second ballot were needed, Alabama, the first state alphabetically and first to vote, should cast all fourteen for JFK to make it look as if he was gaining momentum. Not only would that be disingenuous, Patterson told Bobby, it would be awkward to explain to delegates who had stuck their necks out for a Catholic Yankee that he didn't need their first-ballot vote. "And [Bobby] said, 'Well, do it. I want you to do it,'" Patterson recalls. The governor did as he was instructed, and "some of them held that against me all their lives."

Remembering Jack's narrow loss for the second spot in 1956, Bobby took nothing for granted at the convention. Pledges made in the smoke-filled back rooms of that era lasted only until a more tempting offer arrived. So Bobby choreographed whatever he could, which was more than any campaign manager ever had. His staff prepared dossiers on each delegate. Volunteers tracked their movements and used a network of phones and walkie-talkies to report hourly on any and all disturbing developments. The arm twisting and preplanning paid off. Jack won, on the first ballot, before delegates could defect to LBJ or anyone else. His tally of eight hundred six votes was twice Johnson's and within ten of Bobby's prediction. With the nomination secure, Bobby let himself show a few minutes of emotion, dancing around the room with Pierre Salinger in what the press assistant called a French-Irish jig. He hadn't had any real sleep in days and hadn't let himself or his troops relax even an inch, knowing that if the polling went beyond that first ballot, Jack was sunk. It was, Bobby would say later, the best day of his life, but the celebration was short-lived and so was the joy. The following day would be one of his worst.

Jack still had to find a running mate before the convention wrapped up and the general election campaign could begin. Seldom has the choice of a vice presidential nominee caused so much consternation or sparked such prolonged historical debate. Bobby preferred Senator Henry Jackson of Washington State, whom he knew and liked from their days chasing the Teamsters. Jack liked Humphrey until Hubert balked at endorsing him. The name of another Minnesotan, Governor Orville Freeman, was raised, but not too high. Senator Stuart Symington of Missouri was everybody's second choice for the number two spot, and he was so convinced Kennedy would pick him—he had drawing power in the South and Midwest and support from labor, liberals, and, it seemed, both Kennedy brothers—that he held a family conclave the night of JFK's nomination. "Dad called us up to his room and said, 'I have a big decision to make: Do I accept the vice presidency?'" his son James remembers. "We went to bed that night absolutely convinced that was going to happen."

Candidates prevaricate. Nothing Jack said really counted until he formally won the nomination and made a definitive offer to a running mate. Each previous promise was aimed at giving one more ambitious politician a stake in the Kennedy candidacy. All the vice presidential hopefuls understood that reality, just as they knew that the man among them least mentioned—except to rule him out to nervous liberals—made the most sense. Lyndon Johnson had more backing among the delegates than anyone but JFK, having garnered four hundred nine votes compared to eighty-six for Symington, forty-two for Humphrey, and none for Freeman. Johnson perfectly complemented Kennedy. He was an artful insider who could corral his Senate colleagues while Jack rallied the nation. His fatherly demeanor might comfort voters put off by JFK's youth and glamor, and his lackluster public presence would never threaten Kennedy's place in the spotlight. Better still, Johnson came not just from the South, where a northerner like Kennedy was suspect, but from Texas, which had more electoral votes than all but five other states. "Helps with farmers, Southerners and Texas," the speechwriter Ted Sorensen wrote two weeks before the convention in a memo to Jack and Bobby that put LBJ's name atop a list of vice presidential possibilities. The party's left wing might not have liked him, but its only alternative in the general election would be a Republican. LBJ seemed just the man to keep conservative Democrats in the Kennedy frame. Although Sorensen was one of the few Kennedy advisers who wanted Johnson, the ever-pragmatic Joe Kennedy did as well, and had for years.

While Johnson had a family champion in Joe, he had an enemy in Bobby, who had a memory like an elephant when it came to family slights. For years, LBJ had been regaling listeners with the story of how his friend Franklin Roosevelt gleefully sacked Joe Kennedy as ambassador to Great Britain. For years, Joe's attack dog son Bobby had been seething. The two finally met in 1953 in the Senate cafeteria, where Bobby was sitting with his new boss Joe McCarthy and others when LBJ stopped by to shake hands. Kennedy was the only one at the table not to stand, with his glower speaking for him. "Bobby could really look hating, and that was how he looked then," said an LBJ aide who was there. "He didn't want to get up, but Johnson was kind of forcing him to."

Each new encounter had fueled Bobby's resentment. In 1955, Joe Kennedy passed word to LBJ that if he would run for president with Jack as his running mate, Joe would finance the campaign. When LBJ quickly declined, Bobby was "infuriated," thinking it was "unforgivably discourteous to turn down his father's generous offer," according to Tommy Corcoran, a Washington insider who was the intermediary between Joe and Johnson. The hunting incident at the ranch four years later convinced Bobby that the Texan was, in addition to his other faults, a brute. LBJ had taken to calling Bobby "Sonny Boy" to his face, while behind his back he was "a snot-nose" and "that little shitass." Worse was his slurring of Joe early in the convention. "[I] never thought Hitler was right," Johnson told delegates from Washington State, whereas Joe Kennedy was a "Chamberlain umbrella man."* Just after that, Bobby Baker, an

---

* British prime minister Neville Chamberlain, who habitually carried an umbrella, pursued a policy of appeasing the Nazis before World War II, when Joe was America's ambassador to Britain and a supporter of Chamberlain. "Umbrella man" is another way of saying boot-licker.

LBJ intimate, ran into Bobby Kennedy at the convention hotel coffee shop. Kennedy "immediately grew so red in the face I thought he might have a stroke," Baker recalled. "'You've got your nerve,' he snapped. 'Lyndon Johnson has compared my father to the Nazis and John Connally and India Edwards lied in saying my brother is dying of Addison's disease.' . . . He was leaning forward, clenching his fists, thrusting his face into mine. I was shocked."

That history would form a backdrop to the most acrimonious and consequential relationship in political Washington over the next decade. But for the Kennedys, family overrode everything, and in this case that meant giving Jack the best possible shot at the White House. To that end, Joe, the target of LBJ's most relentless name-calling, was the most bullish about putting him on the ticket. Jack came to see the logic, if not the poetry, in that choice. Eventually, so did Bobby. He would later say that JFK "really hadn't thought about it at all" as to who'd be number two on the 1960 Democratic ticket until it was certain he'd be number one. Perhaps, but that seems more like Bobby's recasting history than the behavior of his candidate brother, who had been running for at least four years and had planned for every contingency. Surely he had thought about this critical one. Equally certainly, Bobby had, too.

Here is what we know. On July 14, less than twelve hours after he accepted the nomination he coveted, JFK took the back stairs from his corner suite on the ninth floor of Los Angeles's Biltmore Hotel to LBJ's suite in the same corner two floors down. He did not stop on the eighth floor, where Bobby had a set of rooms, or at those of any vice presidential contender, where clusters of reporters were camped out. JFK got to the point quickly: Would LBJ be "available" for the vice presidency if it were offered? Johnson was interested. The conversation was over in thirty minutes. In the peculiar mating dance of two master politicians, feelers were extended and intentions signaled, but offers were neither made nor answered.

Piecing together what happened during the bewitching half day that followed that first meeting provides an object lesson in subjective memory and historical legend building. Governors and senators, labor bosses, and campaign aides all offered their recollections, shaded by time, festering hatreds, and other reminiscences they had read or heard. If each was

to be believed, several people were two places at once, offering contradictory advice to people they had never met but who took it nonetheless.
Were there two, three, or four meetings between Bobby and the Johnson
team, and was each an octave angrier? Was the kingmaker *Washington
Post* publisher Phil Graham, House Speaker Sam Rayburn, future Texas
governor John Connally, or Lady Bird Johnson? Did an LBJ aide really
hide in the closet taking notes while Lyndon was meeting with Bobby?
Was Johnson shaking and teary-eyed when he thought JFK might be
backing out of his offer?

What mattered to JFK was not the theatrics but the raw politics. LBJ
had proved in the primaries what a nettlesome if ultimately ineffective
adversary he could be. Better to have him as a vice president who could
be controlled than a Senate majority leader with the capacity to stymie
the president's legislative program. "Embrace your enemy" had always
been at the top of the list of Kennedy commandments. Knowing how
wary his aides were of Johnson, JFK offered this fateful assurance: "I'm
forty-three years old, and I'm the healthiest candidate for President in
the United States. You've traveled with me enough to know that. I'm not
going to die in office. So the Vice-Presidency doesn't mean anything."

LBJ was unsure about his own health after his cardiac attack, and he
knew of all the other men in his family tree who'd died too young thanks
to weak hearts. The vice presidency and the presidency itself would be
less stressful than the job of majority leader, Lady Bird told him. Knowing what he did about JFK's health, Johnson thought it unlikely that
Kennedy would survive two full terms. Johnson had actually had his staff
pore through history books to determine how many vice presidents had
become president (ten) and how many presidents had died in office
(seven). He had been angling for the White House even longer than JFK
had, and it remained his driving ambition, but the closest he could come
for now was the office next door. He wouldn't have to give up his Senate
seat to run with JFK. Even his mentor Sam Rayburn, who started out
saying "never" because he thought the vice presidency mattered less
than being majority leader, now thought he should, because having LBJ
on the ticket seemed like the only way for the Democrats to reclaim the
White House.

The morning of his visit to LBJ's suite, Jack had asked Bobby for an equally sober-minded calculation: If you added the votes of New England to those of the solid South, how many more would be needed to win the election? (The arithmetic was so convincing that Bobby couldn't find a way around it.) Still, JFK had nagging doubts about LBJ, which grew as the day of decision advanced. So in the middle of the afternoon Bobby trekked to the seventh floor, where he had already been at least once before that day, this time to see if LBJ might want to avoid an angry battle on the convention floor by taking his name out of consideration. He offered to make Johnson chairman of the Democratic National Committee, one of the biggest patronage plums in Washington and one that would let him hold his job as majority leader while playing a crucial role in the election. That last pilgrimage to the Johnson suite became the most hotly debated of the day's muddled events. Jack would say that by then he had resolved to take Johnson, having made up his mind at the same time Bobby was trying to change LBJ's. Lyndon and his defenders would speculate that Bobby was acting on his own, out of hatred.

Bobby flatly denied that: "Obviously, with the close relationship between my brother and I, [I] wasn't going down to see if he would withdraw just as a lark on my own." His denials couldn't always be taken at face value, as he proved when he lied about Jack's Addison's disease. But here it fit a pattern. JFK used Bobby for the toughest assignments, even though he knew that Bobby's passion might spell trouble. He never sent his brother on a fool's mission. Testing how much LBJ wanted the job served Jack's purpose. If he pulled out, Kennedy could still tell conservatives that he had tried, while reassuring liberals that he was on their side. Then he'd pick a vice president he actually liked, such as Missouri senator Symington. If LBJ said yes to the second spot, Jack could save face, which is exactly how it turned out. "I didn't really offer the nomination to Lyndon Johnson. I just held it out to here," JFK told reporter Charles Bartlett, stretching his hand several inches from his jacket pocket and suggesting that LBJ had grabbed for it. When the Massachusetts Democrat made his choice official at a press conference late that afternoon, the news was greeted with what *The New York Times* called "gasps of surprise." The next day, Kennedy fed his buddy Bartlett this postscript: "I hear your editors are upset because you said that Symington was going to be the vice president. Well, you can tell them if they're surprised, so am I."

As for Bobby, he got the short straw. Reporters and historians specu-
lated that he was at best his brother's errand boy, at worst an enforcer
whom Jack had to keep on a leash. JFK *was* the decider, but Bobby func-
tioned as his alter ego and master tactician. He would never be cut out on
a matter this essential. As if to confirm the point, the newly anointed
nominee picked his brother as the liaison that day, first with liberals,
then with big labor, and finally with LBJ. Yet it served Johnson's ego to
blame the second thoughts not on his good friend Jack, but on snot-
nosed Bobby. It was, as even he sensed, an unfair judgment, which helps
explain why he remained so insecure both as JFK's vice president and as
his successor. It also doomed any chance that LBJ and RFK would get
along. Bobby was too loyal to Jack to question his brother's spin on picking his vice president, but that allegiance is precisely why the younger
brother never would have defied the elder once he made that decision.
"Even if Jack wanted to give the Vice-Presidency to Eleanor Roosevelt,"
said family friend Dave Powers, "Bobby probably would have said all
right."

Only Joe Kennedy, the unsentimental patriarch, managed to maintain perspective. Not long after the vice presidential pick was finalized,
Jack and Bobby drove to the Spanish mansion in Beverly Hills that their
father had borrowed from the film star Marion Davies, far from the media
spotlight. The two sons were downcast, but not Joe. He greeted them in
the doorway in a velvet smoking jacket and slippers, offering these prophetic words: "Don't worry, Jack. In two weeks they'll be saying it's the
smartest thing you ever did."

————

FOR THE THREE-AND-A-HALF-MONTH general election campaign, Bobby
relied on the playbook he had been fine-tuning since Jack's first run for
Congress, now applied in fifty states and four hundred thirty-five congressional districts. As the race geared up, Bobby dropped in at headquarters, which was housed in three large buildings in Washington. He
was shocked that so many staffers were isolated in offices, removed from
voters and the grassroots campaign, and he ordered everyone to "stop
what they're doing and get out on the road," recalled Milton Gwirtzman,
a young lawyer who was meeting him for the first time and would be-

come an aide to all three Kennedy brothers. "No one told them where to go, they just were told that they all had to go on the road. Of course, very few did." Outbursts like those made their way back to the press, leading one national magazine to conclude that Bobby ran Jack's campaign "the way Captain Ahab ran the *Pequod*."

Time was the enemy now, with so much to do. "We can rest in November," he told anyone he thought wasn't working at his hurricane speed. He wanted everything done *now*. He was especially intolerant of the lazy political pros that Boston called Dearos and whose counterparts he was finding in every city he visited. After three days of powwows with fragmented Democrats in New York, he ran out of patience. "Gentlemen, I don't give a damn if the state and county organizations survive after November, and I don't give a damn if you survive. I want to elect John F. Kennedy," he told the reformers. He had an equally unequivocal message for the bosses: "The only thing I'm interested in is electing Senator Kennedy for president." He loved to deliver speeches like that standing on a chair. His audiences everywhere reacted with undisguised horror followed by frantic action. In New York, the factions from Tammany Hall joined forces with Eleanor Roosevelt reformers just long enough to help Jack carry the Empire State's forty-five electoral votes, the most in the nation.

Issues mattered less than they should have in 1960, and less than they had in any presidential campaign in memory. America was on the cusp, not quite ready to say goodbye to the reassuring do-nothingness of the Eisenhower boom nor to welcome the sexual, cultural, and political revolutions that would become the hallmarks of the 1960s. So it had it both ways, embracing *The Flintstones* and *Ben-Hur* along with the Twist, the Playboy Club, and the Pill. The Kennedys likewise hedged their bets. Bobby pushed for a strong civil rights platform in Los Angeles, which was either a change of heart or opportunism, since on more than one key civil rights vote, Vice President Nixon had stood up to Southern Democrats while Senator Kennedy stood with them. On foreign policy, the Democrat called for closing an imagined missile gap with the Soviet Union, backing "liberty-loving Cubans who are leading the resistance to Castro," and otherwise outpacing the Republicans in waging a Cold War against Communism. "Of course I preferred JFK to Nixon, but I was not bowled over," said Harrison Salisbury, who had headed *The New York Times*'s Moscow bureau. "I am afraid I took to calling Jack 'a lace curtain Nixon.' It was not unfair. Under the skin the politics of the two men did not differ much."

Bobby cared about solving problems but believed the time to talk about that was after you'd won. He also knew that if the election were decided on experience, Nixon's eight years as vice president would trump anything either candidate had done in the House or Senate. So he tried to frame the campaign around style and hope, themes that had worked against Lodge, Humphrey, and Johnson, all of whom, like Nixon, presented as weighty, steady, and boring. Leaflets that described Jack as fresher and bolder couldn't get him far enough fast enough, however, and the country was too big for personal appearances to work the way they had in Massachusetts. Bobby realized almost as early as Jack that they had to get him on television side by side with his unhandsome opponent.

Debates have become so central to American politics that it is easy to forget that 1960 was not just the first time the Democratic and Republican presidential nominees had faced off on television, but the first time major party nominees had debated anywhere. Still, Richard Nixon was no TV neophyte. In 1952 he salvaged his place on Eisenhower's ticket when sixty million Americans tuned in to hear him try to defend his $18,000 political slush fund and instead were beguiled by his story of a gift he wouldn't give back: a cocker spaniel named Checkers. But Nixon hadn't grown up around cameras as Jack and Bobby had, with their dad taking home movies to make his children comfortable around a medium he realized would dominate politics.* Nixon couldn't match Jack's affable style. And Nixon wasn't the master of chicanery, not yet, although he would learn from the Kennedys.

Shortly before the candidates went on the air for their first of four debates, as seventy million viewers were warming up their sets, Jack declined a CBS producer's offer of theatrical makeup. Nixon heard that and, not wanting to seem less manly, he declined as well. He hadn't no-

---

* While Jack always was a natural on television, Bobby never was, and he taught his children that watching TV was a waste of time.

ticed that Kennedy had a deep tan after campaigning in the California sunshine. He couldn't know that a TV-savvy aide was about to apply makeup in Kennedy's dressing room. All Nixon managed was a dab of Lazy-Shave powder procured at a nearby drugstore. When a Nixon aide asked how his candidate looked, Bobby carefully appraised the vice president's beard stubble, his pallid skin, and a haggardness that bore witness to his recent hospitalization for a knee infection. "Terrific! Terrific! I wouldn't change a thing!" Bobby dissembled. Then he turned to Jack with one last snippet of advice: "Kick him in the balls."

The debates reversed the relative positions of the contestants, pushing Nixon from the role of presumptive president to that of marginal underdog. Jack not only belonged on the same stage as the vice president, he shone much brighter. The senator spoke to the cameras and to America while the vice president played to a nonexistent panel of judges. Kennedy was relishing the encounter, or made it seem so; the vice president glowered, his shirt hanging loose around his still sickly torso, looking nothing like his trademark combative, confident self. Pollsters agreed that most voters who decided based on the TV duels picked Jack. The Massachusetts Democrat "maintained an expression of gravity suitable for a candidate for the highest office in the land," the obsessively fairminded *New York Times* wrote after the first debate. By contrast, "Mr. Nixon, wearing pancake makeup to cover his dark beard, smiled more frequently as he made his points and dabbed frequently at the perspiration that beaded out on his chin." But while the rest of Team Kennedy celebrated, Bobby knew that three and a half weeks remained in the campaign and the postdebate bounce was sure to flatten out. He relentlessly prepared for election day, repeating his mantra that the stakes were nothing less than life and death. More quietly, he decided it was time to open his bag of tricks.

The opposition research that Bobby stage-managed in 1960 set the standard for every election that followed. Frank Sinatra, a pal of Jack's, hired a private investigator who found out that Nixon periodically visited a psychiatrist, which still carried a stigma and could have stirred up a hornet's nest if Bobby had made it public. He didn't. He also kept hush-hush information leaked to the campaign by two credible sources—the governor of Alabama and a journalist turned Kennedy aide—that anti-

Castro exiles backed by the CIA were getting ready to invade Cuba. In both cases, knowing was enough, and feeling he could fire back if Nixon made an issue of Jack's medical records or of Castro and Cuba. It was Bobby the way he was on the football field and in the Hoffa hearing room: better armed for battle than anyone else, and ready to fight dirty if his adversary struck the first low blow. Kennedy staffers, meanwhile, compiled a big black binder they dubbed the Nixonpedia that cataloged every detail of the Republican's public life, with special attention to flip-flops, smears, controversial votes, and other potential embarrassments.

Bobby did uncork at least one dirty trick: leaking documents showing that the billionaire businessman Howard Hughes had secretly lent Nixon's brother $205,000. Hughes, who received millions in government largesse, presumably sought to curry favor with the candidate. National columnists Drew Pearson and Jack Anderson ran the story not once but in six separate columns, and in case anyone missed those, Pearson took to the airwaves to charge that "Mr. Nixon has been talking about experience. It now develops that his experience, which began with an $18,000 personal expense fund, has progressed to a $205,000 loan. . . . This is the kind of experience the American people can do without." Coming on the eve of the election, it hurt. Bill Haddad, an investigative reporter working for Bobby, says his contacts in the Hughes organization supplied the information and that Bobby, while he didn't say "go do this, go do that," was anxious to see what Haddad and his colleagues came up with. Author Mark Feldstein, who did extensive interviews with Anderson shortly before his death in 2005, said he uncovered evidence that the Kennedy campaign went several steps further—paying $16,000 to an informant ($128,000 in today's dollars), accepting documents that were pilfered or burgled, then slipping the incriminating paperwork to the press. In his post-Watergate memoir, Nixon, who had been pinned with the nickname Tricky Dick as far back as 1950, called Bobby and his brethren "the most ruthless group of political operators ever mobilized for a presidential campaign. . . . I vowed that I would never again enter an election at a disadvantage by being vulnerable to them—or anyone—on the level of political tactics."

The real master of political hardball was Joe Kennedy, who stayed out of sight for most of the campaign, as he had in 1952. "Jack and Bob will run the show," reporters joked, "while Ted's in charge of hiding Joe." But the press didn't appreciate that Joe trusted Bobby completely by now, since he had schooled him, then arranged apprenticeships for him with the hardheaded Joe McCarthy and the even fiercer John McClellan. And Joe was never out of reach of a phone that he could use to advise or buck up Bobby or Jack, or to call in a favor from an old-pal mayor, congressman, or governor. "If Jack had known about some of the telephone calls his father made on his behalf to Tammany-type bosses during the 1960 campaign, Jack's hair would have turned white," said Kenny O'Donnell. But Joe had the wisdom to avoid becoming a distraction, as he told Bobby's campaign assistant John Seigenthaler: "I don't want my enemies to be my sons' enemies or my wars to be my sons' wars." As for the cash Joe contributed, "no one will ever know what was spent on the Kennedy campaigns," said campaign chronicler Teddy White. "John F. Kennedy probably did not then know himself. Later I learned that even Robert Kennedy did not know. Perhaps only Joseph Kennedy knew."

———

WITH THE CAMPAIGN nearing its finish, confidence grew in every part of the Kennedy entourage except at the top. Bobby was living on nerves, plain to see in the dark rings under his glacier-blue eyes and the old-man stoop to his shoulders. He knew he was pushing too hard but felt that doing "one bit less of anything" might mean defeat. He could control the organization's internal dynamics, but not real-world events like the arrest of Martin Luther King, Jr. That required quick wits and high-wire improvisation, at which he and Jack excelled. The campaign had jeopardized its standing with Negroes first by the choice of Lyndon Johnson, who was as unnerving to blacks as he was soothing to Southern whites. Almost as tone-deaf was Bobby's sparring with the race hero Jackie Robinson, who backed Humphrey, then Nixon, and—when Bobby questioned his motives—denounced the campaign manager as a man "who will not hesitate to use lies, innuendos and personal attacks on those who disagree with him to get his candidate into the White House." That is why the Kennedy brothers' back-to-back phone calls following King's jailing mattered so much.

Those calls came at a moment when the campaign and the civil rights movement were both reaching a rolling boil. The activist minister from Montgomery had long been a favorite target of the Dixie establishment, which saw its chance when he was arrested on October 19 with a group of students sitting in at the whites-only lunch counter at Rich's Department Store in Atlanta. Everyone went to jail, and everyone but King was released. His problem, a judge in neighboring DeKalb County explained, was that his arrest violated the terms of an earlier suspended sentence for driving without a Georgia license three months after moving to the state (he had one from Alabama). His real offense was that he and his wife had been driving with the white novelist Lillian Smith, which was enough for a patrolman in Ku Klux Klan–friendly DeKalb to stop them for questioning and, when he realized who King was, to slap him with a summons. Now the judge revoked the probation and sentenced the reverend to four months of hard labor on a road gang, commencing immediately. That news was bad enough for Mrs. King, who was six months pregnant, but not as frightening as the call she got the next day from Martin. He had been transferred in the middle of the night, in handcuffs and leg chains, to a rural prison that his supporters feared was a setting ready-made for a lynching.

The full story of what happened next has filtered out bit by bit over the decades, with the final details revealed here for the first time. As soon as they heard about King's fate, Bobby and Jack started making calculations about how they could help him and themselves. They knew the civil rights leader wouldn't have ended up on a chain gang for a traffic misdemeanor if the judge weren't trying to make a point. They also were counting on the segregationists who ran Georgia to deliver the state to them in the next month's election. Standing up for King could cost them in the Peach State; doing nothing would cost them with black voters nationwide and Northern liberals. The solution was classic Bobby: Have it both ways.

The Kennedys quietly started making long-distance calls. The first was to Georgia governor Ernest Vandiver, who was known for his "no, not one" stance against letting black children into all-white schools— and then for not standing in the way when a federal judge ordered two black students admitted to the all-white University of Georgia. Vandiver was just the watch-what-I-do, not-what-I-say kind of Southerner to whom the Kennedys could relate. Jack "asked the assistance of the governor's office in seeking the release of Martin Luther King," Vandiver recalled. The governor knew just which strings to pull. He first called his brother-in-law Bob Russell, who called Georgia Democratic Party secretary George Stewart, who called his pal the DeKalb sentencing judge, J. Oscar Mitchell. During this back-and-forth, Vandiver added, "I had three or four conversations with Bobby Kennedy in Washington."

Harris Wofford, Kennedy's civil rights liaison, knew nothing about that intrigue, but he did know the campaign needed to do something. He contacted Sargent Shriver, urging him to persuade the candidate to make a sympathy call to Mrs. King. Shriver waited until he was alone with Kennedy in his hotel room at O'Hare Airport, made his pitch, and was taken aback when his brother-in-law said, "Why not? Get her on the phone." When Shriver did, the senator said in his most sympathetic telephone tone, "I understand you are expecting a baby, and I just wanted you to know that I was thinking about you and Dr. King." It lasted less than two minutes, but the call "was like a shot of lightning in the middle of the night," Shriver said, giving Mrs. King hope about her husband's prospects and about Kennedy as a potential president. Yet when Bobby heard what his aides had done behind his back, he turned on them: "Do you know that three Southern governors told us that if Jack supported Jimmy Hoffa, Nikita Khrushchev, or Martin Luther King, they would throw their states to Nixon? Do you know that this election may be razor close and you have probably lost it for us?"

The truth was that Bobby was outraged not at Wofford and Shriver's instinct, but at their making an impetuous and token gesture when he himself had been meticulously hatching a plan that could actually free King. Not long after he chewed out his assistants, Bobby made his own call to Judge Mitchell, a move he would insist was impromptu when in fact it had been prearranged by Governor Vandiver and Party Secretary Stewart. Nor did he lecture King's sentencing judge about any moral or legal lapses, as he later claimed. To underscore the political importance of King's release, Bobby told the judge that without it "we would lose the state of Massachusetts." He also said Mitchell would be a welcome visitor in a future Kennedy White House, an offer the judge would cash in.* Stewart already had convinced the judge he could legally release King pending an appeal, which meant that he and Bobby could reach an accommodation. Mitchell understood just what was being asked of him. Not only did he release on bail the fiery black minister, he hinted to reporters that Bobby had pushed for that to happen—and, by implication, that Vice President Nixon had not.

Even that wasn't by chance. Before he'd dialed the judge, the evercautious campaign manager eliminated any possibility that his support for King would backfire and hurt his brother by instructing his aide Seigenthaler, who was from Nashville, to ask every Democratic state chairman in the South his reaction to Jack's earlier call to Mrs. King. When they voiced less opposition than expected, Bobby knew he could chance his conference with Mitchell and the likelihood the judge would sing to the press. The only thing he didn't let bother him was the propriety of a lawyer like him calling a judge on a matter pending before his court, which the Bar Association regards as an ethical breach.

The Kennedys' gamble paid off bigger than even Bobby could have foreseen. Stories on the King calls appeared in the mainstream press, but the one describing Jack's that could have frayed white Southern nerves was buried as deeply as the brothers hoped, on page twenty-two of *The New York Times*. While Bobby's call made page one, the only controversy it sparked was when four honorary colonels resigned from Vandiver's staff.† In the black world, by contrast, the grapevine telegraph lit up. The Kennedy calls, and the Kings' reaction, were splashed across the front page of newspapers like the *Washington Afro-American* and shouted out on radio stations targeting black listeners. As he was leaving prison, Martin Jr. said he was "deeply indebted to Senator Kennedy, who served as a great force in making my release possible." Martin Sr. was more

---

* Mitchell said his visit was a political one, to assist Carl Sanders in his bid for governor of Georgia, and that Bobby agreed to help even though that meant not sending in federal voting registrars to enforce civil rights laws. Bobby told a different version, saying Mitchell "never asked for anything." (Bass, *Taming the Storm*, 171; RFK OH, December 4, 1964, 348, JFKL.)

† The colonels served as aides-de-camp to the governor's staff and their titles, scores of which had been bestowed by governors, date back to a time when the state was hard-pressed to find educated Georgians willing to serve.

graphic if less broad-minded: "I had expected to vote against Senator
Kennedy because of his religion. But now he can be my President, Catholic or whatever he is. . . . I've got all my votes and I've got a suitcase and
I'm going to take them up there and dump them in his lap." To ensure
that black voters across the country heard those and other words of tribute, the campaign printed up three million leaflets—called "blue bombs,"
a reference to the color of paper they were printed on and their impact
on black voters—that were handed out two days before the election at
churches, barrooms, and other "coloreds-only" settings. To be sure nobody could trace the effort back to the Kennedys, the fanciful Freedom
Crusade Committee was listed as the sponsor.

The story behind those Kennedy phone calls remained unknown for
more than twenty years, until a journalism professor from South Carolina tracked down Vandiver, then in his sixties and anxious to make
amends for his segregationist past.* To have told the truth back in 1960,
the ex-governor explained, would have been "political suicide, with the
temper of the times as it was." So he lied, doing his damnedest behind the
scenes to boost Jack Kennedy's candidacy while telling reporters that "it
is a sad commentary on the year 1960 and its political campaign when
the Democratic nominee for the Presidency makes a phone call to the
home of the foremost racial agitator in the country." When he came
clean he did it full blast, claiming he had engineered King's release and
Kennedy's triumph.

New threads in the reconstruction suggest that the history-making
intervention had even more architects than realized. Wofford says that
Byron "Whizzer" White, counselor to both Kennedys who later served
on the Supreme Court, confessed to him—without elaboration—that "I
am the one that told [Bobby] to call the judge." The latest to fill out the
narrative and put himself at the center of the affair is Carl Sanders, who
succeeded Vandiver as governor. He says he called the judge "and told
him that Martin Luther Jr. really had no business being in [jail] to begin
with. . . . Word came back from the court, from the judge, that he

---

* While that was the first time the public heard the governor's version, he actually had laid
it out in 1967 in an oral history for the Kennedy Library. It went unnoticed in part because
Vandiver wanted it to, asking that his disclosure be placed on a different tape from the rest of
his interview (Kuhn, " 'There's a Footnote to History!'," *Journal of American History*).

wouldn't consider releasing [King] unless Kennedy called and told him
that they'd like him to be released. And Bobby Kennedy did that. . . . It
was a situation that could have exploded into some horrible things, but
it turned out all right." Whatever marionettes actually appeared in the
show, it was the young campaign manager pulling the strings.

Bobby hinted at his back-channel orchestrations in a 1964 interview
for the Kennedy Library, saying that Vandiver made it clear "that if I
called the judge, that he thought that the judge would let Martin Luther
King off." He didn't reveal that in 1960, he added, "because I thought it
would destroy the governor." Even in that interview, however, Bobby was
obfuscating. He said he wasn't sure he knew about his brother's call to
Mrs. King when he made his to the judge. Seigenthaler set that part of
the record straight shortly before he died, saying Bobby not only knew,
but had him sound out the political fallout of Jack's call before he made
his. The two brothers had coordinated early on their approach to the
King jailing, the way they did on everything that mattered in the campaign. And Vandiver wasn't the only one who reaped a political dividend
by hiding the full facts. Bobby and Jack Kennedy were lionized for seeming to spontaneously redress a wrong.

Bobby did the right thing in the end, for reasons that were more complicated and self-serving than he admitted. His racial consciousness was
still embryonic, but nobody understood better than he did the potent
symbolism of helping spring Martin Luther King from prison on a charge
that was shaky from the start. Now, more than ever, Bobby was an entangled blend of Machiavellian contriver and man of conscience. King
seemed to get that when he said, just after his release, "there are moments when the politically expedient can be morally wise." Bobby may
have understood it, too. Asked by a reporter just after the election
whether he was glad he had called the judge, he replied, "Sure I'm glad,
but I would hope I'm not glad for the reason you think I'm glad."

While the brothers made those and other moves jointly, anyone following the campaign knew that Bobby always worried more and worked
harder. Early on, when they passed each other at an airport in West Virginia, Bobby yelled, "Hi, Johnny, how are you?" Jack: "Man, I'm tired."
Bobby: "What the hell are you tired for? I'm doing all the work." So it was
that on election night—after Jack, the sixteen telephone operators, the

pollster Louis Harris, and everyone else had headed to bed—shock-headed Bobby remained at the makeshift command post in his cottage at Hyannis Port. His long-distance phone bill for the night reached $10,000, as he checked and rechecked results from Texas, California, and Illinois. In truth, the Rubicon had been crossed much earlier that evening, although there were no French-Irish jigs to mark the moment. Jack was sound asleep when he locked down the ultimate prize in politics, and Bobby was too bone-tired to dance even if he'd had a partner. The only victory lap he allowed himself was a toll call to Liz Moynihan, a campaign volunteer in upstate New York. The two had agreed early in the campaign that if Jack won Republican Onondaga County, home to Syracuse, he would win the nation. When no one was watching, on the longest and tensest night of his life, Bobby checked in with Liz. "It was nine o'clock on the dot," she remembers. "I say, 'Hello.' He says, 'Didn't we?' I say, 'Yes!' Then he hung up."

When a margin of victory is as narrow as it turned out to be in 1960—Kennedy won 49.7 percent of the popular vote to Nixon's 49.6 percent—analysts inevitably debate why. Was it the telegenic JFK's dazzle, versus Nixon's five o'clock shadow, in the televised debates? Was it Kennedy's money and hardball tactics, or Nixon's failure to focus on swing states? Those factors mattered, but what counted more were the Kennedy phone calls. "This one unfortunate incident in the heat of a campaign served to dissipate much of the support I had among Negro voters," Nixon wrote in his first memoir.* He left unsaid the suggestion that Eisenhower had botched a chance to help him when he failed to release the statement drafted by his Justice Department that deplored

---

* This was a touchy subject for Nixon, who had more to say on the matter: "[Campaign Press Secretary] Herb Klein, in response to inquiries from the press, asked me what comment I had on Robert Kennedy's action. I told him: 'I think Dr. King is getting a bum rap. But despite my strong feelings in this respect, it would be completely improper for me or any other lawyer to call the judge. And Robert Kennedy should have known better than to do so.' Under the circumstances, Klein answered the press query by saying that I had 'no comment' on the matter." Nixon then took the matter to Attorney General Bill Rogers, one of his campaign advisers, and Rogers strongly recommended that the White House say it had ordered the Justice Department to investigate whether King's constitutional rights had been violated. "Had this recommendation been adopted," Nixon wrote, "the whole incident might have resulted in a plus rather than a minus as far as I was concerned. But Rogers was unable to get approval from the White House for such a statement" (Nixon, *Six Crises*, 362–63).

King's imprisonment. Teddy White, the dean of balloting analysts back then, made clear the meaning of the resulting drop in black support: "It is difficult to see how Illinois, New Jersey, Michigan, South Carolina or Delaware (with seventy-four electoral votes) could have been won [by Kennedy] had the Republican-Democratic split of the Negro wards and precincts remained as it was, unchanged from the Eisenhower charm of 1956." And capturing those seventy-four electors would have meant that Nixon, rather than Kennedy, would have moved into the White House. The worsening recession had helped push black voters away from their historic allegiance to Abraham Lincoln's Republican Party and toward Kennedy and the Democrats, White added, but so did the "master stroke of intervention in the Martin Luther King arrest."*

The Kennedy brothers seldom said thank-you for masterful strokes like that or anything else—and they never said it to each other. It was understood. Voicing it would sound syrupy, and they made so many decisions jointly that it would be unclear who should thank whom. But throughout the last year Bobby had gone so far beyond any call of duty that over Christmas, Jack wrote out what he couldn't say face-to-face, in the teasing meter that the brothers often used. "For Bobby—The Brother Within—who made the easy difficult," the president-elect inscribed in a richly bound red leather copy of Bobby's book *The Enemy Within.* Jackie added, just above, "To Bobby—who made the impossible possible and changed all our lives."

---

* After the campaign, some reporters and Republicans charged that the Kennedys had stolen votes in Illinois, with help from everyone from the Mafia to Chicago mayor Richard Daley. But the Prairie State hadn't decided the election, and the Kennedy tally wasn't heavier than normal in districts where unions loyal to the Mob or Daley had allegedly pulled votes out of thin air or graveyards. Whatever underhanded techniques Cook County Democrats did use were balanced by equally shady manipulation by downstate Republicans.. "Elections then were not as clean as we think they are today," says Bill Daley, son of the legendary mayor and a former chief of staff to President Obama. "The only thing I can state is that at the end of that, my dad said, 'Recount every ballot in the state. We'll pay for half of it. The Republican Party can pay for half of it.' And they refused to pay for half of it" (Author interview with Bill Daley).

Chapter 4

GETTING JUSTICE

N OBODY HAD STRIVED more tirelessly than Robert F. Kennedy to
make John F. Kennedy president, with the possible exceptions of
the candidate himself and their father, Joseph P. Kennedy. Jack's
future was set now, for four years at least, and probably eight. Joe, too,
had what he wanted: a son in the White House. But what about Bobby?

Joe had been contemplating the question nearly as long as he had the
paths of his eldest sons. He made plain his goals three years before in a
Saturday Evening Post profile entitled "The Amazing Kennedys," which
envisioned "the day when Jack will be in the White House" and "Bobby
will serve in the Cabinet as Attorney General." The article continued, "If
this should come to pass, of course, the joy of the senior Kennedy would
know no bounds."

Making that dream a reality would strain even Joe's capacities. How
would the country and the Congress react to the most politically conflicted job in government going to the president's campaign manager
and brother, who was just turning thirty-five? Senior political aides had
run the Justice Department before, but never had so close a relative of
the president been named to the cabinet or any top administration posting. Only twice had a younger man been U.S. attorney general—one was
the former attorney general of Pennsylvania, whose father had been a
signatory to the Declaration of Independence, the other was a veteran of
the Delaware Legislature and U.S. House of Representatives—and both
held office in the early 1800s, when the job was part time, there was no
Department of Justice to oversee, and the salary was meager because the
attorney general was expected to take on private clients.

More intriguing were the family dynamics that surrounded Bobby's appointment. These played out far from public view, in tones so whispered that even siblings weren't sure who was saying what to whom. The easiest to read was Joe, who paced nervously around his winter manse in a custom-made white suit and horn-rimmed glasses. He wanted someone in the cabinet to protect Jack's flank and tell him the hard truth, especially since most of his other nominees were strangers to him. Joe knew the attorney general's expansive portfolio would let Bobby dabble in foreign as well as domestic affairs, offering advice where needed and fattening his own résumé for high office. As a business tycoon who lived his own life on the edge of lawlessness, Joe also grasped how useful it could be having America's chief law enforcement officer at his dinner table. And he had no illusions about his eldest surviving son. The capital teemed with the enemies, both Republican and Democratic, that Jack had made during his swift climb to power, while skeletons continued to pile up in his bedroom closet. Nobody had shielded Jack more effectively from himself and his adversaries than Bobby, even when that meant lying. It was Bobby who squashed rumors not just of Jack's being distressingly ill but of his having had a secret earlier marriage (the first was true, the second not). Now they needed a bulwark more than ever at the same time that Bobby needed the right job. Joe would not be easily denied. "Fuck public opinion," his father coolly instructed the president-elect. "He'll do a good job."

What Jack wanted was less obvious. He was a master at reading popular sentiment, and he confided to Jackie late one evening his worry that the public would decry as nepotism his naming Bobby and it would wipe out his postelection honeymoon with the press and lawmakers. He also knew his brother was no soft touch, having watched him manhandle election foes and grill roughneck Teamsters, and he realized the qualities that would enable Bobby to bring the Justice Department to life might make it tough to keep him in line. So even as he was telling a journalist friend that "Bobby's the best man I can get," Jack quietly explored his options for the post. Connecticut governor Abraham Ribicoff preferred and got Health, Education, and Welfare; Adlai Stevenson preferred State and got the United Nations. Over the course of the campaign JFK had become increasingly comfortable standing up to his dad—but he wasn't sure he wanted to do that on a matter like naming Bobby attorney general, on which Joe felt so strongly and made so much sense.

In trademark fashion, Jack tried to have this difficult conversation through surrogates. First he enlisted his Senate buddy "Gorgeous George" Smathers to see whether the old man might be open to Bobby's taking another job. Jack and Smathers were sitting next to the oversized Kennedy swimming pool in Palm Beach, with Joe at the far end enjoying his morning newspapers. "Excuse me, Mr. Ambassador, Jack and I have just been talking about Bobby," Smathers said. "I thought he could be assistant secretary of defense, and then in a year or so, he could move up." Ignoring Smathers, Joe summoned to his side the soon-to-be leader of the free world and let him have it: "Your brother Bobby busted his ass for you. He gave you his life blood. You know it, and I know it. By God, he deserves to be attorney general of the U.S., and by God, that's what he's going to be. Do you understand that?" Jack responded as he had been taught, "Yes, sir." JFK tried again a short time later, this time via the Washington power broker Clark Clifford. Thinking it "truly a strange assignment—the President-elect asking a third party to try to talk to his father about his brother. Only the Kennedys!"—Clifford flew to New York and did as asked. Joe still wouldn't budge. "*Bobby is going to be Attorney General.* All of us have worked our tails off for Jack, and now that we have succeeded I am going to see to it that Bobby gets the same chance that we gave to Jack," Clifford recalled Joe telling him. "I would always remember the intense but matter-of-fact tone with which he had spoken—there was no rancor, no anger, no challenge." Joe's determination surprised Smathers and Clifford, but not Jack, who knew when to surrender.

Bobby's own wishes were the most difficult to untangle. Even he couldn't decipher them or admit having ambitions of his own after a lifetime of indoctrination that the family came first. Starting just after the election, he and Jack parsed every scenario as they walked barefoot along the deserted beach in Hyannis Port, their unruly hair swept straight up by the late-autumn breeze, their focus finally on what was best for Bobby. "He wanted to know what I wanted to do," Bobby recalled. One by one, then and later, Jack mentioned government posts he felt made sense and Bobby countered with jobs that drew him to other

realms entirely. What about something at the State Department involving Latin America, or that secretary-in-waiting spot at Defense? Terrific
training, the brothers agreed, but awkward for either secretary to be
second-guessed by the president's little brother. The White House staff
was another possibility, but it was awfully close for JFK's comfort, and
Bobby worried that "I had been working with [Jack] for a long time, and
I thought maybe I'd like to go off by myself." For brothers, he added, "or
at least for the two of us—we had to have our own areas. I had to be
apart from what he was doing so I wasn't working directly for him and
getting orders from him as to what I should do that day." Neither law nor
business held any more appeal for Bobby than they had before. Lying in
bed next to Ethel he ticked off other possibilities—he could run a nonprofit (he already was president of the Joseph P. Kennedy, Jr. Foundation), run a newspaper (he enjoyed courting reporters and had briefly
been one himself), or teach, travel, or simply spend a year reading (he
relished the thought of each but never seriously considered any). Jack
also mentioned that he could arrange for Bobby to serve out the remainder of his term as senator from Massachusetts. Annoyed, Bobby made
clear that he didn't want a hand-me-down. The only way he would be a
senator, thanks very much, was to win the office on his own.

The attorney general idea kept reeling him in. It was the first option
Jack had offered, but Bobby was torn. He worried that "nepotism was a
problem." He reasoned that "I had been chasing bad men for three years,
and I didn't want to spend the rest of my life doing that." He told the
about-to-be head of state, "I didn't want to be in government." This
young man who rarely vacillated in making difficult calls during his
brother's campaigns couldn't make up his mind when it came to thinking about himself. A similar indecision would plague him years later
when he weighed running for the Senate, then the presidency. He had a
stunning array of options available to few men in history, but he felt, too,
the onerous expectations of his parents, siblings, and public. He wanted
to do what was right but couldn't say for sure what that was. Could he
handle being the nation's top legal authority and cop? Doubts like those
had never stopped him when he was diving into Cape Cod's deepest water
to test whether he could swim, or calling out the British for trading with
Red China. Part of him yearned to stop being a Kennedy for once and

withdraw into the family he was building with Ethel. He also wanted his big brother to seek him out, and any sign that Jack was having doubts would crush Bobby.

During a desperately needed vacation in Acapulco, Bobby tried to focus on anything but his future. When he got back, Jack needed him as a sounding board and emissary in the frenetic search to fill other key jobs in the administration before the inauguration. As for who'd run the Justice Department, "we just vacillated back and forth," he remembered, "almost like we did on the Vice President." Finally, five weeks after he had sat up monitoring the votes that made his brother president, he realized it was time to make a choice. So he drove himself on an asking-and-listening tour of Washington, stopping to see everyone whose opinion he valued or felt he should.

"Nothing but headaches," advised William P. Rogers, the outgoing attorney general who, to underscore his point, would leave his successor a large bottle of aspirin. "Do it," countered FBI director J. Edgar Hoover, although not long after Bobby left, he told others he hadn't meant it. Supreme Court justice William O. Douglas knew Bobby better and cared about him more, and over lunch they analyzed options ranging from running for senator or governor in Massachusetts to making his home and career in Maryland. "I told him I thought he would make a fine Attorney General, but that at some juncture in his life he should start a course that was wholly independent of Jack," Douglas said. "It was now time to think of himself."

Bobby agonized over his decision one last time at home that evening with Ethel and his friend John Seigenthaler. Acknowledging that "this will kill my father," he picked up the telephone and called Jack to say no. No, he didn't want to be attorney general. No, he couldn't be talked into it. Jack listened, then invited him to breakfast the next morning at his redbrick townhouse in Georgetown. Over bacon, eggs, and strong coffee, the elder brother used the same "ask what you can do for your country" reasoning that would rally the nation the following month. "If I can ask Dean Rusk to give up a career; if I can ask Adlai Stevenson to make a sacrifice he does not want to make; if I can ask Bob McNamara to give up a job as head of that company [Ford Motor]—these men I don't even know—if I can ask them to make this sacrifice, certainly I can expect my own brother to give me the same sort of contribution. And I need you in this government," Jack said, according to Seigenthaler, whom Bobby had brought along for moral support. As soon as Jack went back into the kitchen, Bobby started assembling a point-by-point rebuttal, but Seigenthaler reminded him that it hadn't been his brother talking, it was the president-to-be. The conversation was over. Jack reappeared and announced, " 'So that's it, general. Let's go.' [Bobby] sort of laughed, and maybe cussed a little. And that's it, and we went."

Like most Kennedy stories, that one has romance and enough truth to make it live on. The full story is even better. Bobby wasn't quite the object of the last-minute dragooning that he and his friends suggested. Justice Douglas recalled the lunch he had with Bobby, which took place well before that breakfast with Jack, saying that "by the time he left my office, he had made up his mind to be Attorney General." Senator Smathers remembered that he had acted as Jack's emissary twice regarding the attorney general's job—once with Joe Kennedy and the other time with Bobby, who, according to Smathers wanted the posting as much as his father wanted him to have it. It was Jack who balked, Smathers told the *Miami Herald,* and the Florida senator agreed to try to persuade Bobby to take a job at the Defense Department. His response was as ice-cold as his father's had been, Smathers said: "Whenever I want your advice, I will call you. And you might tell my brother if he has anything to say to me he can call me direct." By the time Jack finally made his choice, Bobby's was clear. He did what he had done with each of his earlier jobs— following the advice of his father, then explaining it with a flourish that buried the qualms and burnished the legend.

His enemies said his hesitation was an act from the first. "Kennedy people try to make out that when Jack became president, he and their old man insisted that Robert become the attorney general. That's a lot of crap," Teamsters boss Jimmy Hoffa wrote in his memoir. "The spoiled brat blackjacked John into giving him the job." Hoffa cited as evidence the *Miami Herald* story quoting Senator Smathers, but the union leader also knew what drove Bobby almost as well as Bobby did. Attorney general was the only job that made sense for him. It tapped his legal and investigative expertise. It let him pursue social justice while handling political matters for his brother. And it gave him the tools to fight the fights he had promised never to abandon—against Roy Cohn, Lyndon Johnson, and, highest on his list of evildoers, James Riddle Hoffa.

Jack knew that what he was proposing for Bobby was unprecedented and perhaps preposterous. Newly elected presidents often kept their campaign managers around to help with the political challenges of running the country, but the tradition was to make them postmaster general, not attorney general. Eisenhower broke the pattern in 1953 by naming Herbert Brownell, Jr., one of his key political operatives, as attorney general, but that president kept his brother Milton in the low-key role of special ambassador. Woodrow Wilson had thought about making his only brother a postmaster in Nashville in 1913, but decided "it would be a very serious mistake both for you and for me." The whole government would eventually come around to that thinking, and in 1967 Congress passed and the president signed an antinepotism statute that banned such hiring.

But neither Eisenhower nor Wilson had been as brazen as Jack in running for president as an untested leader. And neither had a brother as artful as Bobby. The Kennedys believed that together, they could take the sting out of the anticipated charge of nepotism. They took the first step a full month before they made the appointment official, during a round of golf in Palm Beach. Jack let slip the idea of Bobby's running the Justice Department to William H. Lawrence, the same friendly reporter at *The New York Times* to whom they had leaked embarrassing information on Hubert Humphrey's draft records. An even chummier journalist, Joseph Alsop, had opined three weeks before that "it seems both ridiculous and unjust that Robert Kennedy's relationship to John F. Kennedy should be widely thought to debar him for the kind of post he could otherwise count on." Those trial balloons served two political purposes: to see whether appointing Bobby attorney general would generate a firestorm of protest (it didn't), and to minimize the shock by gently letting the public in on the secret. (It worked so well that, the day Bobby and Jack shook hands over breakfast, they again leaked to Lawrence that there would be a formal announcement the next day.)

A dash of Kennedy wit helped, too. Asked by *Newsweek*'s Ben Bradlee how he would announce the appointment, a straight-faced JFK said, "I think I'll open the front door of the Georgetown house some morning about 2:00 A.M., look up and down the street, and, if there's no one there, I'll whisper, 'It's Bobby.'" Just before he did make it official, Jack advised Bobby, "Don't smile too much or they'll think we're happy about the appointment." A week later, during a talk in Washington, the newly inaugurated president joked, "I don't see anything wrong with getting [Bobby] a little legal experience before he goes out to practice law." Bobby had heard the line before and didn't see the humor. "You've got to make fun of yourself in politics," Jack lectured him. Bobby: "You weren't making fun of yourself. You were making fun of me."

Bobby had never left anything to chance as a congressional staffer or campaign manager, and he took the same scrupulous approach in preparing for the anticipated battle over his appointment. A Kennedy staffer scoured the records of all past attorneys general to see if any had entered office with less legal experience than RFK, who had never actually tried a case in a court of law. "Even though I went back to the very, very beginning, I could find no one who hadn't practiced law," recalled John Reilly, who worked on JFK's campaign and would oversee the U.S. attorneys in Bobby's Justice Department. "But we finally came up with the fact—or I finally came up with the fact—that Harry M. Daugherty, who was attorney general during the Teapot Dome scandal, had practiced law for thirty-some-odd years, so that we decided that experience wasn't much of a qualification anyhow. So at the time of the hearing we planted that question with [Senator] Phil Hart."

Those preparations paid off especially with political reporters, who after eight dull years under Eisenhower took delight in the Kennedy brothers' whimsy and boldness. Analysts and editorial writers were less easily charmed. Wallace Carroll wrote in *The New York Times* that Bobby's appointment "struck the first jarring note today in five weeks of masterly political orchestration." Legal scholars registered their own doubts, with the Yale law professor Alexander Bickel laying out in *The New Republic* a blistering critique of Bobby's record as a Senate investigator. "Mr. Kennedy appears to find congenial the role of prosecutor, judge and jury, all consolidated in his one efficient person," Bickel concluded. "On the record, Robert F. Kennedy is not fit for the office."

That denunciation might have undone other nominees, but not Bobby, who had spent his life purposefully defying the low expectations others had of him. While many of the senators whose confirmation he needed had concerns at the outset of his hearings, there was but one dissenter in the end. That overwhelming endorsement may have come courtesy of Bobby's least favorite person in the new administration, Lyndon Johnson. Senator Richard Russell, a powerful conservative from Georgia, had secured enough votes to kill the nomination and planned to use them, said Bobby Baker, the secretary of the Senate and LBJ's longtime lieutenant. "Johnson called and said . . . 'This will be the most humiliating defeat I, as Vice President, could suffer if I don't have enough influence in the Senate to confirm the President's nominee,'" remembered Baker, who loathed RFK as much as LBJ did. "So I took Senator Russell over to the Secretary of the Senate's office and I really poured heavy drinks in him. I said, 'Your best friend and my best friend is pleading with me to talk to you to see if you'll let us have a voice vote.' Between my persuasion and the booze, he agreed. That's the only way he was confirmed. He would have been defeated if there had been a roll-call vote.* The Republicans and Southern Democrats had enough votes to defeat Bobby Kennedy to be Attorney General."

What Russell, Bickel, Carroll, and all the other skeptics failed to see was how much Bobby had grown by then. He was determined to show not just that he was up to the job, but that he could do it better than anyone before. He would exceed even the forecasts of his brother, who at times would have appreciated an attorney general less driven to go wherever the politically embarrassing facts led. Jack had learned during his yearlong presidential campaign just how capable Bobby was, and how resolute, which is why he risked so much in naming him to the trailblazing role at the Department of Justice. As for Bobby, he quickly forgot the to-ing and fro-ing that had brought him there. "Once I had made up my mind," he wrote, "I was glad it was all behind."

———————

* Voice votes often leave it unclear who voted which way, giving senators political protection on matters such as confirming controversial nominees. Formal roll calls, by contrast, record each lawmaker's ballot. In Kennedy's case, he was approved by something in between called a standing vote, in which, to clarify the outcome of a voice tally, all those voting yes are asked to stand, then the noes—but the votes still aren't recorded.

BOBBY MIGHT CLAIM that he'd had enough of chasing bad men, but it wasn't true. Not yet, and never entirely. Tracking down malefactors was what this pseudo-policeman did best and enjoyed most, and it was the only area of law in which he had any expertise when he arrived at the Department of Justice on January 20, 1961. So it became his highest priority in his early days as attorney general. At the Rackets Committee, Bobby had helped educate America about the existence of a Cosa Nostra crime syndicate. But back then he had to rely on the Eisenhower Justice Department to put them behind bars, and he'd been mad as hell at how few ended up there. Now he had a chance to put things right. The mission fit with the way he still viewed the world—in moral absolutes, with good people struggling to root out an enemy that Ethel, with characteristic directness, called the "baddies."

Frank "Screw" Andrews, a poster-child baddie, entered the world as Frank Joseph Andriola in 1911 in Cincinnati's Little Italy. He began his career peddling moonshine beer and whiskey to blacks in the West End. As he matured he realized the real money was in the numbers game, known in Little Italy as the "Italian lottery" and in the West End as the "nigger pool." It ran like today's lotteries, except that mobsters, rather than the government, managed the buying, selling, and skimming. With help from his brother "Spider" and his nephew "Junior," Screw expanded across the Ohio River into Newport, Kentucky, a city of thirty thousand where, for the right money, the police refrained from asking embarrassing questions. In Newport, Frank earned his nickname by turning the screws on fellow racketeers, especially the black ones whose numbers businesses he coveted. Only one, Melvin Clark, refused to be intimidated, so Screw killed him. The police, buying his improbable plea of self-defense, didn't investigate why Andrews had shot Clark not once but several times.

That history earned Screw a spot on Bobby's list of America's top forty racketeers. His vicious numbers operation—and the famously corrupt government in Newport that let it thrive—was just the kind of setup Bobby meant to take down. Known as Sin City, Newport had been servicing Cincinnati's cravings for vice since the Civil War, when it furnished prostitutes to Union soldiers garrisoned across the river. Local reformers hoped the new attorney general would succeed where others hadn't. Despite his hesitancy to wade into provincial politics, Bobby dispatched to Kentucky an investigator who convened a grand jury. The Internal Revenue Service planted an informant in Screw's syndicate, then staged a commando-style raid of his club, uncovering not just illegal slot machines but a safe full of guns and cash. The agents also found evidence that Screw's gang had rigged the supposedly random selection of winning daily numbers to ensure the smallest payouts. Bobby's men made sure the public knew about the fix. Lower-level operatives received immunity in return for testifying against kingpins. Finally, eleven months after Kennedy became attorney general, Screw, Spider, Junior, and six of their henchmen were indicted for evading nearly four hundred thousand dollars in gambling excise taxes on their two-million-dollar-a-year numbers caper. They went on trial the following summer, and just when prosecutors were starting to panic about the length of deliberations, the jury returned a verdict: guilty for Screw, Junior, and six of the other seven defendants. Screw was sentenced to five years in prison, and Bobby's point was made.

Attorneys general had been declaring war on lowlifes like Screw ever since Al Capone ran rampant in Chicago during Prohibition, but finally one was actually waging that war. The organized crime unit that Bobby inherited had seventeen lawyers; he added forty-three. Before Bobby took over, organized-crime lawyers spent 1,963 days in the field and 283 in court. Two years in, those numbers soared to 7,359 and 809. His card file of bad guys had begun with just forty names. By the time he left office he had amassed records, filling two large rooms, on twenty-three hundred triggermen, gangsters, and swindlers. Each file contained the most up-to-date information from the FBI, Secret Service, Internal Revenue Service, Coast Guard, and twenty-three other agencies that gather intelligence. A month after taking over, Bobby summoned to the Justice Department representatives of each essentially autonomous agency and laid down the laws: *We need to be as single-minded as the Mafia, so get used to collaborating; criminal enterprises are firmly implanted, so dig up the roots after you chop down the tree; and this war matters to me so, needless to say, it matters to the president.* The last dictum went unstated but not unheard.

The only agency that balked was the one that should have been leading the onslaught. For years, J. Edgar Hoover's FBI had refused even to acknowledge the existence of a Cosa Nostra. It was one thing to track down Bonnie and Clyde: Lock 'em up or gun 'em down, and close the case. But the Mafia was a web that would take manpower and time to unravel. That meant more corrupt politicians for Hoover to confront, more chance his G-men would be compromised by the underworld's drugs or money, and more uncomfortable questions about the director's own relationship with Meyer Lansky and other mobsters. The FBI boss had more important wars to wage, like his long-running crusade against Commies and other subversives. Whatever the reason, the result was that in 1958, when the FBI's own top crime researcher issued a report on the Mafia's far-reaching influence, Hoover retrieved and destroyed every last copy, calling the findings "baloney." A year later the FBI office in New York, the epicenter of mob power, had four hundred agents investigating Communists and only four tracking down racketeers. The director understood that Bobby was demanding change, but he assumed he could stonewall the new attorney general the way he had his predecessors.

Kennedy would not be denied, even by a seasoned infighter and survivor like Hoover. The attorney general was a crusader on a mission, and he was the president's brother. G. Robert Blakey, a young member of Justice's Organized Crime Section, witnessed Bobby confronting FBI officials on their inaction: "He said, basically, 'get off your asses . . . Get me some evidence so I can prosecute these people.' The bureau didn't have anything but newspaper articles in these mob guys' files." And it wasn't just that once. Bobby "pushed, ordered, cajoled and successfully enticed the FBI into the fray so that eventually it was a full-fledged if somewhat eccentric participant in the fight to destroy the syndicates," said Victor Navasky, author of the most exhaustive review of the Kennedy-era Justice Department. The price Bobby paid, Navasky added, was that while Hoover entered the battle, he did it not as a team player but on self-serving terms. The bureau managed to accrue more resources, more power, and more latitude to use bugs and wiretaps, all of which would come back to haunt the attorney general.

If Hoover was a reluctant convert, IRS commissioner Mortimer Caplin was an evangelist from the first. The IRS had helped bring down Al Capone, ultimately on charges of tax evasion, and Caplin was anxious to bring investigative accounting once again to the war against high-profile lawbreakers. He also grasped, in a way the FBI chief didn't, that by the early 1960s gangsters and mobsters posed more of a threat to America than did fifth columnists and insurrectionaries. That the anticrime campaign was being marshaled by his old law student, Bobby Kennedy, only increased his resolve. "The tax returns of major racketeers to be identified by the Department of Justice will be subjected to the 'saturation type' investigation," Caplin wrote in a directive issued just after Bobby's February 1961 interagency conclave. He had already given Jack's and Bobby's top aides access to the tax files of Jimmy Hoffa and other primary targets. Now he increased tenfold the number of IRS agents working on crime cases. As a final sign of Caplin's readiness for battle, he authorized his men to carry guns, something "brand new" that he knew even before he asked had the "blessing" of his former student.

Did this flurry of government action actually pose a serious threat to the Mafia? No question, said Carlos Marcello, boss of the New Orleans crime family. "That fucking Bobby Kennedy is making life miserable for me and my friends." Another chieftain who felt under siege was Sam "Mooney" Giancana, who started out as Al Capone's wheelman and ended up running the Chicago mob. Mooney thought he had a deal with Joe Kennedy to leave him alone in return for supposed favors done during the 1960 election, his brother Chuck Giancana wrote, but it soon became clear that "Bobby Kennedy, now ensconced as the attorney general, was orchestrating what would become the largest attack on organized crime in the nation's history. . . . Mooney came to the conclusion that the man he'd envisioned slaving away behind a desk in some obscure legal office after the election was to be his nemesis." Every step he took, the feds were there in the shadows. The Chicago don finally got a judge to rule that only one FBI car at a time could stake out his house or follow his pink Cadillac, and that when an FBI foursome tracked him on the golf course there had to be at least one other group between them and the Mob leader's party.

Bobby himself wanted to be judged by his results, which were impressive but not decisive. The number of indictments of organized-crime figures rose from nineteen the year before he took over to 687 as he was leaving. His conviction rate was close to 90 percent. He and his allies went after the Bonnano family in New York, the Patriarca gang in Rhode Island, and the De Cavalcante operation in New Jersey. In Newport, Kentucky, he took down Screw Andrews and, in the process, helped spur a cleanup that indicted the mayor, councilmen, policemen, and the sheriff. Mooney was right, it was the most relentless attack on organized crime not just then but ever. Still, it didn't come close to nabbing all the mafiosi on Bobby's list, and it didn't get Mooney himself. Once Bobby left office, Organized Crime Section lawyers quickly returned to their old level of productivity, spending half as much time in the field and in court, and demonstrating how difficult it was to institutionalize the war.

The Mafia made an easy target, but skeptics wanted to see what the hard-knuckled ex-campaign manager would do when justice intersected with politics. He said all the right things in the first meeting with his assistant attorneys general: "No politics—period. You don't attend political functions, you don't speak on political matters, you don't get involved in any way." Convincing words, but the department held its collective breath, waiting to see if he could back them up.

In the spring of 1961, the new attorney general faced his first politically sensitive case. Justice Department investigators compiled evidence that J. Vincent Keogh, a judge on the New York Supreme Court, had accepted thirty-five thousand dollars to fix the sentence of a jukebox operator convicted of bankruptcy fraud. The bribery case, however, was not as straightforward as it first appeared. The witnesses against Keogh were the convicted jukebox man and the supposed bagman, neither of whom had anything like the credibility of a member of the judiciary. The alleged payoff wasn't simply trading money for a lighter sentence, since the case wasn't Keogh's, but involved his agreeing to get the judge handling the case to reduce the punishment. Most complicated were the politics. Vincent Keogh didn't matter to Bobby or the White House, but his brother Eugene, a Democratic congressman from Brooklyn, had been instrumental in delivering the reluctant New York delegation to JFK in Los Angeles. Eugene was one of "the five people who were most helpful to the president in the election," Bobby said. Weaknesses in the legal case against Vincent could have let the attorney general off the political hook with Eugene. "If the judge is indicted, even if he is acquitted, his usefulness as a judge will be over," Bobby cautioned the aides gathered in his office. "I'd hate to have that on my conscience." JFK, meanwhile, made clear where he stood. "The President asked me if Bobby was going to indict Vincent Keogh," recalled the attorney general's new administrative assistant, John Seigenthaler. "I said, 'I honestly don't know, but I know that there are some problems.' And the President said, 'My God, I hope that he doesn't.'"

He did, in a style that would become characteristic. First he replaced the young firebrand handling the case with a more seasoned lawyer who, as an Eisenhower holdover, added a bipartisan hue to the prosecution. After confirming with his legal team that there was enough evidence to indict, he took personal responsibility for the decision rather than disqualifying himself, which might have helped him with his brother, the Keogh brothers, and the public. He went so far as to call Eugene to give him a heads-up about the impending charges against his brother, a move of questionable legal ethics but consistent with his personal code of decency. And he never hid from his investigators his nervousness about their pursuing allegations that the congressman, too, was dirty, although he never interfered with their probe. He closed with an unrehearsed and revealing touch of humor. After giving the green light to prosecute, he placed his face on his oversized desk, wrapped his elbows around his head, and said to the aides who were with him, "Goddamn-it, I told my brother I didn't want this job." He half-joked with another assistant, "If you guys indict one more Democrat [JFK]'s going to put me on the Supreme Court to get rid of me." And before the Keogh trial began he warned William Hundley, the Republican he had made lead prosecutor, "Remember, if we lose this case, you and I are going to look like a couple of real shits."

Hundley won, sending Keogh to prison for two years. Political operatives at the White House were furious. The treasurer of the Democratic National Committee approached Bobby's longtime investigator Walter Sheridan at a party "and said, 'I can't believe that you couldn't have fixed that case,'" Sheridan remembered. "And I said, 'Of course we could have, but that's the difference [between] you and us.'" That difference was evident to nearly everyone at the Justice Department, especially the career attorneys, who from that instant were Kennedy men. "It said to us at the time that Kennedy would do whatever he had to do as attorney general, regardless of the political situation," says Henry Ruth, then a young lawyer in the Organized Crime Section. "A lesser Attorney General might have stepped in and said, 'I don't want to indict this fellow,'" agreed Hundley. "While he was Attorney General, I think [Kennedy] probably indicted more people like this than any other Attorney General."*

It was true. In 1962 he indicted, convicted, and sent to prison as part of a kickback scandal George Chacharis, the mayor of Gary, Indiana, who had delivered 70 percent of his city's votes to JFK and was being considered as ambassador to Greece. He indicted and won a nolo contendere plea from the gossip columnist Igor Cassini, who wrote under the pseudonym Cholly Knickerbocker. Cassini was a friend of Joe Kennedy's, and he got in trouble when his public relations firm represented the Dominican dictator Rafael Trujillo without telling the U.S. government about it. Bobby was at his best in such sensitive cases. During his three years as attorney general, his office prosecuted two congressmen, three state supreme court justices, five mayors, two chiefs of police, and three sheriffs—all Democrats. Bobby understood the politics involved in each, and he insisted that the arguments be airtight and the accused be treated respectfully. JFK expressed anger at times, and more often annoyance, but he gave Bobby a wider berth than anyone else in government and on occasion used his brother's scrupulousness to get himself off a particularly sharp hook. When a fat-cat donor to the Democratic Party complained to the president that Bobby was investigating him for antitrust infractions, Jack told him, "You're a good

---

* Not everyone was a fan. The firebrand lawyer he took off the Keogh case says that while Bobby often was overzealous in pursuing his prey, on other occasions he was too obliging of criminals. The scuttlebutt, reports Jay Goldberg, was that Congressman Keogh was as dirty as his brother but too close to the Kennedys to be charged. There were three things Bobby cared about when he was attorney general, Goldberg adds: what was good for JFK, what was good for the Democratic Party, "and only then what was best for the citizenry." Edwyn Silberling, a more seasoned attorney who headed the Organized Crime Section, was also critical of Bobby's handling of some sensitive cases. With Judge Keogh, he said, "My own impression was that if it were at all possible to avoid going ahead with this case he would have avoided it." Kennedy decided to prosecute, Silberling added, in part because local newspapers knew about the investigation and would have been suspicious if nothing was done. By the time he gave that interview to the Kennedy Library, however, Silberling, like Goldberg, had a personal reason to resent Bobby, who had fired him from his job overseeing the attack on organized crime. (Author interview with Goldberg; Silberling OH, March 24, 1971, 57–58, JFKL.)

friend and I'd like to help you. But I'm afraid we have an attorney general we can't fix."

· Nobody saw anything funny about the case of James M. Landis, the former dean of the Harvard Law School who was as close as anyone to the Kennedy clan. Landis served with Joe on the Securities and Exchange Commission, succeeded him as chairman, acted as his lawyer, and assisted with his memoir. He helped Ted get into law school and helped Jack pilot his political career, first in Congress and continuing into the White House. Landis's favorite was Bobby, whose confidence he boosted back when Joe used to ignore his third son, and whose merits he touted often enough to make Joe start to take notice. A brilliant academic and regulator, Landis drank too much and was pathologically absentminded, forgetting to bill Joe for legal services and letting slip the filing of first a single year's income tax return, then a full five. The fact that he set aside in a separate checking account the money he owed made clear he hadn't meant to cheat. But the Justice Department concluded in 1963 that it had no choice but to prosecute, and Bobby felt he had no choice but to disqualify himself from the case and watch his friend be sentenced to thirty days in prison.

"If grandfather is so close to President Kennedy, why didn't he stop the trial?" asked Landis's six-year-old granddaughter, voicing the chagrin shared by the adults who knew him, including Bobby. The attorney general didn't stop the trial, but he did act—first to ensure that Landis would serve his time at a psychiatric hospital rather than a prison, then to transfer him from a public health hospital on Staten Island, where he was barely surviving, to the better equipped and more humane Columbia Presbyterian. Even that had consequences. Nicholas Katzenbach, the deputy attorney general who took over the case when Bobby bowed out, said it would open Bobby to charges of cronyism. Bobby shot back: "If any goddam reporter wants to say that the Kennedy administration, having prosecuted one of the best friends they've ever had—somebody who's been practically a father to me . . . if they want to say that, having prosecuted him, having exposed him to the public through this, that we are now soft on criminals by having him serve that stupid thirty days in some degree of comfort, they can just go to hell!" With fifty years of hindsight, Katzenbach concludes that "Bobby had the power to do something that he thought was the right thing to do and there was no legal reason why he shouldn't do it. The only reason why he shouldn't do it, which I was probably oversensitive to, was that he would be criticized for doing it, which he was. He was always willing to be criticized."*

If his handling of Keogh and Landis suggested that Bobby generally went where the facts and his heart took him, his handling of Frank Sinatra showed he didn't always. Sinatra, who by then had Oscar and Emmy awards to go with his chart-topping record albums, had raised millions and campaigned nationwide for Jack in 1960. He had even recorded a version of his hit "High Hopes" with lyrics like "Everyone wants to back Jack, Jack is on the right track." Bobby's brother-in-law Peter Lawford, an original member of Sinatra's Rat Pack,† loved palling around with Frank. So did Jack. The problem was that Sinatra had another pack of friends that included mobsters Mooney Giancana of Chicago, Lucky Luciano of New York, and half the casino operators in Las Vegas. That was no surprise to the FBI, IRS, or the Federal Bureau of Narcotics. Sinatra's name also turned up in enough probes by Bobby's own Organized Crime Section that he ordered it to prepare a memo detailing Sinatra's Mafia ties and recommending action.

Bobby had been suspicious of Frank from the beginning of the 1960 campaign. As attorney general, he urged his father to rescind an invitation to Sinatra to visit him on the Riviera. Likewise, he advised JFK to cancel a planned weekend stay at Sinatra's compound on Frank Sinatra Drive in Palm Springs. Frank was devastated and, said Lawford, "he called Bobby every name in the book." After all, the crooner had expanded his home with just such a presidential visit in mind, adding cottages for the Secret Service, constructing a heliport, even raising a flagpole like the one at the Kennedy compound in Hyannis Port. To make

* Many friends, relatives, and journalists concluded that the disgraced Landis had committed suicide when he was found drowned in his backyard swimming pool. The coroner said Landis died of a heart attack, and his biographer, Donald Ritchie, agrees (Ritchie, *Landis*, 201).

† The core members were Sinatra, Dean Martin, and Sammy Davis, Jr., with Lawford and Joey Bishop also part of the pack that appeared together onstage, in films, and palling around at nightclubs.

matters worse, the president ended up staying at the Palm Desert home of Bing Crosby, Frank's rival and an avowed Republican.

Bobby wasn't bothered by the singer's tirades, but he had to have been unnerved by the series of reports he got from his aides in 1962 and 1963 spelling out Sinatra's business and personal relationships with a bevy of underworld figures. Justice's lead investigator had been allowed to talk to Sinatra associates "but was precluded from any immediate contacts with SINATRA or his staff," according to the FBI, which in a trademark Hoover ploy was quietly keeping tabs on the Justice probe. Still, department lawyers managed to assemble enough damning material that the head of the Organized Crime Section recommended a full-blown inquiry. Katzenbach scribbled in the margin "makes sense to me." Bobby disagreed, and no investigation was launched.

Did he back off out of gratitude to Sinatra for his role in electing Jack? Was he afraid of stirring up the hornet's nest that prosecutors had unearthed of Jack's ties to Frank, and Frank's to the women Jack caroused with, some of whom also were sleeping with Mafia men? Or was it, as Kennedy defenders insisted, that the Justice Department had too few resources and more serious crooks to chase? Dougald McMillan, who wrote the reports to Bobby on Sinatra, says the attorney general had a mantra when it came to bringing down the Mob: "Peel the banana, meaning go to the guys on the periphery and turn them as witnesses against those in the center. I thought Sinatra was an ideal candidate for that." But McMillan never got the permission he sought, or even a clear answer. "No one said no, but no one said yes."

Looking back, McMillan gives Bobby the benefit of the doubt while acknowledging the tangled family web that made the attorney general's task so impossible: "I believe that if it had been left to Bobby, he would have opened an investigation on Sinatra. But it appears obvious that the Kennedy election campaign was deeply indebted to Sinatra, and perhaps to Giancana. That's my explanation for Bobby's failure to give me the go-ahead to open an investigation on Sinatra. Because I never, not one time, heard of him killing any other investigation. He was always gung-ho to go after the Mob."

He was even more gung-ho in his pursuit of two enemies of old, Jimmy Hoffa and Roy Cohn. Hoffa earned a team at the department that was virtually dedicated to him. Justice officials labeled it the Labor Rackets Unit, Teamsters operatives called it Operation Big Squeeze, and the world knew it as the Get-Hoffa Squad.* The department had not managed to get him when Eisenhower was president and Bobby was feeding it everything he could dig up at the McClellan Committee. Now Jack was president, Bobby was the country's chief crime buster, and all the resources of the government could and would be mobilized to settle a score and put him away.

The effort expended was unprecedented. Just as Bobby had once subjected Hoffa to the most unrelenting congressional assault ever aimed at an individual, now he made his bête noire the most indicted man in America. Fifteen grand juries were impaneled to consider evidence against the Teamsters president (Hoffa counted twenty-nine). Sixteen lawyers worked exclusively on the Hoffa cases, along with thirty FBI agents and a series of other investigators (Hoffa said it was half of the attorneys at Justice and half of the FBI). While the Get-Hoffa group technically was a unit within a section within a division, Walter Sheridan, its director, reported directly to the attorney general. Sheridan was an ex-FBI man, not an attorney, and his primary qualifications were his close friendship with Bobby and knowing more than anyone else about Hoffa from his days at the Rackets Committee. The depth of Bobby's interest would become clear during the Cuban missile crisis, when, between meetings on the epic confrontation of superpowers, Bobby and Sheridan conferred over the phone on progress in the latest Hoffa trial.

Bobby focused his attention primarily on a case that had stuck in his craw when he first exposed it in congressional hearings five years earlier, in which Hoffa and his partner had made a million dollars from the Test Fleet trucking company for which he once settled a strike. The complaint rested on such arcane legal arguments—involving federal labor law and complicated kickback schemes—that a government lawyer had to explain them after adjournment each day to the court reporter in Nashville, where the trial was held in 1962. The government could muster only misdemeanor complaints, but Bobby was so determined to win that he and his team insinuated within the Hoffa camp an informant named

---

* Hoffa had his own squad of high-priced legal talent that critics dubbed the Teamsters Bar Association.

Edward Grady Partin. Partin had been languishing in jail on charges including kidnapping, rape, and manslaughter, any one of which was more serious than everything facing Hoffa and the accumulated burden of which made Partin anxious to curry favor with prosecutors. His spying turned up stunning allegations, not about the case at hand but about Hoffa's attitude toward Bobby. The Teamsters leader told Partin about three different ways he imagined having the attorney general killed: blown up at Hickory Hill using plastic explosives; shot with a high-powered rifle; or murdered while traveling in the South, with the crime pinned on archsegregationists. "Somebody," Partin quoted Hoffa as saying, "needs to bump that sonofabitch off." Hoffa denied everything and, pointing to Partin's "criminal records from coast to coast dating from 1943," branded his accuser a "fraud and liar."*

The Nashville trial was historic. "Never," Navasky pointed out, "had the government devoted so much money, manpower and top level brainpower to a misdemeanor case." When the proceedings ended in a hung jury and a mistrial, the government cried foul. Hoffa, it said, hadn't trusted his fate to luck or jury discretion. He tried to bribe several jurors, sometimes with the offer of a job promotion, other times with easy money. At a trial in Chattanooga in 1964 the bribery evidence stuck and the Teamsters president, who started out facing a mere misdemeanor, stood convicted of a felony. After all the indictments dating to that first arrest in 1957 for trying to buy his way into the Rackets Committee files—and all the acquittals—Bobby had his man. Hoffa was sentenced to eight years in prison for jury tampering, and in a separate case that ended just before Bobby left office, he would get five more years for fraud.

One question continues to hang over the Get-Hoffa Squad: Was Bobby Kennedy conducting a vendetta against Jimmy Hoffa? He surely was, just as federal authorities had against Al Capone, Screw Andrews, and

---

* During a 1963 meeting at the Justice Department, Hoffa became so enraged that he "started choking Bobby with two hands and hollering, 'I'll break your fucking neck! I'll kill you!'" said Frank Ragano, Hoffa's attorney, who was there. "The combined efforts of Bobby, Danny, Jack, and myself finally broke his chokehold. I am positive Robert Kennedy would have died before our eyes if we had not intervened." Selwyn Raab, an ex–New York Times reporter and coauthor of Ragano's memoir, says he checked the story and is convinced Ragano's account is credible. (Ragano and Raab, Mob Lawyer, 142–43, and email from Raab, April 15, 2014.)

other organized crime targets. With each of them, the justice system worked in reverse: Instead of starting with a crime and searching for the criminal, it started with a presumed criminal and looked for a crime to justify locking him up. Few second-guessed that approach with villainous masterminds like Capone or callous murderers like Andrews. Hoffa is more ambiguous. No doubt he broke some laws and bent more. But Teamsters members had elected him, then reelected him, because he won contracts nobody else could and made drivers proud of their work. Dedicating a crack unit of lawyers and investigators to Jimmy Hoffa meant fewer resources to chase mobsters, blue-collar criminals, and other enemies of justice. Bobby was convinced that nobody was more dangerous than Hoffa for corrupting not just the Teamsters but the labor-management equilibrium and our democracy itself. Yet his idealism had cost him his objectivity. So single-minded was his pursuit that he accomplished the unthinkable: He made people feel sorry for Hoffa. "If you indict someone enough, you're probably playing Russian roulette," says Jimmy's son James, the current president of the Teamsters. "Eventually you're going to find a jury" that will convict.

"It's like Ahab and the whale," agrees Navasky, who studied the case in depth. "[Bobby] became fixated on this evil guy who stood for absolute evil and then it became a macho contest. He was going to show him, and his own sense of self was at stake as long as this evil guy was at large." Jimmy himself, in a rare moment of self-awareness, offered this reflection on his long grudge match with Bobby Kennedy: "A corrupt Jimmy Hoffa is no great danger to the United States of America. There are police forces and law-enforcement agencies to take care of a Jimmy Hoffa, courts of law to try him and jails to incarcerate him, if he truly violates the laws. The real menace is a vindictive cabinet officer with power over the courts, who by threat or coercion can force weak men to do his bidding and thus make [a] mockery of the forces of law and order."*

Bobby would have dismissed that meditation as malarkey, but he was genuinely conflicted over the fate of his archfoe. In the years since their

---

* Jimmy was more straightforward in 1962 when, at a rally of his supporters in Detroit, he took a swipe at Bobby's manliness. Asked by a wisecracking Teamster whether Bobby was a "doxy," or immoral woman, Hoffa answered, "He's worse than that—he's a touch football player" (Russell, *Out of the Jungle*, 216).

get-acquainted dinner, Bobby's us-versus-them rendering of the world
had begun to soften. The upshot with Hoffa was that the attorney general "was delighted with the conviction and unhappy that he was going
to go to jail," Kenny O'Donnell surmised, adding, "1957 was one thing,
seven years later Bobby had grown up an awful lot and I don't think
anybody exulted in anybody going to go to jail that had been around that
much, seen enough jails, seen enough prisons."*

Roy Cohn was the other old enemy Bobby revisited from his perch at
the Justice Department. Their simmering hatred had never subsided and
tensions flared anytime they encountered each other. Three rows apart
on a plane from Hyannis to New York, they didn't speak or even glance
at each other. When Bobby was seated near Cohn at Orsini's, an upscale
restaurant in New York, Cohn turned to him and said, "Who's going to
move, you or me?" (Bobby had the headwaiter change his table.) When
they had worked for Senator Joe McCarthy, Cohn had the senior title and
the upper hand, and he wielded them to keep Bobby in his place and
doing his bidding. Now their positions were reversed.

"It's a toss-up between you and Jimmy Hoffa as to who's number one
on [Bobby's] list," another old McCarthy staffer, Jim Juliana, told Cohn
after Kennedy was named attorney general. Juliana advised Cohn to "get
out of town." Neil Gallagher witnessed their battle up close in the early
1960s when he was a congressman from New Jersey. When Cohn offered
to use his press contacts to help win support for the Kennedy administration's civil rights bill, "Bobby went nuts," Gallagher says. "He said, 'I

---

* Years later, when he was running for president, Bobby offered conflicting evidence on
whether he had mellowed on Jimmy. Teamsters officials approached Ted Kennedy to see
whether, in return for their campaign help, Bobby would push for Jimmy to be "transferred
from the [prison] mattress factory to the farm, so he could get outdoors," recalled Dave
Burke, an aide to Ted. Bobby's response: "As far as I'm concerned, Jimmy Hoffa can stay in
the mattress factory forever. And if I'm ever elected president of the United States, he has a
darn slim chance of ever getting out of jail." But William Hundley, who ran Justice's Organized Crime Section under Bobby, recalled that during that 1968 campaign, Bobby told him:
"If I become president I'm going to let [Hoffa] out." Hoffa's biographer Lester Velie offered
one more unlikely twist on the Hoffa-Kennedy relationship, writing that in the spring of
1964, Bobby offered Jimmy a quick parole if the Teamsters boss agreed to cut his ties with the
union. Jimmy flew into a rage: "That son of a bitch [Kennedy] is trying to take my union
away from me." (Burke OH, December 8, 1971, 55, JFKL; "Legend in the Law," *Washington
Lawyer: Why Jimmy Hoffa Had to Die*, 95–96.)

don't want anything to do with that son of a bitch.' . . . Kenny O'Donnell picks up Bobby and pushes him against the wall. He says, 'What the hell's more important, the civil rights bill or your hard-on for Roy Cohn?' "

In 1963 Bobby gave the green light to sue Cohn for perjury and obstruction of justice. The government alleged that Cohn had rigged a grand jury to prevent his friend and three associates from being indicted for swindling a company they had invested in, then lied about it. Cohn said Bobby's lawyers had "unleashed all the power they had" against him by, among other things, subpoenaing "every client I had," calling "a thousand witnesses before grand juries, concerning me," and monitoring not just his mail but his attorney's. Indeed, the trial judge decried the mail watch as something "that smacks of Russia rather than the United States." It also was precisely the kind of tactic Cohn had used so effectively against alleged subversives earlier in his own career, in the very New York courthouse where he now stood as a defendant. Was it, as Cohn and others charged, a simple case of making a personal dislike a federal matter? Bobby's hatred of Cohn is not in doubt, nor is his prodigious capacity for holding a grudge. But in this instance, says the government attorney who handled the case, the attorney general was wary of how it would look to bring an indictment against his old adversary. Gerald Walpin says he was summoned to Hickory Hill on a Saturday afternoon to lay out for the attorney general his "clear" evidence that Cohn "had lied and had obstructed justice," along with any doubts Walpin might have about winning a conviction. "He said to me at the end of the session, 'I realize I may get mud thrown at me in the media. I don't care. I'll take it. We should do the right thing. You believe they're guilty, that the indictment is well founded, you go ahead.' And we did."

Cohn was acquitted, twice. He believed those verdicts vindicated him and he pointed an accusing finger back at Bobby for bringing the case. Walpin disagrees, explaining that the entire jury was dismissed in the first trial when one juror's father died. After they were discharged, Walpin adds, "the foreman said, 'Your Honor, we had been eleven to one for conviction earlier this afternoon, and then the last holdout agreed to conviction. But we thought, with such an important matter, that we

oughta sleep on it overnight to make sure everybody's still in agreement.' The judge said, 'I'm sorry, there's nothing we can do about it. I
have discharged you.' "

As the head of a bureaucracy with thirty-two thousand employees and
a $400 million budget, Robert Kennedy could and did set broadly ambi-
tious goals like attacking organized crime and rooting out political corruption, which reverberated across the worlds of law enforcement and
politics. At the same time this attorney general had the capacity to look
down as well as up, focusing on the individual stories of people desperate
for justice. Junius Scales was one of those small stories that reflected
Bobby's tender side.

Born to an affluent family in Greensboro, Scales loved books as much
as he hated the Jim Crow system of racial segregation that governed life
in the South in 1920. At the young age of sixteen he enrolled at the University of North Carolina, and the day he turned nineteen he joined the
Communist Party. Over the next eighteen years he became a local organizer, then chairman of the state party, positions from which he could
battle Jim Crow, then Joe McCarthy. On the evening of November 18,
1954, the FBI arrested Scales on a quiet street in Memphis, binding him
in leg irons and carting him off to stand trial in Greensboro. The charge:
violating the Smith Act of 1940, which made it a crime to belong to
any group that advocated the violent overthrow of the United States
government. The verdict: guilty, which his hometown paper said was
"what he deserved." After more than six years of new trials and appeals,
the Supreme Court upheld his conviction by a five-to-four vote and he
began serving a six-year sentence at the Lewisburg Penitentiary in
Pennsylvania.

The Smith Act itself seemed un-American, outlawing the advocacy
of ideas rather than the commission of misdeeds, and reflecting the
anticommunist fever of postwar America. Scales's punishment, in turn,
seemed an especially poor fit for his supposed crime. He was the only
American ever imprisoned for merely belonging to the Communist Party,
as opposed to participating in a violent or subversive activity. His sentence was longer than that of anyone who had been convicted of actual

political violence or subversion. By the time he was jailed under the Smith Act's "knowing membership" provision, he no longer belonged to the Communist Party, having become disillusioned first by the Soviet invasion of Hungary, then by revelations of the murderous crimes of his onetime idol, Joseph Stalin. His real crime, the FBI made clear, was refusing to name names of other former or present party members. On the bureau's say-so, Robert Kennedy's Justice Department weighed in against a reduction in Scales's sentence. That disappointed but didn't surprise the growing groundswell of Scales supporters, which included the civil libertarian Roger Baldwin, the labor leader David Dubinsky, the *New York Times* editorial page, and nine of the twelve jurors who had convicted the curly-haired North Carolinian. The only thing that annoyed the attorney general more than the Communist Party was being told what to do by smug liberals or *The New York Times*.

But Bobby was changing. He had begun to distinguish saying provocative things from actually doing something wrong. He was more open to admitting a mistake. He was also less afraid to break with the unbending J. Edgar Hoover, who insisted Scales stay behind bars until he named his ex-comrades. *The New York Times*'s Anthony Lewis remembers first raising the Scales case with Bobby just when the administration was trying to persuade Southern senators, who were as fervidly anticommunist as they were pro-segregation, to dial back Jim Crow. The attorney general turned on him angrily, saying, "'You liberals, you think we can just do anything we want and it will all come out your way. But if we did anything for Junius Scales I can tell you that it would be the death of our civil rights legislation.' I said, 'Okay, okay. You know more about it than I do.'" A month later, at his own birthday party, Bobby took Lewis aside and in an "almost shy way, he said, very briefly, 'We're going to let your friend Scales out of prison.' That's what he was like. It bothered him. All the things he said to me, he was angry because he knew it was wrong, and he didn't think he could do anything about it. But then he thought he would do something about it. And he did." What he didn't tell Lewis was that in order to get JFK to commute Scales's sentence, he had to buck not just Hoover but three other citadels against the Red Menace—the Senate Internal Security Subcommittee, the House Committee on Un-American Activities, and his own Internal Security Division. He also didn't mention that Scales would be let out of jail on December 24, 1962, with a guard on duty yelling to him, "We just got a telegram from Bobby Kennedy, and he says we gotta get you home by tonight in plenty of time for Christmas."

The attorney general's turnaround on Scales signaled a man in transition, much as his nation was. Bobby was slowly shedding the Cold War persona of his McCarthy days, but he hadn't yet become the liberal icon we remember. He cracked down on Communist Party members who failed to register as agents of the Soviet Union, indicting them and the party. He had a union leader in San Francisco arrested for being a Communist. Yet he intervened to grant visas to leftists such as the Mexican painter Juan O'Gorman when he was invited to speak by several American universities. He turned down a request from the shah of Iran, and the U.S. State Department, to ship back to Iran thirty students the shah accused of being Communists. And he hounded from office an obscure bureaucrat named Otto Otepka, who had overseen security vetting at the State Department since the McCarthy attacks. Otepka angered the attorney general by leaking classified files to Congress suggesting that the administration was lax in cracking down on subversives, and by refusing to clear appointees whom Bobby trusted but Otto didn't. By the time he was fired in November 1963, Otepka had become a cause célèbre for anticommunists. "The lesson of the Otepka case is plain," wrote the conservative scribe Frank Kluckhohn. "The State Department security against penetration by Communists and against other security risks has been smashed." That smashing, Kluckhohn said, was done "at the personal order of Bobby Kennedy."

If those moves alienated his old anti-Red allies, at least some of his liberal critics applauded the changes they were seeing, starting with his pledge to give meaning to the phrase "equal justice." "I have a strong feeling that the law, especially in criminal cases, favors the rich man over the poor," Bobby said in his first interview after taking office. Tame language by today's standards but not so then, and not for the head of the Justice Department. The inequality was particularly glaring on the issue of bail. The rich could afford it, the poor could not, and Bobby took critical first steps to make the system fairer. He also helped pass a law ensuring that destitute defendants could get a lawyer in federal criminal cases.

And he set up the Office of Criminal Justice to explore other equity issues in law enforcement, including something as simple as ensuring that poor people could get transcripts of their trials in order to file appeals. Hoover dismissed such moves as the "maudlin proposals" of "misguided sentimentalists." Patricia Wald, former chief judge of the influential U.S. Court of Appeals for the District of Columbia Circuit, saw them differently. "Criminal justice was just not that much of a focus for any previous attorney general," Wald says. Kennedy's sensitivity to these human-sized issues as well as the headline-generating ones—and his determination not just to talk but to act—was, according to Wald, "very unusual."

More unusual still was a cabinet officer engaging with issues facing American Indians, which even liberals had not yet done. The Justice Department's Lands and Natural Resources Division handled compensation claims for territory that the Indians maintained had been stolen from them when federal treaties were broken. The department's stock answer to any claim had been "no," after which the cases headed to trial. Bobby instructed Ramsey Clark, who ran the division, to settle as many suits as possible even if that cost the government more, which he knew it would. His bond with Indians would intensify over time, and would come to be about much more than land. "That such conditions can be allowed to prevail among a people uniquely entitled to call themselves first Americans is nothing less than a national disgrace," he said at a 1963 meeting of the National Congress of American Indians. He would later confide that "I'd like to be an Indian, but it's too late." Maybe not. The Congress's ninety tribes bestowed on him a war bonnet and the name Brave Heart. The Senecas gave him their own tribal title: Above the Crowd. "You asked me why he had this thing about Indians," said Clark. "It didn't have anything to do with the law, it had to do with justice with a small j, with doing right and being fair by these people that we had pushed around for so long." John Nolan, a Justice Department aide, offered a less high-minded explanation: Indians were like Bobby—soft-spoken until you riled them up, at which point they raised hell.

Bobby knew that justice denied and Indian rights were part of a more pervasive problem of poverty in America. Bureaucratically, that was the jurisdiction of the Secretary of Health, Education, and Welfare. Politically, the attorney general cared too much and was too close to the president to be denied. Realistically, nobody in government understood enough about the origins of poverty to know how to root it out, so nobody really objected when he jumped in. Bobby's approach was to call on anyone he needed in government no matter where they worked and to try everything. He started with the kids he cared about most and entrusted the leadership to a childhood buddy he knew wouldn't be deterred. Dave Hackett knew even less than Bobby about the problem, but both believed that kids in trouble were more like the misunderstood gangbangers in the red-hot movie *West Side Story* than the "beastly punks" that Hoover had branded them. With Bobby overseeing it, Hackett's Committee on Juvenile Delinquency funded programs in Harlem, on New York's Lower East Side, and in fifteen other cities. Each treated youth crime as a matter of poverty, not individual misbehavior. The key was to seed the projects with federal money and keep the control local, with poor people helping decide their own fate. Funding went to preschools, vocational training, and any other governmental fix Bobby and Hackett could conjure up. Public money helped attract private. The attorney general was so committed that in 1963, he invited every cabinet member but the secretary of state to meet with Hackett and his insurgents, locking them in his office for four hours of brainstorming on ways to battle poverty. The most enthusiastic participant was Secretary of Defense Robert McNamara, who agreed that this was the single most important challenge facing America. Bobby wasn't in office long enough to test a domestic Peace Corps and other dreams, but when Lyndon Johnson picked up the vision of a War on Poverty, his building blocks were precisely the pilot projects set in motion by Bobby and Hackett.

Those initiatives further showcased the evolving Bobby Kennedy. He had grown up an outsider and underdog within his family and would always identify with both. Campaigning in places like West Virginia had shown him firsthand what poverty and delinquency looked like. As attorney general he had the resources and grabbed the authority. There was no stopping him once mistreatment of Indians, child poverty, or any other cause had earned his favorite judgment word: "unacceptable." To him the most unconscionable of sins was indifference. Bobby's drive and enthusiasm were infectious, instilling in those around him the feeling that they had the power to change the world and the responsibility to try.

But as ever, he was impatient and sometimes callous in the way he treated flesh-and-blood humans as he battled on behalf of humanity. Patrick Anderson, an information officer for Hackett, saw his best and worst instincts on display in a down-and-out neighborhood of Washington where, thanks to Bobby, a school swimming pool would for the first time stay open through the summer. "As he inspected the pool," recalled Anderson, "a blustering bureaucrat from the recreation department approached him, hoping for commendation. Instead, he was met with a machine-gun burst of questions:

Q. How deep is the shallow end of the pool?
A. Three feet.

Q. What about children under three feet tall?
A. They can't use the pool.

Q. Why not use a wood platform to raise the shallow end?
A. It would rot.

Q. Why wasn't the pool to be open on Sundays?

A. None of the pools was ever open on Sundays . . .

"By then, the poor man, suddenly become an enemy of tiny tots and Sunday swimming, was almost incoherent. Kennedy turned and walked away without a word," said Anderson. "Minutes later, as he left the pool, hundreds of Negro children ran after him, shouting his name and reaching out to touch him. Kennedy moved among them slowly, smiling, rubbing their heads, squeezing their hands, reaching out to the smaller ones who could not get near him. This was not done for show—there were no reporters or photographers along—but because he loved those slum children, loved them as much as he disdained the fool of a bureaucrat who could not give him the answers he wanted."

He loved crippled children, too. What politician didn't? Upon meeting a ten-year-old girl in a wheelchair at the Washington Horse Show, he invited her and her classmates to visit him at work. "Her teacher didn't believe her," says James Clayton, who covered the Justice Department for *The Washington Post*. "She kept pushing and finally the teacher telephoned up Bobby's secretary, Angie Novello, and Angie said, 'Oh, we've been waiting for your call.' So late one evening, after the press was gone, a school bus pulled up and all these kids, handicapped kids, were brought up to Bob's office. He said to them, 'Would you like to talk to the president?' They said, 'oh.' He picked up the hotline to the White House. . . . The president said two or three sentences to them and those kids went out floating." Stories like that, Clayton adds, are one reason the press warmed to the attorney general. "He didn't want it published. He would have objected if we published it."

He never stopped advocating for the impaired and the impoverished, but he was less fearless in policing the errant rich. Antitrust lawsuits are traditionally the best weapon an attorney general has to keep big business in line. Bobby said that bigness worried him, but while he threatened to sue the most brazen of the monopolists, big oil and big steel, he never followed through. Instead he took the politically safe road of attacking price fixing while doing less actual trust-busting than the business-friendly Eisenhower administration had done. And at times he even appeared in court on the side of megacorporations like the dominant pipeline company in the Far West, drawing this rebuke from his old friend Justice William O. Douglas: "The Department of Justice knuckled under to the El Paso Natural Gas Company." Business frankly bored Bobby, as it did all of Joe Kennedy's offspring. But the attorney general knew he could neither afford to look like a toady to the robber barons, especially since his father was one, nor seem antibusiness at a time when the economy was sluggish. So he vacillated, one day telling the Economic Club of New York that "this administration and any administration has no choice but to be 'pro-business,' " then assuring the public that "we've done a good job" in trust-busting "and we've done it with vigor."*

Ask any businessman in the 1960s, and the abiding memory of Bob-

---

* In Kennedy-speak, "vigor" was a favorite word, pronounced "vigahhh."

by's days at Justice is sure to be his "Gestapo-like" tactics during the great steel face-off of 1962. The crisis was sparked when the major American steel companies announced price increases just after the Steelworkers Union, under pressure from a White House worried about inflation, had agreed to forgo wage hikes. The Kennedys felt double-crossed. An outraged Bobby vowed to "play with a hard ball"— convening a grand jury, issuing subpoenas, and even scouring expense accounts to determine whether U.S. Steel and the other giants had colluded. "It was a tough way to operate," the attorney general acknowledged, "but under the circumstances, we couldn't afford to lose." His probes included whether Bethlehem Steel president Edmund Martin had in fact said one day that prices should be lowered and the next that they should be raised, hinting that he had switched gears to fall in line with his fellow conspirators. With newspapers differing on what Martin had said, Bobby asked the FBI to talk to the reporters and to the Bethlehem president.

Bobby meant to get rough but not to unleash a tempest. The agents couldn't reach Martin until 11:00 that night. After talking to him they placed a call to Courtney Evans, the FBI's liaison with Bobby, to ask how they should handle the reporters. "It woke me up out of a sound sleep" at 2:00 A.M., Evans recalled. "The question asked was whether these reporters should be interviewed at once or whether this could be put off till the following day. Unfortunately, I didn't check with anybody. I just made a decision predicated on the fact that if we could interview the president of a steel company at eleven or twelve o'clock at night, perhaps we could at least call three reporters on the phone, recognizing that we would have to wake them up." The agents roused one reporter by telephoning at 3:00 that morning, met a second at his office at 6:30 A.M., and questioned a third later in the day. Reporters routinely phone sources in the middle of the night, but they don't like it when anyone— most of all federal policemen—does the same thing to them, as they let the world know. The public's understanding of the facts quickly snowballed into fantasy, with suggestions of not just journalists but steel executives getting woken, and not by the telephone but by agents violating the sanctity of their homes. Even the normally unflappable *New York Times* published a page one story with this screeching headline: STEEL: A

72-HOUR DRAMA WITH AN ALL-STAR CAST AND PLOT OF MANY SURPRISES.
The chairman of the Republican National Committee called it "reminiscent of the days of Hitler and the Gestapo when the German people lived
in fear of the knock on the door in the middle of the night." Others suggested a conspiracy to embarrass Bobby, orchestrated by J. Edgar Hoover,
who, according to Evans, learned about the calls from him the next
morning and told him they never should have been made.

In fact, Bobby and Jack were finally getting tough with big steel and it
was working, with the companies backing down from their proposed
price increases. Then the Kennedy brothers backed down from the grand
jury and subpoenas that Bobby had promised, with the president reasoning that keeping the peace with the steel companies trumped finding out
whether they had illegally fixed prices. Bobby blamed his brother for that
retrenchment, saying that JFK felt "it was important to make up to business so that they would not consider him or the Administration antibusiness." But the attorney general accepted full responsibility for the
late-night telephone calls, even though he hadn't ordered them and
knew the calls would reinforce his image as ruthless. "Robert Kennedy
didn't try to wiggle out of this by saying: 'Somebody—a minor FBI
official—made that decision,'" said Evans. "He indicated that this was a
decision of the department and was his responsibility. Of course, he
didn't know anything about it." As for Bobby, he never regretted the
White House's flexing its muscles during the steel crisis, but he was more
reflective than his critics realized about the "rather scary" potential that
such power could be abused. "That potential, as far as the attorney general of the United States [is concerned], rests in a thousand ways," he
added. "If I started an investigation of you in your community, you're
ruined."

Most of what he did as attorney general, whether it was going all out
to put Hoffa and Cohn behind bars or snuffing out fires like the steel crisis, fit into his grand scheme. Occasionally he acted only because something or someone caught his notice, offering a glimpse into his heart. So
it was with Sergeant Alvin York, the celebrated hero of World War I.
York and the seven soldiers under his command had silenced deadly German machine gun nests and captured 132 enemy troops. That story won
an Oscar for Gary Cooper, and it brought fame but not fortune to York, a

subsistence farmer from Tennessee. Bobby learned that the seventy-three-year-old invalid owed $172,000 in federal taxes on the royalties from the book and movie about him, which he had donated to build a Bible school and a high school. Bobby was a sucker for a story like York's and asked his staff, "What can we legally do to help?" Then he did it, getting the IRS to reduce what York owed, helping plan a fundraiser to cover the rest, and kicking in a thousand dollars of his own.

Jack had joked two years before that the job of attorney general would give his little brother some legal experience, but even he would have found it a stretch to imagine that Bobby's first courtroom appearance would be before the nine justices of the U.S. Supreme Court in one of the most consequential cases in American history. *Gray v. Sanders* challenged Georgia's apportionment system that gave rural voters disproportionate clout in primary elections for such statewide offices as governor,* a setup Bobby felt was unfair as well as unconstitutional. Before he could make that argument to the court, however, he needed to persuade his own solicitor general, Archibald Cox. A luminous legal mind burnished at Harvard made Cox perhaps the most influential and intrepid solicitor general in U.S. history, and he was unconvinced that federal court was the forum in which to challenge these state voting systems. Bobby knew that without Cox's support the justices would look skeptically at anything he said. He also knew that ordering Cox to yield wouldn't work and might impel him to quit. So the attorney general first invited the president's top political aides to meet with him, Cox, and other Justice officials. When JFK's men started talking politics, Bobby stopped them, saying it didn't matter which party would gain, "malapportionment was simply wrong." When Cox protested that there was no way to make a convincing argument for Kennedy's "one man, one vote" approach, Bobby ended the meeting by saying, "Archie, I know you'll find a way." That closing remark was preplanned and "one of the shrewdest things I've ever heard somebody say," said Bruce Terris, a smart young lawyer whose job with Cox gave him a front row seat at the

---

* Georgia used a County Unit System that made the number of counties a candidate won matter more than the number of votes. While the system gave more weight to urban than rural counties, it wasn't nearly enough more to account for the population differences.

backroom drama. As he and Cox returned to their offices, Terris added, "Cox said to me, '[Bobby] doesn't understand.' While I diplomatically did not reply, I thought about how much Kennedy did understand. He not only understood the fundamental legal-political issue but he understood his man, Archibald Cox." The solicitor general ended up writing a magnificent brief, which was one of the very few he did entirely on his own and provided a compelling framework for Bobby's presentation to the justices on January 17, 1963.

The attorney general brought along a cheering section that included his mother, wife, two sisters, younger brother, nephew, four of his seven children, and two sisters-in-law, one of whom was the First Lady. But all eyes were on Bobby, wearing the uniform of morning coat and striped trousers customary for government attorneys arguing before the Supreme Court. Most recent attorneys general had argued at least one case before the high court, but surely he was the first for whom it was his inaugural case. And he was one of the few lawyers who would actually invite the justices to interrogate him. All that made it the toughest ticket in Washington, remembered Terris. "Everybody in town wanted to see Bobby Kennedy get his teeth knocked out."

With no text or even notes, the attorney general made what amounted to a four-page opening argument. Having deftly marshaled the solid support of the government behind his arguments, Bobby displayed a confidence that belied his inexperience and shone a rare spotlight on his legal brainpower. He reminded the justices what was at stake: "[Election] districts have been so arranged in certain areas of the United States that an individual in one area has 10, 15, 50 or 100 times the vote strength of an individual in another area." He challenged the court to admit that the Georgia system "strikes at the very heart of the United States." He drew laughs from the nine men in black robes by telling them, "We used to have, and I repeat used to have, a saying in my City of Boston which was vote early, and vote often. If—if you live in one of the small counties in the State of Georgia, all you have to do is vote early and you accomplish the same result." As he sat down, Bobby bowed slightly to the bench, which included two old friends and a former deputy. Fourteen months later the justices, in a landmark eight-to-one decision, struck down the Georgia system and sanctified the principle—extolled so eloquently by the attorney general—that the vote of every American should count equally.

Archie Cox should have intimidated Bobby Kennedy. At Harvard Law School, he had served on the law review, a spot reserved for top achievers. He clerked for Learned Hand, one of history's most-quoted judges, and came to Justice as a Harvard professor and the nation's leading scholar on labor law.* Bobby came from a less esteemed law school where he finished in the middle of his class and had, since graduating, impressed many with his zeal and few with his scholarliness. He understood that, and he compensated brilliantly by filling the top ranks of his Justice Department with men more accomplished than himself—Rhodes Scholars and Yale Law graduates Byron White, Nicholas Katzenbach, and John Douglas as deputy and assistant attorneys general; Yale Law grad and Supreme Court clerk Louis Oberdorfer to run the Tax Division; Phillips Exeter, Yale, and Yale Law intellectual Burke Marshall to run Civil Rights; and Edwyn Silberling of Harvard Law overseeing the crackdown on organized crime. Even junior lawyers such as Terris carried impressive credentials: summa cum laude from Harvard College and magna cum laude from Harvard Law School.

Early on, surrounding himself with such a gifted staff backstopped Bobby and deflected insinuations that he wasn't up to the job. Over time he learned how to manage his position in ways that made him and the government look good, such as getting Cox to author just the right brief in the one person, one vote case. Not knowing the legal fine points helped Bobby slice through legal argot and arrive at more fundamental truths affecting policy and politics. "I wouldn't characterize Bobby as an intellectual," said Teddy White. "I'd characterize him as something more important: the guy who can use intellectuals." Bobby also was smart enough to know that filling a staff just with Ivy League gentlemen like Cox and Katzenbach would have made his department too high-minded and plod-

---

* Cox would be back in the spotlight a decade later when he was named special prosecutor in the Watergate case. But five months into the job the Nixon White House fired Cox as part of a cover-up of the cover-up that became legendary as the Saturday Night Massacre. What set Nixon off was Cox's insistence that the president turn over tapes of Oval Office conversations that ultimately proved a conspiracy to hide the administration's ties to the Watergate burglary.

ding, and not necessarily primed for action or change. So he recruited
what Victor Navasky called "home-grown activists"—crusading journalists like Edwin Guthman and John Seigenthaler, street-smart investigators like Walter Sheridan, hard-nosed auditors like Carmine Bellino,
and quietly savvy Washington hands like Joe Dolan.

JFK's New Frontier* would become known for attracting what the
journalist David Halberstam called America's "best and brightest," but
within the Kennedy circle it was RFK's Justice Department that drew
envy for embodying Shakespeare's "band of brothers." Bobby's staff
took on his passions. They became his avenging angels. "It was really
kind of like a love affair—for myself and for everybody else in the Civil
Rights Division," said John Doar, who helped run the division. "Justice has emerged as the most yeasty of all the Departments in the
Administration—and by far the most important power base," the journalist and former JFK speechwriter Joseph Kraft pronounced in *Harper's
Magazine.* "The Department has been made available as a kind of emergency reservoir of talent and know-how, ready to serve the Administration wherever occasion requires. As one Justice Department aide put it:
'We are the riot squad for the New Frontier.' "

The image of a riot squad would have horrified buttoned-down cabinet secretaries such as Dean Rusk at State and Douglas Dillon at Treasury, but it suited Bobby at Justice. He was mounting nothing short of a
crusade, with dragons to slay, and he needed to be surrounded by knights
disposed to assail, not to accommodate. He didn't merely issue instructions to his aides; he led by example. He wandered the back corridors,
opening office doors, extending a hand, and announcing himself to career Justice lawyers, as if they didn't know, "I'm Bob Kennedy. What are
you working on?" He did the same in every city he visited, introducing
himself to assistant U.S. attorneys, street-level FBI agents, and prison
guards. He didn't make small talk. He couldn't. When he asked what
they were working on he actually wanted to know and waited for their
answers. Each division chief had to file detailed written dispatches each

---

* In accepting his party's nomination for president, JFK had promised to chart a "new frontier" that pushed scientific limits, attacked poverty, and promoted peace. The phrase resonated enough that it became the slogan for the Kennedy administration.

night. Every senior staffer had to come to lunch every Tuesday and Thursday, ready to report. He granted his assistants more latitude than they had ever had—and he offered his help and the White House's—but the job had to get done. He set the tone at his very first meeting: "Do your homework. Don't let there be anything in your department that you don't know. Know every damn thing!"

"The Kennedys didn't wait. . . . You learned as you went," said press aide Ed Guthman, who had won a Pulitzer Prize before coming to work for Bobby. "I learned the first week, the first couple of days I was there that nobody was going to invite me to do anything. . . . I could never go to Robert and say, 'Gee, I didn't know that.' It had to be my business." John Reilly, who was in charge of the U.S. attorneys, said Bobby's "entire philosophy" boiled down to these favorite phrases: "Don't tell me what you're going to do. Tell me what you've done, and until you've done it, it really doesn't mean anything." Another favorite, according to Katzen-bach: "Cut the shit, just do it."

Bobby had picked his staff with that kind of mental toughness in mind, and most who didn't have it didn't last. It was no accident that so many of his deputies had been to war—Ramsey Clark with the Marines, Katzenbach as a navigator and prisoner of war, Byron White as an intel-ligence officer and winner of two Bronze Stars. These were square-jawed warriors with an instinct for executing a mission and impatience with flabby bureaucracy. Few, however, had Bobby's stamina, as they learned in the winter of 1963. It had started with a joke, when one day the Ma-rine Corps Commandant showed the president an old order from Presi-dent Teddy Roosevelt saying that every Marine should be able to walk fifty miles in twenty hours. JFK wondered aloud whether contemporary Marines were up to the challenge, and it soon became a national craze, with civilians from Boston to Burbank trying to see how far and fast they could walk. Never to be outdone, Bobby invited four unlucky aides to join him before dawn on a Saturday morning when the mercury was hovering at twenty and their path was covered with ice and snow. Some had the sense to wear hiking shoes, but the attorney general had on penny loafers. By late afternoon three had dropped out as a helicopter swooped in for a closer look. "Maybe there's an emergency and I'll have to go back?" Bobby said hopefully to Guthman, his remaining companion. The copter turned out to be a photographer from *Life* magazine anxious to see the attorney general's progress. At mile thirty-five, Guthman's legs stiffened to the point where he had to stop. "You're lucky your brother isn't president of the United States," Bobby whispered as he pushed on. His final time—recorded in *Life* under the headline A LITTLE STIFF FOR A MAN OF 37 and a picture of him recuperating in stocking feet—was seventeen hours and fifteen minutes.

The new mood was conspicuous in Bobby's fifth-floor office. There actually were two walnut-paneled offices, with most of the previous attorneys general working out of the private back one and reserving the bigger, more baronial one up front for ceremonial purposes. Bobby did the opposite. The old setup was like "being on a desert island without girls," he complained. The new one let him keep open his door so any staffer could walk in. When he shouted, as he liked to do, a secretary or administrative assistant could hear him and run in. The back office was reserved now for lunches with staff or family and to display his endless photographs of Kennedys at play. Adding to the new sense of informality were his tie and hair that were always askew, and an open shirt collar with sleeves rolled up.* Sitting behind his desk, he looked less like the attorney general than a copyboy hamming it up while the boss was away. Comfortable sofas replaced old, stuffy furniture. Each richly paneled wall had a unique motif. Scotch-taped to the one nearest his desk were the children's watercolor sketches and a crayoned Mona Lisa. A stuffed sailfish caught off Acapulco hung over the hearth and a stuffed tiger guarded the stone fireplace that blazed all winter, sometimes providing the occasion to roast hot dogs and marshmallows. Formally framed photographs of his predecessors still hung there, along with the WPA-style allegorical murals, but they suddenly looked fusty. Bobby jettisoned his autographed picture of boxer Floyd Patterson when the heavyweight champ lost his title. Kennedys had never liked losers.†

---

* Jack joked that Bobby "still wears those button-down shirts. They went out five years ago. The only people I know who still wear them are Chester [Bowles] and Adlai [Stevenson]" (Sidey, *John F. Kennedy, President*).

† He never liked watching sports as much as playing them. That was consistent with his preference for doing rather than observing, no matter the activity, but ironic given how many famous athletes he counted as friends.

Ethel helped with the renovation. It was her idea to put picnic tables, awnings, chairs, and a snack bar in the courtyard of the Justice building, and to pipe in music at lunchtime. A gym went in on the roof. Groups of new lawyers who had never been on the fifth floor were ushered up to meet the boss. Randomly selected messengers, file clerks, and telephone operators, whom past attorneys general might or might not have acknowledged, got invitations to the annual judicial reception at the White House. For Evelyn Wright, an elevator operator he loved to gossip with, Bobby sent his chauffeur to make sure she and her husband arrived in style. Then he introduced them to the president. None of this surprised his new secretary, Jayne Lahey, who was on crutches and in a full leg cast after a terrible car accident. Bobby had her driven home the night of the presidential inaugural—but only long enough so she could change into her gown and be driven back to the galas. "He had a tremendous feeling for people in need," Lahey said. Bobby also invited secretaries and clerks to sit in when he was delivering testimony they had typed or copied. "Although I have served under ten Attorneys-General, no one before you has ever seen fit to reach this far down the ladder and include a person of my position in 'The Mainstream of History,'" Bessie M. Greene, who ran the mimeograph room, wrote in a thank-you note. "This is what sets you apart from other men. You have a heart and you use it."

He did have a heart. He also led a more princely life than ever, which some saw as fitting for America's new royal family. He was driven to work in his powder-blue convertible by Clyde Herndon, a government-supplied chauffeur who, when he wasn't driving Bobby, sometimes took the Kennedy kids for ice cream. When Bobby brought to work his beloved Brumus, the black Newfoundland who was the size of a pony and could drool at will, he let nature call in the courtyard and trusted that the guards would clean up after him. A wood-paneled elevator reserved for the attorney general and anyone he gave a key to whisked him to his office, where, if he felt moved, he could settle in to the private apartment with its sitting room, bath, shower, bedroom, and kitchen with its own chef. Other retainers ensured a supply of laundered dress shirts (often still with frayed collars), and to feel fresh he changed his three or four times a day and sometimes took another shower. His front office was almost big enough to be a football field and he relaxed by tossing one during meetings, which ensured that staff members learned to catch it. Darts were lobbed absentmindedly toward a board tacked to the wall.*

The offices were ideal for receptions, too, and one winter afternoon Bobby was hosting students from abroad. He and Ethel were on the way in the limousine when they passed the syndicated columnist Mary McGrory emerging from a Justice Department interview. "Are you coming to my party?" Bobby bellowed through a rolled-down window. She needed to get back to work, she explained, and kept walking down Tenth Street. Seconds later the attorney general was on the sidewalk, scooping the middle-aged McGrory off the ground and hoisting her over his shoulder. "You *are* coming to my party," he roared as he carried her back up the steps of his building. Were it anyone else she might have called it assault, but with Bobby it was fun, and the story quickly made the media rounds.

One person who didn't appreciate the informality—especially the darts that sometimes missed the board and the dogs that weren't supposed to be in government buildings—was J. Edgar Hoover. "He was like a child playing in a Dresden china shop. It was pure desecration," railed the FBI chief, who favored starch in his white shirts and a greasy tonic slicking back his hair, and lamented the day he'd encouraged Bobby to take the job. "Desecration of government property" and "the most deplorably undignified conduct . . . ever witnessed on the part of a cabinet member." Ethel made clear what she thought of Hoover and his quibbles. Knowing how much he despised Los Angeles police chief William Parker, she cornered Hoover at an office Christmas party and asked, "Don't you think Chief Parker is a wonderful man? Don't you think that if you ever retired, he'd be the man to replace you?" The beet-red G-man stammered, "Yes, Ethel."†

---

* It wasn't just the Justice Department that was his playroom. After his swearing-in as attorney general, Bobby took his children for a tour of the White House, where he led them in sliding down the long curving balustrade.

† The FBI chief was notorious for his likes and dislikes. The former included dark suits with a folded handkerchief in the breast pocket, shirts with French cuffs, and underlings who bought his book, *Masters of Deceit: The Story of Communism in American and How to Fight It.* The list of things he didn't like ran from sweaty palms and the smell of tobacco to both Kennedy brothers (Report on the FBI from Jack Levine to Herbert J. Miller, Jr., January 23, 1962, President's Office Files: Justice Department, JFKL, 34–36).

More so than his dartboard, the way he used his desk reflected how Bobby worked and thought. Made of mahogany, it weighed three hundred pounds and looked like a railroad boxcar without the wheels. The desktop was nearly big enough to play Ping-Pong on. Its original user was Amos T. Akerman, the second of five attorneys general appointed by President Ulysses S. Grant. Archivists excavated it from a government warehouse at Ethel's urging. Bobby kept the bottom drawer empty and open so he could prop one foot on it, with the other on the desk or under his other leg. At birthday parties and other special occasions he climbed atop it to give his remarks extra emphasis. Several phones sat on the desk—a red one installed upon Bobby's arrival that went directly to the White House, a standard line, and a third unit routed to the FBI director. That last phone became a bone of contention when the attorney general made clear he wanted Hoover himself, not his secretary, to answer it. Next to the phones were a pair of mementoes with special meaning: a dented helmet worn by a U.S. marshal during the race riots at the University of Mississippi, and a rifle taken from a dead Vietcong. Pointing to the helmet and rifle, Bobby would tell visitors, "These are two things we have to watch."

Skeptics inside and outside the government were watching him. They felt he got the attorney general's job merely because he was the First Brother, and they couldn't get past their earliest bad impressions. "I just don't like that boy, and I never will," former president Harry Truman confided to his biographer after taking Attorney General Kennedy on a tour of his library in Independence, Missouri. "He worked for old Joe McCarthy, you know, and when old Joe was tearing up the Constitution and the country, that boy couldn't say enough for him."* Now the doubters had a record to check, and a surprising number grudgingly conceded that seldom, in memory or in history, had there been an attorney general better at rallying not just his troops but the nation. Staff morale had soared. By ignoring its rules he had managed to harness the federal bureaucracy in a way few cabinet secretaries could. Americans who barely knew there was a Department of Justice now heard and cared about its

---

* Truman had earlier explained that his doubts about JFK didn't have to do with his religion but his genes: "It's not the pope I'm afraid of, it's the pop!"

battles to uproot organized crime, turn around juvenile delinquents, and unmask corrupt politicians. Half a century later, nearly all of his surviving band of brothers say working for Bobby was the high point of their professional lives, even when those lives later included becoming attorney general themselves. "He may be the best," says Katzenbach, Bobby's successor. "He was absolutely unwilling to believe you could not solve problems of employment, poverty, that you could not solve problems of education. . . . The fact that he might not succeed never deterred him. He didn't not do something because he might not succeed." Even the irascible Truman seemed to be coming around: "They say young Bobby has changed for the better . . . and maybe he has."

There were overreaches, as with the Hoffa and Cohn cases. But over the years Bobby's mythos would grow to the point where he became a model for successors to his right and left. John Ashcroft, President George W. Bush's arch-conservative attorney general, renamed his headquarters the Robert F. Kennedy Department of Justice Building and praised Bobby for the way he'd "arrest mobsters for spitting on the sidewalk." Eric Holder, President Barack Obama's ultra-liberal attorney general, cited Bobby as his inspiration for believing the department "can and must always be a force for that which is right." Kennedy's most glaring Achilles' heel going into the job was a reputation for trampling on civil liberties when he was a congressional investigator, and the American Civil Liberties Union continued to oppose him on issues such as his reach for more wiretapping authority. But Francis Biddle, a venerated liberal and civil libertarian who had served as FDR's attorney general for four years, saw more hopeful signs than disquieting ones in the young attorney general, even on eavesdropping. "I should have been happy, looking back," Biddle wrote Bobby in January 1962, "to think that I had done as much for civil liberties when I was Attorney General as you have done in your first year."

BOBBY HAD LESS time for life outside work during these years, with the strains of being a cabinet secretary and perpetual travel, overseas and cross-country, and he regretted the hours away from his family. The first creases appeared on his forehead, and his mop of straw-brown hair showed flecks of gray. But for Bobby, each new child added to the fun of being a parent—a good thing, since by the time he left office he would have eight, with a ninth due shortly. He did well enough with them as infants but, like many dads, he related to them best when they got old enough to play games that he understood. Ethel loved them as little babies and loved having babies with Bobby, although she teased him with this postscript to her before-supper prayer: "And please, dear God, make Bobby buy me a bigger dining-room table."

She got not just a table but a whole new wing with four bedrooms and a formal drawing room, along with a barn furnished with paddocks for the horses and a bathhouse that doubled as a movie theater. Hickory Hill was becoming a virtual country club and amusement park, much like Hyannis Port, letting the Kennedys have fun without having to expose themselves to the public. It was a casual brand of beautiful, built with children in mind, down to the pint-sized toilets and sinks. There was a big swimming pool for adults and bigger kids, a small one for the toddlers, and for everybody a Coke machine that dispensed free soft drinks and a jukebox that generally blared at full volume. The pool house had a kitchen as well as separate changing rooms for men and women, each the size of a gymnasium locker room. Ethel smashed tennis serves at anyone who was game. Five swings and a rope ladder let Bobby test how high he could push Kathleen, Joe, and Bobby Jr. as they yelled, "Higher, go higher!" When it rained, the games continued in the wood-paneled playroom, which had dolls along one wall and at the other end a huge terrarium. Sam Adams, a friend from Milton Academy and Harvard, remembers the scene a day after Bobby's swearing-in at the Justice Department: "Sinatra kept calling to find out what was going on, and getting the cold shoulder. Kim Novak was here being very attractive. We played touch football in four inches of snow and did some tobogganing. Bobby asked who wants to go horseback riding, and Novak and I volunteered. We weren't a block away when Dave Hackett called, 'Hey Bobby, your brother is here.' The president got on a toboggan and ended up in the bushes, with his bad back, but he survived it."

The compound was never empty. Pop star Andy Williams might be there with quarterback Don Meredith. The satirist Art Buchwald stopped by regularly, John Lennon less often. Ethel called celebrity guests "sparklies" and funny ones "jollies." Bobby collected people, and ones who never would have fit in elsewhere did at his estate in McLean. Staff from Justice came, too, but only when invited and often mixing a swim in a borrowed bathing suit with talk about the latest Hoffa probe. CBS's Roger Mudd, one of Bobby's favorite journalists, remembers his first visit, in 1963: "Ethel was at the door, making sure we met those of her children who were old enough to be up. When she introduced me to Bobby Jr., then nine years old, he exclaimed: 'Roger Maris!' 'No, no,' I said. 'Roger Mudd.' 'Oh,' he said." Mudd recalls, too, weighing how to address the attorney general. "'Mr. Attorney General' or 'Attorney General Kennedy' was cumbersome; 'General' was correct but sounded inaccurate and misleading. So, before I started our first interview, I asked the attorney general what I should call him. He said, 'How about Bobbsie?'"

Names had always been serious business for the Kennedys. The president was still Johnny or Jack to Bobby and his siblings, but only in family settings. In public, Bobby used the more respectful "Mr. President" and pressed the others to follow. Journalists started calling JFK by his initials as soon as he was elected president, which was an unusual sign of intimacy. Not long after, they took the unprecedented step of substituting RFK for Bobby. Reporters balked, however, when the attorney general's publicity people tried to get them to use Bob instead of the more breezy Bobby. Ted called him Robbie; Bobby returned the gesture with Eddie. To Ethel, he always was and remains Bobby. Staffers who were friends, like Seigenthaler, or of nearly comparable rank, like Katzenbach, used Bob. Lower-level government workers turned to the titles that Mudd found ponderous, mainly Mr. Attorney General. Jimmy Hoffa called him Bob at first, when there was a chance of cordiality, then Bobby, uttered with dripping sarcasm. Lyndon Johnson did the same. Bobby called Hoover by his middle name, Edgar, which Hoover, who was thirty years older, found inappropriately familiar. Each new media profile offered another sobriquet for this unfolding man of myriad parts—from Saint Francis to No. 2 Man, Deputy President, Pied Piper, Hero of Irish Folk Tales, Villain of a Shakespearean Drama, Crown Prince, Tiberius Gracchus, Savonarola in Short Pants, Little Brother, and, with a nod to Fidel Castro's younger brother and trusted minister, Raul.

Their children's names commemorated people who had singular meaning for Bobby and Ethel at milestone moments. The oldest, Kathleen Hartington and Joseph Patrick, were in memory of his older siblings who were killed in airplane accidents. Robert Jr. was Bobby's namesake. David Anthony, the most fragile and most like his father, honored Saint Anthony along with Bobby's oldest pal Dave Hackett and David Ormsby-Gore, a family friend and British diplomat. Mary Courtney was for the Holy Mother and a college friend of the baby's mother. Michael LeMoyne took his unusual middle name from LeMoyne Billings, Jack's buddy who became everyone's, and his first name from Saint Michael the archangel. The Mary in Mary Kerry was for Jesus' mother, the Kerry for the county in Ireland. Christopher George was named for the martyred Saint Christopher and for Ethel's favorite brother. Matthew Maxwell Taylor was for Saint Matthew, author of the first Gospel, and General Maxwell Taylor, a friend and hero of Bobby's. Douglas Harriman was for Treasury Secretary Douglas Dillon and New York governor W. Averell Harriman. Rory Elizabeth Katherine, born after Bobby died, took her two middle names from two of Ethel's close friends, while her first name is an Irish version of Robert. While Bobby joked about forgetting where all those names came from, Ethel remembered the derivations into her late eighties.

The children were always welcome at the many Hickory Hill cookouts their parents hosted, and they got served first. Bobby manned the grill, where he smothered his steaks with mustard. The Kennedy diet, indoors or out, for guests or family, was as no-nonsense and all-American as it had been when Bobby was growing up: chops and roasts; chicken broiled, fried, or roasted; baked potatoes; salad; and, on Fridays, chowder thick with clams, the way they made it on Cape Cod. Bacon and poached eggs were breakfast staples, and what Bobby ordered even at fancy French eateries. If he was drinking beer it was Heineken. On rarer occasions, he'd indulge in a daiquiri or an old-fashioned. His drink of choice was milk, ideally out of a bottle that had been chilled in the freezer for precisely fifteen minutes.

Politics infused the life of this Kennedy household even more than it had Bobby's childhood homes. The attorney general brought back to his kids yarns about Jimmy Hoffa and J. Edgar Hoover. Colleagues and journalists were frequent visitors, for briefings and fun. Most dads "go to work, they come home. Home is home, work is work," recalls daughter Kerry. "But he had a very holistic approach. . . . There were always civil rights activists and Justice Department people at our house, playing football with us, swimming in the pool, coming over for breakfast, lunch, and dinner." To preserve the amiable atmosphere, Bobby fine-tuned an artful maneuver in the water: Whenever a reporter or other guest raised an awkward question, their host would glide underwater, reappearing at the pool's far end, recovering his wind, and deftly changing the subject.

The after-dark pool parties in particular became legendary. The Kennedy children would climb out of bed in their nightclothes and peek over the hedges at guests arriving in black ties and the little black dresses that Audrey Hepburn made famous in *Breakfast at Tiffany's*. One or two tables might be set on a board stretching the length of the pool, daring diners to stay dry. That was a special challenge one night when the guests included John Glenn, recently back from his orbit around the earth; Byron White, named two months before to the Supreme Court; and Harry Belafonte, who had performed at JFK's inaugural gala. Dancers dipped and swayed to the syncopated rhythms of Lester Lanin and his band. "Suddenly Ethel's chair, with Ethel on it, slipped quietly into the pool," recorded Arthur Schlesinger, the informal White House historian who was seated next to Ethel on the plank. "I helped her out from the side; and, while I was still contemplating this, was suddenly (I believed) nudged into the pool myself, carrying Ethel back with me." Bobby was not the culprit this time, testified Schlesinger, who "found that Bobby's clothes fitted me perfectly and stayed till five." Astronaut Glenn was creating his own whimsy on the other side of the pool, scribbling on a paper napkin a message—"Help! I'm a prisoner at the Kennedys'!"—then tying it to a balloon that the wind carried into the night.

Hickory Hill had become the social nerve center of the New Frontier and deliciously fertile ground for Washington gossip columnists. "When Bobby Kennedy sends out invitations to a formal party, they read 'black tie and snorkel,' " joked Senator Barry Goldwater, who knew Bobby from the McClellan Committee and was gearing up to challenge Jack in 1964. It was great sport—and a growing embarrassment to the president, who was sensitive to his own image as rich and spoiled and to his slumping

poll numbers.* He did not relish seeing headlines like POOLSMANSHIP AT
HICKORY HILL splashed across front pages from New York to Rome. This
wasn't how Jack himself socialized. He seldom attended Bobby's parties,
and he rarely invited Bobby and Ethel to the more demure gatherings
Jackie hosted at the White House or on the Cape. "Kid," Ethel explained
to a friend who was on her way to the president's place, "we don't come
over unless we're invited over." Schlesinger, a guest at both brothers' soi-
rees, described the president's as "chic, decorous, urbane," while Bobby's
were "raffish, confused, loud." That was incongruous because Bobby
had always been the reticent brother. At Jack's insistence, he started ton-
ing down his gatherings and seeing that his guests stayed dry.

But it was more than pool parties that drew visitors to Hickory Hill in
the early 1960s. Bobby knew he lacked the intellectual gravitas not just
of his brother Jack, but of the administration's bigger thinkers such as
John Kenneth Galbraith, the Bundy brothers McGeorge and William,
and Bobby's own Harvard- and Yale-trained deputies. During a ski trip to
Colorado he and Ethel had attended seminars at the Aspen Institute,
where contemporary leaders learned from older, more established sages
including Mortimer Adler. Joe had pushed his boys to do precisely that
through their dinner-table dialogue and world travels. Why not bring
the same spirit of probing and self-education, Bobby wondered, to Hickory Hill and the Kennedy crowd? Nobody had better contacts. No one
was more anxious to move beyond the immediate concerns of the office
in-box and explore philosophy, antiquity, and literature. He realized he
had neither listened nor learned enough in prep school or at Harvard,
and he was grateful for this chance at reeducation.

They dubbed the monthly seminars Hickory Hill University. The faculty consisted of Schlesinger, a Pulitzer Prize–winning historian from
Harvard, and Walt W. Rostow, a former MIT economist now working at
the State Department. Speakers ranged from the cartoonist Al Capp to
the philosopher Sir Isaiah Berlin and the ecologist Rachel Carson. Topics
could be anything from whether there was a God to why poverty was so

---

* The president's popularity was sinking in the summer of 1962 in large part due to the
plummeting stock market, dubbed the "Kennedy Slide," and to lingering resentment over
the steel crisis the previous April.

persistent. The salons generally were accompanied by dinner and drinks, and they were held at other homes in addition to Hickory Hill. Participants included such top administration guns as Treasury Secretary Dillon, Defense Department chief McNamara, and Edward R. Murrow, the former CBS newsman whom Bobby had forgiven for helping topple Joe McCarthy and who now ran the government's overseas propaganda agency. At one prophetic seminar in the White House living room, President Kennedy asked the Princeton historian David Donald whether President Lincoln's place in history would have been assured if he hadn't been assassinated. While the attorney general typically "confined his role to interrogation," Galbraith recalled, "you had the feeling that if you were shabby on any important point you could pretty well count on Bobby to come in and press you on it." The writer and socialite Alice Roosevelt Longworth, Theodore Roosevelt's oldest child, said the seminars "sound rather precious, but there was nothing precious about those lectures. It was all sorts of fun, that was all." Not everyone was a fan. Marian Schlesinger, Arthur's wife then, called them "an intellectual quick fix. . . . No doubt a harmless exercise, but so Kennedyish, the whole of Western Thought in eight hour-long seminars."

It was a miracle that Bobby found time for any intellectual exercise at all, given his burdens as attorney general and father of eight children, all preteen or younger. But he managed to fit into his schedule one last thing: voice lessons. He was a relentless self-improver and this may have been a way to get better at giving the speeches he delivered across the country. Or maybe it was with an eye on the White House or some other elective office. With Bobby it was always more than one thing. He knew that he and Jack spoke with a similar Boston accent, but that while people found Jack's softly reassuring, his came across as nasal and jarring. So for a few weeks in 1963 he took lessons from a respected New York speech therapist. But, said press aide Ed Guthman, "he became increasingly bored doing the repetitive exercises she required and stopped when he got the woman's first bill and thought it was outrageously high."

He was funny about money. He probably had more of it than any of his siblings, given Ethel's wealthy family, but he also spent more, given all his kids and the cost of sustaining Hickory Hill. His $25,000 salary as attorney general went to charity. He was a soft touch for staffers in a squeeze, and for strangers like Sergeant York whose stories touched him. Yet his staff and friends got used to the fact that while he never carried cash, he expected them to, and to spring for meals, tips, shoeshines, and other expenses that seemed negligible to a man of means. "We'd stop by a newsstand, and he'd hit me for a quarter for this or that; or if he wanted *Life* or *Time*, or a candy bar at Schrafft's. He tried to *charge* a sandwich at Schrafft's once," said the journalist Peter Maas. The funniest incident, Maas added, occurred when they were at a service together at an Army chapel: "The collection plate started coming up the aisle towards us, and I could see him starting to look around. I knew what was going to happen. The basket got closer and closer, and finally it was just one pew away, and he nudged me, and I reached in my pocket and pulled out a dollar and gave it to him. He looked at it, and he turned around to me and nudged me again and whispered, 'Don't you think I should give more?'"

Joe had left Bobby a fortune that by then exceeded ten million dollars, and he praised his son by calling him "the stingy one in this family." He also relished needling Bobby about that. It was "Joe's favorite joke about the family," the journalist and Kennedy friend Arthur Krock recalled. "Bobby was penurious, which [Joe] 'corrected' at Metropolitan Club luncheons with me in Washington by ordering the most expensive dishes either of us could find on the menu and signing Bobby's name to the check."

Having grown up comfortable but not rich, Joe understood the average American's scramble to get by. That was something his children had to learn. One day press aide Jack Rosenthal was driving to Hickory Hill with Bobby to work on the attorney general's testimony. "His driver drove us. It was like four o'clock on a summer afternoon. . . . We were stalled in traffic and inched along, and he was getting visibly agitated. And he finally says with real impatience, not directly to me, just sort of to the world, 'What do you suppose all these people do when they get home so early?' And I knew at the moment I shouldn't say and didn't say, 'Well, they go pick up their dry cleaning and they get their kids from school; they do all the things that you've got people to do for you.' But the point was, he wanted to be doing something productive and useful and was furious at having to waste time."

Joe had spent much of his life plotting to get a Kennedy into the White House, but once that happened, the proud patriarch generally refrained from joining in the seminars, parties, and rest of the Kennedy scene in Washington. He had accepted a front row seat in the viewing stand at Jack's inauguration, tipping his top hat and receiving a tip back, the only person Jack so honored. But he didn't stop at the White House before leaving Washington, and he visited just once that whole first year. He had already taught his boys all he knew about how to attain power and what to do with it. While he relished Jack's calls and advised him when asked, he wondered whether his counsel was welcomed and held himself in check. "Jack doesn't belong any more to just a family," conceded Joe, whose family had been his purpose. "The family can be there. But there is not much they can do sometimes for the president of the United States." As elated as he was at seeing his dreams realized, Joe was depleted. "I have had it," he confided to a *Life* magazine editor in explaining why he wouldn't grant an interview in December 1961, a few months after he turned seventy-three. "The future reputation of the Kennedys will be made by the President, the Attorney General, and I am very hopeful, by Ted."

Eight days later, Joseph Patrick Kennedy suffered a massive stroke, after a round of golf in Palm Beach, on day 322 of the presidency he had helped orchestrate. By the time Jack and Bobby got to his bedside the news was dismal. "The doctors came to the family and said, 'Look, this strong, virile man is going to be imprisoned in a body that won't work even if he recovers,'" recounted Lem Billings. "It was an opportunity to pull the plug. But Bobby said no, let him fight for his life." His doctors were right in their prognosis. Joe lost the use of the right side of his body and would spend the remainder of his life in a wheelchair, unable to speak, write, or otherwise make his thoughts clearly known. Yet those around him believed he was taking in all that he heard, saw, and read. There was one word he could manage, although he used it to affirm as well as deny: "No."

All his children were shaken, but none as deeply as Bobby. Joe had continued to dispense career advice to his third son, telling him only the previous Thanksgiving that "he should move to Maryland and become governor—then president [in] 1968." The boy he had taken longest to come to know now understood Joe better than any of his offspring. The more his father retreated to the background, the more Bobby accepted that he had been tapped to take over the roles of patriarch and protector. It wasn't just because Jack was too busy being president. Family never had meant to him what it did to Joe and Bobby. And Bobby would need to take care of much more than practical matters like executing the family trusts. Joe counted on him to watch out for Jack and Ted, mend whatever needed fixing, and keep the clan as one. The stroke formalized the transition.

As busy as he was, the attorney general managed to visit Joe nearly every weekend on Cape Cod or in Florida. "Bobby would fly down to Palm Beach at 6 A.M. and be back at noon, just to say hello for fifteen minutes," recalled Tish Baldrige, the First Lady's social secretary. He searched in vain for possible cures for the paralysis. He supervised Joe's caretakers and swam alongside when his father was getting therapy in the pool, yelling, "Attaboy, Dad. Keep it up and you'll be walking out of here in no time." He told his father, as he always had, about developments that mattered in the family and the world. Only now it was a monologue, with no biting responses or certainty his father was even hearing. It was Bobby's way not just of being there, but of saying goodbye. Once, when Joe staggered as he tried to get out of his wheelchair alone, "Bobby grabbed his father," recalled Rita Dallas, Joe's nurse. "Mr. Kennedy tried to struggle loose and began swatting at him with his cane. We were horrified! The Secret Service men sprung to attention and moved in. The President wisely refrained from getting involved. . . . [Bobby] gambled a blow to the face and kissed his father. 'That's what I'm here for, Dad.' He smiled. 'Just to give you a hand when you need it. You've done that for me all my life, so why can't I do the same for you now?' "

Joe's incapacitation was a loss and a gain for Bobby. He desperately missed turning to his father for bucking up and for razor-sharp advice. "His interest in life has been his children—not his business, not his accomplishments, not his friends, but his children," Bobby wrote about Joe. "Any lasting contributions we might have made have been in a large part due to the effect he had on our lives." But his father's sidelining made Bobby independent and self-confident in ways he never had been, freeing him not just from Joe's firm grip but from the limits of seeing himself, and being seen, merely as Joe Kennedy's son. The axiom that no man is ever fully grown while his father is in the picture rang truer for Bobby than for most.

———————

BOBBY HAD ACTED as his brother's keeper throughout his campaigns, and he took that role even more seriously now that Jack was in the White House. Often, that entailed helping make the right picks for key posts such as secretary of state. The president wanted Senator J. William Fulbright of Arkansas, an enlightened internationalist, but Bobby knew that having a staunch segregationist represent the United States would be grist for the Soviet propaganda mill. "I really stopped Fulbright," he claimed. Others wanted Adlai Stevenson, but JFK had "never liked him," Bobby said, and neither had he. (Stevenson's son and namesake says his father had, in effect, been offered the job, and having it pulled back "finally killed him.") The ultimate choice, Dean Rusk, turned out to be Bobby's least favorite cabinet member, and he used his 1964 oral history with the Kennedy Library to take a last swipe. JFK "was his own secretary of state," Bobby said, and after the '64 election the two Kennedys had been planning on "moving Rusk out, perhaps to the United Nations, and appointing Bob McNamara secretary of state."

The attorney general continued vetting appointments throughout the administration, everywhere from the cabinet to the Supreme Court. He troubleshot for JFK around the globe, from Brazil and Japan to the Ivory Coast. He also jumped in on issues as diverse as the Berlin Wall, the space program, tax reform, a nuclear test ban treaty, and whether to build a dam in Ghana. Bobby said no to this last project, pointing out that the Ghanaian president was "playing 'footsies' with the Soviet Union" and that the proposed aid had "no strings attached." JFK said he could "feel the cold wind of [RFK's] disapproval on the back of my neck," but he approved the loan anyway. It was one of the few times the brothers publicly and strongly disagreed, but even then Jack appreciated that Bobby had in mind the country's best interests and his. He gave his brother the broadest portfolio any president had given not just his attorney general, but any cabinet officer.

That brief included politics, despite Bobby's vow that it shouldn't.

Politics was an inherent part of governing: A president and his cabinet had to rally support from Congress and the public. Politics also informed the dual nature of the office of attorney general: on the one hand, the guardian of the sacred rule of law, as embodied in the blind lady of justice; at the same time, a counselor to the president, setting legal and, inevitably, political guidelines. Bobby steered well clear of shameless politics, as he demonstrated by indicting friends and insulating himself behind incorruptible aides. But he also fused, more effectively than most, the dual traditions of high purpose and string pulling.

With more than four hundred thousand jobs to dispense, the U.S. postmaster general historically had the most political position in Washington. Not so under the Kennedys. "The chief political manager of the Kennedy Administration was also very much in charge of the political aspects of the Post Office Department. That man was not Democratic National Chairman John Bailey, who was largely a figurehead. The man in charge of both was Bobby Kennedy, the Attorney General," J. Edward Day, Kennedy's postmaster general, reported in his memoir. "One afternoon I talked to him three times by telephone about a single rural letter carrier who was to be appointed in a small town in Mississippi."

Partisan politics came into play when the Kennedys responded to what they felt were unfair attacks on their policies and patriotism from the John Birch Society and other right-wing organizations. Bobby led the counterattack. First his liberal allies formulated a twenty-four-page secret plan for choking off those organizations' appeal and money. In late 1961, he drafted the IRS, already an ally in the war against the Mob, to conduct broad-based audits of "alleged extremist groups" to determine which ones were so political that they violated their tax-exempt status. There were two problems with the initiative, which became known as the Ideological Organizations Project. It employed the same inverted logic as the attack on organized crime: Target the supposed lawbreakers, then look for a tax law they might have broken. That might have worked if the agency had cracked down equally on the left as well as the right. But nineteen of the twenty-four groups it focused on in its final phase were "right-wing," as were fourteen of fifteen whose very existence it threatened by recommending revoking their tax-exempt status. Luckily for the Kennedys, Richard Nixon's later bid to politicize the IRS—

including compiling an "enemies list"—was egregious enough that when Congress got around to investigating, it focused mostly on Republican abuses and less on Bobby's. Luckily for Bobby's enemies, only four groups—three conservative and one liberal—actually received letters of revocation.

Bobby didn't always get his way. His investigators had learned that Sherman Adams, President Eisenhower's chief of staff, had accepted from a Boston textile maker close to half a million dollars in cash in addition to the famous vicuña coat and oriental rug that had compelled Adams to resign in 1958. By the summer of 1963 the Justice Department had enough evidence, in the form of canceled checks, to indict Adams and embarrass the Republicans. "Eisenhower, in retirement, got wind of this," said Bobby Baker, the keeper of Capitol Hill secrets whom Bobby called Little Lyndon. Using Senate Minority Leader Everett Dirksen as an intermediary, Ike offered JFK a deal: Block the Adams indictment, due to be announced the next day, and Eisenhower would owe Kennedy an equally huge favor. Jack called Bobby and ordered him to put the indictment "in the deep freeze," Baker recounted. Bobby balked at playing politics with his judicial process, at which point the president pulled rank: "I'm president. If you can't comply with my request then your resignation will be accepted." Baker's story, which he says came from Dirksen, is corroborated by Herbert Stern, a former federal judge in New Jersey who heard a nearly identical version from Edward Bennett Williams, the attorney for the Boston textile manufacturer who made the payoffs to Adams and tipped off Bobby. "I nearly fell off my chair," Stern recalls. Not long after he made the deal, JFK cashed in his chit not just with Eisenhower but with Dirksen as well. Kennedy's nuclear test ban treaty looked as though it might die in the Senate until the minority leader and ex-president endorsed it.

Nothing was as important to the Kennedys politically as their own electability, and nobody in the family was better at delivering that than Bobby. Jack's Senate seat in Massachusetts became vacant after he took over as president, and Joe insisted it go to Ted. Ted didn't know whether he wanted it, and Jack and Bobby fretted over how it would look with another Kennedy coming to Washington. They had a little time to think it over, because Ted wasn't old enough to be named as Jack's replacement and there would be a new election to fill the seat nine months after he had turned the required age of thirty. In the meantime, the Democratic governor agreed to name the Kennedy family friend Ben Smith as interim senator, and Joe persuaded his older sons it was Ted's turn. Bobby then headed to Massachusetts to help Ted prepare for his maiden debate against a strong primary opponent, Attorney General Eddie McCormack. Bobby trumpeted his arrival with the words "Have no feah, we are heah." His advice was a classic blend of directness and sassiness. If Ted was asked why he wanted to be senator, "Tell them why you don't want to be sitting on your ass in some office in New York." When Teddy had the opportunity to pose a question to his opponent, Bobby advised, "Ask Eddie McCormack what he thinks of the situation in West Irian," a province in Indonesia that Bobby had recently visited. "He'll think it's West Iran and he'll talk about the Middle East and he'll look like a fool."* Ted won the primary by a two-to-one margin and the general election by 10 percentage points.

JFK's planned run for reelection in 1964 represented a more consequential political face-off. At times Bobby adamantly refused to get involved. He would stay on as attorney general and his brother-in-law Steve Smith could run the campaign. Newly released material from the Kennedy Library, however, shows that by the spring of 1963, Bobby had instructed key administration officials to begin assembling material on JFK's accomplishments that could feed into the 1964 election drive. Everything Bobby had done from the time he took office—from deciding how his civil rights programs would affect the votes of Southern whites and blacks nationwide to calibrating the president's moves in hot spots like Cuba—made it clear that he had never taken his eye off the next election. In his official version, presented in his oral history after JFK's death, Bobby said he started talking with his brother in the fall of 1963 about "what basis I could get out as attorney general," because the controversy inherent in that office would be "such a burden to carry in the 1964 election." Jack, he added, said that was "impossible to do because then, also,

---

* Bobby would later offer Ted more sage advice, this time on what to do when you were a guest on the Sunday morning TV news shows: "You decide what you want to say and go in there and say it no matter what the questions are" (Littlefield and Nexon, *Lion of the Senate*, 270–71).

it would make it look as if we were running away from it. . . . The only basis which I could sort of get out was that he wanted me to manage the campaign or something, so that I'd get out at that time."

That kind of loyalty—offering to sacrifice his position for the sake of his brother's presidency—was visible every day to White House and Justice insiders. Outsiders got their look one hot summer day when family and friends were sailing side by side on Joe's boat, the *Marlin*, and the *Honey Fitz*, the presidential yacht that Jack had renamed for his maternal grandfather. Charlie, the president's dog, tried to jump from one to the other and ended up in the deep water. "Without any hesitation, Bobby jumped overboard and swam as hard as he could to the dog," said Rita Dallas. "Bobby couldn't possibly reach him in time—but he kept right on swimming, apparently oblivious to the fact that he also was heading straight into the propellers. . . . The dog was within inches of his death, fighting now to keep himself from being drawn under. He and Bobby went down at the same time. Someone yelled, 'Stop the engines! For God's sake! Stop the engines,' and for what seemed like an eternity we held our breaths. Finally, Bobby surfaced with the dog in his arms. He treaded water, showing Charlie first to the President, then to us! A wild cheer went up! The children screamed and yelled! The adults clapped and whistled! Some of us wept."

Jack himself could never have performed that muscular feat, for reasons that Bobby understood but that he had ensured few others did. He was practiced by then at covering up his brother's physical frailties. During the 1952 Senate race, he had hidden Jack's crutches in the car during campaign appearances and used a sunlamp to give color to his pallid skin. In 1960, he had made light of the adrenal insufficiency. Now Bobby was suspicious of the injections the president was getting from Dr. Max Jacobson, known to his celebrity clients as "Dr. Feelgood." He finally persuaded Jack to send the medications to the Food and Drug Administration for testing. When the agency confirmed the presence of amphetamines and steroids, Jack told his brother, "I don't care if it's horse piss. It works."

The truest sign of Bobby's confederacy with his brother was his willingness to camouflage and sometimes enable the president's sexual deceptions. Joe had been Jack's bulwark early on, prying the then bachelor away from, among others, Inga Arvad, a married Danish journalist and suspected Nazi spy. Bobby stepped in during the 1960 campaign, helping squash old gossip that Jack had been married before he met Jackie—and still was—to the socialite Durie Malcolm. False rumors like that made it easier to get outraged about others that hit the mark. JFK's White House mistresses ranged from Judith Campbell Exner, who would become involved as well with the gangster Mooney Giancana, to Mimi Alford, a nineteen-year-old intern. He is said to have also slept with strippers and socialites, stewardesses and secretaries, before and throughout his marriage and presidency. Bobby's most dramatic brotherly intervention involved Ellen Rometsch, a twenty-seven-year-old German who looked like Elizabeth Taylor and was married to a West German Air Force sergeant stationed at his embassy in Washington. The FBI was convinced she was a high-priced call girl, spy for the East Germans, and mistress to the president of the United States, and the bureau shared its suspicions with Bobby. He couldn't take the chance, and he had her quietly deported to Germany in the summer of 1963, with his old Rackets Committee aide LaVern Duffy riding along. Bobby Baker, who says he had arranged the original liaison between President Kennedy and Rometsch, labeled what Bobby did kidnapping. "Had she been called before the Senate investigating committee," Baker says, "her testimony would have wrecked President Kennedy." RFK branded as "untrue" stories that his brother was involved with Rometsch, but he conceded that if all the rumors were aired about call girls and their relationships with a spectrum of senior elected officials, "it would be very unpleasant."

Historians generally focus on the toll JFK's adultery took on his credibility and his marriage, but they exacted at least as onerous a toll on his brother. Bobby came to see whitewashing for Jack as part of his job as family protector in chief, which meant dirtying himself and, worse for a truth-seeking prosecutor, becoming a practiced equivocator. He convinced himself Jack's sex life was no more of the public's business than the state of his adrenal glands or who said what in the calls to free Martin Luther King. Whether and to what extent his friend Jackie was aware of her husband's betrayal is unclear, but J. Edgar Hoover knew, perhaps even more than Bobby. It became one more area of sparring between the

FBI director and his nominal boss, and it gave Hoover the moral and practical upper hand. If Bobby was unwilling to be Jack's sexual policeman, Hoover would be.

Jack's infidelities were little surprise to anyone familiar with his family history. His father had had a longtime mistress, the silent film star Gloria Swanson, and scores of short-term dalliances. Grandfather Honey Fitz was an impenitent flirt, which helped explain why Rose seemed so unruffled when Joe compartmentalized his life into the time spent with his devoted household and the nearly equal time away with girlfriends. Joe passed down to his children his canons on the sanctity of friendships and family and the evils of cigarettes and whiskey. When it came to sexual mores, his message boiled down to this aphorism: Boys play while girls pray.

It was not just Jack who absorbed those lessons. Ted's first marriage wouldn't survive his playboy lifestyle. Joe Jr., too, had gotten around, although since he was never married, his fidelity gene was never put to the test. But Bobby was different. As an eighteen-year-old, he wrote a former schoolmate lamenting that he lacked his brothers' ways with women. Bobby wedded at a younger age than all but one of his siblings (Kathleen, who was nearly six years older, beat him by two months) and reveled in an unusually stable and robust marriage for a Kennedy. Few doubted that Bobby was the most puritanical and sanctimonious of Joe's boys, but he was also most like his father in so many other ways. Did he take after the old man when it came to marital infidelity? And if so, was he hushing that up the way he did Jack's indiscretions?

Scores of books have proposed answers to those questions, and a cottage industry has sprung up around those who claim to know. The list of Bobby's alleged mistresses starts with the film stars Lee Remick, Kim Novak, and Candice Bergen, ends with the singer Claudine Longet, and includes other names familiar and unknown. No family in American history has been subject to more gossip, hearsay, and embellishment about their private affairs than the Kennedys. Prurient interest aside, they opened themselves to it by asking for the public's trust and votes. JFK's illicit sex and cover-ups confirmed our distrust. The question is fairly asked about Bobby, too, precisely because he publicly prized conjugal faithfulness and chided those who didn't practice it. Many reporters at the time suspected hypocrisy, but journalists operated under different standards then, and they or their bosses declined to publish what they heard or saw.

"He definitely had an eye for pretty women, like every Kennedy man. Like the father. He was a flirt," says Gwen Gibson, a reporter then in the Washington bureau of the *New York Daily News* who wrote about the Kennedys, including a feature on Bobby and Ethel. John Anderson, a California attorney who would help on Bobby's presidential bid, recalls seeing him "smooching" and "nuzzling" with Candice Bergen in the first-class cabin on a campaign plane. Richard Goodwin, Bobby's friend and aide who traveled with him overseas and in America, says there is no question that Bobby had extramarital affairs: "Of course he did. That's a Kennedy family tradition. . . . He wasn't sort of randomly random like his brother [Jack] or Teddy, for that matter. Not at all. He was much more selective and limited. . . . Everyone was doing it, including the press. That's why they never reported it."*

No one knows for sure what happened when the doors were closed. The FBI tried to find out, but its reports on Bobby mainly repeated wild rumors, including those caught on wiretaps and bugs of Mob figures that Bobby easily refuted. What is beyond dispute is that, before his marriage but during his courtship of Ethel, Bobby was seeing a young British actress named Joan Winmill whom he got to know in 1948 while traveling after his Harvard graduation. Joan met Ethel later but didn't know about her budding romance with Bobby. Ethel didn't know he was sending intimate letters to Joan back in London, along with perfume, Whitman's Sampler chocolates, and his sister's hand-me-down green velvet dress. While Joan and Bobby were not officially engaged—she was dating other men and presumed he was seeing other women—"for the first time in my life, I considered myself to be 'in love,'" Joan said. She "couldn't believe [her] eyes" when she got a letter from Bobby, post-

* Author Diane White-Crane worked on Bobby's campaigns and in his office and was a friend of Mary Jo Kopechne, who would drown at Chappaquiddick Island when Ted Kennedy drove his car off a bridge. "The difference between Robert Kennedy and Ted Kennedy is not that he wouldn't have taken Mary Jo out," says White-Crane. "The difference is Robert Kennedy would have drowned trying to get her out of there. . . . And he did. He had affairs" (Author interview with White-Crane).

marked Hyannis Port, announcing his engagement to Ethel. Looking back more than sixty years later, Joan blames her breakup with Bobby on his family, and particularly his father: "His family really didn't care for English people, and they were very upset that I was seeing him."

The most exotic speculation revolved around a relationship between Bobby and Marilyn Monroe, who was said to be having an affair with both brothers, consecutively or simultaneously, depending on who told the story. Again, the accounts were secondhand or based on tape recordings and other evidence that supposedly vanished years before. Marilyn herself seemed to have it every which way—whispering to some friends that there was no affair and to others that Bobby was leaving Ethel to marry her, berating him for dumping her or wondering how to tell him it was splitsville. The accusations don't stop with infidelity. Bobby helped her commit suicide or outright murdered her—to cover up his affair, or JFK's, or her ties and theirs to the Mafia—various authors and journalists have charged, starting in 1964 and continuing nearly unabated. Then he concealed his complicity in her death, so the story goes, with help from the FBI, the Los Angeles police, and his own investigators and aides. The rumors swirled so feverishly that the Los Angeles County district attorney's office reviewed all the claims and counterclaims in 1982, twenty years after the sex siren's death. "Her murder would have required a massive, in-place conspiracy covering all the principals at the death scene on August 4 and 5, 1962; the actual killer or killers; the Chief Medical Examiner-Coroner; the autopsy surgeon to whom the case was fortuitously assigned; and most all of the police officers assigned to the case," the off-the-record report concluded. "Our inquiries and document examination uncovered no credible evidence supporting a murder theory."

That doesn't mean Bobby wasn't entangled with Marilyn, if only to cover up any relationship JFK had with her. Eleanor McPeck, a Massachusetts landscape architect and historian, makes no claims to knowledge of any ties Bobby had to the movie star. She does assert that nearly a decade before he met Marilyn, he was fascinated with her. When McPeck was a teenager living a couple of blocks from them, Bobby and Ethel would have her over for dinner and to play a game of "Who would you rather be with?" You could name anyone you found interesting, she says, and it was all in fun. Ethel's favorite was Andy Williams, who later became a close friend of hers and Bobby's. Bobby's, she adds, was " 'Marilyn Monroe, Marilyn Monroe,' repeated over and over and over again."

Ethel has lived with the rumors for fifty years, and she says she long ago stopped listening to or reading them. She tried to block them out then, too, although they must have hurt. She never disclosed any suspicions. She also understood Bobby's family better than anyone else who wasn't born into it, and she knew that whatever her church and theirs said about sex outside marriage, there was no tradition of monogamy in the Kennedy clan. She loved her husband more completely than she'd dreamed possible and still does. And she knew he always came home, not just to the kids but to her.

Chapter 5

BREAKING BARRIERS

T HE BEST CLUE to where the participants at the historic gathering
stood was where they sat. All eleven Negroes lined up on one side
of the Kennedys' drawing room overlooking Central Park, the
five whites on the other. It was Harlem vs. Hickory Hill. The partition was
a fitting one for the spring of 1963, when demarcation of the races was
written into law across the American South and into practice in the rest
of the land. But it was not an auspicious beginning to an urgent conclave that the black novelist James Baldwin had pulled together, at Bobby's request, to talk about why a volcano of rage was building up in
northern ghettos and why mainstream civil rights leaders couldn't or
wouldn't quell it as summer approached.

A second sign that the meeting was ill-fated was not who had been
invited but who had not. Baldwin assembled a motley collection of fellow artists, academics, and second-tier civil rights leaders, along with
his lawyer, secretary, literary agent, brother, and brother's girlfriend.
Martin Luther King, Jr., wasn't welcome, nor were the top people from
the NAACP and the Urban League, because Bobby wanted a no-holds-
barred critique of their leadership. He also hoped for a sober discussion
of what the Kennedy administration should do, with Negroes who knew
what it already was doing. Having a serious conversation without the
serious players would have been difficult enough, but Bobby made it
even harder: What he really wanted was gratitude, not candor. Baldwin
did his best given those constraints and only one day's notice. Bobby
may not have been inclined to take them seriously, yet everyone
participating—whether a matinee idol or crooner, dramatist or
therapist—had earned their stripes as activists.

After feeding his guests a light buffet and settling them in chairs or on footstools, Bobby opened the discussion on tame and self-serving notes. He listed all that he and his brother had accomplished in advancing Negro rights, explaining why their efforts were groundbreaking. He warned that the politics of race could get dicey with voters going to the polls in just eighteen months and conservative white Democrats threatening to bolt. "We have a party in revolt and we have to be somewhat considerate about how to keep them onboard if the Democratic party is going to prevail in the next elections," said the attorney general. He had already implied that he was among friends by tossing his jacket onto the back of his chair, rolling up his shirtsleeves, and welcoming everyone into his father's elegant apartment. Now he wanted these friends to explain why so many of their Negro brethren were being drawn to dangerous radicals like Malcolm X and his Black Muslims.

The first reaction was polite and tepid. Bobby assumed his audience was naïve about the real world of rawboned politics, while they took him to be too credulous on the even rawer realities of the slums. "He had called the meeting in hopes of persuading us that he and his brother were doing all that could be done," remembered the singer Lena Horne, whose silken voice had earned her center stage at the Cotton Club and whose left-leaning politics had gotten her blacklisted in Hollywood. "The funny thing was that no one there disputed that. It was just that it did not seem enough. . . . He said something about his family and the kinds of discrimination it had had to fight. He also said he thought a Negro would be president within 40 years. He seemed to feel that this would establish some sort of identification, some sort of rapport, between us. It did not. . . . The emotions of Negroes are running so differently from those of white men these days that the comparison between a white man's experience and a Negro's just doesn't work."

Kenneth Clark, black America's preeminent psychologist, came prepared to lay out studies and statistics to document that corrosive racial divide, but he never got the chance. Jerome Smith, a young activist who had held back as long as he could, suddenly shattered the calm, his stammer underlining his anger. "Mr. Kennedy, I want you to understand I don't care anything about you and your brother," he began. "I don't know what I'm doing here, listening to all this cocktail-party patter." The

real threat to white America wasn't the Black Muslims, Smith insisted, it
was when nonviolence advocates like him lost hope. The twenty-four-
year-old's record made his words resonate. He had suffered as many savage beatings as any civil rights protester of the era, including one for
which he was now getting medical care in New York. But his patience .
and his pacifism were wearing thin, he warned his rapt audience. If the
police came at him with more guns, dogs, and hoses, he would answer
with a weapon of his own. "When *I* pull a trigger," he said, "kiss it good-
bye."

Bobby was shocked, but Smith wasn't through. Not only would young
blacks like him fight to protect their rights at home, he said, but they
would refuse to fight for America in Cuba, Vietnam, or any of the other
places the Kennedys saw threats. "Never! Never! Never!" This was unfathomable to Bobby. "You will not fight for your country?" asked the
attorney general, who had lost one brother and nearly a second at war.
"How can you say that?" Rather than backing down, Smith said just
being in the room with Bobby "makes me nauseous." Others chimed in,
demanding to know why the government couldn't get tougher in taking
on racist laws and ghetto blight. Lorraine Hansberry, who wrote the play
A Raisin in the Sun, stood to say she was sickened as well. "You've got a
great many very, very accomplished people in this room, Mr. Attorney
General. But the only man who should be listened to is that man over
there," she said, pointing to Smith.

Three hours into the evening the dialogue had become a brawl, with
the tone set by Smith. "He didn't sing or dance or act. Yet he became the
focal point," said Baldwin. "That boy, after all, in some sense, represented
to everybody in that room our hope. Our honor. Our dignity. But, above
all, our hope." Bobby had heard enough. His tone let everyone know the
welcome mat had been taken up. His flushed face showed how incensed
he was. As his guests were leaving he was approached by Harry Belafonte, the King of Calypso, whom he had considered a loyal friend. "I
said, 'Well, why didn't *you* say something?'" Bobby recounted later. "He
said, 'If I said something, it would affect my position with these people,
and I have a chance to influence them. . . . If I sided with you on these
matters, then I would become suspect.'" Before Belafonte could finish his
thought, Bobby turned away, grumbling, "Enough."

Neither side got nearly what it wanted from the ill-conceived parley. The blacks had grasped the chance to vent their rage, which was one reason they'd come on such short notice. They had also hoped to remake this well-meaning brother of the president into their ally not for his kind of incremental reforms but for breakthrough change. They believed they had not just failed but had burned the bridge they came to build. "We left convinced that we had made no dent or impact on Bobby," said Clark, whose research on how color barriers harmed black children helped push the Supreme Court to outlaw segregated schools. "It may very well have been that Bobby Kennedy was more antagonistic to our aspirations and goals than he was before, because the clash was so violent. . . . This was tragic."

Bobby came away with even less. He had let his temper win out over his compassion. He had asked his guests for candor but had stopped hearing as soon as fingers pointed at him. What Smith and the others said should not have come as a surprise. It mirrored what Baldwin had written six months earlier, and Bobby had read, in an acclaimed *New Yorker* article that explained why, for today's Negro, "it is not hard for him to think of white people as devils"—but the essayist offered hope that "we may be able, handful that we are, to end the racial nightmare." Neither the attorney general nor his guests that night sensed that he would soon be counted among Baldwin's handful. A born fighter, Bobby's first reaction after the meeting was to jab back. "They don't know what the laws are—they don't know what the facts are—they don't know what we've been doing or what we're trying to do. You can't talk to them the way you can talk to Martin Luther King or Roy Wilkins," he told Arthur Schlesinger, forgetting that it was his frustration with King and Wilkins that made him ask Baldwin to gather other black voices. And there was more. "None of them lived in Harlem. I mean, they were wealthy Negroes," Bobby would complain to another interviewer. His own wealth, of course, dwarfed theirs, and their fame didn't exempt them from the humiliations faced by every dark-skinned American. Worse still, to Bobby, three of his black guests that night "were married to white people," which he said exacerbated their insecurities and encouraged them to talk tough. His conclusion: "I should not have gotten involved with that group."

Both sides had agreed not to talk to the press but neither could resist. *The New York Times* reported that the "secret" meeting was a "flop." The attorney general "didn't get the point," Baldwin told the paper, when he and others had urged that JFK address the nation on Negro rights and otherwise step up his engagement. Bobby didn't talk to that reporter but he did speak to a friendlier writer at the *Times*. James Reston positioned him precisely where he saw himself—caught between the rock of "militant white segregationists" like his Democratic allies in the South, and the hard place of "militant Negro integrationists" like those at the Baldwin meeting. Reston worried along with Bobby "that 'moderation' or 'gradualism' or 'token integration' were now offensive words to the Negro, and that sympathy by a Negro leader for the Administration's moderate approach was regarded as the work of 'collaborationists.' "

Reston was partly right. The administration walked a calibrated and overly cautious middle path on civil rights in its first two years. JFK had promised during his 1960 campaign to sign with "a stroke of a pen" an order banning discrimination in housing, but he took so long that protesters launched an "Ink for Jack" campaign, mailing him hundreds of fountain pens. He and Bobby named too many racist judges, took too long to file a serious-minded civil rights bill, and left the black voters who pulled them to victory in 1960 looking for more forceful answers. While moderation might have been the smart approach for a White House hell-bent on reelection, it made less sense for the commander of the New Frontier's riot squad.

In Bobby's earlier years, the disastrous Baldwin meeting might have been the end of the story. But after a couple of days of fuming, Smith's tirade began to sink in for Kennedy. Rather than repeating his refrain of "imagine anyone saying that," Bobby now told friends, "I guess if I were in his shoes, if I had gone through what he's gone through, I might feel differently about this country." It was not empty talk. Earlier on that very day of the Baldwin get-together, the attorney general had urged the owners of national chain stores to voluntarily integrate their lunch counters below the Mason-Dixon Line. Days before that, he had helped broker a settlement on desegregation and employment that partly de-fused ongoing violence in Birmingham.

Bobby Kennedy was stretching himself. He still brooded, but he was learning to channel his rage into outrage. Instead of deriding critics like Baldwin and Smith, which was his first impulse after they attacked him, he found himself identifying with them. He could see the effects of racism and started searching for causes. Instincts like those had led him to spring Junius Scales and Martin King from prison. Increasingly his words and actions on race would take on the very element of moral indignation that Lena Horne and Lorraine Hansberry had pleaded for. He already knew that bigotry wasn't confined to the South, but he now acknowledged for the first time that not just America's laws but its soul needed redemption. Eventually he would emerge as the only white politician who could talk to Black Muslims and to black mothers. Looking back, Clark conceded he had underestimated the attorney general. "Our conclusion that we had made no dent at all," the psychologist said, "was wrong."

———

BOBBY'S FIRST PUBLIC signal of where he stood on civil rights had come in his first formal speech as attorney general, back in May 1961, which was carefully staged to show that justice for Negroes mattered to him and his brother. What better way to make that point than by giving a major address on race in Athens, Georgia, on a campus that just four months before had been racked by riots after a federal judge compelled it to take its first Negro students? The most iconic figure then in the Peach State and surrounding ones was Jim Crow, a song-and-dance caricature played by a white minstrel in blackface whose name had become shorthand for the amalgam of statutes and customs mandating the segregation of the races everywhere from libraries, beauty parlors, and baseball diamonds to public toilets, parks, and bubblers. Even after fighting for their country in two world wars, black men had to endure the indignity of whites addressing them as "Uncle." Even after they were dead, Negroes couldn't reside in the same burial ground as Caucasians. Any marriage between a black and white was automatically void, and interracial sex was forbidden. The U.S. government was slowly striking down such barriers, starting in the armed forces and public schools, but white southerners were even slower to yield and quick to harbor grudges against northern officials they thought were pushy and preachy.

The night before the attorney general arrived in Athens, protesters daubed YANKEE. GO HOME. in white paint on downtown sidewalks. Bobby wasn't sure what to expect when he walked into the auditorium at the University of Georgia packed with sixteen hundred law students, faculty, and alumni. Noticeably absent were the governor and other public officials. "You may ask, will we enforce the Civil Rights statutes?" he told his anxious listeners. "The answer is: Yes, we will." But he also promised that "we will not threaten, we will try to help." Each word had been meticulously culled from seven different drafts offered up by a team of advisers, seeking the precise balance between tough and evenhanded. He feared the worst of reactions—and got the best. "Never before, in all its travail of by-gone years, has the South heard so honest and understandable a speech from any cabinet member," observed Ralph McGill, the anti-segregationist publisher of *The Atlanta Constitution.* Jackie Robinson, never a fan of the Kennedys, called it "most encouraging." Bobby's audience seemed to agree, standing and clapping for a full thirty seconds. That response, according to one student reporter, "was as loud and as long as they gave the football team for winning the [Georgia] Tech game last fall."

A closer listen to the talk, however, revealed that backbone and candor were not the only Kennedy civil rights credos foreshadowed that day. "We are trying to achieve amicable, voluntary solutions without going to court," Bobby told his audience. In those early years the attorney general tended to move cautiously on controversial issues such as race. He reinforced that inclination by surrounding himself with gentlemen lawyers at Justice who, like their boss, favored incremental change over upheaval. Bobby remained a man of politics as well as his brother's protector. He had witnessed President Eisenhower's wrenching decision to send a thousand federal soldiers and ten thousand Arkansas National Guardsmen to enforce the integration of Little Rock's schools, and he said, on that humid morning in Georgia, "we just can't afford another Little Rock." He knew, too, how essential the South had been to Jack's narrow election. "There are a lot of Kennedys in Georgia. But as far as I can tell, I have no relatives here and no direct ties to Georgia, except one," he said. "This state gave my brother the biggest percentage majority of any state in the union and in this last election that was even better than kinfolk." And, in words he hoped would help sustain that political bond between the president from Massachusetts and the Georgia electorate, he vowed that "the problem between the white and colored people is a problem for all sections of the United States."

A comparable push-pull was evident in every civil rights decision Bobby made during his first two years in office, starting with voting rights. Securing the vote for black Americans was priority one because he was convinced that political rights could be a gateway to all the others, from housing to jobs and education. Elect a few Negro congressmen from the South, along with state legislators and county commissioners, he argued, and watch how fast things get better. That might have worked if the Justice Department had been armed with a voting rights law with punch like the one that would pass in 1965. But fighting for a bill like that early in JFK's first term would mean taking on Congress's powerful Southern bloc, whose Senate members chaired the Judiciary, Foreign Relations, Armed Services, and Finance committees. In the House the obstructionists had all they needed in Virginian Howard W. Smith, who, as chairman of the Rules Committee, could bury any bill he opposed. Going up against such clout likely would require sacrificing other critical pieces of the administration's congressional agenda, and civil rights wasn't worth the risk to Bobby or Jack. Not yet.

Instead, Bobby from the first focused on beefing up his Civil Rights Division, eventually adding two hundred young, committed lawyers who did their best to cajole Southern registrars into opening their voter rolls to blacks. When that didn't work, which was most of the time, they sued under the weak-kneed laws passed in 1954 and 1960 that required them to prove that literacy tests, poll taxes, and other barriers disproportionately harmed specific Negroes. That effort was further stymied by FBI investigators who balked at collecting that proof, local election officials who were masters at disenfranchising even those blacks who managed to register, and federal district judges who said no often enough that lengthy appeals generally were needed to win. Bobby's fact finders turned up shocking evidence of obstructionism in places like Macon County, Alabama. Illiterate whites didn't have to recognize the word "registration" to get enrolled. Not so blacks, who were barred from signing up despite being able to write out long sections of the U.S. Constitution. Federal judge Frank Johnson, a trailblazer, ordered sixty-four Negroes enrolled and said that in the future, the standard applied to blacks would be the one used for the least-qualified whites. Yet even that hard-fought victory signified the difficulty of applying these incremental wins on a broader scale. Forty-six lawsuits filed by the department from 1961 to 1963 gave the vote to 37,146 Negroes—but did not cover 511,212 others in the same counties who would not be allowed to exercise the right guaranteed them by the Constitution they were memorizing. "The right to vote is the easiest of all rights to grant," Bobby had assured his audience at the University of Georgia, but defiant registrars across the South were proving cagier than the attorney general and his brigade of voting rights lawyers.

Integrating public schools wasn't any easier. In 1954 the Supreme Court, in its *Brown v. Board of Education* ruling, struck down state laws that set up separate schools for black and white students. Six years later the apartheid-like system remained, with just 0.162 percent of black children in the eleven Deep South states attending integrated schools. Bobby was of two minds. He found "deplorable" and "inexplicable" the resistance to even token integration, but the specter of Little Rock made the idea of using federal force even less acceptable. Caution kept him from fully testing whatever limited powers the law granted him. His intrepid attorneys, once again, did what they could—negotiating behind the scenes to enforce voluntary desegregation rulings, suing on behalf of children of black soldiers, and staging what Bobby's defenders called guerrilla strikes, even as civil rights groups called for all-out war. Why not use his bully pulpit to actively encourage integration? they asked. What about cutting off federal funds to districts that were resisting federal orders? The symbolism of his calls to free Rev. King from prison might have sufficed in the heat of an election, but now he needed to show more substance and a deeper commitment. Remember, King and other civil rights leaders told the politically canny attorney general, it wasn't just white Southerners who had helped his brother squeak into the White House, but also Negro voters in toss-up states from South Carolina to New Jersey.

Bobby demonstrated how far he could have gone in Prince Edward County, Virginia. School officials there responded to a 1959 order to integrate by dismantling the entire public education system and replacing it with a private one to educate white children, with substantial subsidies from the state and county. Black children were on their own, which for many meant no schooling at all. Finally Bobby got angry and creative. In the spring of 1961 he asked the court to reopen the county's public schools, halt tuition subsidies to white students, and punish all of Virginia by cutting off federal education funds. It was the muscular approach that civil rights advocates had been seeking and that Bobby had said he wasn't authorized to undertake. He wouldn't stop there. Seeing that the legal appeals were taking years, in 1963 he rallied teachers from across the country to construct a network of private schools for the county's fifteen hundred black children. JFK had told reporters there were only four places on the planet where children couldn't attend school: North Korea, North Vietnam, Cambodia, and Prince Edward County. It took until 1964 for the Supreme Court to rectify that. In the meantime, Bobby had shown the difference he could make when he got incensed enough and dared to try.*

There was no doubt about the attorney general's legal authority to advise the president on federal judicial appointments. The only uncertainty was who Bobby would listen to—those urging him to use the appointments to affirm his opposition to segregation, or Southern senators who saw it as their historic prerogative to weigh in and saw segregation as part of Southern culture. He vowed to do the right thing and expressed shock when some of the appointees turned out to be unabashed racists. Harold Cox was the most salient example. "We sat on my couch in my own office. . . . I said that the great reservation that I had was the question whether he'd enforce the law and whether he'd live up to the Constitution and the laws, and the interpretation of the Constitution by the Supreme Court," Bobby said in explaining why he named Cox as a federal district judge in Mississippi in 1961. "He assured me that he would." That, and the fact that neither the FBI nor the American Bar Association raised red flags, were enough for the attorney general. But flags were

---

* At the end of his term the share of black children in the South attending integrated schools was up dramatically from when he started, but it still stood at just 2.25 percent (Southern Education Reporting Service, 16th rev., 1966–1967, Nashville).

being raised. After Cox was nominated but before he was confirmed, NAACP boss Roy Wilkins wired the White House to say that "for 986,000 Negro Mississippians Judge Cox will be another strand in their barbed wire fence, another cross over their weary shoulders and another rock in the road up which their young people must struggle." Even more telling, if Bobby really had wanted to know, was the fact that Cox was the college roommate and enthusiastic choice of Senate Judiciary Committee chairman James Eastland, the archsegregationist from Mississippi. "Tell your brother," Eastland reportedly told Bobby, "that if he will give me Harold Cox I will give him the nigger [meaning Thurgood Marshall, a black judge JFK wanted to appoint to the Second Circuit Court of Appeals]." Eastland got Cox, and not long after, he gave the Kennedys Marshall, who would eventually be promoted to the Supreme Court.* As for Cox, he proved to be as bad as Wilkins feared. In clarifying from the bench why he planned to reject the Justice Department's request to register Negro voters, Cox referred to the would-be voters as "a bunch of niggers." Who, he demanded to know, "is telling these people they can get in line and push people around, acting like a bunch of chimpanzees?"

The Kennedys almost made history in 1962 by naming Circuit Judge William Hastie as the first black Supreme Court justice. "It would mean so much overseas and abroad that we had a Negro on the Supreme Court. It could do all kinds of good for the country, as well as the fact that he was qualified," Bobby later explained. But he said that idea died both because Chief Justice Warren was "violently opposed," arguing that Hastie was "not a liberal," and because "a lot of people in the White House were opposed to having a Negro."

Bobby's overall record on judgeships was as mixed as the rest of his civil rights agenda. Cox and four others of the twenty-five federal district judges he named in the Deep South proved to be nightmares for civil rights attorneys and their clients, although eight of his appointees were

---

* The Kennedys originally offered Marshall just a federal district judgeship, and they were offended when he turned it down. Bobby: "It's this or nothing." Marshall: "All I've had in my life is nothing. It's not new to me, so, good-bye." Later, Marshall confided to an interviewer that "Bobby was like his father. He was a cold, calculating character. 'What's in it for me?' . . . He had no warm feelings. None at all. With that big old dog of his, walking around, cocking his leg up on your leg" (Tushnet, *Thurgood Marshall*, 484–85).

committed integrationists. When he left office, the South still had no Negroes on the federal circuit court, none on the district court, and none as jury commissioners or U.S. marshals. "A Negro involved in a federal court action in the South could go from the beginning of the case to the end without seeing any black faces unless they were in the court audience, or he happens to notice the man sweeping the floor," concluded the Southern Regional Council, a respected civil rights group. Bobby did, however, appoint ten Negroes to judgeships in the North. And, outraged at how few black faces he saw in his own Justice Department, he increased the number of black attorneys from six to sixty.

This attorney general was on a learning curve and so, unfortunately, was his chief adviser on civil rights, Burke Marshall. The thirty-eight-year-old Marshall's lack of background on race issues was part of what made him attractive to Byron White, the deputy attorney general who recommended him. That paper-thin record meant that Southern senators had no justification for holding up Marshall's nomination the way they would have the more logical choice for the posting, Harris Wofford. Wofford, whom Bobby had bawled out during the 1960 campaign for his role in getting JFK to call Martin Luther King's wife, was too much of an agitator on an issue the attorney general didn't yet think worthy of agitating. Picking Marshall over Wofford in 1961 was, Assistant Attorney General Nicholas Katzenbach said, "an effort to signal that while the administration was committed to civil rights, miracles should not be expected." Marshall's job interview became famous in the Kennedy world because he and Bobby were both so shy that neither said anything, and each man incorrectly assumed he hadn't clicked with the other. He would ultimately become the most trusted of Bobby's assistants, and perhaps the most effective head ever of the Civil Rights Division, although less so in these early years when Bobby needed prodding more than patience. "It would be comforting to think the Kennedys had a plan," said Katzenbach. "They simply did not. There were ideas, but the sum total of them did not add up to much—certainly not enough to satisfy the growing demands of black leaders like Martin Luther King."

Kennedy and Marshall got their baptism of fire in Alabama. It came in the wake of the Supreme Court's December 1960 ruling outlawing segregation in interstate travel, whether it was aboard a bus or train or waiting in the terminal. Like the 1954 ruling on school desegregation, this one was greeted with delight by civil rights groups but would meet with bitter resistance in the real world of the segregated South. That spring a group of activists, black and white, decided to test their new rights by taking buses across the South in ways that directly challenged the old norms. Interracial pairs sat in adjoining seats while at least one black sat up front, in an area from which they were historically banished. When they got to the station, the black barrier-breakers used whites-only bathrooms and lunch counters. Everyone planned to end up in New Orleans on May 17, 1961, the seventh anniversary of *Brown v. Board of Education*. They called themselves Freedom Riders, and the first fourteen of what would eventually be more than four hundred made it through Virginia, North and South Carolina, and Georgia with what would later look like only minor skirmishes. The real trouble came when they divided into two groups, one on a Trailways bus, the other on arch-competitor Greyhound, and rolled into Alabama.

In Anniston, a city of 33,000 midway between Atlanta and Birmingham, a caravan of angry whites caught up with the Greyhound bus on May 14 and hurled a Molotov cocktail through the window. The rioters used clubs and iron bars to batter the riders as they scrambled out of the burning vehicle. While the injured Greyhound passengers made their way to the hospital* the Trailways bus rolled into the station, where a hostile boarding party waited. Eight white toughs, their shirtsleeves rolled up to display their biceps, snarled, "Niggers, get back. You ain't up North. You're in Alabama, and niggers ain't nothin' here." They backed up their words by raining blows on the blacks sitting up front. One white Freedom Rider who protested was battered into semiconsciousness as a second was lifted over two seats and deposited in the aisle. Simeon Booker, who was covering the ride for the black journal *Jet*, pretended to read a newspaper but actually was bearing witness through a small hole. "A policeman boarded," he said, "grinned at the white thugs, and mumbled, 'Don't worry about any lawsuits. I ain't seen a thing.'" When the

---

* The hospital in Anniston refused to treat them and, with an angry mob gathering outside, they were rescued by a caravan of civil rights workers who drove up from Birmingham (Raines, *My Soul Is Rested*, 98–99).

riders finally got to Birmingham, that city's police were conspicuously missing even though their headquarters was just two blocks from the terminal. For what everyone later learned was a prearranged fifteen minutes, forty white thugs waiting in the loading bay assaulted the activists with baseball bats, blackjacks, and bicycle chains. James Peck, who had been hauled over the seats in Anniston, was attacked again so savagely that it took fifty stitches to close his head wound. Theophilus Eugene "Bull" Connor, Birmingham's police commissioner, said he couldn't prevent the violence because too many of his men were on leave for Mother's Day. FBI agents were on hand, having been tipped off by a Ku Klux Klan informant, but all they did was take pictures and issue a report. None lifted a finger to prevent the ambush.

Bobby later said he "never knew they were traveling down there . . . before the bus was burned in Anniston." But he had to have known. Two months earlier, James Farmer of the Congress of Racial Equality, one of the organizers, had sent him the itinerary. In case he missed that, the next month Booker told Bobby he was joining the ride. "His buoyant response—'I wish I could go with you!'—had surprised me," the reporter recounted. "I told Kennedy the Riders might need protection at some point, and he said to call him if trouble arose."

Now Bobby had no choice but to act, sending in as a troubleshooter John Seigenthaler, his aide from Tennessee. It was an impossible mission. JFK made it clear to Bobby and Seigenthaler that he wanted the marchers to "call it off," which they hadn't been willing to do earlier that week when they were brutally beaten and certainly wouldn't on the say-so of a thirty-three-year-old ex-journalist, no matter whom he was representing nor how pronounced his Southern drawl. Bobby, meanwhile, offered Seigenthaler his encouragement but no federal protection for the protesters or for him. In the minds of both Kennedys, the rides couldn't be taking place at a less opportune moment—a month after their botched Bay of Pigs invasion and weeks before JFK's summit meeting with Soviet leader Nikita Khrushchev, who already was gloating over America's racial strife. Seigenthaler met the beaten and bruised activists in the departure lounge of the Birmingham airport, where, after several bomb threats, they joined him on a flight to New Orleans. Once there, he'd barely laid his head on a hotel pillow when he got a call from Burke Marshall saying that ten replacement riders had shown up in Birmingham determined to make the trip to the state capital of Montgomery.

Bull Connor arrested those riders, and he thought he rid himself of the problem by loading them into cars in the middle of the night and depositing them across the state line in Tennessee. But a third group took their place, and this time Bobby wouldn't take no for an answer from Alabama authorities. John Patterson, who had done more than any other governor in the South to put JFK in the White House, now ducked calls not just from the attorney general but from the president, telling his aides to say he had gone fishing. Seigenthaler, who'd flown back to Alabama, finally managed a face-to-face meeting with the governor, who vented his spleen for thirty minutes on "everybody and everything from the Supreme Court to me, but was heaviest on Bob Kennedy." Patterson declared himself "sick of these spineless people that I supported not standing up," added Seigenthaler, and warned that "if federal marshals come in to Alabama, there'll be blood in the streets." Then the governor reluctantly agreed to ensure the safety of the Freedom Riders.

The next challenge was to find someone at Greyhound willing to take the protesters to Montgomery. The scheduled driver told reporters, "I only have one life to give and I'm not going to give it to CORE or the NAACP." Bobby got on the phone to George Cruit, a bus company superintendent, and made clear the stakes: "I think you should—had better be getting in touch with Mr. Greyhound. . . . I am—the Government is—going to be very much upset if this group does not get to continue their trip." His insistence produced a driver, but Cruit would get his revenge. He had taped the conversation, and critics in Alabama and elsewhere misread Bobby's statement that "we have gone to a lot of trouble to see that they get to [make] this trip" as proof that the attorney general had helped orchestrate the Freedom Rides.

The crisis of the moment involved the riders themselves. State troopers escorted them with cruisers and helicopters to the city limits of Montgomery, where city police were supposed to take over. But Montgomery officials identified with the segregationists, not the integrationists, and like their counterparts in Birmingham, they stayed away from the bus terminal just long enough for the mob to convey its vicious message. Angry whites descended from every direction—some as young as fifteen, most wielding baseball bats, iron pipes, chains, or bottles, and all seeming to scream at once, "Get them niggers!" John Doar, the Justice Department attorney who had been leading Bobby's push for voting rights, watched in horror from a building high above the terminal, providing a blow-by-blow to colleagues back in Washington: "A bunch of men led by a guy with a bleeding face are beating them. There are no cops. It's terrible. It's terrible." FBI agents again snapped pictures and did nothing. Seigenthaler drove up in time to see a young white girl being pummeled over the head with a pocketbook by a "little fat woman who looked like Nikita Khrushchev's wife," while a skinny kid who looked about fifteen "was facing her and dancing backwards like a boxer and smacking her in the face." Seigenthaler tried to intervene, telling the rabble, "Get back, get back. I'm a federal man." That earned him a crack over his left ear so hard it landed him in the hospital with a concussion. Bobby called to ask, "How do you feel?" Seigenthaler: "I've got a small headache. . . . Let me give you some advice. . . . Never run for Governor of Alabama. You couldn't get elected." Told that federal marshals were on the way to restore order, Seigenthaler said, "I hate that. It's sort of like an invasion." Kennedy: "Sooner or later something had to happen. This is what triggered it."

Bobby's wrath was provoked only partly by events on the ground, which were spiraling beyond the beatings at the terminal. Even more important, given the way his brain worked, things had gotten personal. He always knew he'd have to ratchet up his enforcement of civil rights, but as always it was experiences rather than abstractions that pushed him into the fray. His friend Seigenthaler was lying in the hospital, lucky to be alive. Patience and caution now gave way to resolve and rage. Jack was at his weekend retreat in Virginia, content to let Bobby take control along with any heat. Bobby had just thrown out the first ball at the annual FBI softball game when news of the riots reached him. He raced to the Justice Department in blue denim slacks and shirtsleeves, still wearing a baseball cap, and began issuing the orders for which activists had been pleading. He mobilized a force of four hundred U.S. marshals, border patrolmen, prison guards, and revenue agents, some of whom had trained for riot duty. He asked a federal judge in Montgomery to restrain the KKK and National States' Rights Party from interfering with the riders, later expanding the request to include Bull Connor and three other police officials whom he blamed for the mayhem in Birmingham and Montgomery. And he ordered more FBI agents into the area to investigate the riots.

Those actions came just in time to prevent calamity. As bad as the bus beatings had been, the state capital now looked as if it could become the scene of a massacre. Martin Luther King, Jr., who six years before had inaugurated the modern civil rights movement by leading a boycott of Montgomery's segregated bus lines, had returned and rallied fifteen hundred supporters at the redbrick First Baptist Church. Angry whites gathered in a park across the street, howling rebel chants and, to show they meant business, setting fire to a car as they advanced on the church with bottles, rocks, and Molotov cocktails. Byron White, Bobby's deputy attorney general and man on the scene, dispatched his marshals in a surreal caravan of cars, postal delivery vehicles, and a prison truck. The marshals wore business suits (another bid by Bobby and his brother to distinguish them from the paratroopers who were called up in Little Rock), but their armbands, nightsticks, sidearms, and tear gas grenades clearly revealed their purpose. They temporarily fended off the demonstrators, but as the tear gas ran out and their cordon seemed about to be breached, Governor Patterson finally declared martial law and sent in the Alabama National Guard.

Back at the Justice Department, Bobby fielded frantic phone calls and eased the stress by tossing a football with some of his very anxious aides. He sensed that this was the end of his honeymoon, and of his innocence, and he knew that the precedent of federal intervention in Montgomery would set the pattern for everything in this conflict that came after. "It's a bad situation," he murmured. "Trouble could spread all over the South." A month before, he and a handful of advisers had sat down with King for an off-the-record get-acquainted lunch in a private dining room at Washington's Mayflower Hotel, with waiters barred so word wouldn't leak to the press and Bobby assuring Martin he could call "any hour of the day or night" if there was trouble. Now the two were on the phone, and Kennedy was losing patience as he tried to reassure an understandably nervous King. "You shouldn't have withdrawn the marshals. Patterson's National Guard won't protect us," King said. Bobby: "Now,

Reverend, don't tell me that. You know just as well as I do that if it hadn't been for the United States marshals you'd be as dead as Kelsey's nuts* right now!" Minutes later, Patterson called from Alabama to berate the attorney general and insist the melee was Bobby's fault. Holding the phone away from his ear so others could hear the governor's tirade, Bobby finally broke in: "Now, John, you can say that on television. You can tell that to the people of Alabama, John, but don't tell me that." When Patterson complained that sending in the marshals was "destroying us politically," Kennedy claimed the high ground: "John, it's more important that these people in the church survive physically than for us to survive politically."

Yet Bobby never entirely forgot about politics during the crisis. He placed federal troops on standby but did everything in his power to avoid dispatching them to a situation where their numbers and training would have been welcome relief to his ragtag army of law enforcement officers. He wrote to all of Alabama's congressmen and senators, promising to deploy the marshals only as "a last resort" and not for "a minute longer than is necessary" and deceiving them with the assurance that he'd never so much as considered inserting federal troops. He repeatedly urged the Freedom Riders to "cool down," saying they had already made their point. (James Farmer's response: "We have been cooling off for 350 years. If we cool off any more, we will be in a deep freeze. The Freedom Ride will go on.") And in more than thirty calls back and forth with Senator Eastland, Bobby brokered a deal whereby the powerful Mississippi lawmaker would guarantee the riders' safety on the next leg of their journey, from Montgomery to Jackson; in return, the federal government wouldn't raise any objections—under either the equal protection guarantees of the Fourteenth Amendment or the undisputed rights the Supreme Court had guaranteed interstate travelers—when the police arrested the protesters for violating a Mississippi law that made a crime of "refusing to disperse and move on when ordered to do so by any law enforcement official." Days after the Jackson arrests, Bobby took to the

---

* Kelsey's nuts were the secure nuts-and-bolts attachments on wheels made by the Kelsey Wheel Company. In its colloquial usage, "Kelsey's nuts" originally referred to someone who was thrifty to the point of stingy. But Bobby, Richard Nixon, and others used the phrase to mean someone who was powerless and sometimes deceased.

airwaves to try to counter the news on America's racial unrest now splashed across front pages from Nairobi and New Delhi to London and Moscow. While the beatings of Freedom Riders are "a matter that disturbs us tremendously," he said on a Voice of America broadcast beamed in thirty-seven languages to more than sixty countries, the white mobs are "just a small minority group" that "doesn't represent the vast majority of the people in the South. . . . and it certainly doesn't represent the feelings of the United States Government or the American people."

The Freedom Rides were a testing moment for Bobby. He and Jack "wanted to have a record of having some accomplishment in the segregation field . . . this was an opportunity to build a record," argues Patterson, adding that half a century later the name Bobby Kennedy remains a cuss word in his home and many more across Alabama. Patterson says he and other savvy politicians in the South knew they were on the losing side of the race debate but wanted time to help voters adjust. "When he was dealing with me . . . he wasn't dealing with an Orval Faubus," Patterson boasts, referring to the Arkansas governor whose resistance touched off the crisis in Little Rock. "He could have dealt with me reasonably." Bobby's failure to do that, the ninety-year-old ex-governor adds, meant not just that Patterson would never again win elected office but that Alabama politics would mutate from Yellow Dog Democrat to staunchly Republican. Booker, the black journalist, was equally disillusioned yet for precisely the opposite reason: that Bobby was too cautious and accommodating to the reactionary Southern whites. "The Freedom Rides and the ensuing months erased the aura of Kennedy infallibility as far as blacks were concerned," Booker maintained. "The vastly popular attorney general, for all the power of both his family and the department he headed, was now seen as just a human being—a white man caught in a web of racial passion and prejudice."

Bobby angered both sides by walking a middle line, failing to see that the combatants were not morally equivalent and that half-measures were not enough. He proved in Alabama that he was prepared to act against violence, but not against the degrading segregation that spawned it, not even when the Supreme Court was on his side and activists were taking the lead. He took off the table the only leverage he had with Alabama officials when he vowed not to deploy federal troops, and he failed to see how ill-suited the well-meaning marshals were for riot control duty. The night the Freedom Riders reached Jackson safely, Bobby was in his Justice Department office, barefoot and wearing the shorts and dressing gown he'd had on when he was summoned from home. He offered a drink to the pair of sleepy aides there with him, pouring himself an Old Grand-Dad over ice and reflecting on his newfound appreciation that race really was the story of America. "These situations are something we're going to have to live with," he told his companions. "This is going on and on."

The Freedom Rides did not go on and on, thanks largely to a behind-the-scenes move suggested earlier by King and initiated by Bobby just nine days after the marshals had marched into Montgomery. He asked the Interstate Commerce Commission to order an end to segregation in interstate bus terminals. While the famously slow-moving commission was independent of the White House, nudging bureaucracies was Bobby's specialty, especially when he understood that it could save lives as well as soothe feelings. Less than four months later, the ICC agreed. Although some cities were slow to comply, Jim Crow all but vanished in bus stations, and shortly afterward in airports and train stations. Signs proclaiming WHITES ONLY or COLORED sections became collectors' items. The only question was why it took the attorney general so long. The answer activists came away with was not one Bobby intended: that the way to pressure the Kennedys to act was to stage street-level protests, fill Southern jails, and shed their own blood the way the Freedom Riders had.

Mississippi had looked like friendly territory to Bobby as he did battle in Alabama in the spring of 1961. "The fact that there was no violence in Jackson, Mississippi, shows that local authorities can keep order when they accept their responsibilities," he said then. Sixteen months later he would see the Magnolia State for what it was: the most stubbornly segregated of the fifty states. And he came to regard Ross Barnett, its frosty-eyed governor who had seemed so reasonable next to Alabama's John Patterson, as the most brazenly racist politician in Mississippi and "genuinely loony." Entrenched southerners who resisted integrating their bus terminals held their all-white schools even more sacred. That is why every public school district in Mississippi remained segregated eight years after

the Supreme Court declared the practice illegal. No school was closer to
the heart of Mississippians than the hundred-fourteen-year-old, whites-
only state university in Oxford fondly known as Ole Miss. That is why
twenty-nine-year-old James Meredith, the grandson of slaves and a proud
native of Mississippi, spent eleven months fighting in the courts until the
highest in the land said he could enroll there in the fall of 1962.

Bobby was determined that it happen, too, and hoped to quietly work
out an arrangement with Governor Barnett. He tried, in twenty-two
separate phone conversations over a two-week period that tested his san-
ity as well as his endurance. Each call only strengthened the sixty-four-
year-old Barnett's conviction that he could talk his way around the
thirty-six-year-old attorney general. Sometimes the exchange was over
esoteric issues of federalism and how far a state could go in challenging
federal authority:

Kennedy: Governor, you are a part of the United States.

Barnett: We have been a part of the United States but I don't know
whether we are or not.

Kennedy: Are you getting out of the Union?

Barnett: It looks like we're being kicked around—like we don't belong
to it. General, this thing is serious.

Kennedy: It's serious here.

Barnett: Must it be over one little boy—backed by a Communist front—
backed by the NAACP, which is a Communist front?

Kennedy: I don't think it is—

Barnett: We know it is down here.

Two days later the conversation turned to how the attorney general
and governor could choreograph events to get Meredith registered without Barnett's looking as if he was backing down:

Kennedy: I will have the head marshal pull a gun and I will have the rest of them have their hands on their guns and their holsters. And then as I understand it [Meredith] will go through and get in and you will make sure that law and order is preserved . . .

Barnett: Oh, yes.

Kennedy: And then I think you will see that's accomplished?

Barnett: . . . General, I was under the impression that they were all going to pull their guns. This could be very embarrassing. We got a big crowd here and if one pulls his gun and we all turn it would be very embarrassing. Isn't it possible to have them all pull their guns?

Kennedy: I hate to have them all draw their guns as I think it could create harsh feelings. Isn't it sufficient if I have one man draw his gun and the others keep their hands on their holsters?

Barnett: They must all draw their guns. Then they should point their guns at us and then we could step aside.

As deals were made and broken, and plans were executed then canceled at the last minute, Bobby played the one card he had left: threatening to have the president reveal, on national television, the private negotiations to bring Meredith to Ole Miss. Barnett was nearly speechless. "I don't want the President saying I broke my word," he told the attorney general. "That wouldn't do at all. . . . We will cooperate with you." Once they pieced together a new agreement, the governor asked Bobby whether it was okay "if I raise cain about it." Bobby: "I don't mind that; just say law and order will be maintained." That evening Barnett released a statement vowing, "I will never yield a single inch in my determination to win the fight we are engaged in. I call upon every Mississippian to keep his faith and his courage. We will never surrender." Meredith, who knew something about fighting from his nine years in the Air Force, said he "considered such maneuvers as we were going through to be an utter waste of human manpower and intelligence. At the same time I realized their absolute necessity in the process of changing social patterns."

The folly underlying all that back-and-forth was the notion that Barnett could control the crowds he was whipping into defiance. Or that he would even try. Two dozen U.S. marshals quietly moved Meredith into an Ole Miss dormitory on September 30, a sleepy Sunday, one day before angry demonstrators expected him to enroll. The main force of five hundred white-helmeted marshals, with tear gas canisters sticking out of their orange vests, ringed the stately redbrick Lyceum building. That was where Meredith would register and where, the marshals hoped, protesters would assume he was now. It worked. Throughout the afternoon the mob in front of the Lyceum got bigger and grew uglier. Student demonstrators were joined by agitators from as far away as Texas and Georgia, some of whom wore Confederate army uniforms. Many chanted slogans like "2-4-1-3, we hate Ken-ne-dy!" and, scarier, "Just wait'll dark." Most had armed themselves with stones, iron bars, jagged slices of concrete from smashed campus benches, Coca-Cola bottles converted into gasoline bombs, pistols, rifles, or shotguns. Later they added to their arsenal the campus fire truck and a bulldozer. The marshals had orders to fire their tear gas, not their riot guns. The eggs hit them first, then rocks and bullets. They were outmanned from the start, with most of Barnett's highway patrolmen clearing out early or never showing up. The only reinforcements were a sixty-man troop of federalized National Guardsmen commanded by Captain Murry C. Falkner,* whose recently deceased uncle William Faulkner had written so eloquently about Gothic horrors like the one playing out now in his hometown. The informal commander of the racist army was former major general Edwin Walker, who had led the paratroopers who squashed the anti-integration insurrection in Little Rock. This time Walker himself would be charged with insurrection.

Back in Washington, Bobby monitored the action from the White House Cabinet Room via his aide Nicholas Katzenbach, who had called collect from a pay phone at the Lyceum and never hung up.† Bobby knew

---

* This Falkner's family didn't change the spelling of the family name to Faulkner.

† Over the course of the evening, Bobby's men on the scene used that phone line to relay what they were seeing and hearing to Burke Marshall, Bobby, and even President Ken-

that riots were inevitable in Mississippi, unlike in Alabama, and that federal troops would likely be required. But with midterm elections barely five weeks away, he and Jack clung to the hope that Governor Barnett would keep his promises; if he did, they could avoid the need for a federal invasion that would spell disaster at the polls for his fellow Southern Democrats. Throughout the evening, the Kennedys wavered. The president tried to buy time by pushing his speech to the nation back from 7:30 P.M. to 10:00 P.M., but that only assured that much of America would be asleep while Ole Miss was already on fire. Bobby assumed his familiar role as long-distance field commander, and he used his playfulness to boost the morale of his beleaguered and blood-splattered men on campus. "It's getting like the Alamo," press aide Ed Guthman reported. Bobby: "Well, you know what happened to those guys, don't you?" Yet each phone conversation made it clearer that it really was like the Battle of the Alamo. First a French newspaperman was killed by an execution-style shot in the back, then a jukebox repairman, a mere bystander, took a deadly bullet to his forehead. The marshals came under increasingly heavy fire and repeatedly sought permission to fire back, but the Kennedy brothers said no, not unless Meredith's life was imperiled. They worried that unleashing the marshals, who had modest arms and minimal training, would turn a melee into a disaster. "We could just visualize," Bobby said, "a lot of marshals being killed, or James Meredith being strung up." As the endless evening dragged on, a total of 166 marshals and 40 guardsmen were injured, with one shot in the throat and Captain Falkner suffering two broken bones from a flying brick. Now was the time, Katzenbach told his boss, to call in the Army.

It was a few minutes' drive from the Oxford airport where the troops were supposed to be to the campus where they were needed, but after they heard JFK's reassuring message on television the soldiers had returned to their barracks, eighty miles away in Memphis. Then they had to wait for rifles and ammunition. The secretary of the Army had promised to have his men at Ole Miss within two hours, and he repeatedly assured the pres-

---

nedy. The connection was clear enough that listeners in Washington could hear the amplifying violence in Mississippi. "In a very real sense," Katzenbach said, "it became our lifeline" (Katzenbach, *Some of It Was Fun,* 77).

ident and attorney general that they were on their way when they weren't. It would be a full five hours before twenty-five thousand soldiers rolled onto campus, where they were greeted by rocks and firebombs. "The planning wasn't that bad, but the execution was disastrous," Bobby would say. "The idea that we got through the evening without the marshals being killed and without Meredith being killed was a miracle."

Miracle or not, history would portray the battle of Ole Miss as the federal government standing up not just for the rule of law and against mob violence, but for racial justice. It was a kinder verdict than the Kennedys deserved. Rather than learning from his mistakes during the Freedom Rides of the previous year, Bobby compounded them in Mississippi. He continued to misread the lesson of Little Rock. It wasn't to resist using federal troops, but to recognize early when they'd be needed and send them in numbers overwhelming enough to quell the violence. Eisenhower, the ex-general, understood that and had avoided the toll of deaths and injuries in Little Rock that made Oxford into an object lesson in how not to execute a federal intervention.* Bobby also let himself be played by Governor Barnett in Mississippi even more than he had been by Governor Patterson in Alabama. The attorney general's vacillation on how to register Meredith was read by the governor and most Mississippians as weakness. His threats notwithstanding, Bobby had let Barnett get away with private barter while at the same time remaining publicly defiant. Worst of all, Bobby's actions at Ole Miss suggested that he still considered racial injustice another in a string of crises he would confront only when forced to. Although President Kennedy deserved much of the blame for the administration's missteps and indecision in Oxford, Bobby, true to form, shouldered full responsibility for the mess. "It was a nervous time for the president," Bobby explained, "because he was torn then between, perhaps, an attorney general who had botched things up, and the fact the attorney general was his brother." The bloody battle at Ole Miss, he said in its wake, was "the worst night I ever spent."

----

* Eisenhower had an advantage the Kennedys didn't: The mayor of Little Rock had invited him in.

IN THE RICH white communities where Bobby grew up—Hyannis Port, Riverdale, Bronxville, and Palm Beach—race wasn't a topic of dinner-table conversation. "What we did grow up with [was] the idea that there were a lot of people that were less fortunate . . . this was during the 1930s," he said. But "as far as separating the Negroes for having a more difficult time than the white people, that was not a particular issue in our house." True as that was, his siblings said Bobby was a bit less sheltered than he suggested. Jackie Bell, the son of the Kennedys' white laundress in Hyannis Port and her black husband, lived three blocks away and was one of Bobby's closest friends as a child. In law school, Bobby overcame opposition from the Virginia legal code and the University of Virginia student government to bring in as a speaker diplomat Ralph Bunche, the first black Nobel laureate. Racists tossed fiery missiles into their yard when Bobby and Ethel invited Bunche to sleep in their attic. "They were all over the lawn," Ethel recalls. "We just thought, why would anybody get that exercised because of somebody's skin color?"

All the Kennedy kids knew that being Irish and Catholic brought their own kinds of prejudice. It was less overt than in Patrick Kennedy's day, when signs warned that "no Irish need apply" for jobs or housing, or in Joe's time, when neither his money nor his influence could fully erase lingering prejudice. "I was born here. My children were born here. What the hell do I have to do to be called an American?" Joe bristled when Boston papers persisted in calling him an Irishman. Bobby bristled, too, when the Spee Club at Harvard blackballed an Irish American classmate and when Jack's Catholicism looked as if it might keep him from the presidency.

Disabilities were not considered a civil rights issue in the mid-1900s, certainly not on a par with discrimination against Negroes or even Irish Catholics. But in the Kennedy home the afflictions of Rose Marie, the oldest daughter, gave her siblings their first up-close lesson in misfortune. What it was that afflicted Joe and Rose's third child, known as Rosemary, remains unclear.* Her parents initially told her brothers and sisters that

---

* One old theory, fleshed out in a new biography of this "hidden Kennedy daughter," is that the obstetrical nurse helping with Rosemary's home birth was determined to wait until the doctor arrived even though Rose was in labor. The nurse reportedly held the baby's head and forced it back into the birth canal for "two excruciating hours," which could have resulted in a damaging loss of oxygen (Larson, *Rosemary*, 3–4).

she was shy and, as Rose put it, "a little slow." They hoped that, with encouragement and special schooling, she could live a normal life. For a while that seemed possible. At Cape Cod, she crewed a sailboat steered by Bobby and her younger sister Eunice. She traveled to Switzerland unchaperoned at age nineteen with Eunice, and she kept a diary that reflected the active life of a Kennedy. "Went to luncheon in the ballroom in the White House," she wrote in 1937. "James Roosevelt took us in to see his father, President Roosevelt. He said, 'It's about time you came.'" But by the time she was twenty-one, Joe decided his Rosie, who had been at convent boarding schools since she was fifteen, was better off staying there over vacations, too. Within two years even that became problematic. She began experiencing what her mother called "tantrums, or rages, during which she broke things or hit out at people." There were convulsions, too, which may have indicated epilepsy and which Rose said made clear "there were other factors at work besides retardation." She would wander off from school, and her parents worried that something terrible could happen to such an attractive young woman with so limited an IQ.

Joe had been searching for medical remedies since Rosie was a child, trying everything from glandular injections to two years of one-on-one tutoring. In 1941 the "miracle cure" was a lobotomy, an experimental procedure in which doctors removed or destroyed part of the brain's prefrontal lobe as a way of calming distraught patients, often at the price of their personalities. Rosemary was among the first patients with presumed retardation to be lobotomized, and the outcome was calamitous. Her mild mental defect now presented as severe. She lost much of her memory and speech, along with the use of her left arm and hand. "The operation eliminated the violence and the convulsive seizures," Rose wrote in her memoir, "but it also had the effect of leaving Rosemary permanently incapacitated. She lost everything that had been gained during the years by her own gallant efforts and our loving efforts." For most of the next sixty-three years, until her death in 2005, she lived in a ranch-style house that Joe had built on the grounds of the St. Coletta School in rural Wisconsin. A pair of nuns oversaw her round-the-clock care. The remote location kept her out of the reach of prying reporters, and those who asked were told that she "cares for and teaches 'exceptional' children." Few knew she herself was exceptional and, with the family focused on Jack's soaring fortunes, none knew about her failed lobotomy. "The solution of Rosemary's problem has been a major factor in the ability of all the Kennedys to go about their life's work," Joe wrote to a St. Coletta nun in 1958.

Bobby and his younger siblings knew only marginally more than the public did about the fate of their big sister, gleaning what they could from their father's overly upbeat updates. Only Joe visited her, and he stopped going once she got settled at St. Coletta. Everyone in the household had a different way of responding to what Rose called "the first of the tragedies that were to befall us." Joe made mental retardation—and the Wisconsin convent caring for his daughter—the centerpiece of his philanthropy. Rose began going to see Rosemary again after Joe's stroke in 1961, but she never told him. Eunice was the driving force behind the creation of the Special Olympics, and she took Rosemary in as a regular visitor at her home. Jean resumed contact, too, and founded Very Special Arts, an education program for youths with disabilities. While Bobby was less close to Rosemary than his sisters were, he took to heart as much as they did the lessons of her disability and the failed attempt to treat it. He never blamed his father but attacked with special vengeance programs that didn't deliver promised care to the mentally ill and retarded. Having a sister who was the ultimate underdog helped him identify with people who faced bias and bullying.

Not all the lessons that Bobby grew up with were ones of tolerance. There has been an ongoing debate over the last seventy years as to whether or not Joe Kennedy was an anti-Semite. Critics point to his habit of slurring Jews as "sheenies" and "kikes"; defenders say (as if it's a defense) that he was equally unenlightened in calling Italians "wops" and fellow Irish Americans "micks." In 1938 the new German ambassador to London met with Kennedy, who was then the American ambassador, and reported back to Berlin that Joe had said, "It was not so much the fact that we wanted to get rid of the Jews that was so harmful to us, but rather the loud clamor with which we accompanied this purpose. He himself understood our Jewish policy completely." Kennedy insisted that account was distorted and pointed to his record of pushing Britain to open its colonies to Jews fleeing Hitler's Germany, which had prompted the Arab National League of Boston to brand him a "Zionist Charlie

McCarthy." Joe said his dislike of Jews was not categorical but individual, but the truth was just the opposite: Although he had Jewish friends, and liked to boast that he was "the only Christian member" of a Jewish country club in Palm Beach, his letters and diaries made clear that he stigmatized Jews as vindictive, ambitious, and self-pitying.

Joe was always looking for someone to blame for his failed tenure as ambassador. His favorite culprits were President Roosevelt's Jewish advisers, as he suggested in this diary entry from 1941: "The four men who followed me to Europe: *Hopkins* had a Jew wife and 2 Jew children. *Harriman* a Jew wife. *Cohen* a Jew. *Fahey*—lawyer—a Jew mother."* In an unpublished interview in 1944 with a Boston journalist, Joe explained that "whenever I have been asked for a statement condemning anti-Semitism, I have answered: 'What good would it do?' If the Jews themselves would pay less attention to advertising their racial problem, and more attention to solving it, the whole thing would recede into its proper perspective. It's entirely out of focus now, and that is chiefly their fault." A year later, just after FDR died, Joe wrote in a long letter to his daughter Kathleen: "The Jews are crying that they've lost their greatest friend and benefactor. It's again a clear indication of the serious mistake that the Jews had [made] in spite of their marvelous organizing capacity." He sent someone—who it was is unclear—a copy of that letter with a note at the top reading, "Please destroy this after you've read it."

The most disturbing evidence of anti-Semitism comes from an exchange of letters in 1934 between Joe and Joe Jr., who was just back from Hitler's recently installed Third Reich. The younger Kennedy expressed regret at the Nazis' scapegoating of Jews, but quickly added that "this dislike of the Jews, however was well founded. They were at the heads of all big business, in law etc. It is all to their credit for them to get so far, but their methods had been quite unscrupulous. . . . It is extremely sad, that noted professors, scientists, artists etc. so should have to suffer, but as you can see, it would be practically impossible to throw out only a part of them." The Nazis' brutality, he added, "was a horrible thing, but in every

---

* Harry Hopkins was in charge of the Lend-Lease program, Benjamin Cohen co-crafted the Lend-Lease legislation, and Averell Harriman helped coordinate that plan and other U.S. war efforts. Charles Harold Fahey was assistant solicitor general.

revolution you have to expect some bloodshed." He sounded just like his father, which was his intention. Joe responded that he "was very pleased and gratified at your observations of the German situation."*

There is no evidence that Bobby shared those feelings, but neither he nor Jack could escape the whispers that they, too, had been influenced by their father's hostility toward Jews. At times Bobby's disdain for the liberal establishment, and for *The New York Times*, seemed to grow out of his belief that both were dominated by Jews. Why, he wondered, were they so quick to denounce anti-Semitism and so untroubled by anti-Catholicism? (He loved the political philosopher Peter Viereck's musing that "anti-Catholicism is the anti-Semitism of the intellectuals," and he joked that the *Times*'s ideal headline would be MORE NUNS LEAVE CHURCH.) But there also were signs that Bobby admired the Jews as a people. In college he went out on a limb to attack the Jew-bashing demagogue Father Leonard Feeney. In a series of stories from the Middle East that he wrote for *The Boston Post* in 1948, he gushed about the "immensely proud and determined" Jewish race and called the new State of Israel "a truly great modern example of the birth of a nation with the primary ingredients of dignity and self-respect." With Jews as with blacks, Bobby was a work in progress. He started from a place of little interaction or understanding, but he came to identify with their collective suffering and to earn their trust.

That can't be said for his feelings about homosexuals. His bias was evident to gays, whether or not he got along with them as individuals. A two-minute confrontation with Gore Vidal at the White House in 1961 would be recounted so often, with such embellishment, that it spawned a lawsuit for libel, a settlement in which the libeler admitted he had lied, and a christening by the acerbic novelist as "the intervention." Vidal was kneeling next to Jackie Kennedy, whose stepfather had married his mother. "I started to stand. To steady myself, I put my hand on her shoul-

---

* While Joe acknowledged that "it is still possible that Hitler went far beyond his necessary requirements in his attitude towards the Jews," it was his fellow Catholics that Kennedy was most worried about. "If [Hitler] wanted to re-unite Germany, and picked the Jew as the focal point of his attack, and conditions in Germany are now so completely those of his own making, why then is it necessary to turn the front of his attack on the Catholics?" (Kennedy and Smith, *Hostage to Fortune*, 133).

der," Vidal recounted. "A hand pulled my hand off her shoulder. I looked up. There was Bobby. . . . I said something like, 'What the fuck do you think you're doing?' . . . Bobby looked startled: 'What's wrong, buddy boy?'" Vidal, who believed all humans are bisexual, was convinced that his "same-sex sex" was off-putting to Bobby.

Truman Capote, another gay writer and public intellectual, had the same sense. "I always felt that [Bobby] was asking himself, 'Well, what is this all about?'" Capote shared an apartment building in New York with Bobby and the two would have drinks together, or chat when they walked their dogs. But Capote was sure "there was something exotic about me that he couldn't entirely accept." In later years, when he was a senator, Bobby worked on a book with "a copy editor who was a drunken homosexual"—and he "absolutely could not deal with this," recalled Peter Edelman, his aide and friend. "The Kennedys are male chauvinists and Robert Kennedy could not understand why anybody would want to be a homosexual, and it made him extremely uncomfortable."

Bobby was ahead of the tolerance curve in so many areas that it was surprising how conservative he was, especially in his younger years, in other realms of propriety and morality as taught by his church and family. All the Kennedy men publicly shied away from anything perceived as womanly and proudly asserted their machismo on the athletic field and everywhere else. Trying to explain JFK's dislike of Adlai Stevenson, Bobby said it was because he "acted like a girl, looked like a girl, complained like a girl, cried like a girl, moaned, groaned, whined like a girl." Later, when LBJ was president, he told Bobby that FBI director Hoover had told him you could tell a homosexual by the way he walked. "What does that mean, that you'll watch the cabinet carefully as they walk into the cabinet meeting?" Bobby asked. He added, "Well, one thing I can assure you of, Mr. President, it isn't me."*

If the Kennedy boys were held to a clear standard when it came to gender roles, so were the girls. They benefited from Joe's trust funds like

---

* It was a sign of the bigoted times that Hoover, who himself was sexually closeted, would be telling homophobic jokes to the president and spreading raw gossip about people's alleged homosexuality, including the Kennedy brothers'.

their brothers, but they were subject to tighter restrictions that presumed they would be taken care of by their husbands. Joe encouraged his daughters to give back to society, as he had the boys, but he presumed their primary role would be minding their families, as Rose's had been. "I think women should stay at home and raise children," Bobby once half-joked to his colleague Nicholas Katzenbach when they were discussing a presidential statement on equal rights for women.

There were different assumptions, too, about extramarital relationships. Joe's sons had free rein, while his daughters had to hew to a far more puritanical standard and to atone if they transgressed. When Bobby's sister Jean reportedly was romantically involved with the lyricist Alan Jay Lerner,* a man Lerner was convinced was Bobby telephoned to warn him off. The threat—"we'll fix your gondola"—scared Lerner, and he and Jean eventually broke it off, according to Lerner's assistant. It was just the sort of sexual policing that might have benefited the country as well as the family if Bobby had done it with Jack.

And while civil rights wasn't much discussed in Joe and Rose's household when the children were young, the patriarch let slip his attitude in sideways comments like one in his diary referring to black Pullman porters as "nigger porters." He also was averse to interracial marriages, including Sammy Davis, Jr.'s. That sensitivity was shared not just by many whites and blacks of the day, but by President Kennedy, who refused to be photographed with Davis and his white wife at a Lincoln's birthday celebration at the White House in 1963. Bobby hinted at a similar intolerance after his meeting, three months later, with Lena Horne and other friends of James Baldwin who were married to whites. But he showed how much he had changed several years later, when Peter Edelman, who is white, said he planned to marry Marian Wright, who is black. Not only had Bobby encouraged the romance, but when Peter mentioned some flak he was getting, Bobby understood immediately and said to his young aide, "'Let me just tell you, the first time somebody in my family married

---

* Lerner had other connections to the family: He was Jack's boyhood pal at Choate and Harvard, and he wrote the lyrics to "Camelot," which would become a metaphor for the Kennedy administration.

somebody who wasn't Irish, it was just terrible. And then somebody married someone who wasn't Catholic, and that was just terrible again.' And [Bobby] said, 'You know what? It all worked out.' "

———————

THE RIOTS IN Montgomery and Oxford had stirred a small voice within Bobby that would amplify over the second half of his tenure as attorney general. He offered a hint of that evolution in his first public speech after Ole Miss. Civil rights had always been one of too many domestic issues competing for his attention, but now he was beginning to see it in a different context. "James Meredith," he told his audience that October 1962 evening in Milwaukee, "brought to a head and lent his name to another chapter in the mightiest internal struggle of our time."

The next chapter in that struggle played out back in Alabama, at the state university's main campus in Tuscaloosa. The new governor, George Wallace, had made two seminal vows on his long road to election. First, back in 1958, when he ran as a racial moderate and was beaten by the tougher-talking John Patterson, he promised, "I'll never be out-niggered again."* Second, he vowed in the heat of his successful 1962 campaign that he would block with his own body the door to any segregated schoolhouse that was ordered to enroll black students. Lest anyone still doubt his intent, he made himself even clearer in his inaugural address. Noting that he was standing on the sacred ground where Jefferson Davis had been sworn in as president of the Confederate States of America, Wallace paraphrased a secret KKK pledge: "I draw the line in the dust and toss the gauntlet before the feet of tyranny, and I say segregation now, segregation tomorrow, and segregation forever."

The way to fulfill all three promises, Wallace decided, was to go head-to-head with Bobby Kennedy over a federal judge's order to admit two black students—Vivian Malone and James Hood—to the university's summer session in 1963. Wallace's neighbor Ross Barnett had done that

———

* There is an ongoing debate over whether Wallace said "out-segged" or "out-niggered." Wallace defenders insist it was the former, but others who heard him have no doubt he used the more offensive wording. (Berger, "George C. Wallace," *Anniston Star*; Trammel, *George Wallace*, 5; and author interview with Edwin Bridges of the Alabama Department of Archives.)

in Mississippi and seen his poll numbers soar. But the Alabama governor underestimated Bobby's capacity to learn from his mistakes in Oxford. Before the court in Alabama even issued its opinion, Bobby traveled there to demonstrate his interest and take the measure of his adversary. Greeting him at the state capitol were forty riot-trained state troopers—Confederate flags were painted on their helmets, while a real Navy Jack had been hoisted above the building—one of whom poked Bobby in the stomach with his stick, while another refused to shake his hand. The governor, the attorney general said, was using his lawmen to make a point: "that my life was in danger in coming to Alabama because people hated me so much." Bobby took away a different message: that Wallace was "acting like a raving maniac" because he was "scared" by a judge's threat to toss him in jail if he blocked the students' enrollment. That impression was reinforced when Kennedy and Wallace met face-to-face in a session that lasted an hour and twenty minutes and, with the governor taping it, was aimed at trapping Bobby into saying something shocking and letting Wallace play to public opinion. Typical was this exchange:

Kennedy: Do you think it is so horrifying to have a Negro attend the University of Alabama?

Wallace: I think it is horrifying for the federal courts and the central government to rewrite all the law and force upon people that which they don't want.

Kennedy: But Governor, it is not the central government. We are not rewriting the laws. It is the federal courts that have made a decision, and a determination—

Wallace: The federal courts rewrote the law in the matter of integration and segregation. For a hundred years they said we could have segregated schools, and then all of a sudden, for political reasons, they pull the rug out from under us. . . . I will never myself submit voluntarily to any integration in a school system in Alabama.

Bobby's trip to the Heart of Dixie convinced him to plan for the worst at the university even as he calculated ways to exploit Wallace's various soft spots. He prepared to federalize the Alabama National Guard and had real federal troops standing by at nearby Fort Benning. State business leaders, meanwhile, had been shocked out of their instinctive support for the ways of the Old South by the white mob's savage reaction to the Freedom Riders in Montgomery and by withering pressure from the White House; they let Wallace know that the only acceptable outcome was a peaceful one. The University of Alabama president also quietly conspired with federal officials, determined to keep his campus from becoming a riot-torn replica of Ole Miss. In charge on the scene was the Justice Department's Katzenbach, who this time had orders to avoid any face-off that would make Wallace into a hero and, if possible, "to make him look foolish." The table and floor in Bobby's office in Washington were covered with maps of Tuscaloosa, letting him not just monitor the action but pilot it.

D-Day in Tuscaloosa fell on June 11, but instead of an invasion, Bobby ran an end run. He had been tipped off about something few in Alabama were aware of then: that four years before, then Circuit Court judge George Wallace had worked out a "secret deal" in the "darkest hours of the night" with federal judge Frank Johnson to turn over voter registration records even as he publicly proclaimed he wouldn't. Knowing about that and other historic backtracking, Bobby gambled that Wallace would give a repeat performance now. The attorney general let the governor make his theatrical stand in the schoolhouse door. White crayons marked where Wallace should stand, TV and radio crews had been pre-positioned, and the diminutive governor raised his hand in the universal symbol of the traffic cop as he denounced the federal interference. The only people he was blocking, however, were Katzenbach and two law enforcement colleagues, with Malone and Hood a safe distance away. The National Guard was mobilized but saw no combat. The two students checked in to their dormitories and quietly registered that afternoon. Wallace's performance as defender of the South was beamed across the land and stoked his national ambitions, but those on the scene knew his script had been carefully crafted to suggest defiance but deliver acquiescence.

"The show is over. Obviously the Kennedys have won," said Seymore Trammel, Wallace's former finance director and friend. The governor "wanted the fires of integration fanned in order to build the issue to a fever pitch among the emotional voters. We figured there were 30 emotional voters, especially in the South[,] to every 1 objective voter," Trammel recounted in an unpublished memoir. Bobby, too, used the events in Tuscaloosa to present the exact mix of conciliation and persuasion that he needed after his disasters with the Freedom Rides and Ole Miss. "All eyes of integration were on Bobby," said Trammel, who eventually had a bitter break with Wallace. "And all eyes of segregation were focused on Wallace."

That week in June 1963 turned out to be one of the most pivotal in the narrative of the civil rights movement. The same day Malone and Hood made history in Alabama, JFK went on national TV to define racial justice as "a moral issue. It is as old as the scriptures and is as clear as the American Constitution." Rarely had any president captured so concisely and precisely what was at stake. John Kennedy—who wanted his presidency to redefine America's place in the world, not just to remake America's ghettos—had never come close before. He also promised, the next week, to push Congress to pass broad civil rights legislation. As sure as he sounded that night, all of the president's political advisers "except me" opposed his giving the speech or filing his bill, Bobby said, and JFK worried that civil rights could be "his political swan song." The attorney general shared that concern, but at long last he was convinced that "the mightiest internal struggle of our time" justified the risk. Baldwin and the others who'd met with Bobby three weeks earlier at his father's New York apartment now celebrated, having advocated just this sort of national call to arms. Their jubilation, however, was brief. Hours after Americans shut off their television sets, Medgar Evers, the NAACP's field director in Mississippi, was hit in the back by a sniper's bullet that ripped through his heart. His assassination—in his driveway, his arms loaded with T-shirts reading JIM CROW MUST GO—made clear how deep racial hatreds ran and how difficult it would be to enforce a new civil rights law in the unlikely event that Congress approved it. Nobody understood that better than Bobby, who attended Evers's funeral, offered support to his widow, and became the closest of friends with his brother.

The eventful week ended on an upbeat note. Three thousand Negroes and whites marched through Washington peacefully and circled the Jus-

tice Department building with placards asking WHY AN ALMOST LILY
WHITE JUSTICE DEPARTMENT? IT'S NOT EASTER. Administrators closed the
doors but Bobby reopened them, jumped onto a makeshift platform, and
spoke to the crowd through a megaphone. His tone was partly defensive—
talking about the tenfold increase in black lawyers and saying "I'm not
going out and hire a Negro just because he's not white"—but he took the
wind out of the protesters' fury just by showing up, and he drew cheers
for what he'd done in Tuscaloosa and beyond.

Days later Bobby came out swinging over the slow pace of black hiring. The setting was the Committee on Equal Employment Opportunity,
the first federal agency to take "affirmative action" to ensure that Negroes got a fair shot at federal jobs. JFK set up the committee, LBJ chaired
it, and RFK was its perpetual gadfly, grousing that the snail's pace of
government progress in cities like Birmingham undercut White House
calls for private employers to integrate their workplaces. At its June
meeting, Bobby stormed in midway and took over. "He wanted to know
what agencies had how many Negroes, how many vacancies there were,
who had done what to get more jobs. He wanted to know what defense
industries were located in Birmingham, what their employment patterns
were, and what the compliance reports were showing. . . . [He] was beginning to be shrill," recalled Judge Marjorie McKenzie Lawson, a committee member. Then, in the middle of a staffer's reply, "Bob got up
without saying a word to excuse himself, and Burke Marshall got up behind him, [and] they stomped out of the room." No one there that day
doubted Bobby's true target: the vice president he'd never wanted to see
get the job, whose face had turned dark red and voice was nearly inau-
dible. LBJ wouldn't forget.

If the first two years of his civil rights work felt as if he was taking two
steps back for every one forward, as Harry Belafonte complained, now
it was two steps ahead for every one of slippage. August's March on
Washington,* the biggest demonstration ever held in the capital, drew
an estimated quarter million people to press not just for liberty but for
employment, which even more than the vote was now seen as the gateway to racial justice. A. Philip Randolph, grandfather of the civil rights

* What was first conceived as a March for Jobs was expanded to Jobs *and* Freedom.

movement, had been imagining a show of strength like this since the New Deal. Now the country was finally ready. But Bobby, while committed to jobs and justice, feared it could prove catastrophic to bring hundreds of thousands of Negroes to Washington just as the administration was building a case for its civil rights bill. What if the Communists, who had been trying for years to attach themselves to the civil rights movement, co-opted the march? What if the peaceful protest that Randolph dreamed of turned violent? What if, as President Kennedy worried, members of Congress said, "Yes, I'm for the bill, but I am damned if I will vote for it at the point of a gun"?

If they weren't able to stop the march—and Bobby knew that if they tried, it would look as if he and Jack didn't support its goals—the attorney general was determined to control it. He couldn't do that publicly, in case it turned into a disaster, and he couldn't even work backstage with the organizers, for fear Bayard Rustin and the others would think he was trying to supplant them. But for a full five weeks, five of Bobby's trusted assistants at Justice had their hands in everything essential to the rally's success. They started by making a list of all that could go wrong, including a planned protest by the Nazi Party getting out of hand. (The Nazi demonstration was moved to 7 A.M. at a safe location, and law enforcement authorities singled out seventy-five or so suspected subversives and assigned an undercover agent to each of them.) They persuaded concessionaires to open even in the face of a potential riot, because the marchers had to be fed. (Records were set for sales of hot dogs and Cokes.) Bobby's aides educated the D.C. police about the public relations risk of using their twenty-seven dogs to control a crowd to whom dogs like those symbolized police oppression. (Marchers, pouring through the Baltimore tunnel that morning at the rate of one hundred buses an hour, policed themselves in a way that set a model for crowd control.) They persuaded the owners of bars and liquor stores to close, and they let marchers know they were welcome for the day but shouldn't spend the night. (The Department of Justice said it was a matter of logistics; organizers knew better.) At the last instant, John Lewis, a student leader and the youngest speaker, agreed to remove from his speech the dig that the Kennedy legislation was "too little, too late" and his threat to lead the next march "through the Heart of Dixie, the way Sherman did"; in return, Washington archbishop Patrick O'Boyle—with behind-the-curtain prodding by Bobby—agreed to deliver the opening invocation he had threatened to withhold. (James Baldwin, deemed too inflammatory, was simply excluded from the roster of speakers.) The Kennedys helped ensure that whites marched, too, to show that the crowd was all-American. They even had a plan for what would happen if a speaker got too incendiary: The Army Signal Corps had installed a cutoff switch that would let the Justice officials—manning a secret outpost at the Washington Monument—activate a turntable queued to play Mahalia Jackson's "He's Got the Whole World in His Hands."

The march came off with no visible hitches and no need to switch on the turntable. Mahalia Jackson instead made her presence felt in person, urging Rev. King to "tell 'em about the dream, Martin," as he set out his vision for a day when "black men and white men . . . join hands and sing in the words of the old Negro spiritual, 'Free at last! Free at last! Thank God Almighty, we are free at last!' " Black activists were joined on the dais by leaders of the Catholic, Protestant, and Jewish faiths, along with Big Labor's Walter Reuther. TV networks set up more cameras than at JFK's inauguration and preempted regular programming, expecting fireworks that, thanks to the meticulous planning, never went off. Seeing so many blacks and whites assemble harmoniously on the National Mall gave hope to a civil rights movement consumed by images of carnage from Montgomery and Oxford. But back at the Justice Department, Bobby and the senior staff watching on TV with him held their breath as King uttered his iconic words. "Oh my God," Katzenbach said, giving voice to everyone's worries. "He'll get that crowd revved up and then we're gonna really have a problem." Burke Marshall later offered this footnote to the history of the celebrated march: "Bayard Rustin and A. Philip Randolph may have taken a good deal of credit, and they should—but the person that organized it, as a matter of fact, was the attorney general."

OPERATING FROM THE shadows was becoming a pattern for Bobby. His brother used him to take on not just the stickiest jobs in government, but those with the highest stakes, facing off against presumptive allies along with unmistakable enemies. Martin Luther King bridged that gap. The attorney general's relations with the Southern preacher had always been stilted. King was lyrical and loquacious, a style as foreign to Kennedy as his literalness and prickliness were to King. Bobby couldn't forgive him for that spring's Children's Crusade in Birmingham, when King summoned high school and college students to the streets, where they were set upon by Bull Connor's high-pressure hoses and snarling police dogs. (Bobby acknowledged that public disgust at such viciousness was the main reason his civil rights bill had a shot, yet he couldn't understand why King had jeopardized those young lives; King felt Bobby should have understood that the youth faced even greater peril from the day-to-day racism they were protesting.) But what really doomed the relationship between Robert F. Kennedy and Martin Luther King, Jr., were the warnings J. Edgar Hoover had been sounding about King since early 1961.

Hoover had learned precisely which buttons to push with Bobby, and he pushed them all in the King affair. Stanley Levison, King's aide and closest white friend, had been a senior operative in the Communist Party in the 1950s, and Hoover insisted that he was still active. The FBI director said the same about another King aide, Jack O'Dell. While Hoover's warnings that King was being influenced by Levison and O'Dell made an impression on an old cold warrior like Bobby, the attorney general's politics had grown more nuanced and he had more pressing worries during the first two years of the administration. By the summer of 1963, however, the Kennedys had put their careers on the line to promote a civil rights bill and they now depended on King, the most popular Negro in America, to help. They took Hoover's alarms seriously enough that even the president tried to warn King away, during a walk in the Rose Garden. Couldn't he see the risk posed by his leftist friends, not just to the cause, but to the White House? King said he did, but he also saw Hoover using outdated information to manipulate the Kennedys. The civil rights leader disdained his white allies' assumption that he could be outfoxed either by them or by supposed Communists. Hoover proposed breaking the standoff by installing wiretaps that would reveal in their own voices the civil rights leaders' true ambitions.

Bobby authorized the FBI to listen in on Levison's office phone in

March 1962, and eight months later he added the home phone to the warrant. But Hoover wanted more. He already had King on his roster of dangerous people to be rounded up during a national emergency. He leaked incriminating information on O'Dell to the press that fall, and King eventually severed his tie with O'Dell. In July 1963 Bobby added to the wiretap list King's lawyer, who was an intermediary with Levison, and he requested the permission form for King, too, but hesitated about signing it. It wasn't that he objected to wiretapping, which he saw as a necessary tool of law enforcement. And, by God, he had to know whether he could trust King. Governor Barnett already was alleging that Bobby and his brother were part of a "world Communist conspiracy to divide and conquer" America by fomenting racial strife, and he couldn't afford the chance that a critical ally like King was conspiring with Marxists. But if saying no to Hoover was dicey, saying yes could be even more perilous. Whatever the wiretap revealed, the FBI director could use the mere fact of its existence to undermine the Kennedys' standing with liberals, who abhorred such invasions of privacy, and with blacks, who a recent poll showed were backing JFK by an unheard-of thirty-to-one margin over any Republican opponent. This green light to snoop was just the sort of ammunition that Hoover relished, and long after Jack was gone, he would exploit it to the full against Bobby.

In October, just two months after the March on Washington, Kennedy gave Hoover what he wanted. First, he approved the phone taps at King's home and office in New York, then on his Atlanta office line. All were subject to reevaluation in thirty days but none was stopped. All were justified as vital to national security, which stretched credulity, not to mention the law. All were supplemented by electronic bugging of hotel rooms and other venues, which the FBI and local police undertook without Bobby's approval. No evidence was unearthed of any ongoing relationship between Levison and the Communists, or of any attempt to subvert King or his movement. The surveillance did unearth embarrassing information on King's extramarital sex life that Bobby tried to retrieve but couldn't. The FBI, it was clear in hindsight, had been asking the wrong question—what mattered most was not whether King was anticommunist, but that he was antiviolence, which it didn't take secret recordings to reveal. Most of all, the taps reinforced a lesson Bobby already knew: that rather than enabling Hoover, he and Jack should have replaced the FBI director early in the administration, when he had less dirt on them and everyone in their orbit.*

Any regrets about how he'd treated King added to Bobby's determination to press ahead on the civil rights bill. The legislation would open to blacks all lunch counters, hotels, movie theaters, and other public accommodations. It would ease the way for them to vote in national elections and for the attorney general to sue for integrated schools. Two and a half years into the administration, it would make good on most of the Kennedy rhetoric from the 1960 campaign, although not on the job protections that Bobby knew were vital. But first, the bill had to win approval from a skeptical Congress, and nobody worked harder on that than the president's brother. Other big initiatives that he and the White House cared about were put on hold for months. Bobby bartered with Southern Democrats who wanted no part of the changes and with northern ones who wanted more than he believed southerners would accept. He made allies of top Republicans in the House and Senate and absorbed accusations from civil rights allies that he was selling them out. Frustrated by the shellacking he was taking, he told reporters, "What I want is a bill, not an issue." He held meeting after meeting with national organizations of chain store owners, clergy, college presidents, lawyers, and others the administration thought could help. He made nine exhausting appearances before the Senate Judiciary Committee alone, leading Ethel to tease one senator who was particularly tough on her husband, "What have you been doing to Bobby? He came home and went straight to bed."

Bobby knew that this bill—more than anything he did in Mississippi, Alabama, or anywhere else—would define the administration's legacy on civil rights. Much as conflict was his natural state, he was tired of managing crises. He was as much a dreamer as he was a realist, and here was a chance not just to imagine a brighter future but to bring it into being. He hadn't lost his determination to take down the Mob and Jimmy Hoffa, but nothing consumed and inspired him more now than civil

---

* Bobby and Jack almost surely would have fired Hoover at the start of a second Kennedy administration. Knowing that, Hoover used all his wiles to gather material on the brothers that he could use to control them and his own fate.

rights. To Jack, racial justice was an abstract ideal. To Bobby, it was about the real lives of flesh-and-blood people. He was his brother's superego as well as his alter ego, the way Eleanor Roosevelt had been for Franklin. "These are moral issues, not legal ones. . . . The stifling air of prejudice is not fit to be breathed by the people of a nation that takes pride in calling itself free," he told his audience at Philadelphia's Independence Hall in June. "This is a national crisis, and it is immediate." In July, testifying before the Senate, Bobby posed a question that echoed the one the young activist Jerome Smith had asked him two months before in James Baldwin's drawing room powwow: "How can we say, to a Negro in Jackson: 'When a war comes you will be an American citizen, but in the meantime you're a citizen of Mississippi and we can't help you'?"

Being on the warpath the way Bobby was, he naturally made enemies. There were constant reminders that segregationists blamed him, more than they did the president, for the assault on their color-coded way of life. In Anniston, Alabama, Bobby was hanged in effigy alongside three FBI agents and a civil rights leader, with his dummy bearing the moniker "Robert Bobby Sox Kennedy." In Birmingham, the outgoing mayor said of the attorney general, "I hope that every drop of blood that's spilled he tastes in his throat, and I hope he chokes on it." And in tiny Winona, Mississippi, policemen cursed Bobby's name aloud as they beat a civil rights worker until her head was bloody, her tooth chipped, and her eye knocked out of alignment. A person, Bobby would tell his oldest daughter Kathleen, could be judged by the enemies he made. Still, he was baffled by the intensity of the hatred his foes felt toward him.

By the end of his tenure, Bobby Kennedy had become the kind of attorney general that the Baldwin group had urged him to be, and that Martin Luther King had had faith he would become. The ideologue in him was yielding more to the idealist. Asked to chart Bobby's growing awareness on civil rights, Burke Marshall shot his right arm sky-high. "The more he saw," said Marshall, "the more he understood." King recognized that potential sooner than most, and patiently endured the slow way in which Bobby's growth was stoked by the furnace of experience. No matter that Bobby was neither as patient nor as trusting with King, and had never even sat down with him one-on-one. "Somewhere in this man sits good," the preacher told his lieutenants early on. "Our task is to find his moral center and win him to our cause." But neither Marshall nor King had suffered the way Jack O'Dell did from Bobby's shortsightedness, which made the civil rights soldier pay for his past flirtations with Communism by derailing his career as a King confidant. Fifty years later, O'Dell has forgiven Bobby for all of that: "I saw him mature to something different. We are all human and we all start somewhere."

Chapter 6

CUBA AND BEYOND

THIRTEEN DAYS, BOBBY Kennedy's memoir of the Cuban missile crisis, is the inside story of the most nerve-shattering two weeks in human history. It tells how the Soviet Union, spinning "one gigantic fabric of lies," smuggled half of its entire stockpile of ballistic missiles onto our island enemy a mere ninety miles south of Florida. It recaptures the dread our nation felt in realizing that "within a few minutes of their being fired eighty million Americans would be dead." It reminds us that in the final days of October 1962, the world abruptly found itself poised at a crossroads where Armageddon seemed not just possible, but likely.

Fortunately, America's most lionhearted men took charge. Deliberating around an egg-shaped table in the president's cabinet room, with George Washington peering down from his picture frame, steely-eyed peacemakers outargued and outvoted fire-breathing generals. There would be no bombing raids on the missiles and no invasion of the Communist archipelago. We would begin with a naval blockade, keeping out new weapons and demanding the withdrawal of those already there. But would the Soviet vessels steaming toward our armada of warships reverse course? "We're eyeball to eyeball, and I think the other fellow just blinked," Secretary of State Dean Rusk declared when the blockade held and the Soviets acquiesced to U.S. demands. So riveting was the tale Bobby told, and so artful was his narration, that it became the basis not just for the acclaimed docudrama *Missiles of October,* but for how a generation of Americans understood its scariest moment. A generation of Russians, too.

His story, however, is laced with fictions. As with much of Bobby's public take on history, *Thirteen Days* is a fundamentally self-serving account that casts him as the champion dove he would like to have been, rather than the unrelenting hawk he actually was through much of those two weeks. To reinforce that scenario, he mischaracterized many of his fellow deliberators and concealed the fact that U.S. leaders had ignored repeated warnings about the Russian missile buildup. It was the kind of embellishment and misdirection that might be excused if the consequences hadn't unsettled America's foreign policy for years to come. It also was the sort of skillful myth building that Bobby had learned from mentors like Joe Kennedy and Joe McCarthy.

The biggest deceit in Bobby's narrative of the missile crisis is his failure to level with readers about how we got into it. The actual confrontation wasn't a story of the devious Russians acting out of the blue and guileless Americans responding with what Bobby called "shocked incredulity." The buildup was a predictable response to American aggression. In April 1961, just three months after President Kennedy's inauguration, we had armed, trained, and bankrolled an army of émigrés who tried to reclaim Cuba by staging an invasion at a swampy inlet on its southern coast known as Bahía de Cochinos, or the Bay of Pigs. When that failed, Bobby personally steered a campaign to sabotage Cuban agriculture, incite political upheaval, and chart new schemes for invading the island and deposing its leaders. The myopic attorney general failed to consider how his plotting would be perceived in Havana and Moscow. Cuban prime minister Fidel Castro logically concluded that the United States was hell-bent on eliminating his regime.* It was foreseeable that his primary protector, Soviet premier Nikita Khrushchev, would come to his aid, especially when doing so would underscore Soviet resolve in other Cold War hot spots like Berlin and Laos. "We had to think up some way of confronting America with more than words. . . . The logical answer was missiles," Khrushchev wrote in a memoir spirited to the West

---

* Former defense secretary Robert McNamara would concede the point at a conference in Havana in 1992 attended by Castro as well as his former Soviet allies and American foes. Based on the Bay of Pigs attack, U.S.-backed covert operations, and the bellicose anti-Castro voices in Washington, the former defense secretary said, "If I had been a Cuban leader, I think I might have expected a U.S. invasion" (Blanton, "Cuban Missile Crisis Isn't What It Used to Be," *Cold War International History Project Bulletin*).

for publication in 1970. "The installation of our missiles in Cuba would, I thought, restrain the United States from precipitous military action against Castro's government." It worked. America should have understood that sort of gambit, since we had signed similar mutual defense pacts—backed up by nuclear weapons—with our allies in Europe.

While the Cuban missile crisis wasn't Bobby's shining moment, as his book suggested, it did transform him. He hadn't yet shed his cold-warrior instincts, but spending thirteen days on the brink of extinction sobered him forever. He proved so adept at appropriating other men's wise ideas that it barely mattered how few were his own. He learned as he went, as he had in Montgomery and Oxford, with the same growing pains. His foreign policy portfolio, which was there from the beginning of the administration, swelled in a way not seen before or since in the office of the attorney general.

The change that mattered most, yet was least noticed at the time, was how those two weeks in October helped Bobby become his own man even as he continued serving as his brother's adjutant. That process of separation and self-realization had started with his father's stroke ten months earlier and would accelerate with the death of his brother fourteen months later. "Exposure to danger strips away the protective covering with which each of us guards his inner thoughts—it quickly and dramatically displays a man's character," Robert McNamara, the secretary of defense back then, wrote in an introduction to Bobby's book. The missile crisis had precisely that effect on the attorney general. He perceived more clearly than ever the essential parts he played for Jack—as sounding board and stand-in, guardian and conscience—and imagined in a way he never had before one more role for himself: successor.

————

THE SEEDS OF the missile crisis were planted three Octobers earlier, before the Kennedy brothers even announced Jack's bid for the White House and before they or anyone else had heard of the Bay of Pigs. President Eisenhower was growing increasingly anguished about developments in Cuba, where Fidel Castro and his guerrilla bands had deposed the president-turned-dictator Fulgencio Batista on New Year's Day in 1959. At first the U.S. administration wanted to believe that Castro would be a democrat and a capitalist, and he fostered those beliefs, but both knew it wasn't to be. Batista had mortgaged his country to American mining firms, utilities, agribusiness, and mafiosi who had remade it into what a Harvard professor rightly called "the whorehouse of the Western Hemisphere." Castro's revolution was more concerned with reclaiming Cuba's culture and redistributing its wealth than with open elections or free speech, and he realized early on that he would find more support for that in Moscow than in Washington. In October, Eisenhower signed off on a State Department proposal to quietly back Castro's homegrown opposition. By the end of March 1960, the president had given the green light to a Central Intelligence Agency plan to train and equip a paramilitary force of exiles that would be deployed to the island nation to recruit an army of resistance. Secrecy was paramount, insisted Ike, who knew how to run a war: "Our hand should not show in anything that is done."

Eisenhower's anxiety about Cuba was political as well as strategic. As worried as he was about protecting American multinationals and keeping the Russians from gaining a foothold, he was at least as concerned about the Democrats. When the Republic of China was remade into the People's Republic while Democrats occupied the White House, Republicans demanded to know "Who lost China?" Now, Ike knew, toughminded Democrats like the Kennedys would ask the same about Cuba. Jack proved him right early in that fall's campaign, attacking the incumbent administration for letting "a Communist menace . . . arise under our very noses, only ninety miles from our shore."

While it was fair for the Kennedys to ask why President Eisenhower and Vice President Nixon hadn't pushed their friend Batista to redress the complaints of the Cuban people, Jack and Bobby knew full well—from official CIA briefings and unofficial leaks—that the administration was trying to unseat Castro. But smart politics dictated that the Democrats make it seem that the Republicans had no such plans, and the need for secrecy kept Nixon from saying otherwise. "If you can't stand up to Castro, how can you be expected to stand up to Khrushchev?" Kennedy asked of his Republican opponent in an October speech. Days later he ratcheted up the rhetoric, charging that "these [anti-Castro] fighters for freedom have had virtually no support from our government."

Their hard line helped the Kennedy brothers win the White House, but it boxed them in once they got there. They knew they had to do something, and a force of Cuban expatriates already was being trained in Guatemala courtesy of the previous administration. JFK got his first full briefing on the scheme just eight days after taking office, with regular updates thereafter. The new president was determined to act, both because he believed Cuba needed rescuing and because he'd publicly promised he would. All of which made him ignore the red flags raised by his civilian aides and even some military men. For one thing, the well-meaning army of refugees—aristocrats and chauffeurs, students and soldiers, disillusioned Castro allies and Catholics who deplored his suppression of the Church—was too ragtag and out of touch to prevail on the battlefield or in the struggle for Cuban hearts and minds. The only way to win was with more planes, beach craft, and troops than JFK was willing to commit, and with more realistic contingency plans than the rose-colored ones drawn up by the trigger-happy CIA. There was no way to keep the U.S. role secret, with *The New York Times* speculating about it and Castro anticipating it. As for the Cuban strongman, he was more entrenched militarily—and more popular—than the exiles or the CIA would admit. Even Vice President Nixon had recognized Castro's appeal when the two met in Washington back in 1959, telling Eisenhower that the new Cuban prime minister "has those indefinable qualities which make him a leader of men." White House aide Arthur Schlesinger laid out all the reasons for caution in a memo to President Kennedy on April 5, 1961, warning that JFK would be branded the aggressor if he went ahead with the invasion and worrying that "Cuba will become our Hungary."*

President Kennedy read the situation differently, telling Bobby that "I'd rather be an aggressor than a bum." And so it was that at dawn on April 15, eight B-26 bombers from the anti-Castro Cuban Expeditionary Force took off from a friendly airfield in Nicaragua under orders to disable Castro's air force before the ground invasion got under way two days later. That was half the number of attacking aircraft that was originally planned, and they missed most of their targets. The media pub-

---

* The Soviets crushed the Hungarian uprising of 1956, fortifying their control over the East Bloc but alienating Marxists across the world.

lished pictures of the thinly disguised planes, which were obsolete CIA-supplied B-26s painted to look like Cuban Air Force jets, and an embarrassed President Kennedy canceled the second and third air strikes. The invaders, fourteen hundred CIA-trained exiles that Castro called *gusanos*, or worms, were doomed the moment they came ashore at the Bay of Pigs shortly after midnight on April 17. Not only were they strafed by the real Cuban Air Force and pursued by twenty thousand ground troops, but the anticipated popular uprising never materialized. By the time JFK sent in six unmarked fighter planes to provide air cover, it was too late and too little. Nearly twelve hundred of the attackers surrendered, more than a hundred were killed, and the rest got away by boat. The Cuban émigré community blamed the Kennedys for failing to back up the invaders even as much of the world condemned them for underwriting the assault on a sovereign nation. Not even the skeptics had dreamed things could go this badly.

The first eighty-five days of the Kennedy administration had been a cakewalk for the young and handsome president. He and his brain trust promised not just new faces but can-do thinking that reminded many of the breathless early days of Franklin Roosevelt's New Deal. In the wake of the Bay of Pigs, however, John Kennedy seemed more green than fresh, and perhaps in over his head. Cuba was the Kennedys' problem now, and they'd made a mess of their first bid to intervene. Nobody had to remind JFK of all he'd done wrong or that the buck stopped with him. "There's an old saying that victory has a hundred fathers and defeat is an orphan," the president said at a press conference on April 21. What matters, he added, is "I am the responsible officer of the government."

As for Bobby, he had played little part in planning or executing the Bay of Pigs raid. The CIA briefed the attorney general days before the assault, and as it started going sour, Jack called him in Williamsburg, Virginia, where Bobby was giving a speech to journalists. "Why don't you come on back," the president said, "and let's discuss it." RFK remained at JFK's side as things played out during those tense days in the spring of 1961. He assured his brother he was doing the right thing ("there really wasn't any alternative"), vacillated along with everyone else over whether to approve the CIA's request for air cover for the invaders ("we didn't really have enough information to know"), and could be heard muttering to himself as it became clearer that things were going very wrong ("we've got to do something, we've got to do something"). Edwin Guthman, Bobby's press aide, ran into him the afternoon of the April 17 landing and asked whether there was anything he could do. "Well, there's one thing you can do," Bobby said. "You can start praying for those poor fellows on the beach." He was more explicit when he encountered Senator Smathers the next evening at the White House congressional reception: "The shit has hit the fan. The thing has turned sour in a way you wouldn't believe!"

Immediately after the invasion, Bobby assigned himself a familiar task: doing whatever was needed to protect his brother's flank. JFK had accepted full blame, but the way Bobby saw it, everyone on the team shared responsibility whether or not they had supported the incursion. That posed a problem for Chester Bowles, the former governor of Connecticut now serving as number two at the State Department. First, he "came up in a rather whiny voice and said that he wanted to make sure that everybody understood that he was against the Bay of Pigs," Bobby recalled. A week or so after the invasion, Bowles presented the National Security Council with a go-slow plan on Cuba that Bobby branded as "worthless." What, he asked Bowles in front of their colleagues, "can we do about Cuba? This doesn't tell us." Bowles agreed the encounter was a travesty, but he pinned the fault on an out-of-control attorney general who was "slamming into anyone who suggested that we go slowly. . . . I left the meeting with a feeling of intense alarm, tempered somewhat with the hope that this represented largely an emotional reaction of a group of people who were not used to setbacks or defeats and whose pride and confidence had been deeply wounded." It wasn't just Bowles. Walt Rostow, another senior JFK adviser, was alarmed by Bobby's combativeness. "If you're in a fight and get knocked off your feet," he advised, "the most dangerous thing to do was to come out swinging. Then you could really get hurt." Bobby, Rostow added, "looked up expressionless. He finally said: 'That's constructive.' "

The Kennedys' pride had been wounded at the Bay of Pigs, and they were determined to find out what had gone wrong and ensure the mistakes weren't repeated. Bobby started referring to his brother as "the President before Cuba and after Cuba," saying he now was "a different man." JFK named a four-member investigatory panel chaired by retired General Maxwell Taylor, with Bobby second in charge and acting as pseudo-prosecutor. Their Cuba Study Group interrogated close to fifty witnesses over a six-week stretch in the spring of 1961, piecing together for the first time a more complete story of an invasion plot that had been deliberately compartmentalized to maximize secrecy. "Never would have tried this operation if knew that Cuba forces were as good as they were and would fight," Bobby noted in longhand. "Political limitation on military activity. This should be known and understood by those who are planning project. If impossible to succeed with these limitations project should be canceled . . . 19 requests for help from guerrillas which were not satisfied because of lack of planes . . . Amazing that [Joint Chiefs of Staff] approved plan with no air strikes prior to D day." To Bobby, that lack of planning and follow-through was a personal affront.

Taylor worried that the panel would sugarcoat its findings, since its other members represented the very people who had blundered—Bobby, as a proxy for his brother, along with the director of the CIA and the chief of naval operations. Compared to his fellow panelists, however, "Bob was in favor of bearing down harder on the misdeeds committed," Taylor concluded. "There was no question of his wanting to participate in a snow job or a whitewash of any sort." That, the general learned to his delight, wasn't how this unbending attorney general worked. Yet rather than questioning the goals or ethics of the invasion, the committee zeroed in on the narrower questions of flawed tactics and slack bureaucracy, then it encouraged the president to redouble his engagement in the Cold War. "We feel that we are losing today on many fronts," Taylor wrote, "and that the trend can be reversed only by a whole-hearted union of effort by all Executive departments." Bobby agreed, and he told JFK and anyone else who asked "that a good deal of thought has to go into whether you are going to accept the ideas, advice and even the facts that are presented by your subordinates." President Kennedy embraced that advice and never again fully trusted his generals and spies, which proved wise during the Cuban missile crisis. The one aide the president would rely on more than ever, in the most sensitive foreign as well as domestic affairs, was his brother. Jack talked about making Bobby director of the CIA, replacing Eisenhower holdover Allen Dulles. But Bobby, whose Hickory Hill estate was around the corner from the new CIA headquarters, already had a seat at the spy agency's table and "thought it was a bad idea . . . because I was a Democrat, and [JFK's] brother." He ended up adding unofficial job functions that mattered even more, as the president's personal envoy and troubleshooter.

Those weren't easy roles for him to play. Bobby's strong suit was domestic affairs, and the extra workload couldn't have come at a more harried time for him or the country. That spring and summer of 1961 he was consumed by dealing with the Freedom Riders, even as the Justice Department's war on organized crime was going full throttle. In Vienna in June, Jack had his first face-to-face meeting with Khrushchev, and afterward he confided to the *New York Times* columnist James Reston that the older, more battle-tested Soviet leader had "savaged me." Two months later East Germany began installing an eighty-seven-mile barbed-wire fence separating socialist East Berlin from the democratic West—the East called it the Anti-Fascist Protection Rampart, while the West would know it as the Berlin Wall—that constituted an overt challenge to America and its allies. Bobby's six weeks studying the Bay of Pigs established a work pattern that allowed him to juggle his expanded portfolio, and it helped explain why issues like civil rights never became the priority they might have in the early Kennedy administration. He met his fellow invasion panelists early every morning, working out of a special office at CIA headquarters. Then he'd stop by the White House to consult with the president or attend a policy briefing. Late in the afternoon, when other bureaucrats were plotting ways to beat rush hour traffic home, he headed to the Justice Department and stayed until ten, with a lineup of aides briefing him on decisions that had piled up there. He was learning to get by with less sleep. His seven children were learning that when Daddy wasn't home for dinner, it probably meant the country was facing some new crisis.

It might also have meant he was meeting with his curious new friend Georgi Bolshakov, a faintly cloaked Soviet spy posted to the USSR's embassy in Washington as bureau chief for the *Tass* news agency. Theirs was one of the most beguiling relationships of the Cold War. The buttoned-down attorney general and the hail-fellow secret agent got together an average of three times a month for a year and a half, starting in the spring of 1961. They conferred sitting on the lawn near the U.S. Capitol, in the back office at the Justice Department, and at Hickory Hill, where the Russian dazzled the Kennedy children by dancing on his haunches, Cossack-style. The subject of conversation ranged from crises in Berlin and Laos to the upcoming superpower summit in Vienna. Why, agents at the FBI and elsewhere wanted to know, was the president's brother risking these unprecedented cloak-and-dagger encounters with a known Soviet spy? To the Kennedys, however, they were just the thing. What better conduit for messages to be passed between JFK and Khrushchev without the misinterpretation, second-guessing, and risk of leaks of regular diplomatic channels? Who better to do it than Bobby, who wasn't bound by rules of spycraft or diplomacy yet could be trusted with anything? No need to share any confidences with J. Edgar Hoover, or to write anything down. Politics had always been personal for Bobby, no matter that the arena now was the globe. This informal channel of exchange with the Soviets worked brilliantly until the missile crisis in 1962, when Bolshakov either didn't know about Khrushchev's true plans for Cuba or lied about what he did know.*

Bobby, meanwhile, had taken a different message than Jack from the Bay of Pigs rout. To him, the solution was fighting back the way the enemy did, furtively and strategically. He became such a believer in this so-called counterinsurgency that a senior national security aide credited him with coining the term, which Bobby defined as "social reform under pressure." He saw counterinsurgency as embracing everything from land reform to building schools, roads, clinics, labor unions, and an impartial judiciary. He also was convinced that butter like that could only work if it was backed up by guns. To better understand his revolutionary enemies, he plowed through the writings of Mao Zedong and Ho Chi Minh. Green Berets came to Hyannis Port to show rather than just tell the attorney general about their unconventional warfare techniques

---

* Either way, Bobby was heard to say, "That son of a bitch has got to go." Khrushchev got the message and recalled Bolshakov, which was just fine with the new Soviet ambassador, Anatoly Dobrynin, who felt he should be Bobby's channel to Moscow. Before he went, Bolshakov warned Bobby that Dobrynin had been dangerously "undercutting" what Bolshakov was reporting to Moscow—including Bobby's insistence that "the United States would fight under certain circumstances." (Brugioni, *Eyeball to Eyeball*, 178; and RFK Oral History, February 13, 1965, 5, JFKL.)

such as swinging through trees and climbing over barricades. Bobby and Jack were both leery of the American military and intelligence brass, but they believed in military force and espionage as practical tools. The younger brother was determined to make Khrushchev pay for daring to bully America and the Kennedys. He knew that, having blamed Vice President Nixon for the loss of Cuba in 1960, Jack would be blamed in 1964 if his administration didn't do more to take it back. Castro may have won Round 1, but the Kennedys weren't paper tigers, no matter what the Republicans said, and they didn't give up that easily. Paying Castro back would become Bobby's obsession.

———————

THE KENNEDYS' CLANDESTINE war against Castro's Cuba needed a name, and a CIA officer had just the one: Operation Mongoose. It was proposed as a handle without a point, but to the men involved, it conjured up the image of a sleek and agile carnivore out to catch a cobra. Every agency that mattered in Washington had a part to play, but nobody could breathe a word to anyone outside the brotherhood. It officially lasted just a year, from the fall of 1961 to shortly after the missile crisis, although it didn't truly cease operations until the end of the Kennedy administration. On paper, it was overseen by a committee of the president's senior military, intelligence, and foreign policy advisers, with day-to-day control in the hands of Edward Lansdale, a brigadier general who had earned his anticommunist stripes in the jungles of the Philippines and Vietnam.* In practice, Mongoose was Bobby's operation. He left no doubt what he had in mind at a January 1962 meeting of the Operation Mongoose team, according to CIA notes on the session: The "Cuban problem" is "the top priority in the United States Government—all else is secondary—no time, money, effort, or manpower is to be spared."

Bobby got what he asked for. Two weeks after that meeting, the Defense Department started proposing a series of increasingly outlandish

———————

* The Kennedy White House's counterinsurgency bureaucracy was three-headed: Special Group was a committee, chaired by National Security Advisor McGeorge Bundy, that oversaw covert operations. The Special Group (Counter-Insurgency) helped friendly foreign governments resist insurrection. The Special Group (Augmented) focused on Cuba. Bobby was a member of the last two.

schemes for undermining the Caribbean nation. Operation Free Ride would airdrop into Cuba one-way plane tickets on Pan American or KLM to Mexico City, Caracas, and other "free-world" destinations. Operation No Love Lost called for harassing Cuban Air Force pilots by having refugees contact them by radio. "Argument could go, 'I'll get you you Red son-of-a-gun.'" Operation Good Times imagined undermining Castro's domestic support by disseminating fake pictures of him with "two beauties" in a room "lavishly furnished, and a table briming [sic] over with the most delectable Cuban food." The caption would read, "My ration is different." Another U.S. military official offered up an even quirkier scheme. Knowing Cuba's shortage of toilet paper, he wanted to airdrop across the island cases of the white rolls. "To make it an effective psychological impact, my recommendation was to print a picture of Fidel Castro and Nikita Khrushchev on alternate sheets," he recounted. "The idea was accepted and plans were made to carry it out, until President Kennedy put the squash on it."

While most of the bizarre blueprints met that same fate, some were embraced by the CIA, which knew it had a lot to make up for after the Bay of Pigs. It assembled its largest peacetime spy operation ever, with six hundred agents and nearly five thousand contract workers devoted to Mongoose. The agency's relatively modest Miami station became its biggest, with its own polygraph teams, gas station, and warehouse stocked with everything from machine guns to caskets. Every major CIA office worldwide had one or more case officers specializing in Cuba. The agency's secret flotilla of yachts, fishing craft, speedboats, and other vessels—all modified for spying or sabotage, and docked in Florida—qualified as the region's third-largest navy. Agents were recruited on the island and an interrogation center was established in Florida to pry information from Cuban refugees. (The U.S. government maintained a similar operation in West Germany.) Some of what this army of spies did was merely annoying, like pouring untraceable chemicals into lubricating fluids bound for Cuba to make equipment wear out faster. But there were paramilitary missions, too, which got bigger, more frequent, and grizzlier, targeting resources critical to the Cuban economy such as sugar mills and petroleum refineries. In one raid, commandos blew up a railroad bridge and watched a train career off the ruptured rails. In another, a CIA han-

dler joked to Ramon Orozco, a commando recruit, that he'd pay fifty dollars "if you bring me back an ear" of a Cuban. "I brought him two,"
remembered Orozco, "and he laughed and said, 'You're crazy,' but he
paid me $100, and he took us to his house for a turkey dinner."

Bobby pushed ahead like a man possessed. However much the CIA
bosses promised in their efforts to undermine the Cuban leader, this truer
believer wanted more, and he wanted proof that the operations were
more than just smoke and mirrors. "Every time we didn't succeed we got
blasted by Robert Kennedy," said Samuel Halpern, a CIA Mongoose organizer who was convinced the attorney general was beyond his portfolio and out of his depth. "To make Cuba the number-one priority of the
agency, at the expense of everything else; then to put Bobby in charge of
the operation and this—well, this boy, really, this hot-tempered boy—to
try to run it and do the personal bidding of his brother. Unbelievable."
Traditionally the CIA had been the one hatching harebrained schemes,
with civilian administrators restraining the gung-ho agency. Mongoose
reversed those roles. Richard Helms, the agency's chief of clandestine
services, said he tried to explain the difficulties to Bobby but "his consistent response was, 'Yes, Dick, I do understand.' A short pause would follow, and then, 'But let's get the hell on with it. The President wants some
action, right now.'"

And it wasn't just Cuba. Bobby worried about Communism spreading
across Latin America. He recognized sooner than most that long-term
solutions depended on solving underlying social problems, from poverty
so severe that children scavenged at landfills to the inevitable disenfran-
chisement that followed when oligarchs owned the land and monopo-
lized the government. In the short run, however, he put his faith in
strong-arm tactics such as arming the police so they could control rioting leftists and supporting leaders, including dictators, who stood firm
against Communism. In places such as Brazil, Venezuela, and Bolivia,
Bobby saw the dissidents as proxies for Castro. His suspicions were right
sometimes, but not always. The subtly nuanced perspective that would
become a hallmark of his approach to the region when he was a U.S.
senator, and would make him a hero among its poor, hadn't fully developed in the early 1960s. Instead, he was the administration's ramrod
and enforcer. He played those roles with special relish in the Dominican

Republic when, a month after the Bay of Pigs, strongman Rafael Trujillo was assassinated. Bobby saw an opening for the United States to ensure that Trujillo's successors were not just democrats but anti-Castro. With the U.S. president and secretary of state both in Europe, the attorney general stepped in and advocated a limited but direct intervention in the Dominican Republic by U.S. troops. Chester Bowles, his old adversary and now the acting secretary of state, advised that such a move would be illegal and imprudent. Bobby again verbally assaulted Bowles, calling him a "gutless bastard." Bowles got the last word when JFK, reached by telephone in Paris, sided with him, opposing such an intemperate intervention. Told by the president that he was in charge, Bowles replied, "Good. Would you mind explaining it to your brother?"

Bobby's fixation with keeping Communists out of Latin America was understandable in the context of the early 1960s, when America really was engaged in an ongoing undeclared war with the Soviet Union and the stakes seemed to be the very future of both capitalism and democracy. Castro represented not just a Russian toehold in our hemisphere but a launching pad for leftist revolutions as far away as the African Congo. His Get Castro vendetta, however, made Bobby lose sight of broader goals and values just as he had with his Get Hoffa campaign. Operation Mongoose was based on logic as flawed as the Bay of Pigs incursion—that the Cuban population would rally to the anti-Castro cause, and that America's secret army of CIA-trained Cuban exiles could vanquish anybody. Bobby had spent enough time studying the failed invasion to know better. Yet he couldn't see that every botched American bid to topple Castro made the Cuban leader more of a hero for defying the Yanqui imperialista. The attorney general was employing precisely the methods that he had condemned in actions by the Soviet Union: subverting another country's government, underwriting guerrilla armies, and operating under the cloak of darkness rather than in the light of day, where Bobby said democracy did best. Rather than discouraging Moscow from backing Cuba, Mongoose—coming on the heels of the Bay of Pigs and other muscle flexing by the Americans—helped convince Khrushchev he was doing the right thing by installing missiles to defend the island against U.S. aggression.

Operation Mongoose mirrored the Bay of Pigs in one more key aspect:

Both flopped. Instead of learning from the administration's earlier mistakes, Bobby repeated them to the same inglorious end. Mongoose "proved to be a rather futile exercise," says Richard Goodwin, who chaired a White House task force on Cuba and was close to JFK and Bobby. "Castro outwitted us at every stage." Richard Helms reached a similar conclusion, saying that all the planning and scheming "never amounted to more than pinpricks."

The result may have been pinpricks, but the intent was deadly serious, as Helms knew. The only way to bring down the Communist regime, most Mongoose planners agreed, was to eliminate Fidel Castro. The CIA hatched at least eight separate plots to do just that, Senate investigators reported in 1975 as part of a probe of assassinations of foreign leaders. Knowing how much Castro treasured cigars, the agency laced a box of his favorites with a strain of botulism so toxic he would have died hours after he smoked one. The Cuban ruler loved scuba diving, too, so there was a plan to give him a diving suit dusted with fungus that would produce a chronic skin condition and a breathing apparatus dusted with bacteria that would infect him with tuberculosis. U.S. spies also rigged a pen with a hypodermic needle that a high-placed mole in the Cuban government could insert into Castro without his noticing until he keeled over. It was the kind of stuff Ian Fleming, so admired by the Kennedy brothers, invented for his agent 007, James Bond. The CIA went so far as to recruit as assassins the same Mafia kingpins Bobby's Justice Department was trying to put in jail. The Mafia plan was one of the few schemes to get beyond the planning phase, with teams bearing CIA-prepared poison pills dispatched to the island.

The question is, did Bobby Kennedy issue an order to kill Fidel Castro? The investigating senators could say that he was briefed about the Mafia plot, but after the fact and after he thought it was terminated. They couldn't say whether he knew beforehand, but they were left with the same nagging doubt we have all these years later, about this and other of Bobby's darkest secrets: How could he not have known? As Chairman Frank Church and his fellow senators put it, "The Attorney General indicated his displeasure about the lack of consultation on such assassination planning rather than about the impropriety of the attempt itself. There is no evidence that the Attorney General told the CIA that it must not engage in plots like that in the future." A series of CIA officials insist his body language made clear what he wanted even if he never mouthed the words. "With all of the customary Kennedy 'vigor,' and in the most forceful language, Bob informed us that Castro's removal from office and a change in government in Cuba were then the prime foreign policy objectives of the Kennedy administration," wrote Helms. "The repeated blunt references to 'eliminating' Castro brought us once again to the moral aberration of political assassination in peacetime."* Others are equally convinced that a man with Bobby's religious conviction and moral clarity never would have gone that far, and never did. He told several aides, including Richard Goodwin, that not only hadn't he endorsed Castro's murder, "I saved his life," although he never explained how. A Kennedy Library interviewer asked him explicitly whether the assassination of the Cuban president was attempted or even contemplated. Without hesitating, he answered no to both questions.

We know now that both answers were untruths, given the revelations about Mongoose and related operations. The U.S. Senate probe made that clear, as did the declassification of a secret document prepared eight years earlier entitled "CIA Inspector General's Report on Plots to Assassinate Fidel Castro." It's also clear that Senate investigators, Kennedy Library interviewers, and others who have sought answers the last half century have been posing the wrong questions. It's highly unlikely that Bobby directly authorized Castro's killing. He had learned well at least one lesson from the Bay of Pigs: Don't leave fingerprints. The government left itself no deniability in that invasion, with evidence everywhere that Americans had trained, equipped, and encouraged the invaders, which is why the president had little choice but to accept blame. Bobby wanted to ensure that Jack never had to do that again. The question wasn't even whether Bobby wanted Castro dead. There's a chance that he didn't, for moral or practical reasons. But intent isn't necessary to establish culpability.

Bobby, an intrepid interrogator, never asked the CIA operatives who

---

* "I heard [my husband] talking to various people," says Helms's wife, Cynthia, about how "Robert Kennedy really wanted to get rid of Castro. Dick said he was adamant about this, and said you could see the welts on his back where he had been lashed by the Kennedys to get rid of Castro" (Author interview with Cynthia Helms).

briefed him about their failed Mafia plot whether more deadly conspiracies were in the works, which they were. We also know, from what he said and did, that the attorney general never wavered on wanting Cuba's revolutionary hero out of power—and that he knew that would never happen via the ballot box or other peaceful means. He knew deaths could result from schemes he did explicitly authorize, including blowing up bridges and refineries, and he got angry when the CIA couldn't carry out more of them. War meant casualties. Nobody who worked for Bobby on Operation Mongoose doubted, as General Lansdale made clear from the first, "that we are in a combat situation—where we have been given full command." Speaking on the attorney general's behalf, the general was asking not just for "a change from business-as-usual," but for scalps. None mattered more to their commander at the Justice Department, his men in the field knew, than Fidel Castro's. Goodwin, the senior Cuba adviser, said that "it would have been like Henry II asking rhetorically, 'Who will free me of this turbulent priest?' and then the zealots going out and doing it."

The Kennedys' Cuba obsession and the underhanded tactics that it spawned became a legacy that long outlived JFK and RFK's administration. Veterans of the Bay of Pigs and Mongoose operations would help engineer the 1972 Watergate burglary, the 1976 bombing of a Cuban airliner that killed all seventy-three passengers, the assassination that same year in Washington of Orlando Letelier, the former Chilean ambassador to the United States, and a rash of other terrorist acts. The precedent of the Kennedys' underwriting a secret war in Cuba emboldened future American presidents to pursue undeclared wars of their own. Richard Nixon did it in Laos and Cambodia; Ronald Reagan did the same in Nicaragua. Bobby "was out-CIAing the CIA," worried Harris Wofford, who was helping launch the Peace Corps. The scariest suggestion of all, posited but never proven, is that the Kennedy administration's attempts to assassinate Fidel Castro encouraged him or his zealous disciples, like Lee Harvey Oswald, to murder Bobby's brother Jack.

———

CUBA WASN'T THE only place where Bobby pushed the borders of his job as attorney general, advancing the president's overseas agenda and broadening his own worldview. His first foreign mission their first summer in office seemed purely ceremonial. The occasion was the celebration of the first anniversary of independence for Ivory Coast, which had come in such a headlong rush that there wasn't time then for festivities. The land that Francophones called Côte d'Ivoire had spearheaded the anticolonial drive among, and remained a leader of, Africa's dozen former French colonies, all of which generally sided with the West and against Soviet-friendly states such as Ghana. Sending not just the attorney general but the president's brother to represent the United States conveyed a message to Africa and to Moscow: America was grateful to its Cold War friends. "Just as George Washington fought to free our country, President Houphouet-Boigny has rallied the people of this land to establish in the Ivory Coast a free and united nation," the attorney general said in French. *Travail bien fait.*

Bobby's Africa trip was aimed at an American as well as a global audience. He hoped the Freedom Riders and other civil rights supporters in the United States would recognize that the Kennedy administration cared about the problems of Negroes, at home and everywhere. "The United States government and the vast majority of people are trying to do something about this [racial] problem," he said at a news conference in Abidjan that drew forty reporters from Africa and Europe. But as he would in every land he visited, he made it clear that America wasn't alone in facing such intractable troubles, no matter what Soviet propagandists said. "Visiting your country and part of the world where there are tremendous problems," he explained, "points up the fact that any time you try to overthrow a system or a set of mores you are bound to have problems." It helped, in getting his messages across in Africa, that the press knew that Bobby had opposed restrictions on African diplomats at a fashionable club in Washington and would do the same with establishments throughout Jim Crow America. What the press didn't know was that on visits like this, Bobby was gathering intelligence on what it took to "overthrow a system" that he would apply in Cuba.

His Africa travels, like all his international expeditions for the administration, were a whirlwind. Most embassy staffers had never been to the places he was determined to go. "We took Kennedy out of Abidjan into the real Africa. He loved being in a village in the rain forest where he was

greeted by cheering crowds, even though few, if any, understood who
Robert Kennedy was," said Brandon Grove, the young foreign service officer who helped him execute this and other trips. "He waved, clasped
hands, and passed out his brother's PT-109 tie clips, which must have
seemed mysterious to Africans who never wore neckties." It didn't matter: "They recognized charisma when they saw it." Grove was torn. He
had never met anyone in government so genuinely drawn to people, yet
he'd never seen anyone with so little patience for officialdom. Things got
done—"he was driven, tackling everything with New Frontier 'vigah' "—
but fellow diplomats, including the U.S. ambassador, whom Grove liked,
got trampled on and eventually replaced, thanks to Bobby's verdict that
he was too stuffy and hidebound.*

The attorney general was back on a plane early in 1962, this time
heading with Ethel on a goodwill trip around the globe that began with
fireworks in Japan. His visit came at a time of stress between the two
countries. America had bombed the island nation into submission during World War II and then occupied it for seven years. In the ensuing
decade, Japan had grown increasingly proud of its economic comeback
and resentful of what it saw as ongoing U.S. domination. Japanese anger
built to such a level that President Eisenhower felt the need to cancel his
planned trip there in 1960, and President Kennedy was anxious to rescue the relationship. First, he appointed as ambassador Edwin Reischauer, a Harvard scholar who understood the respect the Japanese
craved and set out to equalize the partnership. Next, he dispatched
Bobby to take Japan's pulse and smooth the way for a trip the president
planned to make during the 1964 campaign, when he would dramatically reunite his PT-109 torpedo boat crew with that of the Japanese destroyer that sank it during World War II.

Bobby was a novelty to the Japanese. In Tokyo, he sat on the counter
of a working-class bar and, after discussing world affairs with other pa-
trons, serenaded them with "When Irish Eyes Are Smiling." Told of his
drinking habits, the proprietress poured him two glasses of milk, but

---

* The ambassador to the Ivory Coast and three other former French colonies was R. Borden
Reams, a career diplomat. "This played out," Grove said, "by Reams' returning home, retir-
ing, and playing golf, at which he excelled" (Author email from Grove).

they remained undrunk as he opted for sake. At a steel mill, picketers outside the gates held signs saying KENEDY STOP OPPRESING CUBA (the misspellings were the same everywhere he went) while workers wearing yellow helmets cheered him with chants of "banzai!" He chatted with housewives, patted babies, ate whale meat and seaweed, and spoke a Japanese so crude that his audience assumed it was English and waited for the translation. The newspapers published everything he said. "They were interested in him because he is young—a point he kept emphasizing," reported the *New York Times* correspondent A. M. Rosenthal, who was three years older than the attorney general. "All by himself Mr. Kennedy received more attention than did half the Kennedy Cabinet when it visited here in November. Part of the reason was that Mr. Kennedy jumped into the Tokyo frenzy, instead of encouraging the Japanese bureaucracy to take him off to a guarded mountaintop, as did Secretary of State Dean Rusk and his colleagues."

The trip was primarily a charm offensive, but this statesman in the making chose just the right moments to demonstrate his tough side. One came at a meeting with the head of Japan's four-million-member leftist labor union, whom Bobby challenged to see for himself whether America really was an "imperialist" land of "monopoly capital." When the union man persisted in referring to J. P. Morgan, the Rockefellers, and other robber barons of old, Bobby told him, "You are talking about the United States of a hundred years ago." That was tepid compared to the set-to during his address at Waseda University, where Communist hecklers yelled, "Kennedy, go home." He invited the group's twenty-one-year-old leader to the platform, where the young man denounced the United States. When Bobby took back the microphone, someone pulled the plug and shut off the lights, creating chaos. Reischauer finally restored order, and, led by the school cheerleader, the audience of two thousand extended a gesture of conciliation by serenading the U.S. attorney general with its school anthem. Thanks to TV crews covering the talk, millions of Japanese viewers witnessed a reversal of stereotypes: a famously well-mannered country treating its guest rudely, while an American leader renowned for ruthlessness responded with what the Japanese called "low posture," speaking softly and behaving courteously. "It was the best thing that happened in my trip," Bobby said. "It was very, very successful from that point because everybody was so humiliated and embarrassed that I'd been invited and then couldn't speak."

If his trip to Japan helped cement a friendship with an old enemy, he used his two-hour refueling stop in South Vietnam to scope out a future adversary. Washington already knew Bobby as Mr. Counterinsurgency, and he saw Vietnam as a test of his approach. Would his tactics work better than France's use of conventional warfare to battle an enemy it couldn't see and didn't understand? Bobby had sensed the futility of the French mission eleven years before, when he visited Indochina with Jack and their sister Pat. Now Bobby sought to buttress the president's increasing involvement in Southeast Asia. Although a tight schedule prevented his leaving the Saigon airport, the attorney general found time to brief the press. "We are going to win in Vietnam. We will remain here until we do win," he vowed. When a British reporter asked whether America approved of its boys' dying in Vietnam, Bobby shot back: "I think the United States will do what is necessary to help a country that is trying to repel aggression with its own blood, tears and sweat." But even as he hewed to the official line, he worried—the way he had after the Bay of Pigs—that he and his brother weren't getting the full story. "He was supposed to be briefed at the airport terminal by the top members of the [U.S.] mission," recalled the *New York Times* reporter David Halberstam, who would earn a Pulitzer Prize for his coverage of Vietnam. " 'Do you have any problems?' [Bobby] asked. No, said everyone in unison, there were no problems. He looked at them somewhat shocked by the response. 'No problems,' he said, 'you've really got no problems? Does anyone here want to speak to me in private about his problems?' And then one by one they talked to him at length and it all came pouring out." While it took years for his critique on Vietnam to fully congeal, Halberstam said encounters like that helped cement Bobby's reputation as "the best man in government to bring an unconventional idea to."

Every stop posed unique challenges. In Jakarta he listened to Indonesian president Sukarno rail about why Dutch-held Western New Guinea was his. In The Hague he heard the Dutch rant back. In both capitals he counseled talking, not fighting. He saw the king and queen in Thailand, spent forty minutes with President Charles de Gaulle in Paris, and had a private audience at the Vatican with Pope John XXIII, who afterward blessed the "pens, hearts and tongues" of the newspapermen traveling with Bobby. Hong Kong was blanketed with fog when he arrived, but he still boarded a launch and visited four U.S. Navy ships in the harbor. Nearly everywhere he went he declined formal sessions with the mission's country team and only thumbed through his briefing book, preferring private updates from the ambassador and CIA station chief. "He was an oral man who preferred face-to-face encounters," explains Grove, his State Department aide. "He believed that having to listen to someone lecture him diminished him." Free of the embassy, Bobby visited landmarks to understand a country's history, talked to local officials to gauge its present thinking, and caucused with students to get a look into the future. A realistic optimist, he perceived what he called "a tremendous reservoir of goodwill toward the United States which will disappear if the potential is not realized." The way to realize it, Bobby added, is by "keeping ourselves prepared militarily, but also building our strength in the domestic areas, such as civil rights, economic productivity and Social Security."

He made news again in Berlin, another Cold War flash point. Arriving at Tempelhof Airport, he declared, "Ich bin ein Berliner," a gesture of kinship to the isolated city that his brother would famously echo the following year. More than 150,000 West Berliners were waiting for Bobby in front of the city hall on a day so cold he could barely get his words out. "An armed attack on West Berlin is the same as an armed attack on Chicago, or New York, or London, or Paris," he assured his listeners. "You are our brothers and we stand by you." At the Potsdamer Platz, he got his first look at the wall of masonry and wire separating the city's free and entrapped halves, and he saw several women peering back from windows in East Germany. "As I turned, several of the women slowly and carefully waved their hands without moving their arms," he wrote in the inevitable book that grew out of the trip, this one called *Just Friends and Brave Enemies*.* "It was a poignant moment and I felt a chill in the back of my neck."

* That the word "enemy" made it into the title of two of his books was a sign of Bobby's black-and-white take on his world. But this time it was a signal that he was recognizing subtler shadings, that his enemy was brave, whereas in his first book it was dark enemies like Jimmy Hoffa lurking within our unsuspecting society.

The way he traveled said a lot about this attorney general and his times. He always flew on commercial carriers, and always first class. There was no security, but a handful of reporters tagged along. Bobby tried to sleep on the planes with the help of an eye mask that advertised his mischievousness: painted on the veil were one eye that was shut, as in sleep, and the other wide awake, giving the impression that he was permanently winking. "Passengers returning to their seats from the toilets were startled by this image of the Attorney General," recalls Grove, "and probably voted for any Republican in the next elections."

Bobby arrived back in Washington on February 28, after twenty-eight days abroad, having logged thirty thousand miles and touched down in fourteen countries. The press had always been beguiled by him, especially when Ethel was by his side, and journalists threw bouquets instead of asking why an attorney general was jetting around the globe. "The joyful Christian couple who are obviously enjoying every minute of their travels may help convince the world that it is possible to be happy and an American at the same time," opined the columnist Mary McGrory. Republicans in Washington asked the questions reporters didn't, sounding like embittered old men even when the words came out of the mouth of an ambitious young luminary like Congressman John Lindsay of New York. "We question whether it is necessary for you and your office to be either burdened or embarrassed by free wheeling foreign missions on the part of highly placed amateurs who do not have the background, training, language ability, or capability to carry on the enormous burden of diplomacy in the context of today's long struggle," Lindsay groused in a letter to Dean Rusk, who would later voice identical concerns in his memoir.

The boyish congressman and middle-aged diplomat missed the point. Bobby's freedom from the cumbersome rituals of statecraft is precisely what let the attorney general take his resonant message to the jungles of Africa and the walled-in streets of Berlin. America was engaged in a struggle of cultures and visions with its Cold War nemeses, and Bobby saw that it would be won not by giving speeches at private embassy parties but by using a public megaphone to trumpet his fiery love of country. The United States had no more effective propagandist than its good-looking, irrepressible attorney general. Those who met him, including even the young socialist who ranted against him at Waseda University, would remember his visit half a century later and would be grateful he'd come. They remembered Ethel, too, whose instincts were even better than Bobby's on whom to like and who was "just awful," and whose spiritual nourishment energized him during their nonstop travels. Moreover, Bobby's crusade didn't end when he got home. When young Americans travel overseas they have a duty, he told them, to explain to everyone they meet that "the state exists for the individual." Unless they know enough to talk about what is right and wrong in America they would do the country a favor if they "stayed in bed at home."

If domestic opponents couldn't see the difference he was making, the embassy staffs he'd run ragged did. In Japan, for example, his visit "commanded the attention of more people and elicited a more positive response from the Japanese public than any good will visit in Japan's history," the legation in Tokyo said in a confidential report to the State Department, even though the authors knew their words wouldn't win favor with Secretary Rusk, who had made such a goodwill visit himself. "The initial (and perhaps also the most lasting) impression on the Japanese people at large was made less by what the Attorney General said than by what he (and Mrs. Kennedy) did, the pace at which they did it, and their attitude and personality—and by the unprecedented efforts that all Japanese mass communications media made to convey these things to their audiences. Japanese generally received a new and vivid sense of the dynamism and vigor of the United States Government and the American people."

The change of mind went both ways. At the outset of the trip, Bobby had shared his father's conviction that the State Department lacked the creativity and agility to deal with the crises it faced. His travels helped him see otherwise, in enough cases, to assume a more refined stand about not just the diplomatic corps but the planet. If standing in the shadow of the Berlin Wall hardened his views of the Soviet Bloc, the frightened hand wavers in East Berlin gave his enemy a human face. Likewise, the leftist students who accosted him in Tokyo made him determined to replace their diet of Soviet propaganda with New Frontier optimism. This was how he learned, the same way he had on his trip to the Soviet Union with Justice Douglas. World affairs, to Bobby, were less a global chess game than a latticework of bonds between humans, much as they had been for Ben Franklin two centuries before. The extraordinary outpouring of human response to him, quite apart from his charismatic brother, suggested to the young attorney general new possibilities for what he could do in the world.

He was growing personally, too, as Brandon Grove saw. It was Grove who had to absorb Bobby's grousing about the unreliable CIA, his complaints about the fat and flabby State Department, and his sophomoric restlessness at having to stand in receiving lines behind chiefs of state from what he considered second-rate countries. In Islamic Indonesia, Bobby humiliated Grove by making him dance the Charleston in public, with an equally embarrassed friend of Ethel's, to reward their hosts who had dazzled them with a traditional candle dance. The Kennedy entourage caught its flight to Saigon only because Grove took it upon himself to pack Bobby and Ethel's bags, explaining to them in exasperation that "this is a real world with real people and real airplanes. Pan Am isn't going to hold the plane for us!" Grove was therefore surprised and delighted when, back in Washington, "Ethel, with a sweet smile, slipped a small leather box into my hand and said, 'Bobby and I want you to have this.' Inside were two gold cufflinks, one inscribed 'Real World,' the other 'Real People.' On their backs were the initials BHG and RFK. . . . He and Ethel were saying an affectionate 'thank-you.'"

IT WAS NATURAL to assume that Bobby Kennedy didn't know much about life's realities given his age—not quite thirty-seven in October 1962—and how boyish he sounded and looked. He was the youthful president's kid brother, old Joe Kennedy's pampered son. If experience was the measure, however, few in the cabinet or country could match Bobby's. He had seen more of the world by his early twenties than many secretaries of state do in a career, thanks to his father's money and insistence that his children be broadly informed. As a globetrotting attorney general he consorted with presidents and prime ministers, kings and autocrats, and a pope who would achieve sainthood. Yet for all his interest in domestic issues as pressing as civil rights and crime control, and foreign ones as far-reaching as East-West relations, it was that crocodile-shaped island in the Caribbean that would grip him, from the earliest days of the Kennedy administration to its very last.

That grip felt like a noose during the two crisis-laden weeks in October 1962 when the United States was demanding that the Union of Soviet Socialist Republics remove its nuclear missiles from Cuba and the Soviets took their time weighing whether to comply or face the likelihood of war. The public was unaware of this brinkmanship until six days into the crisis, on October 22, when President John F. Kennedy went on national television with three sobering revelations: America had "unmistakable evidence" that the Russians were installing atomic warheads in Cuba capable of striking the Western Hemisphere; President Kennedy was insisting that Chairman Khrushchev "halt and eliminate this clandestine, reckless, and provocative threat"; and, to show we were serious, American warships would set up a "strict quarantine on all offensive military equipment" bound for Cuba. Even as JFK was speaking, his government was placing all U.S. forces around the globe on high alert. The public reaction to the president's words was a collective shudder. Parents emptied the shelves of supermarkets and gun stores as they outfitted their fallout shelters. Children tried to remember the duck-and-cover drills they'd learned in school, in which they were told to hide under their desks as a shield against falling glass and debris. The planet quickly picked sides, with the West backing America, 650 million Red Chinese standing by their comrades in Cuba, and Pope John beseeching the two superpowers to "save peace." Everyone everywhere, God-fearing or not, prayed that America's young president knew what he was doing as he faced off against the more worldly-wise Soviet leader.

They had to take the last part on faith since the next seven days of moves and countermoves took place out of public view. People could follow the debate playing out in the United Nations, but even the U.S. and USSR ambassadors who were spitting venom at one another in New York weren't in on all the nerve-testing maneuvering in Washington and Moscow. It was entirely unlike more recent traumas such as the September 11, 2001, attacks on the World Trade Center, which viewers watched play out in real time on television. Not until October 28, 1962, the thirteenth and last day of the missile standoff, did America and the rest of mankind learn enough to finally relax. Khrushchev affirmed in writing that he would withdraw his missiles in exchange for the United States pledging not to invade Cuba. "In view of the assurances you have given and our instructions on dismantling," the Soviet premier wrote in a four-and-a-half-page letter to the American president, "there is every condition for eliminating the present conflict." President Kennedy, in a three-paragraph response, called the Soviet stand-down "an important and constructive contribution to peace."

Having lived in the dark while its fate was being decided, it is no wonder that the world was so interested in the first-ever inside story of the crisis as told by Bobby Kennedy. His slender book *Thirteen Days* said that humanity had come even closer than it knew to the dreaded nuclear holocaust. (He put the odds at "one chance in five or so," adding that "everybody thought there was a good chance of getting blown up.") The presumptive star of Bobby's narrative is President John F. Kennedy, who parsed conflicting advice, talking down the warmongers and settling on a less confrontational nautical quarantine of the island nation. The thinly veiled hero, however, was the author himself. In his account, Bobby played Lancelot to Jack's King Arthur, deftly steering an exhausted cabinet toward an elusive consensus, acting as interlocutor with the Soviets, and offering his brother not just guidance but solace at the tensest junctures.

October 24, day nine of the crisis, was D-day. Shortly before 10:00 A.M. on the twenty-fourth, as Russian ships neared our line of destroyers and JFK and his counselors faced the fateful choice of whether or not to intercept, Bobby emboldened his commander in chief. "I sat across the table from the President. This was the moment we had prepared for, which we hoped would never come. The danger and concern that we all felt hung like a cloud over us all and particularly over the President," Bobby recalled in his book. "We stared at each other across the table. For a few fleeting seconds, it was almost as though no one else was there and he was no longer the President."

The brothers had never shared an experience like this. It wasn't just the imminence of catastrophe, but how, when he wrote about it years later, Bobby for the first time claimed a major slice of the credit. He had consciously underplayed his role in steering Jack's path to the White

House, just as he did when he took the heat for miscues with the steel titans and melees over civil rights. During the impossibly tense days in October 1962 he once again acted as his brother's moral bell ringer, only now he wanted everyone to know what he had done. As an early call was sounded for U.S. air strikes, "I passed a note to the President: 'I now know how [Japanese prime minister Hideki] Tojo felt when he was planning Pearl Harbor.'" Later, Premier Khrushchev boxed in the Americans by sending them contradictory messages—an encouraging private one on Friday, October 26, suggesting the Soviets would withdraw their missiles if the United States merely promised not to invade Cuba, and a public one the next day, "Black Saturday," that upped the ante, saying the Soviet missiles would go only if the United States dismantled its atomic warheads pointing at Russia from Turkey.* It was Bobby, he told us, who suggested an elegantly simple way out: Accept the offer they liked and ignore the other one. "I said that there could be no quid pro quo" to swap missiles "made under this kind of threat or pressure." The word "I" appears 158 times in Bobby's 105 pages of text in *Thirteen Days*, alongside 231 "we"s. This unrivaled alliance of brothers, the author added, ensured that Black Saturday gave way to Sunny Sunday.

His account was riveting but not completely honest. Bobby portrayed himself as the artful pacifist in his book, an image first introduced by two journalist friends in a *Saturday Evening Post* article that called him the "leading dove" in the White House brain trust. In fact, he began as an outspoken hawk. In his first comments in the cabinet room on October 16, day one of the crisis, he doubted that an air strike on the missile sites would be enough and pondered whether it should be followed by an all-out invasion. Seeing war as inevitable, he wondered aloud if "we should just get into it, and get it over with, and take our losses." He even suggested staging an incident at our Navy base in Guantánamo Bay—"sink the *Maine* again"—creating the kind of pretext that had ignited the

---

* Circumstantial evidence leads some historians to believe that several days before, Bobby had inadvertently signaled to Khrushchev—through a meeting between the Russian spy Bolshakov and two U.S. journalists briefed by Bobby—that America would be open to the missile swap JFK hoped to avoid, which emboldened the Soviet leader to add that as a last-minute demand (May and Zelikow, *The Kennedy Tapes*, 468–69).

Spanish-American War in 1898 after the mysterious sinking of the USS *Maine* in Havana Harbor.*

By day five he began to waver, suggesting instead that we start with a blockade while making it clear to the Russians that air strikes would follow if they didn't halt work on the missile installations. That would avoid a Pearl Harbor–like surprise, which to Americans had been the ultimate treachery, yet it would still allow for an attack. "Now," he argued, "is the last chance we will have to destroy Castro and the Soviet missiles deployed in Cuba." Once the president decided on the blockade, nobody did more to rally support than his brother, out of loyalty and knowing that his reaction would set the tone for the rest of the cabinet and even the military.† But ten days into the quarantine he was still asking whether it "might be better to go ahead and knock out the missiles with an air attack rather than confront the Soviets at sea." Two days later the focus had switched to the missile swap deal that would, in just twenty-four hours, bring the crisis to an end, but Bobby remained unsettled. With half the president's aides gone and those remaining indulging in gallows humor, Bobby said, "I'd like to take Cuba back. That would be nice." An unidentified colleague responded, "Suppose we make Bobby mayor of Havana?"

We can track his push and pull not because of what Bobby wrote in his book, but because his actual words were picked up by microphones implanted in the wall of the cabinet room and connected to a tape recorder in the basement. The recordings were one of Bobby's and Jack's "non-sharables," and nobody else had a clue they were being taped. The public didn't find out until 1973, as part of Watergate-inspired disclosures, and it took another twenty-four years for the last of the Cuban crisis tapes to be released. Unlike Richard Nixon's sound-activated recording system, this older set of tapes required the president to push a

---

* He'd been proposing a staged attack like that since at least August, when he asked a small group meeting in the secretary of state's office "the feasibility of provoking an action against Guantanamo which would permit us to retaliate, or involving a third country in some way" (John McCone's memo on the conversation, August 21, 1962, *Foreign Relations of the United States*, vol. X, 947–49).

† At times during the crisis the generals seemed out of control, Bobby said afterward: "If we hadn't had [Joint Chiefs of Staff chairman] Maxwell Taylor over there we would have had a revolt, a revolution within the military" (RFK OH, February 13, 1965, 38).

hidden button and let him turn the recorder on or off at his pleasure. The picture of what happened during those torturous thirteen days in 1962 was filled in over time thanks to memoirs by Soviet and American leaders, anniversary gatherings of the participants, the declassification of government records, and the opening of the last of Bobby's archives in 2014. The real story is more interesting if less heroic than Bobby rendered it, reflecting his shifting understanding of both himself and his relationship to his brother.

The Russians, it turns out, got precisely the quid pro quo that Bobby said they hadn't, and that he initially was dead against. His proposal to accept Khrushchev's offer of a no-invasion pledge and ignore his demand for a missile swap would be enshrined in history as an ingenious solution and given a lyrical name, the "Trollope ploy," a reference to Victorian novelist Anthony Trollope's marriage-hungry maiden who interprets an innocuous squeeze of the hand as an offer of matrimony.* To the world, it looked like the Soviet leader was as desperate as Trollope's maiden for a way to reconcile with the Americans, and the wily Kennedys exploited Khrushchev's vulnerability. The true deception, however, was Bobby and Jack's hoodwinking of some of the cabinet and all of the public into thinking it really was a Trollope ploy when in fact America had acceded to both demands made by the Russian premier. The two superpowers had stood on the brink, each looking for a way out. The attorney general offered it at a one-on-one meeting with Soviet ambassador Dobrynin, who rode the private elevator to Bobby's office at about 8:00 on the evening of Black Saturday. The Kennedys were convinced that a tit-for-tat on the missiles was inevitable, and that the Jupiter rockets the United States had in Turkey were inconsequential to Europe's defense. They also knew an explicit swap like that would cause an uproar, not just among hawks in America but from the Turks and other allies. So they made Khrushchev the offer on the condition that Russia keep that part of the deal secret. They promised that America would unilaterally remove its Jupiters four or five months later, in what would be described as

* Llewellyn Thompson, the former U.S. Ambassador to the Soviet Union, was the one who came up with the Trollope approach, said Rusk. "Bobby got the credit because he proposed it at the ExComm meeting," the secretary of state added, "but it was Thompson's idea" (Rusk and Papp, *As I Saw It*, 240).

a modernization of the NATO nuclear deterrent rather than a payback to the Russians for withdrawing their nuclear warheads from Cuba.

Bobby emphasized to the Soviet ambassador that "the White House was not prepared to formalize the accord, even by means of strictly confidential letters, and that the American side preferred not to engage in any correspondence on so sensitive an issue," Dobrynin recalled in his memoir. The attorney general also confided to the ambassador in the wake of the crisis another reason why stealth was imperative: "That some day—who knows?—he might run for president, and his prospects could be damaged if this secret deal about the missiles in Turkey were to come out." Bobby offered a stick along with his carrot: If the Soviets didn't agree to the arrangement, the United States would likely attack Cuba in short order.

The rest of the world didn't learn about the deal until twenty-seven years later when, at a conference in Moscow, Dobrynin challenged John Kennedy's speechwriter and confidant Ted Sorensen to come clean. Sorensen publicly confessed that, after Bobby died but before *Thirteen Days* was published, he removed from the text Bobby's "very explicit" admission about the missile swap. "At that time it was still a secret even on the American side, except for the six of us who had been present at that meeting,"* he said, "so I took it upon myself to edit that out." Sorensen maintained the cover-up not just to protect himself and his co-conspirators, but to safeguard the hard-line reputation of the president he cherished, whose role in the missile crisis needed no burnishing.

Thirteen Days indulged in another self-interested untruth. As the book describes it, the Soviet placement of missiles in Cuba took America by total surprise. "No official within the government," Bobby wrote, "had ever suggested to President Kennedy that the Russian buildup in Cuba would include missiles." Saying otherwise would have made the president look derelict for ignoring what were, in fact, repeated warnings. Some came from CIA director John McCone, who, in September 1962, took time from his honeymoon on the French Riviera to pass on his

---

* National Security Advisor McGeorge Bundy remembered nine participants in that critical meeting, not six, adding that "we agreed without hesitation that no one not in the room was to be informed" (Bundy, *Danger and Survival*, 432–33).

growing suspicions that the Soviets were installing offensive weapons in Cuba. (Bobby would later say that if McCone had been serious, "he should have come home and worked on it, not be sending a letter from Cannes, France.") Other alerts came from Republican senator Kenneth Keating of New York, who claimed to have "fully confirmed" evidence of missile sites under construction in Cuba nearly a week before pictures taken by a U-2 spy plane documented their existence. Bobby's reaction to the U-2 photographs was typically blunt: "Oh shit!, Shit!, Shit! Those sons a bitches Russians." He was infuriated not just by the weapons installations, but because the Soviets had promised not to take any precipitous actions before the upcoming congressional elections. He also had seen this confrontation coming and perhaps blamed himself for not doing enough to head it off. For it was Bobby himself who had sounded the earliest and strongest warnings eighteen months before, when he ended a memo to the president by saying, "If we don't want Russia to set up missile bases in Cuba, we had better decide now what we are willing to do to stop it."

As was his wont, Bobby used his book to reward his friends and to undermine his enemies. Robert McNamara, a "goodie" in Bobby's and Ethel's vernacular, became the blockade's "strongest advocate" and someone JFK considered "the most valuable public servant in his Administration." He was both, by the end, but there is no mention of his earlier insistence on "nothing short of a full invasion." Baddies were cut no such slack. Bobby had never had any use for Dean Rusk, his idea of the quintessential deskbound, overstarched bureaucrat. The secretary of state, he said, should have chaired meetings during those thirteen days but often arrived late, left early, or didn't show up. He later added that Rusk "was impossible. . . . He would always adjust. No matter what the subject was. Never argue. Never take a position that was different. . . . He collapsed physically and mentally during that period of time—just because of the strain."* The tapes, however, prove that Rusk attended nineteen of the twenty critical meetings during the crisis, and McGeorge

---

* After the crisis, Bobby said, Rusk approached him "and offered to resign. And was humiliated at the way he handled himself. . . . The president knew he wasn't effective but he was his own secretary of state and he was going to let him stay through to the election in '64 and then replace him" (RFK OH, February 13, 1965, 30–31).

Bundy, JFK's national security advisor, put Rusk's role in the critical missile swap on par with Bobby's.* The attorney general also thrashed the vice president, telling a Kennedy Library interviewer that Johnson "was against our policy on Cuba in October of '62 . . . although I never knew quite what he was for." As for Adlai Stevenson, the Kennedys' ambassador to the United Nations but not their friend, Bobby called him "courageous" but wrong in proposing the blockade-and-negotiate strategy that became the consensus choice. "We have to get someone better at the UN or put some starch in the son of a bitch's back," Bobby told Jack loudly enough for others to overhear.

Embellishments and score settling notwithstanding, Bobby did have a compelling case to make for his own contributions during those history-making thirteen days. He drew on his skills as an interrogator and listener to recognize the best ideas being voiced in the White House Cabinet Room. Acting as de facto chairman of the meetings, he ensured that the president heard the full spectrum of views as the crisis was building, then he mobilized support for JFK's decisions. Who better to conciliate than someone who had been both hawk and dove, and who among cabinet officers had less to prove to the commander in chief? He also was effective enough as an intermediary with the Soviets that Khrushchev later paid him a compliment: "In our negotiations with the Americans during the crisis, they had, on the whole, been open and candid with us, especially Robert Kennedy."†

Nobody worked harder during those two weeks than Bobby. He met with cabinet officials during the day, the Russians at night, and found time in between to check on Jimmy Hoffa and other matters at the Justice

---

* Rusk gave Bobby one more reason to dislike him during the crisis: The secretary of state was the only key presidential adviser to consistently stand up to the attorney general during his hawkish phase. Bobby also disparaged Bundy's performance during the crisis: "[He] flip flopped so many times in such an extreme way that—it was complete deterioration of an individual before one's eyes." (Stern, "Beyond the Smoke and Mirrors," *A Critical Reappraisal*, and RFK OH, February 13, 1965, 31.)

† The Soviets were impressed enough by his diplomatic skills prior to the missile crisis that they had floated the notion of his coming to the USSR as U.S. ambassador, an idea that JFK at least considered. But Bobby balked. "In the first place," he said looking back, "I couldn't possibly learn Russian because I spent ten years learning second-year French, and secondly . . . I don't think the amount of good that it would have done would have remained" (RFK OH, April 30, 1964, 209–10, JFKL).

Department. "I watched him walk slowly up the stairs, briefcase in hand, his shoulders hunched," one aide recalled. "When I think of him now, that is the image that comes to my mind again and again: the lean figure standing in the late-afternoon sun near the top of the steps, arm outstretched, waving." While the tape recordings exposed his self-important habit of thinking out loud, they also let us see the intellect and wit that helped his colleagues clarify their thinking. Bleak as those days were, Bobby still cracked jokes, asking the officials who showed him the U-2 photos, "Will those goddamn things reach Oxford, Mississippi?" Ever conscious of snooping reporters, he got fellow National Security Council members to pile into his limousine on one another's laps so as not to arouse suspicions by having a lineup of limos pull up to the White House during the earliest days of the crisis, when the public didn't know what was happening. Told later of the plans to evacuate top officials to a bunker in West Virginia if things got bad, he instructed his aide, "I'm not going. If it comes to that, there'll be sixty million Americans killed and as many Russians or more. I'll be at Hickory Hill." The night of Black Saturday, eating a warmed-over dinner of broiled chicken in the upstairs living room at the White House, JFK recounted to a friend all the ways that RFK had helped during the crisis. Such an open display of affection for his brother was so unusual, Dave Powers added, that years later he remembered precisely the president's last words on the matter: "Thank God for Bobby."

Why, given all that he did right, wasn't Bobby more forthright in his book? It was partly genetics. Joe Kennedy had warned his children, "Don't put it in writing," and while many of them published books, none bared their souls or secrets. Politics played an even more critical role, as Bobby had hinted to Ambassador Dobrynin. The goal when he first conceived of *Thirteen Days* was to polish the president's image around what both brothers considered the singular accomplishment of his first term as he campaigned for reelection in 1964. The crisis had already demonstrated its political punch when JFK's approval rating soared to 74 percent in November 1962, and Democrats did better than anyone dreamed in the midterm elections, with a net gain of four Senate seats and a loss of just four in the House. After Jack was killed, however, Bobby set the book aside.

When he finally picked it up again in 1967, Bobby reimagined *Thirteen*

Days as the literary foundation for his own race for the White House. Jack had pointed the way with his 1956 bestseller, *Profiles in Courage*, which was half history treatise, half a way of introducing the senator to America. Bobby would run in 1968 as an antiwar candidate, and he wanted to underscore his peacemaking credentials and paper over his cold warrior past. He couldn't tell the true story of his uneven performance in October 1962, not if he had his eyes on the presidency. Robert McNamara, who understood Bobby's ambitions, helped by writing an introduction to *Thirteen Days* that extolled the author for "a most extraordinary combination of energy and courage, compassion and wisdom." When JFK crony Kenny O'Donnell got a look at an early draft, he teased, "Bobby, I thought your brother was president during the missile crisis." Bobby: "Yeah, but he's not running and I am." The CIA reviewed a later draft, after Bobby was dead. "I listed a number of errors or inaccuracies. From what I was to understand, others who read the galley did the same," said Dino Brugioni, a longtime senior intelligence official. "When these were shown to the publisher, it was decided not to correct the errors but to allow the book to stand as written."

It is tempting to blame those errors on faulty memory, but Bobby knew about the tape recordings documenting what he and others had said, and he apparently used an early and rough four-hundred-page transcription to refresh his memory. National security might have been an excuse for some of the secrecy surrounding deliberations at the time of the crisis, but it wasn't five years later. And it is legitimate to blame Sorensen for editing out the truth, but only about the missile swap. What Bobby picked and chose was the version he wanted to tell. He wasn't worried about being contradicted because he trusted that the tapes had been the president's private property and would never be made public, or at least not before the 1968 election. It was not unlike the miscalculation Richard Nixon would make four years later, during Watergate.

What Bobby wrote mattered because, grave as he and we thought the crisis was, later revelations by the Soviets and the Cubans made clear that the perils were substantially worse. The Russians had more missiles than America believed, with greater capability to take out short-range targets like the U.S. base in Guantánamo Bay in addition to long-range objectives like Manhattan. There actually were forty-three thousand Soviet soldiers on hand, not the ten thousand we thought. Scarier still was the fact that Castro had encouraged Khrushchev to launch a preemptive nuclear strike against America if America invaded Cuba. Castro and his Russian benefactors also had lightweight rocket launchers in the field to repel any attackers with atomic weapons. The Soviet submarines we were tracking and harassing each carried a nuclear-tipped torpedo, and their commanders had orders to use them to break the blockade if war broke out. All of which made it even more essential that, after the fact, policymakers soberly study what happened over those thirteen days—what went wrong as well as right, what we did and didn't know.

Instead, based in part on Bobby Kennedy's watered-down and self-referential rendition of events in his book and elsewhere, we drew the wrong lessons from this first-ever nuclear showdown. Dean Rusk's "eyeball to eyeball" quotation, reported in a December 1962 *Saturday Evening Post* article that the Kennedys helped shape, would become the defining image of the crisis—although by the time it was uttered the Russian ship captains had already put seven hundred fifty miles between them and the naval blockade as they headed back toward the Soviet Union. And Bobby's telling of the wider story would become the accepted one—that we had stared down the enemy—when what really saved the day was that both sides blinked.

Getting that wrong had ramifications. In Vietnam, President Lyndon Johnson was determined to prove that he was every bit as hard-nosed as the Kennedys had been in Cuba. He wasn't in on the behind-the-scenes bartering, so he didn't know that it was compromise, not steeliness, that got the United States out of the missile crisis. None of his advisers who did know—not Rusk, nor Bundy, nor McNamara, nor even Bobby—broke his vow of secrecy and shared that information with LBJ as he got increasingly mired in the quagmire of Southeast Asia. "Instead," as the former Kennedy Library historian Sheldon Stern notes, "Johnson went to his grave in 1973 believing that his predecessor had threatened the use of U.S. military power to successfully force the Soviet Union to back down."* An analogous misreading of history helped topple Khrushchev

---

* McNamara and Ted Kennedy worried that President George W. Bush was making a similar mistake by invading Iraq in 2003, and both tried unsuccessfully to warn him off. One of

from power. The syndicated columnist Joseph Alsop wrote that the crisis was resolved in a way that gave America "a remarkable victory," and most Americans agreed. So did most of the rest of the world. The Soviet Presidium and Bobby both knew better, but his rivals blamed the aging Communist Party leader for making Russia lose face, and Bobby preferred the America-is-remarkable version of the missile crisis story. Two years later Khrushchev was deposed and counted himself lucky to hang on to his pension, his *dacha*, and his life.

Thirteen Days, which has sold half a million copies and never been out of print since its release in 1969, got one thing right: The Cuban missile crisis was John Kennedy's shining moment. He had believed his generals and spies about the likely success of the Bay of Pigs invasion, and he refused to be fooled again. He stood tough when he had to and made the necessary concessions even if he didn't admit them. It helped that he had fought in World War II and seen its casualties, whereas Bobby had spent the war wishing he were old enough to fight and had spent the years since then proving he was as tough as any warrior. It also helped that of all the old hands and bright lights in his cabinet room, the president exhibited more patience and wisdom than anyone else.* None of that would have mattered, however, if President Kennedy hadn't had an equally heroic leader with whom to barter. Nikita Khrushchev nimbly shifted from tough guy to conciliator much as JFK did, but he took the sacrificial step the Kennedys demanded by making his withdrawal of the missiles look like a one-sided deal. It wasn't just his generals who felt betrayed but also his ally Fidel Castro. Getting us into the crisis was Kennedy and Khrushchev at their worst, but they revealed the best in themselves by getting us out without going over the brink. "The two most powerful nations of the world had been squared off against each other, each with its finger on the button," Khrushchev said looking back.

---

those who did understand the lessons of the missile crisis was Castro, whose long reign was in part enabled by the pledge made by JFK during the crisis, and honored by his successors, not to invade the island.

* Bobby underlined the point to a Kennedy Library interviewer: "The ten or twelve people who would participate in all of these [missile crisis] discussions were bright and energetic people. We had perhaps amongst them the most able in the country, but if any one of the half dozen of them were president, the world would very likely have been plunged into a catastrophic war" (RFK OH, February 13, 1965, 39).

"You'd have thought that war was inevitable. But both sides showed that if the desire to avoid war is strong enough, even the most pressing dispute can be solved by compromise."

As for Bobby, aspects of his behavior during and after the missile crisis are even more puzzling now that we have the pieces he left out of *Thirteen Days*. The afternoon of October 16, just hours after JFK shared with him the photographic evidence of the Russian missile installations, the attorney general summoned the Operation Mongoose planners to his office. Their work so far was "discouraging," he chided, because "there had been no acts of sabotage, and . . . even the one which had been attempted had failed twice." He didn't say anything about the missiles, but he did vow to "give Operation MONGOOSE more personal attention" by holding a meeting at 9:30 every morning with key representatives from participating agencies. That pledge was strange in two ways: His missile-crisis-related meetings left him less time than ever, yet he was committing an hour a day to Mongoose, and he apparently failed to see any incongruity in plotting such destabilizing operations in the midst of a nuclear crisis.

Once the crisis had passed, Bobby's role with Cuba was reduced, but he remained determined to pick a fight with Castro. In April 1963 the attorney general encouraged fellow national security planners to commission three studies. One would review what the United States should do if something dramatic happened such as "the death of Castro or the shooting down of a U-2" spy plane. A second would spell out a program for "overthrowing Castro in eighteen months." The last would explore ways to "cause as much trouble as we can for Communist Cuba." All such efforts would violate the spirit and letter of the deal reached with Khrushchev the previous October, but that didn't bother the Kennedys, nor did it keep them from trumpeting breaches by the Soviets and Cubans. Richard Helms, the CIA's espionage czar, recalled that "although as part of the negotiation [with Khrushchev] President Kennedy had forsworn attempting any invasion of Cuba, he and his brother remained absolutely determined to trounce Castro once and forever. . . . The MONGOOSE operation came slowly back to reality." Bobby himself recounted that in the summer and fall of 1963, "we were also making more of an effort through espionage and sabotage. . . . It was better organized than it had been before and was having quite an effect. I mean, there were ten or twenty tons of sugar cane that was being burned every week through internal uprisings."

———

THERE WAS NEVER just one side of Bobby, as he showed when he vacillated between hawk and dove during the nail-biting days in October 1962. Likewise, in their aftermath, he worried about the human cost of an earlier covert operation against Cuba even as he plotted new ones. He had never been able to get out of his head the more than one thousand Cuban expatriates captured after the botched raid at the Bay of Pigs, who had been rotting for eighteen months in Castro's jails despite repeated attempts by the United States to ransom them. Castro at first offered their release in exchange for five hundred bulldozers. A Tractors for Freedom Committee was created, headed by President Eisenhower's brother Milton and quietly encouraged by JFK. The committee bartered with Castro to provide farm tractors rather than the military-grade excavators he wanted, then to substitute $28 million in cash, which Castro said was the value of the tractors and the least he would consider. But congressional Republicans and much of the public resisted any payout to the Communists, and the deal fell through. Castro got his revenge by staging a show trial early in 1962 that condemned the prisoners to thirty years of hard labor. Having used his stick to maximum effect, the Cuban leader dangled another carrot. He would release his captives, but for twice the original ransom. To show his goodwill, he let go sixty of the sickest prisoners—for a payment of $2.9 million that he said could be made later—and they arrived in Miami a year to the day after they had left Nicaragua bound for the Bay of Pigs. With talks on getting out the rest of the detainees stymied, Castro presented a shopping list as thick as a telephone book, detailing the medicines and food he would accept in lieu of cash. The gambit might have worked but for the timing: The offer arrived two days before the president made public his discovery of Russian missiles in Cuba.

The abuse the Bay of Pigs prisoners were suffering became clear a month after the missile crisis, when one of their fathers visited the jail where the Castro regime was holding them. "I'm a cattleman, Mr. Attorney General, and these men look like animals who are going to die," Alvaro Sanchez, Jr., warned Bobby. "If you are going to rescue these men, this is the time because if you wait you will be liberating corpses." Bobby replied, "You are right. I think this is the moment." It was the moment, too, to come to Bobby with a plea like that. He was anxious not just to make up for the botched Bay of Pigs fiasco, but to embrace a mission that put him back on the side of the angels after his relentless bids to depose Castro and clandestine trading of missiles. Once he told Sanchez what he wanted to hear, Bobby-the-evangelist showed it was more than a politician's lip service. Nobody was better than the attorney general at mobilizing people. Drug firms were cajoled into donating the morphine and other medicines Castro demanded, and the Bureau of Narcotics said not to worry about dispensing controlled substances. Food companies were persuaded to kick in food supplies. The AFL-CIO paid the tab for operational expenses, while organizers packed cases of Budweiser, Castro's favorite beer. The IRS did its part by ruling that all $53 million in donations were tax deductible, a decision it reached in two hours rather than the normal two months. Justice Department regulators said they would give the firms a pass, this once, for violating antitrust laws by collaborating on pricing and shipping. Castro rightfully suspected that the American companies would try to unload their expired baby food and moth-eaten bins of clothing, so he dispatched four agents to Florida to inspect the goods. Bobby let his team do its work, but he checked in twice a day, asking, "How much have you got in drugs? Can we get it to Cuba? What can I do? What can the president do?"

They called it Operation Habeas Corpus, a nod to its focus on springing prisoners. It was accomplished within three weeks and on the q.t., because U.S. critics were poised to pounce and Castro had threatened to up the ante again if he suspected the direct involvement of the American government. The Cuban leader also insisted, mid-deal, on the $2.9 million promised when the sick prisoners were released the previous year. Bobby made two phone calls that only he could make—to Richard Cardinal Cushing of Boston, a friend of Joe Kennedy's who delivered $1 million that night, and to General Lucius Clay, the organizer of the Berlin

Airlift, who signed a personal note guaranteeing the rest.* Castro, meanwhile, was fattening up his captives and showing them his Soviet-built fighter planes to convince them how easily he could repel any future attacks. The press knew some of the deal's details but breathed barely a word until afterward, just as Bobby asked. He did tip off one refugee leader, telling him "that guy with the beard has accepted."

Five aircraft carrying 1,113 liberated prisoners touched down in Miami on Christmas Eve 1962, with many of the grateful returnees kissing the ground as they deplaned. Mission accomplished, complete with holiday drama designed to mute any criticism and with more than two hundred journalists there to bear witness. As for his staff, Bobby offered a "Thanks, fellows, and Merry Christmas." Pause. "Now let's go get Hoffa!"

Not all loose ends could be tied up that easily, and not all the families were reunited with their Bay of Pigs veterans. In Pete Ray's case, it took the government thirty-seven years even to acknowledge that he and his colleagues from the Alabama National Guard had been there. The CIA had selected the Alabama squad because it used B-26s similar to those flown by the Cuban Air Force, and the agency wanted to disguise the American planes to look like Cuban ones being flown by defectors instead of by U.S.-trained émigrés. The CIA got not just planes but Ray and other Americans who wanted to help at the agency's secret bases in Nicaragua and Guatemala. The cover story was that wealthy Cubans had hired the Americans to fly cargo planes. They weren't supposed to participate in the actual invasion, but they jumped in to relieve their exhausted émigré confederates. Ray was on his way to bomb Castro's headquarters when his plane was shot down. He survived the crash and a gun battle with Castro's troops, but was executed with a point-blank shot to his temple while he was lying on his back, says his daughter, Janet

---

* A more modest contribution ($25,000) allegedly came from John "Jake the Barber" Factor, a notorious swindler and half brother of the cosmetics mogul Max Factor. Not long after that donation was logged, JFK—who knew of the mobster from his earlier largesse to the 1960 Kennedy presidential campaign—pardoned Jake for a mail fraud conviction that would have resulted in his being deported to a prison cell in England (Touhy, *When Capone's Mob Murdered Roger Touhy*, 250–54).

Ray, who has spent the past half century tracking what happened after her dad left home that day in 1961 when she was six years old.

Janet doesn't blame the U.S. government for sponsoring the invasion, or for her dad's involvement, but she remains outraged by the lies that followed. JFK couldn't deny having trained the Cuban invaders, but he and Bobby were loath to admit that a handful of Americans were fighting alongside them even when Castro said he had the corpses to prove it. Janet says she discussed this with Richard Bissell, Jr., the CIA's point man for the Bay of Pigs, just before he died. Bissell remembered very clearly what Bobby said upon learning that Pete Ray's plane and another piloted by an Alabama guardsman had been shot down: "Those American pilots had better God damn well be dead or we're going to have another Francis Gary Powers* on our hands." Janet believed Bissell because his words were consistent with Bobby's actions. "I think Bobby Kennedy did a very commendable job in getting the [Cuban] prisoners released," Janet says, but she can't forgive him for not retrieving her father's remains. "The United States didn't ask for the body back due to political reasons: to protect JFK, the 1964 elections, CYA [cover your ass]." Her family and three others were eventually paid compensation and even given medals, but they had to keep that secret for decades, not just to protect America's security but to shield the Kennedys. "These four Alabama men's reputations," Janet says, "were sacrificed for political reasons."

Politics also was likely behind Bobby's preoccupation, nearly two years after the Bay of Pigs, with downplaying mistakes his brother had long ago put behind him. Had the president backed out on a vow to provide vital air protection for the invaders? "There never was any plan to have U.S. air cover," Bobby told a *Miami Herald* reporter in one of several "exclusive" interviews he gave on the topic. "There never was any promise." Bobby was nitpicking and reopening a controversy that everyone else considered closed. Having interviewed every witness and read every

---

* Powers was an American pilot whose CIA U-2 spy plane was shot down over the Soviet Union in 1960. Unable to activate the jet's self-destruct mechanism, and unable (some said unwilling) to use his suicide device, he and his plane were captured, causing a crisis in U.S.-Russian relations.

document as part of his review of the invasion, the attorney general knew that the refugees were convinced they'd been promised more air support. "Jets are coming!" brigade commander Pepe San Roman said he was told by his American contact in the midst of the battle, reassuring him of help that never arrived. There had also been a clash of views in the White House over what commitments had been made and how to keep them. Secretary Rusk said the promise was not to use American forces; the CIA and military said the reverse; and the president's national security advisor argued midinvasion that "the right course now is to eliminate the Castro air force, by neutrally painted U.S. planes if necessary." JFK decided on a compromise of having U.S. jets provide cover for the émigrés' B-26s, but even that didn't happen because the B-26s, including Pete Ray's, arrived early and met with disaster. Senator Richard Russell, the Democratic chairman of the Armed Services Committee, tried to fend off GOP attacks on the suddenly loquacious attorney general, but he admitted to being puzzled as to why Bobby would rehash "this sad episode" in newspapers and magazines. "I don't think there's any doubt," the senator said, "that the people who made the invasion thought they had air cover arranged for." Drew Pearson had his own explanation for Bobby's fixation on the long-past invasion: that the Kennedy administration was "the most PR-minded in American history."

Pearson was right, but he didn't know the full story. Bobby was eager to paper over past mistakes, but he was also exploring creative and politically risky ways to defuse hostilities with Castro. Those subterranean initiatives started in the spring of 1963 and continued until the day JFK was assassinated. James Donovan, the New York superlawyer who had helped negotiate the release of the Bay of Pigs prisoners, used that relationship with Castro to probe the Cuban leader's willingness to reconcile with America.* William Attwood, a U.S. official at the United Nations, was trying to set up his own meeting with Castro, and Bobby suggested it be somewhere remote like Mexico to ensure privacy. The attorney general even used journalists to test Castro's openness to negotiate. This "sweet approach" recognized that Castro was furious at

---

* Donovan also negotiated the exchange of Francis Gary Powers for the Russian spy Rudolf Abel, a dramatic story retold in the 2015 movie *Bridge of Spies*.

Khrushchev for taking away his nuclear missiles without consulting him, and what a coup it would be to push Cuba out of the Soviet orbit. The president and his brother knew that anything but a hard-line approach to Castro would cost them votes in Florida and elsewhere, but they seemed willing to take the gamble in an anticipated second term. What would happen, they asked themselves for the first time, if they simply left Cuba alone? Better still, what if Castro could be remolded into another Tito, leader of not just Yugoslavia but of the twenty-five-nation Non-Aligned Movement?*

In the days before his death, JFK made still more overtures. "Nothing is possible" in forging new relations so long as Cuba remains a Soviet pawn, he said during a speech in Miami, but if those ties were severed, "everything is possible." The president also encouraged the French journalist Jean Daniel to raise the idea of rapprochement when he interviewed Castro in late November. Daniel did, and got a positive reception, but a Castro aide interrupted the meeting to report that Kennedy had been shot. Whether those explorations would have led to real détente is impossible to know, although Castro later said that "Kennedy would not have received a rebuff from us." The Kennedy administration's intent is tougher to read, since it was pursuing war and peace at the same time—simil-opting, in the jargon of security officials. "It is likely that at the very moment President Kennedy was shot," the CIA inspector general reported later, "a CIA officer was meeting with a Cuban agent in Paris and giving him an assassination device for use against Castro."

What we do know is that after his brother's death, Bobby pushed Secretary of State Rusk to lift the ban on U.S. citizens traveling to Cuba, arguing that it "would contrast with such things as the Berlin Wall and Communist controls on such travel." As for a more history-bending initiative, Bobby said he and Jack had been "trying to work it out," which is more than any subsequent American administration did until President Obama's normalization agreement with President Raúl Castro in December 2014. Ethel Kennedy is convinced that Jack and Bobby could have achieved a comparable breakthrough with Fidel Castro, based on

---

* Castro did eventually try to become another Tito, taking on a leadership role in the Non-Aligned Movement and loosening but never severing his ties with the Soviet Union.

five or six private meetings she has had with him in recent decades.* Fidel, she says, saw her husband as a practical man with whom he could have struck a deal.

In the end, Cuba proved to be Bobby's biggest misstep as well as a milestone in his turnaround. He helped the U.S. government recover from the Bay of Pigs fiasco but never understood that the fault for the invasion's failure lay in its conception, not its execution. Operation Mongoose repeated those mistakes, in the process reinforcing Castro's image as David doing battle with the American Goliath and pushing Russia to protect him with a missile shield. Bobby did help his brother find a way out of the missile crisis, but only after the president rejected the attorney general's earlier call for an air strike. In rare moments, Bobby discussed his role with candor, although the story he generally told was more aspirational than factual. But he also matured during the Cuban crises—slowly seeing that a leader could be tough without being bellicose, finding his voice on foreign affairs as he had at home, and stepping out of his brother's long shadow even as he remained his closest and most loyal confidant.† Each new role he assumed on Jack's behalf was preparing Bobby to be his own man. The process wasn't complete, but the course was set.

---

* At their first meeting, Ethel says; Castro "embraced me. And, you know, in the Continental way, he kissed both cheeks. And then, and then he held me away from him, and his eyes filled with tears, and then the tears came down his cheeks. He had a very tough time recovering." His meetings with Ethel suggest how entranced Fidel is with the family, despite Jack and Bobby's bids to eliminate him, and how he realizes that the Bay of Pigs and missile crisis were his defining moments (Author interview with Ethel Kennedy).

† One small sign of that maturation came in the summer of 1963, when Brandon Grove consulted Bobby on whether to accept Chester Bowles's offer of a job in India, where Bowles was doing a second tour as ambassador. Kennedy had called Bowles's performance during the missile crisis "whiny," branded him a "gutless bastard" for not intervening in the Dominican Republic, and helped get him fired as undersecretary of state. Now, as Grove remembered, Bobby's "surprising reply was: 'Do it. [Bowles] is a good man'" (Grove, *Behind Embassy Walls*, 78).

Chapter 7

THE INTERREGNUM

T HE NEWS THAT would shatter his world couldn't have come from less sympathetic lips. Bobby had brought two colleagues back to Hickory Hill for lunch after an exhausting day and a half of meetings on how to ratchet up the war against the Cosa Nostra. Before heading back to the Justice Department he treated himself to a quick swim on what was an unseasonably mild afternoon for November 22. Then he changed into dry shorts and joined Ethel and their guests near the shallow end of the pool for a Vatican-sanctioned Friday menu of tuna fish sandwiches and creamy clam chowder. The calm was broken by ringing in the green wooden phone box that housed the direct line to the White House, a sound that generally signaled trouble. Ethel answered, hoping to shield her husband from the interruption, but when the operator insisted it was urgent she held out the white receiver and announced, "It's J. Edgar Hoover."

"I have news for you," Hoover told Bobby. "The president's been shot." The FBI director's monotone made his ghastly meaning difficult to fathom. Bobby's mind hurtled back to two nights earlier, when he'd been laughing with Jack about the president's impending trip to Dallas to forge a peace between feuding Democrats. After a moment of stricken silence he refocused to reply: "Is it serious?" Hoover: "I think it's serious. I am endeavoring to get details. I'll call you back when I find out more." The director's words and expression, as the attorney general would later say, were "not quite as excited as if he were reporting the fact that he had found a Communist on the faculty of Howard University."

To Bobby, the news was cataclysmic. His hand instinctively clasped his mouth as his face stretched tight, telegraphing his horror. Ethel saw his expression from the far side of the pool and sprinted to his side, embracing him. "Jack's been shot," he choked out. "It may be fatal." An emotional onslaught catapulted him between despair and disbelief even as he carefully realigned his countenance into an emotionless mask. The reflexes of crisis were by now a well-known body memory and he forced himself into action. There were too many roles to play, too much that only he could do. Grieving would have to wait.

Tensely, he dialed Defense Secretary McNamara on the black house phone and requested a plane to fly him to his brother's side. Then he bounded up the stairs to change clothes and make arrangements. Everywhere he looked were framed reminders—Jack addressing a joint session of Congress, Jack holding hands with Jackie, Jack striking a pose with the rest of Rose and Joe's brood. Bobby called the hospital in Dallas, peppering the Secret Service detail with queries. Were the president's injuries serious? (Very.) Was he conscious? (No.) How was Jackie holding up? (Not well.) Had they summoned a priest? (Yes.) Dashing between phone extensions in the upstairs study, downstairs library, and outdoor pool and tennis court, Bobby muttered to himself, "There's been so much hate." Thirty minutes later, Taz Shepard, JFK's naval aide, called back with word that the president had died.

In an instant, Bobby shifted from First Brother to First Son. His thoughts went not to his loss, but to his siblings' and parents'. Ted had heard about the shooting and rushed home, but with the telephone exchanges jammed he had to ring the doorbells of neighbors he didn't know until he found one with a working phone and could call Hickory Hill. "He's dead," reported Bobby, whose house was becoming an impromptu command center. "You'd better call your mother and our sisters." The attorney general knew who was capable of what and handed out assignments. Ted and Eunice would fly to Hyannis Port, where he'd persuaded Rose to wait until they arrived to tell Joe about his son's murder. Jean agreed to come to Washington to attend to her sister-in-law and friend Jackie. Patricia was tracked down in California, and Jackie's sister, Lee Radziwill, in London. Sargent Shriver was already arranging the funeral with help from another brother-in-law, Steve Smith. Ethel stayed close by her husband, squeezing out between tears, "Those poor children!" Bobby had been the de facto head of the Kennedy clan for two years, since his father's stroke. With Jack gone, it became official.

Barely an hour after the Secret Service confirmed that the president was dead, his successor telephoned Bobby from Dallas. "A lot of people down here think I should be sworn in right away. Do you have any objections?" Lyndon Johnson asked, tone-deaf to his bad timing and adding another bone for Bobby to pick with him. At Hickory Hill, meanwhile, a crowd was gathering. Bobby asked John McCone for clues about the killer, but the CIA chief said he had none. To press aide Ed Guthman, Bobby confided, "I'd received a letter from someone in Texas last week warning me not to let the President go to Dallas because they would kill him. . . . I never thought it would happen. I thought it would be me." Guthman thought the same thing, and shortly after the assassination, he quietly posted a dozen Fairfax County police officers around the crowded Kennedy compound. His red-rimmed eyes concealed by sunglasses, Bobby bucked up his guests by saying, "We don't want any gloomy faces around here." He bear-hugged his children when they got home from school, reminding them that Uncle Jack "had the most wonderful life." It would become his refrain.

By early evening his focus had switched to Jackie. A military helicopter whisked him to Andrews Field, where he wanted to be on hand to meet Air Force One, which was carrying home his brother's corpse and widow. Bobby jumped into the back of an empty Air Force truck and sat in the darkness, where he could avoid the swarming reporters. It was the same solitary setting where, thirteen months before, he had waited for Jack to fly home from Chicago during the tense early moments of the missile crisis. "Tears were streaming down his eyes, down his face, his cheeks. It really got to me, I had never seen the man cry," remembers David Kraslow, a reporter with the *Los Angeles Times* who'd escaped the press cordon and found a hiding spot near Bobby's.

The moment the plane touched down, Bobby ran up the steps even as they were being rolled into place, intent on finding Jackie. He barely acknowledged LBJ, which Johnson would remember. "I'm here," he told his brother's widow, draping his arm around her as millions of Americans watched on live television. "Oh, Bobby," she whispered, reassured that, as always, her brother-in-law was there when she needed him. The two rode to Bethesda Naval Hospital curled in the back of the ambulance with Jack's body. Jackie recounted every detail Bobby dreaded hearing about the motorcade, the assassination, and the aftermath. "It was so obvious that she wanted to tell me," he would recall, "that whether or not I wanted to hear it wasn't a factor." Then he asked a Secret Service agent riding with them, "Did you hear they'd apprehended a fellow in Dallas. . . . It was one man." All day and night he was forced to deal with the unthinkable and the unspeakable. He made the key choices on everything, from the size of his brother's bier and hearse to picking a Navy hymn for his funeral. When they arrived at the White House in the small hours of the morning there was one more question to answer: Should the casket be open or closed? Bobby asked everyone to leave the East Room so he could view the body. It was his first look at Jack since the shooting, and he nearly collapsed. "Close it," he ordered. Cosmetics made the president look waxlike and made up, too little like the majestic leader America knew and the brother he wanted to remember.

The most pressing duties finally done, Bobby was alone for the first time since he took the FBI director's call twelve hours before. An entire nation was mourning its president, but nobody—not Bobby's mother or siblings, nor even his sister-in-law Jackie—would grieve as deeply or as long as Bobby did. None of the losses that had come before could prepare him for this one. Jack had taken Joe Jr.'s place as Bobby's revered older brother, then Joe Sr.'s as a father figure. The two were closer than any brothers had been at high levels of government, talking in a private code, perpetually interrupting each other and finishing one another's sentences. Gone now were the dreams of what they could accomplish side by side. Gone, too, was Bobby's seat at the table of power—J. Edgar Hoover and Lyndon Johnson had already made that clear. From his years with the Rackets Committee to his time at the Justice Department, Bobby's career and life had been hitched to his brother's. The sniper's bullet that had penetrated Jack's skull shattered Bobby's own vision even as it broke his heart.

Such were the thoughts swirling in his mind as he headed to the Lincoln Bedroom, where he would spend the few remaining hours before dawn. Charles Spalding, a scriptwriter who was close to both brothers, looked for and finally found a sleeping pill for the attorney general. "It's such an awful shame," Bobby said softly. "The country was going so well. We really had it going." Spalding closed the bedroom door and started to walk away, then turned to listen: "He just gave way completely, and he was just racked with sobs and the only person he could address himself to was 'Why, God, why? What possible reason could there be in this?' "

Bobby would never find a reason, but he would find a way to get it going again. His upbringing had instilled in him a steely drive. Joe Kennedy loved his boys, but he wasn't a sentimentalist. He had trained them all for public service and high office and would not be denied. When he lost his firstborn, in whom he had invested his highest hopes, Joe saw to it that Jack stepped in to fulfill those dreams all the way to the White House. Now, by the laws of primogeniture, it was Bobby's turn. Nobody had articulated the way the Kennedys worked better than JFK, who back when he was a senator said, "Just as I went into politics because Joe died, if anything happened to me tomorrow, my brother Bobby would run for my seat in the Senate, and if Bobby died, Teddy would take over for him." When he won the presidential nomination, Jack gave Bobby a cigarette box inscribed, "When I'm through, how about you?"*

Bobby was readier than anyone realized. Jack had been training him to take his place from the start of his term, although he didn't expect the succession to take place until 1968 at the earliest. He not only gave his brother the legal experience he had joked about, he let him try on more hats than anyone else in the administration. At various times Bobby had acted as the virtual secretary of defense and the CIA director. He had offered advice on political affairs, diplomatic affairs, and press affairs, and he had set so many policies on poverty and juvenile delinquency that the secretary of Health, Education, and Welfare wondered aloud if Bobby wanted his job. So did the postmaster general, who knew that in the Kennedy administration, the attorney general was the true prince of patronage. Bobby had signaled his latest intentions before the assassination by ordering for his senior staff cufflinks with an inscription that marked his

---

* Rose is reported to have said, just three months after her son Jack's assassination, "The next president of the United States will be my son Bobby" (Beale, *Power at Play*, 270).

time at the Department of Justice as 1961 to 1963. The rumor floated around Washington that Angie Novello, his personal secretary, had already been to the State Department to measure the curtains and that Bobby was heading there to oversee U.S. relations with Latin America or perhaps the whole world.

It was not just affairs of state Bobby was privy to, but all of Jack's dark secrets. Only Bobby had access to every segment of the president's rigidly compartmentalized life. Now only Bobby knew how much truth lay behind the whispers about bids to steal votes from Richard Nixon or to assassinate Fidel Castro. He also knew enough about his brother's marital and extramarital affairs to guess the rest. That's why, in the midst of the two busiest and worst days of his life, Bobby took time out to quietly issue orders nobody would learn about until years later. The National Security Advisor changed the combinations on JFK's locked office files and secured the rest of his personal papers. The Secret Service removed secret listening devices from the Oval Office and Cabinet Room. And doctors overseeing the president's autopsy made sure not to mention embarrassing information like the state of his hotly debated adrenal glands. Here was the brutally efficient, fraternally devoted Bobby coexisting somehow with a man enveloped by a blanket of sadness.

Perhaps sensing his own vulnerability and his brother's blossoming, Jack had drawn Bobby even closer near the end. Since the Bay of Pigs, his presidency had come as close to a collaboration as the nation had ever seen. It was visible in the battery of White House phones installed around Hickory Hill, from the study to the tennis court and swimming pool, compared to the single line to LBJ's home. In the two days before he left for Dallas, the president was on the telephone to the attorney general seven times. Friends of both also noticed that the older brother had stopped needling the younger the way he had throughout their campaigns together. He was more respectful. Yet even as he had become Jack's second self, Bobby was emerging as a prime force. He was growing up fast and putting aside the colder, tougher incarnation that he had assumed partly for the sake of his father and brother. With the president's passing, that process continued with an intensity and in directions that would have surprised even John Kennedy. Relegated to a supporting role by birth order and his brother's oversized presence, Bobby now would step into a limelight of his own.

AMERICA WAS AS one in its shock, outrage, and heartache over the assassination of President John F. Kennedy. Those who lived through it can remember where they were when they heard, and they will never forget the date November 22, 1963. But for most the pain subsided bit by bit as his casket was viewed by a select audience in the East Room of the White House, by hundreds of thousands who passed by as it lay in state at the Capitol, by millions who lined his funeral route, and by nearly everyone else in the country who watched on television the requiem mass at St. Matthew's Cathedral and the burial at Arlington National Cemetery.

For Bobby it was just the opposite. He was the steadiest of the stricken during the public observances, rallying to face the world and lending his hand in every critical decision. It was he who mediated between those who insisted the president be entombed in his native Boston and others who preferred the nation's cemetery. He picked the precise spot, the hillside below Arlington House that his brother had visited and liked, announcing, "This is where we'll bury the president." He decided that Joe couldn't handle the strain and kept him away from his son's funeral. When Jackie dressed little John in white gloves, Bobby took them off, deciding it was unmanly even for a boy of three. Attentive to his own children, he took time the day he buried his brother to write to each, reminding them of their responsibility, as Jack's nieces and nephews and as Kennedys, to serve their country. Then he reminded his siblings to pen similar letters to their own offspring. "It was natural for Bobby to take charge," said his younger brother Ted. "He's always been a sort of second father to us."

Bobby stepped gracefully into the role of premature patriarch, having trained nearly his entire life to handle tragedy. At eighteen, he was at Hyannis Port that mild August afternoon in 1944 when chaplains broke it to the family that Joe Jr. wouldn't be coming home from World War II. Nobody took the news harder than Bobby, who idolized his oldest brother. Four years later a plane crash took his big sister Kathleen. A stroke had banished his father to a wheelchair, and a failed lobotomy left his sister Rosemary under round-the-clock care in faraway Wisconsin. Both calamities were agonizing for Bobby. He had consoled Ethel through the loss of both of her parents in yet another airplane accident, and he comforted Jack and Jackie after the loss of their two-day-old son, Patrick. Tragedy struck the family so often that it acquired a name: the Kennedy curse. The very worst of times brought out the best in Bobby.

He would come unstrung, however, just as others were beginning to pull themselves together. Journalist Haynes Johnson described him after the funeral: "I remember Bobby standing on the steps. I looked at him and he looked at me and his eyes" were haunted. "It was deep, deep, deep black despair." John Seigenthaler, who had taken a leave from journalism to work at the Justice Department, went back to Hickory Hill after the burial: "[Bobby] opened the door and said something like this, 'Come on in, somebody shot my brother and we're watching his funeral on television.' Which was sort of the sardonic humor I was talking about earlier. I said, sort of with a half laugh, 'Bob, that's not funny.' And he looked me dead in the eye and said, 'Don't you think I know that?' " Ethel says that in the days after the assassination her husband was like the marathon runner who somehow finds the energy to make it 26.2 miles "and then it takes you a little while to slow down and maybe just walk, and then maybe to lie down, and [then you] crash."

That his grief was different is no surprise. Everyone else, even his siblings, returned to familiar routines that distracted them from their loss. But Jack had been a part of every piece of Bobby's life and reminders were everywhere, from the red phone on his desk to the new occupant of the Oval Office. Forgetting, even temporarily, wasn't an option, as he was pulled into a deeper, darker stage of mourning. That difference became apparent over the Thanksgiving holiday. Celebrating in Hyannis Port was a Kennedy tradition, and with Thanksgiving Day in 1963 falling a week after the assassination, everyone felt it was especially important to be in the embrace of family. Everyone but Bobby. "It was something he could not quite do," explained Rose. "He had reached a state, I suppose, of almost insupportable emotional shock." Instead he headed to Florida with Ethel, their older children, and friends including White House press secretary Pierre Salinger. "He was the most shattered man I had ever seen in my life," Salinger said. "He was virtually non-functioning. He would walk for hours by himself. . . . From time to time, he'd organize a touch football game. . . . They were really vicious games. I mean it seemed to me the way he was getting his feelings out was in, you know, in knocking people down. Somebody, in fact, I think either Ed Guthman or somebody broke a leg during one of those games."

Back in Washington it was Bobby who crumpled, retreating into himself. Unable to sleep, he would drive off in his convertible on frigid nights under a pitch-black sky. The U.S. marshals now patrolling his property could hardly keep track of him. Other mornings he was up at four riding his horse or wandering the grounds, his huge Newfoundland at his heels. He stayed away from the Justice Department for most of the rest of 1963, returning occasionally for partial days in which he couldn't maintain his focus. He was unable to make himself read official documents that he typically would have devoured. Staffers noticed his trousers were missing a belt and his socks were mismatched. In meetings, his expression would go blank as he stared out the window. His colleagues' sense that they were an elite crew on an extraordinary mission—Bobby's band of brothers—faded after Dallas. "I don't think there is much left for me in this town," he told friends. He talked about going away—to England for a year to write, or to a university to teach—but couldn't make himself do it. He also couldn't refer directly to Jack's murder, instead using the euphemism "the events of November 22, 1963."

Ed Guthman begged journalists to "just come over. Ask him anything. . . . Draw him out of the damned shell he's in." One who did was journalist Simeon Booker. "Entering the dark paneled room, I found Robert Kennedy at his desk, his head in his hands," Booker recalled. "When he looked up, I could see that he'd been crying. His eyes were red and moist. 'Come on, now,' I told him lightly, 'You're Irish. You're supposed to be tough. I'm Negro and you think you can push me around.' My ribbing made him laugh. 'Booker,' he said, smiling, 'you always know how to knock somebody off balance.'" Charles Spalding, another writer who stayed close, borrowed images from Bobby's treasured sport of sailing to capture his devastation: He "was just the picture of a boat, if you will, under such full sail and breezes just perfectly pitched and the sails set right and everything going and suddenly—it sinks."

Jack was no longer in Bobby's world but still governed his life. The attorney general quietly built a shrine to his slain brother in a corner of his office, with JFK's photos, books, and other talismans. He donned Jack's tweed overcoat and his leather bomber jacket with the presidential seal, and he continued to wear a black mourning tie far longer than tradition dictated. He had to drive past Arlington Cemetery at least twice a day and would stop often, climbing over the wall, kneeling in front of the gravestone, and praying. (Bobby called it "visiting the President"—as if Jack still were alive.) Faith failed to comfort him the way it did Ethel, who was sure her brother-in-law was in heaven alongside his big brother and little sister, keeping watch. Jack's ambitions had been Bobby's, and now the hero-brother was gone and any earthly goals seemed ephemeral. The president's assassination was, as journalist and friend Jack Newfield observed, "like an amputation that never healed."

The Kennedy family trait of holding feelings behind a wall of silence had often frustrated friends who wanted to help. Jack himself was famous for putting misfortune in his past, be it the death of a sibling or even a child. Teddy, too. Bobby, however, could neither open up nor let go. "I think often of Bobby's grief over the loss of Jack," Ted said looking back. "It veered close to being a tragedy within the tragedy. Ethel and my mother feared for his own survival; his psychic survival at least. . . . He would spend hours without speaking a word. . . . Hope seemed to have died within him, and there followed months of unrelenting melancholia. He went through the motions of everyday life, but he carried the burden of his grief with him always. I was so worried about Bobby that I tried to suppress my own grief."

Bobby's symptoms were those of a wounded warrior, uncertain whether he could make it back to battle or even through the day. He lost weight and felt depleted. He couldn't sleep or focus for long. His eyes were swollen, his hands trembled more than normal with fingernails bitten to the quick, while his movements and speech seemed tentative. He had always been brooding and even sad, but now the despair wouldn't let up. To Seigenthaler, it looked as though his friend was suffering from what today would be diagnosed as clinical depression and back then was whispered to be a nervous breakdown. Seigenthaler resisted confronting him, knowing Bobby would never admit weakness or accept assistance.

Finally he asked, "Have you gotten some help?" Bobby: "You mean from a psychiatrist?" Seigenthaler: "Yes." Bobby "didn't get angry, but he was very brusque in saying no," Seigenthaler added. "That ended the conversation."

Only children could lift him out of his self-absorption, as happened during a Christmas Eve party at an orphanage in Washington. It was the first time Bobby had been out in public since the assassination, and he went because it was a tradition. "The moment he walked in the room, all these children—screaming and playing—there was just suddenly silence," remembered the journalist Peter Maas. "A little boy—I don't suppose he was more than six or seven years old—suddenly darted forward, and stopped in front of him, and said, 'Your brother's dead! Your brother's dead!' Gosh, you know, you could hear a pin drop. The adults, all of us, we just kind of turned away. . . . The little boy knew he had done something wrong, but he didn't know *what;* so he started to cry. Bobby stepped forward and picked him up, in kind of one motion, and held him very close for a moment, and he said, 'That's all right. I have another brother.' "

The other perpetual mourner was Jackie. Like Bobby, she had shown superhuman strength throughout the public memorials, only to crash once she was out of view. The night of the funeral, Bobby asked Jackie, "Shall we go visit our friend?" The two dropped to their knees in front of Jack's gravestone, offering silent benedictions, then walked hand in hand through the wet grass. Bobby tried to soften the blow of losing their father for John Jr. and Caroline, spending as much time as he could with his nephew and niece and bringing them to Hickory Hill to play with their cousins. Over Easter, Bobby and Jackie joined friends at a hilltop villa lent to them in Antigua, without Ethel or any of the kids. They had been close before but not intimate confidants like this. While Ethel had always had issues with Jackie, until now they hadn't included jealousy.* Whether JFK's brother and widow were having an affair nobody can say for sure, but there was speculation enough to fill a book with the indelicate title *Bobby and Jackie: A Love Story.* (It was published in 2009, when

---

* In the aftermath of the assassination Ethel actually told her grieving sister-in-law, "I'll share [Bobby] with you" (*Robert Kennedy: His Life,* 278).

neither of the supposed lovers was alive to refute that contention or to sue for libel.) What is clear from interviews with sources close to each is that both were devastated by their loss and each was determined to help the other through. Bobby "always came, unasked, at times like that," Jackie would say later. "Because of him, no one ever gave up." And fifty years after the fact, Ethel concedes it might well have been Jackie who lifted Bobby from his haze.

There was one memory about Jack that Bobby couldn't share even with Jackie and that tormented him on his sleepless nights: He suspected that Jack's assassination was motivated by actions he had taken as attorney general, in public or, worse still, out of sight and with questionable authority. He had no doubt that the gunman was Lee Harvey Oswald—or "Harvey Lee Oswald," as the press first called him and as Bobby would always remember him—but he didn't know who might have put Oswald up to it. Was it payback from Fidel Castro? Was it Oswald acting alone but thinking he was doing the bidding of the Cuban leader he idolized? Was it anti-Castro Cubans—with help, perhaps, from their CIA handlers who were master liquidators—who hated the Kennedys for abandoning them at the Bay of Pigs? Could it have been the work of "Screw" Andrews or some other hoodlum Bobby had locked up, or more likely a mob higher-up like Mooney Giancana? What about Jimmy Hoffa, who had promised to get even and knew just the hired guns to do it? What if the Teamsters boss had decided that the sweetest revenge was making Bobby's life a living hell by murdering the person he loved the most and making Bobby feel responsible? Hoffa called the notion "nonsense," which it likely was, but Justice investigator Walter Sheridan told the attorney general that Hoffa was at a restaurant when he heard about the assassination and "he got up on the table and cheered."

There is no way to know how much those suspicions bedeviled Bobby, but questions he put to Sheridan, John McCone, Haynes Johnson, and others leave little doubt they were on his mind. So did his saying, to people he trusted such as Guthman, "It should have been me." Yet the FBI and other agencies involved weren't interested in pursuing such conspiracy theories, nor was the new president. The only way left for Bobby to resolve the underlying who and why of his brother's assassination

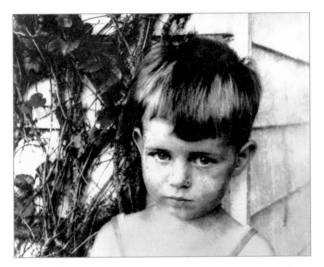

A freckle-faced Bobby, when he was small and shy enough that his father discounted him as the runt of the litter even as he was his mother's pet. COURTESY OF ETHEL KENNEDY

Joe and Rose Kennedy with their nine children. Bobby is wearing a light-colored suit and standing behind Ted, who is sitting on his father's lap. PHOTO BY ULLSTEIN BILD/ULLSTEIN BILD VIA GETTY IMAGES

Dockside with his mother and his sisters Eunice and Kathleen, on New Year's Day 1942, shortly after Bobby turned sixteen.

Bobby and Ethel on their wedding day, June 17, 1950. The ceremony was at St. Mary Roman Catholic Church in Greenwich, Connecticut, the reception was at Ethel's family home nearby, the honeymoon was in Hawaii, and Bobby's best man was his brother Jack.

Bobby converses at a 1954 congressional hearing with his boss, Republican senator Joseph McCarthy, as Democratic senator Henry Jackson looks on from Bobby's left. PHOTO BY HANK WALKER/THE LIFE PICTURE COLLECTION/GETTY IMAGES

For six weeks in 1955, Bobby and Supreme Court Justice William O. Douglas tour factories, libraries, and any place they can talk their way into throughout Turkmenistan, Uzbekistan, and other outposts of Soviet rule. PHOTO BY ULLSTEIN BILD/ULLSTEIN BILD VIA GETTY IMAGES

Ethel was Bobby's second self. Her lightness relieved his heaviness and her love was the kind he had craved—without conditions. They even looked alike, from protruding front teeth to thick mops of hair that made them seem like teenagers. Courtesy of Ethel Kennedy

Seven kids and counting at bedtime, when the Kennedy children assembled to recite as one "Now I lay me down to sleep." Courtesy of Ethel Kennedy

Team Kennedy huddles to plot the next play in touch football, the signature game for Ethel and Bobby's offspring as it had been for Rose and Joe's. COURTESY OF CHRISTOPHER KENNEDY AND ALAN DABBIERE

Horsing around with his oldest boys—Joe, Bobby Jr., and David—at Hickory Hill, where RFK and his brood frolicked as friends rather than as father and children, which was the right fit for this man-sized child.

COURTESY OF CHRISTOPHER KENNEDY AND ALAN DABBIERE

Bobby and Ethel's Hickory Hill estate in McLean, Virginia, whose fourteen rooms
included marble fireplaces, crystal chandeliers, and the space to expand should they
keep making babies, as they knew they would when they moved there in 1957.

Counsel Robert Kennedy sketches the alleged pattern of Teamsters corruption at a 1957
hearing of the Senate Permanent Subcommittee on Investigations.

The Kennedy family and campaign aides anxiously watch election returns in 1960 at Bobby and Ethel's place in Hyannis Port. After Jack, the sixteen telephone operators, the pollster Louis Harris, and everyone else had headed to bed, Bobby remained at his makeshift command post. COURTESY OF ETHEL KENNEDY

The newly elected president announces his brother's nomination as attorney general. Just before he did, Jack kidded Bobby, "Don't smile too much or they'll think we're happy about the appointment." PHOTO BY KEYSTONE-FRANCE/GAMMA-KEYSTONE VIA GETTY IMAGES

Bobby takes a moment with his firstborn, Kathleen, named after his sister who had been killed in a plane crash. COURTESY OF ETHEL KENNEDY

A month after JFK's swearing-in, he and Bobby meet at the White House with the man who would become their nemesis, FBI director J. Edgar Hoover. PHOTO BY ABBIE ROWE/ PHOTOQUEST/GETTY IMAGES

Ethel and Bobby have a private audience at the Vatican in 1962 with Pope John XXIII, who afterward blessed the "pens, hearts and tongues" of the newspapermen traveling with the attorney general. COURTESY OF ETHEL KENNEDY

Peering over the Berlin Wall in 1962 with Willy Brandt, the governing mayor of West Berlin, who went on to become chancellor of West Germany and winner of the 1971 Nobel Peace Prize. PHOTO BY KEYSTONE-FRANCE/GAMMA-KEYSTONE VIA GETTY IMAGES

Bobby and Ted grieve for their brother Jack, with fellow mourners Jackie, Caroline, and John Jr., outside St. Matthew's Cathedral in Washington, D.C. Photo by Consolidated News Pictures/Getty Images

Their grim expressions mirror their mutual contempt, as President Lyndon Johnson joins the newly elected Senator Robert Kennedy in December 1964 at the ground-breaking for the John F. Kennedy Center for the Performing Arts in Washington, D.C. PHOTO BY FRANCIS MILLER/THE LIFE PICTURE COLLECTION/GETTY IMAGES

Ted called the older brother he adored "Robbie"; Bobby returned the gesture with "Eddie." COURTESY OF ETHEL KENNEDY

The classic RFK hairstyle, thick on the top with an unruly cowlick flopping onto his forehead. Bobby loved that haircuts from the Senate barber were free, although nobody could tell the difference after he'd had one, and he seldom had coins to tip the shoeshine boy or barber.

Senator Robert F. Kennedy visiting with the children who were his favorite constituents, this time at a playground in Brooklyn. Photo by Buyenlarge/Getty Images

Bobby showing off his formidable forehand, which he perfected on the Kennedy tennis courts in Hyannis Port and Palm Beach and at Hickory Hill. Ethel is in the background.

Courtesy of Ethel Kennedy

Bobby rides through Los Angeles in 1968 in his typical campaign pose: standing in an open-air car, smiling and reaching out to touch the endless hands that greet him.

Photo by Lawrence Schiller/Polaris Communications/Getty Images

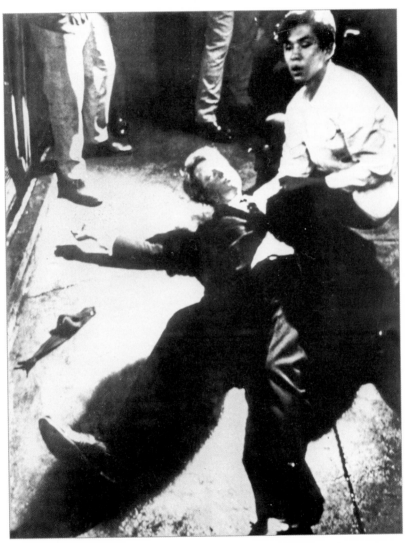

Just after Bobby is shot at the Ambassador Hotel in Los Angeles, busboy Juan Romero places rosary beads in his hand and tries to cushion his head as Ethel pleads with the pressing crowd to "give him room to breathe." PHOTO BY ULLSTEIN BILD VIA GETTY IMAGES

More than a million Americans turn out along the Penn Central tracks to say their last goodbyes as a train carries Bobby's body from his funeral at St. Patrick's Cathedral in New York to his burial at Arlington Cemetery outside Washington. Photo by Declan Haun/Chicago History Museum/Getty Images was to unmask the very stories he was determined to hide forever. And as difficult as it was to comprehend the senseless act of a crazed assassin, a purposeful one that bore his fingerprints would have been intolerable.

––––––––––

BOBBY NEVER HAD to speculate about where he stood with LBJ, who would play even more of a defining role in his life than earlier enemies like Jimmy Hoffa. The animus was evident from the instant they met in the Senate cafeteria a decade before, and it was reinforced during their brushes the day after JFK's assassination. Every time the two had interacted during the Kennedy administration, their relationship suffered. New Frontiersmen mockingly referred to the vice president as Uncle Cornpone. He was invited to Hickory Hill parties at the last minute if at all, and he was consigned to what Ethel called the losers' table. During one fete he didn't attend, the attorney general's friends gave Bobby a Lyndon Johnson voodoo doll and a set of pins. Bobby also had a long list of substantive gripes against the vice president—from his advising JFK to delay filing civil rights legislation, to his failing to mediate between dueling Democrats in Texas, which is why Jack made his fateful trip to Dallas. LBJ blamed Bobby for displacing him as JFK's second in charge and never missed a chance to belittle the attorney general. "John Kennedy and I had achieved real friendship," Johnson wrote in his memoir. "I doubt his younger brother and I would have arrived at genuine friendship if we had worked together for a lifetime. Too much separated us—too much history, too many differences in temperament."

That gulf was on graphic display after a White House dinner dance in 1961, when a group of officials gathered in the First Family's upstairs kitchen to scramble some eggs. LBJ crowded in on RFK, saying, "Bobby, you do not like me. Your brother likes me. Your sister-in-law likes me. Your daddy likes me. But *you don't like me*. Now, why? Why don't you like me?" Charles Spalding, who was standing nearby, remembers that "Bobby agreed to the accuracy of all that" and "was enjoying" watching LBJ grovel. Finally the vice president tried a new tack: "I know why you don't like me. You think I attacked your father [at the 1960 Democratic Convention]. . . . I never did attack your father and I wouldn't and I always liked you and admired you. But you're angry with me and you've

always been upset with me." Doubting his own memory, the next morning Bobby asked Seigenthaler to check old newspaper clippings that confirmed that LBJ had in fact smeared Joe Kennedy as thinking "Hitler was
right." Bobby's conclusion, as he told an interviewer later, was that LBJ
"lies continuously about everything. In every conversation I have with
him, he lies. As I've said, he lies even when he doesn't have to lie."

Bobby was right that Johnson perpetually shaded the facts, but so did
Bobby. LBJ came closer to the truth when he said the two men were simply too different to get along. Although each had been weaned on the old
politics of party loyalties and backroom deals, that had remained LBJ's
comfort zone while Bobby, seventeen years his junior and an early ad-
herent of the New Politics movement, enthusiastically embraced new
media such as television, new ways of reaching voters such as scientific
polling, and building an entirely new base of support among America's
rambunctious youth. Bobby had to learn by observation about the plight
of the poor and minorities, whereas both were in the bones of LBJ, who'd
grown up dirt-poor in the Texas Hill Country. The bombastic Texan
pawed and hugged his listeners as he exercised his electric capacity to
persuade, moving into just that personal space that the restrained New
Englander felt should not be violated. The attorney general, meanwhile, ·
disproved the new president's self-justifying theory that intellectuals
couldn't get anything done. Bobby was a thinker as well as a doer, glib
along with direct. Perhaps what separated the two came down to Southwest Texas State Teachers' College versus what LBJ called "the Har-
vards," his dismissive term for the Kennedys and their East Coast chums.
In the end, each made the other recoil.

But Bobby shared more than he admitted with Lyndon, as was the
case with all of his enemies. Both knew well how to count votes, and how
to double-deal when they had to. Each would disarm and dismay conservative allies by moving to the left on issues like civil rights and poverty.
Both were strong-willed and thin-skinned. Neither forgot a slight or forgave an adversary. Each seemed to have been put on earth to annoy the
other. LBJ blamed Bobby for blocking his getting closer to JFK, failing to
see that JFK had been amused by his vice president but had never embraced him. For RFK, Johnson became the scapegoat for his grief and
anger over losing his brother, and he failed to see that no successor could

ever have filled that sacred space. One last thing united America's two
most closely chronicled political personalities and as a consequence divided them: Both saw themselves as the legitimate heir to the JFK legacy.
The other, by definition, became the wicked usurper.

For the 1,036 days of JFK's presidency, Bobby had the upper hand if
not the senior title, with LBJ chafing, in the words of his young aide Bill
Moyers, like "a great horse in a very small corral." Gunshots in Dallas
flipped those roles. LBJ was now the one with the power and the capacity
to make underlings quake, leaving RFK with only the authority the president chose to confer. It wouldn't take long for that turnaround to mani-
fest itself, beginning with a series of run-ins the day after the assassination.

LBJ's advisers pushed him to move into the Oval Office that morning, even as JFK's secretary Evelyn Lincoln was trying to move out the
dead president's belongings. When Bobby stopped by to see how things
were going, Lincoln wailed, "Do you know he asked me to be out by
9:30?" To Bobby, whose world had been upended less than twenty-four
hours before, that was as inconceivable as LBJ's earlier inquiry about
his swearing-in. "Oh, no!" he said to Lincoln, then he found the president in the hallway. Johnson tried to reassure Bobby that he needed
him in his cabinet even more than Jack had. Bobby said there was
something more immediate to address: the time it would take to remove JFK's furniture. "Can you wait" until noon? he asked. LBJ: "Well,
of course." Johnson in fact delayed three full days, but the encounter
made him see himself through Bobby's eyes—as an unfeeling oaf. To
the president, that was strike one against the attorney general.

Strike two came that afternoon, when Johnson held the first gathering of the cabinet. Bobby hadn't planned to go. "By this time I was rather
fed up with [Johnson]," he explained. But "I went by and Mac Bundy said
it was very important that I come in. So I went." It was an impossible
situation, with JFK's furniture still strewn across the corridor and his
corpse half a building away. Sitting in his chair was an imposter who had
had no presence at all in earlier cabinet meetings.* Bobby entered the

---

* Bobby's charge that as vice president LBJ had been useless at cabinet meetings was a bit
hypocritical. Bobby himself considered most cabinet meetings a waste of time and often sent
Nick Katzenbach in his place.

room looking nearly as forlorn as he felt. Several presidential aides stood, one reaching for his hand, another patting his back. LBJ was in the middle of remarks that he continued, still seated, as soon as Bobby sat. "None of us in this room can really express the sadness we all feel," Johnson said. "Yet we have work to do. And must do it. . . . I want you all to stay on. I need you." He knew how rough it must be for the attorney general, but he was convinced that Bobby had come late intentionally and with the aim of upstaging him. "During all of that period," LBJ would say later, "I think [Bobby] seriously considered whether he would let me be President, whether he should really take the position [that] the Vice President didn't automatically move in."

The third perceived affront occurred that same Saturday, in connection with the issue of when the president should deliver his televised address to a joint session of Congress. LBJ wanted to do it that Tuesday, to reassure a nervous nation of the continuity of its government and to get senators and representatives home in time for Thanksgiving Day. RFK preferred waiting an extra day—"at least one day after the funeral," as he put it. When Bundy told him the president's preference he exploded: "The hell with it. Why do you ask me about it? Don't ask me what you want done. You'll tell me what it's going to be anyway. Just go ahead and *do* it." When Sargent Shriver relayed Bobby's reaction, LBJ again backed down and made a mental note. Strike three.

Payback took assorted forms, starting with presidential appointments LBJ knew would rankle Bobby. One was Thomas Mann, the new point man for Latin America and a diplomat who opposed Communists no matter their dogma or context, supported dictators so long as they were friendly to American commerce, and had little use for the Kennedys' cherished Alliance for Progress. In another passive-aggressive move, Johnson named Shriver supreme commander of the new War on Poverty. Bobby's brother-in-law had proved himself when he launched the Peace Corps for JFK, and he had demonstrated his loyalty to the new administration in the two months since President Kennedy's assassination, but LBJ was less interested in his bona fides than in making him a pawn in the relentless chess match with RFK. He knew that Bobby would love to have been offered the job himself, that he would resent its going to a second-tier in-law, and that the public would credit the president for naming a Kennedy. Checkmate.

Bobby understood that his influence would wane with Jack gone, but he hadn't anticipated how fast or cold-blooded the reversal would be. J. Edgar Hoover, a pro at reading political winds, ordered his direct line to the attorney general moved back to his secretary's desk, "where it belongs," and dropped Bobby as a middleman in his dealings with his old friend and neighbor Lyndon. "As far as Hoover was concerned," said Guthman, "it was like [Bobby] had been transplanted to the moon." And it wasn't just the FBI director. "People who had called him every day and whom he would call on the phone and the reply would come back in about twenty seconds [now] never returned the call at all," remembered Kenny O'Donnell. "I'm more callous than he is. I understood that. The transition of power is the transition of power. It was all over." The phone from the White House stopped ringing because the new commander in chief wasn't interested in consulting his attorney general on foreign affairs and other matters outside his brief, and he inquired about issues at Justice only when it was absolutely necessary. We can't know what the response would have been had Johnson asked, given how forlorn Bobby was, but the one overseas assignment he was sent on suggests that more involvement might at least have been a helpful distraction. The president wasn't eager to oblige even that once, but his advisers persuaded him to dispatch Bobby to Asia in January 1964 to calm tensions between Indonesia and the newly christened Malaysia. Using a blend of charm and hardheadedness, the attorney general got their leaders to okay a temporary cease-fire. He also stopped at Waseda University in Tokyo, where, instead of the heckling that had greeted him two years before, he drew wild cheers. The world seemed to understand Bobby and his loss, but back home the State Department and LBJ would go only so far. "The President may have been sincere in giving Bob the mission to help him out of the doldrums," said Guthman, who went along on the expedition. "But Bob concluded otherwise." Even so, the attorney general said that while "I hadn't wanted to go on that trip . . . afterwards I was glad I had."

Nowhere was Bobby's diminished status clearer than in politics, LBJ's favorite sphere. Not long after Kennedy got back from Asia, Johnson summoned him to the Oval Office and told him to fire Paul Corbin, the dirty trickster and Bobby friend who, even as he was on the payroll of Johnson's Democratic National Committee, had been organizing a campaign in New Hampshire to write in Kennedy's name for vice president. The president didn't care who might have been pulling Corbin's strings: "Get him out of there. Do you understand? I want you to get rid of him." Bobby: "I don't want to have this kind of conversation with you . . . [Corbin] was appointed by President Kennedy, who thought he was good." That was all the new president needed to hear. In his mind Corbin was a symptom and the Kennedys the syndrome, and he could no longer contain his Texas temper: "Do it. President Kennedy isn't president anymore. I am." Bobby: "I know you're president, and don't you ever talk to me like that again." Looking back, Bobby would call the president's remarks "bitter, mean . . . the meanest tone that I've heard anybody talk."*

LBJ got even meaner, although not within earshot of Bobby. When he was growing up in Texas, the president told Pierre Salinger, "I used to know a cross-eyed boy. His eyes were crossed, and so was his character. . . . That was God's retribution for people who were bad and so you should be careful of cross-eyed people because God put his mark on them. . . . Sometimes I think that, when you remember the assassination of Trujillo and the assassination of Diem, what happened to [President] Kennedy may have been divine retribution." In telling Bobby's close friend Salinger, LBJ had to know the story would get back to the attorney general, whom it was likely intended for. Rather than backing off from his retribution theory, Johnson stoked it over the years as he learned more of the Kennedys' bids to bring down Castro. "Kennedy tried to get Castro," LBJ would say, "but Castro got Kennedy first." Later he would charge that Jack and Bobby "had been operating a damn Murder Inc. in the Caribbean."

Bobby knew this couldn't go on. Through the fog of his depression he could see that his allies in the government, a hundred or so of them scattered throughout the senior ranks, would have to make a choice. So would he. LBJ repeatedly said he wanted them to stay, especially JFK's world-tested White House aides like Salinger, O'Donnell, O'Brien,

---

* LBJ fired Corbin and RFK hired him not long after, putting him on the Kennedy payroll.

Schlesinger, and Goodwin. But Bobby realized early on that those invitations, and his, had an expiration date. "Our power will last for just eleven months. It will disappear the day of the election. What we have to do is to use that power in these months to the best permanent advantage," he cautioned Goodwin and Schlesinger in the aftermath of the assassination. "We must all stay in close touch and not let them pick us off one by one. . . . My brother barely had a chance to get started—and there is so much now to be done—for the Negroes and the unemployed and school kids and everyone else who is not getting a decent break in our society. This is what counts. The new fellow doesn't get this. He knows all about politics and nothing about human beings."

It was classic Bobby Kennedy reasoning as well as wording. To him, LBJ would remain "the new fellow," "Johnson," "Lyndon," "Lyndon Johnson," or "this man." Bobby wouldn't call him "LBJ," which was too embracing, and rarely referred to him as "the president"—that would always be his brother. Equally emblematic was his inability to decide not just whether to stay on as attorney general, but whether to push for the open second spot on the ticket with a man he considered "a very mean, mean figure." Decisions about his own future had never come easily. He knew that teaming up with LBJ would make for "an unpleasant relationship," but he wanted to remain a political player—for the sake of voters who'd elected Jack, the White House aides and cabinet men who continued to believe in the New Frontier, and his own outsized if interrupted ambitions, which still included the dream of following his brother to the presidency. He realized he couldn't go on provoking Johnson if he wanted to run with him, yet he was too transparent and willful to mask his contempt. General Douglas MacArthur knew what it was like to be pulled in just those competing directions, and when he and Bobby met in New York five weeks before the old warhorse died, MacArthur offered this advice on LBJ and the vice presidency: "Take it! Take it. He won't live. He gambled on your brother and won. You gamble on him and you'll win!"

Bobby couldn't take a job that hadn't been offered, and LBJ had been careful never to do that. Yet he felt trapped by what his staff called "the Bobby problem." The new president was enough of a pragmatist to know that if his Republican opponent was a moderate like Governors William Scranton of Pennsylvania or Nelson Rockefeller of New York, he could get a huge boost from having as his running mate a Yankee and a Kennedy, especially the one who had looked so tragically heroic during the national mourning for JFK. But he resented Bobby more than he did anyone else in Washington, as he would confide to his biographer: "I'd given three years of loyal service to Jack Kennedy. During all that time I'd willingly stayed in the background; I knew that it was *his* presidency, not mine. . . . And then Kennedy was killed and I became custodian of his will. I became the President. But none of this seemed to register with Bobby Kennedy, who acted like *he* was the custodian of the Kennedy dream, some kind of rightful heir to the throne. It just didn't seem fair. I'd waited for my turn. Bobby should've waited for his." Even more consequential, as he acknowledged, "with Bobby on the ticket, I'd never know if I could be elected on my own." Weighing those pros and cons left him not with an answer but with a sense of being cornered, much the way Bobby and Jack had felt when they reluctantly chose him four years before. Yet thanks to the goodwill generated by the assassination, LBJ was substantially stronger politically than JFK had been in 1960, with polls showing him winning in a landslide against any would-be Republican foe.

The reality was that Lyndon Johnson would never have picked Bobby Kennedy, however much he toyed with the idea. Bobby got it right when he told *Newsweek's* Ben Bradlee, "I should think I'd be the last man in the world he would want . . . because my name is Kennedy, because he wants a Johnson administration with no Kennedys in it, because we travel different paths, because I suppose some businessmen would object, and because I'd cost them a few votes in the South." But he mused that Johnson might take him anyway, "because most of the major political leaders in the North want me. All of them, really." LBJ, meanwhile, was telling friends that "if they try to push Bobby Kennedy down my throat for Vice President, I'll tell them to nominate him for the Presidency and leave me out of it." Equally certain, however, is that while Bobby might have taken it, he would have been miserable as vice president. LBJ himself had been, and having delivered Texas and much of the South to the Democratic ticket in 1960, he had substantially more clout with JFK than Bobby would with him. "As vice president, I'm not going to have any influence," conceded the attorney general, who was used to being deputy president.

"He's not going to have to pay any attention to me whatsoever anymore."

The matter was settled in mid-July when the Republicans picked as their nominee Senator Barry Goldwater. Whatever strength the Arizonan had was in the South, where Bobby would be a liability, and Goldwater had no shot in Northern states where Kennedy could have helped. LBJ broke the news to Bobby soon after in a congenial forty-five-minute one-on-one in the Oval Office. The only disagreement in their versions of the meeting was over what jobs the president had offered Bobby as a consolation prize. Kennedy said they included any open cabinet post, the ambassadorships of Moscow, Paris, or London, or running LBJ's presidential campaign. Johnson said all he offered was an unspecified role in the campaign or possibly representing the United States at the United Nations. Both agreed that Bobby's parting words were, "I could have helped you, Mr. President." What neither saw, then or later, was how much the vice presidential merry-go-round had helped Bobby, taking his mind off the loss of JFK and focusing it, laserlike, on his career and his archenemy.

Things might have ended relatively amicably if either combatant had been willing to let it drop there. But that wasn't in the nature of their relationship. When Bobby wouldn't agree to fudge by saying he had voluntarily withdrawn from being considered for vice president, the president came up with what he thought was the ideal cover story—that it had been a matter not of singling out Kennedy, but of ruling out "any member of the Cabinet or any of those who meet regularly with the Cabinet." Even that wasn't enough. The next day the president invited in three White House correspondents and, over a four-hour lunch of broiled lobster, watermelon, and sherry, he joyfully recounted how Bobby had taken the news. "When I got him in the Oval Office and told him it would be 'inadvisable' for him to be on the ticket as the vice-presidential nominee, his face changed, and he started to swallow. He looked sick. His adam's apple bounded up and down like a yo-yo." To make sure his guests got the picture, LBJ demonstrated by letting out a fat gulp.

In the meantime Johnson dangled the vice presidency in front of the one man he knew Bobby couldn't accept, Sargent Shriver, who found the prospect tantalizing. The attorney general was outraged. First he gave reporters his version of the Oval Office meeting, which was less colorful and more believable. LBJ, he said, had bad-mouthed his own most trusted advisers ("I was shocked to hear him being so critical to me of people who had been so loyal to him"*) and trashed his protégé Bobby Baker ("he said God must have been watching over him because he did not have financial dealings with Bobby [Baker]"). Then the attorney general let the White House know that "if you are going to take a Kennedy, it's got to be a *real* Kennedy"—not "a half a Kennedy."† It was bad enough, Bobby said, that LBJ broke his vow to keep their meeting private, but then he denied the flagrant leaks. Over the course of the following weekend, Bobby's anger gave way to humor and he shared with Arthur Schlesinger, who was with him in Hyannis Port, possible answers if the press asked about LBJ's exclusion of his entire cabinet. His favorite: "I swear to the best of my knowledge I am not now and have never been a member of the cabinet on the ground that it might tend to eliminate me."

That decision made, LBJ and RFK both had reason to look forward to the August nominating convention in Atlantic City. Lyndon knew he would win by acclamation, and Bobby would be introducing a film honoring his brother. But Johnson still was worried to the point of paranoia: Would the Kennedy forces, flush with fondness for their fallen king, railroad the convention into nominating his princely brother as vice president? The president wasn't taking any chances. The JFK tribute film, scheduled for day two of the convention, was pushed back to the fourth and final night, after the choice of the vice president. The president also

---

* LBJ named names of the aides he couldn't count on—Walter Jenkins, Jack Valenti, George Reedy—and added that Bill Moyers "was good but his most useful function was rewriting what other people did" (*Robert Kennedy and His Times*, 660).

† Shriver, an immensely talented man, was learning that marrying into the Kennedy family closed almost as many doors as it opened for him. It would take both Jack's and Bobby's deaths before he could accept an invitation onto a national ticket, this one in 1972 from George McGovern. Everyone has a theory about why Bobby scorned his brother-in-law, but it came down to Sarge's being everything Bobby didn't like—a liberal, a Catholic intellectual, a savvy businessman, and a goody-two-shoes. Their different takes on life were on display one day in the mid-1960s when Joe and Rose's grandchildren were playing football on the lawn in Hyannis Port. Little Bobby Shriver fell and began crying. Bobby Kennedy offered his familiar rebuke: "Kennedys don't cry!" Sargent Shriver walked straight to his son, lifted him up, and said, "It's okay, you can cry! You're a Shriver!" (Mark Shriver, *A Good Man*, 46.)

got a dozen or so FBI agents dispatched to Atlantic City to provide him with early warning about "any last-minute surprises from the Kennedy camp," said William C. Sullivan, who ran the agency's Domestic Intelligence Division. Kennedy boosters might have been capable of mounting an insurrection, but Bobby remained too shell-shocked from the assassination and too ambivalent about the vice presidency to let that happen. In a last and unsubtle sign of their place in the new Johnson order, key JFK and RFK aides including O'Donnell and O'Brien were banished to motels as far away as possible from the convention site.

Bobby was escorted backstage just before his JFK testimonial, to an area so dark and remote that he joked to John Seigenthaler, "I think Lyndon may just have put us back here with orders to forget us. They'll probably let us out day after tomorrow." He reviewed his notes, then headed to the runway behind the platform, where the milling politicians treated him like "a bastard at the family reunion." Finally he was introduced to the delegates, and "it hit," remembered Seigenthaler. "I mean, it really hit." Seven times Bobby began, "Mr. Chairman"; seven times the clapping drowned him out. The applause radiated in waves and emanated from Alabama, Wyoming, and states in between. The only ones not standing were the delegates from Texas, who were glad the matter of the vice presidency had already been settled. Even the Texans yielded when their fellow delegates from Massachusetts, seated behind them, chanted "Up in front." The ovation lasted a record sixteen minutes. It was not the staged cheering that is a trademark of political conventions, but spontaneous and cathartic. Standing on the podium in his black tie and dark suit, tears welling, Bobby looked more boyish than ever. He was embarrassed and he was touched. "Some people in that hall wanted desperately to let him know that they share his palpable grief," Mary McGrory wrote. "Some wished passionately to express their regret that he had lost the big prize. And some may have wanted to cheer him on in his political future. . . . A convention totally dominated by Lyndon B. Johnson had been captured by a Kennedy."

Finally he began to speak, trusting more to memory than to script. He thanked the delegates for all they had done for his brother, saying that "when there were difficulties, you sustained him. When there were period of crisis, you stood beside him. When there were periods of happiness, you laughed with him." He recounted the New Frontier's best moments—from its work to "do something for the mentally ill and the mentally retarded" to its efforts on behalf of "our fellow citizens who are not white and who had difficulty living in this society." Yet it wasn't his reminiscences that made the audience most nostalgic, but his urging that "we must look forward. When I think of President Kennedy, I think of what Shakespeare said in *Romeo and Juliet*:

> *When he shall die*
> *Take him and cut him out in little stars*
> *And he will make the face of heaven so fine*
> *That all the world will be in love with night,*
> *And pay no worship to the garish sun.*

Had he ended on this emotional high point it would have been enough. It also would have had the world speculating—as many did anyway— whether, if JFK was the dead hero who lit up the heavens, Lyndon Johnson must be the garish sun. But Bobby was at his generous best that night, intending not to demean but to honor, and not just his brother but his brother's chosen number two. So, in lines that the history books have forgotten, he went on to implore the delegates and the nation that "the same efforts and the same energy and the same dedication that was given to President John F. Kennedy must be given to President Lyndon Johnson and Hubert Humphrey." Afterward, he begged off talking to the press and sat for fifteen minutes on a fire escape outside the convention hall, quietly weeping.

———

JOURNALISTS TRUMPETED THAT Democratic National Convention appearance as the moment when Bobby began to arise from his post-assassination despair and despondency, and they were right. "He had, in a way, become his own man in the sunshine of Atlantic City," wrote Stan Opotowsky in the *New York Post*. "Bobby Kennedy seemed to be trying to talk himself out of the trance of grief that has held him since November," agreed McGrory, who was herself shaken enough by the murder to declare that, with JFK gone, "we will never laugh again." His raucous embrace by the delegates surely registered, and helped him dry his wounded tears. Yet misery that crushing couldn't vanish that fast. Anyone who followed Bobby during those blackest months of his life observed many such moments that together pointed a way out.

The first turning point had come the previous March, when he reluctantly agreed to speak at a Friendly Sons of St. Patrick dinner at the Hotel Casey in Scranton, Pennsylvania. He hadn't delivered a talk before a large domestic audience since Jack's death and he wasn't sure he was ready. But the ten thousand women, men, and children who lined his route were, and proved it by standing in place for an hour despite the wet snowfall. Bobby had planned to address his brother's legacy, closing with a poem written when Ireland was in comparable mourning over the death of its patriot Owen Roe O'Neill in 1649. The ballad ended,

We're sheep without a shepherd
When the snow shuts up the sky —
Oh! Why did you leave us, Owen?
Why did you die?

Ed Guthman scratched the poem from Bobby's notes and the attorney general asked why. Guthman: "Because you'll never get through it." Bobby: "I've been practicing in front of a mirror. I can't get through it yet—but I will!" And he did, Guthman recalled, "just barely." So touched was the attorney general by his audience's reaction, with many husky sons of Erin openly weeping, that on his plane ride home "he made an irrevocable decision about his future," Guthman said. "Somehow, he would remain in public service."

Bobby didn't know precisely what he would do, but he was slowly remembering what it was that moved him, as the journalist Ben Bradlee observed that summer when he traveled halfway across the country with him. "We spent two hours at the dedication of a Catholic Home for the Aged in Kansas City," Bradlee recalled. "Almost half of that time Bobby spent upstairs (away from TV cameras and other reporters) in a ward for the terminally ill, sitting alone at the bedside of a woman whose eyes were tight shut, whose death rattle was the only sign that life still existed in her frail body. I watched with tears in my eyes as the 'ruthless'

Bobby Kennedy stroked this unknown woman's hand, and spoke to her in a near whisper."

Shortly afterward, Bobby was off on another trip that reminded him of his engagement with the world. The Polish People's Republic wasn't quite prepared for this Kennedy brother who stormed onto its scene in the summer of 1964. Like the rest of the Soviet Bloc, Poland was on tenterhooks then, with the relatively liberal Khrushchev about to be deposed and reformers certain that whatever apparatchik came next wouldn't be good. Bobby, by contrast, personified the brash, fresh leader most Poles dreamed of as he climbed onto the roof of whatever car he was riding in, including the limousine of a flustered U.S. Ambassador John Moors Cabot, often lifting Ethel and their eldest children up with him. He serenaded crowds that never left his side with an improvised "When Polish Eyes Are Smiling." He met with the Catholic primate, the government's principal adversary, and reached out to disaffected youths after Cabot had specifically warned they were a "nightmare to Polish Communist leadership." His trip was "nonofficial" and there was no need to pretend he cared about protocol now that his brother wasn't president and he was on the outs with the new leader of the Western world. Asked in Cracow if he wanted to be president of Poland, Bobby quipped, "No . . . I think I'll run for mayor of Cracow." In the short run "the Kennedy visit certainly did harm to Polish–United States relations," wrote Arthur J. Olsen, the *New York Times* correspondent in Eastern Europe and later a diplomat himself. "In the long run the Kennedy invasion of Poland may well be remembered as an act of unorthodox statesmanship. Using deliberate shock tactics, he assaulted the complacencies of diplomats and Communist functionaries. . . . It was a bold and conscious response to his brother's appeal: 'Let us begin.'" It also bolstered Bobby in finding his own new beginning.

Religion helped, too, but on his terms, not the Church's. He kept a missal beside him in the car and thumbed through to prayers he found consoling. Instead of attending mass mainly on Sundays and days of obligation, as had been his adult routine, he was in the pew nearly every day. His faith helped him internalize the assassination in a way that, over time, freed his spirit. Shortly after Jack's death, a friend and former president of the University of Notre Dame, Father John Cavanaugh, came to

Hickory Hill for dinner. Ethel asked him, "If there is someone who has lived a great, good, wonderful life and died suddenly, and has no opportunity for confession, don't we know that God is good enough for that person not to have to deal with purgatory?" She wanted assurance that Jack was in heaven, but the prelate equivocated. That wasn't good enough for Bobby, recalls Seigenthaler, and he said "not in anger but not in a friendly way, 'I don't think that's how God gets his kicks.' . . . Bobby was saying, 'Ethel and I agree that Jack's sitting up there on the right hand of the throne. He's not suffering in purgatory.'"

Bobby continued as attorney general, but he found it difficult to reconnect with most of his old passions. The war on organized crime had lost its appeal and its commander. So, too, the campaign to dislodge Castro was fizzling out. The one issue that mattered enough to pull him out of his mist even temporarily was civil rights. Months after the assassination, LBJ deputized Bobby to steer a beefed-up version of JFK's bill through a viciously divided Congress, knowing not only that his presence would remind reluctant legislators how much his brother had wanted the law, but also that if it died on Capitol Hill, Bobby would have to share the blame. (That seemed fitting, since JFK had involved LBJ for the same reasons.) The new president kept his word, giving Bobby free rein in setting the tactics for passage and working out with congressional leaders the final legislative language. At that summer's signing ceremony the president gave a handful of pens to the attorney general, although neither could disguise the awkwardness of what should have been a triumphal moment.

That law, the most far-reaching ever on civil rights, demonstrated what LBJ and RFK could do when they worked together, but it also highlighted the tragic conflict that kept them from doing more. "Had they ever been congenial to paving over past wounds, and real or imagined slights, and if from this congeniality there had been built an alliance between the two," lamented LBJ's confidant Jack Valenti, "it is likely that these two men, linch-pinned together, could have constructed a political combination unbeatable by any known political force."

Much of Bobby's energy in those months went to his family. He spent time with his grieving mother and infirm father, although not as much as he had in the past or would in the future. He was an uncle and surrogate father to Jack's two young children as well as father to his own eight, the youngest of whom was born just four and a half months before JFK died. He was a friend and perhaps more to Jackie. He was also polishing his brother's legacy, the way he always had. To Jack, the New Frontier existed mainly as a campaign slogan; to Bobby it became a rallying cry for the young, here and abroad, whom he urged to reach for "new frontiers of education, science and technology." Where the inheritance was even thinner, Bobby made whatever leaps were required. Finding a notepad on which JFK, at his last cabinet meeting, had scratched the word "poverty" several times and circled it, Bobby said it was a sign of the president's determination to make the poor the priority they hadn't been in his first three years. He saved the note, framed it, and displayed it in his Justice Department office.

There were, however, two matters even Bobby avoided. One was the notion that the Kennedy administration had achieved the glory of King Arthur's Camelot. Jackie wanted to believe it, and Bobby was too gallant to contradict. "At night before we'd go to sleep . . . we had an old Victrola. Jack liked to play some records . . . the song he loved most came at the very end of this record, the last side of *Camelot*, sad *Camelot*: . . . 'Don't let it be forgot, that once there was a spot, for one brief shining moment that was known as Camelot,'" the widow told Teddy White, who wrote it into legend in *Life* magazine. So, White added, "the epitaph on the Kennedy administration became Camelot—a magic moment in American history, when gallant men danced with beautiful women, when great deeds were done, when artists, writers and poets met at the White House, and the barbarians beyond the walls held back." While the Kennedy administration did offer hope, White later admitted that comparing it to Arthur's enchanted reign was "a misreading of history. The magic Camelot of John F. Kennedy never existed."

The dream, however real it was, ended with an assassin's gunshot. The President's Commission on the Assassination of President Kennedy— known as the Warren Commission, after its chairman, Chief Justice Earl Warren—was determined to explain the who, how, and why of the killing, and Bobby was equally determined not to help. Aside from LBJ and Defense Secretary McNamara, he was the highest-ranking official who was let off the hook, presumably in deference to his grief, although Jackie did testify. Bobby said publicly that he didn't believe there had been a conspiracy, that he hadn't read and wouldn't read the Warren Commission report but had been briefed on it, and that he agreed with the commission that "Oswald was solely responsible for what happened." That apparently satisfied Warren and the other seven commissioners, at least two of whom, according to LBJ, had been named at Bobby's behest.

Half a century later there is still a torrid debate over what Bobby thought and felt. "He publicly supported the Warren Commission report but privately he was dismissive of it," said Robert F. Kennedy, Jr., who was nine when his uncle Jack died. The attorney general, his son added, was "fairly convinced" that others were involved, maybe the Mafia. Ted Kennedy saw it differently. After a four-hour briefing by Warren, Ted "reported to Bobby that I accepted the commission's report and thought he should too. Bobby agreed readily. He did not want to continue to investigate Jack's death." Others say, with conviction but without proof, that Bobby privately briefed Warren, launched his own quiet investigation, and would have done more if he ever became president. His silence made such speculation inevitable. There is no question he was hurting, but so were Jackie and Ted. To do their job, the commissioners needed to know everything Bobby could tell them about the enemies he and Jack had made—from Cuba to the Cosa Nostra—and where to look for conspirators. With the president dead, nobody but the attorney general had all that knowledge, and he wouldn't share it.

Just as the Warren Commission was making its last edits before presenting its 889-page opus to President Johnson, on September 3, 1964, Bobby handed the president his resignation as attorney general.* Three years and nine months had passed since his brother named him to the post, which was longer than he had planned to stay and tested the limits of his and LBJ's mutual tolerance. He got a five-minute standing ovation that morning from thirty-five hundred students at Washington's Cardozo High School, who had heard the news and greeted him with signs plastered across their stadium reading WE SHALL MISS YOU BOBBY and,

---

* The nicest thing Bobby could find to say about Lyndon was that he had "consolidated" JFK's accomplishments. In an equally frosty response, LBJ acknowledged RFK's "very vital role in the conduct of public affairs" (Beschloss, *Reaching for Glory*, 26).

even better, WE'LL MEET AGAIN. He then spent an hour with the president and shared a farewell lunch with fellow cabinet members. At day's end he met in the Justice Department courtyard with a thousand staffers. Their task, he told them, was "to tame the savageness of man and make gentle the life of the world." His choice of words and themes suggested the transformation in this man, who had come to the department baring his own savage determination and barely recognizing the name of Aeschylus, the Greek playwright he was quoting now.

Reading the Greeks was Jackie's idea but something Bobby was ready for. Their tragic and skeptical view of the world fit his needs now better than his more stoic and rigid Catholic faith. So did the French philosopher Albert Camus's existentialism (Camus preferred to call it absurdism), which helped make room for doubt in an Irish American known for his self-certainty. Both men's epitaphs could have read "Live fast, die hard." Aeschylus, meanwhile, seemed to be speaking directly to Bobby when he wrote, "Take heart. Suffering, when it climbs highest, lasts but a little time." Bobby would now sit alone in his room reading until the pages were dog-eared in Edith Hamilton's *The Greek Way*. He and Jack had kept a daybook of quotes that moved them for use in speeches. Now Bobby did it on his own from readings that had progressed beyond his old war and adventure tales to biography and history. There was more poetry now and less football. For the rest of his life he would habitually stuff a paperback into his coat pocket or briefcase, some new to him and others that he liked enough to reread repeatedly, his lips moving as he did. Aides thought he was staring into his lap until they looked closer and saw the essays of Emerson or Thoreau, or poetry by Shakespeare or Tennyson. It was one more thing to which he came late—"Hey," a journalist friend imagined him saying, "they've got books now?"—yet once he did he couldn't get enough.

The readings were a search for missing meaning. For the last dozen years, since that first Senate campaign, Joe Kennedy's ambitions for Jack, and Jack's for himself, had defined Bobby. He had become a masterful coach, but the game plan had been laid out long before, from seeking ever higher offices to giving back to the country. Bobby rallied the loyal minions, garnered votes, and suppressed his own competitive drive for the sake of the family. He hated on its behalf, too, although never as

ruthlessly as his father. Life was often cruel, as when it took too young
Joe Jr. and Kathleen, but everyone, Bobby especially, ritualistically
stepped up a notch in response to calamity. Even Joe's stroke was surmountable; by then Bobby had internalized his father's aspirations, and
the ways and means of getting there.

Jack's death was different. It seemed more arbitrary and unfair, plung-
ing Bobby into a pit out of which he thought he'd never climb. It took
away the one friend to whom he could tell everything. Nearly every day
had begun and ended with a call to his brother. "It's strange," he confided to a journalist, "to think that you can't just pick up the phone." Lee
Harvey Oswald's bullets ruined that and everything else. Lyndon Johnson was president now, and the Kennedys, not just Jack but Bobby, too,
were part of the past. He lost his sense of purpose and his clout. The Get
Hoffa and Get Castro squads lasted for a while, but the trauma had loosed
Bobby's moorings, quelled his passions, and made him question even his
faith. This was the one death he couldn't help but admit into his life. Part
of his soul had succumbed in Dallas.

Still, he wasn't rebuilding entirely from scratch, however much it felt
that way. "Bobby Kennedy, after November 1963, was like a landscape
riven by an earthquake, familiar landmarks shattered," said his friend
Goodwin. "Yet the reconfigured land is composed of the same elements
of stone and soil that abided there before the earth shook." The values
and qualities that would define him were present from the beginning, but
they fully bloomed only after his father's disability and his brother's
death. Since childhood, he had been quietly incorporating aspects of
those closest to him—Joe's determination, Rose's grace, Jack and Joe Jr.'s
ambition, and the warmth of the Kennedy girls. Now this man so shaped
by others was reshaping himself, the way the existentialists said he could.
He could finally ask what *he* wanted and needed. His public persona finally began to reflect the gentleness that family and friends say they had
always known.

Most people have this kind of identity crisis in their teens. The questions are harder when they are raised at age thirty-eight by a man un-
used to internal dialogue. "Jack has traveled in that speculative area
where doubt lives. Bobby does not travel there," their friend Charles
Spalding had said the summer before the assassination. Now Bobby had

more doubts than he believed he could handle, and he looked for answers not just in books but in his heart and his actions. The introspection and retrospection would be ongoing, and what he found freed him, for the first time, to be himself.

The Bobby Kennedy who emerged from that season of gloom was more fatalistic, having seen how fast he could lose what he most cherished. Rather than leading him to give up, sensing his mortality made him even more impatient to get things done while he had time. He understood the influence he had forfeited with the president's death, but he knew, too, that becoming the number one Kennedy meant an opening to the kind of national leverage exercised by his father and brother. The loss of his brother also left him more nuanced. A palette that had been entirely blacks and whites now included shades of gray that reflected the ambiguities of the real world. "The pendulum," said Larry O'Brien, "just swings wider for him than it does for most people." Added Kenny O'Donnell: "He was not a simple man but many different simple men."

He still had enemies, but even the guilty verdicts for Jimmy Hoffa that spring and summer brought none of the "euphoria" they would have before, remembered O'Donnell. "He had enough tragedy of his own now." Bobby's loss and suffering made him "retreat into himself for quite a while," says Rose Styron, a friend who had helped her husband, the author William Styron, navigate a similar voyage through darkness. "Bobby came out as a gentler, more expansive person." He still had no patience for lost causes and remained a tough-minded pragmatist, but he had been enlarged in measurable ways that are unusual for adults and almost unthinkable for politicians. He questioned truths that he had taken as gospel—from an unflinching loyalty to the Democratic Party to an assumption that socialism was an unqualified evil—and softened his edges and his righteousness. There was more empathy now, more humility, more capacity to identify with delinquent children, dispossessed minorities, and others who were suffering.

The legend that would define his life after Jack wasn't *Camelot* but *Man of La Mancha*, which he would see three times. Whereas *Camelot* was built around a fabulous world of chivalrous kings on noble quests, Don Quixote sensed that all of that was chimerical, yet continued to dream. For Bobby, the public purpose that went along with being a New Frontiersman had left him when Jack died. He had spent his first twenty-five years with the world seeing him as Joe Kennedy's boy, and the next dozen as John Kennedy's brother. Now he would be his own man, one who was both more tempered and fiercer. Like the character he loved in *Man of La Mancha*, Bobby Kennedy would tilt at windmills that his more cautious brother and father would likely not have noticed.

Chapter 8

OFF AND RUNNING

════════════

W ILL HE OR won't he? No one ever asked that question about John Kennedy, whose career course was charted from the day his older brother died and the family mantle fell on his shoulders. The path was equally clear for brother Teddy, the most instinctive politician in the Kennedy clan with the exception of the patriarch, who would claim and never let go of Jack's old seat in the Senate.

Bobby was different. Everything was a struggle for this most passionate and least polished of the Kennedy boys. He had made his acceptance of the post of attorney general seem like a riddle when, as his father and brother let him know, it was the only logical fit. It was true, too, for earlier jobs, whether it was working for the Republicans, then the Democrats, on the Permanent Subcommittee on Investigations or running his brother's campaigns. He agonized over outcomes that were preordained. The point was to convince himself and those around him that he was less predictable than the evidence said, and less a pawn of his family.

By the summer of 1964, with neither Joe nor Jack to guide him, Bobby's career and life choices felt even knottier. He had only just begun to dig himself out of a post-assassination grief that had left lines on his face and his collar a size too large. He told friends everything was on the table, and this time he meant it. Maybe he would use Joe's millions to buy and run the *New York Post*. He contemplated traveling, studying and teaching, or writing a book. He'd ruled out running for governor of Massachusetts, a position with too little real power and too many sewer contracts to hand out, or governor of New York, which, since he didn't meet the residency requirements, wasn't actually an option. Neither were U.S. ambassador to the Soviet Union or proconsul to Latin America, two jobs he had considered when Jack was president and he could have had anything. In June, with the matter of the vice presidency still unsettled, Bobby had offered LBJ and himself a way out. "If you wished me to go to Viet Nam in any capacity I would be glad to do so. It is obviously the most important problem facing the United States and if you felt I could help I am at your service," he handwrote in a note that began with the difficult-to-concede "Dear Mr. President." LBJ explained later that "I did not accept his offer because I feared, as did Secretaries Rusk and McNamara, that the potential danger to the late President's brother was too great."

Bobby had come to a crossroads and a crisis point. The breadth of the choices he was weighing reflected the reality that for the first time, he didn't know what he should do. Could he really walk away from the family business and the Kennedy name? He already had all the advantages—influence, renown, and riches—that typically lured people into public life. "What I *really* want to do is leave the government in January and go away to study for a year at some university, probably in Europe," he told a journalist that summer. "I want to take Ethel and all the children with me so I can be with them every day for that whole year." But he was torn: "I *do* have a responsibility to a lot of people to try to stay in Washington. There's Jackie, and a lot of others who depend on me." He also was self-aware enough to realize the implausibility of his impasse: "It's a hell of a thing, isn't it? Thirty-eight years old and no place to go." Reporter: "You'll be back." Bobby: "Yes, I'll be back."

Coming back meant more than simply coming to terms with Jack's assassination. He had to know whether he had value in his own right or was just a brother and son, husband and father. He had to decide not what JFK's New Frontier stood for but what RFK stood for. Experience had stretched him. Tragedy made him more introspective. Now he had to grow up fast and on his own. "He never verbalized anything about that being the transforming moment of his life; he never said anything like that. But I believe it was. I think there were these early dawnings while he was still Attorney General of change and growth. But I think until President Kennedy was assassinated, he didn't really think about what's the goal in his life," said Jack Newfield, a Bobby biographer. "To think for the first time . . . 'Who am I?' 'What do I believe?' 'What is the meaning of life?' 'What is the meaning of my faith?'"

Those weren't questions that Kennedys ordinarily asked, and Bobby looked for answers during his solitary afternoons spent reading at Hickory Hill. The Greeks and the existentialists spoke to him about the mystery of suffering and the danger of hubris, in both of which he was as versed as they were. But the passages he underlined, reread, and quoted to friends also suggested a way forward. "A journey of a thousand miles must begin with a single step," wrote Lao-Tzu, the ancient Chinese poet. Camus advised, "Perhaps we cannot prevent this world from being a world in which children are tortured. But we can reduce the number of tortured children. And if you don't help us, who else in the world can help us do this?" Francis Bacon put it more simply: "In this theater of man's life, it is reserved only for God and for angels to be lookers-on."

Dropping out never was an option for Bobby, no matter how much he mused about it. His response to trauma had always been to try harder, not to give up. During that summer of his indecision he cobbled together a philosophy that was part Francis Bacon and part Joe Kennedy. While Jack's death and Joe's incapacitation had liberated Bobby to make his own career choice, in the end he reached the same decision they would have made for him. Public service was his calling as well as his inheritance. Yet Bobby was neither Joe nor Jack. He had greater depth and compassion, as would become clear. It wasn't just Jack's agenda that he wanted to see through, but one of his own that was more specific and more radical. "I like this kind of life better than basking on the beach at Acapulco," he would say about his decision to stay in the spotlight. "It is the only life worth living for me . . . my reason for being alive."

With the general direction set, the particulars of the route remained to be filled in. Jack was no longer there to appoint him to anything, and he had burned his bridges with his brother's successor. To remain in the public realm, Bobby would have to run for an office of his own. That would mean leaving the security of the backstage and facing voters' embrace or rejection. It also meant a shift from the executive arena, where he could order things done the way he liked, to a world of conferring with voters and collaborating with fellow officeholders. He had always joked about his ruthlessness, but it was very real to countless critics and would require softening or explaining. It would have been easier to own a newspaper that he could run from behind the scenes, or to hide out in academia. Maybe in retirement.

Only one job made sense now, that of U.S. senator. He understood the institution from his days with Joe McCarthy and John McClellan. He had spent nearly all of his career in Washington, and few knew better how to run a campaign for the upper chamber, as he showed with the ones he orchestrated for Jack in 1952 and for Ted ten years later. Most important, the Senate would restore his national platform and provide a launching pad for the White House that all the Kennedys craved. The only remaining question was which state to run in. The U.S. Constitution and Bobby's personal fortune gave him fifty options. He thought about moving to Maryland but ruled that out when his friend Joseph Tydings said he was planning to run there. There was a Senate election in Virginia in 1964, but that would have meant taking on the incumbent Democratic titan Harry Byrd, who'd held the seat for more than thirty years and was a scion of one of the first families of Virginia. The Kennedys were the first family in Massachusetts, but the seat there that was up in 1964 was Ted's.

That left New York. As he would point out repeatedly to voters, he had moved there before he turned two and, depending how you counted, had lived there even longer than he had in Massachusetts. More to the point, the New York metropolitan area was as cosmopolitan and cocksure as Bobby himself, home to America's titans of money lending, merchandising, and labor guilds. It had a history of embracing outsiders as its own and elevating them to the nation's stage. But Bobby was too savvy a politician to ignore the risks. While New York had half a million more registered Democrats than Republicans, the GOP held both U.S. Senate seats, the governor's mansion, both houses of the state legislature, and a majority of the congressional delegation. Despite the years he had spent in upscale Riverdale and Bronxville, and the real estate his family still owned and rented in New York, it didn't take an investigative reporter to determine that his true home was Hickory Hill in Virginia and his voting address was still Cape Cod in Massachusetts. Toughest of all, the state seemed to like just fine its courtly, silver-haired incumbent senator Kenneth Keating, a born-and-bred New Yorker who had won all seven elections he had contested. Bobby sent a young lawyer across the state to assess his chances, and the news he brought back wasn't good: Keating, the seventy-eight-page report predicted, would trounce Kennedy by 650,000 votes.

The press relished Bobby's guessing game, and since May it had been parsing every sign that he'd jump in and every hint that he wouldn't. A strong vote in favor came from President Johnson, who delighted in the prospect of Bobby's focusing on an office other than his own, ideally in a place that required a moving van to get to. But *The New York Times* weighed in against such a bid, editorializing in mid-May that "there is nothing illegal about the possible nomination of Robert F. Kennedy of Massachusetts as Senator from New York, but there is plenty that is cynical about it. . . . If he became a candidate, he would merely be choosing New York as a convenient launching-pad for the political ambitions of himself and others." That tongue-lashing from a broadsheet he saw as anti-Catholic and anti-Kennedy made Bobby want to run even more.*

Just when he seemed ready to declare, the Kennedy curse struck again that June. This time the victim was Ted, whose plane crashed into an orchard in Western Massachusetts, killing the pilot and a Senate aide and hurling Kennedy's corkscrewed body into the cockpit. Ted emerged with a broken back and a lung punctured by the tip of one of several cracked ribs. Luckily, he wasn't paralyzed, but doctors had to suction water and air from his chest to keep him from suffocating. "I guess the only reason we've survived is that there are too many of us. There are more of us than there is trouble," Bobby told the columnist Jimmy Breslin after rushing to Ted's bedside, where he stayed for two days. "If my mother did not have any more children after her first four, she would have nothing now."† And to aide Ed Guthman: "Somebody up there

---

* The *Times* was being disingenuous. Three weeks before, it had urged a run by Adlai Stevenson, the former governor of Illinois, whose roots in New York ran only as deep as the time he spent there as United Nations ambassador, which was less time than Bobby had lived there. Bobby made clear how he felt about the *Times* when, in a Kennedy Library interview with the paper's longtime reporter Anthony Lewis, he said editors there were an "irritant" to him and JFK. His brother, he added, would often call from the White House to ask, "Did you read what those pricks said today?" ("Stevenson vs. Keating," *New York Times*, April 24, 1964, RFK OH, December 4, 1964, 459.)

† Rosemary, Rose and Joe's third child, was alive but—like her deceased siblings Joe Jr., Jack, and Kathleen—no longer part of Kennedy family life.

doesn't like us." Soon after, Breslin and his colleagues reported that Bobby was canceling any plans to run for the Senate.

Ted's accident reminded Bobby of the responsibility he already bore for his own eight children and Jack's two. Yet even as Bobby was worrying, Ted quickly got better and began encouraging his older brother to reengage with the world. The civil rights bill had passed and LBJ made clear that if Bobby chose to run, nobody would block his way to the New York Senate nomination. He needed to focus on something other than Lyndon's Washington and Jack's memories, and he was already spending more time in Manhattan with Jackie and other family. Yes, he had told the press and public he wasn't going to run, but circumstances had flipped and, as he would prove repeatedly, he could, too, on a dime and without a flinch. "Bobby typically addressed his career decisions in that manner," Ted said. "He lived and made decisions in the moment and not in the cold, calculating way that some critics have tried to attribute to him." Or as Bobby himself had put it, "These things have a way of solving themselves . . . all of a sudden everything is obvious and right."

Joe Kennedy understood that better than anyone else. Although he was mute by then, and unable to find the words to tell Bobby how he felt about his running for the Senate, "he was still actively giving instructions and advice," said his nurse and interpreter Rita Dallas. Bobby "hunched and strained to hear every garbled word, almost as if he expected clarity to burst forth. There were times when I felt he was actually trying to pull words from his father's mouth. . . . It was apparent that Mr. Kennedy sanctioned and approved of Bobby's decision to run. He still yelled at him and shook his fist under his nose, but it was in a different way, for he knew that in this son rested the hope and future of the Kennedy image."

So it was that on August 25, standing before a podium crowded with broadcasters' microphones at Gracie Mansion, the mayor's official residence, Bobby Kennedy announced to New York and the world that the campaign was on. "There may be some who believe that where a candidate voted in the past is more important than his capacity to serve the state," he said in a Boston accent and feisty phrasing that were unmistakably his and an undisguised challenge to skeptics like those at *The New York Times*. "I cannot in fairness ask them to vote for me, even though my mother and father have had a home in New York since 1926 and I attended New York schools for six years before my father became Ambassador to Great Britain, and I have once again established residence in this state. But I do not base my candidacy on these connections. I base it on the belief that New York is not separate from the nation in the year 1964. I base it on the conviction that my experience and my record equip me to understand New York's problems and to do something about them. I base it on the fact that the greatest state in the union must play a leading role at the Federal level in solving these problems. And I wish to play a part in that effort." He was elated to have finally made up his mind and eager to share his thinking, but his 755-word message that magnificent summer day could have been boiled down to two: I'm back.

————

THE FIRST STEP on the road to the Senate was to secure the Democratic nomination. Smoke-filled back rooms were more than a metaphor back then, and Bobby was the consensus choice of the political bosses everywhere from the Bronx, Brooklyn, and Harlem to suburban Nassau County and upstate in Buffalo and Albany. Those same power brokers had helped JFK, and Bobby was old-school enough that he had no hesitation about paying them the deference they demanded (his favorite expression was "He was awfully good to us in 1960"). Even when he'd been publicly saying he wasn't running, ex-governor Averell Harriman had been quietly lining up for him influential liberals across the state. Kennedy in-law Steve Smith was doing the same with key political operatives, reporting back that "if it's there, it's there. It was there for us." But Bobby knew that New York City contributed half the votes in the state, and that reform-minded city dwellers would resent his back-slapping his way to the nomination. That meant winning the blessing of Robert F. Wagner, Jr., the three-term mayor of New York and, recently at least, a critic of Tammany Hall and a champion of reform.

Wagner was, more than anything else, a man of ambition, which meant he could easily sniff out an equally hungry and more celebrated figure like Bobby Kennedy. The mayor "welcomed Kennedy's arrival into New York much as the fifth-century Romans welcomed the entry into Italy of Attila," observed the journalist and author William V. Shannon.

Wagner had coveted that Senate seat, but he'd been distracted by the recent loss of his wife to lung cancer. With little time left, the mayor couldn't see a way to snag the nomination for himself or, with LBJ lobbying for Bobby, for someone he would have preferred, such as Adlai Stevenson. Still, Bobby knew he remained anathema to many progressives, and he never trusted to chance. First he wheedled a last-minute endorsement from William Fitts Ryan, the only reform member of Congress; then he made two trips to Gracie Mansion to personally pitch the reluctant mayor. The upshot: Just four days before Bobby made his announcement speech, Wagner accepted the inevitable and welcomed to his city and the Senate race his "good friend, Bob Kennedy."

One New York Democrat didn't get the message that the nomination was a deal already sealed. Sam Stratton, an ex-broadcaster and now a congressman from Schenectady, was conservative enough to have won in a heavily Republican district and cantankerous enough to demand that he be heard at the upcoming state Democratic convention on the first of September. With the bands, banners, and bunting ready for a coronation, Kennedy trounced Stratton by 968 to 153 on the first and only ballot. The delegates roared out "Hello, Bobby," echoing the "Hello, Lyndon" theme of the national convention a week before and the "Hello, Dolly" being sung a dozen blocks away on Broadway. There was only one sour note: Rather than reacting graciously to Stratton, who had declared his candidacy before Bobby did and might have won but for the Kennedy blitzkrieg, the nominee was angry that his challenger had refused to bow out early. When it came to politics, "Robert Kennedy tended to see things in terms of people 'for me and against me, for us and against us,'" said Milton Gwirtzman, who worked for Jack, Bobby, and Ted. "I remember him saying, 'Stratton's really making things hard for me.' That was hard for me to understand, because I saw how he had made things much harder for Stratton." That Bobby couldn't see was a sign of two things—a blinding self-focus that was typical of the Kennedys, and his rightful conviction that he was the candidate most likely not just to win but to make a difference.

The six thousand shirtsleeve delegates and spectators at the sweltering Armory on East Thirty-Fourth Street left convinced that the Kennedy political machine was as well lubricated as it had been when paving

JFK's way to the White House. But the fact that few if any of them made their way to the postconvention reception at the air-conditioned Sheraton-Atlantic suggested that the machine had some rust to shake off. The bartenders were at the hotel ready to pour while placards made clear who was being toasted. The problem: Nobody had invited the convention delegates. The nascent campaign had plenty of senior strategists like Harriman and Smith, but too few of the nuts-and-bolts types Bobby had put in place for Jack's early runs. Alarmed at the nearly empty ballroom, Kennedy staffers scattered to nearby department stores to corral anyone they could. "I was just coming out of Stern's and all of a sudden this girl grabs me," explained one woman with a canapé in her mouth. "The next thing you know I'm shaking hands with Bobby!" Told what had happened, Kennedy quipped, "I knew there was something wrong. Not enough people were wearing delegate badges and too many were carrying boxes marked Macy's."

Bobby, meanwhile, had proved that while nobody was better than he at managing campaigns, he was unseasoned and unsteady as a candidate. It seemed that everyone in New York knew him, or thought they did, and most had a reason to resent him, starting with Italian Americans. They represented the state's biggest voting bloc, at a million and a half, in an era when ethnic and religious identities mattered more at the ballot box than they do today. "There is the suspicion that anybody who makes a big case out of the Mafia, as Bobby Kennedy did when he was in Washington, is going to meet resentment in Italian neighborhoods," wrote Jimmy Breslin. "These people look on the Mafia a little bit the way the Irish here regard the IRA. They are outside the law, but blood counts ahead of any law." Bobby's support for civil rights also stuck in the craws of at least some Italian Americans, who saw blacks and other minorities as competitors for scarce jobs. "All he talks about," one such critic told *The New York Times*, "is niggers and spics." Bobby didn't make things easier when, in a visit to the city of Oneida, one hour west of the Adirondacks, he was presented with a pizza pie. "He looks down," recalled advance man Jim Tolan, "and he says, 'Where's the fork?' I think it's the first time he ever had pizza in his life. . . . Finally he got the idea you're supposed to eat it with your hands." Bobby's Republican opponent, meanwhile, was doing whatever it took to lure Italians into his camp. "We developed the issue of what we felt was his smear of the Italian community with his Mafia views and probe on that, and we were able to develop a good following in the Italian community," recalls Eugene Rossides, Keating's campaign manager. "We had leading Italian Democrats come out for Keating."

Jewish New Yorkers, of whom 1.3 million were on the voting rolls, had their own reservations. During his six terms in the U.S. House and one in the Senate, Keating had attended umpteen bar mitzvahs, Jewish weddings, and fundraisers for Israel, a yarmulke planted on his skull. He had just the right Yiddish phrases in his lexicon, and fellow Empire State senator Jacob Javits or New York attorney general Louis Lefkowitz regularly appeared at his side. For anyone who didn't know that Israel had named a fifty-acre forest after him, a sign at a Lower East Side deli reminded, KEATING AND ISRAEL GO TOGETHER LIKE BAGELS AND LOX. Keating made no secret of his disdain for his party's presidential nominee, Barry Goldwater, which made it easier for Jewish Democrats to justify splitting their votes. Bobby tried his own ethnic politicking, with the same clumsiness he displayed in the pizza parlor. At a kosher deli he asked for a glass of milk. At a Lower East Side eatery he eschewed bagels and blintzes in favor of melon and split pea soup. He couldn't grasp why Jews were so determined to remember their enemies, whether it was the Irish toughs who beat them up as kids or the U.S. ambassador to Great Britain who slurred them as "sheenies" and "kikes." "Why are they against me? Was it because of what my father did?" Bobby asked Gwirtzman. *"That was twenty years ago."*

He didn't have to wonder why other old rivals harbored a grudge. Roy Cohn was back in New York practicing law and letting everyone know the gripes he had against his former colleague from the McCarthy Committee. Jimmy Hoffa's list was even longer. He pressed the House Judiciary Committee to investigate Bobby's crusade against him, but Bobby's congressional allies forestalled that effort. Teamsters magazines railed against a "Kennedy dynasty" and urged union members to back Keating. A Hoffa front group—Committee of Democrats for Keating-Johnson-Humphrey—distributed in Harlem five hundred thousand flyers attacking Bobby's civil rights record, with other pamphlets attacking him as antilabor, anti-Italian, and anti-Semitic. Hoffa himself told *The New York Times* that Kennedy was "temperamentally and morally unfit" for public office. Thankfully for Bobby, the union's 175,000-member New York chapter, already disillusioned with Hoffa, split with its national leader and endorsed the Democrat for senator.

Liberal New Yorkers didn't need Jimmy Hoffa or Roy Cohn to encourage them to form their own Democrats for Keating group. Gore Vidal had detested Kennedy ever since their altercation at a White House dinner, and so had Paul Newman ever since the two argued about Joe McCarthy. Barbara Tuchman was no fan even though Bobby and Jack let everyone know they were crazy about *The Guns of August*, her book on World War I. Another surprising defector was Arthur Schlesinger, Sr., whose son and namesake was an aide to and eventual biographer of both Kennedy brothers. Jackie Robinson wasn't a Democrat but he was back criticizing Bobby, explaining that whatever this Kennedy's glamor, "it cannot be truthfully said that his record is spotless or perfectly consistent in defense of the rights of the Negro people." Keating made it easy for the liberal critics, having helped pass the Civil Rights Acts of 1957 and 1964, and on foreign affairs outshining even JFK by serving heroically in both world wars and sounding an alarm on the Cuban missile threat months before the missile crisis.

Other attacks on Bobby crossed ethnic, religious, and party lines, such as the one branding him a carpetbagger. His bids to cast himself as a New Yorker rang hollow and reinforced his image as rootless and rich. He leased from a wealthy designer a twenty-five-room Dutch Colonial house in Glen Cove on Long Island, staging his family there for press events but seldom staying himself. He pointed out the apartments the Kennedys had rented in Manhattan and said that their homes on Cape Cod and Palm Beach were for vacations, which offended people struggling to afford a single mortgage. He dug up evidence that New York's first senator, Rufus King, also hailed from Massachusetts, as if that experience from the early 1800s was relevant or King's carpetbagger status justified Bobby's.* "Bobby was Massachusetts," said the author and

---

* John Kennedy was also accused of being a carpetbagger when he first ran for office in Massachusetts, having spent much of his young life living elsewhere. Bobby boasted about having grown up in New York, gone to school there, and held his first job there, all of which was true. But he sometimes got carried away, adding "I was born here," which would have been a surprise to his mother, who gave birth to him in the Bay State (Shannon, *Heir Apparent*, 29).

journalist Harrison Salisbury. "He hadn't learned the Kennedy accent in Riverdale. Every time he opened his mouth he reminded you of that." Keating, who was born in New York and lived his life there, offered his own reminder every chance he got, joking that "there have been people waiting in line at the World's Fair longer than Kennedy has been in this state."

His early attempts to fight back against those and other charges made clear not just the steepness of Bobby's learning curve but the tenacity of his grief. "He'd be very quiet when we were in the plane or in a car; he often wouldn't talk at all, he'd just stare out the window. Those of us who were around him much knew enough not to try to strike up a conversation; we'd wait until he would," remembered John Burns, who was mayor of Binghamton and cochair of Bobby's campaign. "He was obviously still depressed about his brother's death and he really, I think, was wondering to himself if he was doing the right thing by running for Senator. . . . He was not a happy man in those days." Justin Feldman, the campaign scheduler, agreed that Bobby was "a dreadful candidate" at the start. "I think he was sorry he'd gotten involved. I think that he was sorry that he couldn't indulge himself and wallow in his own grief."

But if his normal high energy was missing, so were his characteristic sharp edges, which made him more sympathetic to many. "Everybody was sitting there waiting for this ruthless, aggressive man to come in, and they were filled with resentment," Ronnie Eldridge recalled of the first time Bobby met her fellow reformers. "The doorbell rang. . . . This scared little guy came in. And he, really, just looked so out of it all . . . very shy, his eyes down on the floor all the time, and it just took everybody by such surprise because they were really there to eat him up, and there really wasn't anything, you know, to eat up. And it was very sad."

He performed only marginally better in public, where his style amounted to JFK redux. He compulsively reminded voters what President Kennedy had wanted for the country and which of his missions remained unfulfilled. He mimicked his brother's gestures, chopping the air with his right hand to make a point and tucking his left one into his jacket pocket. He smoked the short, slender cigars that Jack had favored. He embraced John Kennedy's precept that issues mattered *after* you were elected. Until then they should be ducked, especially controversial ones like compulsory busing to desegregate public schools, or Congress's Gulf of Tonkin resolution that gave LBJ the free hand he wanted in Vietnam. The would-be senator even borrowed the former president's manner of driving home a point by quoting (or misquoting) wise men of the past, although Bobby overused it to the extent of citing, in a single fifteen-hundred-word statement, Andrew Jackson, Dante, Thomas Carlyle, Lord Tweedsmuir, Bonar Law, Francis Bacon, and John F. Kennedy himself. To some the aping seemed staged and even offensive. To Bobby it was natural and unavoidable. "We grew up together and some of what he was rubbed off on me, and some of what I was rubbed off on him. For me to change any of myself now would be phony," he explained to a reporter. "I don't talk of him as my brother for campaign purposes."

It worked at first, because New Yorkers missed their dead president almost as much as his brother did and saw Bobby as Jack's avatar. That was apparent in his first prolonged foray into Republican territory upstate, with fifty-one stops in twenty-one cities over three punishing days in early September. He ended in Glens Falls, population twenty-one thousand. He was running late, as always, only this time it was nearly 1:00 A.M. when he arrived, certain that everyone would be in bed or their pajamas. He was half right. Three brass bands and a thousand booming voices greeted him at the airport, with four thousand more waiting downtown. Many had taken a dinner break, then come back for the vigil—the men in T-shirts, the women in nightgowns, the kids in their PJs. "I'd like to make my very first commitment of the campaign," Bobby told them. "I promise that win or lose, the day after election day, I'm coming back to Glens Falls."

Every stop brought more of the same. Women grabbing for a tuft of hair. Children mobbing him as he stood waving from his convertible. Newspapermen filing stories flush with superlatives. In Rochester, Keating's birthplace and residence, the crowd was so thick and zealous that it took thirty policemen to move Bobby the thirty feet from his car to the Civic Center, where four thousand fans had been waiting for three hours. It wasn't his oratory they were after; few even listened. They were there to see and hopefully touch him. "It's sex appeal," said one reporter. "He stands there, stooped and diffident, with that sad Bugs Bunny smile of his, and they love him." Another gushed that he was bigger than the

Beatles, the rock band that was then leading the British Invasion of the U.S. popular music market. "If I send in one more story about the unprecedented crowds," said *The New York Times*'s Johnny Apple, "my editor will crown me." But even editors who spent their lives on the political desk had to admit they had never seen anything this tempestuous, with overflow audiences swarming the candidate from six in the morning to eleven at night, day after day. Before long Bobby's right hand looked like raw meat, while his left was swollen and bruised. Both were too sore to shake.

"This is something new in American politics. It is not to be explained by mere curiosity," the veteran politics watcher Joseph Alsop wrote. "It can only be explained, in truth, by admiration and indeed by love—the same love and admiration that still brings thousands to Washington every weekend with the prime purpose of visiting President Kennedy's grave." Murray Kempton, who had covered New York politics almost as long, captured the voice of those thousands when he wrote in *The New Republic*, "If the Attorney General has a wound so great that, not to heal him but just for a little while to relieve him, he must be made a Senator, then we owe him nothing smaller." Bobby understood what was happening. Thinking of Jack in a rare moment of quiet during his tour upstate in September, he muttered, "These crowds should have been his." Even as he soaked in the warmth and absorbed the jostling, he was too much of a realist and too canny to believe it could last. He confided to Ed Guthman, his aide at Justice and now on the campaign staff, how he thought the election would play out: "I'll draw huge crowds as I go to different parts of the state for the first time. All the attention will be on that, and it will last for about three weeks. I'll hit a low point around the first of October. The question will be whether I can turn it around and regain the momentum."

Right on schedule, internal polls by both campaigns in late September showed Kennedy's lead evaporating and Keating pulling even or slightly ahead. While some doubted those results—was Bobby a bit too anxious to take on the mantle of an underdog and Keating too anxious to look as if he could lose?—the *New York World-Telegram* telegraphed the change of fortunes a week later, with the public opinion analyst Samuel Lubell writing that "Robert Kennedy is running well behind Sen. Kenneth

Keating." Many Kennedy admirers, Lubell added, are saying, "It's not fair to kick out a man like Keating even for a Kennedy." At just that moment—with the election just six weeks away—the incumbent took his hardest shot yet at Bobby, charging that as attorney general, he had "made a deal" to turn over more than $60 million in assets of a government-held company to a front for a "huge Nazi cartel."* The implication was obvious: Kennedy was a chip off his father's anti-Semitic block, and New York's Jewish voters had better beware.

The accusation struck a raw nerve in Bobby, rallying him to defend not just his brother's administration but his father's integrity. Coming on the heels of the discouraging polls, it was a wake-up call: Unless he focused, he could actually lose. To a warrior like him—and a Kennedy—that prospect was unfathomable. First he punched back against the Nazi slander with the same appeal to Americans' sense of fair play that had worked so well for JFK when he fended off anti-Catholic bigotry in 1960. Bobby pointed out that it was Keating himself who had introduced the bill making the $60 million sale possible, adding that he had "never heard of a charge as low as this one. . . . I lost a brother and a brother-in-law to the Nazis. I'm not making any deals with Nazis." The pro-Keating *New York Times* agreed, chastising the senator for raising "a fake issue" and making clear that "Attorney General Kennedy did not make 'a deal with Nazis'; he settled an incredibly complicated lawsuit." But Bobby wasn't done. He flew in from Mississippi Charles Evers, brother of the martyred civil rights leader Medgar, to tell New York Negroes why they'd be making a mistake to support Keating. Harry Golden, the legendary publisher of Charlotte's *Carolina Israelite*, did the same with New York Jews. "[Bobby] had been reluctant to attack Keating directly, fearing that, with his reputation for toughness and aggressiveness, he might create sympathy for the white-haired, well-meaning Senator," recalled

---

* In 1942, the U.S. government seized the General Aniline and Film Corporation, claiming the chemical maker was a Nazi asset. A Swiss company, Interhandel, insisted that it was the rightful owner and that General Aniline was not a German front. After decades of arguments, Bobby's Justice Department reached a settlement in 1963 that provided for General Aniline's sale, with U.S. taxpayers getting 70 percent of the proceeds and Interhandel the rest. While Keating's belated doubts about the deal didn't stick, if he had probed deeper he would have found questionable ties between Interhandel and both Bobby's father and JFK's brother-in-law, Prince Stanisław Albrecht "Stash" Radziwiłł.

Guthman. "That ended when Keating accused him of being party to a deal with Nazis. . . . His strategy shifted, and he was free to carry the fight to Keating." What could have been a knockout punch for the Republican incumbent had turned into a boomerang.

Bobby showed off his new feistiness to more than two thousand people at Columbia University's Wollman Auditorium on the evening of October 5. Standing onstage alone in the glaring TV lights, a microphone in his hand, he looked younger and smaller than the student interrogators who threw him one hardball question after another for eighty-five minutes. Why run for office here in New York instead of Massachusetts or Virginia? "If it's going to be judged on who's lived here in the state of New York longer, then my opponent has. But then maybe you should elect the oldest man in the state of New York." Are you using New York as a launching pad for the White House? "I have [had] really two choices over the period of the last ten months . . . My father has done very well and I could have lived off him. Or I could have continued to work for the government. . . . Frankly I don't need this title [of senator] because I [could] be called General, I understand, for the rest of my life." What about Vietnam? "I don't have an easy solution. . . . The social effort to do things for the villages and the people who live in the city, is really going to be the key."

These were questions he had been asked before, and ducked. Tonight his answers were sharper, his mouth stretching into a familiar half smile before he delivered a self-mocking response, the laughter louder and the applause more sustained. His audience was filled with students from the most politically active generation ever in America, who four years later would help ignite the nation in protest over everything from the war in Vietnam to crumbling U.S. ghettos. For now, these fans of Bob Dylan and the Rolling Stones sensed that Bobby was as authentic as a politician got. He might have entered their auditorium in a stupor of bereavement, but now they watched him come alive. Even a question about the Warren Commission—did he accept its verdict on who murdered Jack?—couldn't undo him. "When I, ah, spoke to the students in Poland, I said, uh, that the death of my brother was the work of, ah, one individual," he said, barely audible as silver tears collected on his lower lashes. "I think the Warren Commission Report shows that conclusively."

It was the performance his admen had prayed for, knowing he had been underperforming but sensing he was about to break out, which is why they were there filming him. This was the wry, passionate Bobby who had faced down student leftists in Japan and Teamsters thugs in Washington. This was the man friends and relatives loved dearly but whom too few New Yorkers knew or understood. Now they would. The advertising experts culled segments to air on television for thirty minutes, fifteen, three, and one, along with spots of just twenty seconds and ten. "That was absolutely the turning point. His TV had been stiff. His speeches hadn't come through," said Feldman, the scheduling guru. "Those kids peppered him with every conceivable question, and he fielded them and answered them and treated them in an incredibly sensitive and responsive way." The only one who couldn't see that was Bobby himself. "'It didn't work,' he said, 'did it? You blew it. That was a lousy session. They were lousy questions. They were lousy answers.' He had absolutely no sense of appreciation of what he had done. It was really the most fantastic and moving performance you can imagine." When Bobby saw the TV spots and finally realized how good he'd been, Feldman added, he changed as a candidate: "It brought him to a realization that he could talk substantively, he could talk about the Kennedy period . . . and do it in real terms. He could dream a little for the people; he wasn't just Jack Kennedy's brother."

His hands still trembled, his knees moving up and down as he tapped his front tooth with his finger. But he finally displayed bits of the old joy not just with crowds of voters, but with the kids whom he had always touched and been touched by. After a rally in Brooklyn's Borough Hall he was shaking hands when he noticed Cathy Troy, a ten-year-old so self-conscious about the freckles dotting her face that she hated being in public. "He had no idea who she was," recalled Feldman, "and reached out to her and took her face in his hands and he said, 'You're beautiful. I hope you don't ever lose those freckles. I have a daughter with freckles. I used to have freckles. My sisters used to have freckles, and I think that girls with freckles are absolutely beautiful. I think you're beautiful,' and he walked on." He never knew that what he'd done sent Cathy "prancing around this house like no one you've ever seen," according to her mother.

"He was no more capable of doing that in the beginning of that campaign," added Feldman, "than he could fly."

His rekindled fire brought out both sides of Bobby, the one who could sling mud as instinctively as he could bring a bashful girl out of her shell. Taking the high road, painting himself as an upstanding former attorney general, hadn't been working, so he set his investigators loose on his opponent's record. A widely disseminated leaflet titled "The Myth of Keating's Liberalism" branded the senator an unabashed conservative on issues ranging from the minimum wage to civil liberties. "I was trying to destroy Keating as a liberal," conceded Bill Haddad, who coordinated the research. The truth was that Keating had supported Kennedy administration bills more often even than Senator Mike Mansfield, the Democratic majority leader. *The Reporter,* an influential magazine that did its own comparison of Kennedy's charges and Keating's record, concluded that "the Kennedy forces have not been above inventing the nonexistent bill or amendment for Senator Keating to have voted against on the more important issues." That sort of "clipping and cropping," the magazine added, had a "vaguely McCarthyesque quality." It also harked back to Jack's broadsides against "Lodge's Dodges" when he ran against the equally moderate Senator Henry Cabot Lodge, Jr., in 1952, and it anticipated today's no-holds-barred opposition research. Whatever the ethics, it worked: Keating's supposed right-wing tendencies, rather than Bobby's, became the issue in liberal New York.

Bobby did admit that his campaign staff had overstepped the bounds of fairness when it misrepresented Keating's record on the Nuclear Test Ban Treaty. Yet he opted not for an apology but for a counterattack, which was the Kennedy way as preached by Joe and perfected by Bobby. The head of the bipartisan Fair Campaign Practices Committee had condemned Bobby for "dishonest and unfair distortion" of Keating's position, making it seem that he opposed the treaty when in fact he "strongly supported" it. But Bobby framed the issue in self-serving terms, going after the committee for inadvertently leaking to the press its letter criticizing him. "The tactical results of the Kennedy counter-foray were impressive," acknowledged Bruce Felknor, the committee chief who was so wounded by the contretemps that he eventually resigned his post. A leak "that was unfair to the Attorney General," Felknor added, "wound up as a net plus for him." Bobby himself later conceded that if he hadn't gone after the committee the way he did at that late stage of the race, "that would have been the whole campaign right there. Gone."*

Early in the campaign Bobby had been reluctant to debate, not wanting to look like a bully beating up on his older (by twenty-six years), more courtly (by every measure) opponent. Keating sought to exploit that refusal. Late in October he bought a half hour of TV time and set up next to him an empty chair to remind viewers of what he called Bobby's "utter contempt for the voters of New York." The Kennedy campaign bought its own air time for later that night. But thirty minutes before Keating was due to go on, Bobby told his aides, "I can't let him debate an empty chair. I'm going down there and sit in that empty chair." And so he tried, with guards at the TV studio barring his way. No matter, he had turned the tables: Instead of stories about Kennedy ducking out on a debate invitation, TV stations had live footage of Bobby knocking on the studio door, with Keating later fleeing the scene as his aides hurled furniture and fake palm trees in the path of pursuing journalists.

Gone, too, in the last month of the campaign was the flaccid slogan, "Let's Put Robert Kennedy to Work for New York." In its place was one tying him to the popular president: "Get on the Johnson-Humphrey-Kennedy team." Bobby's pride at not wanting to ride anyone's coattails—especially those of a politician he loathed—gave way to his fear of losing. He also received an endorsement from former president Harry Truman, who had never hidden his distrust of "that boy." He campaigned alongside Adlai Stevenson, who Jack had said "acted like a girl," and Mayor Wagner, who he knew considered him an interloper. He embraced those left-leaning intellectuals willing to embrace him—such dons of salon society as Jules Feiffer, Paddy Chayefsky, and Lillian Hellman—forgetting his lifelong disgust at mushy liberals. Like any successful coach, Bobby

---

* There were more dirty tricks on election day, when Kennedy operatives helped steer voting machine repairmen in New York City to areas where they thought they'd do well and to delay them in other areas, said Philip Ryan, a former assistant U.S. attorney and Kennedy aide. When a voting machine in one area was locked and nobody could find the key, "we sent somebody out" to break the machine open, which Ryan acknowledged "was strictly against the law. . . . Now that we haven't been caught, I guess it was I that did that" (Philip Ryan OH, December 13, 1973, 82–84).

knew how to regroup midgame. He also knew it didn't matter that Keating three years before had backed his nomination for attorney general, calling him "a longtime personal friend," and had been his guest at Hickory Hill. They were rivals now, and Bobby would do what it took to win. That included embracing, figuratively and in the flesh, a president with whom the contempt was mutual.

LBJ made two trips to the state and dispatched Hubert Humphrey, his running mate, on three more. "You don't often find a man who has the understanding, the heart and the compassion that Bobby Kennedy has," Johnson said at a rally in Buffalo. Bobby gushed back, calling LBJ "already one of the great presidents of the United States." The words didn't come easily to either of them, or ring true to their aides. At the same time that LBJ was singing the Senate candidate's praises, the White House was trying "to shaft Bobby in every conceivable fashion," reported Kenny O'Donnell, who said the only way he got the president to make that trip was by pretending to try to talk him out of it. Perfect psychology. It was no easier from Bobby's side. "Johnson would get up on the platform, put his arm around [Bobby] and say, 'This is mah boy. I want you to elect mah boy,'" recalled Richard Wade, a Kennedy campaign adviser. "You could see the whites of Bobby's knuckles, as this would go on."

One last factor tipped the scales in the election: Joe's millions. Wade, who lived in Chicago, was shocked when the campaign gave him a book of tickets on American Airlines so he could fly in as often as he liked: "I never even heard of such a thing." Neither had New York assemblyman Al Blumenthal, who said, "We had cars, volunteer cars. We had babysitting services. We had an escort service for the elderly." Bobby's staff was so big that it filled five separate suites in office buildings and hotels across Manhattan, with more young volunteers than there were jobs or there had been for JFK's Senate races. TV ads alone cost a million dollars, a record for a Senate race in New York and probably anywhere else at that time.

Terence Smith, who covered the campaign for the *New York Herald Tribune* and studied its marketing, said the clear challenge was to dispel the candidate's longstanding image "as a Little League ogre." The strategy was equally straightforward: Film him unrehearsed, talking to voters in shopping center parking lots, on the Staten Island Ferry, in the auditorium at Columbia. Every night two planes shuttled that day's footage free of charge to every TV station across New York so they could run it on the evening news, which conferred infinitely more credibility than any paid commercial. Every day, interspersed among ads of Bobby on the trail, were shorter ones with this soft sell: "Think about it for a minute. Which of the candidates running for United States senator has the better chance of becoming a great United States senator? A *great* United States senator. On November third, vote for Robert Kennedy." Did that barrage, unleashed during the campaign's final weeks, work? Bobby, who had been skeptical, became a believer. "The TV spots," he said, "showed that I was something more than a Beatle." Smith agreed: "There's no question his image softened. . . . It was a major remaking, not only of an image, really, but of a person."

Even as he freely spent his inheritance, Bobby held onto one rich man's idiosyncrasy that he drilled into his aides: no Cadillacs or other limousines for his campaign caravan, no matter how generous the local car dealership was. He might ride around in a family plane and bounce between mansions, but he also was sensitive about appearing highfalutin, which is one reason why he wore frayed chinos and drove beat-up jalopies. "This was just a Kennedy thing," explained Smith. "I remember on one occasion Bob coming to the top of the stairs of the plane, looking out, seeing that line of half a dozen shiny black cars, and just absolutely recoiling and backing off, and saying, 'No, no, no, no.' "

There is no denying that Bobby's Senate campaign helped set a new paradigm for image building, but in the end his most effective tactic was the simplest one: tying his opponent to the Republican presidential nominee, Barry Goldwater, whose popularity was sinking even faster in New York than in the nation as a whole. Keating tried to counter that by enlisting assistance from GOP stalwarts like Richard Nixon and Thomas Dewey and tapping the personal treasury of billionaire governor Nelson Rockefeller, whose bandwagon had helped carry Keating to victory in his first Senate campaign in 1958. But this wasn't 1958. Going up against Bobby, the affable Keating seemed too hoary and slow, too Republican no matter his disclaimers, and too little interested in a post he would gladly have traded for the one he really relished: commissioner of baseball. Just before the election, the respected *New York Daily News* straw poll predicted that Kennedy would carry 57.4 percent of the vote, a forecast so rosy that it worried Bobby the cautious campaign manager at the same time that it delighted Bobby the candidate. Lubell, the *World-Telegram* poll taker, intensified that unease when he said that while Kennedy "should win," Keating had "an underdog chance."

———

THE KENNEDY FAMILY jumped into Bobby's race with even more fervor than it had Jack's and Ted's, because Bobby was less of a natural campaigner and needed their help more. It also offered them the same catharsis it did Bobby. Winning another campaign could help convince everyone that the dynasty Joe had shaped could be brought back to life in the wake of Jack's loss. And just trying helped them forget their torment.

Rose, now seventy-four and the biggest draw of any Kennedy, set the pace. "I realized Bobby could stand a little coaching and further that if he and I were on the platform together I could make him feel somewhat more at ease. I had a special utility also, as his mother, in meeting the charge that he was a 'political carpetbagger,' " she explained. "We had a little routine worked out. . . . He brought up the charge that he was an outlander, then turned to me and said, 'Tell them, Mother.' Which I would do, chapter and verse, about moving from Brookline to Riverdale and to Bronxville when Bobby was only two years old . . . and then even afterward we always had a residence in New York City, and that the city had always remained the headquarters for my husband's business interests, and Bobby and all the others had gone for some years to schools in New York, and so forth—and what more identification with the state could anyone want? All of which seemed to soothe people's fears." So devoted was she to this favorite son that on her fiftieth wedding anniversary, she left Joe's side to campaign for Bobby in the faraway Hudson River Valley.

Joe, too, supported Bobby wholeheartedly, as he'd made clear from the earliest days of the campaign in spite of his difficulty speaking intelligibly. "When we were in New York, Bobby would always arrive at the apartment very early in the morning to have breakfast with his father," said Joe's nurse, Rita Dallas. "Mr. Kennedy's voice would rise in excite-

ment and then fall into a low, confidential whisper, while Bobby listened
carefully. . . . I can see [Bobby] sitting with his hand in a pan of warm salt
water trying to relieve the swelling that was caused from hours of shaking hands. . . . His voice would lift and explode. 'I'll make changes, Dad,'
he'd say. 'You know I'll make changes. Millions of people need help. My
God, they need help.' Mr. Kennedy would nod his head solemnly, then
reach out his hand to his son."

The Kennedy girls, Jean and Pat especially, offered their help along
with their money. Steve Smith, Jean's husband, spent his days on his
cream-colored telephone in his oversized office in the Pan Am Building,
raising cash and setting up a campaign organization. He made himself
indispensable, although he wasn't the alter ego Bobby had been for Jack.
Ethel, who was five months pregnant, campaigned alongside her husband and assembled the family when asked to in Glen Cove, their pretend
home. The kids jumped in, all eight of them, for special events like the
convention. "We were campaigning in New York with all my siblings
and we were on a stage someplace and he said, 'Now I'm just going to
introduce my children,'" recalls Kerry, who was barely five. "And he
went down the line, and he was pretending he couldn't remember everybody's names. We were laughing and reminding him, and then we were
switching places and making him reintroduce the same ones again and
again. I don't know how you put that into a book and make it funny but
it was, to me it was. . . . You were going to be happy, enjoying yourself,
because that's the way he was. . . . It was just really fun to be with him."

The one relative missing from those events was the former First Lady,
although she was one of those who had encouraged him to stay in public
life. "There was an abundance of suggestions on ways in which Jacqueline Kennedy could be used in the campaign," said Gerald Gardner, an
RFK speechwriter who wrote a book about the campaign. "They included everything from television commercials to joining the candidate
at Mass at St. Patrick's Cathedral. [Bobby] said no to all of them." It was
partly that he didn't want to sully her, and partly that she was preoccupied with John, Caroline, and reclaiming her life. He also didn't want to
look as if he was playing politics with his brother's memory and widow.

Even without Jackie, the national and foreign media couldn't get
enough of the race. The 1964 presidential campaign that year lacked

both suspense and appealing candidates. Goldwater never stood a chance, and Johnson was neither eloquent nor likable despite his popularity. American culture was in transition, hovering somewhere between its 1950s-like fascination with the new Mustang muscle cars and the heavenly Mary Poppins on the one hand, and on the other LBJ's call to create a Great Society that would root out poverty and racism. The struggle for the Senate seat from New York offered an early hint of that generational battle and pivot in the country's tastes and worries. Here was Bobby Kennedy, a boyish-looking thirty-eight-year-old, making his maiden run against a less politically astute sixty-four-year-old incumbent whose ruddy complexion and bulging girth made him seem even older. One critic called the former attorney general a "glamour puss." Everywhere he went he would draw stares, then a dawning recognition, and finally a shriek: "It's Bobby!" Keating, by contrast, was seldom noticed and never hailed by his constituents or the army of reporters based in Manhattan. The national stakes, however, were what really made the press and public pay attention. Bobby bore the mantle of a prince in exile, and a win here would be interpreted as a first step toward reclaiming the White House. A loss by Keating, in a year when the GOP had taken a sharp turn rightward, could be a death knell for his breed of Republican moderate.

The Washington Post and other faraway news outlets were editorializing on the race as early as August, and many others weighed in as it neared its end in November. From the isolated perches of their newsrooms, editorial writers saw Bobby more as a ruthless carpetbagger and an echo of his brother than as a flesh-and-blood politician. New Yorkers and the nation might have been swept up in Camelot nostalgia but not these stalwart editors, who would prove their independence by sounding their warnings. "We believe that a man who is not entitled to vote in the state has no business being elected to the U.S. Senate from that state," wrote *The Saturday Evening Post*. "If Robert Kennedy had really wanted to further the plans and ideals of his late brother," scolded the liberal *Nation* magazine, "he could have served them gallantly by running against Harry Byrd, who is out for a sixth term in Virginia and who stands as a roadblock to most of the things John F. Kennedy cherished. Robert has been living in Virginia; he could have stayed there and been above reproach." And the grayest of ladies, *The New York Times*, endorsed Keating, explaining that "nothing that has happened in the campaign thus far has altered our previous estimate of Robert F. Kennedy as an able, purposeful young man who has rendered distinguished service as Attorney General, but who is now attempting to use New York and the Senatorial office in a relentless quest for greater political power."

Most of the street reporters covering the campaign rendered a decidedly different verdict. The more they saw him, the more they trusted him, and they liked that he broke the familiar molds of politicians. He was less polished and more spontaneous. The hard-as-nails shell they had heard about protected a deep, reassuring tenderness. He listened, learned, and changed in ways journalists believed were nearly impossible for officeholders. It had been that way with beat reporters at the Justice Department, and it would be that way during his run for the White House. The scribes took care not to reflect that embrace too overtly in their stories, for fear of violating their pledge of neutrality, but they subtly conveyed it anyway, in books, interviews, and between the lines of newspaper columns. In the process they reinforced the evolving adage that Bobby was easy to hate at a distance and difficult not to love up close.

"Who is he, this rich man's son who happened to be the brother of a President and now wants everything in sight because of it? Who is he to be coming in to New York just because Lyndon Johnson didn't make him Vice President?" asked Jimmy Breslin, the dean of up-close journalism. The New York–based columnist answered his own question: "Where is there a Democrat in the whole state worth running for an office as big as Senator? Where is there one? There isn't. . . . Why shouldn't we have a man like Bobby Kennedy around here?" Norman Mailer, even crustier than Breslin and less likely to jump on any bandwagon, made known his feelings in the weekly *Village Voice* that he cofounded: "I think something came into him with the death of his brother. I think Bobby Kennedy has come a pilgrim's distance from that punk who used to play Junior D.A. for Joe McCarthy and grabbed headlines by riding Jimmy Hoffa's back. Something compassionate, something witty, has come into the face. Something of sinew. . . . I'd rather go this way and be wrong, than vote the other way trying to stop a possibility with a non-entity."

FOR MOST CANDIDATES, election day is a time for sleeping in, biting nails, and looking for something to occupy them at the end of a campaign filled with preoccupations. That was one more way Bobby stood out. He was up at dawn for breakfast with the West Side Democratic Club, many of whose members still hadn't warmed to him, then off to thank his young headquarters staff on Forty-Second Street. A trip to the zoo with Ethel and their eight children showed that this family weaned on politics hadn't lost its sense of humor. "Please do not feed the candidate," Ethel chided when Bobby bought a bag of peanuts for the kids. When Kerry, who'd just turned five, planted a kiss on her father's cheek, he laughed: "I told you—only when there are cameramen around!" No matter his lightness, there were two things this candidate knew better than anyone else: Kennedys didn't lose elections that mattered. And for all his amazing track record in managing elections, he had yet to prove he could win one for himself.

Thankfully for Bobby, more New Yorkers agreed with columnists Breslin and Mailer than with their editorial-writing colleagues. He beat his Republican rival by 719,693 votes,* which was 335,000 more than Jack's margin of victory in the state in 1960. He captured just 60 percent of the Jewish vote, a full nine points less than Keating's opponent in a closer Senate race six years earlier, but he made up for that by winning easily in black and Puerto Rican areas and stanching the defection of Italian Americans. He did less well than expected in New York City but better than Democrats generally did in Republican counties upstate. Overall, his majority was the biggest a New York Democrat had managed, for senator or governor, since 1934. "This vote," he said that night, "is a mandate to continue the efforts begun by my brother four years ago." It was that, but it was also a demarcation between his past as Jack's kid brother and his future as his own man.

The White House didn't have to claim credit for Bobby's win, since the numbers seemed to speak for themselves, and pundits echoed that message. Johnson beat Goldwater by 2.7 million votes in New York State, a historic edge and, more to the point, nearly four times bigger than Ken-

---

* His margin of victory was smaller—about half a million—when one adds votes cast for the conservative and two socialists.

nedy's. "If it was a race just between the two of them, and no Goldwater, Keating would've won easily," says Eugene Rossides, campaign manager for the spurned incumbent. The *New York Times* editorial board agreed, arguing that it was the "anti-Goldwater sentiment resulting in a Johnson landslide that carried [Kennedy] to victory." The paper couldn't resist getting in a last dig: "This was a victory not only over the incumbent, Senator Kenneth B. Keating, but also over the old tradition that a member of Congress should come from the state or district he represents."

Bobby's boosters read the results differently. "Kennedy did not need the Johnson landslide to win," said Gwirtzman. "The difference between the Johnson and the Kennedy vote . . . was comprised exclusively of *Republican* voters who bolted the Goldwater ticket to vote for Johnson, and then returned to their party to vote for Keating. Kennedy did not get these voters, did not expect to get them; and thus there was no coattail effect in the Senate election in New York in 1964."

Bobby himself had it both ways, as was still his wont. When LBJ took time out of his historic election triumph to call and congratulate the senator-elect, RFK was gracious. Johnson: "Let's stay as close together as [JFK]'d want us to. . . . Ain't nobody going to divide us. . . . I'm proud of you." Kennedy: "Thanks for your help. . . . [It] made a hell of a difference." But in a look-back with a reporter dissecting all the factors that had aided his campaign, Bobby mentioned just about everything—the empty-chair debate, his TV commercials, Keating's abortive bid to paint him as a Nazi sympathizer—but not the visits by the president or vice president. In his nationally televised victory speech on election night he thanked just about everyone, from Ethel to former New York governor Averell Harriman to Steve Smith. But he made no mention of the man he'd thanked privately minutes before for making a hell of a difference, and who had. "As Bobby looked up from his notes, I found myself silently urging him to speak: *C'mon, Bobby, let's hear it.* [But] the name I wanted so much to hear never came," recalled Jack Valenti, a Johnson aide who had traveled to New York with the president and now was watching the election results with him on TV at a hotel in Austin. "President Johnson made no outward sign that the omission had registered. . . . But I certainly felt the absence of Bobby's appreciation for the hard stumping the president had done on his behalf. To be honest, I felt ill."

If that was an example of the soon-to-be senator at his least forgiving, the rest of his victory lap that night revealed his genial best. He made a sentimental visit at 3:30 in the morning to the Fulton Fish Market in Lower Manhattan, where the campaign had kicked off nine weeks before. The fishmongers gave him a halibut to hold and he joked that "it smells better here than it did two months ago." After three hours' sleep he was off and running again, this time to catch a flight to Glens Falls. "Well, it's all over," the reporter Terence Smith said as Bobby was climbing aboard the plane. Bobby: "Yes, now I can go back to being ruthless." When he finally landed in the upstate town that had waited up half the night for him in September, and that he'd promised to revisit win or lose, the crowd was nearly as large. "You befriended me," he said, and they had, giving him a 555-vote margin. "Bobby said you looked nice in your pajamas," Ethel added. "But you look nice dressed too." His next-to-last stop was Boston, where he spent two hours at the hospital bedside of his brother Ted, who'd been reelected by 900,000 votes even as he lay in an orthopedic frame with a broken back. A photographer chided Bobby for standing so close to the bed that he cast a shadow on his brother, prompting Ted to chime in: "It'll be the same way in Washington." Bobby: "He only says that because he got a bigger vote than I did."

Bobby had one more person to thank, this time like all the others. Joe had come back to Manhattan to be near his boy on election day, and Bobby insisted on taking his father to dinner before the Kennedy elder returned to Cape Cod. With help from his nurse, Joe dressed in black tie and dinner suit and slicked back his silver hair. When his son arrived he bowed his head low in his wheelchair and extended his hand to the senator-elect. Bobby bent down for a hug, whispering, "We made it, Dad! We made it!"

They had made history. The Kennedys were the first family ever to send three brothers to the U.S. Senate, and the second to have brothers serving simultaneously*—a tribute not just to Joe and Rose's ambitions but to their sons' talents. His two and a half months of campaigning had also transformed Bobby, who, unlike Ted, was a reluctant candidate and

---

* The first were the Fosters, Theodore from Rhode Island and Dwight representing Massachusetts, in the early 1800s.

an unlikely politician. Having to ask the public for their votes proved the
best therapy for his broken life, tugging him out of the last of his post-
Dallas depression and unlocking him in ways that surprised even him.
He loved battling Republicans again, not to mention old enemies such as
Jimmy Hoffa and Roy Cohn. He enjoyed being the front man, and would
have enjoyed it even more if he hadn't had to double as campaign manager. "Being clawed and pushed by the crowds" was the least fun part, he
said, not surprising for a man who loathed being touched and was energized by the idea, but not the bruising reality, of the mobs he drew. His
favorite election experience? "Getting away from Washington. Getting
to know upstate New York and the people who live here." Coming from
any other candidate that would have sounded disingenuous, but Bobby
offered his reflections under an agreement that they'd be published *after*
the election. This ultimate product of Washington really did loathe its
phoniness. This naturally reticent man had actually learned to like inter-
acting with a public that couldn't get enough of him.

He hadn't lost his sharp edges during those nine weeks barnstorming
the Empire State, but he bantered in a way that made it clear he took his
message more seriously than himself. Told that California had displaced
New York as America's most populous state, "I turned to my wife and I
said, 'What can we *do*?' So I moved to New York, and in just one day I
increased the population by ten and a half. . . . My opponent has just
sixty days to match that record." He threw this bone to the tradesmen at
the Fulton Market: "I have eight children, and we eat fish every Friday.
From now on, we'll eat fish twice a week. That's what we're going to do
for the fishing industry of New York." The ethnic politics that had confounded him now brought him joy as he marched with the Italians to
honor Christopher Columbus, with the Poles on behalf of General Pulaski, and alongside the Germans for General von Steuben. He put on a
yarmulke during a visit to the Lubavitcher Rebbe, and emerging from a
meeting with a dozen rabbis he quipped, "Are you sure those guys were
rabbis? I didn't see a single beard in the crowd."

He was changing in deeper ways, too. Defining his own public identity
meant clarifying his own beliefs, as opposed to those that had come from
Jack. Few could see those critical differences even when the two were
working side by side. Both men were pragmatic, but Bobby was more

willing to experiment with radical solutions and spend political capital. Both talked about promoting Negro rights and battling poverty, but Bobby felt the injustice on a gut level and lost sleep over it in ways that his imperturbable and cerebral brother never did. Bobby also embraced contradiction in ways that neither Jack nor Teddy wanted to or could. His realism butted up against his romanticism even as the existentialist in him looked for ways to coexist with the politician. He was half ice, half fire. How, observers wondered, could someone so shy be so intimidating? Was it possible to love both Albert Camus and roughhouse football? "Robert Kennedy's motto," said the *Village Voice*'s Jack Newfield, "could have been, 'Do not understand me too quickly.' . . . His most basic characterics were simple, intense, and in direct conflict with each other. He was constantly at war with himself."

That conflict and growth were there to read in Bobby's latest book, a thin volume called *The Pursuit of Justice* that, with help from a Cornell professor, had been rushed out in time for the 1964 campaign but had no impact on it.* Like all his writings, this book steered clear of personal disclosures and lacked even the candor of his Kennedy Library interviews on Jack's presidency. It had a pontifical style and political purpose, but still managed to be revealing between the lines. He remained an anticommunist, but he wrote that "the Communist Party as a political organization is of no danger to the United States." He had not changed his mind on Vietnam, but he said, "As long as the instruments of peace are available, war is madness." He remained a child of the establishment, but an increasingly rebellious one. "Change," he explained, "means that someone's professional feathers will be ruffled, that a glass-topped desk might be moved to another office or abandoned, that pet programs might die. Progress is a nice word. But change is its motivator. And change has its enemies."

---

* Most of his books were compilations of old speeches or diary notes, and most were written with the help of a friendly ghost. In the case of *Pursuit of Justice*, Bobby's collaborator was a young professor whose wife had just had a baby and who therefore wasn't anxious to take on the project. But "with somebody like [Bobby], you can't simply say no," explains Theodore Lowi. He never had regrets, however, since he got more credit than he'd expected (his name went on the cover as editor), more money than he'd counted on ("he was so decent"), and more cooperation than he'd dreamed possible (Bobby responded to most of his suggestions with "That's a damn good idea") (Author interview with Lowi).

Because it was in an unremitting state of becoming, Bobby's ideology was challenging to pin down at any given moment. The evolution had begun when he toured the world with Justice Douglas in 1955 and continued as he traveled the country during the 1960 campaign, talking to and trying to understand the disenfranchised people of the Soviet Caucasus and the poverty-stricken residents of West Virginia. His developing worldview took shape in his years as attorney general, when he learned not just how bad things were for Negro Americans but that he could help. He would make these people and issues his cause as a United States senator and later as a candidate for president.

There was one more lens through which to follow the permutations in Bobby Kennedy: the men he called heroes. Paladins had always been important to him, starting with his father and continuing with his brothers, Joe Jr., then Jack. The two Roosevelts—Teddy and Franklin—were on his list from the first; he saw them as tough leaders who got things done. He revered soldiers, too: Maxwell Taylor, for his willingness to back JFK and defy his fellow chiefs of staff; Douglas MacArthur, for his courage and showmanship; and Francis Marion, the Swamp Fox, for showing how to wage guerrilla warfare. But while he still defended Joe McCarthy, he no longer considered him a hero. The same went for Cardinal Francis Joseph Spellman, an ally of both McCarthy and Joe Kennedy who was known as the American pope and whose archconservative views of politics and the Church were now less appealing than those of the real pope, the Vatican II reformer John XXIII. Bobby was split on the Hoovers, continuing to admire Herbert but coming to hate J. Edgar, whom he called "senile" and "rather a psycho." There was room now on his mantel and bookshelf not just for the transcendentalists Ralph Waldo Emerson and Henry David Thoreau, but for revolutionaries such as Mao Tse Tung and Che Guevara.

As he prepared to take his seat in the U.S. Senate, he held in less regard his early mentors there like McClellan and McCarthy. His new exemplars were from an earlier era, and none were still alive. George Norris, a Nebraska Republican, backed the New Deal, helped create the Tennessee Valley Authority, and confounded Democrats and Republicans with his fierce independence. Another Republican New Dealer, Robert La Follette, Jr., was an ally of labor and civil libertarians and a founder of the

Wisconsin Progressive Party. And the Democrat Robert Wagner of New York, an anti-Nazi German whose son would become New York City's mayor, authored bills to outlaw the lynchings that were rampant across the South and to create a National Labor Relations Board. All three senators were Bobby's kind of insurgent. All were patient enough to do the gritty work Bobby knew was needed to make a difference in that deliberative body. Most important to Robert F. Kennedy, all set a standard nobler than the norm for politics and politicians—as crusaders against what Norris characterized as "wrong and evil" in the affairs of the government and the nation.

Chapter 9

SENATOR KENNEDY

N OBODY HAD TO tell Senator Robert F. Kennedy that the world was filled with starving children. He'd met them—toddlers with the telltale swollen bellies, oozing sores, and persistent listlessness—in Africa, Latin America, and Southeast Asia. But surely not in America's richly fertile Mississippi Delta, whose sugar, rice, and soybeans fed the world. Not after the billions we'd spent waging a War on Poverty, a war that the Kennedys helped kick-start. Not *our* babies.

What he heard about hunger at a Senate hearing on Capitol Hill in March 1967 so alarmed him that a month later he flew to a field hearing in Jackson, where his airport greeting party included a gauntlet of KKK protesters shrieking "nigger-lover" and carrying a sign reading LET LBJ SEND RFK TO HANOI, NOT TO MISSISSIPPI. The next day he and fellow senators listened intently as witnesses gave human faces to the figures recited in Washington. Black sharecroppers were surrendering their jobs to crop-picking machines, then being chased out of the state by white oligarchs who were petrified they'd lose power now that Negroes had the vote. Two-parent families were ineligible for welfare and, with zero income, could not scrape together the monthly fee of two dollars per person for food stamps. Bobby knew better than to take seriously Mississippi governor Paul Johnson's sneer that "all the Negroes I've seen around here are so fat they shine!" But surely Marian Wright, the young civil rights activist, was being equally hyperbolic in testifying that scores of her fellow Mississippians were "starving. They're starving, and those who can get the bus fare to go north are trying to go north. . . . I wish that [senators] would have a chance to go and just look at the empty cupboards in the Delta and the number of people who are going around begging just to feed their children."

"I want to see it," Bobby said. The following day, while other senators on the Poverty Subcommittee flew home to the perquisites of Washington, he and Chairman Joe Clark ventured into the region that once was the dominion of King Cotton. Their first stop was a black outpost in the bowels of the Delta, at a shotgun shack where daylight shone through cracks in the floor and ceiling and the only item in the refrigerator was a jar of peanut butter. Fifteen people called it home. The stench was a nauseating brew of mildew and outhouse. Children huddled out front, clad in rags that barely covered the open sores on their arms and legs. "What did you have for breakfast?" Bobby asked a young boy. "Molasses." he said. "For supper?" "Molasses." "For lunch?" "Don't have no lunch." A large, ancient-looking woman in baggy clothes thanked the senators for their offer of help but explained that she was too old to wait. How old was she? Bobby asked. "I'm thirty-three."

"I've been to third-world countries and I've never seen anything like this," Bobby whispered to his aide Peter Edelman as they trekked across a field of uncut grass to another weather-beaten hovel. Clotheslines crisscrossed one room. Bricks propped up a bed where an infant sucked on a bottle. An open toilet out back had no plumbing. There were no tables in the house, nor any knives, forks, or spoons. Annie White, mother of seven, was in the kitchen doing laundry over a washboard and zinc tub that could have been her grandparents'. Her twenty-month-old son sat nearby in a tattered diaper, his tummy bloated from too little food rather than too much. The boy picked at bits of cornbread and rubbed spilled kernels of rice in circles, around and around in a hypnotic motion. Bobby knelt beside him on the dirt floor, silently stroking his cheek. It was the way this tactile senator communicated—a pat and tickle delivered at the child's eye level, where adults seldom ventured. A minute went by, then four more. The boy remained transfixed by his scraps, oblivious to the flies swarming overhead or the senator with tears streaming down his cheeks, trying desperately to make a human connection.

Quietly shattered, Bobby stepped through the back door and told those within hearing, "We spend $75 billion a year on armaments and $3 billion a year on dogs. We have to do more for these children who didn't ask to be born into this." Cliff Langford, editor of the local weekly newspaper and a longtime Kennedy hater, shouted back that the two senators were being brainwashed and "I don't know of anybody starving down here." Bobby: "Step over here and I'll introduce you to some."

The reassembled motorcade—a pair of senators, a dozen reporters from state and national newspapers and the three TV networks, along with a squad of U.S. marshals, state highway patrolmen, and local police—headed toward Clarksdale, where a crowd of a thousand young blacks waited. But Bobby wasn't quite ready. He insisted on stopping at one more roadside shack, where he was greeted by an out-of-work farmer named Andrew Jackson, who invited him in, unsure who he was. Jackson said he was supporting his family of six on twelve dollars a month. His house had no electricity, running water, or toilet. On the wall were two photographs—of the Glorybound Singers and John F. Kennedy. "Is you really Mr. Bobby Kennedy?" Jackson inquired. "Yes," said Bobby, as he grinned and clasped his host's hand, "and are you really Mr. Andrew Jackson?"

That trip to the Delta is often cited as Bobby's epiphany regarding the depth of poverty in America, and proof of his ability to focus a laserlike spotlight on a hidden issue like starvation. It was both. Only four of nine subcommittee members deigned to travel halfway across the continent for hearings on issues afflicting the hungry and poor, most of whom didn't vote or matter in Jackson or Washington. Fewer still—two senators, to be exact—stuck around to see the horrors they had heard about. Once there, not even the big-hearted Chairman Clark would plant his tailor-suited self on a grimy kitchen floor to talk to an underfed toddler. Bobby wasn't putting on a show; he didn't know anyone was watching. He sought out human misery, then sought to ease it. Even the battle-hardened Marian Wright saw something that changed her opinion of the senator from New York. "I'd formed an image of him as a tough, arrogant, politically driven man from the Joseph McCarthy era," she said. "These feelings dissolved as I saw Kennedy profoundly moved by Mississippi's hungry children." It had the same effect on Curtis Wilkie, who covered the trip for the *Clarksdale Press Register:* "You've seen these guys phony up emotions, and this was genuine. It had an emotional impact on me like it would anybody who was watching."

But declaring himself a ministering angel was hardly enough. This New England patrician realized that Mississippians and others would judge him by what he could deliver. So the very next day, he and Edelman met with Agriculture Secretary Orville Freeman. "Orville," Bobby said, "you have got to get some food down there." Freeman balked: "Bob, there isn't anybody in America who has no income." Kennedy: "I'll tell you what. I'll send Peter here back down there with some of your people. . . . Will you agree that you'll change the regulations if your people are convinced there really are people in Mississippi who have no income?" Freeman said he would and, when the evidence came in, he loosened the food stamp rules. Kennedy also got the nonprofit Field Foundation to dispatch doctors to examine hundreds of children like those he'd seen; they documented kwashiorkor,* rickets, and other signs of actual starvation in what the doctors deemed a "national disaster." Mississippi's segregationist senator John Stennis was so embarrassed that he proposed $10 million in emergency funding for food and medical services. Newsmen at CBS were so startled that they produced a first-of-its-kind documentary titled *Hunger in America*. "He didn't go away," said Marian Wright, the first black woman admitted to the Mississippi bar. "Robert Kennedy's pushing, passion, and visibility set in motion a chain of events that culminated years later in the virtual elimination of hunger in America during the Nixon years." It also ended in Wright's marrying Edelman, with Bobby's encouragement.

Kennedy scholars often write off those Senate years as a prosaic interlude between Bobby's action-packed attorney generalship and his exhilarating run for the White House. He wasn't nearly as eloquent a senator as his brother Jack, they say, or as effective an insider as Ted. True enough, but that was not nearly the complete story. Jack got to the Senate because he and Bobby ran a brilliant campaign paid for by Joe, while Teddy made it there on Jack's and Bobby's coattails. The Kennedy name and money helped Bobby, too, but unlike his brothers, he had done his

---

* Kwashiorkor, caused by too little protein in the diet, is the most common nutritional disorder in developing nations.

homework. He learned the Senate's arcane ways a decade before when
he played decisive roles in the Army-McCarthy hearings and the rackets
probe. He helped steer America's domestic and foreign policies for nearly
three years as attorney general and de facto deputy president. He discovered how to connect with voters at the same time as he ran his own campaign. Bobby was readier for his new role not just than Jack and Ted, but
than all but a handful of senators in the institution's 178 years.

That groundwork paid quick dividends. Bobby was from the beginning a national senator even if parliamentarians didn't recognize such a
thing. His older brother had steered clear of controversy to seed his run
for president, and it took Teddy half a century to earn his crown as Lion
of the Senate. Not Bobby. He didn't have the patience to serve a long ap-
prenticeship, and if all he cared about was restoring a Kennedy to the
White House, he wouldn't have been moving to the left on issues such as
ending poverty when much of the country was reacting to the culture
wars by tilting rightward. He delivered his first speech in the Senate just
three weeks after his swearing-in, compared to Jack's five months and
Ted's sixteen. He attended hearings on issues that mattered, like hunger,
with his very presence ensuring that reporters would come. When peti-
tioning the White House could help, he held his nose and did it. Few in
Congress made better use of their full palette of tactics and strategies—
from model programs to the bully pulpit—than the very junior senator
from New York. Even so, liberals said he was providing an illusion of dissent, while conservatives worried he was all heart and too subversive.
Neither could see at first that he was crafting a new creed—grasping at
the bits of FDR and his father's New Deal collectivism that still worked,
and borrowing from heroes such as Herbert Hoover and Ralph Waldo
Emerson who saw the centrality of self-reliance. He also was hardheaded
enough to disdain rebellion without results, which set him apart from
most 1960s activists.

This was no Saint Bobby. He was as headstrong as ever. He trumpeted
his self-sufficiency in an institution that turned on collegiality. But the
odyssey he had been through—the painful deaths of three siblings, the
loss of his father's guiding hand, crises over Cuban missiles and campus
race riots—brought to the surface his senses of irony and empathy. It
happened not in a single transformative moment but in subtle, incre-

mental stages. Most people harden as they add years and accumulate power, but Bobby's sanctimony and starchiness increasingly yielded to his introspection and idealism. He had firmly and finally become one of James Baldwin's handful of righteous warriors. "I hope I've learned something in the last ten years and understand some things better," he told a journalist seven months after he'd taken office, with characteristic understatement. He realized that elective office wasn't merely a means to claim the thrones Joe Kennedy had dreamed of for his sons. His mission, from early in his career as a senator, was to be the tribune of America's outcasts. Jack may have won a Pulitzer Prize for writing about senators with the courage to go against the grain, but Bobby came closer to living that profile.

IF THE MISSISSIPPI Delta served as a metaphor for the troubles that moved Bobby as a senator, the impoverished Bedford-Stuyvesant neighborhood of New York City offered a microscope to examine and test his preferred solutions. Like most of his good ideas, this one grew not out of a reasoned blueprint but a seat-of-the-pants sensibility that he had to try something, anything, to keep America's ghettos from imploding. Young blacks felt so trapped that when an off-duty white police lieutenant in New York shot a fifteen-year-old Negro under disputed circumstances in the summer of 1964, the incident ignited race riots not just in Harlem but in Philadelphia, Chicago, Rochester, and Jersey City. Black parents were frightened, and so was nearly all of white America. Lyndon Johnson responded with a set of New Deal–like education, health care, and welfare programs that he called the Great Society—lifting millions of Americans out of poverty, but not treating underlying social and racial ills. By the summer of 1965 the violence had spread to the West Coast, with the Watts district of Los Angeles going up in flames, leaving thirty-four dead. America seemed on the cusp of another civil war, this one pitting slum dwellers in the North and South against everyone else. At the end of his first year as a senator, Bobby instructed Peter Edelman and Adam Walinsky, his closest and smartest aides, to formulate some new approaches.

Their suggestions formed the basis of three provocative speeches that he delivered to three very different gatherings in New York on consecutive days in January 1966. To an assembly of Jewish fundraisers, many of whom had abandoned their urban neighborhoods as blacks moved in, he insisted that integration—economic as well as racial, of neighborhoods, schools, and jobs—was essential "to assure that every American comes to know the full meaning of the truths that we held to be self-evident for the rest of America almost 190 years ago." The next day he told a black audience to get realistic. Ghettos weren't going away, but they could be made safe and livable if community leaders did less finger-pointing and more soul-searching. "None of this can happen," he lectured, "unless you will it to happen, and unless you can and do make the hard and sometimes unpopular decisions which come with responsibility." Speech three offered the most novel ideas to his most skeptical listeners, the mainly white members of the United Auto Workers union. Rather than battling with ghetto Negroes, Bobby explained, blue-collar Caucasians had to see their shared need for better education, better jobs, and a better life. "We are only at the beginning of a beginning," he said in appealing for the black-white alliance that had become his obsession. If anyone other than a Kennedy had been saying those things, his audiences would have walked out before they finished their chicken à la king. He succeeded in jump-starting the discussion, with them and with the wider public, but it was still just words. Talking about something made Bobby eager to do it. So he handed Walinsky and Edelman two new assignments: tell him what laws and programs were needed, and find a place to put those visions to a real-world test.

Thus was born the Bedford-Stuyvesant experiment, which aimed to recast America's biggest ghetto into its most ambitious proving ground for slum busting. If change could happen in this 653-block neighborhood—known in Brooklyn as Bed-Stuy and invisible to the world beyond—it might work anywhere, or so the senator had reason to believe. Bed-Stuy had rioted alongside Harlem in the overheated summer of 1964, but it lacked that neighborhood's finances, clout, and renowned cultural ambassadors like Langston Hughes and Billie Holliday. Eighty-four percent of Bed-Stuy's 450,000 residents were black, another 12 percent were Puerto Rican, and nearly a third of its families subsisted on $3,000 or less a year. No place in America had as high a rate of infants dying or toddlers being poisoned by lead. Whites, who fifteen years before had composed half the community, had fled in fright, with legend having it that one family on Hart Street was in such a hurry that they left their furniture behind. By the time the senator discovered it, said writer and activist Michael Harrington, "Bedford-Stuyvesant was on the well-greased road to economic and sociological hell."

To Bobby, Bed-Stuy represented more than the sum of its afflictions. This son of Irish Boston hadn't forgotten how an impoverished neighborhood known as Eastie had provided a launching pad for a onetime stevedore named Patrick Joseph Kennedy. In college, Bobby had collected rents at tenements owned by his father's bank, and he came home with wide-eyed tales of how big families lived in four cramped rooms and slept on the fire escapes on hot nights. Bobby knew that in Bedford-Stuyvesant, the brownstones generally were solid and could be made elegant again, and that with one in five of them owner-occupied, residents had a stake in the community. Its history of neglect by federal, state, and local governments was to him another irrefutable argument for equalization.

Any doubts that this was the greenhouse where he should plant his seeds were erased when he walked the neighborhood's streets one freezing afternoon in mid-February 1966. Neon signs offered loans and liquor. Forsaken cars rusted in front of boarded-up houses crawling with roaches, rats, and human squatters. Out-of-work fathers congregated on street corners while their children played outdoors in winter without coats. The journalist Jack Newfield, a Bed-Stuy native whose family left with the rest of the whites, remembered Bobby asking, "Show me the house where you grew up." The structure was abandoned by then, the block drug-infested. Newfield: "What would have happened if you grew up on this block, Senator?" Kennedy: "I either would have been a juvenile delinquent or a revolutionary." As for Newfield's roots in the run-down neighborhood, Bobby said, "I'm jealous of the fact you grew up in a ghetto. I wish I did. I wish I had that experience."

His ideas for attacking poverty weren't revolutionary, but no other politician was so willing to contravene political orthodoxies. Washington would pay for training unemployed adults, constructing a cultural complex, and other classic liberal initiatives. Tax breaks would lure big

business to build industrial plants and shopping centers, an idea that
drew raves from the conservative standard-bearer William F. Buckley, Jr.
And borrowing an approach from the New Left protest movement, local
residents would exercise unprecedented self-governance. "We must
combine the best of community action with the best of the private enterprise system," Kennedy said. "We are striking out in new directions, on
new courses, sometimes perhaps without map or compass to guide us."

Integration remained the long-term goal, but Bobby knew that getting white businessmen to work with black activists was a nonstarter for
now. So he set up side-by-side bureaucracies—an all-black corporation
to run the jobs and cultural enterprises, and an all-white one to raise
cash and recruit industry. The dual structures, the head of the blacks-
only group later said, ensured "that at the first meeting of the board, if
somebody said motherfucker, the white guys wouldn't all get up and
run." It worked, with Bobby cajoling and charming onto his business
board such titans of commerce as IBM chairman Thomas Watson and
CBS chief William Paley. He put the community group in the hands of
one of the city's most promising black leaders, Franklin Thomas, who'd
grown up in Bed-Stuy, served as New York City's deputy police commissioner, and would later run the Ford Foundation. Bobby gave political
credit to John Lindsay, the new Republican mayor of New York, whom
Bobby despised but knew could undermine the enterprise. He let another
Republican, Senator Jacob Javits, claim more credit than was deserved.
And he devoted more time to this project than to any other in his adopted
state, visiting three times a week and biting his tongue when Bed-Stuy
leaders gave him a hard time. "We've been studied to death," Elsie Richardson, a community activist, told him at the first neighborhood meeting in February. "The writers of sociology books have milked us of all the
information." Rather than getting defensive, as he had with Baldwin and
Belafonte in 1963, Bobby sat quietly as he was harangued, then asked for
a chance to prove himself. He agreed that too many studies had been
done already, adding, "The fact is, there has to be coordination, direction
and leadership." Richardson, his most vocal critic, left the meeting saying she'd been won over by Kennedy's "good intentions."

The first initiative involved patching sidewalks, repairing iron gates,
and repainting façades to make a difference that people could see. The

project provided work for three hundred locals who were unemployed and, with criminal records ranging from drug offenses to murder, unhirable anywhere else. Residents responded warily when, in an effort to give them skin in the game, they were asked to contribute $25 to renovations valued at $325, keep their sidewalks clean, and buy garbage cans marked with a green R for restoration. But the organizers persisted, eventually signing up 98 percent of owners in the eleven-block test area. It spread from there, with twenty-two hundred units of housing built or renovated, twenty thousand people placed in jobs, and the neighborhood becoming more sanguine and stable. "Driving past the brownstones, savoring the calm of the place," Harrington wrote in *New York* magazine, "one can see an immense and important fact: The blight of urban decay is not inevitable; there are alternatives. Something is happening in Bedford-Stuyvesant."

In hindsight, the record looks mixed. The Kennedy initiative did lure an IBM plant that employed five hundred people, but rather than signaling a trend it remained an isolated case of an entrepreneur willing to invest in the ghetto. The Bedford-Stuyvesant mini-model helped spur federal and foundation funding for similar neighborhood-specific revitalization bids, and today thousands of community development projects nationwide can trace their roots to Bed-Stuy and to Bobby Kennedy. But it took half a century and New York's changed demographics to remake Bedford-Stuyvesant, and the restoration still isn't complete. The project's most lasting effect wasn't in bricks and mortar but in how Bobby and his collaborators helped change America's thinking about poverty. Jobs mattered even more than education and housing, he said in what then was an avant-garde idea and today is accepted wisdom. So were the notions that control should be vested not in Washington but in communities like Watts and Harlem, with a public-private partnership the best way to draw funding. And he saw sooner than most that America's racial challenge was no longer Southern segregationists but Northerners who were seldom in conflict with blacks because they almost never encountered them.

The senator understood from the first the limits of what he was trying to do in Bedford-Stuyvesant and other ghettos. "I'm not at all sure this is going to work," he said days before unveiling his ideas. "Even if we fail, we'll have learned something. But more important than that, something has to be done. People like myself just can't go around making nice speeches all the time. We can't just keep raising expectations. We have to do some damn hard work, too."

Other politicians called them hopeless causes. But Bobby refused to believe there weren't remedies, not just for urban poverty but for the problems that for generations had bedeviled the miners who drilled into the Appalachian hills for an increasingly elusive supply of coal; the Indians who were this country's earliest and most invisible inhabitants; and, a group he came to know early in 1966, the migrant workers who picked but didn't share in the bounty of lettuce, grapes, and other harvests of America's agribusinesses. In the last instance, especially, he resisted getting involved. He was busy with Bed-Stuy and a hundred other things, and attending a hearing of a committee he didn't serve on, on an issue he didn't know anything about involving a strike by farmworkers against California grape growers, would mean another trip across the country. But his friends at the United Auto Workers had said he should go, and Edelman agreed. So Bobby found himself on a plane out West asking his aide, "Why the hell am I dragging my ass all the way out to California?" Shown where the mainly Filipino workers lived and labored—in housing that often lacked running water and heat, without a minimum wage or protection from pesticides, with their children picking beside them in the fields—he quickly sized up the situation. "This," he told the UAW's Paul Schrade, "is worse than Mississippi."

Then it was a matter of how to help. These were the days before college students and suburban liberals had begun to rally support for the farmworkers. Political friends were hard to come by, particularly among elected officials who lined up on the side of the wealthy growers. Bobby showed whose side he was on at the March hearing in the grape-growing town of Delano, California, held by the Senate's Migratory Labor Subcommittee. The local sheriff, who was the migrants' archfoe, testified that he had arrested forty-four picketing workers to protect them from strikebreakers who were threatening violence, which the sheriff thought could touch off a riot. It didn't take long for the senator from New York to read the situation and revert to his familiar form as an outraged prosecutor. Bobby: "How can you go arrest somebody if they haven't violated the law?" Sheriff: "They're ready to violate the law." Bobby: "I suggest during the luncheon period that the sheriff and the district attorney read the Constitution of the United States."

That alone made him a hero to the farmworkers, who had never seen anyone question the arbitrariness of local law enforcement. But he also forged a connection that day with Cesar Chavez, the farmworkers' leader. "They're standing in a parking lot and they just start talking to each other," remembers Edelman. "There starts to be this circle of people around them, and then it's two deep and three deep. . . . Neither one of them was somebody who used words extensively. It just took a five-minute conversation and they were friends for life." For Bobby, that friendship meant helping Chavez raise money, supporting laws that gave the nascent union a chance, and standing behind his friend's hunger strikes and La Causa. Migrant workers had supported JFK in 1960, "but with Bobby it was like an entirely different thing," Chavez recalled. "It was like he was ours." This Kennedy brother related to the poor—and to migrants in particular—the way the novelist John Steinbeck had in *The Grapes of Wrath*, trying to see the world through their eyes. "Robert didn't come to us and tell us what was good for us," said Chavez deputy Dolores Huerta. "He came to us and asked us two questions. All he said was, 'What do you want? And how can I help?' That's why we loved him."

He didn't have to travel across the country to witness the abuse of farmworkers. It was happening just outside Rochester, New York, at a fruit farm that he and Senator Javits visited as part of a Senate investigation in the fall of 1967. A sign there warned, ANYONE ENTERING OR TRESPASSING WITHOUT MY PERMISSION WILL BE SHOT IF CAUGHT. That stopped most of the government, press, and union entourage. But Bobby proceeded to an abandoned bus that was home to three migrant families, including six children under ten years old. Like those he had met in Mississippi, all were black and covered with running scabs. The parents looked older than their ages and, as one woman told Bobby, they earned a dollar an hour picking celery. The bus seats had been replaced with filthy mattresses, the windows with cardboard and wood. Bobby trembled with rage as he confronted the owner of the camp, Jay DeBadts, who was carrying a gun and looked as if he meant what his sign said. "You had no right to go in there," DeBadts yelled at the senator. "You're just a

do-gooder trying to make some headlines." Bobby looked back in disbelief, then raged in a near-whisper: "You are something out of the nine-
teenth century. I wouldn't put an animal in those buses."

Bobby never forgot what he saw at the fruit farm, and he added to his
list of causes afflicting Neanderthals like DeBadts and uprooting the
abuses at migrant camps. While that was the kind of politics he relished,
what he hated was the pressure to promote the careers of well-meaning
hacks like Francis X. Morrissey. Morrissey, a municipal judge in Boston,
was for decades Joe Kennedy's friend, factotum, and informer. He helped
Jack in his early runs for Congress and oversaw JFK's Boston office, then
steered a politically naïve Ted through Massachusetts's legal and political rites of passage. Joe had wanted Jack to name Morrissey to the federal
bench—the only favor of that kind he ever sought—but the president
held off as long as he could, and the events of Dallas intervened before he
could act. Two years later a conscience-ridden Ted resurrected the idea,
to the delight of his infirm father and with the assistance of the new
president. Bobby knew Morrissey's limits and realized that some of the
blackest marks on his record as attorney general were the archsegregationists and other politically expedient judges he had named to the
bench. But he felt boxed in by his familiar fealty to his father and brother,
which was reinforced rather than relieved by his new role as chief of the
tribe. That was just how LBJ had hoped it would play out, delighting at
making Bobby squirm and perhaps denting his credentials as a reformer.
Just in case, the president ordered J. Edgar Hoover to go all out in digging
up dirt on Morrissey, saying, "I don't want him to get that judgeship."

It wasn't the FBI that torpedoed Morrissey, however, but *The Boston
Globe*, which questioned the Horatio Alger narrative the Kennedys had
spun for the nominee. It was true that he was one of twelve children who
grew up in a house without electricity, but after that the story got muddy.
Morrissey had attended not Boston College Law School but its extension
school. He got his law degree from a diploma mill in Georgia. His credentials were so weak that the normally compliant American Bar Association withheld support and the Boston Bar branded him "entirely lacking
in the qualifications of education and training necessary to carry out
the duties of the office of a Federal judge." The battle won the *Globe* its
first-ever Pulitzer Prize. It gave Ted a lesson in the limits of Senate colle-

giality, when he was abandoned by his friend and Bobby's, Senator Joe Tydings of Maryland. As for Bobby, the Morrissey affair made clear that while he still wouldn't buck his father on something that mattered that much to him, he had the good judgment to let Ted spearhead this drive. Bobby offered support only when pressed, and he told his younger brother when to yield in a fight they couldn't win. He also managed to get in a last lick, not forewarning anyone of their surrender plans. Ted delivered a long speech in the Senate defending Morrissey, then, in the last paragraph and with Bobby's prodding, he stunned listeners by raising the white flag. Bobby didn't want Tydings and the other Morrissey foes "to have the satisfaction of knowing they had won, without at least being surprised," said Milton Gwirtzman, Ted's aide. The older senator brother then offered this postmortem on the debacle: "I think we've more than fulfilled our commitment to Frank Morrissey."

If his support for Morrissey placed Bobby back in the role of old-school politician, the next spring he saw an opportunity to seize the grail of reform in New York City. The 1966 race that caught his eye was a primary for the obscurest of offices, Surrogate's Court, charged with the routine processing of wills and using that authority to hand favored lawyers bloated fees. As if such patronage weren't egregious enough, Democratic and Republican bosses had quietly agreed that instead of squandering money contesting the election, both parties would endorse the Democrat Arthur Klein in return for the Democrats' endorsing a Republican for the state trial court. Bobby cried foul and found a candidate of his own, Samuel Silverman, a pasty-faced justice of the state supreme court whom the senator had never met and who ran only because Bobby insisted. It was, as Kennedy in-law and Silverman campaign coordinator Steve Smith said, "two unknowns running against each other for a job nobody understood." But all that mattered was that Bobby was pulling out all the stops for Silverman and the reform cause. He raised a million dollars, set up a phone bank, and even called in the Kennedy sisters, which is something Jack wouldn't have done for any candidate not named Kennedy. For the last ten days of the campaign, the Empire State senator with the Boston accent and newfound ease was at Silverman's side every afternoon. "How many here have heard of Surrogate's Court?" Bobby asked his school-aged audience as he and Silverman stood atop a station wagon on a hot night at a Lenox Hill housing project. A few hands rise. "How many of you study hard and obey your parents?" More hands. "How many of you are going to go home tonight and tell your mothers and fathers to vote for Judge Silverman for Surrogate?" All arms shoot up as Bobby says, "Silverman, Silverman, remember that name. Now let's go over it again. What are you going to tell your fathers and mothers?" Kids: "Vote." Bobby: "Vote for whom?" Children: "Kennedy."

Win or lose, Bobby knew that just making this fight would generate goodwill with New York liberals. Their image of him as Peck's Bad Boy had been reinforced the previous fall when he backed the Democratic machine's candidate, Abe Beame, in his losing race for mayor against the Republican reformer John Lindsay. His support for Silverman put him on the side of widows and orphans against greedy lawyers and, rarer for a Kennedy, allied him with *The New York Times*. The *Times* and other papers had cast the race simply as Kennedy versus the Tammany political organization—and they noted the irony that the candidate of the bosses was now taking on those bosses. The race also gave him a chance, as he said, to "stick it to John Lindsay," who was trying to stay on the sidelines. When Silverman won—by an overwhelming 56 to 38 percent—the *Times* crowned Bobby a "hero of the Reformers" and said his "prestige as the most influential Democrat in this state has now been considerably enhanced." As ever, however, the paper insisted on the last word: "This does not mean that he has become a Reformer himself. Senator Kennedy is a very practical politician who in the past has dealt with some pretty distasteful holders of power and will doubtless continue to do so."

Bobby did, in fact, continue to work with political power brokers the way the Kennedys always had. But the newspaper failed to see that he'd always been a reformer, although never a "squishy" one, and that he would continue to push for changes that he felt would help the state as well as himself. That was what he'd done in 1965, when he tried to get more reform-minded legislators into leadership positions in Albany; he failed when Republican governor Nelson Rockefeller teamed up with entrenched Democrats. Both Rockefeller and Kennedy were sons of corporate titans, both had their eyes on the White House, and, while they waited, both wanted to call the shots in New York. In Bobby's first speech in the Senate, he pushed to make thirteen New York counties eligible for an aid program benefiting poverty-stricken Appalachia, a move the governor said would damage those counties' reputation at a time when he was trying to attract new businesses. The limits of Bobby's clout in state politics were apparent in the summer of 1966 when he couldn't find a strong challenger to Rockefeller and gave lukewarm support to the Democratic nominee, Frank O'Connor. He also couldn't persuade Franklin Roosevelt, Jr., not to run on the Liberal ticket, where he pulled enough votes to ensure Rockefeller's victory.

Even more nettlesome to Bobby was the mayor of New York, another glamorous and ambitious rival. Bobby thought Lindsay was an intellectual lightweight and a threat to challenge him for the Senate seat in 1970 or the White House in some future year. Lindsay, who was smart enough and shared Bobby's visions for Bedford-Stuyvesant and other urban projects, thought Bobby was a publicity hound. Some of their antagonism went back to their days together in Washington, when Congressman Lindsay had challenged the Kennedy administration on everything from its record on civil rights (not enough) to the attorney general's role in foreign affairs (too much). Now each was too stubborn to cut the other any slack. "One thing that Lindsay was trying to do was trying to look like he was a Kennedy," said John Burns, chair of the New York State Democratic Party and a Bobby crony. "The newspapers kept saying, 'There's another John Kennedy type.' . . . I don't think that Senator Kennedy appreciated that very much."

Bobby also continued to defy political handicappers on where he'd land on any issue. The liberal Americans for Democratic Action gave him a perfect score on his voting record his second year in office, one of just four senators to rate that high. Less noticed was that he also notched a 33 percent rating from the conservative Americans for Constitutional Action. That wasn't just a matter of his protecting his flank, but of seeking solutions that defied an easy liberal-conservative delineation, the way he always had. Bobby believed in a social safety net—but he envisioned it as a trampoline, helping recipients bounce back to jobs that made them self-reliant rather than fostering dependency. He broke with his church by endorsing birth control and voting to fund family planning in countries that wanted it. The Defense Department wanted to prevent the American Communist Party boss Robert Thompson from being buried in Arlington National Cemetery despite his Distinguished Service Cross from World War II. Bobby thought that was ludicrous. "I don't think anyone now buried in Arlington would object to having Thompson buried there," he explained, "so I don't see why all these living people are objecting."

In later years, the conservative Jack Kemp and the liberal Barack Obama would both embrace Bobby's ideas on fighting poverty. The columnist Murray Kempton called him "the first significant post–New Deal American politician," adding that "[Franklin] Roosevelt was historic because he betrayed his class, the old rich; Robert Kennedy could be historic for betraying his class, the new rich." Asked by another journalist whether he was a liberal or conservative, Bobby balked: "I don't go for analyzing myself."

———

JOURNALISTS DIDN'T SHARE his reluctance. Only the president got anywhere near the coverage that Bobby did in the mid-1960s, with profiles, commentaries, and even armchair psychoanalysis showing up everywhere from the daily newspapers and newsweeklies to *Look*, *Life*, and *Good Housekeeping*. The issue scrutinized most, by diplomatic and political reporters as well as feature writers, here and overseas, was the senator's stance on Vietnam. The questions were straightforward even if his answers were everything but. How and why, the scribes and their readers wanted to know, had the brother of the president who got us into Vietnam morphed into the war's most emphatic critic? Was his turnaround a matter of conscience or expediency? When would he stop pretending to back LBJ?

Bobby's evolution on Vietnam took place in three stages. His hawkish phase started with his first trip there in 1951 with Jack and lasted until a year and a half after his brother's death. He believed the United States could win and had to try, not just to save the Vietnamese from the scourge of Communism, but to show the Soviets we would make the same stand against their expansionism in Indochina that we had in Berlin and Cuba. He wrote that in his book *Just Friends and Brave Enemies*. He drilled it into his colleagues on the Kennedy administration task forces on counterinsurgency. He also said it as clearly as he knew how in speeches such as the one he gave at the North Carolina Cold War Seminar in the spring of 1963. The struggle, he told his Asheville audience, would be "long and hard," but "I believe the tide has turned. I believe it is within our ability to keep world Communism on the defensive, and we intend to do just that." The war wasn't an issue during his 1964 Senate campaign, but the few times he was asked about it, he expressed confidence that the South Vietnamese would rally and win. A month after he took office he reiterated, in a speech in Ithaca, that "the United States has made a commitment to help Vietnam. . . . If our word means anything, we must remain as long as it is evident that the people favor it."

His resolve grew out of bedrock beliefs. He'd been an unwavering anticommunist even before he went to work for Joe McCarthy or traveled across the Soviet Union with Justice Douglas. The provocateur in him remained convinced that the counterinsurgency's black pajamas and green berets were the way to battle back against leftist insurrectionists. He was determined to keep faith with his dead brother, who had steadily increased the number of military advisers in Vietnam from 685 when he came into office to 16,732 at the time of his assassination. But even during this hawkish period, Bobby wasn't blind, as many of his New Frontier colleagues were. He recognized the importance of winning not just battles but the minds and hearts of the people we were fighting to save, saying, "Ultimately, Communism must be defeated by progressive political programs which wipe out the poverty, misery, and discontent on which it thrives." He had seen firsthand the embarrassing failure of the French despite their overwhelming military superiority. Better than anyone else, he knew how an overconfident CIA had led JFK to a humiliating drubbing at the Bay of Pigs, and how out of touch the State Department was with the third world. He was born a skeptic and had learned to ask hard questions as a congressional investigator and the nation's top prosecutor. So even as he was underlining in North Carolina that the war was winnable, he insisted that America would triumph only if it was "ready to meet war by guerrillas, subversives, insurgents, assassins, war by ambush instead of combat." And in Ithaca, he added the caveat that he was "not in favor of staying a minute more than is necessary."

His certainty that the United States could prevail and should try started to give way in the spring of 1965, as Bobby entered the in-between phase of his Vietnam progression. In April he urged LBJ to temporarily suspend his bombing of North Vietnam, but the president pushed ahead with troop increases and heavier bombardments. The next month, Bobby supported Johnson's request for another $700 million in military spending on Vietnam, but he took to the Senate floor to argue for "honorable negotiation"—a middle course, he said, between the unacceptable options of abandoning or escalating the war. By July he signaled another leap in a speech to the International Police Academy in Washington, writing that "if all a government can promise its people in response to insurgent activity is ten years of napalm and heavy artillery, it would not be a government for long." The written text of that talk made its way to the press, but when Bobby saw the reaction, and realized that making a break then would be especially embarrassing to an old administration friend who was on the same podium,* he took a softer approach in his delivered remarks. Then, without hesitating, he misled the media about the changes. "I'm going to lie," Bobby confessed beforehand to Sherwin Markman, the young LBJ aide assigned to get the senator to tone down his criticism. "I'm going to say it's not the speech that my staff handed out—it's the speech I give—that counts, and nobody influenced me, that sort of thing."

He generally managed to stay on his tightrope in prepared remarks but not in press conferences, where candor often trumped caution, as it did at the University of Southern California that November. "What," a journalist asked, "about giving blood to the North Vietnamese?" Bobby: "I think that's a good idea." Reporter: "Is that going too far?" Bobby: "If we've given all the blood that is needed to the South Vietnamese, I'm in favor of giving [to] anybody who needs blood." The press couldn't believe its good luck, nor could Barry Goldwater, who branded the remarks as "closer to treason than to academic freedom." Rather than backing off, in February 1966 Bobby called in his top advisers and Jack's to discuss just what America might be willing to give up to get a negotiated peace.

---

* That friend was David E. Bell, a Harvard professor of economics who served as administrator of the Agency for International Development from 1963 to 1966. Like many administration officials, Bell was caught between his friendship with the Kennedys and his allegiance to his new boss, President Johnson.

His new middle-way option—outlined in a seven-page statement that he read to the media just before leaving for a family ski trip to Vermont—was to offer the Communist insurgents in South Vietnam a carrot along with the continuing stick of our troops and guns. Just as withdrawing from Vietnam was "impossible for this country" to contemplate, he argued, the only way to lure the Vietcong to the peace table was "to admit them to a share of power and responsibility."

The White House saw that as a step too far, and as the opening for which it had been waiting. The administration's friends in the press pounced first, with the *Chicago Tribune* titling its editorial HO CHI KENNEDY and calling Bobby "the senior senator from communist North Viet Nam—Ho Chi Minh's Trojan horse in the United States." Vice President Humphrey reached for every metaphor he could find to lambaste the man for whom he had recently campaigned. Bobby's proposal, Humphrey said, would be like putting "a fox in a chicken coop; soon there wouldn't be any chickens left." It amounted to putting "an arsonist in a fire department." In case those didn't sink in, the vice president couldn't resist this warning: that the Kennedy prescription for the ills of South Vietnam "includes a dose of arsenic." Bobby was bruised enough by the backlash that, although his mind didn't waver, he kept his mouth shut on Vietnam through the rest of 1966.

This neither-hawk-nor-dove period frustrated not just the press that was trying to decipher his messages, and a White House that never doubted his ill will, but the senator himself. While Bobby was better than a meteorologist at reading the political currents and forecasting storms ahead, all that data was immobilizing. He recognized the twin trap that history had set for him as he waded into the quagmire of warfare: being the guy who committed our troops to a deadly and unwinnable mission, like the French he had met in Vietnam in 1951, or being blamed for losing Southeast Asia, the way Harry Truman had been condemned for losing China in 1949. Any overt break with the White House would be read as a launching pad for a presidential bid, not to mention a rejection of his brother and the Kennedy brain trusters still working in the White House. "I'm afraid," he told an antiwar journalist, "that by speaking out I just make Lyndon do the opposite, out of spite. He hates me so much that if I asked for snow, he would make rain, just because it was me."

But how could he not stand up against a war he felt was increasingly futile, with an ally who was corrupt as well as inept? The moral issues were eating at him even more than the political ones. He asked himself what Joe and Jack would have done. His father had always been an isolationist, if not a dove, but his brother had been more inscrutable. The late president's loyalists said he had planned to pull out of Vietnam, but not until after the 1964 election, when it would be less controversial. LBJ believed otherwise, and insisted he was staying true to JFK by standing up to North Vietnam and the Soviet Union.

Bobby wasn't the only one on the fence. It was a wrenching time for the nation, with U.S. troop strength rising by 150,000 over the course of 1966, to 350,000. America's casualty count for the year climbed to 9,378 dead and 62,024 wounded, which set a terrible new record and was higher than the South Vietnamese losses for the first time. Students were burning draft cards and staging rallies even as more of Bobby's fellow senators were speaking out against the bombing and wider war, including Mike Mansfield, LBJ's successor as Senate majority leader. Yet the vast majority of Congress, the country, and even college students still backed their president on Vietnam, at least for the time being. Bobby wanted to do the right thing and be a leader, but he didn't want to be marginalized or sacrifice his political future. "If I became convinced that by making another speech that I could do some good," he said in mid-December, "I would make it tomorrow."

Vacillation like this was how Bobby changed. It had taken him longer than most to recognize the perils of McCarthyism, and he never fully severed his ties with McCarthy himself. He had learned slowly at the start of the civil rights struggle, having had to suffer through riots in Montgomery and at Ole Miss before grasping what Martin Luther King, Jr., and James Baldwin had been telling him. He followed a similar pattern during the Cuban missile crisis, although that metamorphosis from militant to moderate was accomplished in just thirteen days. His evolution on Vietnam took only slightly less time than America's, which is what helped make it convincing. Bobby was neither a quirky individualist like Senator Wayne Morse of Oregon nor a longtime liberal like Senator George McGovern, both of whom LBJ could easily dismiss as out of touch. He was an old cold warrior whose anticommunist credentials matched up against anyone's. And he was a Kennedy.

An especially nasty meeting with the president in February 1967 finally pushed him over the edge. Bobby was just back from Paris, where a French diplomat had told him that the North Vietnamese were ready to talk peace in return for an unconditional halt in the bombing. When word filtered to the press about a "peace feeler," LBJ was outraged, telling his pals that it was a ruse and that Bobby was the self-serving leaker. Bobby tried to explain that it came "from someone in your State Department." Leaks were habitual in Washington, especially involving Vietnam, and this one might not have registered if the president and the senator hadn't been so ready to explode at each other. "It's not *my* State Department, God damn it. It's *your* State Department," said LBJ, who was paranoid about JFK holdovers throughout his government and incongruously saw Bobby, but not himself, as part of the old Kennedy administration. As for the war, the president insisted it would be over by summer and told Bobby, "I'll destroy you and every one of your dove friends in six months. You'll be dead politically in six months." Bobby tried yet again, as he recounted for his press secretary Frank Mankiewicz, pushing LBJ to end the bombing and begin negotiations. "There just isn't a chance in hell that I will do that," the president said, "not the slightest chance in the world." Bobby shot back: "Look, I don't have to take that from you."

But he knew he did, unless he spoke out. On March 2, 1967, Bobby made his moves. First he apologized to the packed Senate gallery and chamber: "Three presidents have taken action in Vietnam. As one who was involved in many of those decisions, I can testify that if fault is to be found or responsibility assessed, there is enough to go round for all—including myself." That was more candor than he had shown with regard to his mistakes with Joe McCarthy or Fidel Castro. Then he bore the kind of witness that scarcely any politician did to the horrors of the faraway war in Southeast Asia, showing concern for not just American soldiers but Vietnamese civilians. "To the Vietnamese," the Catholic senator said, "it must often seem the fulfillment of the prophecy of Saint John the Divine: 'And I looked, and beheld a pale horse; and his name that sat on him was Death.'" Last, he spelled out what had to be done to end the nightmare: halt the bombing, reform South Vietnam's political and social systems, negotiate with the enemy, then phase out U.S. and North Vietnamese troops and replace them with international monitors to police the cease-fire and supervise elections in the South. LBJ tried to trump his critic by delivering two hastily arranged speeches and staging a news conference at which he confirmed the gossip that his daughter was pregnant. The press might have been amused, but it had waited too long to be distracted. Fascinating as Luci's parturiency was, the lead stories were Bobby's.

Finally unleashed, Bobby would do for Vietnam what he had done for civil rights and antipoverty programs: give opponents of the war the political credibility they had lacked, because no one could grab the public's attention the way he did. Nobody, with the exception of Rev. King, was stitching together all of it—race and poverty, the twin plagues of colonization by the Communists and by us—with the tone of outrage and hope that Bobby was voicing. Few consulted as wide a range of opinion on Vietnam as did the Democratic senator from New York, from his old friend Robert McNamara to a new one, the antiwar radical Tom Hayden, whom he'd met recently at the suggestion of the antiwar journalist Jack Newfield.* The ideological breadth of Bobby's friendships was reminiscent of his father's, which ranged from Senator McCarthy to Justice Douglas, but not even Joe Kennedy had been so far outside the mainstream of his party and country. Today's youth "are the children not of the Cold War, but of the Thaw," Bobby wrote in his 1967 book, *To Seek a Newer World.*† "However the war may seem to us, they see it as one in which the largest and most powerful nation on earth is killing children (they do not care if accidentally) in a remote and insignificant land. We speak of past commitments, of the burden of past mistakes; and they ask

---

* "That was an attempt on [Bobby's] part to build relationships," says Hayden. Hayden's purpose was even more straightforward: "Whether Kennedy would get us out of Vietnam . . . I thought it was a good conversation" (Author interview with Hayden).

† The titles of Bobby's books always had a special resonance. This one was borrowed from Alfred, Lord Tennyson, who in his poem *Ulysses* wrote, "'Tis not too late to seek a newer world." *Just Friends and Brave Enemies* echoed the words Thomas Jefferson wrote to Andrew Jackson in 1806: "We must meet our duty and convince the world that we are just friends and brave enemies."

why they should now atone for mistakes made before many of them were born."

Daniel Ellsberg had top secret evidence of those mistakes, some in the past and others America was about to make in a bid to rescue a war effort on the verge of collapse. The military analyst at the Rand Corporation think tank had never shown president's-eyes-only documents like these to anyone without clearance, but now he felt that that was the only way to keep the Pentagon from getting the 206,000 extra soldiers it wanted to ship to Vietnam. The only question was whom to leak them to, which turned out to be the easy part. Bobby was "the one person who had the passion and commitment to do something," says Ellsberg, who would later be persecuted, prosecuted, and eventually have the charges against him dismissed for releasing a much more comprehensive secret history of Vietnam titled *The Pentagon Papers.* "I thought of Bobby Kennedy as being in a category of his own." Ellsberg wasn't the only one who had reached that conclusion. McNamara was talking to Bobby, once a week at least, and, says Peter Edelman, the defense secretary was giving the senator "figures, classified material, or at least, you know, unreleased material." Few noticed the irony that this man who once was the keeper of the nation's deepest secrets was now helping to expose them.

The senator from New York's involvement with the Republic of South Africa was different. Unlike Vietnam, it didn't matter to the White House or to most Americans. And in South Africa, it wasn't Bobby but millions of oppressed blacks and thousands of their white allies who were desperate to speak out but had gagged themselves for fear of the consequences. Traveling there in 1966, Bobby gave them a voice in a way that nobody else had. The trip also freed him from the politics that clouded everything he did in America and brought him back to first principles.

The multiracial union representing college students had invited him to give the keynote address at its annual Day of Reaffirmation of Academic and Human Freedom, but no one expected the South African government to let him in. It was an especially tense moment for the country, with apartheid segregating the races everywhere except in a few church and student groups. The activist Nelson Mandela had been jailed for life; television was prohibited, along with books by Ernest Hemingway and Mary Shelley; and the political opposition had been crushed or driven underground. A year before, when the students had invited Martin Luther King, Jr., to speak, the government refused him a visa. Saying no to a man who could someday be the American president was more problematic. So, after a month of hemming and hawing, South Africa said Bobby could come, but it also slapped a banning order on Ian Robertson, the student union president who had planned to host the senator.* Even the White House took notice of the trip, with LBJ delivering his first and last address on Africa the week before Bobby left.

Bobby made clear his attitude about his hosts on the flight over, when he was asked to register as black, white, or other: "I didn't fill out the card." The government had refused to let in the thirty American newsmen who'd planned to accompany the senator, thinking it could control the coverage and choreography of a visit it viewed as a publicity stunt. Just how little the efficiently authoritarian regime understood its own people became clear at Johannesburg's Jan Smuts Airport when the plane carrying Bobby, Ethel, and two aides touched down just before midnight on June 4. Four thousand students hoisted him onto their shoulders and marched him into the terminal. "The airport was swarming with white, black, brown, Indian, every hue of skin," remembered Margaret Marshall, vice president of the student union who stepped in as host after Robertson was banned.† "I don't think I had ever seen anything like that in my life. And so, that very first night we began to get an inkling of what this visit was going to entail."

The first speech, at the all-white but liberal University of Cape Town, remains one of Bobby's most memorable, beginning with one of his favorite devices of leading listeners in one direction and then taking them somewhere else entirely. "I came here," he said, "because of my deep interest [in] and affection for a land settled by the Dutch in the mid-seventeenth century, then taken over by the British, and at last

* In their bid to maintain the racial status quo, the South African government banned publications and organizations along with individuals, placing them under severe restrictions intended to shut them up. Robertson was in eminent company, with Steve Biko, Winnie Mandela, and the entire African National Congress. Robertson's banning, like the others, was for five years, although he left the country three months after Bobby's visit and didn't return for twenty-two years.

† Marshall, Robertson, and most of the other officers and members of the student union were white, as were most South African college students then.

independent; a land in which the native inhabitants were at first sub-
dued, but relations with whom remain a problem to this day; a land
which defined itself on a hostile frontier . . . a land which once imported
slaves, and now must struggle to wipe out the last traces of that former
bondage. I refer, of course, to the United States of America." His audience understood instinctively their speaker's point: that he had not come
as a pious missionary but as someone struggling with his own country's
racial shame.

But it was his odic lines halfway through the talk that proved defining
for the sixteen hundred students in the lecture hall, the eighteen thousand huddled in the cold and wind listening via loudspeakers, and the
millions who read transcripts or heard recordings of what would be
called the Ripple of Hope Speech. "Few will have the greatness to bend
history itself, but each of us can work to change a small portion of
events, and in the total of all those acts will be written the history of this
generation," Bobby said. "Each time a man stands up for an ideal, or acts
to improve the lot of others, or strikes out against injustice, he sends
forth a tiny ripple of hope, and crossing each other from a million different centers of energy and daring, those ripples build a current which
can sweep down the mightiest walls of oppression and resistance. . . .
Only those who dare to fail greatly, can ever achieve greatly. It is this new
idealism which is also, I believe, the common heritage of a generation
which has learned that while efficiency can lead to the camps at Auschwitz, or the streets of Budapest, only the ideals of humanity and love can
climb the hills of the Acropolis."

Those lines—"the most stirring and memorable address ever to come
from a foreigner in South Africa," according to the *London Daily
Telegraph*—had been carefully scripted by Bobby's wordsmiths Adam
Walinsky and Richard Goodwin, but only after the anti-apartheid activist Allard Lowenstein "blew the whole thing up with impassioned de-
nunciations of the speech and everything in it," recalled Walinsky.
Lowenstein, Walinsky added, complained that the early version of the
talk "wasn't 'attentive to the struggles of the people' there and how ma-
ligned and dreadful the government was. [Lowenstein's critique] was a
really good corrective. It certainly acted as a jolt for us." It also was how
Bobby did things, drawing on outside voices to shake up even his most

valued aides and saving for himself any last edits. That speech, like his other four in South Africa, anticipated his critics and disarmed them with humor and rhetoric toned to the right pitch, neither too fiery nor too minced. Wording was revised on the run by Walinsky, or by the senator as he sensed an audience's mood.

The day after his Ripple of Hope talk, Bobby addressed Stellenbosch University, the Harvard of Afrikaanerdom, making clear that he was there "less to lecture than to learn." But that was only half true. He admonished his listeners that "as the skilled and professional people of South Africa and the world, you will be largely removed from contact with the hungry and the deprived, those without ease in the present or hope in the future. It will require a constant effort of will to keep contact, to remind ourselves everyday that we who diet have a never ceasing obligation to those who starve." There and elsewhere, students fired back with challenges. Had Bobby's failure to crack down on Communism contributed to his brother's death? The audience gasped and the senator grew quiet. What about the Bible's admonition that Negroes were created to serve? Bobby: "But suppose God is black. What if we go to Heaven and we, all our lives, have treated the Negro as an inferior, and God is there, and we look up and He is not white? What then is our response?" His audience's response was unexpected applause.

Between speeches, Bobby did what he had done in all of his foreign travels, going wherever it took to uncover what people were thinking and how they lived. In Cape Town he visited the student leader who'd invited him in the first place, bringing a copy of *Profiles in Courage* inscribed by Jackie. "He asked what it was like being a banned person and I told him that. He asked about South Africa and I told him," recalls Robertson. "As soon as he walked in he asked, 'Is this place bugged?' I said, 'I assume so.' He said, 'Do you know how to handle a bugging mechanism? You can either play music very loud or jump up and down like this.' It was a wooden floor and that made a big banging noise. That kind of set me at ease right away."

Just after dawn on his last day in the country, the senator called on another banned leader, Albert Luthuli, on the farm north of Durban where he was living in exile. The Zulu tribal chieftain was president of the anti-apartheid African National Congress, the first African to win the Nobel Peace Prize, and as popular as Mandela would be later. Bobby's seventy-minute visit sent powerful signals—to the government that he was defying its bid to make Luthuli invisible, and to black South Africans that the leader they hadn't heard from in five years was okay and still mattered to the world. Bobby brought gifts along on the helicopter that took him to Luthuli—a letter from Martin Luther King, Jr., and a record player on which he and the chief listened to President Kennedy's 1963 civil rights speech. "When [Luthuli] talked of the future of his country, of his people, of the relationship between the races, [he became] intense and hurt and hard, all at once," Bobby wrote about the man he would add to his list of heroes. Luthuli asked his American guest, "What are they doing to my country, to my countrymen? Can't they see that men of all races can work together—and that the alternative is a terrible disaster for all of us?"*

Bobby and Ethel's last big excursion was to the sprawling township of Soweto, where half a million blacks were crowded into matchbox houses behind wire fences. Never before had a prominent politician from abroad included them on his itinerary. Few whites had ever mingled so easily, addressing residents from the rooftop of his car. The Bantus here knew that shaking hands with a white man could spell trouble, but they also knew about Bobby's visit that morning with the venerated Luthuli and few refused when the senator extended his hand. As he approached, the crowd surged forward as one, shouting, "Master, Master." It was their way of warmly greeting an important personage, but to Bobby it was embarrassing. "Please," he implored, "don't use that word."

Press reviews of his trip agreed that it was momentous, but whether that was for better or worse depended on where the newspapers stood along the racial divide. "Is it too difficult for [Americans] to grasp that if their non-White population had consisted of more than half a dozen different nations which together were four times more numerous than the White Americans, the enthusiasm for integration there would have been as limited and politically powerless as here?" *Die Burger* asked in Afri-

---

* Luthuli died a year after Bobby's visit. The government said he had been struck by a train, a story widely disbelieved since he walked in that same area every day and knew the schedule of the trains.

kaans. The English-language *Rand Daily Mail* countered that "Kennedy's visit is the best thing that has happened to South Africa for years. It is as if a window has been flung open and a gust of fresh air has swept into a room in which the atmosphere had become stale and foetid." The only common ground was captured by the one American reporter who had defied the government's ban on foreign press. "Neither Kennedy nor any other politician like him will ever be welcome again in their apartheid state," George Laing wrote for the *New York Daily News.* "Once is more than enough."

That single visit, lasting barely six days, was the most important ever made to South Africa by an American and a watershed in the lives of many whom Kennedy encountered. "If you're in an environment where somebody is telling you over and over and over again that you are the tool of Communists, that you're out of line, that it's not the way the world operates, and somebody who is as respected as he is comes and says, 'No, no, no, no, no, no, there's a whole world out there that thinks the way you do. In fact the whole of history thinks the way that you do.' . . . That has a really powerful impact," explains Margaret Marshall, who emigrated to America, married Bobby's friend Anthony Lewis of *The New York Times,* and became chief justice of the Massachusetts Supreme Judicial Court.* As for black South Africans, they have a custom of naming their eldest son after a famous person they admire. Kennedy Malibusha, Robert Kennedy Makalima, and Kennedy Gowgela Kilokibi Nakala are among the hundreds who honor Bobby's memory.

The visit had an equally powerful impact on Bobby. Exhausting foreign trips like that reenergized him for the battles back home, whether it was rebuilding Bed-Stuy or electing a new judge to the Surrogate's Court. South Africa reminded him how insidious racism could be and, while he never said so, what he did there was partly to make amends for his belated response to racial injustice in America. His Senate years turned out to be as peripatetic as those he had spent as attorney general and Senate investigator. There were trips to Latin America and Europe, visiting with peasants and another pope. Joe had made his children citi-

---

* Thirty-seven years later, Marshall would strike her own blow against bias by authoring the first state ruling in the nation affirming the constitutional right to same-sex marriage.

zens of the world and given them the means to see it. Everywhere Bobby went, and especially in South Africa, he said he was reminded of his power, and America's, to be a beacon not just for capitalism and democracy but for the elusive ideal of justice.

———————

EVEN WITH ALL the travel overseas and trips to New York, Bobby's years as a senator gave him his most relaxed time with the children and the life he relished at Hickory Hill. He had more control over his hours than he had during the JFK administration, when foreign crises pulled him to the White House or CIA at any hour and he spent late nights plotting deployments of U.S. marshals to racial hot spots. Senators, especially ones on the outs like Bobby, were seldom consulted by the president or his aides on anything.

Ethel had given birth to eight children by the time Bobby was sworn in on January 3, 1965, with Max arriving eight days later and Douglas two years after that. The only way around the bedlam was to develop routines. Bobby tried to be in bed by 10:30 and to get up when the sun did for a horseback ride and sit-ups. While shaving he'd listen to a long-playing record of a play by Shakespeare or act out his own drama with the kids. The youngest loved smearing lather all over him and themselves, mimicking him with a bladeless razor as he attacked his beard. The ritual at the other end of the workday was for his brood to swarm him the instant he drove up. He'd toss a football or play tickle-tumble, a game in which everyone rolled on the grass squealing and pretending to resist. They frolicked together as friends rather than as father and children, which was the right fit for this man-sized child. Remembering what it felt like to be in the second tier, he made certain never to leave out his youngest (Kerry and Chris, and later Max and Doug) or his frailest (David). He also found time for a walk across the grounds with Ethel most nights after dinner. "It was," she recalls, "a nice habit to be into."

Having so many people share the same tent made Hickory Hill seem like the Big Top, with multiple acts going on at the same time. Youngsters played charades in one room while aides typed Bobby's latest manuscript. You could hear the Kennedy convertible approaching before you saw it as towheaded passengers belted out the fight songs of Army and

Navy along with Harvard and Notre Dame. In the kitchen, their long-time cook Ruby Reynolds might be preparing Bobby's favorite dessert, a chocolate roll layered with sponge cake, ice cream, and gooey chocolate sauce. Twelve people would be asked to lunch and twenty would turn up; thankfully the four refrigerators were well stocked. "The kids were a pain in the ass," grumbled Art Buchwald, the humor columnist. "They were fighting all the time and throwing peanut butter at each other. The lunches were pretty bad, as far as everyone dunking each other in mayonnaise and things like that. But that also was part of it, and water fights the whole time. You just have to get in the spirit of it or you become a blithering idiot too."

No circus was complete without animals, and Bobby's menagerie was growing as fast as his progeny. The most notorious was Brumus, the malodorous Newfoundland who peed once on Senator Harry Byrd's spaniel and twice on two ladies picnicking at Hickory Hill, and who got his name and mug shot on the lyric sheet of the Jefferson Airplane's *Crown of Creation* album. Others who would call Hickory Hill home were the Irish spaniel Freckles, who loved campaigning with Bobby, the English sheepdog Panda, who spent every summer spread-eagled on the floor panting, a St. Bernard and an Irish setter aptly named Bear and Rusty, and two hunting Labradors called Battle Star and Firecracker. Sandy, a California sea lion, lived in the swimming pool. A red-tailed hawk named Morgan Le Fay, after the sorceress in the Arthurian legend, took up residence in Bobby Jr.'s room, near the posters of Lenin, Stalin, and Cardinal Spellman. Also coming and going were homing pigeons, iguanas, raccoons, possums, cockatoos, squirrels, mice, rats, ducks, rabbits, parakeets, hamsters, geese, chickens, roosters, guinea pigs, lizards, a 4-H calf, and a leopard tortoise brought from Kenya in a suitcase that was unusable afterward. Snakes were okay, too, for the children and parents if not the staff. Every child had his or her own horse, and for serious riders like Kathleen there was a paddock with jumping hurdles.

Bobby sometimes used his pets to make a point, as he did with his favorite, the antisocial but entirely devoted Brumus. "He knew everyone hated the dog, and it was like a haircut," opined Buchwald. "He also had a perverse thing about a haircut. And he once said to someone, 'If somebody would stop telling me to get a haircut, I'd get one.' I think it was the same about Brumus. If somebody would stop telling him that Brumus was a mean dog, he might get rid of him."

The animals were Ethel's to oversee, along with the children and a staff consisting of a laundress, governess, wet nurse, yard man, and a pair each of maids, cooks, and secretaries. There was also a groom for the animals, whom Ethel once enlisted to rescue a starving horse from a neighbor's yard. A jury acquitted her of horse theft, and Bobby, who was then attorney general, joked, "You're not going to be let out again without your keeper." She didn't get off so easily when she was showing two journalists Bobby Jr.'s latest acquisition, a raccoonlike coatimundi. He pounced, digging his sharp claws and doglike teeth into the heavily pregnant Ethel, who shrieked, "Get him off me! He's biting me! Oh, God, he's biting me!" One newspaperman lifted her atop a cabinet while the other kicked the Latin American mammal across the room. After a doctor bandaged her leg, she saw Bobby off as he headed to the Senate to deliver his speech breaking with LBJ on Vietnam. "If these are all the scars the Kennedys end up with by five o'clock," she said playfully, "it'll be all right."

As with Rose, Ethel's affluence ensured that all she had to budget was her time. She ad-libbed where her mother-in-law had been methodical, but she exercised enough control over the chaos that Bobby never had to focus on it, especially when he was distracted by grief or work. She lived by the dicta she and Bobby preached to the kids—Kennedys don't whine, they don't give up, and they don't abide tattletales—which helped her tune out the gossip and manage their marriage through stressful stretches. The children knew they had to arrive at meals on time, hair combed, fingernails clean, teeth brushed, vitamins taken. During summers at Hyannis Port, the older ones were required to join her at 8:00 A.M. mass; when they overslept, they stayed late for private prayers. Calling herself Old Moms, she greeted Bobby at breakfast with a royal "Hail, Caesar," which sounded even more ironic when he was wrapped in his monogrammed blue robe and she in her habitual purple maternity dress.

There was no levity the April evening in 1967 when he returned to his Hickory Hill estate from his visit to starving children in the Mississippi Delta. "We had sat down to dinner in the dining room, with the crystal chandelier hanging from the ceiling, the table set with a linen tablecloth and china," remembered his daughter Kathleen. "He talked to us about the Delta. 'Families there live in a shack the size of this dining room,' he said. . . . 'Do you know how lucky you are, do you know how lucky you are?' " He was asking the question as much of himself as of his offspring, the oldest of whom was fifteen. His answer was the one he gave them that warm spring evening: "Do something for our country. Give something back.' " And it wasn't just his children he begged to give a damn, but wealthy friends he persuaded to ship soup and other foodstuffs to the poor people he'd met in Mississippi.

This senator worried about the world even when he was sleeping, but one way he temporarily forgot was by getting adults to act like kids when they visited Hickory Hill. He loved games, and he insisted all his guests learn to play Prisoner's Base, Murder, and Kick the Can. His and Ethel's favorite was Sardines, a variation of Hide-and-Seek in which just one person is concealed, the others jam like sardines into that hideaway when they find it, and the loser is the last person looking. The twists at Hickory Hill were that the hiders included luminaries such as the secretary of defense and a future Supreme Court justice, and it often ended with fifteen men tumbling out of a closet with Ethel. For Averell Harriman's seventy-fifth birthday, the Kennedys gave a surprise costume party. Bobby dressed in the kind of overcoat and fedora Harriman wore when he was ambassador to Moscow, and on the terrace were life-sized statues of Winston Churchill, Franklin Roosevelt, and Josef Stalin, borrowed from a wax museum. Liz Stevens, a guest who was due to deliver in days, wore a sign saying MAKE LOVE, NOT WAR. Bobby sent her a photo of herself afterward with the inscription, "I will if you will." Liz's husband, George Jr., founder of the American Film Institute, says that Bobby "had that kind of sweet humor." It was midlife nurture more than Kennedy nature that nourished that sweetness. "My father really had the weight of the world on him," said Kerry Kennedy, "and Mummy was funny and fun and full of laughter."

Neither his time in the self-important Senate nor his expanding family responsibilities tempered Bobby's daring. The Canadian government had named in honor of President Kennedy its highest unscaled peak, where the Yukon Territory meets the Alaska panhandle, and Bobby and Ted were determined to be the first to reach its top. With Ted's back still

healing, Bobby barreled ahead in March 1965 with expert mountaineers. No matter that he hated heights, that he had no experience with
rope or snowshoes, or that his only preparation, as he said, was "running up and down stairs and practicing hollering *Help!*" Over the course
of two days he climbed out of crevasses chest-deep in snow, trudged up
a sixty-five-degree ridge, and counted his steps to make himself relax.
This adventure, like others in which he pushed the edge, brought him
alive. Four and a half hours after leaving high camp, he reached the
13,900-foot summit. Head bowed, he made the sign of the cross, then
planted in the snow a black-bordered flag with the Kennedy crest. He
came back down so fast that Jim Whittaker, the first American to summit Mount Everest and Bobby's guide, had to egg on his fellow professionals: "For God's sake, this guy is a Senator from New York. You're
going to let him run you into the ground?" What Bobby never said about
the climb, but his friends did, is that he spent the last of his disabling grief
on Mount Kennedy.

He hoped his children would develop that same fearlessness, which is
why on family vacations they rafted on Idaho's "river of no return" or
skied the steepest slopes at Stowe or Sun Valley. It wasn't just his brood of
ten but seventeen nieces and nephews who often came along, with most
adoring Uncle Bobby and internalizing his vision of what it meant to be
a Kennedy. Always do what you are afraid to do. Only mama's boys collect wildflowers. Don't expect special treatment when the game is on the
line. "Bobby and I were the pitchers on our teams" during one such
game in Hyannis Port, recalls Fred Harris, an Oklahoma Democrat who
started in the Senate two months before Bobby. "Right up until the last
inning, each of us slack-pitched slow balls to the little kids like Kerry. But
in the last half of the ninth, with the score tied, two people on base, and
two out, Kerry Kennedy stepped up to bat for our team, and Robert
pitched her three sizzling fast balls in rapid succession—and *struck her
out!* . . . That night we had dinner over at his house and his mother was
there and so was Jackie Kennedy. I said, 'Gee, isn't it an awful thing that
your son just ruthlessly struck out his daughter?' He said, before Rose
could answer, 'Can I help it if she's a sucker for a high inside fastball?'"

On every trip to Hyannis Port, Bobby visited Joe in his room just before
dinner and engaged in a spirited monologue that often lasted thirty min-

utes. He was convinced his father could hear, but he would have talked to him regardless. Bob and Ted also took their father to the opening game of the 1967 World Series at Fenway Park between the Red Sox and the St. Louis Cardinals. Joe didn't last long, collapsing in his seat and needing oxygen before his sons took him home. There also were new tragedies in Ethel's family, with a plane crash killing her brother George Jr. on his way to a hunting trip in Idaho in the fall of 1966. That was eleven years after her parents died in a similar accident and a year before George Jr.'s wife would choke to death when a piece of meat went down the wrong way during a family dinner. Nobody could and did offer more credible consolation than a practiced mourner like Bobby.

Jackie, meanwhile, continued to absorb a disproportionate share of Bobby's time and energy. Just as she was adjusting to Jack's being gone, William Manchester was finishing his meticulous examination of the assassination, *The Death of a President.* The Kennedys had recruited the journalist to the project, and Manchester agreed to let them review the book before publication. The manuscript ended up treating JFK adoringly, but both Bobby and Jackie—neither of whom had read it, asking friends to undertake that painful process and report back—voiced major concerns. Jackie's were personal, having to do with the author's gruesome details about her husband's murder, which was too raw for her to relive. Bobby's were political, fearing that Manchester's depiction of LBJ made him look so brutish and unassimilated that it would come across as a Kennedy hatchet job. Bobby first tried to work out the changes amicably, then he got tough. Finally, at Jackie's insistence, the Kennedy lawyers sued in December 1966 even as Manchester, who had devoted two years to the project and done more than a thousand interviews, was threatening to kill himself.

The NBC anchor David Brinkley called the dust-up "the biggest publishing story since the New Testament," and gossip columnists couldn't get enough. If the assassination and its aftermath showed the Kennedys at their noblest, this was the family at their smallest-minded. Each new revelation of the behind-the-scenes machinations made Jackie seem more imperious, with one in three Americans saying they thought less of her now. Bobby suffered worse. Liberals called him a book burner. Intellectuals denounced him for rewriting history. Democrats said he was threatening party unity. The old charges of ruthlessness were dredged up, as Bobby knew they would be, but he could neither abandon his sister-in-law nor look as if he was backing down.* In the end the lawsuit was resolved, the serializations were published in *Look* magazine, and the book was released, but none of that helped the junior senator from New York. A poll by Louis Harris revealed that among those who had followed the controversy—an impressive seven in ten Americans—59 percent preferred LBJ for president in 1968 compared to 41 percent for Bobby. With those who had not been paying attention, Bobby led 54 to 46 percent. Ironically, while the public was blaming him for his bad behavior, Manchester was forgiving him. "Amicable relations with Bob Kennedy were quickly restored," wrote the author, who wanted the Kennedys to like him and understood Bobby's zeal in protecting his brother's reputation and widow. "And in the spring of 1968, after he had announced for the Presidency, I was campaigning for him."

NEVER HAD THERE been a Senate office quite like Bobby's. He had one of the biggest staffs ever, starting with about forty in 1965 and building three years later to more than seventy, which was more than double Ted's and four times as many as Majority Leader Mike Mansfield's. Others worked part time and without pay while the salaries of some official staff came at least partly from his own purse; he was kicking in a hundred thousand dollars a year by 1968. He received seven hundred fifty letters on an average day and twelve hundred when an issue was hot, both surely high-water marks for a freshman lawmaker. So were his daily calls from seventy-five journalists and fifty invitations to speak. The traffic to his office was so heavy that a doorway threshold that normally lasts a decade had to be replaced after six months. All of which was extraordinary for a senator who chaired no committees or subcommittees,

* "Bob doesn't represent me," Jackie told the men from *Look*. "He sort of protects me." Also trying to protect her—although she never appreciated that—was Manchester's editor at Harper's, Evan W. Thomas II, who also edited JFK's *Profiles in Courage* and RFK's *The Enemy Within* (Corry, *Manchester Affair*, 121).

led no geographic or ideological blocs, and sat with three other junior members in a newly created back row that he joked was closer to the men's room than the dais.

The explanation was axiomatic: Never had there been a senator quite like Bobby Kennedy. It wasn't just his money, fame, and power, although each elevated him beyond any other freshman in memory. So did his apparently permanent title as attorney general and the knowledge that he'd been the martyred president's most trusted lieutenant. Twenty-two books had been or were being written about him (he never read them, but did look at the picture books), and he wrote five of his own (with help, and with the hope of making them bestsellers). His mail bore postmarks from Burbank and Missoula along with Poughkeepsie and Schenectady, with other senators' constituents seeking assistance with everything from missing Social Security checks to how to extricate us from Vietnam (or make sure we stayed). It was as if Bobby belonged to all fifty states and 195 million Americans. The same way reporters had dubbed him assistant president when JFK was alive, they now dreamed up new epithets, from "probable president" and "exiled prince" to "a happening." The most apt was "heir apparent." When a Senate colleague complained to a committee chairman that "you're giving Kennedy preferential treatment," the chairman quipped, "I treat him the same way I'd treat any future president."

Bobby knew that those expectations created an opportunity beyond the reach of a normal senator, and he had set up his office in a way meant to capitalize on that. The plotting and politics were delegated to old New Frontiersmen like Richard Goodwin and Ted Sorensen and family faithful like Steve Smith and Ted Kennedy. His mission in the Senate was to change the country and the planet, for which a quartet of staffers was key. Adam Walinsky, who internalized his boss's mettle and cadence as he drafted speeches on everything from Bed-Stuy to Vietnam, was the irascible bomb thrower Bobby fantasized becoming. Peter Edelman shared that passion but with the gentler edges needed for ferreting out novel solutions to problems like poverty. Both were Jewish intellectuals who rose from the lower levels of Bobby's Justice Department, elbowed their way onto their hero's Senate campaign, and had the Ivy League pedigrees that made the Kennedys comfortable, Adam having graduated from Yale Law School and Peter from Harvard Law. Both also understood that Bobby would follow them out onto ledges, but he counted on them to pick ones with footing solid enough to justify the risk.

"If you're making speeches about, you know, redevelopment on the Upper West Side or something like that, then who cares what you say? But if you're messing around with the lives of people in Vietnam or something of that magnitude, then you better have it right, not wrong," explains Walinsky, who grew so frustrated with Bobby's indecision on the war that "I told him he had a month to find a replacement for me. . . . I loved him, actually, but I just felt that was necessary." It was one of a dozen pressures on the senator to finally make a break, and knowing that he would, he advised his fiery aide, "When you go home and tell your wife, don't get her real upset."

Joe Dolan was like his boss in different ways. A pragmatic Irishman, Dolan hired and nurtured the staff, filtered unrealistic demands from the pathologically impatient senator, and communicated with Bobby in the same private language of gestures, pauses, and monosyllables that assistant attorneys general like Burke Marshall had mastered. Angie Novello was a blend of mother hen and Mother Superior. She'd been with Bobby since the Rackets Committee. The scores of advisers, lobbyists, and even family members who wanted to reach him had to get by her. They also had to satisfy her standards. The senator could be late, but not anyone hoping to meet with him. What one fellow staffer called "pretty young things" perpetually circled, but Angie wouldn't let them in without a serious reason, and without hems and necklines she considered appropriate. She also didn't let in anyone who looked menacing, and she wasn't shy about pressing the security buzzer by her knee. She was the only one able to read the senator's pinched script and the only one who dared to call him "boss" or "Bob"; to everybody else he was "Senator."

Angie was unique in one more respect. Nearly all the women in his office were smart enough that they knew their jobs without being told, were as determined to make a difference as Walinsky or Edelman, and went on to impressive careers as lawyers, literary agents, or professors of, among other things, feminist theology. But Angie was the only one with real power. The remainder of the mainly female staff answered phones and mail and responded to visitors' questions, requests for tea, or, for the luckiest, complaints from constituents. That was partly a reflection of that *Mad Men* era, with barely a dozen female legislative aides on all of Capitol Hill. It was also a Kennedy thing. Joe held his wife and daughters to standards of propriety he and his sons never tried to meet, while in the Kennedy White House, there was a saying that "women belonged in the parlor, in the kitchen, in the bedroom, and behind the typewriter." Bobby was able to imagine a black in the White House but not a female. Ethel helped her husband in most everything he did but saw herself in a subsidiary role. "I would never use the word 'partner,' " she says. "That refers to equality." Anne Hudson Shields worked for and admired Bobby when he was a senator but says, "One can only answer so many legislative mail letters before you begin to go nuts." Shields, who later became a lawyer, then chief of staff to the secretary of the interior, quit her job with Bobby because "there was obviously a glass ceiling. You were not going anywhere, and so what was the point?"

The rest of the staff, female and male, swallowed what reporters joked were loyalty pills.* Most were young and unscarred by cynicism or battle fatigue. They volunteered to work six long days a week and felt privileged to be part of Kennedy World. No big deal when he asked them to fetch his favorite chicken and rice soup and Hershey bars with nuts, or requested that they get the china coffee cup from his office so he didn't have to drink from the thick ones in the cafeteria. No complaints, either, working shoulder to shoulder in offices too small for that big a staff, spread across two buildings, with few windows, none of which opened. It felt like a campaign and paid as poorly. When you were drooled on by Brumus—or one of the boss's toddlers—you wiped it off and went on. Bobby still borrowed cash that he meant to but didn't pay back. Same for pocket combs, and everyone knew he preferred long ones. He loved that haircuts from the Senate barber were free, although nobody could tell the difference after he'd had one, and he seldom had coins to tip the shoe-

---

* Bobby had always said that loyalty was the most important ingredient in politics. In 1966, his Christmas gifts for the twenty-five office clerks were small gold bracelet charms shaped like aspirin. On the front was engraved "One a Day—RFK," and on the back, LOYAL was spelled out horizontally and vertically ("Robert Kennedy Staff Gets Gold Loyalty Pills," *New York Times*).

shine boy or barber. It was the millionaire's casualness about money that he'd had from the start.

So why did they put up with it? Why not move on, as Shields did? They loved Bobby's resolve to be a Jeremiah, afflicting the comfortable, at a time when most congressmen preferred the reassuring role of Pollyanna. He had an acrobat's ability to juggle twenty issues at once and a motivational magic that convinced the aide assigned to each issue that it was the senator's number one priority. His office was the same kind of intellectual open shop that it had been at Justice. He accepted his assistants' mistakes so long as they confessed and didn't make them all the time. Like Bobby, most staffers preferred field visits to folders of statistics, especially when they were punctuated by his familiar entreaty: "Tell me what I can do." The forgotten legions in the mail and copy rooms appreciated that he trooped through regularly, trying to make small talk and succeeding in letting them know that he cared. Such things, his longtime advance man Jerry Bruno said, are what "made me really want to knock myself out for him; I hated to see him unhappy."

But that was only the public half of the explanation for why his aides believed in Bobby in a way they never had or would in anyone else. He was the rare senator who had no social armor and the uncommon politician who was generous to people who didn't matter. His staffers learned those secrets when he reached out to them specifically and confidentially, revealing the tenderness he worked so hard to disguise. "A friend of mine's brother died and he wrote a several-page handwritten letter . . . about what the loss of a brother was. She was incredibly moved," recalls Esther Newberg, a New York literary agent who, like Bobby, was not known for sentimentality. With Jeff Greenfield, it was the senator's response when the young aide warned that he planned to resist if he were drafted. Whereas other senators might have fretted about how that would reflect on them, Bobby joked, "I used to be attorney general and I have some important friends in the federal correctional system. And anyway, some writers have done their best work in prison." Later, just after Martin Luther King was killed, Bobby arrived at his campaign hotel in the middle of the night and found Greenfield passed out on the bed. "He tucked me in, which was why I said to him, 'You aren't so ruthless after all.' He said, 'Don't tell anybody.' " Wes Barthelmes, his first Senate press secretary, remembered when a Negro National Guardsman from Washington, D.C., was ambushed and killed in Georgia. The soldier's wife died shortly after of natural causes. Bobby contacted a relative of theirs in Syracuse who agreed to take the couple's children, "and [the senator] made arrangements to provide for them financially," said Barthelmes. Bobby also insisted that nobody know what he'd done, telling his aide, "I don't want it to get out. I'm not winking when I say it. I don't want it to get out."

He'd done even more for Ena Bernard, although she never told the story. The Costa Rican nursemaid went to work for the Kennedys when Kathleen was an infant and stayed for forty-four years, helping raise ten more children and keep the household going. Eventually Ena brought over her daughter Josefina, who had had a rough time in Costa Rica, living first with a family friend who was abusive, then at a strict boarding school. Josefina's life was transformed here in big ways, because Bobby and Ethel gave her a home, and in two small ones that mean even more to her looking back. Once, when the teenager returned from a party at 2:00 A.M., she found Bobby waiting in the den. "These," Josefina says, "are the words I remember: 'Your father is not here, and I am your father away from home.' That has stayed with me to this day, and I am seventy-four years old. In that family I felt loved. I never had love." She also recalls how Bobby would empty the coins from his pocket onto a table. Twice, she filched a quarter. "I was the only one that was around and he asked me, 'Josefina, did you take a quarter from me?' 'No, no, no, sir, I didn't,' I lied, lied, lied, lied like a rug. . . . If I did anything wrong back in Costa Rica, man, I had the daylights beaten out of me with belts, with soap and urine. I never admitted it. I knew Mr. Kennedy knew I took it. But he never punished me for it, and that was the cure. That was the cure."

If he surprised his staff with his benevolence, he surprised colleagues with his mood swings. "One day he would crack jokes for an hour, the next day he would chop you off," recalls Democrat Walter Mondale, a seatmate in the Senate's back row. "At first I got mad, but I just figured that's the way he was. . . . I'm not sure that he realized how some people were hurt by that." Republican Javits was torn, too—drawn in by Bobby's "passion for life," yet put off by a sense of entitlement "which one associated more with royalty." Frank Mankiewicz, Bobby's longest-lasting press secretary, found a way to manage the choler that he knew had a short half-life.* He did nothing to discourage the determined senator from dictating an angry letter, whether it was to the editor of *The New York Times* or the ski resort that hadn't been friendly enough to a Kennedy kid. But "about a week later I'd say to him, 'Remember the letter you wrote to Abe Rosenthal or the ski resort?' He'd say, 'yah.' I'd say, 'I didn't send it.' He'd say, 'fine.'"

The one senator he didn't have to explain himself to was Ted, who was his only real friend in Congress and, after Jack died, a trusted confidant. There was competition among their staffs, with Bobby's whiz kids hiding neither their ambition nor their disdain, same as their boss, and Ted's more nuts-and-bolts aides resenting that. Ted himself was accustomed to it. He'd grown up with Bobby's sharp elbows and the clan consciousness of a pecking order based on age and accomplishment. He'd also grown up adoring his brother, and he said, "Our new proximity brought with it the spirit of the old times; the laughter and teasing and optimism of our boyhoods; the easy intimacy of our autumn garage weekends at the Cape house." While the Senate was a step up for Ted, it was a comedown for the former attorney general. Each helped the other adjust. Ted knew he had to do his homework, learning every detail of each bill and of parliamentary procedure, in order to be accepted as something other than Bobby and Jack's little brother. Bobby saw Senate folkways as something to be circumvented and had an unusual capacity to teach even as he was learning. Reaching out to colleagues came easily to Ted but remained painful for Bobby. Whereas the older brother asked why, the younger cared only about how. Neither could have been the other if he tried, and neither did.

In practice, that meant dividing the issues both cared about, with

---

* Mankiewicz also knew that at seven in the morning, weekends along with weekdays, he could expect a call from Bobby. "He had, of course, already read the papers and expected that I, too, had done so before I answered the telephone," the press secretary recalled half a century later. "With rarely a cursory greeting, he would be speaking as though in mid-thought or mid-sentence. 'Bombing pause in Vietnam. Looks like Johnson's about to end it. Should I call now for continuance?' Or, 'Possibility of new unrest like Watts last summer'" (Mankiewicz, *So As I Was Saying*, 152).

Bobby getting first crack at the hottest ones, like Vietnam, and Teddy focusing on civil rights and immigration. Bobby instinctually took more responsibility for Jack's children, just as he took over the center seat in the family plane, known as the President's Chair. The two often walked back to their offices together after a vote in the Senate, consulting and laughing, and they had special phone numbers that let them get through to each other almost as fast as the old White House hotline.* Fellow senators adored Ted and feared Bobby. At parties the younger (by six years), taller (by five inches), better-looking (by most benchmarks) Kennedy would regale the crowd, while his brother was in a corner conspiring one-on-one. Their personalities seemed defined by their size, as one friend noticed: "Ted was always big trying to be little, Bobby was always little trying to be big." The spotlight that shone on Bobby gave Ted cover to learn and mature. In the end the Massachusetts senator would have a staff bigger than and as brainy as Bobby's had been, and he became an equally effective advocate for the afflicted. Whatever rivalry existed now was expressed mainly through humor, which was the Kennedy way. In talks on the West Coast, Bobby deadpanned that he'd gotten a telegram from Washington reading, LYNDON IS IN MANILA. HUBERT IS OUT CAMPAIGNING. CONGRESS HAS GONE HOME. HAVE SEIZED POWER. TEDDY. Ted countered, "Everyone here knows that if I ever did seize power the last person I'd notify is my brother."

There wasn't much kidding with LBJ during these Senate years, although Bobby had a favorite joke about him: "You know how to tell when Lyndon Johnson is lying? Well, when he wiggles his ears, he's not lying. When he twitches his nose, he's not lying. But when he moves his lips, he's lying." The president and senator both made occasional gestures of goodwill. In January 1966, Bobby sent Lyndon a copy of Bruce Catton's *Never Call Retreat*, a book that explored Abraham Lincoln's agonizing loneliness in waging the Civil War. In an accompanying note, Kennedy handwrote, "I thought it might give you some comfort to look

---

* The brothers had nearby Senate suites and they'd hold their own private caucus several times a week. "Bob always went to Ted's office; it was never the other way around," recalled Mankiewicz. "'He's been here longer than me, and even if he hadn't, he knows his way around much better,' RFK once told me. But I knew it was much more: a consistent, unplanned effort to show special respect" (Mankiewicz, *So As I Was Saying*, 157).

again at another President, Abraham Lincoln, and some of the identical problems and situations that he faced that you are now meeting." Johnson responded in an equally warm tone: "You know better than most the gloom that crowds in on a President, for you lived close to your brother. Thus, your letter meant a great deal to me and I tell you how grateful I am for your thoughtfulness."

Lulls like that were the exception in a relationship that had grown even stormier. LBJ kept track of Bobby's every move, here and abroad, political and personal, through news clippings and memos from White House aides, diplomats, state party apparatchiks, and others anxious to feed the fears. The files' titles bespoke their tone: KENNEDY—THE CONSERVATIVE, OTHERS ON KENNEDY—COLUMNISTS, and KENNEDY—THE UNCROWNED PRINCE. Liz Carpenter, Lady Bird's chief of staff and LBJ's political ears and eyes, suggested early in 1966 that the president "start working to soften up the Kennedy columnist set . . . subvert them from 'buying' everything Bobby does. We ought to be able to move in with them when Bobby makes an error as he did on Viet Nam." Another way to undermine the senator on his favored ground would be for the president to take "a dramatic poverty installation tour." LBJ read the memo, which had to delight him since it mirrored his own thinking but also made him nervous lest it become public. "Tear this up," he scribbled at the bottom, "and flush it down the toilet."

Johnson's preoccupation with Bobby had become a distraction to his presidency, all the more curious because he was now ensconced in the White House after a landslide victory while Bobby was a mere senator who'd sailed in partly on the president's slipstream. But LBJ's popularity was sagging because of riots in the cities and a growing backlash against his open-ended escalation in Vietnam. Bobby was a convenient scapegoat, since he embodied everything LBJ hated, and his poll numbers were rising in inverse proportion to LBJ's slide. The president now required three things from every potential appointee: "First, of course, skill and capability. And second, absolute loyalty." The third, he admitted, was an assurance "that you are not going to work for Bobby Kennedy down the line." Harry McPherson, Jr., one of LBJ's most loyal counselors, was worried enough by this fixation that he wrote a four-page memo entitled "Thoughts on Bobby Kennedy and Loyalty." The first three pages sympa-

thized with the president's concerns, noting that liberals and journalists
will see Bobby as "St. George slaying the conservative dragon" and that
he would appeal to intellectuals, who "are as easy a lay as can be found."
On page 4 he zeroed in on his real concern: the president's over-the-edge
suspicions about the senator, which was causing him to question the loyalty of even the most talented and loyal JFK holdovers. "You have the
office, the policies, the personal magnetism, the power to lead and inspire, and above all the power to put good ideas into effect," McPherson
wrote. "An obsession with Bobby and with the relationship of your best
people to him may, I believe, distort policy and offend the very men you
need to attract." Instead of achieving its goal of getting LBJ to back off,
the missive "imperiled McPherson's own place in the president's inner
circle," according to Jeff Shesol, who wrote a 591-page book on the LBJ-
RFK relationship that he titled *Mutual Contempt.**

Bobby kept his own tabs on who among JFK's advisers was getting too
close to "this man" in the White House. The senator's feelings about the
president never softened, but they didn't harden into a fetish the way
LBJ's about him had. LBJ was "mean, bitter, vicious, [an] animal in many
ways," Bobby told a Kennedy Library interviewer in 1964, "which makes
it very difficult, unless you want to kiss his behind all the time." After his
swearing-in as senator he asked Richard Goodwin, who'd stayed on temporarily in the White House, "Why does he keep worrying about me? I
don't like him, but there's nothing I can do to him. Hell, he's the president, and I'm only a junior senator." Goodwin: "That's the reality. But
we're not talking about reality. In Johnson's mind you're the threat. If he
had to choose between you and Ho Chi Minh [to succeed him as presi-
dent], he'd pick Ho in a minute."

Bobby escaped from the D.C. intrigue by flying to New York as often as

---

* A clear sign that LBJ didn't heed McPherson's warning was his treatment of Roger Wilkins,
whom he named to run the Community Relations Service in January 1966. Wilkins, the
nephew of NAACP head Roy Wilkins, had been lukewarm about Bobby, but since he was
living in New York it was natural that Kennedy would introduce him at his Senate confirmation hearing. That was too much for LBJ, who snubbed Wilkins at his swearing-in. "[John-
son] spoke to my mother, my step-father, my wife, my kids, my mother-in-law, to my uncle,
to my aunt," Wilkins recalled. "*But he did not speak to me!*" There was no doubt in the appointee's mind why the president was furious: "pure hatred of Robert Kennedy" (Shesol, *Mutual
Contempt*, 321–23).

he could—to check in on Bed-Stuy, see Jackie, and just get away. He almost never used his office there, preferring to meet staff or friends at his new apartment with its floor-to-ceiling windows overlooking the East River. Always short on time, he'd caucus with his visitors while bathing, shaving, or walking around the three-bedroom suite wrapped in a towel. He bought the unit just north of the United Nations when he gave up the Long Island mansion he'd rented during the election to counter charges of carpetbagging. Its living room shelves were stocked with volumes by Dickens, Kipling, and the Kennedys, with former friend Frank Sinatra playing on the stereo. Steve Smith would bring in a closed-circuit tape machine that let Bobby test-run his speeches, and staffers filled him in on the difference between express trains and locals, a mystery to this senator who generally was chauffeured or walked. He complained about the perpetual noise and polluted air but loved that New Yorkers were so harried that at least some of them didn't recognize him.

BOBBY, A LEGITIMATE cultural icon, rarely went unnoticed. He was half James Cagney, half James Dean, only this tough-guy rebel had more causes than anybody else. While liberals remained as suspicious of him as he was of them, the War on Poverty pioneer Daniel Patrick Moynihan offered this reassurance: "Kennedy has worked for his liberalism. It's not something he learned at the Bronx High School of Science. The things he learned first were conservative things. The things he learned second were liberal things. He is an idealist without illusions. . . . You might want to call this higher liberalism." But Bobby hadn't shed all of his conservatism. He still hated Russia, even if he had come to see Saigon as the wrong place to make a stand. He questioned New Deal shibboleths of federal paternalism and remained as devoted as his father and grandfather had been to blue-collar truisms like honoring hard work and self-improvement.

That ideological progression was confounding. Instead of following a straight line from conservative to liberal, he had skipped straight to revolutionary. The man who had waged a holy war against Cuban Communists answered "I know it" when a friend opined that he "should be in the hills with Castro and Che." He wrote that "a revolution is coming—

a revolution that will be peaceful if we are wise enough, compassionate if we care enough, successful if we are fortunate enough, but a revolution that is coming whether we will it or not." His political evolution also ran counter to the normal pattern of Americans' becoming more cynical as they age, the way Ronald Reagan did in going from card-carrying New Dealer to icon of the right. The insurgent had always been there in Bobby. But having lost his father, his brother, and much of his power, there was less to bind him to convention. He had seen close up the darkest sides of this country's underbelly, from the Mob to the Teamsters, so his optimism was never starry-eyed. He'd experienced America's problems and internalized what he had seen and felt. He told Native Americans in Oklahoma that he wished he were an Indian. He meant it no less when he said the same thing to sugarcane cutters in Brazil, blacks in Bedford-Stuyvesant, and children everywhere. In today's derisive political context he'd be decried as a flip-flopper. But his transformation was heartfelt and transcended politics, as Jack Newfield saw, reflecting a "private, internal change, from rigidity to existential doubt, from coldness to an intuitive sensitivity for sorrow and pain, from one-dimensional competitiveness to fatalism, from football to poetry, from Irish-Catholic Boston's political clubhouses to the unknown." For those who knew him as a boy it seemed less a remake than a purposeful return to an earlier gentleness, when he had been the bashful runt of Joe and Rose's litter.

Conveniently for Bobby, America was undergoing its own upheaval in the mid-1960s. An old politics dominated by big-city machines and labor unions was yielding to a new one whose touchstones were television, grassroots organizing, and a distrust of anything old. The Cold War and New Deal seemed archaic to the generation of the Thaw and the New Left. Race riots were igniting the cities and Vietnam was widening the split between parents and children. Even the Catholic Church was riven and trying to reform. There was no national consensus anymore—but there were few figures in American politics more able and determined to build bridges between the alienated and the mainstream than Bobby, who had lived on both sides. He sensed the changes early and they pulled him ahead even as he gave them voice and direction. He was halfway between the old and the new, adjusting on the run and with conviction.

The journalist who best captured that push-pull wasn't a political writer or a columnist but the cartoonist Jules Feiffer, who saw Bobby Kennedy's constellation of contradictions not as old versus new but as good versus bad. He called his schizophrenic senator the "Bobby twins," explaining that "the Good Bobby is a courageous reformer. The Bad Bobby makes deals. The Good Bobby sent federal troops down south to enforce civil rights. The Bad Bobby appointed racist judges down South to enforce civil rights. The Good Bobby is a fervent civil libertarian. The Bad Bobby is a fervent wire tapper. The Good Bobby is ill at ease with liberals. The Bad Bobby is ill at ease with grownups."

The caricaturist's confusion was understandable given the conflicting signals Bobby was sending. Which was the real RFK—the archangel come to rescue the children of the Mississippi Delta or the sonofabitch who verbally assaulted quiet-spoken Walter Mondale? Was he a hawk or peacemaker, sheriff or outlaw, Captain America or Dennis the Menace? The truth was he was all of that at one time or another. His first instinct had always been to lash out, but then he would step back, listen, and find a middle ground missed by others. He'd been both a Shakespearean scoundrel and an Irish folk hero. He was changing in deeper and more authentic ways than politicians generally did, which laid bare his inconsistencies and regrets. Being simple and at the same time sophisticated, he was easy to misunderstand and difficult to stereotype. "Bobby wasn't typical of anything or anybody . . . [he] was sui generis," says the political journalist Elizabeth Drew. "That was and is his draw." Bobby himself understood the paradox he presented. "It seems as if everybody [is] engaged in psychoanalyzing me and the Kennedy family," he told a reporter. "Is he an angel or a devil? A saint or a Bengalese tiger? . . . When I am asked questions about myself, I am incapable of answering." Later he confided to a friend that "no matter what I do, people think I am doing something else." Whether he engendered fierce devotion or ferocious distrust depended on the beholder's prism, since there was compelling evidence for the existence of both a Good Bobby and a Bad.

It also depended on the timing. During his Senate years he tilted more soft than ruthless and was more at home with pacifism than with fighting hot or cold wars. There was less moralism and more morality. The willfulness and cunning remained, but they were harnessed to causes such as ending apartheid and remaking ghettos. He'd laid claim to a rare piece of political ground as a pragmatic idealist, which was the same terrain JFK had hoped to plow. While some remained skeptical, others were dazzled by the possibilities of a standard-bearer with that blend of tenaciousness and gentleness. "One of the reasons, I suspect, that some people are puzzled by Senator Kennedy is that he is a tough-minded man with a tender heart," said Senator George McGovern, who stood with Bobby against both hunger in America and American involvement in Vietnam. "He is, to borrow Dr. King's fitting description of the good life, 'a creative synthesis of opposites.' "

Chapter 10

LAST CAMPAIGN

═══════

FOR A POLITICIAN considered the master strategist of his era, Bobby Kennedy's plunge into the 1968 race for the White House was so melodramatic and ham-handed that it was painful to watch. But there was nothing ruthless about it, although that's the rap he took.

Running for president had been at the back of Bobby's mind since the earliest days of JFK's administration. Jack joked about it in ways that seemed designed to plant the idea in the minds of the public and of his brother.* Joe didn't find it funny. He never doubted that the son most like him should succeed the one most different. Bobby was the last to buy in. While he was perhaps readier for the White House than anyone who hadn't lived there, he remained mesmerized by the prospect of writing, teaching, and freeing himself from the public arena and the Kennedy limelight. But down deep he knew that that wouldn't do for the designated heir.

JFK's assassination shattered dreams of a Kennedy dynasty, but only temporarily. As Bobby pulled out of his despair, he reengaged with the nation's problems in a way that made clear that despite having served half as long, he was twice the senator and reformer that Jack had been. Whereas Senator John F. Kennedy had plotted a course to the White House by gathering chits and avoiding conflicts, Senator Robert F. Kennedy had made himself a lightning rod for controversy. Whether the

---

* "When old Bob gets to be president, why then I think I could best serve him as secretary of state," Jack said, adding with a smile, "I don't know whether I'd enjoy taking orders from lovable old Bob" (Paul Fay OH, November 11, 1970, 215, JFKL).

issue was Vietnam or tobacco ads, auto safety or a minimum tax on the rich, the junior senator from New York consistently positioned himself to the left of the Johnson administration and most of his fellow lawmakers. LBJ and others had rightly wondered whether Jack had sufficient gravitas as a senator to qualify for the White House, but few doubted Bobby's resoluteness. Instead, critics within the opposition party and his own reproached him for brazenly orchestrating a shadow government capable of experimenting with ghetto busting in Bedford-Stuyvesant and putting out peace feelers in Paris.

His achievements added up to a sturdy platform from which to take on LBJ, whose poll numbers had been sliding almost since the day of his historic landslide victory. Nearly every new speech Bobby made suggested not just an alternative policy but an alternative president. The winds were turning against the war and in his direction, and he felt them blowing as he barnstormed the country in the 1966 midterm elections on behalf of a mind-boggling seventy-six candidates for the Senate, House, and state houses. His convoy was of presidential proportions, with limos, a police escort, buses bearing newsmen, and a crowd with signs reading KENNEDY IN '68 and KEEP HARASSING LBJ. The love even crossed the border. During a three-week trip through Latin America at the end of 1965, a Chilean newspaper had referred to him as "the future president," Indians in Peru chanted, "Viva Kennedy," and Bobby joked that he was running for "President of the World." But it was the office of president of the United States that focused the mind of the antiwar activist Allard Lowenstein, who helped launch a Dump Johnson campaign in the summer of 1967 and that fall approached Bobby to pick up the baton. It was a presumptive candidate's dream scenario—being drafted to run by a grassroots movement he agreed with, making them, rather than him, look like schemers and disrupters.

A lone dissenter stymied that challenge-the-president scenario: Bobby himself. He never seriously questioned the goal, just the year. He had the scars to attest to the whatever-it-takes tactics this sitting president would use to maintain his grip on the Democratic Party and the White House, no matter what the pollsters said about the softness of his support. A brash bid to topple Johnson would dredge up charges that everything Bobby had done as a senator was Machiavellian, motivated by politics

rather than ideals. With Kennedy as the champion of the anti-LBJ crusade, the president might actually dig in deeper in Vietnam. Running in
1968 would divide the Democrats and could help Republicans retake the
White House and make gains in the Senate. It could also ruin Bobby's
chances in 1972, when LBJ would be constitutionally excluded from running again and there'd be a clearer path to 1600 Pennsylvania Avenue.
So overwhelming were his doubts that he told Lowenstein that while he
endorsed his objective, "someone else will have to be the first one to run.
It can't be me because of my relationship with Johnson." He told the
press that he planned to run for reelection to the Senate and to support
President Johnson for a second term.

Bobby was again asking himself Hamlet's famous question, as he had
when he weighed whether to be attorney general in 1961 and to run for
senator in 1964. Just as characteristically, he sought to dig out of his
paralysis by consulting everyone he knew, and some he didn't. The two
Teds, Kennedy and Sorensen, were dead set against his jumping in, convinced the timing was wrong. Not so Adam Walinsky, Peter Edelman,
and other young turks on his staff, who had signed up for precisely this
kind of battle of ideologies. The factions met and deliberated, with and
without Bobby, and in the process managed to reinforce his indecision
and inaction. In December 1967, Jack Newfield wrote in *The Village Voice*
that "if Kennedy does not run in 1968, the best side of his character will
die"; three weeks later Joseph Alsop countered in *The Washington Post*
that if he does run, "He will destroy himself. He will destroy his Party."
The lobbying continued at home, where Ethel and the kids were rehears-
ing for the role of First Family while Rose was having what she called
"profound misgivings." Jack wasn't there to cast a vote, so Ted spoke for
him: "He might have cautioned against it . . . but he probably would
have made the run himself in similar circumstances."

The central struggle, of course, wasn't between Bobby and his advisers or his relatives, but between his dueling natures. The demarcation for
this highest-of-stakes decision was no longer the cartoonish Good Bobby
versus Bad, but Old Bobby versus New. Was he the cautious political pro
who had stayed in the background of the civil rights struggle and vacillated on Vietnam? That had been the hardheaded Bobby whom Joe
reared, serving his country but doing it judiciously and betting mainly

on sure things. Or was he the hot-blooded insurgent he'd become once
he recognized the failures of Jim Crow and counterinsurgency? Torn yet
again between what he thought and what he felt, he would telephone
acquaintances late at night, without introduction, asking, "Should I run
for President?" Before they could answer he'd rant on: "They keep telling
me I should run, my friends, my sisters; Ethel thinks I should run. But
that's not so bad, it's what I hear from myself at five o'clock in the
morning—the country can't stand four more years of this." In the end
the question that haunted him most was one raised by the students who
greeted him at Brooklyn College that winter with a placard asking, BOBBY
KENNEDY: HAWK, DOVE OR CHICKEN?

Events early in 1968 pulled him closer to his inevitable run for the
White House. At the end of January, at the beginning of the Vietnamese
new year, known as Tet, the North Vietnamese and Vietcong unleashed
simultaneous attacks against a hundred South Vietnamese cities and
hamlets that shocked the public there and in America. The next month
George Romney, the governor of Michigan and an antiwar Republican,
withdrew from the race, essentially clearing the field for Kennedy nemesis and Vietnam hawk Richard Nixon. LBJ ignored the findings and rec-
ommendations of his own Kerner Commission on Civil Disorders, which
had warned that America was splitting into "two societies, one black, one
white—separate and unequal," and had called for new jobs, new housing, and a new drive to end segregation. Then Bobby learned that the U.S.
commander in Vietnam was asking for a huge infusion of soldiers even as
the president was firing that commander's boss, the increasingly skeptical defense secretary Robert McNamara. Bobby had tried reasoning with
the president in private. He tried pressuring him in public. He knew there
was one route remaining if he hoped to change things.

But the political world continued to spin while he was making up his
mind. Lowenstein and his anti-LBJ plotters were turned down by Bobby's
favorite senator, George McGovern, and ended up with one Kennedy
didn't much like, Eugene McCarthy. The Minnesota lawmaker had always believed that Jack and Bobby were less Catholic than he was, less
intelligent, and less worthy of high office. Bobby thought McCarthy vain,
lazy, and "not moral" because he "votes one way in the Finance Committee to help his special interests, and then he votes the other way on the

floor when the press is watching."* Yet McCarthy filled the vacuum that Bobby's hesitation had created, and the young and alienated who would have rallied to Kennedy turned instead to the only opposition campaign. Bobby had walked straight into a trap he set for himself: Diving in now would raise suspicions that a lust for power compelled him to take on not just his brother's legitimate successor but that president's brave challenger.

Fully aware of the risk, Bobby privately resolved to declare his candidacy as early as March 4, eight days before the all-important New Hampshire primary. That same Monday he quietly ordered California Assembly speaker Jesse Unruh to make sure he made the March 6 deadline for getting on the presidential primary ballot out there, adding, "Don't get caught at it."† On Tuesday, over a three-hour lunch with Ted Kennedy and other advisers, the talk was about how rather than whether to get in. Two days later he told Ted to warn McCarthy, but Ted balked and the message wasn't delivered until the night before the New Hampshire balloting, fueling McCarthy's hard feelings.‡ By Friday, the nascent Kennedy campaign was starting to churn. Washington aides were researching LBJ's record while New York staffers were lining up that state's delegation. *The Washington Star*'s Haynes Johnson met that day with Bobby and later scribbled a note to himself saying, "March 8, 1968—Spent 1½ hrs. with RFK. Certain he will run."

It was more than the weight of recent events that had changed the

---

* Bobby joked to *The Boston Globe*'s Marty Nolan that "Gene's mother was German. That's why he's so mean." Nolan: "What's your excuse?" Looking back, Nolan says, "RFK was mightily pissed for about 5 minutes. Later, he told the story himself to his friends" (Nolan email to author).

† Not getting caught would become a theme of the 1968 campaign, as it had been in earlier Kennedy races. It meant not getting caught using Senate staff for campaign duties. It also meant not getting caught setting up phony campaign committees, which staffer Barbara Coleman knew about because "I was treasurer of one." They said everyone did it, which was true, but few did it better than the Kennedys. (Peter Edelman OH, July 29, 1969, 185–87, JFKL; and Barbara Coleman OH, January 9, 1970, 63, JFKL.)

‡ There are several reasons why Ted might have refused. He didn't want to be the bearer of such unwelcome news at the eleventh hour, he still hoped to change his brother's mind, and he worried that McCarthy would lash back at Bobby. Bobby then got his old friend Richard Goodwin, now working for McCarthy, to pass on word of a Kennedy run (Schlesinger, *Robert Kennedy and His Times*, 847–48).

senator's mind. He was still a political animal, but one now bent on over-turning the reigning order at least enough to feed the children he had met in the Mississippi Delta and thaw the Cold War he had once fueled. It wasn't that he was a remade man, exactly, but he was responding more to gut instincts than to strategic calculations. "It is a much more natural thing for me to run than not run. When you start acting unnaturally, you're in trouble," he explained to friends. Then he dictated a pair of telegrams. The first—to the novelist and reporter Pete Hamill, who had written from Ireland imploring him to run—read, HAVE TAKEN YOUR AD-VICE. AM IN TROUBLE. PLEASE COME HOME. The other—to the editorial board of *The Harvard Crimson*, the only newspaper to endorse him that early—asked playfully, ARE WE ALONE?

All these early steps took place out of public view. For most reporters, McCarthy backers, and anyone else paying attention, only two events mattered: On March 12, Gene McCarthy embarrassed LBJ in conserva-tive New Hampshire by drawing 41.9 percent of the Democratic votes and a full half when Republican write-ins were counted. A mere four days later, Bobby Kennedy leaped into the race to unseat the suddenly vulnerable president. The case for cause and effect seemed incontrovert-ible. "We woke up after the New Hampshire primary like it was Christ-mas Day," one young McCarthy supporter said. "When we went down to the tree, we found Bobby Kennedy had stolen our Christmas presents." McCarthy was enraged, telling an aide, "That Bobby; he's something, isn't he?" In one stroke, Kennedy had resurrected every doubt ever voiced about him and transformed McCarthy into a martyr. "Your brother's announcement makes clear that St. Patrick did not drive out all the snakes from Ireland," the columnist Murray Kempton said in a telegram to Ted. Fellow scribe Mary McGrory took her own swipe: "Ken-nedy thinks that American youth belongs to him, at the bequest of his brother. Seeing the romance flower between them and McCarthy he moved with the ruthlessness of a Victorian father, whose daughter has fallen in love with a dustman, to break it up."*

---

* Bobby observed of McGrory, "Mary is so gentle—until she gets behind a typewriter." Theirs was a feud between Irish, he added, and they'd work it out (Norris, *Mary McGrory*, 103 and 109).

Bobby's entrance made great copy—"It took Bobby Kennedy seventeen years to come out against McCarthy and then it was the wrong one," Lady Bird Johnson's press secretary would quip—but his critics got things backward. Bobby's decision to challenge the president was anything but swift and calculated. He had been thinking about running for years, was tormented for months, and made his mind up the week before a single anti-LBJ ballot was cast in wintry New Hampshire. Bobby didn't need McCarthy's success to know how vincible LBJ was; reports he was getting a week before predicted the election day outcome almost to the number, and his spies in the McCarthy and Johnson camps had pushed him to jump in before the primary. Waiting until afterward multiplied the risk, as was apparent to any self-respecting snake or avenging father. By the time Bobby did announce, he had missed not only the New Hampshire primary but the deadlines to enter the other critical early primaries, and he had just three months to prepare for the remaining six. He had failed to build the staff, organization, or bankroll that he had put in place for Jack two months before his announcement in 1960 and five months before that campaign's first primary. Just two days before Bobby made his candidacy official, he was waiting to hear the results of one last butterfingered maneuver: a proposal that LBJ name a commission to reevaluate his Vietnam policy top to bottom. While he correctly predicted that the president would reject the overture, Bobby had made clear he wouldn't run if Johnson accepted it.*

Those machinations nearly buried his campaign before he could find his footing. The image of reluctant hero could have enhanced his allure, but instead his tag became one he abhorred: "Bobby-come-lately." Worse, he never even tried to get the true story out to critical journalists like Kempton and McGrory, convinced they wouldn't believe it and would see him as wishy-washy. But both had been his friends and might at least have seen that while his campaign kickoff was emotionally tortured and politically naïve, the last thing it was was ruthless.

---

* The proposal, the brainchild of Ted Sorensen and Mayor Richard Daley, was one Bobby advanced but had little faith in and that LBJ couldn't accept for fear it would look like a backroom deal to keep Bobby out and would brand America's Vietnam policy as a failure when the president didn't think it was. Still, Bobby was swept along to the point where he had his staff type two speeches, one saying that he would run for president, the other that he wouldn't.

THE OFFICIAL CAMPAIGN announcement on March 16 was half Jack
Kennedy, half Bobby. It was staged in the same ornate Senate Caucus
Room with granite columns and gold leaf where JFK had debuted his
candidacy eight years earlier, at the same age of forty-two.* Their opening sentences were identical. Both candidates appealed to the promise of
a nation whose byways they said they had traversed, listening to its citizens, learning its problems, and responding to its noblest yearnings. For
Jack, that meant "leadership" that answered "the hopes of the globe
around us for freedom and a more secure life"; for Bobby, it was exercis-
ing "our right to moral leadership of this planet." The similarities weren't
surprising, since half of Bobby's speechwriters had worked for Jack. Nor
were they accidental: The younger brother was running not just to complete the interrupted agenda of the older, but to restore the missing
magic. If JFK's death meant Paradise Lost, RFK's election promised Paradise Regained.

But this wasn't 1960 and Bobby wasn't Jack. America was a more
turbulent and uncertain place in 1968, with young people more rebellious and their parents more terrified. *The Magnificent Seven* and Chubby
Checker had given way to *The Graduate* and the Grateful Dead. And the
circumstances of the brothers' campaigns couldn't have had less in
common, as was clear to anyone paying attention to the words rather
than the atmospherics of his speech to a room packed with journalists,
staff, and nine of Bobby and Ethel's ten little Kennedys. "My decision
reflects no personal animosity or disrespect toward President Johnson,"
Bobby said, although the bid to unseat him surely reflected both. His
candidacy, he said, "would not be in opposition to [Gene McCarthy], but
in harmony," which no one believed and only served to remind everyone that he was climbing onto the Minnesotan's coattails. While he defined his vision more concretely and compellingly than Jack had—from
ending a disastrous war and addressing the crisis in the cities to remov-

---

* The Caucus Room is also where Bobby had listened to testimony against Joe McCarthy
during the Army-McCarthy hearings and faced off against Jimmy Hoffa. The room was so
associated with the Kennedys that in 2009, after Ted's death, it was renamed the Kennedy
Caucus Room.

ing a sadly out-of-touch president—he failed to point out that the war, the festering ghettos, and Lyndon Johnson were all part of Jack Kennedy's legacy.

For most candidates, the rollout of a presidential campaign is a high point of their lives. Not for Bobby. Nearly all the questions from reporters focused on the politics vis-à-vis McCarthy or LBJ instead of on his platform. Things didn't get any better on day two of the campaign, when he was on what should have been friendly ground at St. Patrick's Day parades in New York and Boston. For every shrieking teenage girl shouting "We're with you, Bobby," there were boos and chants of "coward" and "opportunist." The candidate maintained his composure and even his humor, dodging political questions and shouting to the throngs, "Happy St. Patrick's Day. I hope some of you bothered to have a drink." Then he did more evading on *Meet the Press*, saying again that "I want to cooperate in every way that I can with Senator McCarthy . . . both of us together will do better than one of us as individuals." He desperately wanted to change the subject, but neither angry McCarthy boosters nor the press would let him.

The fun part began the next day in Kansas. Bobby had reminded Walinsky that when writing his speech, he needed to bear in mind that they weren't in the East anymore, where bearded and braless anti-Vietnam activists would buy his no-holds-barred attacks on the president and the war. "These people," Bobby warned, "are very conservative." That made it all the sweeter when he gazed out at the 1,450 students jamming the seats and the rafters at the Kansas State field house. His maiden campaign address opened with humor, some of it ad-libbed. Maybe it was a mistake to say he was "reassessing" his stand on Vietnam, Bobby said, because "yesterday there was a man from the Internal Revenue Service out reassessing my home." Then he laid out for his heartland audience his primary reason for running. The Vietnam War "has divided Americans as they have not been divided since your state was called Bloody Kansas," Bobby said. "It must be ended, and it can be ended in a peace for brave men who have fought each other with a terrible fury, each believing that he alone was in the right. We have prayed to different gods, and the prayers of neither have been answered fully. Now, while there is still time for some of them to be partly answered, now is the time to stop." He was like a lion finally freed from his cage, and his listeners roared their approval. The enclosed arena amplified the noise, making it sound, in the words of one journalist, "as though it was inside Niagara Falls; it was like a soundtrack gone haywire." Stanley Tretick, a photographer for *Look* who'd been covering this Kennedy since he was a Rackets Committee investigator, momentarily forgot he was supposed to be nonaligned. "This is Kansas, fucking Kansas!" Tretick yelled to the senator's staff. "He's going all the fucking way!"

If his central campaign theme was No More Vietnams, a close second was unleashing a second War on Poverty. He explained how he'd do that to a record-setting crowd of twenty thousand at the University of Kansas, where the entire enrollment was just sixteen thousand and classes had been canceled for his appearance. He talked about starving Mississippians, desperate Indians, unemployed Appalachian coal miners, and others who belied the dream of America. This evolving Bobby saw the schism that mattered most now not as black against white but as rich versus poor. "We must," he told his overflow gallery, "begin to end the disgrace of this other America." They listened and they cheered, interrupting him thirty-eight times. "It doesn't matter what he says," said one man who was watching. "He could recite 'Mary's Little Lamb' and they'd still go wild."

Bobby and his advisers knew audiences would be easiest to assemble and friendliest on college campuses, even ones whose girls wore skirts that covered their knees and boys sported buzz cuts and neckties. Geographic choices seemed haphazard—from Kansas to Tennessee, Alabama to California—but the campaign had a point to make. "Any who seek high office this year must go before all Americans: not just those who agree with them, but also those who disagree," Bobby told nine thousand listeners at the University of Alabama, where he'd defied the governor and public opinion only five years before. "I come to Alabama to ask you to help in the task of national reconciliation." He was determined to show he was a national candidate for reasons of politics as well as principle. He couldn't afford to give up even on regions like the Deep South, where his name was mud, if he was to have a chance of winning the nomination. Bobby had concocted a methodical strategy for Jack in 1960—wooing delegates one by one in primaries and in person, outhustling and outflanking his opponents—but he didn't have time for that in 1968. He had entered the race late, and the president had the upper hand in that kind of insiders' game. His only hope was to make an explosive enough impact, in the remaining primaries and public appearances in other states, that the convulsions would be felt by the men who, in that pre-reform era, still manipulated the delegations. Governors, senators, big-city mayors, and union power brokers had to be convinced that Bobby was not just the Democrat most likely to win in November, but the one most likely to let them preserve their power. That was less a matter of delegate counting than of psychology.

Crowds were the most emphatic way to make that point, and the ones he drew were even bigger and more supercharged than in his uproarious campaign for Senate. In 1964, it took just one aide to steady him as he stood and waved from his convertible; now three were needed, with one holding his belt. Hands perpetually reached out not just to grab him but to collect a tie clasp or cufflink, a shoelace or even one of his London-made shoes.* Bloody knuckles and bruised knees had been the main physical toll in the earlier race. This time he was pulled so hard that he tumbled into the car door, splitting his lip and breaking a front tooth that required capping. He ended up on a regimen of vitamins and antibiotics to fight fatigue and infection. If he kept screaming, his doctors warned, his laryngitis would become permanent. Gone was the firm handshake he regarded as a sign of manliness, replaced by a limp mackerel at the end of a wrist too often tested. For most politicians, the challenge was to attract crowds; for Bobby, it was to survive them.

None of the other candidates in 1968 generated the polarized responses that Bobby did. For every voter who wanted a lock of hair, another wanted his scalp. And for each bumper sticker or poster urging RETURN TOUCH FOOTBALL TO THE WHITE HOUSE, there were ones scolding BOBBY AIN'T JACK, NONE OF THE WAY WITH RFK, and STERILIZE BOBBY

---

* In Los Angeles, a Mexican American teenager took both shoes and told a reporter, "I'm going to wear them to the senior prom this year, and then I'm going to have them bronzed." Bobby took such incidents in stride, putting his stockinged foot on the armrest of a reporter's chair and joking, "Don't tell me the people of this country don't love me. . . . On the other hand, perhaps all they wanted was a shoe." (Stein and Plimpton, *American Journey*, 300, and Clarke, *Last Campaign*, 248.)

KENNEDY. No presidential aspirant since Franklin Roosevelt had drawn that level of adulation—and loathing. George Wallace, other segregationists North and South, and the Teamsters had always hated him, as did most members of the Chamber of Commerce and the American Legion. But now he was arousing antipathy from Gene McCarthy's left-wing boosters who remembered his ties to Joe McCarthy and machine politics, along with right-wingers who felt he had sold out his cold warrior roots. "While I have a choice between Kennedy and McCarthy, it's the latter. Easily," the liberal commentator Nat Hentoff wrote in *The Village Voice.* "Kennedy, like his brother, will manufacture the illusion of change, co-opting as he goes." The conservative columnist Westbrook Pegler, a friend of Joe's, welcomed the chance that "some white patriot of the southern tier will splatter [Bobby's] spoonful of brains in public premises before the snow falls." So did Clyde Tolson, J. Edgar Hoover's protégé and companion, who in 1968 said at an FBI briefing, "I hope someone shoots and kills the son of a bitch." At a loss to explain the animus, Bobby kidded that "I'm the only candidate who has ever united business and labor, liberals and Southerners, party bosses and intellectuals. They're all against me."

It was no joke to reporters covering him. He set off particular alarms at the end of March, with a speech at the Greek Theatre in Los Angeles that Richard Goodwin had originally prepared for Gene McCarthy.* "For almost the first time," Bobby said, "the national leadership is calling upon the darker impulses of the American spirit—not, perhaps, deliberately, but through its action and the example it sets—an example where integrity, truth, honor, and all the rest seem like words to fill out speeches rather than guiding beliefs." It was what Bobby believed and had bottled up for the four and a half years since Jack's death, watching a successor he deemed unworthy. Whether or not his audience understood the gauntlet he was throwing down to the president, on everything from Vietnam to racial tensions, the national press did, and they felt it was rabble-rousing gone too far. "When a war becomes a flaming political

---

* Goodwin worked in the White House for JFK, stayed on as one of LBJ's prized speechwriters, then signed up with McCarthy when he was the only antiwar candidate. Nobody, including McCarthy, was surprised when he jumped to Bobby's campaign weeks after Bobby announced.

issue, the line between debate and demagoguery becomes a thin one," Robert Donovan wrote in the *Los Angeles Times*. "A candidate can easily be carried across it in the ardor of the fight."*

Bobby and his team never settled on how far they could go in criticizing the president because on March 31, a week after the Greek Theatre speech, the president dropped a bombshell near the end of his televised speech to the nation on Vietnam. "I shall not seek, and I will not accept," he said that Sunday evening, "the nomination of my party for another term as your president." In a single sentence he had changed history and upended the entire logic of the Kennedy campaign. Bobby was now a dragon slayer without a dragon. LBJ's withdrawal also took the war off the table as an issue when he gave as his reason the desire to devote himself to forging a peace. Johnson's likely replacement as the candidate of the Democratic establishment, Vice President Humphrey, was someone Bobby liked. LBJ had been musing about quitting for years, but neither Bobby nor anyone else had taken him seriously. "You're kidding" is all Bobby could say as he got the news after landing in New York. Then: "I wonder if he would have done it if I hadn't come in." Ethel was more transparent, breaking out a bottle of Scotch and announcing, "He never deserved to be president anyway."

The Old and New Bobbys collided at times like this. The angry insurgent yielded here to the backroom operator, as he telegraphed the president with praise for a move that "subordinates self to country and is truly magnanimous," then stayed up until three in the morning telephoning influential politicians who'd been in Johnson's camp. Two days later, Bobby and LBJ had a private conversation at the White House, the last between them and one of the more cordial. As always, both men were playacting. LBJ, upon getting Bobby's telegram days before, had told an adviser, "I won't bother answering that grandstanding little runt." Afterward he encouraged Humphrey to jump into the fray. Bobby, meanwhile, knew Johnson would do anything he could to undermine

---

* Richard Harwood, who was voicing similar concerns in *The Washington Post*, was reminded that Bobby still didn't like being second-guessed and that Ethel was as protective as ever. "When I went back to the airplane to take off on the next leg of the trip," recalled Harwood, "Ethel Kennedy came down the aisle with my story wadded up, and threw it in my face" (Whitehead, "Kennedys," *American Experience*).

his effort, which is why he or his aide brought to the White House meeting a scrambling device that thwarted LBJ's bid to tape it and had the president fuming over being outfoxed.*

If LBJ's withdrawal knocked the Kennedy team off its axis, Martin Luther King's assassination just four days later gave it an unexpected clarity of purpose. It happened on the evening of April 4, as Bobby was kicking off his campaign in Indiana for the first of the big presidential primary tests. He got word of the shooting as he was boarding a plane from Muncie to Indianapolis; by the time he landed, King was dead. An outdoor rally had been planned for the heart of Indianapolis's ghetto at Seventeenth and Broadway, but the mayor and chief of police told Bobby not to go, fearing for his safety and their city's.† Bobby wouldn't hear of it—"I'm going to go there," he said, "and that's it"—continuing on to the black neighborhood and asking his police escort to peel off just before he arrived. When an aide handed him scribbled notes he stuffed them into his pocket, preferring to extemporize but unsure what the nearly all-black crowd of a thousand knew about King's condition and what it would be open to hearing from a white politician.

"I'm only going to talk to you just for a minute or so this evening, because I have some—some very sad news for all of you . . . Martin Luther King was shot and was killed tonight," he said from the flatbed truck that served as his platform, his black overcoat pulled tight against the raw cold as his audience gasped as one: "No! No!" He continued, louder but his voice still tremulous, "For those of you who are black and are tempted to fill with—be filled with hatred and mistrust of the injustice of such an act, against all white people, I would only say that I can also feel in my

---

* In covertly taping their meeting, LBJ wasn't doing anything different from what JFK had done repeatedly. But he forgot that Bobby knew all about that kind of recording and, always suspicious of LBJ, had brought along an electronic device that would interfere with the signal. When he learned afterward that his tapes were blank, "Johnson exploded," his biographer said, "not because he needed to know the content of the meeting, which his aides Walt Rostow and Charles Murphy had dutifully captured through copious notes, but because he had been outflanked" (Updegrove, *Indomitable Will*, 272).

† The assistant chief of police, who was black, had a different message for Kennedy advance man Jim Tolan: Bobby was so well liked in the ghetto that he "could sleep all night in the middle of Seventeenth and Broadway and not be hurt" (James Tolan OH, June 27, 1969, 43, JFKL).

own heart the same kind of feeling. I had a member of my family killed, but he was killed by a white man. . . . What we need in the United States is not division; what we need in the United States is not hatred; what we need in the United States is not violence and lawlessness, but is love, and wisdom, and compassion toward one another, and a feeling of justice toward those who still suffer within our country, whether they be white or whether they be black. So I ask you tonight to return home, to say a prayer for the family of Martin Luther King—yeah, it's true—but more importantly to say a prayer for our own country, which all of us love—a prayer for understanding and that compassion of which I spoke."

His remarks, lasting barely five minutes, were pitch perfect. No one else had Bobby's credibility in talking about the pain of a loved one gunned down, or about racial reconciliation. It was the first time he had opened up that way about Jack and his listeners sensed it, wanting to comfort him even as he tried to soothe them. "To do it that night was an incredibly powerful and connective and emotionally honest gesture," said John Lewis, a Freedom Rider who knew the strains in Bobby's relationship with Martin and had taken heat for joining the Kennedy campaign. "I said to some of my friends, 'Dr. King may be gone but we still have Robert Kennedy.'" Not only did Bobby prove wrong the mayor and police chief, but the crowd—some carrying knives and homemade bombs—dispersed as he'd asked. Indianapolis would be hailed as an island of calm during that Holy Week Uprising that saw riots break out in more than a hundred U.S. cities. The way Kennedy held his audience spellbound would have been unimaginable for Johnson, Humphrey, or McCarthy. If the King murder and its aftermath put urban unrest back on the front burner of the 1968 campaign, it also reinforced that Bobby was the one Caucasian in America trusted by Negroes. As the signs in the ghetto said, KENNEDY WHITE BUT ALRIGHT.

Back at his hotel, Bobby couldn't unwind. Indianapolis mayor Richard Lugar, who had been waiting to make sure the presidential candidate made it out of the ghetto, recalls him as "shaken." Lewis said Bobby "broke down on a bed, lay there on his stomach and cried." This Kennedy brother also knew from experience and from asking her just what King's widow Coretta would need, and he arranged for a plane to bring her to Memphis to pick up her husband's body, then for three more telephones to be installed at her home that very night. He'd already canceled all campaign appearances except one the next day at the Cleveland City Club, which would be a plea for national calm. He'd met with a dozen local black leaders, with Charles Hendricks of the Radical Action Program conceding afterward that the senator was "completely sympathetic and understanding," and Bill Bell, who ran a youth center, adding that "the cat [Kennedy] was able to relax." Then Bobby prowled the hotel, checking in on aides who years later would recall his stream-of-consciousness remarks that offered a lens into a soul troubled by the nation's problems and his own. "You know," he said to one of them, "that fellow Harvey Lee Oswald, whatever his name is, set something loose in this country." He told another, "My God. It might have been me." The observation that stuck longest with those who heard it was, "You know, the death of Martin Luther King isn't the worst thing that ever happened in the world." Speechwriter Jeff Greenfield said, "I could not for the life of me understand that callousness until, of course, I realized he had been thinking of the death of his brother."

Over the next week Bobby made clear how, for the rest of his campaign and his life, he would be the racial healer that Lyndon Johnson wanted to be but couldn't, despite authoring a record number of civil rights laws. More than any of King's would-be successors, Kennedy inherited the slain leader's mantles of prophecy and advocacy. "Some look for scapegoats, others look for conspiracies, but this much is clear," Bobby told his mostly white and wealthy listeners in Cleveland. "Only a cleansing of our whole society can remove this sickness from our soul." Two days later he was back in Washington, where troops in armored carriers patrolled the riot-ravaged streets that he insisted on walking. "A crowd gathered behind us, following Bobby Kennedy. The troops saw us coming at a distance, and they put on their gas masks and got the guns at ready," recalled Walter Fauntroy, a minister and city councilor. "When they saw it was Bobby Kennedy, they took off their masks and let us through. They looked awfully relieved."

He was the unexpected center of attention again at King's funeral in Atlanta on April 9, to the dismay of McCarthy, Humphrey, Nixon, and Rockefeller, who were largely ignored, and LBJ, who didn't come. Andy Young, one of King's closest aides, who would later serve as Atlanta's mayor and U.S. ambassador to the United Nations, was a Kennedy skeptic until that day when Bobby met with him and other black leaders. "He said, 'You have to pick up the torch or the cross of the fallen hero and carry it on. There's no slowing down, there's no stopping,'" Young remembers fifty years later. "From that point on, I felt that this was a guy that I could give my life for, like I would have for Martin. I never felt that way about Gene McCarthy or McGovern or anybody else." To the Reverend Frederick D. Kirkpatrick, another civil rights icon, Bobby was the "blue-eyed soul brother."

Black leaders may have been impressed with Bobby's reaction to the King killing, but Eugene Pulliam wasn't. The son of Methodist missionaries and grandfather of future vice president Dan Quayle owned both papers in Indianapolis and others in Muncie and Vincennes. And he hated Democrats, especially Kennedys, and above all Bobby. It wasn't just their ideological divide but that unlike Jack, Bobby made zero effort to woo the hardscrabble newspaperman. He simply wouldn't and couldn't. Pulliam took his revenge through a stream of mocking editorials and cartoons, with headlines branding Bobby as UNFIT, UNSHORN, UNWANTED. Orders went out to the newsroom dictating "whenever Senator [Eugene] McCarthy comes to Indiana that we should give him as full coverage as possible—but this does not apply to a man named Kennedy."

Pulliam's naysaying was a window into why Indiana was an unfortunate choice for Bobby's first primary test. Its politics traditionally were right-wing enough that it once boasted the largest Ku Klux Klan chapter in America, and Indiana was where Robert Welch, Jr., had founded the John Birch Society. Jack lost the state to Nixon by more than two hundred thousand votes in 1960, and George Wallace captured close to 30 percent of the Democratic primary tally in 1964. In his primary, Bobby faced not just McCarthy, who had spent months organizing there, but also Roger Branigin, the governor, who four years before had won by the largest margin in Indiana history. Control of the tight-knit state party ensured Branigin the support of all but one of ninety-two county Democratic chairs, along with a war chest filled by what amounted to compulsory contributions from more than twenty thousand patronage workers. The governor had launched his campaign as a stand-in for LBJ, and he ended it as a placeholder for Humphrey or for his own pipe dream of talking himself onto the national ticket. The question in 1960 had been whether a Kennedy could buy Indiana. In 1968, it was whether Indiana would buy this Kennedy.

Bobby seemed oblivious to the challenge at first. In early April he was delivering the same catalog-of-pain speeches he had everywhere else and was buoyed by his huge crowds. But the scenes on the nightly news showed a long-haired, high-voiced candidate being mobbed by fans who were too young and too black for an electorate that was over 90 percent white. Indiana worried more about crime than poverty, and they wanted a father figure, not a fifth Beatle. So Kennedy changed course. By the time he returned to Indiana on April 22 for a pre-primary blitz, his barbers had a green light to crop closer. His schedulers added factories, farm towns, and whistle-stop trains and subtracted universities. He started referring to himself as "former chief law enforcement officer of the United States" instead of "former attorney general," and staffers stopped calling him Bobby, opting for the more grown-up Robert or Bob. His stump speeches focused on crime, hog prices, and his love of Kokomo, Vincennes, and other burgs whose names he could barely pronounce or remember. Even his clothes were toned down. Custom-fit suits from Lewis & Thomas Saltz Clothiers were replaced by one that, in the words of a *New York Times* reporter, "looked as if it had come off the rack of a small-town haberdasher."

Mission accomplished. His audiences now were mirroring the Hoosier State's mid-American electorate, as veteran chronicler Teddy White observed: "The matrons on their porches with their aprons, pin-curlers in hair; the old ladies of Indiana, with their white pinafores over blue dresses, teeter-tottering in tennis shoes to catch a glimpse of him and mothering him from afar. ('He looks so tired, the poor boy, why do they make him work so hard?') Blue-collar workingmen thickened the crowds, a rare sight in daytime political campaigning, and one saw them shyly wipe their hands on overalls or shirts before offering hands to the candidate to shake. One grasped for analogy: Along the highway, as the car swept along, he was, obviously, The Kennedy, of the Family and Blood Royal, the Prince Coming to Town. In a working-class district he was Robin Hood. At night, in such places as Gary and South Bend on the final weekend, he was the Prince, Robin Hood and the Pied Piper all combined."

Some journalists worried that after tailoring his messages to his galleries, he now sounded more like Barry Goldwater than Bobby Kennedy, a charge that resonated with younger staffers. There was no denying that he was a politician, not a prelate, but he was far from the prototypical panderer. Anyone who knew him realized he'd been a law-and-order man since his days chasing down racketeers and mafiosi, just as he'd made Republican-style free enterprise a centerpiece of his Bedford-Stuyvesant experiment. Rural whites "don't want to listen to what the blacks want and need. You have to get them listening by talking about what they're interested in, before you can start trying to persuade them about other matters," Bobby said in siding with his older, more pragmatic advisers. Yet he knew how issues like crime could be used as a wedge between blacks and whites, poor and rich. So he made sure that every speech on crime included a call for justice, and that what he said to chambers of commerce differed in the sequence but not the elements from what he said in the slums.*

Simple evenhandedness was not nearly enough, however. He had come too far to revert to his Bad or Old incarnations, and he'd never learned to mask his emotions. That meant making his audiences squirm. He told college kids everywhere he went that they could change the world, so why the hell weren't they? He warned eight hundred medical students at Indiana University that they'd have to foot the bill for caring for the poor. As boos rang out, a doctor in training asked whether the senator would end medical students' cherished draft deferments. "The way things are going here today, probably yes," he said, smiling but serious. It happened again at a luncheon of Civitans, a men's service club. As his audience chewed on Salisbury steaks, he took the requisite questions on gun control and daylight saving time. Then he turned to his biggest issue—"*American* children, starving in *America*"—and asked,

---

* Asked by a campaign reporter for his views on capital punishment, Bobby said, "I'm against it—in all cases." Reminded that he'd held substantially different views as attorney general, he quipped, "That was before I read Albert Camus." Joking aside, said Frank Mankiewicz, Bobby "had no fear of being accused of flip-flopping, of changing positions once firmly held, or of having earlier been on another side of an issue. He saw, in fact— whether the issue was capital punishment or Vietnam—not vice but virtue in being first on one side, then on the other. . . . That's why so many hated him—and why so many of us loved him" (Mankiewicz, *So As I Was Saying,* 190–92).

"Do you know, there are more rats than people in New York City?" Hearing guffaws, this senator who was kept up nights by images of the hungry children he'd met in the Mississippi Delta grew grim: *"Don't . . . laugh."* Thomas Congdon, Jr., an editor at *The Saturday Evening Post* who had started as a Kennedy cynic, attended the lunch and was struck by what he witnessed: "He was telling them precisely the opposite of what they wanted to hear." It was demagoguery in reverse.

As the candidate was searching for a voice that was sensitive and at the same time genuine, his ad hoc collection of aides was coalescing into a powerhouse of an organization. At its center was Gerard Doherty, the Massachusetts operative who'd parachuted in with an entourage of Vassar girls, Ivy League lawyers from K Street and Wall Street, and other honorary Kennedys.* Onto that unsteady base Team Kennedy grafted thousands of Hoosiers who had resisted joining Branigin's army of professionals and McCarthy's college corps. Back in Washington the campaign set up a "boiler room" like the one in 1960, where female partisans quietly tracked, state by state, everything from the latest count of convention delegates to the allocation of bumper stickers. Money helped. In early April the campaign couldn't afford a mimeograph machine; by early May it was commissioning opinion polls, TV ads, chartered planes with specially stocked galleys, sound trucks, cases of wine, and top-of-the-line hotels and rental cars charged to Papa Joe's credit cards. Cash— tens of thousands of dollars—showed up in suitcases and shopping bags, delivered from the Park Agency office in Manhattan by Kennedy relatives or friends. Richard Corbett, Steve Smith's assistant, was supposed to be keeping track, but when nobody stayed on budget, Corbett appealed to Bobby. "What is the presidency worth?" asked the candidate, whose personal wealth by then was estimated at $10 million. "We will spend whatever is necessary." Rose took the same attitude when one reporter too many quizzed her about buying elections: "It's our money and we're free to spend it any way we please. It's part of this campaign business. If you have money, you spend it to win."

---

* These so-called honorary Kennedys ranged from Bobby's old Justice Department staff to people who'd worked on Jack's campaigns, especially in 1960. "They were awful good to us in '60" was a familiar Bobby refrain, and one that saw him embrace a lot of political hacks who made his current staffers cringe.

Bobby spent the earliest hours of election day doing what he often did, grabbing dinner with staff and journalists at the nearest greasy spoon, in this case Sam's Attic in Indianapolis. Boyish no more, he looked like the wreck he was after a grueling first primary battle—lines on his forehead deepened to crevasses, puffy eyes bloodshot and haunted rather than blue and hostile, and skin blotched like an older man's. He'd rub his hands over his face in a fruitless bid to banish the exhaustion. Yet campaigning was also restorative. "I loved the faces here in Indiana," he told his supper mates, "on the farmers, on the steelworkers, on the black kids." After a couple of hours' sleep he relieved the stress of waiting by quarterbacking a football game on the front lawn of his Holiday Inn, playing tough enough that an aide twisted his ankle and a journalist was sidelined with a bloody nose.

By nightfall Gene McCarthy's nose would be bloodied, too, with Bobby scoring a bigger victory than anyone in his camp had hoped at the start. He took 42.3 percent of the vote—compared with Branigin's 30.7 and McCarthy's 27—and won nine of eleven congressional districts along with fifty-six of the state's sixty-three delegates. Kennedy beat Branigin in his home county, city, and precinct; doubled McCarthy's take among Catholics, laborers, and younger voters; and won every substantial municipality except the college towns of Bloomington and Evansville. In black districts, he scored a crushing 85 percent of the votes, on the same night that he thrashed Humphrey nearly two to one in the primary in predominantly black Washington, D.C. He also carried the seven largest counties in Indiana where Wallace, the racial-backlash candidate from Alabama, had done best in 1964. Bobby did less well in white precincts of Gary and in upper-income suburbs and small towns, where his opponents benefited from Republican crossovers. TV analysts focused on the negative, and it was true that his rivals had won three of every five votes cast. But it also was true that Bobby had trumped McCarthy's showing in New Hampshire—42.3 percent versus 42.2—which the television networks and everyone else had scored as an epic triumph. Most newspaper reporters were more upbeat. Kennedy's chief goal, David Broder wrote in *The Washington Post*, "is to expand the electorate—by bringing out many ordinary non-voters—on the sound theory that those additional voters will give a big margin—to the man who has captivated their interest. In Indiana—despite the obstacles of a late start and strong opposition—that formula worked to perfection."

Watching the televised results that night from his headquarters at the Sheraton-Lincoln Hotel, Kennedy heard McCarthy say that who came in first, second, or third wasn't what counted. Really? "That's not what my father told me," Bobby said, laughing as he talked back to the TV set. "I always thought it was better to win. I learned that when I was about two." But he also offered a sober reading of the voters' verdict: "I really have a chance now, just a chance, to organize a new coalition of Negroes, and working-class white people, against the union and party Establishments."

His day wasn't quite done. From the first he had been envious of McCarthy's legions of college supporters, who he joked were the idealistic A students as compared to his campus dopes. He was sure they'd have been with him if he had gotten in earlier, and no matter how many delegates he won, he never got over their rejection. So when he saw two young McCarthy campaigners that night at the Indianapolis airport, he had to engage: "I wonder why so many of you bright, eager young students are here for McCarthy." It was nearly midnight, but all three had to wait for an early morning flight, and their conversation went on for two hours at an airport restaurant on a night when he'd had no rest but couldn't turn off his motor. "He was puzzled that anybody could think that McCarthy could be a good president," recalls Taylor Branch, one of the student pair, who later wrote the definitive biography of Martin Luther King, Jr. Bobby told them he accepted responsibility for helping get us into Vietnam "and that's why I want to get us out." He said he knew part of his attraction was just being a Kennedy, adding, "I can't help what my name is, all I can do is try to do the best with it for the country." He didn't change the mind of either McCarthy backer, "but we were profoundly impressed, so much so that after we had hashed all this out forever and told him how much we admired him," Branch remembers, "we decided we didn't say it, you know, respectfully enough. So we stayed up and wrote him a long letter . . . then walked across and dropped it off at his airport motel."

THE BEST JUDGES of a candidate's merits or character are not the opposition aides who get paid to find him lacking. His own staffers are even less credible, since they're already adoring, and crowds are around only long enough to hear a single speech or shake a hand. The best arbiters are the national political reporters who are on hand around the clock, day after day, on buses, trains, and airplanes, parsing any discrepancies between what the aspirant says in farm states and urban ones, to black audiences and white, and when his poll numbers are up and down. No group of journalists is more battle-hardened except ones who cover real wars. These so-called boys on the bus—and most were still male in 1968—generally had been around long enough to have heard every political promise, seen every permutation of pandering and strong-arming, and lost whatever starry eyes or infatuations they might have started with.

Bobby couldn't charm them the way JFK had with his intellect, his wit, or his sleek and sophisticated wife. It wasn't his style, either, to intimidate reporters or buy their favor the way Joe did. Nor did he have his brother Ted's disarming way of passing on kudos not just for fawning stories but for ones in which he was skewered, then inviting the reporter in for a Chivas and soda. What Bobby could do, in a manner that still amazes those who were on that campaign trail, was make rhinoceros-hided scribes fall in love with him to an extent not seen since Franklin Roosevelt or perhaps his distant cousin Teddy.

Helen Dudar, a prolific reporter at the *New York Post*, was won over when Bobby took time in Nebraska to visit the Beatrice State Home for the mentally defective. "The superintendent twittered: 'Would you like to see the wards?'" Dudar wrote. "Kennedy, in the flat, imperious voice he uses for people who fawn, replied: 'I would like to see the children.'* We went to the nursery floor. . . . Lying inert in a playpen was a hydroce-

---

* Labels mattered to Bobby. On the one hand, he was one of the least politically correct figures in politics, to the point of offending the faint-hearted. Yet he saw that calling impaired youngsters "wards," as opposed to "children," affected the way they were treated. So it was, said Frank Mankiewicz, that Bobby in the mid-1960s became the first white elected official to use the word "black" at a time when that was what African American activists preferred, and when most white politicians favored "Negro," "colored," or other terms that were coming to be seen as degrading (Mankiewicz, *So As I Was Saying,* 187).

phalic, a child with a head the size of a basketball. Kennedy leaned in and scratched its stomach for a while. I cannot tell what its response was, because I found I could not look at that child. Then he patted a vacant-eyed little girl who grabbed his hand and began chewing its fingers. He let her gnaw for a while. Finally he picked her up and carried the slobbering child as he walked about touching other children—a vegetabloid creature slumped unseeing in a chair, a baby with a grapefruit-sized lump on its head that made it look two-headed, all those pathetic grotesques hidden away from the world, suddenly and compulsively objects of Kennedy's charity and compassion."

"He can be tough, demanding, rude, icy," added Dudar. "But to see him with children is always to wonder how exactly he came to be known as ruthless."

Kristi Witker experienced that tenderness herself. She was getting started at her first job in journalism—working for *American Heritage,* which planned to publish a book on RFK—and the 1968 campaign was her first taste of politics. "Waving my driver's license in a press-cardy sort of way," she talked her way to the front of the hall in New Jersey where Bobby was speaking, then onto the press plane. As she rehearsed how she'd introduce herself to the candidate—"Er—uh, Senator uh—Kennedy, I'm Kristi Witker, and I'm writing a book about you"—she felt a tap on her shoulder: "'Er—uh, excuse me,' a voice said, 'my name is—uh—Robert Kennedy.'" That "really broke the ice. . . . I thought he was wonderful. Absolutely wonderful. And the press corps did, too. Everybody covering him was in love with him. . . . He really believed what he was saying. I think you could have given him a lie-detector test and he would have passed it with flying colors. I don't think any of the others could do that."

Witker didn't have earlier campaigns to compare this one to, but the Pulitzer Prize winner David Halberstam and the legendary muckraker Jack Newfield did. Neither man was close to a pushover, but both were sufficiently beguiled that they wrote books about Bobby that read like valentines. "He would tell you you were full of shit," said Newfield. "I have never found another national politician with his authenticity, his candor, his willingness to express emotions, and his unwillingness to behave in a conventional political manner." Halberstam called him "the most interesting figure in American politics, not only because he was a Kennedy, not only because so much of his education had taken place in the public eye—it could be traced by putting together film clips of this decade—but primarily because he was a transitional figure in a transitional year."

It wasn't just them, and it wasn't always expressed as a panegyric. Bobby had taken to paraphrasing the now famous lines by the playwright George Bernard Shaw—"Some people see things as they are and say why? I dream things that never were and say, why not?"—to signal reporters when he was ending a speech and they should run for the press bus.* Journalists reciprocated by composing an eight-stanza ode to Bobby during their train trip in Indiana that retraced the famed "Wabash Cannonball." They called their parody "The Ruthless Cannonball," and they recited it to the candidate as the trip neared its end:

> *Oh, listen to the speeches*
> *that baffle, beef, and bore*
> *As he waffles through the woodlands*
> *and slides along the shore.*
> *He's the politician*
> *who's touched by one and all.*
> *He's the demon driver*
> *of The Ruthless Cannonball . . .*
> *So here's to Ruthless Robert*
> *May his name forever stand*
> *To be feared and genuflected at*
> *by pols across the land.*
> *Ho Chi Minh is cheering,*
> *and though it may appall,*
> *He's whizzing to the White House*
> *on The Ruthless Cannonball.*

When they finished there was a tense moment of silence, with nobody sure that Bobby would see the humor. He did, addressing the authors

---

* One time he was more explicit, closing a speech with "As George Bernard Shaw used to say, 'run for the bus'" (Halberstam, *Unfinished Odyssey*, 70).

with a poker face: "As George Bernard Shaw once said—the same to you, buddy."*

Not all journalists were joking when they lampooned him. The *Daily News* in Welch, West Virginia, editorialized that "Bobby Kennedy is: un-invited, unwanted, undesirable, unethical, un-American, unfit, unpre-pared, unshorn, unpopular, unloved and overrated." William Loeb, the unyieldingly conservative publisher of the New Hampshire's *Manchester Union Leader*, wrote that Bobby was running for "Dictator of the United States" and that "once installed in the White House, no one and no group of people would be safe from him!" On the other end of the political spectrum, neither Murray Kempton nor Mary McGrory, old RFK and JFK allies, had forgiven him for his oafish entrance into the campaign. Kempton penned a piece in *The New Republic* explaining "Why I'm for McCarthy." McGrory wrote that "Kennedy is not in the large sense a uni-fying candidate because of the deep divisions within himself."

As for his journalist fans, few came from or could relate to an arena of privilege like Bobby's. But they were show-me types, and they could see that this son of Florida's Gold Coast and Massachusetts's Cape Cod was genuinely devoted to an underclass few politicians noticed. Most politi-cal reporters had despaired of finding a liberal with backbone or a con-servative who cared. Bobby was that tough liberal—or humane conservative. "There was something in him that reminded me of some-thing that I had in myself, maybe long ago," says James Stevenson of *The New Yorker.* Norman Mailer was likewise "excited by precisely [Kenne-dy's] admixture of idealism plus willingness to traffic with demons, ogres, and overlords of corruption." Bobby had seen as much of Ameri-ca's dark side as any hard-bitten hack, yet he remained a patriot and an optimist. He started out thinking he could censor the press and ended up listening to and learning from its practitioners. He still reamed out re-porters for stories he felt were overly critical, but now he apologized af-

---

* Most journalists already knew how wry his humor was, although it was situational rather than telling man-goes-into-a-bar jokes. When his campaign plane had problems in Indiana, Bobby turned to reporters and teased, "I don't want to seem immodest, but if we don't make it you fellows are all going to be in small print." When he saw a sign saying NIXON IS THE ONE, he teased the crowd, "Nixon's the one *what?*" (Blackburn, "Personal Thoughts"; *Unfinished Odyssey*, 68; and Mudd, *Place To Be*, 236.)

terward. He made journalists identify with this man who had everything, made them believe, as the columnist Jules Witcover wrote, "that to deny him, at forty-two, the leadership of the most powerful nation in the world would be unjust." The longtime CBS newsman Dan Rather was mistrustful at first but became a believer. Bobby, he says, seemed "tough enough to get elected, and smart and sensible enough to implement what he'd promised to do."

The Nashville Tennessean's John Seigenthaler and Bill Kovach were disciples. Both considered journalism their religion and spent their careers putting politicians in the spotlight, and often in the slammer—but for Bobby, they took a rare hiatus to work on his campaign. "It was the soul of this man," says Kovach. "I have never before, nor since, seen a politician with that core of feeling for other people, especially people who needed his help." Robert Scheer of *Ramparts* helped with speechwriting. Jack Mallon of the *New York Daily News* acted as informal liaison with the labor movement. Roger Mudd became a regular guest at Hickory Hill. All sacrificed their journalistic chastity, but Bobby was worth it. Harrison Salisbury had had few good words for this third Kennedy son when he was reporting for *The New York Times*, but by 1968, when he was an editor overseeing the paper's political coverage, he had become a convert. "The new Bobby was a proud man but a humble one. He was no longer a capo. He was a member of the human race, a man of doubts and uncertainties. This was not the Bobby Old Joe had created in his image," said Salisbury. "Gone was the smart aleck. Gone was the political trickster. Gone was the shallow sureness. Robert F. Kennedy had come of age. . . . I could hardly wait until November. I had not the slightest doubt that Robert F. Kennedy would win."

The journalist whose U-turn resonated most with fellow writers, and with Bobby, was Richard Harwood of *The Washington Post*. Harwood had enlisted in the Marines at seventeen and had scars on his back attesting to his role in the bloody World War II battle to capture Iwo Jima. He brought the same icy resolve to his political coverage, with politicians dubbing him "Black Death Harwood" for fear of what he'd do to them if he smelled malfeasance. With Bobby, he smelled a demagogue on the campaign stump and a bully on the football field, and he shared his doubts with *Post* readers. "I had known Bobby Kennedy slightly prior to the 1968 campaign and found him not to my liking," Harwood said. "That is one of the reasons Ben Bradlee, the *Post*'s executive editor, assigned me to cover his campaign. He thought I would not be seduced, so to speak." Looking back, Harwood acknowledged that Bradlee "was wrong. By the end of Bobby's campaign, I was so fond of him that I asked to be relieved of the assignment."

What turned Harwood around? "We were seduced," he explained, "because [Bobby's] circle was so big that it took us in. It was impossible to draw lines and stay outside. . . . By the time of the Indiana primary— very early in the game—we talked about the Kennedy airplane as 'The Mother Ship.' The airport motel at Indianapolis became 'The Mother Inn.' Those are family concepts which get back to the concept of the Circle. He brought us in by the qualities of his life. . . . A couple of lines from the *Tales of Canterbury* [come] to mind. They were about the poor Parson who had a great gift: '*To drawen folk to hevene by fairnessse, By good ensample; this was his bisynesse.*' That was Bob Kennedy. He did not draw us all to heaven because a lot of us were not capable of that. But he left the good example and made all of us want to try. He drew the circle to take us in and that is why, prodigal or no, we always ached to go home to The Mother Ship."

Elizabeth Drew, then a Washington correspondent for *The Atlantic Monthly*, puts it more concisely: "He was a flame the moths couldn't resist."

———

THE PRIMARY AFTER Indiana was Nebraska, where Kennedy went head-to-head with McCarthy, with no favorite son or other active candidate muddying the contest. Nebraska was an even less promising venue for Bobby than Indiana, with fewer blacks, more farmers, and closer proximity to McCarthy's home in Minnesota. Of all fifty states, Nebraska was where John Kennedy lost to Richard Nixon by the widest margin in 1960. But the same magical connection that JFK developed in 1960 with the coal miners of West Virginia, Bobby forged eight years later with the farmers of Nebraska. One day he was giving a talk and the wind blew away his text. Bobby: "There goes my farm program." His listeners loved it. In Wahoo, on the last day of campaigning, Bobby pointed to a theater marquee reading THE HAPPIEST MILLIONAIRE and told his audience, "I hope that's what you will make me tomorrow." More smiles, from the crowd and the candidate. "There was a kind of communication between him and, you know, almost Grant Wood kind of characters in a sense— leather skinned, very hard working people, very traditional values . . . the *last* people in the world you would imagine Robert Kennedy to have any relationship with," said Jeff Greenfield, an RFK speechwriter who was there. Farmers had "the sense that he was somehow not a part of all those gray, faceless, three-button-suited, crew-cut people that were re- sponsible for a lot of what had driven them crazy."

They were right. Strip away the Kennedy name and privileges, and Bobby really was more like the Americans whose votes he sought than were the professorial Gene McCarthy, the introverted Richard Nixon, and the exasperatingly exuberant Hubert Humphrey. Bobby was smart but as anti-intellectual as any redneck. He relished sports, lacked pa- tience, and loved God. His contradictions were in full view. Pulled by compassion to help the dispossessed, he was tempered by pragmatism and able to see the limits of government. He was less of a conventional politician than McCarthy, even if the college whiz kids couldn't see it, and he offered a palette of bold colors inaccessible to the pallid Hum- phrey and Nixon. When he was bored, his facial expression showed it, the same as when he was angry. What tied everything together for Bobby, as for most adults in this most youthful of nations, was his being crazy about kids. They sensed his magic and loved him back. At his best, the way he was in Nebraska, Bobby Kennedy was open and uncomplicated. And, for the first time in this long campaign, he was having fun.

The proof of the chemistry he'd created came at the polls. On May 14, an impressive 51.7 percent of Democratic Cornhuskers pulled their le- vers for Bobby, compared with McCarthy's 31.2 percent, Humphrey's 7.4 percent, and 5.6 percent for LBJ. That made the New Englander two for two in the Midwest, against his Midwestern rivals.

Those early primaries reinforced how irreconcilable the differences were between the Democrats' two antiwar candidates. Bobby appealed to the blacks and blue-collar whites who lived on either side of the rail- road tracks; McCarthy supporters were suburbanites who drove their cars to catch a train. Bobby was Harold Hill, the Music Man, strutting at the head of a raucous crowd. McCarthy was Marshal Will Kane, striding down a lonely street at high noon. Everything the Kennedy campaign did was oversized, from its boiler room operation to the payouts to poll workers at the going rate of twenty-five dollars; McCarthy did less wooing of delegates and paid his volunteers in peanut butter sandwiches. Each played fast and loose with facts—Kennedy about McCarthy's voting record, McCarthy about Kennedy's part in the Bay of Pigs and Dominican interventions—but Bobby relished hardball politics, whereas McCarthy was easily bruised. No wonder each ended up hating the other and, if he couldn't be the nominee, preferred that the prize go to Vice President Humphrey, an avatar of Old Politics and (out of loyalty if not conviction) of the very Vietnam policies that made McCarthy and Kennedy challenge their sitting president.*

One way Bobby renewed himself and his sense of purpose was by going home—to Hickory Hill on Sundays and to Hyannis Port as often as he could. Jackie sometimes made an appearance at the Kennedy compound, although she and Bobby had grown less close and she was being wooed by the Greek billionaire Aristotle Onassis, whom her brother-in-law detested. Jackie was a big booster of Bobby's campaign, however, and at one family gathering she let her enthusiasm brim over: "Won't it be wonderful when we get back in the White House?" Ethel was normally gracious about sharing her husband, but not this time: "What do you mean 'we'?"†

Bobby visited his parents before heading west for the next primaries in Oregon and California, and he briefed them on the campaign. Afterward, as Joe's nurse recalled, "he hugged Mrs. Kennedy and said, 'How will you feel being the mother of two presidents? That makes you quite a girl, doesn't it?' . . . He bent over to kiss his father good-bye and added, 'I'm

---

* McCarthy suggested early on that if Bobby would drop out in 1968, the Minnesotan would agree to serve just one presidential term, then clear the way for Kennedy to succeed him. Almost as absurd was Bobby's proposal that if McCarthy would drop out, he could serve as secretary of state in a Kennedy administration.

† The antipathy between the sisters-in-law was legendary and true. Jackie called Ethel a "baby-making machine—wind her up and she becomes pregnant." Ethel teased Jackie about her dream of being a ballet dancer: "With those clodhoppers of yours? You'd be better off going in for soccer." (Martin, *Seeds of Destruction*, 375–76, and Adler, *Eloquent Jacqueline Kennedy*, 51.)

going to win this one for you.' [Bobby] stood up straighter than I had ever seen him. Usually his shoulders were hunched over with his head tucked between them, but as he stood before his father, he pulled himself to his full height. Mr. Kennedy held out his hand and they said good-bye with a tight, lingering grip."

Oregon was McCarthy country. The Minnesota senator had a six-month head start there, and he had used the time to raise money and build support from organized labor as well as college students, and from Democratic leaders along with independents and Republicans. The mayor of Portland, the state's biggest city, had never forgiven Bobby for investigating racketeering there a decade before. Neither had the state's mightiest union, the Teamsters. Every media image of Bobby hit the wrong note—diving into the icy Pacific in May, which was nothing unusual for a hearty New Englander but constituted showboating to locals who didn't wade in until August; being mobbed by blacks and Chicanos in neighboring California, which didn't play well in a place where minorities were just 2 percent of the population; pushing for federal gun controls, which were anathema to the many Oregonians convinced it was their God-given right to pack a pistol or shotgun; and being lambasted by Drew Pearson for ordering phone taps five years before on Martin Luther King, Jr., which offended a population passionate about their civil liberties. Oregon Democrats were more turned on by McCarthy's courage in New Hampshire than by any dream of restoring Camelot. They also were better off and more contented with their lot than most of America, with high employment, getaways in the mountains, and few of the urban troubles that were the rationale for the Kennedy candidacy. "This state is like one giant suburb," Bobby said ten days before the primary. "Let's face it, I appeal best to people who have problems."

Those obstacles might have been surmountable if he had run a smarter campaign. It was a Kennedy precept never to let locals make critical decisions, yet he'd vested leadership of the Oregon campaign in Oregon congresswoman Edith Green, who banished from the state Joe Dolan, Dave Hackett, and other first-string Kennedy organizers. A Kennedy commandment he did follow was not sharing his spotlight with a lesser-known opponent, forgetting how misguided that had proved in New York, where he took flak for ducking a debate with then Senator

Ken Keating. He repeatedly refused McCarthy's offer to debate in Oregon, creating the appearance that he was running scared. The root cause of his dilemma was the same one he'd faced early in the New York race: Bobby the candidate needed but didn't have a second in command who could shift tactics on the run and stay focused on the master strategy the way Bobby the campaign manager had for Jack.

A single moment captured all that was going wrong in the Beaver State. The Sunday morning before the primary, both candidates were campaigning in a mountainside park above Portland. A McCarthy speechwriter noticed Bobby's press bus and ran up to his boss yelling, "Kennedy's up there!" While the McCarthy caravan slowly turned to follow Bobby in hopes of a face-to-face confrontation, the young aide, Jeremy Larner, ran ahead to Kennedy's convertible. "Senator McCarthy is coming. Why don't you stick around and have a talk with him?" Bobby snapped back, "Isn't that too baaad!" and then, without looking back, ordered his driver to floor it. The TV crews caught it all, with Larner yelling in Bobby's wake, "Coward! Chicken!" and McCarthy pulling up and shaking hands with reporters abandoned by the retreating Kennedy.

But even Larner later acknowledged there was more to the scene than TV viewers had sensed. Standing next to Bobby, he'd detected "a look of exquisite hurt. . . . He wasn't surprised by the act itself. That wasn't what hurt him. He would have done the same himself, had done the same or worse many times and without hesitation. . . . The hurt look was no cry for pity: it was the registration that something had gone terribly wrong in our fight for the territory. . . . And what did I know, what did I really know, that made me so eager to beat him?" Two candidates who should have been joining forces to take on the establishment had somehow ended up duking it out with each other.*

On election Tuesday, McCarthy capitalized on Bobby's retreat and other stumbles, beating him by a decisive 44 to 38 percent. The press trumpeted it as the first time a Kennedy had ever lost a bid for office, which was only partly true. They had won fifteen straight contested pri-

---

* Larner is one of a series of high-level McCarthy aides who say today that they might have defected to Bobby, because he stood a better chance not just of winning but of keeping the promises he was making (Author interview with Jeremy Larner).

maries and general elections dating back to Jack's first run for Congress in 1946. But JFK had lost his ill-advised try for the vice presidential nomination at the 1956 Democratic National Convention, which analysts left out in their bids to make Bobby feel miserable. It worked. More even than his brothers, Bobby shared Joe's worship of the god of winning. He also understood that how he handled the loss would say even more about him than his victories, and he did it without rationalization. First he sent the winner a congratulatory telegram of the kind he hadn't received when he'd won earlier contests. He also publicly conceded that his campaign had taken "a serious blow . . . I've lost. I'm not one of those who think that coming in second or third is winning." Last, he took aside his chief student organizer in Oregon and said, "I'm sorry I let you down."

The loss was jolting but at the same time liberating. Defeat provided another moment of learning for Bobby. Just as Jack's coming up short at the Democratic convention in 1956 made him refocus on the race that really mattered—for the top spot in 1960—so Bobby's defeat a dozen years later reminded him why he was running and what it took to win. Playing it safe hadn't worked and hadn't been fun. He made clear a day after the Oregon vote that he would debate McCarthy on national TV, a reversal of his earlier insistence that he would agree only if Humphrey did. He announced he'd quit the race unless he won the following week's primary in California, which set up the kind of all-or-nothing odds that Bobby liked. He reminded supporters that his campaign was not the juggernaut everyone had assumed and reiterated that he could win only with their help. He also let journalists know, without having to say it, that this Kennedy might be a bit more fragile and less ruthless than they'd imagined, leading even critic Mary McGrory to concede that he had met defeat "with grace."

———

At stake in California was less whether Bobby could best Gene McCarthy than whether the nation was ready for this Kennedy as its president. The Golden State had recently surpassed New York as the most populous state, and it had always been the most representative demographically and politically. It was going through the same agitation in 1968 as the rest of the nation, over a war that still roiled, riot-torn cities, and tensions between the old and new in everything from electioneering to hair-styles. The question was which presidential aspirant could restore both peace and harmony. Was it law-and-order types like California's governor, Ronald Reagan, and its former senator, Richard Nixon? Or could it be Bobby Kennedy, whose fans imagined him reconciling warring factions here and in Vietnam even as his haters saw him as a juvenile delinquent in a suit? It had come down to a battle not just between right and left, but between despair and hope.

Half of his California advisers implored him to tone things down. Hold fewer rallies in the cities with less crowd frenzy, they said, and focus more on the white working-class Democrats who were escaping to the exurbs. Bobby might have given that same advice in 1960, and he had taken it the month before in Indiana, but not now. He might go down in California, but he'd go down swinging, not playing it safe the way he had in Oregon. "The issues," he told one journalist, "are more important than me now." In the last weeks he imported longtime confidants including his brother-in-law Steve Smith and his Justice Department friend John Seigenthaler, displacing although not replacing Jesse Unruh and the Californians who had been in charge. He also fell back on his instincts, doing more, not less, barnstorming in strongholds of Mexican Americans, urban blacks, wage-earning whites, and other elements of the coalition into whose hands he was thrusting his fate. His fist was once again pounding his open palm, as fans in Los Angeles yelled, "Sock it to 'em, Bobby!" He sounded his new theme at a reception at the Beverly Hilton Hotel: "If I died in Oregon, I hope Los Angeles is Resurrection City." In Oakland, at a secret midnight session with Black Panthers and other minority activists, he listened to them vent in a way he hadn't been able to with James Baldwin and friends in 1963. "These meetings aren't very attractive," Bobby said. "They need to tell people off. They need to tell me off." When that bawling-out got especially nasty, a black Kennedy aide tried to intervene, but the candidate wouldn't let him: "This is between them and me."

All of that served as a prelude to what was supposed to be the big event: an hour-long nationally broadcast TV face-off with McCarthy just three days before the primary. Such appearances had always been Bobby's Achilles' heel. He lacked Jack's quiet grace and McCarthy's poetic intellectualism. He did best in a freewheeling give-and-take, worst in this format, which was more like a joint press conference. But just by showing up he quelled the criticism over ducking debates. He made his case to the thirty-two million Americans who tuned in, most of whom scored the encounter a draw and a yawn, given how often the candidates agreed. There was, however, one exchange that registered. McCarthy, who'd never shown any passion for urban issues, made a compelling pitch for breaking down ghettos so blacks could live where the jobs were and America wouldn't end up with a "practical apartheid." Bobby's Bedford-Stuyvesant approach was just the opposite, acknowledging the dangers of segregation but recognizing that, for now, it was vital to bring good jobs and better housing to where blacks actually resided. Yet the way he put it this time was different. "[You] say that you are going to take ten thousand black people and move them into Orange County," Bobby argued, putting words into his opponent's mouth. "Kick those people out, put them in the suburbs where they can't afford the housing, where their children can't keep up with schools, and where they don't have the skills for the jobs. It's just going to be catastrophic." It was coded phrasing designed less to defend displaced blacks than to scare McCarthy's suburban voters with the specter of an invasion from the ghetto. It also was a rare display—in this phase of his campaign and life—of the bareknuckled Bobby of old.

The day after the debate, Bobby visited Orange County, which he had mentioned the night before and was Nixon's birthplace. His touch this time was light as he asked his audience at a strawberry festival, "Will you all remember to vote for me on Tuesday? Promise? ['Yes, Yes.'] Think of all my children. Think that if I lose, think of all the little tears that will come down all their cheeks." Then he took the six of those children who were with him to Disneyland. Their favorite memory is of the souvenir shop, where they passed up Mickey Mouse ears for a gag gift of cut glass tumblers with holes ensuring that unsuspecting drinkers would get dribbled on. "He loved all that kind of stuff," recalls daughter Kerry. "He loved getting people pushed in the pool." He also realized, even as he faced the most critical election of his life, that the kids were what mattered most.

The day before the primary he traveled twelve hundred miles—from

Los Angeles to San Francisco, Long Beach, Watts, San Diego, and back to Los Angeles. At each stop he railed against the war, against poverty, and against voter apathy, which he believed was his biggest impediment to the nomination. The crowds by now had grown so big that the rallies were held in multiple seatings so everyone could be accommodated, and Bobby barely made it through. It wasn't just bloody hands and wilted vocal cords now. His stomach was roiling and he was dizzy to the point of collapse. "I just ran out of gas," he said in a rare admission after the final rally at the El Cortez Hotel in San Diego. Four bottles of ginger ale helped. So did a rare moment alone sitting offstage, his face buried in his hands as he tried to catch his breath. Seldom, in the long annals of American political history, had a candidate waged as intense and condensed a nomination campaign as Bobby had in the eighty days since his launch.

There was one more incident that Monday that everyone with him remembered. It happened in the teeming streets of San Francisco's Chinatown, in late morning. A large firecracker exploded, near and loud, then a string of them—*Pow! Pow! Pow! Pow! Pow!* Ethel lurched, then crouched in the convertible, frozen. Not Bobby. He continued waving and shaking hands, determined to keep at bay memories of Dallas but quietly asking a reporter to climb in beside Ethel and hold her hand. Random threats had come in throughout the campaign—that the Mob would kill him, or a madman anxious to appear in the history books alongside Lee Harvey Oswald and John Wilkes Booth. Presidential candidates didn't get Secret Service protection then,* and Bobby's only full-time security man was Bill Barry, a former FBI agent. In mid-May, Ethel sounded the alarm with a friend: "He's getting more and more death threats, and I'm worried." Just a day before the Chinatown rally, the Reverend Edwin King of Mississippi received and passed on a warning that if he won the California primary, Bobby would be assassinated by the same unspecified people who had killed JFK. Every week during the campaign, the FBI gave press secretary Frank Mankiewicz pictures of potential assassins, and at every rally he scanned faces in the crowd. Kennedy aides say they tried to work with local police, but there were problems in

---

* LBJ would order such protection for all major presidential candidates after Bobby's shooting, and soon after that, Congress made it the law.

places like Los Angeles, whose mayor, Sam Yorty, hated Bobby. Tom Reddin, the LA police chief back then, says it was the Kennedy people who were the problem in his city and others—staging illegal motorcades, busting through traffic signals, blocking streets, "and just being general 'pains in the ass.'" That, Reddin adds in an unpublished memoir, is why his officers couldn't do their job during campaign rallies and why they weren't on hand to provide proper security at the Ambassador Hotel on election night.

The truth is that Bill Barry and the Kennedy team did their best to protect him, but Bobby got in the way. He had always been a phobophobe, averse to showing fear. Having a brother gunned down would make most people more cautious, but it made Bobby more fatalistic. "Living every day is like Russian roulette," he said. "There's no way of protecting a country-stumping candidate. No way at all. You've just got to give yourself to the people and to trust them, and from then on it's just that good old bitch, luck. Anyway, you have to have luck on your side to be elected President of the United States. Either it is with you or it isn't. I am pretty sure there'll be an attempt on my life sooner or later. Not so much for political reasons. I don't believe that. Plain nuttiness, that's all. There's plenty of that around." If he were elected, he added, he surely wouldn't ride in the kind of bubble-topped, bulletproof limousine that LBJ used: "We can't have that kind of country, where the President is afraid to go among the people."

Primary day in California was cooler than normal for the fourth of June, with smog masking the Los Angeles sun and Bobby allowing himself an indulgent sleep in. The filmmaker John Frankenheimer had lent the Kennedys his Malibu beach house, and after lunch, everyone headed for the water. David, who was just days from his thirteenth birthday, was overtaken by the undertow and Bobby dived in for the rescue. He emerged with a red bruise on his forehead but no deadening of the playful mood.

The early reads on voting were upbeat as more family, friends, and aides gathered throughout the afternoon. That evening, Frankenheimer chauffeured the candidate into the city, taking a meandering route that made Bobby nervous and arriving at his headquarters at the Ambassador Hotel just after seven o'clock.

With the polls staying open until eight, results came in slowly and dif-

ferently on each network. In those days, news organizations could announce partial results before polling stations closed and the final
numbers were tallied. CBS had him ahead; NBC was less sure. South Dakota also held its primary that day, and Bobby was delighted with an
early showing from one district in particular. "You want to hear about
the Indians?" he asked the family and friends in his fifth-floor Royal Suite.
"We've got an Indian precinct in from South Dakota: 878 for Kennedy, 2
for Johnson, 9 for McCarthy. How about that?" The full tally from the
Mount Rushmore State, Humphrey's birthplace, was almost as encouraging: 49.5 percent for Bobby, 30 percent for the vice president, and 20.4
percent for McCarthy. In California, he didn't do quite as well as some TV
analysts predicted or he'd hoped. But buoyed by unprecedented turnouts
and majorities in black and Mexican American districts, in the end Kennedy scored a clear-cut victory with 46.3 percent of the vote, compared
to McCarthy's 41.8 and 12 percent for unpledged delegates. The trend
was encouraging enough for him to go on TV and quietly claim victory,
and for journalists and friends gathered in the suite across the hall to
start the party. Everyone who'd mattered during the previous eleven
weeks was there, including columnist pals Breslin and Hamill, admiring
authors Teddy White and George Plimpton, and activist fans Cesar
Chavez, Charles Evers, and John Lewis.

For the first time since he'd jumped in, Bobby believed he could do it.
The dream—"Make room for the next leader of the free world," he'd
tease as he sprinted from hotel showers wrapped in a towel—seemed less
distant following the day's double win. That very night he held a series of
one-on-ones with Smith, Sorensen, Walinsky, and other trusted lieutenants, and began charting plans for the campaign ahead. There'd be a
single-minded push in his adopted state of New York. A full-page ad in
The New York Times would feature photos of AFL-CIO boss George Meany
and segregationist governor Lester Maddox of Georgia—both staunchly
anti-Bobby and both wielding huge clout in the Democrat Party—asking
rhetorically whether insiders like them should be allowed to pick the
next president. The candidate would head overseas next, showing his
gravitas by meeting with the pope and foreign leaders. Nobody, least of
all Bobby, minimized the obstacles remaining. But after California and
South Dakota he knew that McCarthy didn't matter and that the only

one who could deny him the nomination was Hubert Humphrey, or, as the comedian and mock presidential candidate Pat Paulsen dubbed him earlier that evening, Herbert Humphrey. "I'm going to chase Herbert's ass all over the country," Bobby vowed. "Everywhere he goes I'll go too."

Before he went anywhere, Bobby took a quiet moment. Sitting on the floor of his hotel room, arms around his knees, he lit a victory cigar and contemplated. At the start he hadn't been sure whether he was running as Joe's son, Jack's brother, or LBJ's avowed enemy. He retained a piece of each of those personas, but he had found a voice and two uncomplicated motivations of his own: to end the war and end poverty. Both were doable, he told himself, as aides pressed him to head down to the ballroom. Legions of restless believers were there singing "This Land Is Your Land," the Woody Guthrie ballad that Bobby had promised to make America's anthem. A few minutes before midnight he looked over at Ethel, who was bouncing up and down on the bed. "Ready?" he asked. Then, knowing how McCarthy and others had teased him about campaigning with his dog always at his side, he added impishly, "Do you think we should take Freckles down?"

His valedictory speech began with a nod to Don Drysdale, the Los Angeles Dodgers ace "who pitched his sixth straight shutout tonight, and I hope that we have as good fortune in our campaign." (Bobby was one of the few men in America who actually didn't know who the future Hall of Famer was.) Next came the thank-yous—to Jean and Pat, Rose, "and all those other Kennedys." Also to Freckles—"I'm not doing this in any order of importance," he joked—and Ethel, whose "patience during this whole effort was fantastic." Then he got serious: "I think we can end the divisions within the United States . . . whether it's between blacks and whites, between the poor and the more affluent, or between age groups, or over the war in Vietnam. . . . I intend to make that my basis for running over the period of the next few months." The crowd loved it, shouting, "Bobby Power!" He ended back on a light note, saying that "Mayor Yorty has just sent me a message that we've been here too long already. So my thanks to all of you, and on to [the convention in] Chicago, and let's win there." Giving a thumbs-up, then flashing the V-for-victory sign, he turned to leave for a reception on a lower level followed by a press conference.

But plans had changed. Aides decided to skip the second reception and go directly to the press conference, where reporters were anxious to file their stories. The shortest route was the way he'd come in, through the waiters' swinging doors and into the kitchen and pantry. In the pushing of the crowd Bobby got separated from his bodyguard, Bill Barry, who was helping a pregnant Ethel off the podium. Nobody worried, since the candidate was among friends, with a Mexican busboy reaching for his hand as a cluster of reporters, photographers, and aides trailed behind. Past the rusty ice machine, thirty feet from the media room, a curly-haired, swarthy young man wearing a pale blue sweatshirt was standing unnoticed on a low tray stacker, waiting for his opening. It was shortly after midnight and Andrew West, a reporter for the Mutual Radio Network, was asking Bobby his plans for catching up to Humphrey's delegate lead. Bobby: "It just goes back to the struggle for it . . ."

That was as far as he got. The shooter stepped from his hiding place, reached straight ahead with his right arm, and started firing a .22-caliber revolver. A single shot was followed by a volley—*pop-pop-pop-pop-pop-pop-pop*—that sounded eerily like the firecrackers in Chinatown. Just how many shots were fired, at what range and angle, would become grist for another assassination conspiracy mill. Bobby lurched against the ice machine, then sagged to the ground, lying faceup on the grimy concrete floor. He was conscious, eyes wide open, as blood oozed behind his right ear. "Is everybody okay?" he asked. The busboy, Juan Romero, assured him they were, and Bobby whispered, "Everything's going to be okay." Romero placed rosary beads in Bobby's hand and tried to cushion his head as Ethel pleaded with the pressing crowd to "give him room to breathe." Then she turned to her husband and said softly, "I'm with you, my baby." The scene was bedlam. "Get the gun . . . get the gun," pleaded West, the radio man. "You monster!" a kitchen worker yelled from his perch atop the steam table. "You'll die for this!" The only one who seemed serene was Bobby himself—"a kind of sweet accepting smile on his face," recalled the journalist and Bobby's friend Pete Hamill, "as if he knew it would all end this way." Medics finally arrived and hoisted him by his shoulders and feet. "Oh, no, no," Bobby protested. "Don't. Don't lift me." Then he passed out. As the ambulance drove away, campaign volunteers sobbed and prayed as a large black man pounded a hotel pillar with his bloody right fist, shouting the questions being echoed across America: "Why, God, why? Why again? Why another Kennedy?"

The next twenty-five hours were a hellish whirlwind. When the police showed up at the hotel about fifteen minutes after the shooting— Chief Reddin says they weren't there originally because "we were asked not to be"—they quickly assembled evidence that the gunman was a twenty-four-year-old Palestinian named Sirhan Sirhan who hated Israel, hated Kennedy for supporting Israel, and shot the senator a year to the day after the start of the Six-Day War in which Israel routed its Arab enemies. Sirhan's rampage wounded five others along with Bobby, whose injuries were recognized from the first to be life-threatening. Friends rounded up the children. David, who'd always been terrified that his father would be shot like Uncle Jack, learned by watching the election-night proceedings on TV that his nightmare had come true. Eight-year-old Kerry woke early the following morning to watch Bugs Bunny; "a news flash interrupted the cartoon," she recalled. "That's how I learned my father had been shot." The three oldest—Kathleen, Joe, and Bobby Jr.—were retrieved from their prep schools and flown to Los Angeles in Air Force Two to be with their parents.

Bobby meanwhile was transferred at 1:00 A.M. from Central Receiving Hospital, where he'd been stabilized, to the Hospital of the Good Samaritan, where six surgeons performed an operation that lasted nearly four hours. Machines kept his heart pumping but other machines showed that his brain had ceased to function. At two o'clock the following morning Mankiewicz appeared in the media room across from the hospital with the announcement everyone had been dreading: "Senator Robert Francis Kennedy died at 1:44 A.M. today, June 6, 1968 . . . He was forty-two years old." Back at the Ambassador Hotel, a red rose marked the spot on the blood-stained pantry floor where the senator was felled. On the wall above was a hand-lettered cardboard sign that might have been up for weeks but seemed especially appropriate now: THE ONCE AND FUTURE KING. It was the title of the Camelot novel and had been the glorious epithet of King Arthur. In a way, it didn't matter that Bobby had never assumed the throne and now never would. Millions of Americans already believed in his majesty.

GOODBYES

A MERICA HADN'T SEEN a sendoff like this since Abraham Lincoln's funeral train a hundred and three years before. More than a million people turned out along the Penn Central tracks as the train carrying Robert F. Kennedy's body made its 226-mile run from New York to Washington. The crowds were a panorama of the nation on that sticky Saturday afternoon in June 1968. Girl Scouts came with Little Leaguers. Factory workers stood alongside ragpickers and nuns, stretching on tiptoes to see. Husbands embraced sobbing wives. They arrived in yellow pickup trucks and flotillas of boats, wearing Bermuda shorts and hair curlers, tossing roses. A pair of corpulent policemen stood at attention beside their squad car as the train surfaced in New Jersey. Some climbed water towers and hung from girders to get a better look. Outside Newark, three firemen saluted from the deck of their vessel, *The John F. Kennedy.* There were brass bands, police bands, school bands, Catholic bands. Hands were cupped in prayer or held over hearts, hats off. As the locomotive slowly pulled through the station in Baltimore, seventy-five hundred mourners led by the mayor sang "The Battle Hymn of the Republic" in the same sorrowful tones that had greeted President Lincoln a century before.

It was Bobby's America, bearing, as always, signs that spoke from its collective heart. WE HAVE LOST OUR LAST HOPE. WHO WILL BE THE NEXT ONE? REST IN PEACE, ROBERT. And, hand-lettered and held aloft by Negro youngsters on the platform in Baltimore: WE LOVES YOU, BOBBY.

Michael Harrington looked out the window of the twenty-one-car train for as long as he could bear. "Every time I did, I began to cry. The sorrowing faces along the way were a mirror of my own feelings," said the author whose writings helped launch the War on Poverty and who saw Bobby as "the man who actually could have changed the course of American history." As for those with him inside the railcars—politicians of the old school and new, intellectuals and trade unionists, blacks, Irish, Chicanos, and Jews—they were, said Harrington, "the administration of Robert Kennedy that was never going to be." Frank Mankiewicz was struck by the distinctive ways that different groups grieved during the ride, which took twice as long as its normal four hours: "The Irish were drinking, singing, telling great stories about Bob. 'God, do you remember the time in Butte?' The Jews were sad, weeping. I think in an earlier time they would have been tearing up their clothes, right? The Protestants were just staring straight ahead. You could tell, as you walked through the cars, who was who."

Ethel left the casket and walked down the aisles greeting guests like the generous hostess she had always been. "Nice you were able to make it" to one. To others, "We'll cry later." Pollsters would pronounce her America's most admired woman for how she carried herself in the aftermath. Friends watched as she soldiered through those days and the years that followed, raising eleven children and burying David and Michael,* never removing her wedding ring or contemplating remarrying. It wasn't just that she was an experienced griever, but that her faith let her imagine Bobby in a better place, looking down. It sustains her still. "They're in Heaven, they're in Paradise with the angels," she says of those she has lost. "They can see everything. . . . I feel very, very sure of that."

Bobby had been equally sure. "He asked me one day if I had a choice of dying and going straight to heaven, or of living and taking my chances, which would I choose—I said I would live and take my chances and he said he would choose the other," remembered Kennedy cousin

---

* David died in 1984 of a drug overdose. Michael died in an accident while playing football on the Colorado ski slopes in 1997, the same year that he was accused of having an affair with the family's teenaged babysitter. For all the well-documented woes of Bobby and Ethel's offspring, however, there were the joys of seeing Kathleen elected lieutenant governor of Maryland, Joseph II win the congressional seat held by his Uncle Jack, and nearly all the children engage in the kinds of public crusades that Bobby would have relished and that Ethel has.

Polly Fitzgerald. "It comforts me now to know this and to remember his simple faith in God's promises."

Then there was Rose, seated in the compartment with Bobby's casket in her familiar black mourning dress, ever unruffled as she had been as one after another of her children had impossibly fallen. She waved lightly to the crowds because, as she explained afterward, "I felt that if people cared enough to come out and pay their respects we ought at least to give them some sign of appreciation. As for my being composed—I had to be. If I had broken down in grief I would only have added to the misery of the others. . . . How sad are our hearts when we realize that we shall never see Bobby again, with his tousled, windblown hair, his big, affectionate smile, carrying one child piggyback and leading another by the hand—his dog close behind." Joe, meanwhile, wouldn't let anyone turn off his television set in Hyannis Port, watching and silently weeping as every detail of the murder was reconstructed. "After Bobby's death," Rose remembered, "Joe's condition declined until by the fall of that year he was approaching helplessness." He died a year later, with just one of his four sons alive to mourn him.

Ted tried to step in for Bobby in countless ways, starting with his eulogy. "My brother," he told us, "need not be idealized or enlarged in death beyond what he was in life. He should be remembered simply as a good and decent man who saw wrong and tried to right it, saw suffering and tried to heal it, saw war and tried to stop it." Five months later, in a letter to Bobby's children, he filled in the image: "When I think of Bobby, I shall always see Cape Cod on a sunny day. The wind will be from the southwest and the white caps will be showing and the full tide will be sweeping through the gaps in the breakwater. It will be after lunch, and Bob will be stripped to the waist and he'll say, 'come on, Joe, Kathleen, Bobby and David, Courtney, Kerry, come on Michael and even you Chris and Max—call your Mother and come on for a sail.' . . . The tide is gentle—the sand shifts—the sky is blue—the seagulls watch from above and the breeze is warm. And there will be happiness and love and we are together again."

Jackie continued her transit away from the Kennedy orbit once Bobby was gone. At his urging, she'd slowed her romance with Aristotle Onassis, the Greek shipping tycoon who was twenty-three years older than she and who Bobby thought wanted to exploit her celebrity. Now things were different. Jackie and Ari were married, four months after Bobby's burial, on Ari's private island of Skorpios.

Hubert Humphrey, who captured the Democratic presidential nomination that summer in Chicago, bore the biggest cross politically. "It was after Bobby's death that everything went to pot," he explained. "I said it and I meant it that the bullet that shot and killed Bobby Kennedy fatally wounded me. . . . I felt it from the minute it happened. . . . I think the whole Democratic Party lost momentum. . . . Had Bobby lived I think there'd have been a Democrat in the White House." Monday morning quarterbacking is easy, but Humphrey is right. Had he beaten Bobby for the nomination, Bobby would have supported him in the fall campaign and there might not have been angry demonstrations in Chicago or a bitter third-party bid by George Wallace, who captured 13.5 percent of the vote in an election in which Nixon edged Humphrey by just 0.7 percent. Who better than Bobby to answer Nixon and Wallace on fighting crime and restitching the social safety net into a trampoline?

The questions that everyone asks, and none can answer, are whether Bobby would have been the Democratic standard-bearer rather than Humphrey—and the president instead of Nixon. Nixon himself thought the former, telling his family the night of the California primary, "It sure looks like we'll be going against Bobby." Bill Daley thought so, too, saying that his father, the powerful mayor of Chicago, believed that Bobby "was going to stop in Chicago on his way back from L.A. I would say there was a 70 percent chance [Dad] was going to endorse him. . . . Then the momentum would have shifted to where other people like my dad who were still left would have been hard pressed not to go there." While that is speculation, what is certain is that if Bobby had been the Democratic nominee, he knew Nixon's vulnerabilities better than anybody else, having orchestrated the campaign that beat him eight years before.

Last goodbyes for the slain candidate poured in from across the globe, with Ethel receiving 350,000 letters of commiseration. "Somehow the Kennedys draw the lightning," James Reston said in *The New York Times*. "They seem to be able to save everything but themselves." *The Times* of London wrote that "if American presidents were elected by the suffrage of all countries Robert Kennedy would have gone to the White House next January." Bill Barry, who never forgave himself for not taking the bullets meant for Bobby, said, "I am a much better man for knowing him than I ever was before." TV's Jack Paar quipped that he "would like everything about Bobby's movie but the ending." Fifteen journalists who covered his presidential campaign paid their tribute with an annual award for the best stories on Bobby's constituency of the forgotten and neglected, which is one in a series of memorials to his passions for human rights and justice for children.

Almost on cue with Bobby's prediction that there'd be a black in the White House early in the new millennium, Senator Barack Obama, who was six when Bobby died, remembered more than forty years later that "this man who was never president, who was our attorney general for only three years, who was New York's junior senator for just three and a half, still calls to us today. Still inspires our debate with his words, animates our politics with his ideas, and calls us to make gentle the life of a world that's too often coarse and unforgiving."

Not everyone is sentimental. To this day, Jimmy Hoffa's children, along with Dean Rusk's, can recite the wrongs Bobby did to their fathers. "I kind of dreamed of being invited to one of those Kennedy touch football games on the White House lawn," says Richard Rusk, who was captain of his high school football team. "I would have wanted to catch [Bobby] on the open field and just plant him in the ground. And when he woke, I'd let him figure out why it was that Dean's son had done that to him. You know, he really went after my father in a big way." LBJ was equally unforgiving. He questioned whether RFK had the right to be buried at Arlington Cemetery. He balked at appropriating money to maintain his grave site and at naming the football stadium in Washington after him. He failed to acknowledge Bobby's remarkable odyssey from cold warrior to liberal icon, or to concede that Bobby might have succeeded him in the Oval Office. LBJ's "feelings about Bobby's death were complex," said the president's friend and adviser Clark Clifford. "More deeply than before, Lyndon Johnson feared that history would always trap him between the martyred Kennedys."

The tribute Bobby undoubtedly would have liked best was from his son David. "Daddy was very funny in church because he would embarrass all of us by singing very loud. Daddy did not have a very good voice," the thirteen-year-old wrote as part of a Christmas surprise for his mother at the end of that year of their terrible loss. "There will be no more football with Daddy, no more swimming with him, no more riding and no more camping with him. But he was the best father their [*sic*] ever was and I would rather have him for a father for the length of time I did than any other father for a million years."

ACKNOWLEDGMENTS

"Write a good book, because he's a good man who deserves a good book,"
urged Melody Miller, who had worked for Bobby, Ted, and Jackie and
echoed the advice of nearly everyone I interviewed. The stories they told
me made that challenge infinitely easier. I am grateful to them all, and
especially to John Seigenthaler, who gave me the confidence to push
ahead by telling me that the book his friend Bobby deserves had yet to be
written.

Jill Kneerim, my agent for life, believed in this project from the first
and supported me through the last sentence. Will Murphy, who has edited my last three books, did what he always does: got excited early on,
gave me the freedom I cherish during the research and writing, then
jumped back in with just the right guidance as the final product took
form.

Experts on my various chapter themes offered context and texture
and saved me from more errors than I'll admit. Those able reviewers
were Historian of the Senate Donald Ritchie on the Senator Joe McCarthy years, journalist Victor Navasky on the Kennedy Justice Department
that he wrote a book about, former NAACP Legal Defense Fund lawyer
Michael Meltsner on the Kennedy civil rights record, Cold War historian
James Hershberg on the missile crisis and Operation Mongoose, Terence
Smith on the U.S. Senate campaign that he covered for the *New York Herald Tribune*, Kennedy Senate aide and Georgetown law professor Peter
Edelman on Bobby's career as a senator, and Washington political commentator Elizabeth Drew on RFK's run for president.

Three friends—Bill Kovach, Marty Nolan, and Tom Gagen—read the
complete draft and provided the careful commentary I had counted on.
Sally Jacobs was the writing counselor she has been for all my books and
most of my newspaper stories. Veteran editor David Sobel supplied the

deft word fixes and big-picture critiques that gave me the assurance to hand in the manuscript to Random House. My partner there, in sharpening my thinking and Bobby's voice, was the wise and skilled Mika Kasuga. Thanks, too, to publisher Susan Kamil, for the extra care she gave to this book, and to Evan Camfield and his copyediting team, who again proved how much better a manuscript can become when red pencils are in the right hands.

None of this could have happened—or would have been nearly as much fun—without the backing and feedback of my extraordinary wife and partner, Lisa Frusztajer. My other in-house boosters, Alec and Marina, helped me see what their millennial generation might want to know about Bobby Kennedy and his era. And there with perspective were my pals Teri Bergman, Jerry and Susan Cohen, Gene Dean, Andrew Dreyfus, Kitty and Michael Dukakis, Judy Glasser, Steve Kurkjian, Dick Lehr, Gail Leondar-Wright, Tom Palmer, Phil Primack, Judy Rakowsky, and Phil Warburg.

As part of my research I visited the places that mattered most in Bobby's world—from Hyannis Port, Palm Beach, New York, Washington, D.C., and McLean, Virginia, to the West Coast and Deep South. As I went, I filled in gaps with assistance from hundreds of Kennedy friends, colleagues, and chroniclers, who provided reminiscences, manuscripts, and other materials they hadn't shared before, and whom I list in the bibliography. Those I went back to more often than I had any right to were Bill Arnone, Wendy Cimmet, Ramsey Clark, John Doar, Phil Johnston, Paul Kirk, Sheldon Stern, and Adam Walinsky. I am indebted as well to RFK biographers Arthur Schlesinger and Evan Thomas, whose works still stand out. Bobby's family recently opened up fifty-eight boxes of his papers at Boston's John F. Kennedy Library that had been under lock and key for more than forty years; helping me dig into those and other new and old files were Tom Putnam, Karen Abramson, Stephen Plotkin, and, notably, Michael Desmond. The staff of the LBJ Library in Austin also was terrific, from Claudia Anderson and Barbara Cline to Mark Updegrove.

I hired a stream of student researchers to assist with library and Internet searches, transcribe recorded interviews, and undertake other research. The ones who stayed longest were Katie Abbondanza, Josh

Adams, Mina Asayesh-Brown, Corey Barr, Olivia Boser, Cate Ferson, Lauren Helper, Catherine Lockhart, Maryrose Mesa, Lauren Prescott, Whitney Stohr, and, from first word to last, Nick Catoni. Going back further, Dorothy and Mauray Tye helped me see what was special about the Kennedys and instilled in me the skepticism that every journalist and author needs.

Thanks, too, to Bobby's family and, most of all, to Ethel. She has never stopped talking about her Bobby over this last half century, but she has seldom done so in public. I am grateful for her vetting of my theories on what motivated her husband, both as the unformed young man she fell in love with and the one by whose side she stayed through that terrifying last night in Los Angeles. She welcomed me into her home, helped me see how she was his full partner in the very way she professed not to have been, and let me copy photos that are on public display for the first time in these pages. Other pictures are published here thanks to the generosity of Alan and Ashley Dabbiere, the current owners of Hickory Hill; the Kennedys; and Jonathan Klein, chairman of Getty Images. Bobby's children also were great, especially Christopher, who never tired of my repeated requests for "one more thing," or at least he never let me know that he did.

A couple of notes on sources: My endnotes generally are abridged listings, with the full references in the book's bibliography. I have donated to the Rare Book & Manuscript Library at Columbia University all my research papers, along with recordings and transcripts of my interviews, and I have left to the John F. Kennedy Hyannis Museum my more than five hundred books on Bobby and his family.

NOTES

PREFACE

ix **"Each time a man"**: RFK "Ripple of Hope" speech, University of Cape Town, June 6, 1966. (rfksafilm.org/html/speeches/unicape.php).

x **healing magic**: Guthman and Allen, *RFK: Collected Speeches*, 380; and Kennedy, *Honorable Profession*, 90.

x **less documented car trip**: Newfield, *RFK: A Memoir*, 200–201.

xiii **"Some people see"**: There are different versions of this quote, which RFK and JFK both borrowed from George Bernard Shaw. Shaw began his, "You see." Other variants start with "Some men." The "Some people" rendition used here is from RFK's speech in March 1968 at the University of Kansas.

1. COLD WARRIOR

3 **one man faltered**: Edwin Bayley Oral History (OH), October 10, 1968, 12, JFKL; and David, *Making of a Folk Hero*, 76–77.

6 **Joe at Boston Latin**: Nasaw, *The Patriarch*, 21–22.

8 **all his other deals**: Smith, "Fifty-Million-Dollar Man," *Fortune;* and "Amazing Kennedys," *Saturday Evening Post.*

8 **Joe Kennedy's vision**: "Reform & Realism," *Time;* Joseph Kennedy, "Shielding the Sheep," *Saturday Evening Post;* and Beschloss, *Kennedy and Roosevelt*, 88.

9 **"I have no political ambitions"**: Joseph Kennedy, *I'm for Roosevelt*, 3 and 10.

11 **"I'm willing to spend"**: Lyons, "Kennedy Says Democracy," *Boston Globe.*

11 **"I have four boys"**: Ross, "Joseph P. Kennedy," *New York Post.*

11 **not one to wallow**: Linn, "Truth About Joe Kennedy," *Saga;* and "Amazing Kennedys."

12 **"my plans for my future"**: *The Patriarch*, 572.

12 **simple question of succession**: Author interview with Peter MacLellan.

13 **Rose's mother worried**: Rose Kennedy, *Times to Remember*, 103; and Kennedy and Smith, *Hostage to Fortune*, 535.

13 **"I was the seventh"**: Shannon, *Heir Apparent*, 43; and Thompson and Myers, *Brother Within*, 43.

14 **"I wish, Dad"**: Undated RFK letter to JPK and Rose, JPK Files, Box 5, JFKL.

14 **low expectations**: Visiting Berlin, Ethel confided to students at a German-American school that Bobby had flunked third grade (David, *Ethel*, 151); Thomas, *Robert Kennedy: His Life*, 36–37, 399; and author interview with MacLellan.

14 **In letters home:** "Official Military File of Robert F. Kennedy," National Archives and Records Administration; Schlesinger, *Robert Kennedy and His Times*, 45; Stein and Plimpton, *American Journey*, 37; and author interview with Piedy Lumet.

15 **"what I remember":** Newfield, *RFK: A Memoir*, 41–42.

15 **vacation getaways:** *Times to Remember*, 362.

16 **the Malcolm cottage:** There is disagreement over when Joe bought the Malcolm cottage. Damore suggested it was 1929, Nasaw said it was November 1928, and John Allen, director of the JFK Hyannis Museum Foundation, says, "we use the date 1926 as the date when they bought the cottage and then expanded it in 1928." Damore, *Cape Cod Years*, 19–20; *The Patriarch*, 92; and Allen email to author.

16 **"When are you going":** Undated RFK letter to JPK and Rose, JPK Files, Box 5, JFKL.

17 **Bobby would cower:** Burns, *John Kennedy*, 28.

17 **Bobby's college career:** Viser, "Kennedy Letters," *Boston Globe;* and "Military File of Robert F. Kennedy."

18 **After college:** *Brother Within*, 46–47; *Robert Kennedy and His Times*, 81; and Gerald Tremblay OH, January 8, 1970, 2–3, JFKL.

19 **different with Ethel:** Demerit book, Manhattanville College; "The Tower 1947," Manhattanville College; and author interview with Nan Talese.

19 **star-struck:** Author interview with Ethel Kennedy; Gardner, *Robert Kennedy in New York*, 80; *Ethel*, 70; and William J. Brady OH, November 5, 1974, 2, JFKL.

20 **The next challenge:** *Robert Kennedy and His Times*, 88; Oppenheimer, *Other Mrs. Kennedy*, 126; and author interview with Ethel Kennedy.

20 **a family strikingly similar:** Author interview with Ethel Kennedy.

21 **They were wed:** Rogers, *When I Think of Bobby*, 38.

21 **first significant interaction:** Hersh, *Bobby and J. Edgar*, 128; *Robert Kennedy: His Life*, 65; and *Brother Within*, 100.

22 **his first job:** *Bobby and J. Edgar*, 129; J. Walter Yeagley OH, December 8, 1970, 44–45, JFKL.

22 **1952 Senate race:** *Front Runner*, 170; and *Founding Father*, 432.

23 **Even more impressive:** *Robert Kennedy and His Times*, 97; Krock, *Memoirs*, 338; Stein and Plimpton, *American Journey*, 36 and 45; McCarthy, *Remarkable Kennedys*, 30; and Charles Spalding OH, March 22, 1969, 31, JFKL.

24 **a lot in common:** Ross, "Joseph P. Kennedy"; and *Hostage to Fortune*, 664.

25 **McCarthy played shortstop:** "Campaign: Pride of the Clan," *Time*.

26 **"always and invariably":** Herman, *McCarthy*, 190.

26 **biggest show in Washington:** Oshinsky, "In the Heart of the Heart of Conspiracy," *New York Times; American Journey*, 50; and Executive Sessions, Senate Permanent Subcommittee on Investigations, vol. 1, First Session, 1953, xxvi.

27 **"Joe's *methods*":** Martin, *A Hero for Our Time*, 58; and author interview with Alvin Spivak.

27 **McCarthy couldn't say no:** *Brother Within*, 109; and Herman, *Joseph McCarthy*, 211 and 359–60.

27 **arrangement was confusing:** The first payroll, for two weeks, was $220.09 for Bobby and $517.60 for Cohn (Report of Secretary of Senate, January 7, 1954); Zion, *Autobiography of Roy Cohn*, 87–88; and Von Hoffman, *Citizen Cohn*, 182.

28 **crusade against Communism:** Executive Sessions, Senate Permanent Subcommittee on Investigations, xv.

28 **Greek shipping scandal:** "Control of Trade with the Soviet Bloc," Permanent Sub-

committee on Investigations, Part 1, 66, 130–31, 137, and 140; and Krock, "Large Trade with China," *New York Times.*

29 **worked into the nights:** Lawford, *Shining Hour,* 45–46.

29 **"It seems just unbelievable":** "Control of Trade with the Soviet Bloc," Part 2, 132 and 137.

30 **Eisenhower administration was not amused:** *Robert Kennedy and His Times,* 104; Oshinsky, *Conspiracy So Immense,* 297–98; Reeves, *Life and Times of Joe McCarthy,* 488; and Childs, "McCarthy Letter Contents Revealed," *New York Times.*

30 **earned high marks:** "Large Trade with China"; Pearson, "McCarthy Urged to Push Probe," *Washington Post;* and Francis Flanagan letter to RFK, April 2, 1953, RFK Papers, Box 2.

31 **Not everyone was impressed:** Daniel, "British Defend Stand on Trade with China," *New York Times;* and William David Ormsby-Gore OH, August 27, 1969, 2, JFKL.

31 **"was so strong":** Roy Cohn OH, March 24, 1971, 3, JFKL.

32 **Cohn was half right:** *Robert Kennedy and His Times,* 104; and Pearson and Anderson, "Voters Must Weigh."

32 **letter of resignation:** "R. F. Kennedy Quits," *Boston Globe;* Morris, "3 Democrats Scorn Bid," *New York Times;* and Theoharis, *Secret Files,* 262.

33 **What really scared Bobby:** Evans, *Blacklisted by History,* 450; author interview with Stan Evans; Executive Sessions, Senate Permanent Subcommittee on Investigations, xvii; Kennedy, *Enemy Within,* 307; and author interview with Donald Ritchie.

33 **"I think Roy's homosexuality":** Author interview with Anthony Lewis.

34 **nothing about his departure was simple:** *Enemy Within,* 176; *Life and Times of Joe McCarthy,* 498; RFK letter to Senator Joseph McCarthy, July 29, 1953, RFK Papers, Box 2; "Aide to McCarthy Resigns," *New York Times; Brother Within,* 112; and Reports of the Secretary of the Senate, January 7, 1954 and January 6, 1955.

34 **Bobby's letter:** RFK letter to McCarthy, July 29, 1953; and McCarthy letter to RFK, July 31, 1953, RFK Papers, Box 2.

35 **neither whitewashes nor sugarcoats:** Author interview with Ethel Kennedy.

35 **warmth cooled:** Kelso, "3 Senators Give Praise to Kennedy," *Boston Post; Enemy Within,* 176; and *Brother Within,* 112 and 120.

36 **timing was just right:** Hilty, *Brother Protector,* 82; and *Autobiography of Roy Cohn,* 87.

37 **"but Bob broke in":** O'Brien, *Final Victories,* 45–46.

37 **"That was the period":** *American Journey,* 48.

38 **raising the stakes:** Rovere, *Senator Joe McCarthy,* 206–7.

38 **won the first round:** Roberts, "Dr. Irving Peress," *New York Times;* and *Conspiracy So Immense,* 372.

39 **bastion of the U.S. military:** *Conspiracy So Immense,* 392 and 399.

40 **investigating Annie Lee Moss:** Friedman, "Strange Career of Annie Lee Moss," *Journal of American History;* and "Cohn Scored When Woman Denies," *New York Times.*

41 **their strained introduction:** RFK FBI file, Part 1 of 9, 54; and RFK OH, December 4, 1964, 417.

41 **an unlikely ally:** Dallek, *Camelot's Court,* 45–46.

41 **Army-McCarthy Hearings:** Herman, *McCarthy,* 256; and Army-McCarthy hearings transcript (historymatters.gmu.edu/d/6444/).

42 **simmering animosities:** Rovere, *McCarthy,* 194; and Lawrence, "Cohn Threatens," *New York Times.*

43 **reasons to despise:** Hilty, *Brother Protector,* 88; and Cohn OH, 3–4.

43 **Bobby threw his punches:** Ruth Watt OH, September 21, 1979, 123–24, US Senate Historical Office; and Ritchie, *Landis*, 169.

43 **Senate rendered a decisive verdict:** Rovere, *McCarthy*, 231.

45 **enemies have unfairly:** Lasky, *Myth and the Man*, 79; Ritchie email to author; and Roberts, *Biography of a Compulsive Politician*, 28–29.

45 **It is unclear where:** Author interviews with Ethel Kennedy and Kathleen Kennedy Townsend.

46 **Bobby's defenders:** *American Journey*, 49; *Bobby and J. Edgar*, 128; *Robert Kennedy: His Life*, 65; and author interviews with Barrett Prettyman and Sam Adams.

46 **more nuanced justifications:** Guthman, *Band of Brothers*, 25; Edward Kennedy, *True Compass*, 104; and author interview with Kerry Kennedy.

47 **Bobby himself:** *Robert Kennedy and His Times*, 173; and Stewart Alsop, "Robert Kennedy and the Liberals," *Saturday Evening Post*.

47 **"They had us ten":** Author interview with Ernest Hollings.

48 **When he got word:** *Robert Kennedy and His Times*, 173; and Drury, "M'Carthy Rites Held," *New York Times*.

48 **Bobby retreated slightly:** *Meet the Press*, October 18, 1964; and Kaiser, *1968*, 14.

49 **bully and a con man:** Rovere, *McCarthy*, 8.

50 **"I liked him":** *Brother Within*, 121.

2. CRUSADING

51 **"Cheyfitz kept telling":** Martin, "Struggle to Get Hoffa: Part One," *Saturday Evening Post*.

52 **Hoffa greeted Kennedy:** *Enemy Within*, 41; and "Struggle to Get Hoffa: Part One."

52 **Ethel telephoned for Bobby:** *Enemy Within*, 40–44; and Mollenhoff, *Tentacles of Power*, 148–49.

52 **Hoffa's renderings:** "Struggle to Get Hoffa: Part One"; and Hoffa and Rogers, *Trials of Jimmy Hoffa*, 150.

53 **Five years later:** Hoffa, *Real Story*, 95–98.

54 **McClellan grew close:** Laymon, *Fearless*, 122; author interview with Bobby Baker; Baker interviews, June 1, 2009–May 4, 2010, U.S. Senate Historical Office; and John McClellan letter to JPK, September 11, 1954, JPK Papers, Box 230.

55 **first order of business:** *Robert Kennedy and His Times*, 116.

55 **case of Air Force secretary:** *American Journey*, 54; and *Robert Kennedy and His Times*, 117–18.

55 **Rose Kennedy was surprised:** *Hostage to Fortune*, 666; JPK letter to Ethel Kennedy, July 20, 1955, JPK Papers, Box 4.

56 **But some witnesses:** Baker, "U.S. Woman Aide Testifies on Gifts," *New York Times*; and de Toledano, *Man Who Would Be President*, 69.

56 **Bobby never denied:** Martin, *It Seems like Only Yesterday*, 173; O'Neill, *Man of the House*, 83; and RFK letter to Robert Harriss, January 31, 1955, RFK Papers.

56 **Such ferocity:** Phillips, "McClellan-Kennedy Investigating Team," *New York Times*; and *Tentacles of Power*, 40. It was dramatic, as Mollenhoff wrote, but it wasn't nine years, just five and a half.

57 **Nobody started out:** William O. Douglas OH, November 9, 1967, 17, JFKL; Douglas,

Court Years, 305–6; and Schlesinger notes on interview with Mercedes Douglas, April 26, 1975, JFKL.

57 **he met Douglas:** *Court Years*, 306–7.

58 **The interlude itself:** *Hostage to Fortune*, 669–70; JPK letter to Edward Dunn, July 30, 1955, JPK Papers, Box 218.

58 **Joe got all:** RFK, "Soviet Brand of Colonialism," *New York Times;* "Interview with Robert F. Kennedy," U.S. News & World Report; and RFK, Georgetown University lecture, October 10, 1955, JFKL.

59 **Justice Douglas, not surprisingly:** *Court Years*, 306–7.

59 **KGB kept tabs:** Fursenko and Naftali, *One Hell of a Gamble*, 115.

59 **detailed journal entries:** RFK diary from Soviet Union, 1955, Pre-Administration Personal Files, JFKL; and "Soviet Brand of Colonialism."

60 **filled his journals:** RFK diary from Soviet Union.

60 **revise his opinion:** *Court Years*, 307; and Schlesinger notes, Mercedes Douglas.

61 **Ethel was less worried:** Schlesinger notes, Mercedes Douglas.

61 **Ethel had displayed:** *Ethel*, 50; and author interview with Ethel Kennedy.

61 **Bobby had obsessed:** *Robert Kennedy: His Life*, 70; Buck, *Kennedy Women*, 117–19; Roberta Greene OH, November 4, 1981, 5, JFKL; and *Brother Within*, 82.

62 **Their married life:** *Ethel*, 56–57.

63 **Eleanor McPeck:** Author interview with Eleanor McPeck.

63 **"We were driving":** Spalding OH, 13.

64 **a more sprawling setting:** *When I Think of Bobby*, 10.

64 **this perfect setting:** David, "My Father, Robert Kennedy," *McCall's;* and author interview with Ethel Kennedy.

65 **children at Hickory Hill:** Author interview with Ethel Kennedy.

67 **Kennedy was initially skeptical:** *Tentacles of Power*, 124.

67 **deepest and broadest congressional inquiries:** *Tentacles of Power*, 129–33.

67 **To gear up:** Finding Aid for the Records of the Senate Select Committee on Improper Activities in the Labor or Management Field, 1957–1960; and "Struggle to Get Hoffa: Part Three."

68 **Pierre Salinger went to work:** Salinger, *With Kennedy*, 19; and "Struggle to Get Hoffa: Part One."

68 **Rackets Committee's first target:** "Senators Hear Beck Made Profit," *New York Times;* and *Enemy Within*, 33.

69 **Beck was a warm-up:** *Only Yesterday*, 178–81; and Neff, *Vendetta*, 48–49.

70 **opening salvo:** "Struggle to Get Hoffa: Part One"; and *Vendetta*, 61–62.

71 **Hoffa's trial:** Thomas, *Man to See*, 105; *Real Story*, 112; *Enemy Within*, 58–60.

72 **Kennedy-Hoffa battle was joined:** "Struggle to Get Hoffa: Part Three."

72 **unusual arrangement:** "Struggle to Get Hoffa: Part Three"; and *Enemy Within*, 106.

73 **Hoffa's selling out:** Ibid., 128–31.

73 **typical for Hoffa:** *Enemy Within*, 72; *Real Story*, 107; and *Trials of Jimmy Hoffa*, 163.

74 **combatants made their case:** *Only Yesterday*, 182.

74 **first time Hoffa showed up:** *Vendetta*, 92–93; and ebooksread.com/authors-eng /united-states-congress-Senate-select-committee/investigation-of-improper -activities-in-the-labor-or-management-field-hearings--tin-487/1.

75 **He and Bobby:** *Real Story*, 105; Sheridan, *Fall and Rise of Jimmy Hoffa*, 46–47; Clay, *Hoffa!* 110; and *Myth and the Man*, 107–8.

76 **record number:** *Enemy Within*, 147 and 317.

76   **typical exchange:** Rackets Committee hearing transcript, March 12, 1959 (archive
     .org/stream/investigationofi49unit/investigationofi49unit_djvu.txt).

77   **Kennedy's objective:** *Trials of Jimmy Hoffa,* 148; Clay, *Hoffa!* 85–88; and *With Ken-
     nedy,* 22.

77   **more national attention:** Martin, *Seeds of Destruction,* 217.

78   **it took a toll:** "Struggle to Get Hoffa: Part Four"; and author interview with James P.
     Hoffa.

78   **Kennedy "received anonymous threats":** "R. F. Kennedy Family Threatened," *New
     York Times;* Townsend, *Failing America's Faithful,* 47; author interview with Ethel
     Kennedy; and Paul Fay OH, November 11, 1970, 230–32, JFKL.

79   **no illusions about Hoffa:** *Enemy Within,* 75 and 161.

79   **indulged themselves:** *Vendetta,* 128; *Making of a Folk Hero,* 93–94; *Robert Kennedy:
     His Life,* 88; and *Brother Within,* 195.

80   **Other cases:** *Enemy Within,* 8.

80   **The committee investigated:** Ibid., 297–99.

80   **management as well as labor:** RFK OH, December 4, 1964, 417–18; and *Enemy
     Within,* 252.

81   **The final verdict:** *Trials of Jimmy Hoffa,* 194.

82   **Ironically, all that probing:** Emery, "Why the Teamsters Union Elected Jimmy
     Hoffa," *National Guardian;* and "Struggle to Get Hoffa: Conclusion."

82   **honey-tongued Teamsters lawyer:** Jacobs, "Extracurricular Activities," *California
     Law Review,* 297–98.

83   **Liberals over the years:** Stone, "Why I Would Not Vote for Bobby Kennedy," *I. F.
     Stone's Weekly;* and "Extracurricular Activities," 310.

83   **conservative Barry Goldwater:** Mahoney, *Kennedy Brothers,* 26. One reason the out-
     going Eisenhower Justice Department didn't get tougher with Hoffa, it later became
     clear, was that the Teamsters boss had promised in return to back Vice President
     Nixon in his presidential bid against Jack Kennedy. Both kept their promises to the
     best of their ability (*Vendetta,* 187–88 and 203–4; and Pearson, "Nixon figured in
     Hoffa Delay," *Washington Post*).

84   **Bobby tipped his hat:** "Struggle to Get Hoffa: Conclusion."

84   **an apt postscript:** *Enemy Within,* 162. Teapot Dome was a bribery scandal in the
     early 1920s, during the administration of President Warren G. Harding.

3. BROTHER'S KEEPER

86   **The moment, Ike said:** Lewis, "Protest Over Dr. King's Arrest," *New York Times.*

87   **Bobby's schooling in running a campaign:** *Robert Kennedy: His Life,* 48; Dallek, *Un-
     finished Life,* 126; and Fay, *Pleasure of His Company,* 156–57. Jack probably didn't
     know that Bobby had made a sacrifice for the campaign even before he joined it,
     going AWOL from the Navy for nearly two days so he could be there for the cam-
     paign's kickoff. The stunt earned himself a fine and a ten-day restriction aboard his
     ship, but it didn't compromise his honorable discharge a month later (*Vendetta,* 30).

88   **It was a quintessential case:** *Pleasure of His Company,* 157–58; RFK OH, July 20,
     1967, 638; and Martin, *Front Runner,* 141.

89   **"Lodge was the major figure":** RFK OH, July 20, 1967, 647.

89 **the reluctant brother:** *Unfinished Life*, 172; Goodwin, *Fitzgeralds and Kennedys*, 760–61; and *American Journey*, 41.

90 **To drive home those contrasts:** *Brother Protector*, 68; Tanzer, *Kennedy Circle*, 197; and O'Brien, *No Final Victories*, 30.

91 **a merchandising plan:** *Founding Father*, 432; and O'Donnell and Powers, *Johnny, We Hardly Knew Ye*, 86.

91 **"Yes, Dad":** *Brother Protector*, 67.

92 **Newspaper endorsements:** RFK OH, July 20, 1967, 652; *Hero for Our Time*, 53; *Founding Father*, 425; and Burns, *John Kennedy*, 107.

92 **Joe Kennedy's generosity:** Ross, "Joseph P. Kennedy."

93 **uncompromising declarations:** *Kennedy Circle*, 197.

93 **"I know you're an important man":** *Founding Father*, 421.

93 **the label that stuck:** *Kennedy Circle*, 207; and "Little Brother Is Watching," *Time*.

94 **"It was those damned tea parties":** *Founding Father*, 433–34.

94 **Bobby was less confident:** RFK OH, July 20, 1967, 653 and 655.

95 **"The Ambassador's blue language":** O'Donnell and Powers, *Johnny, We Hardly Knew Ye*, 122.

95 **"This is the luckiest thing":** *Kennedy Circle*, 201.

96 **hardheaded lessons:** White, *Making of the President, 1960*, 160; RFK OH, December 7, 1966, 7, Box 1, John Bartlow Martin Collection, Princeton University; and Martin, *Adlai Stevenson and the World*, 235.

96 **"Bobby had come along":** Salisbury, *Heroes of My Time*, 14.

97 **"All this business about Jack and Bobby":** Laing, *Next Kennedy*, 128–29.

97 **include his younger brother:** *Camelot's Court*, 41; RFK OH, July 20, 1967, 643–45; and O'Brien, *John F. Kennedy*, 236.

98 **"They were kind of twin spirits":** Author interview with Ethel Kennedy.

98 **"Jack has always been":** Schaap, *R.F.K.*, 50.

98 **singularities were easy to spot:** Harold Ulen OH, June 2, 1964, 2 and 5, JFKL; and Collier and Horowitz, *American Drama*, 179.

99 **construct a brotherly alliance:** *Next Kennedy*, 129; Stewart Alsop, "Kennedy's Magic Formula," *Saturday Evening Post*; and McGrory, "Sizeups Begin," *Boston Globe*.

99 **roles belied their characters:** *Robert Kennedy and His Times*, xiii; and *Robert Kennedy: His Life*, 91.

100 **Jackie saw the tender promise:** *Robert Kennedy and His Times*, 98 and 133; Thayer, *Jacqueline Bouvier Kennedy*, 104; and Onassis and Schlesinger, *Historic Conversations*, 192.

100 **softer side was his faith:** *Failing America's Faithful*, 38–39; and Kerry Kennedy, *Being Catholic Now*, xviii–xxi.

101 **"The priests couldn't believe":** Author interview with James Tolan.

101 **the faith's divinity and its hierarchy:** Savadove, "Father Feeney, Rebel from Church," *Harvard Crimson*; author interview with Sander Vanocur; *Ethel*, 111; author interviews with RFK Jr. and Susie Wilson; and *Failing America's Faithful*, 49.

102 **the family vacation retreats:** *Brother Within*, 65–66; and Harris, *Does People Do It?: A Memoir*, 158.

102 **"There is no one in the entire family":** *Pleasure of His Company*, 10–11.

103 **Kennedys had a rulebook:** Knebel, "Bobby Kennedy: He Hates to Be Second," *Look*; "Robert Kennedy and the 1968 Campaign," Kennedy Library Forum, March 16, 2008; and *Pleasure of His Company*, 40.

103 **rules so confused:** Dinneen, *Kennedy Family*, 169–71.

103 **"You're not going to let":** *Ethel*, 79–80.

104 **Kennedys knew from the first:** Caro, *Passage of Power*, 71; Shesol, *Mutual Contempt*, 10; and Vanden Heuvel and Gwirtzman, *On His Own*, 246.

105 **private Kennedy polls:** Krock, "Ban on 'Unfair' Primary," *New York Times*.

105 **Humphrey might have had a shot:** *Making of the President, 1960*, 100–14; Humphrey, *Education of a Public Man*, 151.

106 **Always the Happy Warrior:** *Camelot's Court*, 54; *Education of a Public Man*, 152; Matthews, *Jack Kennedy: Elusive Hero*, 259; *Robert Kennedy and His Times*, 196–97; and Shirley, *Rendezvous with Destiny*, 424.

106 **the next major battleground:** *Making of the President, 1960*, 120–21.

107 **as Bobby put it:** *Robert Kennedy and His Times*, 198.

107 **a master stroke:** *Making of the President, 1960*, 127–28; and William Geoghegan OH, February 17, 1966, 9–10, JFKL.

108 **"Poor Little Jack":** wvculture.org/history/1960presidentialcampaign/article.html.

109 **Kennedy side hit back:** *Making of the President, 1960*, 118–20; William Lawrence OH, April 22, 1966, 5–7, JFKL; Lawrence, "Roosevelt Hits Humphrey," *New York Times;* Fleming, *Kennedy vs. Humphrey*, 51; *No Final Victories*, 73; and Eisele, *Almost to the Presidency*, 148.

109 **Humphrey was equally outraged:** Kilpatrick, "Humphrey Angered by Big Outlays," *Washington Post; Heroes of My Time*, 16; O'Brien, *No Final Victories*, 68–69; and *Kennedy vs. Humphrey*, 152.

110 **"The door opened":** Joseph Rauh OH, December 23, 1965, 71–72, JFKL.

111 **Kennedys were planting doubts:** Peter Lisagor OH, April 22, 1966, 25, JFKL; and Lawrence, "Johnson Backers Urge Health Test," *New York Times*.

111 **LBJ thought his adversaries naïve:** "Johnson Backers Urge Health Test"; and *Mutual Contempt*, 35–36.

112 **It happened at a pool party:** Fletcher Knebel OH, August 1, 1977, 17–20, JFKL.

112 **clear-eyed assessments:** *Jack Kennedy: Elusive Hero*, 255; and author interview with John Patterson.

114 **"Dad called us up":** Author interview with James Symington.

114 **"Helps with farmers":** *Mutual Contempt*, 42.

115 **The two finally met:** *Passage of Power*, 61–62.

115 **Each new encounter had fueled:** *Unfinished Life*, 204; and Baker and King, *Wheeling and Dealing*, 118.

116 **JFK "really hadn't thought":** RFK OH, February 27, 1965, 617, JFKL.

116 **JFK got to the point:** Kennedy, John F., "Day I'll Remember," *Life*.

117 **"I'm forty-three years old":** O'Donnell and Powers, *Johnny, We Hardly Knew Ye*, 193.

118 **equally sober-minded calculation:** *Making of the President, 1960*, 200.

118 **"Obviously, with the close relationship":** RFK OH, February 27, 1965, 619.

118 **exactly how it turned out:** Charles Bartlett OH, May 6, 1969, 36, Lyndon Baines Johnson Library (LBJL); and Lawrence, "Choice a Surprise," *New York Times*.

119 **"Even if Jack wanted":** O'Donnell and Powers, *Johnny, We Hardly Knew Ye*, 191.

119 **Only Joe Kennedy:** Bartlett OH, January 6, 1965, 51, JFKL; and Bartlett OH, May 6, 1969, 35, LBJL.

119 **Bobby dropped in at headquarters:** Milton Gwirtzman OH, December 23, 1971, 2, JFKL; and "Democrats: The Shadow & the Substance," *Time*.

120 **Time was the enemy now:** *Kennedy Circle*, 208; and "Little Brother Is Watching."

120 **Issues mattered less:** huffingtonpost.com/earl-ofari-hutchinson/JFKs-civil-rights
-legacy_b_4290163.html;   ontheissues.org/Celeb/Richard_Nixon_Civil_Rights
.htm; President Kennedy speech, Cincinnati Democratic Dinner, October 6, 1960
(presidency.ucsb.edu/ws/?pid=25660); and *Heroes of My Time*, 17.

121 **Shortly before the candidates:** *Robert Kennedy: His Life*, 106; *Jack Kennedy: Elusive
Hero*, 294–95; *Seeds of Destruction*, 265; *Making of the President, 1960*, 325–27; and
True Compass, 156.

122 **The debates reversed:** *Making of the President, 1960*, 326–33; and "Exchange is
Calm," *New York Times*.

122 **The opposition research:** *Robert Kennedy: His Life*, 106–7; Kelley, *His Way*, 304–5;
Bill Haddad OH, November 2, 1967, 51–53, JFKL; Dean, "Memories with Gov. John
Patterson," *Lake Martin Living*; and author interviews with Haddad and Patterson.

123 **Bobby did uncork:** Nixon, *RN: Memoirs of Richard Nixon*, 225–26; Feldstein, *Poisoning the Press*, 63–72; and author interview with Bill Haddad.

123 **real master of political hardball:** O'Donnell and Powers, *Johnny, We Hardly Knew Ye*,
83; White, *In Search of History*, 465; and John Seigenthaler OH, July 22, 1964, 94,
JFKL.

124 **"one bit less":** *Making of the President, 1960*, 360.

124 **sparring with the race hero:** Rampersad, *Jackie Robinson: A Biography*, 347.

126 **Jack "asked the assistance":** Ernest Vandiver OH, May 22, 1967, 69, JFKL.

126 **Harris Wofford, Kennedy's civil rights liaison:** Branch, *Parting the Waters*, 362; King,
My Life with Martin Luther King, 196; *Kennedys & Kings*, 19; and Shriver, "Kennedy's
Call to King," 24.

126 **Bobby told the judge:** Bass, *Taming the Storm*, 171.

127 **Kennedys' gamble paid off:** "Dr. King Released," *New York Times*; "R. F. Kennedy's
Part in King Case Scored," *New York Times*; "Vandiver Criticizes Kennedy," *New York
Times*; *Taming the Storm*, 171; Bryant, *Bystander*, 185; and *Kennedys and Kings*, 23.

128 **story behind those Kennedy phone calls:** Vandiver OH; and "Vandiver Criticizes
Kennedy."

128 **New threads in the reconstruction:** Author interviews with Harris Wofford and
Carl Sanders.

129 **his back-channel orchestrations:** RFK OH, December 4, 1964, 347; and author interview with John Seigenthaler.

129 **Bobby did the right thing:** *Kennedys and Kings*, 22; and Kempton, "His Brother's
Keeper," *New York Post*.

129 **Bobby always worried more:** Edson, "Restive Brother of President," *Salt Lake Tribune*; *Making of the President, 1960*, 387–88; and author interview with Liz Moynihan.

130 **When a margin of victory:** Nixon, *Six Crises*, 362–63; and *Making of the President,
1960*, 397.

131 **Jack wrote out:** *Robert Kennedy and His Times*, 232.

4. GETTING JUSTICE

132 *Saturday Evening Post* **profile:** "Amazing Kennedys," 48.

132 **never had so close a relative:** President Eisenhower named his favorite brother Mil-

ton to several part-time posts, including special envoy to Latin America, and Milton was a key behind-the-scenes adviser to the president.

132 **Only twice had a younger man been U.S. attorney general:** Pennsylvania's Richard Rush was just thirty-two when he became attorney general in 1814. Caesar Rodney of Delaware turned thirty-five the same month he took office in 1807. (Baker, *Conflicting Loyalties,* 55.)

133 **"Fuck public opinion":** Cassini, *I'd Do It All,* 218. The always practical Joe is said to have advised Jack, "When you get to the White House there are two jobs you must lock up—Attorney General and director of the Internal Revenue Service" (Beschloss, *Crisis Years,* 302).

133 **"Bobby's the best man":** Sidey, *John F. Kennedy, President,* 12.

134 **In trademark fashion:** Kessler, *Sins of the Father,* 389; and Clifford, *Counsel to the President,* 336–37.

134 **Bobby's own wishes:** RFK OH, February 29/March 1, 1964, 15–16; and *Robert Kennedy and His Times,* 228–29.

135 **The attorney general idea:** RFK OH, February 29/March 1, 1964, 15; and *Brother Within,* 14.

136 **"we just vacillated":** *Robert Kennedy and His Times,* 231.

136 **"Nothing but headaches":** Seigenthaler OH, February 22, 1966, 306–7, JFKL; and *Court Years,* 305.

136 **Bobby agonized over his decision:** Seigenthaler OH, February 22, 1966, 307–8 and 325–26.

137 **The full story is even better:** *Court Years,* 305–6; and Beale, "It Wasn't JFK's Idea," *Miami Herald.*

137 **"Kennedy people try to make out":** *Real Story,* 115–16.

138 **Woodrow Wilson had thought about:** Carroll, "Appointing a Relative," *New York Times.*

138 **take the sting out:** Lawrence, "Robert Kennedy Being Considered for Cabinet Post," *New York Times;* and Joseph Alsop, "Religious Issue," *Washington Post.*

138 **A dash of Kennedy wit:** *Robert Kennedy and His Times,* 233; Morris, "Senate Confirms Cabinet," *New York Times;* and *Robert Kennedy: His Life,* 111.

139 **"Even though I went back":** John Reilly OH, October 22, 1970, 18, JFKL.

139 **Those preparations paid off:** "Appointing a Relative"; and Bickel, "Robert F. Kennedy: The Case Against Him," *New Republic.*

140 **courtesy of Bobby's least favorite person:** Baker interviews, Senate Historical Office, 83.

140 **"Once I had made up my mind":** *Robert Kennedy and His Times,* 233.

141 **Frank "Screw" Andrews, a poster-child:** Messick, *Syndicate Wife,* 46.

141 **That history earned Screw:** DeMichele and Potter, "Sin City Revisited," Eastern Kentucky University; "9 in Policy Racket Indicted," *New York Times;* and "Sentencing is Slated for 8 in Tax Fraud," *Marion Star.*

142 **actually waging that war:** Navasky, *Kennedy Justice,* 50–51, 54–55, and 61.

142 **The only agency that balked:** *Kennedy Justice,* 49; and *Robert Kennedy: His Life,* 115.

143 **Kennedy would not be denied:** Author interview with G. Robert Blakey; *Kennedy Justice,* 49–51; Maas, *The Valachi Papers,* 35; and *Robert Kennedy and His Times,* 264–66.

143 **an evangelist from the first:** *Kennedy Justice,* 55; Andrew, *Power to Destroy,* 12; and author interview with Mortimer Caplin.

144 **pose a serious threat to the Mafia:** Ragano and Raab, *Mob Lawyer,* 135; Giancana and Giancana, *Double Cross,* 295–97; and "Silent F.B.I. Man," *New York Times.*

144 **judged by his results:** *Kennedy Justice,* 55; and Goldfarb, *Perfect Villains,* 43 and 313.

145 **"No politics—period":** Harris, "Justice II," *New Yorker.*

145 **first politically sensitive case:** RFK OH, April 30, 1964, 245; *Band of Brothers,* 146; and Seigenthaler OH, February 22, 1966, 393. In this case and others, the attorney general could not indict directly, but had to work through a grand jury. Yet grand juries do what state and federal prosecutors want them to do so regularly that, as Chief Judge Sol Wachtler of the New York Court of Appeals famously said, they'd "indict a ham sandwich."

146 **a style that would become characteristic:** *Kennedy Justice,* 416; author interview with and email from Gerald Shur; and William Hundley OH, February 17, 1971, 30, JFKL.

146 **operatives at the White House were furious:** Walter Sheridan OH, May 1, 1970, 55–56, JFKL; author interview with Henry Ruth; and Hundley OH, 31.

147 **It was true:** *Kennedy Justice,* 413; and *Robert Kennedy: His Life,* 114.

148 **"If grandfather is so close":** *Landis,* 199; author interview with Nicholas Katzenbach; and Justin Feldman OH, October 23, 1969, 19, JFKL.

149 **Bobby had been suspicious of Frank:** Wilson, *Sinatra: An Unauthorized Biography,* 170–71; and Kelley, *His Way,* 329.

150 **Did he back off:** FBI Los Angeles office memo to J. Edgar Hoover, October 7, 1963, File 92-6667, FBI Frank Sinatra records; Gage, "Ex-Aides Say Justice Department Rejected a Sinatra Inquiry," *New York Times;* and author interview with Dougald McMillan.

150 **Looking back, McMillan:** Author interview with McMillan; and "Ex-Aides Say Justice Department Rejected."

151 **effort expended was unprecedented:** *Fall and Rise,* 193; and *Kennedy Justice,* 455–60.

151 **a case that had stuck in his craw:** Parton, "An Insider's Chilling Story," *Time;* and *Trials of Jimmy Hoffa,* 239 and 284.

152 **Nashville trial was historic:** *Kennedy Justice,* 471.

153 **"If you indict someone enough":** Author interview with James P. Hoffa.

153 **"It's like Ahab and the whale":** Author interview with Victor Navasky; and *Trials of Jimmy Hoffa,* 211.

154 **the attorney general "was delighted":** Kenneth O'Donnell OH, May 6, 1969, 37, JFKL.

154 **Roy Cohn was the other old enemy:** Cohn OH, 4 and 7; and *Citizen Cohn,* 261.

154 **"It's a toss-up":** Cohn OH, 5; *Citizen Cohn,* 261; and author interview with Neil Gallagher.

155 **Bobby gave the green light:** Cohn OH, 10-1; Perlmutter, "Cohn Mail Watch Scored," *New York Times;* and author interview with Gerald Walpin.

155 **Walpin disagrees, explaining:** Author interview with Walpin.

156 **his hometown paper said:** Scales and Nickson, *Cause at Heart,* 281.

156 **Scales's punishment:** Goldman, "Junius Scales, Communist," *New York Times;* and Wechsler, "Robert F. Kennedy: A Case of Mistaken Identity," *Progressive.*

157 **But Bobby was changing:** Author interview with Anthony Lewis; "Human Rights and the Legacy of Robert F. Kennedy," Kennedy Library Forum, March 3, 2003; and *Cause at Heart,* 412.

158 **"The lesson of the Otepka case":** Kluckhohn, *Lyndon's Legacy,* 156–57.

158 **liberal critics applauded:** Maas, "Robert Kennedy Speaks Out," *Look; Kennedy Justice* 10–11; and author interview with Patricia Wald.

159 **issues facing American Indians:** Ramsey Clark OH, June 29, 1970, 13–16, JFKL; "Indians Victims," *New York Times;* Mudd, *Place To Be,* 213; and Clarke, *Last Campaign,* 159.

159 **a more pervasive problem:** *Kennedy Justice,* 19; and Edelman, *Searching for America's Heart,* 36.

161 **"As he inspected the pool":** Anderson, "Robert's Character," *Esquire.*

162 **"Her teacher didn't believe her":** Author interview with James Clayton.

162 **policing the errant rich:** Pearson and Anderson, "Big Business Reassured on Kennedy," *Washington Post;* Hailey, "Robert Kennedy Rebuts Critics," *New York Times;* and "Antitrust Cases Defended By U.S.," *New York Times.*

163 **The Kennedys felt double-crossed:** RFK OH, April 13, 1964, 197 and 200, JFKL.

163 **not to unleash a tempest:** Courtney Evans OH, December 18, 1970, 61, JFKL; Carroll, "Steel: A 72-Hour Drama," *New York Times;* and "Miller Hits Steel Probe Tactics," *Niagara Falls Gazette.* Bobby's press secretary then, Edwin Guthman, said the press calls came at the more reasonable hour of 5:00 A.M. (*Band of Brothers,* 233–34.)

164 **In fact, Bobby and Jack:** *Robert Kennedy and His Times,* 405; Evans OH, 61; and RFK OH, April 13, 1964, 200.

164 **So it was with Sergeant Alvin York:** Means, "JFK Joins Drive to Help Sgt. York," *New York Journal-American.*

165 **one of the most consequential cases:** Author interview with Bruce Terris; and Terris, "Attorney General Kennedy versus Solicitor General Cox," *Journal of Supreme Court History.*

166 **"Everybody in town wanted to see":** *Kennedy Justice,* 314.

166 **With no text or even notes:** Oral arguments of *Gray v. Sanders,* 372 US 368.

167 **surrounding himself with such a gifted staff:** *American Journey,* 82; and *Kennedy Justice,* 183–84.

168 **staff took on his passions:** John Doar OH, November 13, 1964, 19, JFKL; and Kraft, "Riot Squad for the New Frontier," *Harper's.*

168 **image of a riot squad:** *Band of Brothers,* 106.

169 **"The Kennedys didn't wait":** Edwin Guthman OH, February 21, 1968, 10, JFKL; Reilly OH, December 16, 1970, 98, JFKL; and author interview with Katzenbach.

169 **Bobby's stamina:** *Shining Hour,* 54–55; and Wallace, "50-Mile Walk," *Life.*

170 **The new mood was conspicuous:** "Justice II"; *Band of Brothers,* 105; and "What Makes Bobby Run?" *Newsweek.*

171 **Randomly selected messengers:** Author interview with Jayne Lahey; and *Band of Brothers,* 106.

172 **"Are you coming to my party":** Norris, *Mary McGrory,* 60.

172 **didn't appreciate the informality:** Schott, *No Left Turns,* 192–93; *Vendetta,* 234; and *Band of Brothers,* 266.

173 **the way he used his desk:** *Making of a Folk Hero,* 127; and author interview with Haynes Johnson.

173 **Skeptics inside and outside the government:** Miller, *Plain Speaking: An Oral Biography,* 409; and author interview with Katzenbach.

174 **Bobby's mythos would grow:** Weiner, *Enemies: A History of the FBI,* 420 (Ashcroft

and President Bush honored Bobby in part to win Ted Kennedy's support for their No Child Left Behind law, although Ashcroft also modeled his war on terror after Bobby's war on crime); Eric Holder briefing September 25, 2014 (whitehouse.gov /the-press-office/2014/09/25/statement-president-and-attorney-general-eric -holder); and Biddle letter to RFK, January 8, 1962. (While Biddle's praise was effusive, he didn't and possibly couldn't offer any examples of Bobby's accomplishments in the realm of civil liberties at that early stage.)

174 **less time for life outside work:** *Robert Kennedy and His Times*, 585.

175 **"Sinatra kept calling":** Author interview with Sam Adams.

175 **The compound was never empty:** *Place to Be*, 209.

178 **Most dads "go to work":** Author interview with Kerry Kennedy.

178 **after-dark pool parties:** Schlesinger, *Journals: 1952–2000*, 158; and *American Journey*, 165.

178 **the social nerve center:** Gibson, "Kennedy Highjinks," *Kansas City Times*; Paul Fay OH, November 10, 1970, 122, JFKL; and *Journals: 1952–2000*, 110.

179 **Hickory Hill University:** Wilson, *The First 78 Years*, 164; *American Journey*, 166–67; and Marian Cannon Schlesinger, *I Remember*, 160–61.

180 **"he became increasingly bored":** *RFK: Collected Speeches*, 5–6.

180 **He was funny about money:** *American Journey*, 149–50.

181 **Joe had left Bobby a fortune:** Arthur Krock OH, May 10, 1964, 11, JFKL; and Kennedy, *Fruitful Bough*, 113.

181 **"His driver drove us":** Author interview with Jack Rosenthal.

182 **proud patriarch generally refrained:** *John F. Kennedy, President*, 21; and *The Patriarch*, 774.

182 **suffered a massive stroke:** *American Drama*, 287; and *The Patriarch*, 774–77.

182 **none as deeply as Bobby:** Perry, *Rose Kennedy: The Life and Times*, 259.

183 **managed to visit Joe:** *Robert Kennedy: His Life*, 190; and Dallas and Ratcliffe, *The Kennedy Case*, 103 and 161.

183 **"His interest in life has been his children":** *Fruitful Bough*, 215.

184 **his brother's keeper:** RFK OH, February 29/March 1, 1964, 5–7 and 20–21; and author interview with Adlai Stevenson III.

184 **build a dam in Ghana:** *Robert Kennedy and His Times*, 561; and Rostow, *Diffusion of Power*, 203.

184 **That brief included politics:** *Kennedy Justice*, 405–6; and "Riot Squad for the New Frontier."

185 **"The chief political manager":** Day, *My Appointed Round*, 9.

185 **Partisan politics came into play:** *Power to Destroy*, 20–44 and 327; and "Investigation of the Special Service Staff of the Internal Revenue Service," U.S. Joint Committee on Internal Revenue Taxation, June 5, 1975.

186 **Bobby didn't always get his way:** *Wheeling and Dealing*, 97–99; author interview with Herbert Stern; and Joseph Alsop OH, June 22, 1971, 45–49, JFKL. In his book, Baker calls Adams "Mr. Jones." In an interview with the author, he confirmed that Jones is in fact Adams.

187 **it was Ted's turn:** Gwirtzman OH, 4–5.

187 **JFK's planned run for reelection:** "'64 Plan Is Denied by Robert Kennedy," *New York Times*; Seymour Harris letter and memo to RFK, May 13, 1963, Box 238, RFK Papers; and RFK OH, December 4, 1964, 353.

188 **"Without any hesitation, Bobby jumped":** *The Kennedy Case,* 137.

188 covering up his brother's physical frailties: *Robert Kennedy: His Life,* 60; and Reeves, *Question of Character,* 295–96.

188 enable the president's sexual deceptions: Author interview with Bobby Baker; and RFK OH, May 14, 1964, 311, JFKL.

190 When it came to sexual mores: Wills, *Kennedy Imprisonment,* 45.

190 But Bobby was different: Viser, "Kennedy Letters."

191 "He definitely had an eye for pretty women": Author interviews with Gwen Gibson, John Anderson, and Richard Goodwin.

191 No one knows for sure: Brown, *No Longer Alone,* 44–51; and author interview with Joan Winmill Brown.

192 Bobby and Marilyn Monroe: Carroll and Tomich, "Death of Marilyn Monroe," 29.

192 he was fascinated with her: Author interview with McPeck.

5. BREAKING BARRIERS

195 "We have a party": Belafonte, *My Song,* 267.

195 "He had called the meeting": Horne and Schickel, *Lena,* 278.

195 Kenneth Clark, black America's: *Band of Brothers,* 220; *My Song,* 267; and *Parting the Waters,* 810.

196 Bobby was shocked: *American Journey,* 120; *My Song,* 268; and Eckman, *Baldwin,* 189.

197 Three hours into the evening: *American Journey,* 122; RFK OH, April 30, 1964, 289; and *My Song,* 269.

197 "We left convinced": *American Journey,* 121.

198 Bobby came away: Baldwin, "Letter from a Region," *New Yorker; Robert Kennedy and His Times,* 334; and RFK OH, April 30, 1964, 289–90.

198 Both sides had agreed: Robinson, "Robert Kennedy Fails to Sway Negroes," *New York Times;* and Reston, "Nation and the Parties," *New York Times.*

198 "I guess if I were": *Band of Brothers,* 221.

199 "Our conclusion that we had": *American Journey,* 121.

200 The night before: Murphy, "Robert Kennedy Was Nice but Firm," *Atlanta Constitution;* RFK Law Day Exercise Speech, May 6, 1961, JFKL, 12–13; McGill, "Robt. Kennedy Gets Ovation," *Atlanta Constitution;* and *Bystander,* 259.

200 A closer listen: Law Day Exercise Speech, 1, 9, and 11–12.

201 Instead, Bobby from the first: Doar and Landsberg, "Performance of the FBI in Investigating Violations of Federal Laws," 13; *Bystander,* 250; Law Day Exercise Speech, 9.

202 Integrating public schools: *Bystander,* 252–60.

203 There was no doubt: RFK OH, December 4, 1964, 402; *Robert Kennedy and His Times,* 307–8; Sherrill, *Gothic Politics,* 195; and "Judge Due to Rule On Suit," *New York Times.*

204 "It would mean so much": RFK OH, December 4, 1964, 411–12.

205 When he left office: *Kennedy Justice,* 276–77.

205 "an effort to signal": Katzenbach, *Some of It Was Fun,* 42.

206 In Anniston, a city: Booker and Booker, *Shocking the Conscience,* 190–92.

207 Bobby later said: RFK OH, December 4, 1964, 370; Farmer, *Lay Bare,* 197; and *Shocking the Conscience,* 182–84.

208 **face-to-face meeting:** Seigenthaler OH, February 22, 1966, 444–45.

208 **next challenge:** Raines, *My Soul,* 103; and *Robert Kennedy and His Times,* 296.

208 **crisis of the moment:** *Band of Brothers,* 171; and Seigenthaler OH, February 22, 1966, 456–61.

210 **Back at the Justice Department:** Sidey, *John F. Kennedy, President,* 142; *Parting the Waters,* 407; and *Band of Brothers,* 177–78.

211 **Bobby never entirely forgot:** RFK OH, December 4, 1964, 384–85; *Lay Bare,* 206; *Bystander,* 274–76; and Loftus, "U.S. Tells World," *New York Times.*

212 **testing moment for Bobby:** Author interview with Patterson; and *Shocking the Conscience,* 203.

213 **The night the Freedom Riders:** " 'Freedom Riders' Force a Test," *Newsweek.*

213 **Mississippi had looked like:** "Bob Kennedy Cites Dire Need," *Chicago Daily Defender;* and *Robert Kennedy and His Times,* 318.

214 **Sometimes the exchange:** Transcripts of phone conversation between RFK and Ross Barnett, September 25, 1962, 12:20 P.M., 6, Burke Marshall Papers, JFKL.

214 **Two days later:** Transcripts of phone conversation between RFK and Barnett, September 27, 1962, 2:50 P.M., 1–2.

215 **As deals were made:** Transcripts of phone conversations between RFK and Barnett, September 30, 1962, 12:45 P.M., 4 and 9; Press Statement by Barnett, September 30, 1962, 11:00 P.M.; and Meredith, *Three Years,* 194.

216 **The folly underlying:** Lord, *The Past That Would Not Die,* 178; and "Though the Heavens Fall," *Time.*

216 **Back in Washington:** *Band of Brothers,* 204; and RFK OH, December 4, 1964, 485.

218 **"The planning wasn't that bad":** RFK OH, December 4, 1964, 484.

218 **Although President Kennedy deserved:** RFK OH, December 4, 1964, 479; and Lewis, "Mississippi: Broader Impact of the Crisis," *New York Times.*

219 **In the rich white communities:** RFK OH, December 4, 1964, 342–43; and author interview with Ethel Kennedy.

219 **"I was born here":** Fenton, "Cabots and Lowells," *New York Times.*

219 **Disabilities were not considered:** *Times to Remember,* 153–55 and 286; Gibson and Schwarz, *Rose Kennedy and Her Family,* 63; and *The Patriarch,* 532–34.

220 **Joe had been searching:** *The Patriarch,* 242–64 and 537; *Rose Kennedy and Her Family,* 60; *Times to Remember,* 286; and "Amazing Kennedys."

221 **"the first of the tragedies":** *Times to Remember,* 286.

221 **Not all the lessons:** *The Patriarch,* 311; *Robert Kennedy and His Times,* 34; *Hostage to Fortune,* 234; and Ross, "Joseph P. Kennedy."

222 **Joe was always looking:** *Hostage to Fortune,* 531 and 615–16; and *Founding Father,* 388.

222 **most disturbing evidence:** *Hostage to Fortune,* 131 and 133.

223 **no evidence that Bobby:** Frank Mankiewicz OH, June 26, 1969, 44, JFKL; author interview with Jeff Greenfield; and RFK, "Jews Have a Fine Fighting Force," *The Boston Post.*

223 **feelings about homosexuals:** Vidal, *Palimpsest,* 393–94.

224 **Truman Capote, another gay writer:** Clarke, *Capote,* 411; and Peter Edelman OH, March 13, 1974, 54, JFKL.

224 **Bobby was ahead:** RFK OH, May 14, 1964, 335; and Eugene Nickerson OH, May 2, 1972, 14, JFKL.

224 **If the Kennedy boys:** *Sins of the Father,* 49; and *Shining Hour,* 56.

224 **Bobby's sister Jean:** Shapiro, *Danced*, 123–24.

225 **And while civil rights:** *Hostage to Fortune*, 531; *Robert Kennedy: His Life*, 241; and author interview with and emails from Peter Edelman.

226 **stirred a small voice:** "Though the Heavens Fall"; and *Band of Brothers*, 205.

226 **next chapter in that struggle:** Berger, "George C. Wallace: His Life and Legacy," *Anniston Star*; and Wallace "Segregation Forever" speech (youtube.com/watch?v=6C -kBVggFrs).

226 **way to fulfill:** RFK OH, December 6, 1964, 518 and 524, JFKL; and civilrights.JFK library.org/Media-Assets/The-University-of-Alabama.aspx#State-vs-United -States—The-Law-is-the-Law.

227 **trip to the Heart of Dixie:** RFK OH, December 6, 1964, 520–21; and *Some of It Was Fun*, 113.

228 **D-Day in Tuscaloosa:** Trammel, *George Wallace: The Self-Inflicted Wound*, 10 and 81.

228 **"The show is over":** Ibid., 73 and 90.

229 **That week in June 1963:** Clymer, "When Presidential Words," *New York Times*; and RFK OH, December 4, 1964, 503–4.

229 **ended on an upbeat note:** Hunter, "Marchers in Capital," *New York Times*; and Casey, "3000 in Peaceful Rights March," *Washington Post*.

230 **Bobby came out swinging:** Marjorie McKenzie Lawson OH, November 14, 1965, 56–57, JFKL.

230 **two steps ahead:** *Robert Kennedy and His Times*, 349.

231 **determined to control it:** *Robert Kennedy and His Times*, 351; Reilly OH, October 29, 1970, 63–64; *Place to Be*, 117; and *Parting the Waters*, 876.

232 **The march came off:** *Parting the Waters*, 882–83; southernspaces.org/2004 /television-news-and-civil-rights-struggle-views-virginia-and-mississippi#section6; RFK OH, December 22, 1964, 591, JFKL; and author interview with Jayne Kobliska.

233 **Bobby authorized the FBI:** *Robert Kennedy and His Times*, 352–61; Garrow, "FBI and Martin Luther King," *The Atlantic Monthly*; *Parting the Waters*, 852–59; "Negro in America," *Newsweek*; and Kenworthy, "Barnett Charges Kennedys," *New York Times*.

235 **Any regrets about:** Whalen and Whalen, *The Longest Debate*, 45; and *Robert Kennedy: His Life*, 260.

235 **Bobby knew that this bill:** *Band of Brothers*, 221; and RFK statement, Senate Commerce Committee, July 1, 1963.

236 **naturally made enemies:** Lowrey, "R. Kennedy, Others 'Hanged' At Rally," *Anniston Star*; Sitton, "50 Hurt in Negro Rioting," *New York Times*; *Parting the Waters*, 819; and *Failing America's Faithful*, 39.

236 **By the end of his tenure:** *Kennedy Justice*, 109; *My Song*, 233; and author interview with Jack O'Dell.

6. CUBA AND BEYOND

238 **Bobby Kennedy's memoir:** RFK, *Thirteen Days*, 27 and 35–36.

238 **"We're eyeball to eyeball":** Stewart Alsop and Charles Bartlett, "In Time of Crisis," *Saturday Evening Post*.

239 **The biggest deceit:** *Thirteen Days*, 27; and Khrushchev, *Khrushchev Remembers*, 493–94.

240 **"Exposure to danger":** *Thirteen Days*, 13.

240 **seeds of the missile crisis:** Wyden, *Bay of Pigs*, 124 (the Harvard professor was John Plank of the Government Department); and nsarchive.gwu.edu/bayofpigs/chron .html.

241 **Jack proved him right:** President Kennedy speech, Cincinnati, October 6, 1960.

241 **While it was fair:** nsarchive.gwu.edu/bayofpigs/chron.html; JFK speech, Johnstown, Penn., October 15, 1960 (presidency.ucsb.edu/ws/?pid=74041); and JFK statement, October 20, 1960 (presidency.ucsb.edu/ws/?pid=74127).

241 **Their hard line:** nsarchive.gwu.edu/bayofpigs/chron.html; and Fontova, "Betrayal at the Bay of Pigs," *TheBlaze.*

242 **President Kennedy read the situation:** Wyden, *Bay of Pigs*, 264; nsarchive.gwu .edu/bayofpigs/chron.html; and "Bay of Pigs," a short history, JFKL (JFKlibrary.org /JFK/JFK-in-History/The-Bay-of-Pigs.aspx).

243 **the Kennedys' problem:** nsarchive.gwu.edu/bayofpigs/chron.html.

243 **As for Bobby:** JFK speech, Democratic Dinner, October 6, 1960; June 1, 1961 RFK memo as reported in *Robert Kennedy and His Times*, 444–45; *John F. Kennedy, President*, 109–11; *Band of Brothers*, 111; and Wyden, *Bay of Pigs*, 269.

244 **protect his brother's flank:** RFK OH, February 29/March 1, 1964, 76–77; *John F. Kennedy, President*, 125; *Foreign Relations of the United States (FRUS)*, 1961–1963, vol. X, April 22, 1961, 314; and Rostow, *Diffusion of Power*, 211.

244 **ensure the mistakes weren't repeated:** June 1, 1961 RFK memo, *Robert Kennedy and His Times*, 447; and "RFK Notes and Memos: Cuban Crisis," Attorney General Papers, Box 215, JFKL.

245 **Taylor worried that:** Maxwell Taylor OH, October 22, 1969, 2, JFKL; Taylor letter to JFK, June 13, 1961, JFKL; June 1, 1961 RFK memo, *Robert Kennedy and His Times*, 446; RFK OH, February 29/March 1, 1964, 58; and author interview with and emails from James Hershberg.

246 **Soviet leader had "savaged me":** Stacks, *Scotty*, 4.

246 **curious new friend Georgi:** Fursenko and Naftali, *One Hell of a Gamble*, 380.

247 **different message than Jack:** Michael Forrestal, who worked for National Security Advisor McGeorge Bundy, said Bobby invented the term *counterinsurgency*, which was both credible and romantic enough that it was repeated over the years; RFK, *Seek a Newer World*, 117; and *Kennedys & Kings*, 386.

248 **no doubt what he had in mind:** January 19, 1962 CIA memo on meeting with RFK re: Cuba, JFKL.

248 **Bobby got what he asked:** William Craig memo to Edward Lansdale, February 2, 1962, National Security Archive—George Washington University; and Bohning, *Castro Obsession*, 102.

249 **embraced by the CIA:** Branch and Crile, "Kennedy Vendetta"; and Helms, *Over My Shoulder*, 202–3.

250 **Bobby pushed ahead:** Blight and Kornbluh, *Politics of Illusion*, 117; and *Over My Shoulder*, 205.

250 **it wasn't just Cuba:** Halberstam, *Best and the Brightest*, 69–70; *Kennedys & Kings*, 372–73; and *FRUS, 1961–1963, American Republics*, vol. XII, 1996.

251 **Instead of learning:** Author interview with Richard Goodwin; and *Over My Shoulder*, 202.

252 **eliminate Fidel Castro:** "Alleged Assassination Plots Involving Foreign Leaders," Senate Select Committee to Study Governmental Operations, 72–108; and "CIA Inspector General's Report on Plots to Assassinate Fidel Castro."

252 **did Bobby Kennedy issue an order:** "Alleged Assassination Plots," 275–76; *Over My Shoulder*, 201; author interviews with Adam Walinsky, Frank Mankiewicz, and Richard Goodwin; and RFK OH, April 30, 1964, 281.

254 **attorney general never wavered:** Edward Lansdale memo to members of Caribbean Survey Group, January 20, 1962, National Security Archive; "Kennedy Vendetta"; and author interview with Richard Goodwin.

254 **legacy that long outlived:** *Castro Obsession*, 258; and *Kennedys & Kings*, 386.

254 **Cuba wasn't the only place:** Halberstam, "Ivory Coast Gets American Hello," *New York Times*.

255 **Bobby's Africa trip:** Halberstam, "Africans Answered by Robert Kennedy," *New York Times*.

255 **a whirlwind:** Grove, *Behind Embassy Walls*, 73–74; and author interview with Brandon Grove.

256 **back on a plane:** Lind, "When Camelot Went," *National Interest*.

256 **a novelty to the Japanese:** Lewis, "Robert Kennedy Tours Hamlets," *New York Times*; Lewis, "Kennedy on the Road," *New York Times*; Lewis, "Robert Kennedy Turns a Bar," *New York Times*; Rosenthal, "His Brother's Voice," *New York Times*; and RFK, *Just Friends*, 50–51.

257 **demonstrate his tough side:** Rosenthal, "Robert Kennedy Debates Leftists," *New York Times*; UPI. "Robert Kennedy's Temper Flares," *Bristol Daily Courier*; Lewis, "Kennedy on the Road," *New York Times*; Rosenthal, "Leftists Heckle Robert Kennedy," *New York Times*; *Robert Kennedy and His Times*, 564–65; and RFK OH, April 13, 1964, 169–70.

258 **scope out a future adversary:** "Robert Kennedy Assures Vietnam," *New York Times*; and *Best and the Brightest*, 274.

258 **Every stop posed:** "Pope Receives R. F. Kennedys," *New York Times*; Grove email to author; Susan Wilson, "Guide to Traveling"; and *Just Friends*, 153.

259 **another Cold War flash point:** *Robert Kennedy: His Life*, 294; and *Just Friends*, 120 and 124.

260 **The way he traveled:** Grove email.

260 **arrived back in Washington:** "Having Wonderful Time . . . Bobby," Mary McGrory, *America*; and John Lindsay letter to Dean Rusk, February 5, 1962, JFKL.

260 **using a public megaphone:** "Text of Address by Attorney General Kennedy Calling on Americans," *New York Times*; and "Robert Kennedy Urges Students," *New York Times*.

261 **the difference he was making:** "Visit of Attorney General to Japan," American Embassy Tokyo to State Department, February 28, 1962, National Archives.

262 **He was growing personally:** *Behind Embassy Walls*, 93–94; author interview with and emails from Grove.

263 **Khrushchev affirmed:** Khrushchev letter and Kennedy statement (microsites.JFK library.org/cmc/oct28/).

264 **"one chance in five":** RFK OH, February 29/March 1, 1964, 100; and RFK OH, February 13, 1965, 33, JFKL.

264 **Bobby emboldened his commander:** *Thirteen Days*, 68 and 70.

265 **he wanted everyone to know:** Ibid., 31 and 108.

265 **not completely honest:** "In Time of Crisis"; and May and Zelikow, *Kennedy Tapes*, 66 and 68.

266 **he began to waver:** *Kennedy Tapes*, 130, 261, and 400.

266 **picked up by microphones:** Naftali, "Origins of 'Thirteen Days,'" *Miller Center Report*.

267 **Bobby emphasized to the Soviet ambassador:** Dobrynin, *In Confidence*. The ambassador also described that conversation in a cable to his Foreign Ministry on October 27, 1962, during the crisis itself, although its contents did not become public for decades (Hershberg, "Anatomy of a Controversy," *Cold War International History Project Bulletin*). Philip Zelikow, an expert on the missile crisis and the Kennedy tapes, says that "JFK is recorded privately telling Admiral Anderson that, on Saturday, the decision had been made to proceed with a strike on Tuesday, October 30. When, on October 30, Max Frankel published a NYT article saying that, in fact, no strike had been imminent, JFK explodes privately to his intimates, saying that Frankel's assertion 'is untrue!'" (Zelikow email to author.)

268 **to come clean:** "Anatomy of a Controversy."

268 **another self-interested untruth:** *Thirteen Days*, 27–28; "Blank Spot in Cuban Picture," *Washington Post*; RFK OH, April 30, 1964, 224; Stern, *Averting 'The Final Failure,'* 30–31; *Eyeball to Eyeball*, 223; and RFK memo to JFK, April 19, 1961, *FRUS, 1961–1963*, vol. X.

269 **undermine his enemies:** *Thirteen Days*, 34, 46, 50, and 120; *Kennedy Tapes*, 82 and 388–89; RFK OH, February 27, 1965, 605–6; RFK OH, February 13, 1965, 22; Stern, *Cuban Missile Crisis in American Memory*, 69–70; RFK OH, May 14, 1964, 322; Bundy, *Danger and Survival*, 431; and *Eyeball to Eyeball*, 318. The Cuba-Turkey deal "had been suggested earlier on Oct 27 in a telegram from Raymond Hare, the US ambassador to Turkey, and then picked up and pressed by Dean Rusk," says Philip Zelikow (Zelikow email).

270 **"In our negotiations":** *Khrushchev Remembers*, 500.

270 **Nobody worked harder:** *Band of Brothers*, 122 and 126; *Eyeball to Eyeball*, 224; and *Johnny, We Hardly Knew Ye*, 283.

271 **"Don't put it in writing":** RFK note to John McCone, May 2, 1962, Attorney General Series, Box 88, JFKL.

271 **Bobby reimagined:** *Thirteen Days*, 16; author interview with Dan Fenn; and *Eyeball to Eyeball*, 570.

273 **by the time it was uttered:** Dobbs, "Price of a 50-Year Myth," *New York Times*.

273 **Getting that wrong:** *Cuban Missile Crisis in American Memory*, 153; and Joseph Alsop, "Gaining the Objective," *Washington Post*.

274 **got one thing right:** Book sales figure is from W. W. Norton, Bobby's publisher, which says *Thirteen Days* was a bestseller and that total sales likely were even higher but not all records are available; and *Khrushchev Remembers*, 500.

275 **even more puzzling:** Memo of Mongoose meeting with RFK, October 16, 1962, National Security Archive; and Hershberg email to author.

275 **Once the crisis had passed:** Mark J. White, *Kennedys and Cuba*, 320; *Over My Shoulder*, 225; and RFK OH, April 30, 1964, 277.

276 **Bay of Pigs prisoners:** *Band of Brothers*, 132; and *Some of It Was Fun*, 94.

277 **Operation Habeas Corpus:** Ottenberg, "Behind the Rescue," *Washington Star*; Oral histories Richard Cull, Richard French, Mario Noto, and Robert Schoenenberg, December 17, 1970, JFKL; and Johnson, *The Bay of Pigs: The Leaders' Story*, 333.

278 **"Thanks, fellows":** *Some of It Was Fun*, 93.

278 **Pete Ray's case:** Author interview with Janet Ray.

279 **outraged by the lies:** Fineman and Mascarenas, "Bay of Pigs: The Secret Death," *Los Angeles Times;* and author interview with and emails from Janet Ray.

279 **downplaying mistakes:** Kraslow, "Bay of Pigs Invasion Errors Detailed," [Yonkers] Herald Statesman; Wyden, *Bay of Pigs: The Untold Story,* 278; McGeorge Bundy memo to JFK, April 18, 1961, *FRUS, 1961–1963,* vol. X; Kenworthy, "Goldwater Asks Senate Inquiry," *New York Times;* and Pearson, "Washington Merry-Go-Round," January 27, 1963.

280 **defuse hostilities with Castro:** Gordon Chase memo, "Mr. Donovan's Trip to Cuba," March 4, 1963, National Security Archive; Gordon Chase memo to William Atwood, November 8, 1963, National Security Archive; and Kornbluh and Lucci, "JFK and Castro," *Cigar Aficionado.*

281 **still more overtures:** JFK address to Inter-American Press Association, November 18, 1963 (presidency.ucsb.edu/ws/?pid=9529); Szulc, *Fidel: A Critical Portrait,* 588; and "CIA Inspector General's Report on Plots."

281 **What we do know:** RFK memo to Dean Rusk, "Travel to Cuba," December 12, 1963, National Security Archive; RFK OH, April 30, 1964, 277; and author interview with Ethel Kennedy.

7. THE INTERREGNUM

283 **The calm was broken:** Manchester, *Death of a President,* 195.

283 **"I have news for you":** *Death of a President,* 196 and 257.

283 **the news was cataclysmic:** *Robert Kennedy and His Times,* 608; and Davidson, "Profile in Family Courage," *Saturday Evening Post.*

284 **"There's been so much hate":** *Death of a President,* 196–97.

284 **First Brother to First Son:** *Death of a President,* 254–58.

285 **Barely an hour:** *Death of a President,* 258 and 269; and *Band of Brothers,* 244.

285 **"Tears were streaming":** Author interview with David Kraslow.

285 **The moment the plane:** *Death of a President,* 387, 391–92, 419, and 442–43; and *Robert Kennedy and His Times,* 610.

287 **"It's such an awful shame":** Spalding OH, 57.

287 **the laws of primogeniture:** "Pride of the Clan," *Time;* and "Democrats: The Shadow & the Substance," *Time.*

288 **rumor floated around Washington:** Jack Rosenthal OH, December 8, 2004, 17, JFKL.

288 **Jack's dark secrets:** *Robert Kennedy: His Life,* 276–80; *Death of a President,* 257–58; and Goldstein, *Lessons In Disaster,* 117–18.

288 **drawn Bobby even closer:** *Death of a President,* 11 and 146.

289 **it was just the opposite:** *Death of a President,* 493–94 and 517; *Robert Kennedy and His Times,* 612; Davidson, "What Has Tragedy Meant," *Good Housekeeping;* and Califano, *Inside,* 128.

290 **He would come unstrung:** Author interview with Haynes Johnson; Seigenthaler OH, June 5, 1970, 7, JFKL; and author interview with Ethel Kennedy.

290 **his grief was different:** *Times to Remember,* 458; and Pierre Salinger OH, May 26, 1969, 2, JFKL.

291 **Bobby who crumpled:** *Shining Hour,* 116; *On His Own,* 2–3; *Making of a Folk Hero,* 217; *Seeds of Destruction,* 475; *Some of It Was Fun,* 134; and Andersen, *Jackie After Jack,* 87.

291 **Ed Guthman begged journalists:** *When I Think of Bobby,* 124; *Shocking the Conscience,* 280; and Spalding OH, 59.

292 **Jack was no longer:** *Making of a Folk Hero,* 219; *RFK: A Memoir,* 29–30; and Davidson, "Profile in Family Courage."

292 **"I think often of Bobby's grief":** *True Compass,* 210.

292 **To Seigenthaler, it looked:** Author interview with Seigenthaler.

293 **"The moment he walked in":** *American Journey,* 146–47.

293 **The other perpetual mourner:** *Robert Kennedy: His Life,* 282; Heymann, *Bobby and Jackie: A Love Story; Shining Hour,* 284; and author interview with Ethel. The notion that Bobby was romantically involved with Jackie offered the latest take on the Camelot legend, with Jackie now in the role of Guinevere.

294 **What about Jimmy Hoffa:** "Hoffa 'Plot' to Kill R. F. Kennedy," *New York Times;* and Sheridan OH, 3.

295 **where he stood with LBJ:** *Robert Kennedy: His Life,* 290; Sidey, "Amid Disorder," *Life;* RFK OH, May 14, 1964, 322; and Johnson, *Vantage Point,* 99.

295 **gulf was on graphic display:** *Robert Kennedy and His Times,* 623–24; *Mutual Contempt,* 9; *Passage of Power,* 229–30; Spalding OH, 64; and RFK OH, February 27, 1965, 623.

296 **on earth to annoy the other:** Goodwin, *Lyndon Johnson and the American Dream,* 200.

297 **"a great horse":** *Robert Kennedy and His Times,* 622.

297 **LBJ's advisers pushed:** *Robert Kennedy and His Times,* 627; *Passage of Power,* 374–75; and *Death of a President,* 453–54.

297 **first gathering of the cabinet:** *Passage of Power,* 375–77; *Death of a President,* 475–78; and LBJ OH, August 12, 1969, 20, LBJL.

298 **third perceived affront:** *Death of a President,* 480.

298 **another passive-aggressive move:** Stossel, *Sarge,* 317.

299 **influence would wane:** Schott, *No Left Turns,* 204–5; Guthman OH, 24; O'Donnell OH, 2–3; *Band of Brothers,* 251; and Kempton, "Pure Irish," *New Republic.*

299 **Nowhere was Bobby's diminished:** Richard Goodwin, *Remembering America,* 248; RFK OH, May 14, 1964, 317; and *Mutual Contempt,* 186.

300 **LBJ got even meaner:** *Robert Kennedy and His Times,* 649; Califano, "Concoction of Lies," *Wall Street Journal;* and Janos, "Last Days," *Atlantic Monthly.* South Vietnamese President Ngô Đình Diệm was assassinated in 1963. Dominican President Rafael Trujillo was assassinated in 1961.

300 **"Our power will last":** *Journals: 1952–2000,* 214–15.

301 **classic Bobby Kennedy reasoning:** RFK OH, May 14, 1964, 324, 327, and 329; and *Band of Brothers,* 256–57.

302 **"I'd given three years":** *Lyndon Johnson and the American Dream,* 200.

302 **The reality was that:** Bradlee, "Bobby Going," *Newsweek; Lyndon Johnson and the American Dream,* 201; and RFK OH, May 14, 1964, 329.

303 **"I could have helped you":** White, *Making of the President, 1964,* 266.

303 **might have ended relatively amicably:** Sam Johnson, *My Brother, Lyndon,* 167–68; *Robert Kennedy and His Times,* 662; *Making of the President, 1964,* 264; and Miller, *Lyndon: An Oral Biography,* 389.

303 **Johnson dangled the vice presidency:** *Sarge,* 377; and *Robert Kennedy and His Times,* 659–62.

305   **FBI agents dispatched to Atlantic City:** Sullivan and Brown, *The Bureau: My Thirty Years,* 58.

305   **before his JFK testimonial:** Seigenthaler OH, July 1, 1970, 46–47, JFKL; McGrory, "They Had Something to Say," *Washington Star;* Opotowsky, "Bobby Stops," *New York Post;* and *Mutual Contempt,* 219–20.

305   **Finally he began:** *RFK: Collected Speeches,* 116–17; and *Robert Kennedy: His Life,* 296.

306   **Journalists trumpeted:** "They Had Something to Say"; and "Bobby Stops."

307   **The first turning point:** *RFK: Collected Speeches,* 103–4 and 110.

307   **slowly remembering what it was:** Bradlee, *Good Life,* 295–96.

308   **off on another trip:** Krock, "Kennedy Interview," *New York Times; Robert Kennedy and His Times,* 655–56; Olsen, "Kennedy Meets Polish Cardinal," *New York Times;* Olsen, "Warsaw Throngs," *New York Times;* Olsen, "Oswald Acted on Own," *New York Times;* and Olsen, "Kennedy's Visit Jolts Regime," *New York Times.*

309   **Ethel asked him:** Author interview with Seigenthaler.

309   **The one issue that mattered enough:** Todd Purdum email to author.

309   **"Had they ever been":** Valenti, *Very Human President,* 123–24.

309   **Much of Bobby's energy:** *Heir Apparent,* 7; and Lemann, *Promised Land,* 142.

310   **the glory of King Arthur's Camelot:** *In Search of History,* 523–25.

310   **determined not to help:** "Kennedy Says He Won't Read," *New York Times;* and *Vantage Point,* 27.

311   **still a torrid debate:** Flick, "Kennedys Make Rare Visit," *Dallas Morning News;* and *True Compass,* 212.

311   **Washington's Cardozo High School:** Casey, "Students Steal Show," *Washington Post.*

312   **Reading the Greeks:** Kennedys, *Make Gentle,* 145; and author interview with Marty Nolan.

313   **"It's strange":** Kempton, "Pure Irish," *New Republic.*

313   **"Bobby Kennedy, after November":** *Remembering America,* 446.

313   **Most people have this kind:** *RFK: A Memoir,* 29–30; and "What Makes Bobby Run?" *Newsweek.*

314   **The Bobby Kennedy that emerged:** "Politics of Restoration," *Time;* and O'Donnell and Powers, *Johnny, We Hardly Knew Ye,* 282.

314   **He still had enemies:** O'Donnell OH, 37; and author interview with Rose Styron.

8. OFF AND RUNNING

317   **Bobby had offered LBJ:** RFK letter to LBJ, June 11, 1964, Family papers, Box 8, JFKL; and *Vantage Point,* 99.

317   **"What I *really* want":** "What Has Tragedy Meant."

317   **"He never verbalized":** "RFK Remembered," Kennedy Library Forum, April 25, 2004, 11–12.

318   **"I like this kind of life":** Fallaci, "Robert Kennedy Answers," *Look.*

320   **Bobby sent a young lawyer:** Philip Ryan OH, December 13, 1973, 3, JFKL.

320   **"there is nothing illegal":** "Another Senator Kennedy?" *New York Times.*

320   **Kennedy curse struck again:** Breslin, " 'I guess the only reason,' " *Boston Globe;* and *Band of Brothers,* 285.

321   **on a dime and without a flinch:** *True Compass,* 228; and "What's Bobby," *Newsweek.*

321 **Joe Kennedy understood:** Dallas, *Kennedy Case*, 280–81.

321 **Bobby Kennedy announced:** Weaver, "Keating Welcomes Kennedy," *New York Times*.

322 **The first step:** Apple, "How Kennedy Did It," *New York Times*.

322 **The mayor "welcomed Kennedy's arrival":** *Heir Apparent*, 21; and "How Kennedy Did It."

323 **"Robert Kennedy tended":** Gwirtzman OH, 23–24.

323 **six thousand shirtsleeve delegates:** *Robert Kennedy in New York*, 18–19.

324 **he was unseasoned and unsteady:** Breslin, "Real Kennedy Handicap," *Boston Globe;* Robinson, "Kennedy in Trouble," *New York Times;* James Tolan OH, December 10, 1969, 243, JFKL; and author interview with Eugene Rossides.

325 **Jewish New Yorkers:** *Making of a Folk Hero*, 249; *On His Own*, 38; and Gwirtzman OH, 38.

325 **old rivals harbored a grudge:** *Fall and Rise*, 378–79; and Wright, "Hoffa Preparing," *New York Times*.

326 **he was back criticizing Bobby:** Robinson, "Kennedy and Keating," *Amsterdam News*.

326 **Other attacks on Bobby:** *Heroes of My Time*, 19; and "Keating Fights the Kennedy Magic," *Time*.

327 **early attempts to fight back:** John Burns OH, December 18, 1969, 57, JFKL; and Feldman OH, November 26, 1969, 39, JFKL.

327 **"Everybody was sitting there":** Ronnie Eldridge OH, April 21, 1970, 6–7, JFKL.

327 **He performed only marginally better:** Hess, *America's Political Dynasties*, 526; and Breslin, "Nobody but Kennedy," *Boston Globe*.

328 **It worked at first:** *Robert Kennedy in New York*, 74–75; Joseph Alsop, "Thousands in Glens," *Washington Post;* and Apple, "4,000 at Glens," *New York Times*.

328 **Every stop brought more:** *Robert Kennedy in New York*, 61–75.

329 **"This is something new":** "Thousands in Glens"; Kempton, "Hosts of Unreason," *New Republic; Robert Kennedy in New York*, 65; and *RFK: Collected Speeches*, 123.

329 **Kennedy's lead evaporating:** Lubell, "Keating in the Lead," *New York World-Telegram;* Halberstam, "Cites Suit on Aniline," *New York Times;* and Wechsler, "Case of Mistaken Identity," *Progressive*.

330 **a wake-up call:** "Nonsense for New Yorkers," *New York Times; Robert Kennedy in New York*, 120–21; *Robert Kennedy and His Times*, 673; and *Band of Brothers*, 303.

331 **his new feistiness:** *Band of Brothers*, 126 and 128.

331 **his answers were sharper:** Feldman OH, 35–36; *RFK: Collected Speeches*, 124–30; and Breslin, "Nobody but Kennedy," *Boston Globe*.

332 **"That was absolutely":** Feldman OH, 35–36 and 40.

332 **he noticed Cathy Troy:** Feldman OH, 40–41.

333 **he set his investigators loose:** Bill Haddad OH, February 27, 1969, 8, JFKL; Greenfield, "Keating Record," *Reporter;* and "Kennedy vs. Keating," *Reporter*.

333 **a counterattack:** "Criticism and Retraction," *New York Times;* Felknor, *Dirty Politics*, 197; *Heir Apparent*, 36–38; and "Kennedy Discusses Campaign," *New York Times*.

334 **reluctant to debate:** *Band of Brothers*, 309–11; *Robert Kennedy in New York*, 137–52; and Bigart, "Keating vs. Kennedy," *New York Times*.

335 **"a longtime personal friend":** RFK confirmation hearing before the Senate Judiciary Committee, January 13, 1961, 34.

335 **LBJ made two trips:** Robinson, "Kennedy Cheered," *New York Times;* O'Donnell OH, July 23, 1969, 85–87, JFKL; Richard Wade OH, December 13, 1973, 19, JFKL; and Robinson, "President Greets Kennedy," *New York Times.*

335 **Joe's millions:** Wade OH, 13; Albert Blumenthal OH, December 14, 1973, 21, JFKL; and Apple, "Kennedy Enlisting A Diversified Staff," *New York Times.*

335 **Terence Smith, who covered:** Smith, "Bobby's Image," *Esquire; Band of Brothers,* 306–7; "Kennedy Discusses Campaign"; and author interview with Terence Smith.

336 **rich man's idiosyncrasy:** "Bobby's Image"; and author interview with Smith.

336 **his most effective tactic:** Apple, "Kennedy Reports Gains," *New York Times;* and Apple, "Kennedy, Keating Close," *New York Times.*

337 **Rose, now seventy-four:** *Times to Remember,* 460; *Rose Kennedy and Her Family,* 249; and Cameron, *Rose: A Biography,* 212.

337 **"When we were in New York":** *Kennedy Case,* 280–82.

338 **"We were campaigning":** Author interview with Kerry Kennedy.

338 **"There was an abundance":** *Robert Kennedy in New York,* 186–87.

339 **One critic called:** Senator Jacob Javits was the critic (Apple, "Calls Campaign 'Arrogant,'" *New York Times*).

339 **news outlets were editorializing:** "Key Republican Candidates," *Saturday Evening Post* (Bobby had always been registered to vote on Cape Cod); "Keating for Sen.," *Nation;* and "Six Key Senate Races," *New York Times.*

340 **"Who is he, this rich man's son":** Breslin, "Nobody but Kennedy," *Boston Globe;* and Mailer, "Vote for Bobby K," *Village Voice.*

341 **Bobby stood out:** *Robert Kennedy in New York,* 186–87.

341 **"This vote," he said:** *Band of Brothers,* 311.

341 **the numbers seemed to speak:** Author interview with Rossides; and "Kennedy Victory," *New York Times.*

342 **"Kennedy did not need":** Gwirtzman OH, 47–48.

342 **Bobby himself had it both ways:** Beschloss, *Reaching for Glory,* 107–8; and Valenti, *This Time, This Place,* 209.

343 **his genial best:** "Bobby's Image"; author interview with Smith; and Bigart, "Kennedy Fulfills Some," *New York Times.*

343 **Bobby had one more person:** *The Kennedy Case,* 285–86.

344 **"Being clawed and pushed":** "Kennedy Discusses Campaign," *New York Times.*

344 **he bantered in a way:** *Robert Kennedy in New York,* 39–40; *America's Political Dynasties,* 526; and Feldman OH, November 26, 1969, 39, JFKL.

344 **He was changing:** *RFK: A Memoir,* 32; and "Robert Kennedy Answers."

345 **That conflict and growth:** RFK, *Pursuit of Justice,* 11, 20, and 69.

346 **hate J. Edgar:** RFK OH, April 13, 1964, 129 and 131, JFKL.

346 **His new exemplars:** "Thousands in Glens Falls."

9. SENATOR KENNEDY

348 **What he heard:** Lapides, "Sen. Stennis, RFK in Clash," *Memphis Press-Scimitar;* Loftus, "Poverty Hearing Set," *New York Times; RFK: Collected Speeches,* 199–200; Kotz, *Let Them Eat Promises,* 36; and Senate Anti-Poverty hearings transcript,

April 10, 1967 (mdah.state.ms.us/arrec/digital_archives/vault/projects/OHtran scripts/AU1060_121027.pdf).

349 **"I want to see it":** *RFK: Collected Speeches,* 200; Booker, "RFK Poverty Probe," *Jet;* and Carr, "With RFK in the Delta," *American Heritage.* The full name of the Labor Subcommittee was Employment, Manpower, and Poverty.

349 **"I've been to third-world":** Wilkie, "Robert Kennedy Meets Hunger in the Delta," *Clarksdale Press Register;* author interviews with Kenneth Dean, Peter Edelman, Charles Evers, George Lapides, and William Minor; *Searching for America's Heart,* 52; Wright Edelman, *Lanterns,* 107; "With RFK in the Delta"; and Lapides, "Two Senators 'Shocked,'" *Memphis Press-Scimitar.*

349 **Quietly shattered:** "Bobby Asks Hike in Aid," *Chicago Tribune;* Wilkie, *Dixie,* 169; and "With RFK in the Delta."

350 **The reassembled motorcade:** "Robert Kennedy Meets Hunger"; *Dixie,* 169; and "Two Senators 'Shocked.'"

350 **That trip to the Delta:** "RFK Remembered," 19; *Lanterns* 106–7; and author interview with Curtis Wilkie.

351 **what he could deliver:** *Searching for America's Heart,* 53; Stewart, "Southern Negroes Starving?" *Boston Globe;* "JFK MLK RFK—1960–1968," Kennedy Library Forum, October 23, 2005, 7; and *Lanterns,* 108.

353 **"I hope I've learned":** Stewart Alsop, "Robert Kennedy and the Liberals," *Saturday Evening Post.*

353 **three provocative speeches:** *RFK: Collected Speeches,* 165–76.

354 **the Bedford-Stuyvesant experiment:** Harrington, "South Bronx Shall Rise," *New York;* Newfield, "Few Rays of Hope," *Life; RFK: Collected Speeches,* 185; and 1968 Annual Report, Bedford Stuyvesant Restoration Corporation.

355 **Bobby had collected rents:** *Remarkable Kennedys,* 43–44.

355 **Any doubts that:** Kennedy Library Forum, April 25, 2004, 19–20; and *RFK: A Memoir,* 90.

355 **contravene political orthodoxies:** *RFK: Collected Speeches,* 189–91.

356 **Integration remained:** "Few Rays of Hope"; Franklin Thomas OH, March, 23, 1972, 7, JFKL; and Blumenthal, "Brooklyn Negroes Harass Kennedy," *New York Times.*

356 **The first initiative:** Edelman, *So Rich, So Poor,* 110–11; and "South Bronx Shall Rise."

357 **"I'm not at all sure":** *RFK: A Memoir,* 96.

358 **In the last instance, especially:** *Searching for America's Heart,* 44; and author interview with Paul Schrade.

358 **Bobby showed whose side:** *On His Own,* 103; and *Robert Kennedy and His Times,* 791.

359 **a hero to the farmworkers:** Author interview with Peter Edelman; Cesar Chavez OH, January 28, 1970, 16, JFKL; Chavez, *Autobiography of La Causa,* 449.

359 **He didn't have to travel:** *RFK: A Memoir,* 82; and Millones, "Kennedy and Javits Are Shocked," *New York Times.*

360 **Bobby never forgot:** *RFK: A Memoir,* 82–83; *Robert Kennedy and His Times* 683–84; and *The Bureau: My Thirty Years,* 59.

360 **It wasn't the FBI:** Doyle, "U.S., State Bar Groups Fight Morrissey," *Boston Globe;* Healy, "BC Law School Records," *Boston Globe;* Doyle, "Bar Assn., Morrissey Conflict," *Boston Globe;* Doyle and Nolan, "Morrissey Furor Mounts," *Boston Globe;* author interviews with and emails from Nolan and James Doyle; and Gwirtzman OH, February 10, 1972, 69 and 74, JFKL. Doyle says the FBI didn't help the *Globe* in its investigation.

361 **seize the grail of reform:** *Robert Kennedy and His Times,* 753; Samuel Silverman OH,

September 3, 1969, 11–13, JFKL; author interview with Peter Fishbein; and Kimball, *Bobby Kennedy and the New Politics*, 87 and 102.

362 **Win or lose:** *RFK: A Memoir,* 154; and "Aftermath of the Primary," *New York Times.*

363 **"One thing that Lindsay":** John Burns OH, February 25, 1970, 79, JFKL.

363 **defy political handicappers:** Glass, "ADA Credits Kennedy Brothers," *Washington Post;* Beran, *The Last Patrician,* 214–15; "Robert Kennedy and Oscar Lewis," *Redbook;* and *Robert Kennedy and His Times,* 733.

364 **both embrace Bobby's ideas:** Kempton, "Monument," *New York Post;* and Stewart Alsop, "Robert Kennedy and the Liberals," *Saturday Evening Post.*

365 **The struggle, he told:** Galloway, *The Kennedys and Vietnam,* 58 and 60–61.

365 **Bobby wasn't blind:** *RFK: Collected Speeches,* 271; and *The Kennedys and Vietnam,* 57 and 60.

365 **entered the in-between phase:** *RFK: Collected Speeches,* 271–80; *The Kennedys and Vietnam,* 63–67; and author interview with Sherwin Markman.

366 **candor often trumped caution:** *RFK: Collected Speeches,* 280; and *RFK: A Memoir,* 125.

367 **a step too far:** "Ho Chi Kennedy," *Chicago Tribune;* Wicker, "Humphrey Scores Kennedy's Plan," *New York Times;* and "Administration Cold Shoulders," *Chicago Tribune.*

367 **"I'm afraid," he told:** *RFK: A Memoir,* 128.

368 **"If I became convinced":** *RFK: A Memoir,* 128.

368 **An especially nasty meeting:** Mankiewicz OH, August 12, 1969, 71–73, JFKL; and *Robert Kennedy and His Times,* 768–69.

369 **Bobby made his moves:** *RFK: Collected Speeches,* 288–98; and *On His Own,* 254.

370 **Today's youth "are the children":** RFK, *Seek a Newer World,* 4–5.

371 **top secret evidence:** Author interview with Daniel Ellsberg; Ellsberg, *Secrets: A Memoir of Vietnam,* 202; and Peter Edelman OH, July 15, 1969, 84–85, JFKL.

372 **Bobby made clear his attitude:** "Kennedy on Africa," *New Yorker;* transcript of *RFK in the Land of Apartheid;* and Laing, "RFK's African Trip," *New York Daily News.*

372 **"I came here":** "Ripple of Hope" speech.

373 **"Few will have the greatness":** Ibid.

373 **Those lines:** Transcript of *RFK in the Land of Apartheid ;* and *Robert Kennedy and His Times,* 746.

374 **Bobby addressed Stellenbosch:** RFK's Stellenbosch University speech, June 7, 1966 (rfksafilm.org/html/speeches/unistell.php); and RFK, "Suppose God Is Black," *Look.*

374 **visited the student leader:** Author interview with Ian Robertson.

374 **another banned leader:** "Suppose God Is Black"; and *Robert Kennedy and His Times,* 747.

375 **last big excursion:** "RFK's African Trip."

375 **Press reviews of his trip:** "Senator Kennedy," *Die Burger,* June 7, 1966; "Kennedy, Come Back," *Rand Daily Mail;* and "RFK's African Trip."

376 **"If you're in":** Author interview with Margaret Marshall.

377 **He also found time:** Author interview with Ethel Kennedy.

378 **"The kids were a pain":** Art Buchwald OH, March 12, 1969, 33–34, JFKL.

378 **No circus was complete:** Cronin and RFK Jr., *Riverkeepers,* 80; and *Ethel,* 92.

378 **"He knew everyone hated":** Buchwald OH, 4.

379 **The animals were Ethel's:** Carroll, "Ethel Kennedy Wins," *New York Times;* and Schaap, *R.F.K.*, 22–24.

379 **Ethel's affluence ensured:** Schaap, *R.F.K.*, 17–18.

379 **"We had sat down":** *Failing America's Faithful*, 42.

380 **he temporarily forgot:** Author interviews with George and Liz Stevens; and Rory Kennedy's documentary *Ethel*, HBO.

380 **first to reach its top:** Whittaker, *A Life on the Edge*, 121–27; Arnold, "Senator Is Praised," *New York Times*, March 26, 1965; RFK, "Our Climb," *Life;* and author interviews with Jim Whittaker and Melody Miller.

381 **"Bobby and I were":** Author interview with Fred Harris; and Harris, *Does People Do It?* 154–55.

381 **on every trip:** *Does People Do It?* 157; and *Seeds of Destruction*, 527.

382 **the dust-up:** Corry, *Manchester Affair*, 176–77; and Manchester, *Controversy and Other Essays*, 65.

383 **Never had there been a Senate office:** Dooley, *Robert Kennedy: The Final Years*, 36, *Robert Kennedy and His Times*, 677; author interview with Melody Miller; and Kiker, "Robert Kennedy and the What-If Game," *Atlantic Monthly*.

384 **Never had there been a senator:** *Heir Apparent*, 74.

385 **"If you're making speeches":** Author interview with Walinsky.

385 **Angie was unique:** Author interviews with Nancy Dutton, Ethel Kennedy, and Anne Hudson Shields.

387 **"made me really want to":** Stevenson, "Talk of the Town," *New Yorker*, June 12, 1971.

387 **why his aides believed:** Author interviews with Esther Newberg and Greenfield; Greenfield OH, December 10, 1969, 27, JFKL; and Wes Barthelmes OH, May 20, 1969, 58, JFKL.

388 **He'd done even more:** Author interview with Josefina Bernard Harvin.

388 **he surprised colleagues:** Author interviews with Walter Mondale and Mankiewicz.

389 **"Our new proximity":** *True Compass*, 229.

389 **In practice, that meant:** Hersh, *The Education of Edward Kennedy*, 276; Fleming, "Kennedy Mystique," *New York Times Magazine;* and Canellos, *Last Lion*, 122–23.

390 **There wasn't much kidding:** Author interview with Nolan; and January 1966 RFK letter to LBJ, with LBJ response, January 27, 1966, White House Famous Names file, Box 8, LBJL.

390 **LBJ kept track:** Liz Carpenter memo to LBJ, April 1, 1966, White House Famous Names file, Box 8, LBJL; and *Mutual Contempt*, 316.

391 **Johnson's preoccupation:** *Mutual Contempt*, 318 and 321; and Harry McPherson memo to LBJ, "Thoughts on Bobby Kennedy and Loyalty," June 24, 1965, Aides file, Box 21, LBJL.

392 **Bobby kept his own tabs:** RFK OH, May 14, 1964, 331; and *Remembering America*, 396–97.

393 **"Kennedy has worked":** Schaap, *R.F.K.*, 40.

393 **That ideological progression:** Warren and Tretick, "Bob Kennedy We Knew," *Look; Seek a Newer World*, 74–75; and Newfield, "What Kind of President," *Boston Globe*.

395 **The journalist who best:** Feiffer, "Bobby Twins," *Village Voice*.

395 **conflicting signals Bobby was sending:** Author interview with Elizabeth Drew;

"Robert Kennedy Answers"; and McGrory, "He Had to Be Explained," *Boston Globe*.

395 **depended on the timing:** Haddad email to author; and McGovern, *Grassroots*, 115.

10. LAST CAMPAIGN

398 **His achievements added up:** *U.S. News & World Report*, "On the Campaign Trail with Robert Kennedy"; "Robert Kennedy for President," *New York Times; Remembering America*, 435; and Glass, "Compulsive Candidate," *Saturday Evening Post*.

399 **he told Lowenstein:** *RFK: A Memoir*, 186.

399 **Bobby was again asking himself:** Newfield, "Time of Plague," *Village Voice;* Joseph Alsop, "Can Bob Kennedy Be Pressured?" *Washington Post; Times to Remember*, 466; and *True Compass*, 262.

400 **telephone acquaintances late at night:** White, *Making of the President, 1968*, 186.

400 **Bobby thought McCarthy vain:** *RFK: A Memoir*, 191.

401 **Fully aware of the risk:** Boyarsky, *Big Daddy*, 183; and Witcover, *85 Days*, 60.

402 **responding more to gut instincts:** *RFK: A Memoir*, 224–25.

402 **only two events mattered:** White, *Making of the President, 1968*, 103; Stout, *People: The Story*, 185; Bradshaw, "Richard Goodwin: The Good, the Bad," *New York;* and McGrory, "Disgust in McCarthy Camp," *Miami News*.

403 **"It took Bobby Kennedy seventeen":** Carpenter, "On the Candidates," *New York Times*.

404 **"My decision reflects":** *RFK: Collected Speeches*, 320–22.

405 **rollout of a presidential campaign:** Schumach, "Kennedy Parades to Mixed Chorus," *New York Times;* and *Meet the Press*, March 17, 1968.

405 **The fun part began:** *RFK: Collected Speeches*, 323–27; *Robert Kennedy and His Times*, 862; and *RFK: A Memoir*, 234.

406 **a second War on Poverty:** *RFK: Collected Speeches*, 328–29; "Charisma Amid the Chaos," kuhistory.com; and Harwood, "First Week's Crowds Elate Kennedy Camp," *Washington Post*.

406 **"Any who seek high office":** *RFK: Collected Speeches*, 334–35.

407 **Crowds were the most emphatic:** *On His Own*, 319–20; and *Making of the President, 1968*, 203.

407 **the polarized responses:** Stevenson, *Robert F. Kennedy Campaign*, 20 and 27; *RFK: A Memoir*, 170; Halberstam, *Unfinished Odyssey*, 96; Knebel, "Las Vegas: It Wins," *Look;* Hentoff, "Help," *Village Voice; Last Campaign*, 25; *The Bureau: My Thirty Years*, 56; and "Robert F. Kennedy Conference," November 18, 2000, 24, JFKL.

408 **set off particular alarms:** *RFK: Collected Speeches*, 338–39.

409 **president dropped a bombshell:** *RFK: A Memoir*, 244; and author interview with Dall Forsythe.

409 **Old and New Bobbys collided:** *RFK: Collected Speeches*, 350–51; and *My Brother, Lyndon*, 252.

410 **told Bobby not to go:** Tolan OH, June 27, 1969, 45, JFKL.

410 **"I'm only going to talk":** RFK remarks on the assassination of Martin Luther King, Jr., April 4, 1968 (americanrhetoric.com/speeches/rfkonmlkdeath.html).

411 **His remarks, lasting barely:** Lewis and D'Orso, *Walking with the Wind*, 407; author

interview with John Lewis; Murray, "Remove Bloodshed from the Land," *Chicago Sun-Times;* Moynihan, "Democrats, Kennedy and the Murder of Dr. King," *Commentary;* and author interviews with Walinsky and Richard Lugar.

411 **Back at his hotel:** Author interview with Lugar; *Walking with the Wind,* 408; Bigart, "Negroes Are Cool," *New York Times;* Boomhower, *1968 Indiana Primary,* 70; Greenfield OH, 27; and Braden, *Just Enough Rope,* 155.

412 **inherited the slain leader's mantles:** *RFK: Collected Speeches,* 360; and *American Journey,* 261.

412 **unexpected center of attention:** Author interview with Andy Young; and *American Journey,* 348.

413 **Eugene Pulliam wasn't:** *Last Campaign,* 81; and Connor, *Star in the Hoosier Sky,* 11.

414 **So Kennedy changed course:** Herbers, "Indiana Seeing a New Kennedy," *New York Times.*

414 **"The matrons on their porches":** *Making of the President, 1968,* 201.

415 **Some journalists worried:** *It Seems Like Only Yesterday,* 287–92; and *85 Days,* 154.

415 **Simple evenhandedness:** *RFK: Collected Speeches,* 342–43; and *Honorable Profession,* 90.

416 **a powerhouse of an organization:** *CBS Reports,* "Robert F. Kennedy"; author interviews with Gerard Doherty and Kaye Martin; *Robert Kennedy: His Life,* 374; author interview with Richard Corbett; and *Times to Remember,* 470. Corbett managed the campaign's finances under Steve Smith, who had been his boss at the Park Agency.

417 **Bobby spent the earliest hours:** *RFK: A Memoir,* 261–62.

417 **By nightfall Gene McCarthy's:** *1968 Indiana Primary,* 115–16; and Broder, "Kennedy Indiana Feat Raises Doubt," *Washington Post.*

418 **Watching the televised results:** *RFK: A Memoir,* 263–65.

418 **"I wonder why so many of you":** Author interview with Taylor Branch.

419 **"The superintendent twittered":** Dudar, "Perilous Campaign," *New York Post.*

420 **Kristi Witker experienced:** Author interview with Kristi Witker; and Witker, *How to Lose Everything,* 24.

420 **both were sufficiently beguiled:** Navasky, "Jack Newfield Talks About R.F.K.," *New Leader;* and *Unfinished Odyssey,* 37–38.

421 **Journalists reciprocated:** *Honorable Profession,* 91–92.

421 **When they finished there:** Ibid., 92.

421 **they lampooned him:** *Chicago Tribune,* "What Bobby Is"; Loeb, "American Dictator," *Manchester Union Leader;* Kempton, "Why I'm for McCarthy," *New Republic;* and McGrory, "Bobby Fights Himself," *Boston Globe.*

422 **his journalist fans:** Author interview with James Stevenson; Mailer, *Miami and the Siege of Chicago,* 93; *85 Days,* 224–25; and author interview with Dan Rather.

423 **were disciples:** Author interviews with Bill Kovach and Seigenthaler; and *Heroes of My Time,* 21–22.

423 **"I had known Bobby":** Harwood, "With Bobby Kennedy," *Washington Post.*

424 **"We were seduced":** *Shining Hour,* 160–63.

424 **"He was a flame":** Author interview with Drew.

424 **The primary after Indiana:** Author interview with Mark Shields; *85 Days,* 191–92; and Greenfield OH, January 5, 1970, 33–37, JFKL.

425 **how irreconcilable the differences were:** Harwood, "McCarthy and Kennedy," *Washington Post.*

426 **"Won't it be wonderful"**: *The Kennedy Case*, 290.

426 **"he hugged Mrs. Kennedy"**: Ibid., 295.

426 **Oregon was McCarthy country**: *85 Days*, 202 and 206.

428 **A single moment captured**: Larner, *Nobody Knows*, 99–101.

428 **But even Larner later acknowledged**: Author interview with Jeremy Larner; and *Nobody Knows*, 101–2.

428 **how he handled the loss**: Dougherty, "Kennedy Has Little to Say," *Los Angeles Times*; and *RFK: A Memoir*, 271.

429 **met defeat "with grace"**: McGrory, "Will Bobby Join Gene?" *Boston Globe*.

430 **go down swinging**: *RFK: A Memoir*, 271; and *85 Days*, 235–37.

431 **one exchange that registered**: *ABC News*, Debate between RFK and Eugene McCarthy, June 1, 1968.

431 **The day after the debate**: *RFK: A Memoir*, 284; and author interview with Kerry Kennedy.

431 **The day before the primary**: *RFK: A Memoir*, 287.

432 **There was one more incident**: *A Life on the Edge*, 135; *Last Campaign*, 118; and Reddin, unpublished memoir.

433 **Bobby got in the way**: *RFK: A Memoir*, 31; Gary, *White Dog*, 194; and *Last Campaign*, 205.

434 **"You want to hear about"**: *85 Days*, 255.

434 **Bobby believed he could do it**: *Unfinished Odyssey*, 214.

435 **took a quiet moment**: *RFK: A Memoir*, 298.

435 **His valedictory speech**: *RFK: A Memoir*, 298–99; and *RFK: Collected Speeches*, 401–2.

436 **That was as far**: *85 Days*, 265–73; *Last Campaign*, 275; Hamill, "Last Hours of RFK," *New York*; Hamill, "Two Minutes to Midnight," *Village Voice*; Lopez, "The Busboy Who Cradled a Dying RFK," *Los Angeles Times*; and *RFK: A Memoir*, 300.

437 **Chief Reddin says**: Reddin, unpublished memoir.

437 **David, who'd always been terrified**: Reddin, unpublished memoir; and *Being Catholic Now*, xvii. Bob Galland, the Kennedy children's caretaker, says he was with David when the teenager heard the televised news about his father; Galland took him for a walk and told him everything would be okay, but David "had seen too much" to be patronized or consoled. Galland also says it was he, not a TV newscaster, who explained Bobby's shooting to Kerry, Courtney, Michael, Christopher, and Max. Bob Galland's unpublished memoir, and emails from Galland to author.

437 **Bobby meanwhile was transferred**: *RFK: A Memoir*, 302; and *85 Days*, 283. Newfield said he was told the sign had been up there for weeks, which suggests it might have had nothing to do with Bobby. Others insisted that the signmaker had the Kennedys in mind, with Jack as the king who was and Bobby the one who would be. Or perhaps both references were to Bobby himself.

EPILOGUE

439 **a sendoff like this**: United Press International, *Assassination*, 197–202; *American Journey*, 46–47; and *Making of the President, 1968*, 213–15.

439 **signs that spoke**: *Robert Kennedy and His Times*, 1; and "In Memory of Robert Francis Kennedy," June 10, 1968, Memorial Church, Harvard University, 6.

439 **twenty-one-car train:** Harrington, *Fragments of the Century,* 214 and 216–17; and author interview with Mankiewicz.

440 **"They're in heaven":** Author interview with Ethel Kennedy.

440 **"He asked me one day":** *Shining Hour,* 51.

441 **Then there was Rose:** *Times to Remember,* 477–79.

441 **Ted tried to step in:** *New York Times,* "Text of Edward Kennedy's Tribute"; *Shining Hour,* 305.

442 **"It was after Bobby's":** Hubert Humphrey OH, March 30, 1970, 40–43, JFKL.

442 **The questions that everyone asks:** *RN: Memoirs of Richard Nixon,* 305; and author interview with Daley.

442 **Last goodbyes for the slain candidate:** Tupponce, "Hickory Hill," *Virginia Living;* "He Stood for Justice," *Times of London;* "Bob Kennedy We Knew"; and *Shining Hour,* 110.

443 **Not everyone is sentimental:** Author interview with Richard Rusk; and *Counsel to the President,* 545.

443 **"Daddy was very funny":** Collier and Horowitz, *The Kennedys: An American Drama,* 363.

BIBLIOGRAPHY

INTERVIEWS AND CORRESPONDENCE

From 2011 to 2016, the author interviewed or exchanged emails with the following RFK authors, colleagues, family, friends, and others familiar with him and his work: Bess Abell, Tyler Abell, Jerry Abramson, Sam Adams, Bill Allard, Graham Allison, Ben Altman, John Anderson, Patrick Anderson, Bill Arnone, Diego Asencio, Richard Aurelio, George Azar, Bob Baime, Bobby Baker, Charles Bartlett, Jack Bass, John Bates, Jr., Birch Bayh, James Beatty, Al Benn, Jim Bennett, Berl Bernhard, Dan Blackburn, Bill Blair, Robert Blakey, Julian Bond, Richard Boone, Bill Boyarsky, Ben Bradlee, William Brady, Taylor Branch, David Breasted, Philip Brenner, Jimmy Breslin, Albert Brewer, Ed Bridges, Tom Brokaw, Hamilton Brown, Joan Winmill Brown, Sam Brown, William Brown, Dino Brugioni, Chris Burch, Fred Burger, Catherine Burks-Brooks, Brian Burns, Angela Cabrera, Gay Campbell, Lou Cannon, Mortimer Caplin, Ted Carey, Rene Carpenter, Mickey Carroll, Hodding Carter III, John Cassidy, Anne Caudill, Donna Chaffee, LeRoy Chatfield, Wendy Cimmet, Ramsey Clark, James Clayton, Adam Clymer, Jerry Cohen, Barbara Coleman, Jack Colwell, Lawrence Connor, Harry Cook, Richard Corbett, Tom Corcoran, Dan Cordtz, Greg Craig, Barbara Crancer, Joe Crangle, Bill Crawford, Gerry Creedon, John Criswell, Judy Cromwell, John Culver, Kerry Kennedy Cuomo, Mike Curzan, Alan Dabbiere, Bill Daley, Chuck Daly, Sid Davidoff, Jackie Davis, John G. Dean, Kenneth Dean, Midge Decter, Cartha DeLoach, Tom Devries, Jim Dingeman, Muriel Dobbin, Gerard Doherty, Sam Donaldson, Norman Dorsen, Jimmy Doyle, Elizabeth Drew, Frank Dunbaugh, Nancy Dutton, Peter Edelman, Ronnie Eldridge, Daniel Ellsberg, Stan Evans, Charles Evers, Myrlie Evers, Paul B. Fay III, Jules Feiffer, Ken Feinberg, Dan Fenn, Peter Fishbein, Jim Flug, Dall Forsythe, Sonny Fox, Neil Gallagher, Curtis Gans, Dave Garrow, Joe Gelarden, Bill Geoghegan, Jack Germond, Gwen Gibson, Frank Gifford, Bill Gigerich, Tommy Giles, John Gilligan, Ben Glascoe, Howard Glickstein, Jay Goldberg, Ronald Goldfarb, Jay Goldin, Richard Goodwin, Victor Gotbaum, Stanhope Gould, Colvin Grannum, Earl Graves, Winifred Green, Jack Greenberg, Jeff Greenfield, Dick Gregory, Brandon Grove, Henry Gwiazda, Judith Hackett, Bill Haddad, Joe Hakim, Lee Hamilton, Tim Hanan, Wayne Hardin, Fred Harris, LaDonna Harris, Laura Harris, V. V. Harrison, Gary Hart, Craig Harvey, Sioux Harvey, Josefina Bernard Harvin, Bea Harwood, Richard Hatcher, Tom Hayden, Katie Healy, Cynthia Helms, Thelton Henderson, Bill Henry, John Herbers, James Hershberg, Ted Hesburgh, Philip Heymann, Arnold Hiatt, Clint Hill, James Hoffa, Tim Hogan, Warren Hoge, Ernest Hollings, John Jay Hooker, Margot Howard, Charlayne Hunter-Gault, Lester Hyman, Andy Jacobs, Eli Jacobs, Doug Jeffe, Sherry Bebitch Jeffe, Haynes Johnson, Charles Jones, Clarence Jones, James Jones, Kirby Jones, Bill Josephson, Jim Juliana, Lew Kaden, Marvin Kalb, Linda Katz, Nicholas Katzenbach, Damian Kearney, Josie Kelly, Jim Kenary, Chris Kennedy, Douglas Kennedy, Ethel Kennedy, Robert Kennedy, Jr., Crickett Kerrebrock, John Kerry, Sergei

Khrushchev, Edwin King, Jim King, Anne Kirby, Gail Kirk, Paul Kirk, Ted Knap, Jayne Ko-
bliska, Peter Kornbluh, Nick Kotz, Bill Kovach, Polly Kraft, David Kraslow, Jerry Kretch-
mer, Jay Kriegel, Jules Kroll, Steve Kurzman, Gerry LaFollette, Brian Landsberg, Lisa
Lansing, George Lapides, Jeremy Larner, Richard Leone, Larry Levinson, Andrew Levison,
Bonnie Angelo Levy, Nat Lewin, Anthony Lewis, John Lewis, Ron Linton, George Lois,
Hector Lopez, Ted Lowi, Richard Lugar, Pidey Lumet, Staughton Lynd, Frank Lynn, Nance
Lyons, Peter MacLellan, Jeannie Main, Jack Mallon, Frank Mankiewicz, Lane Mann, Sher-
win Markman, Dave Marlin, Catie Marshall, Margie Marshall, Gordon Martin, Kaye Mar-
tin, Bobbie Green McCarthy, Eddymarie McCoy, George McGovern, Joe McGowan, Dougald
McMillan, Eleanor McPeck, James McShane, Ellen Meacham, Walter Mears, Michael Melt-
sner, James Meredith, Melody Miller, Wilson Minor, Martha Minow, Newton Minow,
George Mitrovich, P. J. Mode, Walter Mondale, Robert Morgenthau, Robert Moses, Richard
Mosk, Liz Moynihan, Roger Mudd, Irene Murphy, Ralph Nader, Tim Naftali, Victor Na-
vasky, Esther Newberg, Larry Newman, Susan Newman, John Nolan, Marty Nolan, Jack
O'Dell, Fred Ohrenstein, Richard Ottinger, Harold Pachios, Fred Papert, Barbara Parisi,
Carmine Parisi, Bob Pastor, John Patterson, Gwen Patton, Bob Penn, Barbara Perry, Ches-
ter Pierce, Walter Pincus, David Pitts, Stephen Pollak, Barrett Prettyman, Todd Purdum,
Selwyn Raab, Dan Rapperport, Jim Rasenberger, Dan Rather, Henry Raymont, Betty Jane
Reddin, Jewel Reed, Richard Reeves, Edmund Reggie, Robert Reich, Murray Richtel, Marie
Ridder, Mike Riley, Pat Riley, Paul Rilling, Jinx Ring, Donald Ritchie, Ian Robertson, Joe
Robertson, Sean Rogers, John Rosenberg, Roger Rosenblatt, Jack Rosenthal, Sandy Ross,
Eugene Rossides, David Rusk, Richard Rusk, Henry Ruth, Nicole Salinger, Bob Saloschin,
Carl Sanders, Sydney Schanberg, Andrew Schlesinger, Marian Schlesinger, Steve
Schlesinger, John Schnittker, Paul Schrade, Jill Schuker, Michael Schwartz, Frank Schwelb,
Anthony Scotto, Amy Seigenthaler, John Seigenthaler, Patricia Shakow, Don Shannon,
Tony Sherman, Ann Shields, Mark Shields, Larry Shore, Gerald Shur, Charles Smith, Jean
Kennedy Smith, Jerome Smith, Nancy Smith, Terence Smith, Brandy Solomon, Alan Spi-
vak, Elvin Stanton, Herbert Stern, Sheldon Stern, George Stevens, Liz Stevens, Adlai Ste-
venson III, James Stevenson, B. J. Stiles, Herb Sturz, Rose Styron, Adele Sweet, Robert
Sweet, Jim Symington, Gay Talese, Nan Talese, Susan Tannenbaum, Bruce Terris, Evan
Thomas, Franklin Thomas, J. Mills Thornton, Gail Tirana, Bill Tolan, James Tolan, Kathleen Kennedy Townsend, Tom Troyer, Dick Tuck, John William Tuohy, Rick Tuttle, Joe Tydings, Mark Updegrove, John Van De Kamp, Bill vanden Heuvel, Sander Vanocur, Jack
Vaughn, Milton Viorst, Susan Vogelsinger, Nick von Hoffman, Patricia Wald, Adam Walin-
sky, Wyatt Tee Walker, Gerald Walpin, Bob Walters, Susan Wilbur Wamsley, Richard Was-
serstrom, Marvin Watson, Janet Ray Weininger, David Welch, Lee White, Diane White-
Crane, Calvin Whitesall, Jim Whittaker, Phil Wilens, Curtis Wilkie, Roger Wilkins, Susie
Wilson, Jules Witcover, Kristi Witker, Harris Wofford, Lester Wolff, Andy Young, Philip
Zelikow, and Lois Zenkel.

BOOKS

Abernathy, Ralph. *And the Walls Came Tumbling Down: An Autobiography*. New York:
Harper and Row, 1989.

Adams, John Gibbons. *Without Precedent: The Story of the Death of McCarthyism*. New
York: W. W. Norton, 1983.

Adams, Sherman. *Firsthand Report: The Story of the Eisenhower Administration.* New York: Harper, 1961.

Adler, Bill. *Dear Senator Kennedy.* New York: Dodd, Mead, 1966.

_____ (editor). *The Eloquent Jacqueline Kennedy Onassis: A Portrait in Her Own Words.* New York: William Morrow, 2004.

_____ (editor). *The Kennedy Wit.* New York: Bantam, 1964.

Alexander, Herbert E. *Financing the 1968 Election.* Lexington, Mass.: Heath Lexington, 1971.

Allison, Graham T. *Essence of Decision: Explaining the Cuban Missile Crisis.* Boston: Little, Brown, 1971.

Andersen, Christopher P. *Jackie After Jack: Portrait of the Lady.* New York: William Morrow, 1998.

Anderson, Jack. *Washington Exposé.* Washington, D.C.: Public Affairs, 1967.

Andrew, John A. III. *Power to Destroy: The Political Uses of the IRS from Kennedy to Nixon.* Chicago: Ivan R. Dee, 2002.

Aronson, Marc. *Up Close: Robert F. Kennedy, a Twentieth-Century Life.* New York: Viking, 2007.

Attwood, William. *The Reds and the Blacks: A Personal Adventure.* New York: Harper and Row, 1967.

Baker, Bobby, with Larry L. King. *Wheeling and Dealing: Confessions of a Capitol Hill Operator.* New York: W. W. Norton, 1978.

Baker, Nancy V. *Conflicting Loyalties: Law and Politics in the Attorney General's Office, 1789–1990.* Lawrence: University Press of Kansas, 1992.

Banner, Lois W. *Marilyn: The Passion and the Paradox.* London: Bloomsbury, 2012.

Bardach, Ann Louise. *Without Fidel: A Death Foretold in Miami, Havana, and Washington.* New York: Scribner, 2009.

Barron, John. *Operation Solo: The FBI's Man in the Kremlin.* Washington, D.C.: Regnery, 1996.

Bass, Jack. *Taming the Storm: The Life and Times of Judge Frank M. Johnson, Jr., and the South's Fight over Civil Rights.* New York: Doubleday, 1993.

———. *Unlikely Heroes.* New York: Simon and Schuster, 1981.

Bayley, Edwin R. *Joe McCarthy and the Press.* Madison: University of Wisconsin, 1981.

Beale, Betty. *Power at Play: A Memoir of Parties, Politicians, and the Presidents in My Bedroom.* Washington, D.C.: Regnery, 1993.

Belafonte, Harry. *My Song: A Memoir.* New York: Alfred A. Knopf, 2011.

Belin, David W. *Final Disclosure: The Full Truth About the Assassination of President Kennedy.* New York: Charles Scribner's Sons, 1988.

Benn, Alvin. *Reporter: Covering Civil Rights . . . and Wrongs in Dixie.* Bloomington, Ind.: AuthorHouse, 2006.

Bennett, James V. *I Chose Prison.* New York: Alfred A. Knopf, 1970.

Bennett, William J. *America: The Last Best Hope (Volume II): From a World at War to the Triumph of Freedom.* Nashville: Thomas Nelson, 2007.

Beran, Michael Knox. *The Last Patrician: Bobby Kennedy and the End of American Aristocracy.* New York: St. Martin's, 1998.

Beschloss, Michael R. *The Crisis Years: Kennedy and Khrushchev, 1960–1963.* New York: Edward Burlingame, 1991.

———. *Kennedy and Roosevelt: The Uneasy Alliance.* New York: Harper and Row, 1980.

———. *Reaching for Glory: Lyndon Johnson's Secret White House Tapes, 1964–1965.* New York: Simon and Schuster. 2001.

————.*Taking Charge: The Johnson White House Tapes, 1963–1964.* New York: Simon and Schuster, 1997.

Bird, Kai. *The Color of Truth: McGeorge Bundy and William Bundy, Brothers in Arms: A Biography.* New York: Simon and Schuster, 1998.

Bishop, Jim. *The Day Kennedy Was Shot.* New York: Greenwich House, 1968.

Bissell, Richard M., and Jonathan E. Lewis. *Reflections of a Cold Warrior from Yalta to the Bay of Pigs.* New Haven: Yale University Press, 1996.

Blaine, Gerald, with Lisa McCubbin. *The Kennedy Detail: JFK's Secret Service Agents Break Their Silence.* New York: Gallery, 2010.

Blair, Joan, and Clay Blair, Jr. *The Search for JFK.* New York: Berkley, 1976.

Blakey, G. Robert, and Richard N. Billings. *Fatal Hour: The Assassination of President Kennedy by Organized Crime.* New York: Berkley, 1992.

————. *The Plot to Kill the President: Organized Crime Assassinated J.F.K.* New York: Times, 1981.

Blight, James G., Bruce J. Allyn, and David A. Welch. *Cuba on the Brink: Castro, the Missile Crisis, and the Soviet Collapse.* New York: Pantheon, 1993.

Blight, James G., and Peter Kornbluh (eds.). *Politics of Illusion: The Bay of Pigs Invasion Reexamined.* Boulder: Lynne Rienner, 1998.

Blight, James G., and David A. Welch (eds.). *Intelligence and the Cuban Missile Crisis.* London: Frank Cass, 1998.

————. *On the Brink: Americans and Soviets Reexamine the Cuban Missile Crisis.* New York: Hill and Wang, 1989.

Blough, Roger M. *The Washington Embrace of Business.* New York: Columbia University Press, 1975.

Bly, Nellie. *The Kennedy Men: Three Generations of Sex, Scandal and Secrets.* New York: Kensington, 1996.

Bohning, Don. *The Castro Obsession: U.S. Covert Operations Against Cuba, 1959–1965.* Washington, D.C.: Potomac, 2006.

Booker, Simeon, and Carol McCabe Booker. *Shocking the Conscience: A Reporter's Account of the Civil Rights Movement.* Jackson: University Press of Mississippi, 2013.

Boomhower, Ray E. *Robert F. Kennedy and the 1968 Indiana Primary.* Bloomington: Indiana University Press, 2008.

Borkin, Joseph. *The Crime and Punishment of I. G. Farben: The Startling Account of the Unholy Alliance of Adolf Hitler and Germany's Great Chemical Combine.* New York: Free, 1978.

Bowles, Chester. *Promises to Keep: My Years in Public Life, 1941–1969.* New York: Harper and Row, 1971.

Boyarsky, Bill. *Big Daddy: Jesse Unruh and the Art of Power Politics.* Berkeley: University of California Press, 2008.

Braden, Joan. *Just Enough Rope: An Intimate Memoir.* New York: Villard, 1989.

Bradford, Sarah. *America's Queen: The Life of Jacqueline Kennedy Onassis.* New York: Viking, 2000.

Bradlee, Benjamin C. *A Good Life: Newspapering and Other Adventures.* New York: Touchstone, 1995.

Bradlee, Benjamin C., and John F. Kennedy. *Conversations with Kennedy.* New York: W. W. Norton, 1975.

Branch, Taylor. *At Canaan's Edge: America in the King Years, 1965–68.* New York: Simon and Schuster, 2006.

———. *Parting the Waters: America in the King Years, 1954–63*. New York: Simon and Schuster, 1988.

———. *Pillar of Fire: America in the King Years, 1963–65*. New York: Simon and Schuster, 1998.

Brando, Marlon, with Robert Lindsey. *Brando: Songs My Mother Taught Me*. New York: Random House, 1994.

Brandt, Charles. *I Heard You Paint Houses: Frank "The Irishman" Sheeran and the Inside Story of the Mafia, the Teamsters, and the Final Ride of Jimmy Hoffa*. Hanover, N.H.: Steerforth, 2005.

Brauer, Carl M. *John F. Kennedy and the Second Reconstruction*. New York: Columbia University Press, 1977.

Brenner, Philip. *From Confrontation to Negotiation: U.S. Relations with Cuba*. Boulder: Westview, 1988.

Breslin, Jimmy. *The World of Jimmy Breslin*. New York: Viking, 1967.

Brill, Steven. *The Teamsters*. New York: Simon and Schuster, 1978.

Brokaw, Tom. *Boom! Voices of the Sixties: Personal Reflections on the '60s and Today*. New York: Random House, 2007.

Brown, Joan Winmill. *No Longer Alone*. Old Tappan, N.J.: F. H. Revell, 1975.

Brown, Peter Harry, and Patte B. Barham. *Marilyn: The Last Take*. New York: Dutton, 1992.

Brugioni, Dino A. *Eyeball to Eyeball: The Inside Story of the Cuban Missile Crisis*. New York: Random House, 1991.

Bruno, Jerry, and Jeff Greenfield. *The Advance Man*. New York: William Morrow, 1971.

Bryant, Nick. *The Bystander: John F. Kennedy and the Struggle for Black Equality*. New York: Perseus, 2006.

Buchan, John. *The Thirty-Nine Steps*. New York: ImPress, 1915.

Buchwald, Art. *Have I Ever Lied to You?* New York: Putnam, 1968.

Buck, Pearl S. *The Kennedy Women: A Personal Appraisal*. New York: Cowles, 1970.

Bundy, McGeorge. *Danger and Survival: Choices About the Bomb in the First 50 Years*. New York: Random House, 1988.

Burner, David, and Thomas R. West. *The Torch Is Passed: The Kennedy Brothers and American Liberalism*. New York: Atheneum, 1984.

Burns, James MacGregor. *Edward Kennedy and the Camelot Legacy*. New York: W. W. Norton, 1976.

———. *John Kennedy: A Political Profile*. New York: Harcourt, 1960.

Bzdek, Vincent. *The Kennedy Legacy: Jack, Bobby and Ted and a Family Dream Fulfilled*. New York: Palgrave Macmillan, 2009.

Califano, Joseph A. Jr. *Inside: A Public and Private Life*. New York: Public Affairs, 2004.

———. *The Triumph & Tragedy of Lyndon Johnson: The White House Years*. New York: Simon and Schuster, 1991.

Cameron, Gail. *Rose: A Biography of Rose Fitzgerald Kennedy*. New York: G. P. Putnam's Sons, 1971.

Canellos, Peter S. (editor). *Last Lion: The Fall and Rise of Ted Kennedy*. New York: Simon and Schuster, 2009.

Cannon, Lou. *The McCloskey Challenge*. New York: E. P. Dutton, 1972.

Capote, Truman. *Answered Prayers: The Unfinished Novel*. New York: Random House, 1987.

———. *A Capote Reader*. New York: Random House, 1987.

Caro, Robert A. *The Passage of Power*. New York: Alfred A. Knopf, 2012.

———. *The Years of Lyndon Johnson*. New York: Alfred A. Knopf, 1982.

Carson, Clayborne, Tenisha Hart Armstrong, Susan Caron, Adrienne Clay, Susan Carson, and Kieran Taylor, eds. *The Papers of Martin Luther King, Jr., Volume V.* Berkeley: University of California Press, 2005.

Cassini, Igor, and Jeanne Molli. *I'd Do It All Over Again: The Life and Times of Igor Cassini.* New York: G. P. Putnam's Sons, 1977.

Cassini, Oleg. *In My Own Fashion: An Autobiography.* New York: Simon and Schuster, 1987.

Cellini, D.A.S. *Wobby Wennedy, Hero.* Albany: Peter Zenger, 1965.

Chafe, William H. *Never Stop Running: Allard Lowenstein and the Struggle to Save American Liberalism.* New York: Basic Books, 1993.

Chang, Laurence, and Peter Kornbluh (eds.). *The Cuban Missile Crisis, 1962.* New York: New Press, 1992.

Channing, Carol. *Just Lucky I Guess: A Memoir of Sorts.* New York: Simon and Schuster, 2002.

Chayes, Abram. *The Cuban Missile Crisis: International Crises and the Role of Law.* New York: Oxford, 1974.

Chester, Lewis, and Godfrey Hodgson. *An American Melodrama: The Presidential Campaign of 1968.* New York: Viking, 1969.

Childs, Marquis W. *Witness to Power.* New York: McGraw-Hill, 1975.

Cipes, Robert M. *The Crime War: The Manufactured Crusade.* New York: New American, 1967.

Clark, Kenneth B., and Jeanette Hopkins. *A Relevant War Against Poverty; a Study of Community Action Programs and Observable Social Change.* New York: Harper and Row, 1969.

Clarke, Gerald. *Capote: A Biography.* New York: Simon and Schuster, 1988.

Clarke, Thurston. *The Last Campaign: Robert F. Kennedy and 82 Days That Inspired America.* New York: Henry Holt, 2008.

Clay, Jim. *Hoffa! Ten Angels Swearing: An Authorized Biography.* Beaverdam, Va.: Beaverdam, 1965.

Cleaver, Eldridge. *Eldridge Cleaver: Post-Prison Writings and Speeches.* New York: Random House, 1969.

Clifford, Clark. *Counsel to the President: A Memoir.* New York: Random House, 1991.

Clinch, Nancy Gager. *The Kennedy Neurosis.* New York: Grosset & Dunlap, 1973.

Clymer, Adam. *Edward M. Kennedy: A Biography.* New York: William Morrow, 1999.

Cohen, Warren I. *Dean Rusk.* Totowa, N.J.: Cooper Square, 1980.

Cohn, Roy M. *The Autobiography of Roy Cohn.* Secaucus, N.J.: Lyle Stuart, 1988.

———. *McCarthy.* New York: New American, 1968.

Coles, Robert. *Lives of Moral Leadership: Men and Women Who Have Made a Difference.* New York: Random House, 2001.

Collier, Peter, and David Horowitz. *The Kennedys: An American Drama.* New York: Summit, 1984.

Connable, Alfred, and Edward Silberfarb. *Tigers of Tammany: Nine Men Who Ran New York.* New York: Holt, Rinehart and Winston, 1967.

Connor, Lawrence S. *Star in the Hoosier Sky: The Indianapolis Star in the Years the City Came Alive 1950–1960.* Carmel, Ind.: Hawthorne, 2006.

Cook, Rhodes. *United States Presidential Primary Elections, 1968–1996: A Handbook of Election Statistics.* Washington, D.C.: CQ Press, 2000.

Corn, David. *Blond Ghost: Ted Shackley and the CIA's Crusades.* New York: Simon and Schuster, 1994.

Corry, John. *The Manchester Affair*. New York: G. P. Putnam's Sons, 1967.

Cramer, Richard Ben. *Joe DiMaggio: The Hero's Life*. New York: Simon and Schuster, 2000.

Crispell, Brian Lewis. *Testing the Limits: George Armistead Smathers and Cold War America*. Athens: University of Georgia Press, 1999.

Cronin, John, and Robert F. Kennedy, Jr. *The Riverkeepers: Two Activists Fight to Reclaim Our Environment as a Basic Human Right*. New York: Simon and Schuster, 1997.

Crowley, Monica. *Nixon Off The Record: His Candid Commentary on People and Politics*. New York: Random House, 1996.

Cutler, John Henry. *Cardinal Cushing of Boston*. New York: Hawthorn, 1970.

Dallas, Rita, and Jeanira Ratcliffe. *The Kennedy Case*. New York: G. P. Putnam's Sons, 1973.

Dallek, Robert. *Camelot's Court: Inside the Kennedy White House*. New York: HarperCollins, 2013.

———. *An Unfinished Life: John F. Kennedy, 1917–1963*. Boston: Little, Brown, 2003.

Damore, Leo. *The Cape Cod Years of John Fitzgerald Kennedy*. Englewood Cliffs, N.J.: Prentice-Hall, 1967.

David, Lester. *Ethel: The Story of Mrs. Robert F. Kennedy*. New York: World, 1971.

———. *Ted Kennedy: Triumphs and Tragedies*. New York: Grosset & Dunlap, 1972.

David, Lester, and Irene David. *Bobby Kennedy: The Making of a Folk Hero*. New York: Dodd, Mead, 1986.

Davis, John H. *The Kennedys: Dynasty and Disaster, 1848–1983*. New York: McGraw-Hill, 1984.

———. *Mafia Kingfish: Carlos Marcello and the Assassination of John F. Kennedy*. New York: New American, 1989.

Davis, Kenneth S. *The Politics of Honor: A Biography of Adlai E. Stevenson*. New York: G. P. Putnam's Sons, 1967.

Day, James Edward. *My Appointed Round: 929 Days as Postmaster General*. New York: Holt, Rinehart and Winston, 1965.

Dean, John Gunther. *Danger Zones: A Diplomat's Fight for America's Interests*. Washington, D.C.: New Academia, 2009.

Dell, Donald, and John Boswell. *Never Make the First Offer*. New York: Portfolio, 2009.

DeLoach, Cartha "Deke." *Hoover's FBI: The Inside Story by Hoover's Trusted Lieutenant*. Washington, D.C.: Regnery, 1995.

Demaris, Ovid. *The Director: An Oral Biography of J. Edgar Hoover*. New York: Harper's Magazine, 1975.

de Toledano, Ralph. *RFK: The Man Who Would Be President*. New York: G. P. Putnam's Sons, 1967.

Dickerson, Nancy. *Among Those Present: A Reporter's View of Twenty-five Years in Washington*. New York: Random House, 1976.

Dinneen, Joseph F. *The Kennedy Family*. Boston: Little, Brown, 1959.

DiSalle, Michael V. *Second Choice: The Story of the United States Vice Presidency*. New York: Hawthorn, 1966.

Dittmer, John. *Local People: The Struggle for Civil Rights in Mississippi*. Champaign: University of Illinois Press, 1994.

Divine, Robert A. (compiler). *The Cuban Missile Crisis*. Chicago: Quadrangle, 1971.

Dobbs, Michael. *One Minute to Midnight: Kennedy, Khrushchev, and Castro on the Brink of Nuclear War*. New York: Alfred A. Knopf, 2008.

Dobrynin, Anatoly. *In Confidence: Moscow's Ambassador to America's Six Cold War Presidents*. New York: Times, 1995.

Donaghy, Thomas J. *Keystone Democrat: David Lawrence Remembered*. New York: Vantage, 1986.

Donovan, John C. *The Politics of Poverty*. New York: Bobbs-Merrill, 1967.

Dooley, Brian. *Robert Kennedy: The Final Years*. New York: St. Martin's, 1996.

Dorman, Michael. *Payoff: The Role of Organized Crime in American Politics*. New York: McKay, 1972.

———. *We Shall Overcome: A Reporter's Eye-Witness Account of the Year of Racial Strife and Triumph*. New York: Dell, 1964.

Dougherty, Richard. *Goodbye, Mr. Christian: A Personal Account of McGovern's Rise and Fall*. Garden City, N.Y.: Doubleday, 1973.

Douglas, Gregory. *Regicide: The Official Assassination of John F. Kennedy*. Huntsville, Ala.: Monte Sano Media, 2002.

Douglas, William O. *The Court Years 1939–1975: The Autobiography of William O. Douglas*. New York: Random House, 1980.

Draper, Theodore. *Abuse of Power*. New York: Viking, 1967.

DuBois, Diana. *In Her Sister's Shadow: An Intimate Biography of Lee Radziwill*. Boston: Little, Brown, 1995.

Earley, Pete, and Gerald Shur. *WITSEC: Inside the Federal Witness Protection Program*. New York: Bantam, 2003.

Eckman, Fern Marja. *The Furious Passage of James Baldwin*. New York: M. Evans, 1966.

Edelman, Marian Wright. *Lanterns: A Memoir of Mentors*. Boston: Beacon, 1999.

Edelman, Peter B. *Searching for America's Heart: RFK and the Renewal of Hope*. Boston: Houghton Mifflin, 2001.

———. *So Rich, So Poor: Why It's So Hard to End Poverty in America*. New York: New Press, 2012.

Ehrlichman, John. *Witness to Power: The Nixon Years*. New York: Simon and Schuster, 1982.

Eisele, Albert. *Almost to the Presidency: A Biography of Two American Politicians*. Blue Earth, Minn.: Piper, 1972.

Ellsberg, Daniel. *Secrets: A Memoir of Vietnam and the Pentagon Papers*. New York: Penguin, 2002.

English, David. *Divided They Stand*. Englewood Cliffs, N.J.: Prentice-Hall, 1969.

Eppridge, Bill, and Hays Gorey. *Robert Kennedy: The Last Campaign*. New York: Harcourt, 1993.

———. *A Time It Was: Bobby Kennedy in the Sixties*. New York: Abrams, 2008.

Epstein, Edward Jay. *Inquest: The Warren Commission and the Establishment of Truth*. New York: Bantam, 1966.

Evans, M. Stanton. *Blacklisted by History: The Untold Story of Senator Joe McCarthy*. New York: Crown Forum, 2007.

———. *The Politics of Surrender*. New York: Devin-Adair, 1966.

Evans, Peter. *Nemesis*. New York: HarperCollins, 2004.

Ewald, William Bragg, Jr. *Who Killed Joe McCarthy?* New York: Simon and Schuster, 1984.

Exner, Judith. *My Story*. New York: Grove, 1977.

Fairlie, Henry. *The Kennedy Promise: The Politics of Expectation*. Garden City, N.Y.: Doubleday, 1973.

Farmer, James. *Lay Bare the Heart: An Autobiography of the Civil Rights Movement*. New York: Arbor House, 1985.

Fay, Paul B. *The Pleasure of His Company*. New York: Harper and Row, 1966.

Feldstein, Mark. *Poisoning the Press: Richard Nixon, Jack Anderson, and the Rise of Washington's Scandal Culture.* New York: Farrar, Straus and Giroux, 2010.

Felker, Clay. *The Power Game.* New York: Simon and Schuster, 1969.

Felknor, Bruce L. *Dirty Politics.* New York: W. W. Norton, 1966.

Fleming, Daniel B. *Kennedy vs. Humphrey, West Virginia, 1960: The Pivotal Battle for the Democratic Presidential Nomination.* Jefferson, N.C.: McFarland, 1992.

Forman, James. *The Making of Black Revolutionaries.* New York: Macmillan, 1972.

Fox, Sonny. Unpublished memoir, supplied by Fox.

Frankfurter, Felix, and Joseph P. Lash. *From the Diaries of Felix Frankfurter.* New York: W. W. Norton, 1975.

Franklin, Lynn. *The Beverly Hills Murder File.* Tecopa, Calif.: Epic, 1999.

———. *Sawed-Off Justice.* New York: Putnam, 1976.

Freedman, Monroe H., and Abbe Smith. *Understanding Lawyers' Ethics.* Newark, N.J.: LexisNexis, 2004.

Friedman, Stanley P. *The Magnificent Kennedy Women.* Derby, Conn.: Monarch, 1964.

Fursenko, Aleksandr, and Timothy Naftali. *Khrushchev's Cold War: The Inside Story of an American Adversary.* New York: W. W. Norton, 2006.

———. *One Hell of a Gamble: Khrushchev, Castro, and Kennedy, 1958–1964: The Secret History of the Cuban Missile Crisis.* New York: W. W. Norton, 1997.

Gadney, Reg. *Kennedy.* New York: Holt, Rinehart and Winston, 1983.

Galbraith, John Kenneth. *Ambassador's Journal: A Personal Account of the Kennedy Years.* Boston: Houghton Mifflin, 1969.

Gallagher, Mary Barelli. *My Life with Jacqueline Kennedy.* New York: David McKay, 1969.

Galloway, John. *The Kennedys and Vietnam.* New York: Facts on File, 1971.

Garcia, Mario T., and Sal Castro. *Blowout! Sal Castro and the Chicano Struggle for Educational Justice.* Chapel Hill: University of North Carolina Press, 2011.

Gardner, Gerald. *Robert Kennedy in New York.* New York: Random House, 1965.

Garrison, Jim. *On the Trail of the Assassins.* New York: Warner, 1988.

Garrow, David J. *Bearing the Cross: Martin Luther King, Jr., and the Southern Christian Leadership Conference.* New York: William Morrow, 1986.

———. *The FBI and Martin Luther King, Jr.: From "Solo" to Memphis.* New York: W. W. Norton, 1981.

Garson, Barbara, and Lisa Lyons. *The Complete Text of MacBird.* New York: Grove, 1967.

Garthoff, Raymond L. *Reflections on the Cuban Missile Crisis.* Washington, D.C.: Brookings Institution, 1987.

Gary, Romain. *White Dog.* New York: World, 1970.

Gates, Daryl F., and Diane K. Shah. *Chief: My Life in the LAPD.* New York: Bantam, 1992.

Gentry, Curt. *J. Edgar Hoover: The Man and the Secrets.* New York: W. W. Norton, 1991.

Giancana, Sam, and Chuck Giancana. *Double Cross: The Explosive Inside Story of the Mobster Who Controlled America.* New York: Warner, 1992.

Gibson, Barbara, with Caroline Latham. *Life with Rose Kennedy.* New York: Warner, 1986.

Gibson, Barbara, and Ted Schwarz. *Rose Kennedy and Her Family: The Best and Worst of Their Lives and Times.* New York: Birch Lane, 1995.

Gill, William J. *The Ordeal of Otto Otepka.* New Rochelle, N.Y.: Arlington House, 1969.

Gitlin, Todd. *The Sixties: Years of Hope, Days of Rage.* New York: Bantam, 1987.

Glenn, John. *John Glenn: A Memoir.* New York: Bantam, 1999.

Goldfarb, Ronald L. *Perfect Villains, Imperfect Heroes: Robert F. Kennedy's War Against Organized Crime.* New York: Random House, 1995.

————. *Ransom: A Critique of the American Bail System*. New York: Harper and Row, 1965.

Goldman, Eric Frederick. *The Tragedy of Lyndon Johnson*. New York: Dell, 1968.

Goldstein, Gordon M. *Lessons in Disaster: McGeorge Bundy and the Path to War in Vietnam*. New York: Times, 2008.

Goodwin, Doris Kearns. *The Fitzgeralds and the Kennedys: An American Saga*. New York: Simon and Schuster, 1987.

————. *Lyndon Johnson and the American Dream*. New York: Harper and Row, 1976.

Goodwin, Richard N. *Remembering America: A Voice from the Sixties*. New York: Harper and Row, 1988.

Goulden, Joseph C. *Meany: The Unchallenged Strong Man of American Labor*. New York: Atheneum, 1972.

Graham, Katharine. *Personal History*. New York: Alfred A. Knopf, 1997.

Greenberg, Jack. *Crusaders in the Courts: How a Dedicated Band of Lawyers Fought for the Civil Rights Revolution*. New York: Basic, 1994.

Greenfield, Jeff. *Then Everything Changed: Stunning Alternate Histories of American Politics: JFK, RFK, Carter, Ford, Reagan*. New York: Berkley, 2011.

Grier, Roosevelt, and Dennis Baker. *Rosey, an Autobiography: The Gentle Giant*. Tulsa: Honor, 1986.

Griffith, Robert. *The Politics of Fear: Joseph R. McCarthy and the Senate*. Amherst: University of Massachusetts Press, 1970.

Gromyko, A. A. *Through Russian Eyes: President Kennedy's 1036 Days*. Washington, D.C.: International Library, 1971.

Grove, Brandon. *Behind Embassy Walls: The Life and Times of an American Diplomat*. Columbia: University of Missouri Press, 2005.

Guilaroff, Sydney. *Crowning Glory: Reflections of Hollywood's Favorite Confidant*. Los Angeles: General, 1996.

Guthman, Edwin O. *We Band of Brothers: A Memoir of Robert F. Kennedy*. New York: Harper and Row, 1971.

Guthman, Edwin O. and C. Richard Allen (eds). *RFK: Collected Speeches*. New York: Viking, 1993.

Haig, Alexander M., Jr., and Charles McCarry. *Inner Circles: How America Changed the World*. New York: Warner, 1992.

Halberstam, David. *The Best and the Brightest*. New York: Ballantine, 1969.

————. *The Unfinished Odyssey of Robert Kennedy*. New York: Random House, 1968.

Hamby, Alonzo L. *Liberalism and Its Challengers: F.D.R. to Reagan*. New York: Oxford, 1992.

Hamill, Pete. *Irrational Ravings*. New York: G. P. Putnam's Sons, 1971.

Hamilton, Edith. *The Greek Way to Western Civilization*. New York: Mentor, 1948.

Hamilton, Nigel. *JFK: Reckless Youth*. New York: Random House, 1992.

Hardeman, D. B., and Donald C. Bacon. *Rayburn: A Biography*. Austin: Texas Monthly, 1987.

Harrington, Michael. *Fragments of the Century*. New York: Saturday Review, 1973.

Harris, Fred L. *Does People Do It?: A Memoir*. Norman: University of Oklahoma Press, 2008.

Hastings, Max. *The Fire This Time: America's Year of Crisis*. New York: Taplinger, 1969.

Hayden, Tom. *Reunion: A Memoir*. New York: Collier, 1988.

Haygood, Wil. *Showdown: Thurgood Marshall and the Supreme Court Nomination That Changed America*. New York: Alfred A. Knopf, 2015.

Helms, Richard, and William Hood. *A Look over My Shoulder: A Life in the Central Intelligence Agency*. New York: Ballantine, 2003.

Henggeler, Paul R. *In His Steps: Lyndon Johnson and the Kennedy Mystique.* Chicago: Ivan R. Dee, 1991.

Henry, E. William. *Fatal Alliance: The Prosecution, Imprisonment and Gangland Murder of Jimmy Hoffa.* Great Barrington, Mass.: Andover Press, 2012.

Hentoff, Nat. *A Political Life: The Education of John V. Lindsay.* New York: Alfred A. Knopf, 1969.

Heritage, Inc., and Jay Jacobs. *RFK: His Life and Death.* New York: Dell, 1968.

Herman, Arthur. *Joseph McCarthy: Reexamining the Life and Legacy of America's Most Hated Senator.* New York: Free, 2000.

Hersh, Burton. *Bobby and J. Edgar: The Historic Face-off Between the Kennedys and J. Edgar Hoover That Transformed America.* New York: Basic, 2007.

———. *The Education of Edward Kennedy: A Family Biography.* New York: Dell, 1972.

Hersh, Seymour M. *The Dark Side of Camelot.* Boston: Little, Brown, 1997.

Hershberg, James G. *Marigold: The Lost Chance for Peace in Vietnam.* Washington, D.C.: Woodrow Wilson Center, 2012.

Hess, Stephen. *America's Political Dynasties: From Adams to Kennedy.* Garden City, N.Y.: Doubleday, 1966.

Hewitt, Don. *Tell Me a Story: 50 Years and 60 Minutes in Television.* New York: Public Affairs, 2001.

Heymann, C. David. *Bobby and Jackie: A Love Story.* New York: Atria, 2009.

———. *RFK: A Candid Biography of Robert F. Kennedy.* New York: Dutton, 1998.

Hilsman, Roger. *To Move a Nation: The Politics of Foreign Policy in the Administration of John F. Kennedy.* Garden City, N.Y.: Doubleday, 1967.

Hilty, James W. *Robert Kennedy: Brother Protector.* Philadelphia: Temple University Press, 1997.

Himmelman, Jeff. *Yours in Truth: A Personal Portrait of Ben Bradlee.* New York: Random House, 2012.

Hinckle, Warren, and William W. Turner. *Deadly Secrets: The CIA-Mafia War Against Castro and the Assassination of J.F.K.* New York: Thunder's Mouth, 1993.

Hodgson, Godfrey. *America in Our Time: From World War II to Nixon.* Garden City, N.Y.: Doubleday, 1976.

Hoeh, David C. *1968—McCarthy—New Hampshire: I Hear America Singing.* Rochester, Minn.: Lone Oak, 1994.

Hoffa, James R., as told to Oscar Fraley. *Hoffa: The Real Story.* New York: Stein and Day, 1975.

Hoffa, James R., and Donald I. Rogers. *The Trials of Jimmy Hoffa: An Autobiography.* Chicago: Regnery, 1970.

Hoffman, Abbie. *Revolution for the Hell of It.* New York: Thunder's Mouth, 1968.

Horne, Lena, and Richard Schickel. *Lena.* Garden City, N.Y.: Doubleday, 1965.

Horowitz, David. *From Yalta to Vietnam: American Foreign Policy in the Cold War.* New York: Penguin, 1965.

Houghton, Robert A., and Theodore Taylor. *Special Unit Senator: The Investigation of the Assassination of Senator Robert F. Kennedy.* New York: Random House, 1970.

Hryb, William. *Vanished: The Life and Disappearance of Jimmy Hoffa.* Rock Hill, S.C.: Strategic Media, 2013.

Hudson, James A. *RFK, 1925–1968.* New York: Scholastic, 1969.

Humphrey, Hubert H. *The Education of a Public Man: My Life and Politics.* Minneapolis: University of Minnesota Press, 1991.

Hunt, E. Howard. *Give Us This Day: The Inside Story of the CIA and the Bay of Pigs Invasion.* New Rochelle, N.Y.: Arlington House, 1973.

Hunter-Gault, Charlayne. *In My Place.* New York: Vintage, 1992.

Hutchinson, Dennis J. *The Man Who Once Was Whizzer White: A Portrait of Justice Byron R. White.* New York: Free, 1998.

James, Ralph C., and Estelle Dinerstein James. *Hoffa and the Teamsters: A Study of Union Power.* Princeton, N.J.: D. Van Nostrand, 1965.

Jamieson, Kathleen Hall. *Packaging the Presidency: A History and Criticism of Presidential Campaign Advertising.* New York: Oxford, 1984.

Jenkins, Roy. *A Life at the Center: Memoirs of a Radical Reformer.* New York: Random House, 1993.

———. *Nine Men of Power.* London: Hamish Hamilton, 1974.

Johnson, Haynes. *The Age of Anxiety: McCarthyism to Terrorism.* Orlando: Harcourt, 2005.

———. *The Bay of Pigs: The Leaders' Story of Brigade 2506.* New York: W. W. Norton, 1964.

Johnson, Lady Bird, and Claudia T. Johnson. *A White House Diary.* New York: Holt, Rinehart and Winston, 1970.

Johnson, Lyndon Baines. *The Vantage Point: Perspectives of the Presidency, 1963–1969.* New York: Holt, Rinehart and Winston, 1971.

Johnson, Sam Houston. *My Brother, Lyndon.* New York: Cowles, 1970.

Kaiser, Charles. *1968 in America: Music, Politics, Chaos, Counterculture, and the Shaping of a Generation.* New York: Grove, 1988.

Kaiser, David E. *American Tragedy: Kennedy, Johnson, and the Origins of the Vietnam War.* Cambridge, Mass.: Belknap Press of Harvard University Press, 2000.

———. *The Road to Dallas: The Assassination of John F. Kennedy.* Cambridge, Mass.: Belknap Press of Harvard University Press, 2008.

Kaiser, Robert Blair. *"RFK Must Die!" Chasing the Mystery of the Robert Kennedy Assassination.* Woodstock, N.Y.: Overlook, 2008.

Kalb, Madeleine G. *The Congo Cables: The Cold War in Africa—From Eisenhower to Kennedy.* New York: Macmillan, 1982.

Katzenbach, Nicholas deB. *Some of It Was Fun: Working with RFK and LBJ.* New York: W. W. Norton, 2008.

Kavanagh, Julie. *Nureyev: The Life.* New York: Pantheon, 2007.

Kelley, Kitty. *His Way: The Unauthorized Biography of Frank Sinatra.* New York: Bantam, 1986.

Kempe, Frederick. *Berlin 1961: Kennedy, Khrushchev, and the Most Dangerous Place on Earth.* New York: G. P. Putnam's Sons, 2011.

Kempton, Murray. *Rebellions, Perversities, and Main Events.* New York: Random House, 1994.

Kennedy, Edward M. *Decisions for a Decade: Policies and Programs for the 1970s.* Garden City, N.Y.: Doubleday, 1968.

———. *The Fruitful Bough.* West Hanover, Mass.: Halliday Lithograph Graphics, 1965.

———. *True Compass: A Memoir.* New York: Twelve, 2009.

Kennedy, Jacqueline. *Jacqueline Kennedy: Historic Conversations on Life with John F. Kennedy.* Edited by Michael Beschloss. New York: Hyperion, 2011.

Kennedy, John F. *Appeasement at Munich: The Inevitable Result of the Slowness of Conversion of the British Democracy from a Disarmament to a Rearmament Policy.* Thesis, Harvard University. March 15, 1940.

———. *As We Remember Joe* (editor). Cambridge, Mass.: University Press, 1945.

————. *The Kennedy Wit*. Edited by Bill Adler. New York: Bantam, 1964.

————. *Profiles in Courage*. New York: Harper and Row, 1964.

Kennedy, Joseph P. *Hostage to Fortune: The Letters of Joseph P. Kennedy*. Edited by Amanda Smith. New York: Viking, 2001.

————. *I'm for Roosevelt*. New York: Reynal and Hitchcock, 1936.

Kennedy, Kerry. *Being Catholic Now: Prominent Americans Talk About Change in the Church and the Quest for Meaning*. New York: Crown, 2008.

Kennedy, Robert F. *The Enemy Within: The McClellan Committee's Crusade Against Jimmy Hoffa and Corrupt Labor Unions*. New York: Harper and Row, 1960.

————. *I Dream Things That Never Were and Say, Why Not? Quotations of Robert F. Kennedy*. Los Angeles: Stanyan, 1970.

————. *Just Friends and Brave Enemies*. New York: Popular Library, 1962.

————. *Promises to Keep: Memorable Writings and Statements*. Kansas City, Mo.: Hallmark Editions, 1969.

————. *The Pursuit of Justice*. New York: Harper and Row, 1964.

————. *Thirteen Days: A Memoir of the Cuban Missile Crisis*. New York: W. W. Norton, 1969.

————. *To Seek a Newer World*. Garden City, N.Y.: Doubleday, 1967.

Kennedy, Robert F. *Make Gentle the Life of This World: The Vision of Robert F. Kennedy*. Edited by Maxwell Taylor Kennedy. New York: Harcourt, 1998.

————. *Rights for Americans: The Speeches of Robert F. Kennedy*. Edited by Thomas A. Hopkins. Indianapolis: Bobbs-Merrill, 1964.

Kennedy, Robert F., and Edwin O. Guthman. *Robert Kennedy, in His Own Words: The Unpublished Recollections of the Kennedy Years*. New York: Bantam, 1988.

Kennedy, Robert F., Jr., and Dennis Nolan. *St. Francis of Assisi: A Life of Joy*. New York: Hyperion Books for Children, 2005.

Kennedy, Rose Fitzgerald. *Times to Remember*. Garden City, N.Y.: Doubleday, 1974.

Kessler, Ronald. *The Sins of the Father: Joseph P. Kennedy and the Dynasty He Founded*. New York: Warner, 1996.

Khrushchev, Nikita. *Khrushchev Remembers*. Boston: Little, Brown, 1990.

————. *Memoirs of Nikita Khrushchev: Vol. 1, Commissar (1918–1945)*. University Park: Pennsylvania State University Press, 2005.

Khrushchev, Sergei. *Nikita Khrushchev and the Creation of a Superpower*. University Park: Pennsylvania State University Press, 2000.

Kimball, Penn. *Bobby Kennedy and the New Politics*. Englewood Cliffs, N.J.: Prentice-Hall, 1968.

King, Coretta. *My Life with Martin Luther King, Jr.* New York: Holt, Rinehart and Winston, 1969.

Klaber, William, and Philip H. Melanson. *Shadow Play: The Murder of Robert F. Kennedy, the Trial of Sirhan Sirhan, and the Failure of American Justice*. New York: St. Martin's, 1997.

Klein, Edward. *The Kennedy Curse: Why America's First Family Has Been Haunted by Tragedy for 150 Years*. New York: St. Martin's, 2003.

Kluckhohn, Frank L. *Lyndon's Legacy: A Candid Look at the President's Policy-makers*. New York: Devin-Adair, 1964.

Koskoff, David E. *Joseph P. Kennedy: A Life and Times*. Englewood Cliffs, N.J.: Prentice-Hall, 1974.

Kotz, Nick. *Judgment Days: Lyndon Baines Johnson, Martin Luther King, Jr., and the Laws That Changed America*. Boston: Houghton Mifflin, 2005.

————. *Let Them Eat Promises: The Politics of Hunger in America*. New York: Anchor, 1971.

Kraft, Joseph. *Profiles in Power: A Washington Insight*. New York: New American, 1966.

Kraslow, David, and Stuart H. Loory. *The Secret Search for Peace in Vietnam*. New York: Random House, 1968.

Krock, Arthur. *Memoirs: Sixty Years on the Firing Line*. New York: Funk & Wagnalls, 1968.

Laing, Margaret Irene. *The Next Kennedy*. New York: Coward-McCann, 1968.

Larner, Jeremy. *Nobody Knows: Reflections on the McCarthy Campaign of 1968*. New York: Macmillan, 1969.

Larson, Kate Clifford. *Rosemary: The Hidden Kennedy Daughter*. New York: Houghton Mifflin, 2015.

Lasky, Victor. *Robert F. Kennedy: The Myth and the Man*. New York: Trident, 1968.

Latham, Caroline, and Jeannie Sakol. *The Kennedy Encyclopedia: An A-to-Z Illustrated Guide to America's Royal Family*. New York: Penguin, 1989.

Lawford, Patricia Kennedy. *That Shining Hour*. New York: Halliday Lithograph, 1969.

Lawford, Patricia Seaton. *Peter Lawford: Hollywood, the Kennedys, the Rat Pack and the Whole Damn Thing*. London: Sidgwick & Jackson, 1988.

Laymon, Sherry. *Fearless: John L. McClellan, United States Senator*. Mustang, Okla.: Tate, 2011.

Leamer, Laurence. *The Kennedy Men, 1901–1963: The Laws of the Father*. New York: William Morrow, 2001.

————. *The Kennedy Women: The Saga of an American Family*. New York: Villard, 1994.

Leaming, Barbara. *Mrs. Kennedy: The Missing History of the Kennedy Years*. New York: Free, 2001.

Lebow, Richard Ned, and Janice Gross Stein. *We All Lost the Cold War*. Princeton, N.J.: Princeton University Press, 1994.

Lederer, William J., and Eugene Burdick. *The Ugly American*. New York: Fawcett, 1958.

Lee, Raymond Eliot. *The London Journal of General Raymond E. Lee, 1940–1941*. Edited by James R. Leutze. Boston: Little, Brown, 1971.

Leitch, David. *God Stand Up for Bastards*. Boston: Andre Deutsch, 1973.

Lelyveld, Joseph. *Move Your Shadow: South Africa, Black and White*. New York: Penguin, 1985.

Lemann, Nicholas. *The Promised Land: The Great Black Migration and How It Changed America*. New York: Vintage, 1992.

Lesher, Stephan. *George Wallace: American Populist*. New York: Addison-Wesley, 1994.

Levy, Jacques E. *Cesar Chavez: Autobiography of La Causa*. Minneapolis: University of Minnesota Press, 1975.

Lewis, Anthony. *Portrait of a Decade: The Second American Revolution*. New York: Bantam, 1964.

Lewis, John, with Michael D'Orso. *Walking with the Wind: A Memoir of the Movement*. New York: Simon and Schuster, 1998.

Lincoln, Evelyn. *Kennedy and Johnson*. New York: Holt, Rinehart and Winston, 1968.

————. *My Twelve Years with John F. Kennedy*. New York: David McKay, 1965.

Littlefield, Nick, and David Nexon. *Lion of the Senate: When Ted Kennedy Rallied the Democrats in a GOP Congress*. New York: Simon and Schuster, 2015.

Lois, George. *$ellebrity: My Angling and Tangling with Famous People*. London: Phaidon, 2003.

Lokos, Lionel. *Who Promoted Peress?* New York: Bookmailer, 1961.

Lord, Walter. *The Past That Would Not Die*. New York: Harper and Row, 1965.

Maas, Peter. *The Valachi Papers*. New York: G. P. Putnam's Sons, 1968.

MacMahon, Edward B., and Leonard Curry. *Medical Cover-ups in the White House*. Washington, D.C.: Farragut, 1987.

Madsen, Axel. *Gloria and Joe: The Star-Crossed Love Affair of Gloria Swanson and Joe Kennedy*. New York: Arbor House, 1988.

Mahoney, Richard D. *The Kennedy Brothers: The Rise and Fall of Jack and Bobby*. New York: Arcade, 2011.

Maier, Thomas. *The Kennedys: America's Emerald Kings*. New York: Basic, 2003.

Mailer, Norman. *The Idol and the Octopus: Political Writings on the Kennedy and Johnson Administrations*. New York: Dell, 1968.

———. *Marilyn: A Biography*. New York: Warner, 1975.

———. *Miami and the Siege of Chicago: An Informal History of the Republican and Democratic Conventions of 1968*. New York: New American, 1968.

Mallett, William E. *The Reuther Memorandum: Its Applications and Implications*. Washington, D.C.: Liberty Lobby, 1965.

Manchester, William. *Controversy and Other Essays in Journalism, 1950–1975*. Boston: Little, Brown, 1976.

———. *The Death of a President: November 20–November 25, 1963*. New York: Harper and Row, 1967.

———. *Portrait of a President: John F. Kennedy in Profile*. Boston: Little, Brown, 1967.

Mankiewicz, Frank, and Kirby Jones. *With Fidel: A Portrait of Castro and Cuba*. Chicago: Playboy, 1975.

Mankiewicz, Frank, with Joel Swerdlow. *So As I Was Saying: My Somewhat Eventful Life*. New York: Thomas Dunne Books, 2016.

Marshall, Burke. *Federalism and Civil Rights*. New York: Columbia University Press, 1964.

Marshall, David. *The DD Group: An Online Investigation into the Death of Marilyn Monroe*. New York: IUniverse, 2005.

Martin, Gordon A., Jr. *Count Them One by One: Black Mississippians Fighting for the Right to Vote*. Jackson: University Press of Mississippi, 2010.

Martin, John Bartlow. *Adlai Stevenson and the World: The Life of Adlai E. Stevenson*. Garden City, N.Y.: Doubleday, 1977.

———. *It Seems Like Only Yesterday: Memoirs of Writing, Presidential Politics, and the Diplomatic Life*. New York: William Morrow, 1986.

———. *Jimmy Hoffa's Hot*. Greenwich, Conn.: Fawcett Publications, 1959.

———. *Overtaken by Events: The Dominican Crisis from the Fall of Trujillo to the Civil War*. New York: Doubleday, 1966.

Martin, Ralph G. *A Hero for Our Time: An Intimate Story of the Kennedy Years*. New York: Fawcett Crest, 1983.

———. *Seeds of Destruction: Joe Kennedy and His Sons*. New York: G. P. Putnam's Sons, 1995.

Martin, Ralph G., and Ed Plaut. *Front Runner, Dark Horse*. New York: Doubleday, 1960.

Marvin, Susan. *The Women Around RFK*. New York: Lancer, 1967.

Matthews, Christopher. *Jack Kennedy: Elusive Hero*. New York: Simon and Schuster, 2011.

May, Ernest R., and Philip D. Zelikow (eds). *The Kennedy Tapes: Inside the White House During the Cuban Missile Crisis*. New York: W. W. Norton, 2002.

McCarthy, Abigail Q. *Private Faces/Public Places*. Garden City, N.Y.: Doubleday, 1972.

McCarthy, Eugene J. *Up 'til Now: A Memoir*. New York: Harcourt, 1987.
———. *The Year of the People*. Garden City, N.Y.: Doubleday, 1969.
McCarthy, Joe. *The Remarkable Kennedys*. New York: Dial, 1960.
McGinniss, Joe. *Heroes*. New York: Simon and Schuster, 1976.
McGovern, George S. *Grassroots: The Autobiography of George McGovern*. New York: Random House, 1977.
McGowan, Joe, Jr. *From Fidel Castro to Mother Teresa: An Associated Press Foreign Correspondent's Experience Abroad in the 1960s*. Broomfield, Colo.: Lac Amora, 2012.
McGrory, Mary. *The Best of Mary McGrory: A Half-Century of Washington Commentary*. Edited by Phil Gailey. Kansas City, Mo.: Andrews McMeel, 2006.
McNamara, Robert S., and Brian VanDeMark. *In Retrospect: The Tragedy and Lessons of Vietnam*. New York: Times, 1995.
McPherson, Harry. *A Political Education: A Journal of Life with Senators, Generals, Cabinet Members and Presidents*. Boston: Little, Brown, 1972.
McShane, Terence F. *The Death of Jimmy Hoffa*. North Charleston, S.C.: CreateSpace, 2001.
McTaggart, Lynne. *Kathleen Kennedy: Her Life and Times*. Garden City, N.Y.: Dial, 1983.
McWhorter, Diane. *Carry Me Home: Birmingham, Alabama; The Climactic Battle of the Civil Rights Revolution*. New York: Simon and Schuster, 2001.
Mears, Walter R. *Deadlines Past. Forty Years of Presidential Campaigning: A Reporter's Story*. Kansas City, Mo.: Andrews McMeel, 2003.
Mears, Walter R., and Hal Buell. *The Kennedy Brothers: A Legacy in Photographs*. New York: Black Dog & Leventhal Publishers, 2009.
Meltsner, Michael. *The Making of a Civil Rights Lawyer*. Charlottesville: University of Virginia Press, 2006.
Meredith, James. *Three Years in Mississippi*. Bloomington: Indiana University Press, 1966.
Messick, Hank. *Syndicate Wife: The Story of Ann Drahmann Coppola*. New York: Macmillan, 1968.
Meyers, Joan. *John Fitzgerald Kennedy . . . As We Remember Him*. New York: Macmillan, 1965.
Mikoyan, Sergo. *The Soviet Cuban Missile Crisis: Castro, Mikoyan, Kennedy, Khrushchev, and the Missiles of November*. Edited by Svetlana Savranskaya. Washington, D.C.: Woodrow Wilson Center, 2012.
Miller, Alice P. *A Kennedy Chronology*. New York: Birthdate Research, 1968.
Miller, Merle. *Lyndon: An Oral Biography*. New York: G. P. Putnam's Sons, 1980.
———. *Plain Speaking: An Oral Biography of Harry S. Truman*. New York: Berkley, 1973.
Mills, Judie. *Robert Kennedy*. Brookfield, Conn.: Millbrook, 1962.
Minow, Newton N., and Craig L. LaMay. *Inside the Presidential Debates: Their Improbable Past and Promising Future*. Chicago: University of Chicago Press, 2008.
Miracle, Berniece Baker, and Mona Rae Miracle. *My Sister Marilyn: A Memoir of Marilyn Monroe*. Chapel Hill, N.C.: Algonquin, 1994.
Moldea, Dan E. *The Hoffa Wars: The Rise and Fall of Jimmy Hoffa*. New York: SPI, 1978.
———. *The Killing of Robert F. Kennedy: An Investigation of Motive, Means, and Opportunity*. New York: W. W. Norton, 1995.
Mollenhoff, Clark R. *Tentacles of Power: The Story of Jimmy Hoffa*. New York: World, 1965.
Moore, Michael. *Here Comes Trouble: Stories from My Life*. New York: Grand Central, 2011.
Morrow, Robert D. *The Senator Must Die*. Santa Monica, Calif.: Roundtable, 1988.
Moynihan, Daniel P. *Maximum Feasible Misunderstanding: Community Action in the War on Poverty*. New York: Free, 1969.

Mudd, Roger. *The Place To Be: Washington, CBS, and the Glory Days of Television News*. New York: PublicAffairs, 2008.

Murray, Eunice, and Rose Shade. *Marilyn: The Last Months*. New York: Pyramid, 1975.

Nasaw, David. *The Patriarch: The Remarkable Life and Turbulent Times of Joseph P. Kennedy*. New York: Penguin, 2012.

Nathan, James A. *The Cuban Missile Crisis Revisited*. New York: St. Martin's, 1992.

Navasky, Victor S. *Kennedy Justice*. New York: Atheneum, 1971.

———. *Naming Names*. New York: Viking, 1980.

Neff, James. *Vendetta: Bobby Kennedy Versus Jimmy Hoffa*. Boston: Little, Brown, 2015.

Newfield, Jack. *RFK: A Memoir*. New York: Thunder's Mouth, 2003. Originally published in 1969 as *Robert Kennedy: A Memoir*.

Nicholas, William. *The Bobby Kennedy Nobody Knows*. Greenwich, Conn.: Fawcett, 1967.

Nixon, Richard. *Richard M. Nixon's Six Crises*. New York: Doubleday, 1962.

———. *RN: The Memoirs of Richard Nixon*. New York: Grosset & Dunlap, 1978.

Noguchi, Thomas T., with Joseph DiMona. *Coroner*. New York: Simon and Schuster, 1983.

Nordhoff, Charles, and James Norman Hall. *Men Against the Sea*. Boston: Little, Brown, 1933.

Norris, John. *Mary McGrory: The First Queen of Journalism*. New York: Viking, 2015.

O'Brien, Lawrence F. *No Final Victories: A Life in Politic—from John F. Kennedy to Watergate*. Garden City, N.Y.: Doubleday, 1974.

O'Brien, Michael. *John F. Kennedy: A Biography*. New York: Thomas Dunne, 2005.

O'Donnell, Helen. *A Common Good: The Friendship of Robert F. Kennedy and Kenneth P. O'Donnell*. New York: William Morrow, 1998.

O'Donnell, Kenneth P., and David F. Powers. *Johnny, We Hardly Knew Ye: Memories of John Fitzgerald Kennedy*. Boston: Little, Brown, 1972.

Ognibene, Peter J. *Scoop: The Life and Politics of Henry M. Jackson*. New York: Stein and Day, 1975.

O'Neill, Tip, and William Novak. *Man of the House: The Life and Political Memoirs of Speaker Tip O'Neill*. New York: Random House, 1987.

Oppenheimer, Jerry. *The Other Mrs. Kennedy: Ethel Skakel Kennedy: An American Drama of Power, Privilege, and Politics*. New York: St. Martin's, 1994.

Oshinsky, David M. *A Conspiracy So Immense: The World of Joe McCarthy*. New York: Free, 1983.

O'Sullivan, Shane. *Who Killed Bobby?: The Unsolved Murder of Robert F. Kennedy*. New York: Union Square, 2008.

Palermo, Joseph A. *In His Own Right: The Political Odyssey of Senator Robert F. Kennedy*. New York: Columbia University Press, 2001.

———. *Robert F. Kennedy and the Death of American Idealism*. New York: Pearson Longman, 2008.

Parker, Phyllis R. *Brazil and the Quiet Intervention, 1964*. Austin: University of Texas Press, 1979.

Parmet, Herbert S. *Eisenhower and the American Crusades*. New York: Macmillan, 1972.

Paterson, Thomas G. *Kennedy's Quest for Victory: American Foreign Policy, 1961–1963*. New York: Oxford, 1989.

Pearson, Drew. *Diaries, 1949–1959*. Edited by Tyler Abell. New York: Holt, Rinehart and Winston, 1974.

Perry, Barbara A. *Rose Kennedy: The Life and Times of a Political Matriarch*. New York: W. W. Norton, 2013.

Perry, Bruce. *Malcolm: The Life of a Man Who Changed Black America*. Barrytown, N.Y.: Station Hill, 1991.

Peters, Charles. *Lyndon B. Johnson*. New York: Times, 2010.

Petro, Sylvester. *Power Unlimited: The Corruption of Union Leadership*. New York: Ronald Press, 1959.

Pitts, David. *Jack & Lem. John F. Kennedy and Lem Billings: The Untold Story of an Extraordinary Friendship*. New York: Carroll & Graf, 2007.

Poitier, Sidney. *This Life*. New York: Alfred A. Knopf, 1980.

Porter, Darwin, and Danforth Prince. *Pink Triangle: The Feuds and Private Lives of Tennessee Williams, Gore Vidal, Truman Capote, and Members of Their Entourages*. New York: Blood Moon, 2014.

Potter, Charles E. *Days of Shame*. New York: Coward-McCann, 1965.

Potter, Jeffrey. *Men, Money and Magic: The Story of Dorothy Schiff*. New York: Coward, McCann & Geoghegan, 1976.

Powers, Thomas. *The Man Who Kept the Secrets: Richard Helms and the CIA*. New York: Alfred A. Knopf, 1979.

Prouty, L. Fletcher. *JFK: The CIA, Vietnam, and the Plot to Assassinate John F. Kennedy*. New York: Carol, 1992.

Purdum, Todd S. *An Idea Whose Time Has Come: Two Presidents, Two Parties, and the Battle for the Civil Rights Act of 1964*. New York: Henry Holt, 2014.

Quirk, Lawrence J. *The Kennedys in Hollywood*. Dallas: Taylor, 1996.

———. *Robert Francis Kennedy: The Man and the Politician*. Los Angeles: Holloway House, 1968.

Rabe, Stephen G. *The Most Dangerous Area in the World: John F. Kennedy Confronts Communist Revolution in Latin America*. Chapel Hill: University of North Carolina Press, 1999.

Rachlin, Harvey. *The Kennedys: A Chronological History, 1823–Present*. New York: World Almanac, 1986.

Ragano, Frank, and Selwyn Raab. *Mob Lawyer*. New York: Scribners, 1994.

Raines, Howell. *My Soul Is Rested: Movement Days in the Deep South Remembered*. New York: G. P. Putnam's Sons, 1977.

Rampersad, Arnold. *Jackie Robinson: A Biography*. New York: Ballantine, 1998.

Rasenberger, Jim. *The Brilliant Disaster: JFK, Castro, and America's Doomed Invasion of Cuba's Bay of Pigs*. New York: Scribner, 2011.

Raymont, Henry. *Troubled Neighbors: The Story of US–Latin American Relations, from FDR to the Present*. Cambridge, Mass.: Westview, 2005.

Reddin, Thomas. Unpublished memoir, supplied by Betty Jane Reddin.

Reece, Erik. *Lost Mountain: A Year in the Vanishing Wilderness: Radical Strip Mining and the Devastation of Appalachia*. New York: Riverhead, 2006.

Reeves, Thomas C. *The Life and Times of Joe McCarthy: A Biography*. New York: Stein and Day, 1982.

———. *A Question of Character: A Life of John F. Kennedy*. New York: Free, 1991.

Renehan, Edward J., Jr. *The Kennedys at War, 1937–1945*. New York: Doubleday, 2002.

Reston, James. *Deadline: A Memoir*. New York: Random House, 1991.

Reuther, Victor G. *The Brothers Reuther and the Story of the UAW: A Memoir*. Boston: Houghton Mifflin, 1976.

Ritchie, Donald A. *James M. Landis: Dean of the Regulators*. Cambridge, Mass.: Harvard University Press, 1980.

Roberts, Allen. *Robert Francis Kennedy: Biography of a Compulsive Politician*. Brookline Village, Mass.: Branden, 1984.

Roemer, William F. *Roemer: Man Against the Mob*. New York: D.I. Fine, 1989.

Rogers, Warren. *When I Think of Bobby: A Personal Memoir of the Kennedy Years*. New York: HarperCollins, 1993.

Roosevelt, Felicia Warburg. *Doers & Dowagers*. Garden City, N.Y.: Doubleday, 1975.

Ross, Douglas. *Robert F. Kennedy: Apostle of Change*. New York: Trident, 1968.

Rostow, W. W. *The Diffusion of Power, 1957–1972*. New York: Macmillan, 1972.

Roth, Philip. *The Facts: A Novelist's Autobiography*. New York: Vintage, 1988.

Rovere, Richard Halworth. *Senator Joe McCarthy*. New York: Harcourt, 1959.

Rowell, David. *The Train of Small Mercies*. New York: G. P. Putnam's Sons, 2011.

Rusk, Dean, and Daniel S. Papp. *As I Saw It*. New York: W. W. Norton, 1990.

Russell, Thaddeus. *Out of the Jungle: Jimmy Hoffa and the Remaking of the American Working Class*. New York: Alfred A. Knopf, 2001.

Russo, Gus. *Live by the Sword: The Secret War Against Castro and the Death of JFK*. Baltimore: Bancroft, 1998.

Ryan, Dorothy, and Louis J. Ryan. *The Kennedy Family of Massachusetts: A Bibliography*. Westport, Conn.: Greenwood, 1981.

Salinger, Pierre. *P.S., A Memoir*. New York: St. Martin's, 1995.

———. *With Kennedy*. Garden City, N.Y.: Doubleday, 1966.

Salinger, Pierre, Edwin Guthman, Frank Mankiewicz, and John Seigenthaler (eds). *"An Honorable Profession": A Tribute to Robert F. Kennedy*. Garden City, N.Y.: Doubleday, 1968.

Salisbury, Harrison E. *Heroes of My Time*. New York: Walker, 1993.

Sandel, Michael J. *Democracy's Discontent: America in Search of a Public Philosophy*. Cambridge, Mass.: Harvard University Press, 1996.

Scales, Junius Irving, and Richard Nickson. *Cause at Heart: A Former Communist Remembers*. Athens: University of Georgia Press, 1987.

Schaap, Dick. *R.F.K.* New York: New American, 1967.

Schaffer, Howard B. *Chester Bowles: New Dealer in the Cold War*. Cambridge, Mass.: Harvard University Press, 1993.

Scheer, Robert. *How the United States Got Involved in Vietnam*. Santa Barbara, Calif.: Center for the Study of Democratic Institutions, 1965.

Schlesinger, Arthur M., Jr. *Journals: 1952–2000*. New York: Penguin, 2007.

———. *Robert Kennedy and His Times*. Boston: Houghton Mifflin, 1978.

———. *A Thousand Days: John F. Kennedy in the White House*. New York: Black Dog & Leventhal, 1993.

Schlesinger, Arthur M., Jr., and Andrew Schlesinger. *The Letters of Arthur Schlesinger, Jr.* New York: Random House, 2013.

Schlesinger, Marian Cannon. *I Remember: A Life of Politics, Painting and People*. Cambridge, Mass.: TidePool, 2012.

Schlesinger, Robert. *White House Ghosts: Presidents and Their Speechwriters*. New York: Simon and Schuster, 2008.

Schoor, Gene. *Young John Kennedy*. New York: Harcourt, 1963.

———. *Young Robert Kennedy*. New York: McGraw-Hill, 1969.

Schott, Joseph L. *No Left Turns*. New York: Praeger, 1975.

Searls, Hank. *The Lost Prince: Young Joe, the Forgotten Kennedy*. New York: Ballantine, 1969.

Shackley, Ted, with Richard A. Finney. *Spymaster: My Life in the CIA*. Washington, D.C.: Potomac, 2005.

Shannon, William V. *The Heir Apparent: Robert Kennedy and the Struggle for Power*. New York: Macmillan, 1967.

Shapiro, Doris. *We Danced All Night: My Life Behind the Scenes with Alan Jay Lerner*. New York: William Morrow, 1990.

Shapley, Deborah. *Promise and Power: The Life and Times of Robert McNamara*. Boston: Little, Brown, 1993.

Sheehan, Neil, Hedrick Smith, E. W. Kenworthy, and Fox Butterfield, *The Pentagon Papers: The Secret History of The Vietnam War*. New York: Quadrangle, 1971.

Shefferman, Nathan W., with Dale Kramer. *The Man in the Middle*. Garden City, N.Y.: Doubleday, 1961.

Sheridan, Walter. *The Fall and Rise of Jimmy Hoffa*. New York: Saturday Review, 1972.

Sherrill, Robert. *Gothic Politics in the Deep South*. New York: Ballantine, 1969.

Shesol, Jeff. *Mutual Contempt: Lyndon Johnson, Robert Kennedy, and the Feud That Defined a Decade*. New York: W. W. Norton, 1997.

Shestak, Jerome J. *A Mass in Memory of Robert F. Kennedy: A Personal Memoir*. Self-published and undated.

Shirley, Craig. *Rendezvous with Destiny: Ronald Reagan and the Campaign That Changed America*. Wilmington: ISI, 2009.

Shriver, Mark K. *A Good Man: Rediscovering My Father, Sargent Shriver*. New York: Henry Holt, 2012.

Sidey, Hugh. *John F. Kennedy, President*. New York: Atheneum, 1964.

Sidorenko, Konstantin. *Robert F. Kennedy: A Spiritual Biography*. New York: Crossroad, 2000.

Sikora, Frank. *The Judge: The Life and Opinions of Alabama's Frank M. Johnson, Jr.* Montgomery: Black Belt, 1992.

Slatzer, Robert F. *The Curious Death of Marilyn Monroe*. New York: Pinnacle, 1974.

Smith, Jeffrey K. *Bad Blood: Lyndon B. Johnson, Robert F. Kennedy, and the Tumultuous 1960s*. Bloomington, Ind.: AuthorHouse, 2010.

Smith, Joseph Burkholder. *Portrait of a Cold Warrior*. New York: G. P. Putnam's Sons, 1976.

Sorensen, Theodore C. *Counselor: A Life at the Edge of History*. New York: HarperCollins, 2008.

———. *Kennedy: The Classic Biography*. New York: Harper and Row, 1965.

Spada, James. *Peter Lawford: The Man Who Kept the Secrets*. New York: Bantam, 1991.

Speriglio, Milo A., with Steven Chain. *The Marilyn Conspiracy*. New York: Pocket, 1986.

Spoto, Donald. *Marilyn Monroe: The Biography*. New York: HarperCollins, 1993.

Stacks, John F. *Scotty: James B. Reston and the Rise and Fall of American Journalism*. Boston: Little, Brown, 2002.

Steel, Ronald. *In Love with Night: The American Romance with Robert Kennedy*. New York: Simon and Schuster, 2000.

Stein, Jean. *American Journey: The Times of Robert Kennedy*. Edited by George Plimpton. New York: Harcourt, 1970.

———. *Edie: An American Biography*. New York: Alfred A. Knopf, 1982.

Steinberg, Alfred. *Sam Johnson's Boy: A Close-up of the President from Texas*. New York: Macmillan, 1968.

Steinem, Gloria. *Outrageous Acts and Everyday Rebellions*. New York: Owlet, 1995.

Stern, Sheldon M. *Averting 'The Final Failure': John F. Kennedy and the Secret Cuban Missile Crisis Meetings*. Stanford, Calif..: Stanford University Press, 2003.

————. *The Cuban Missile Crisis in American Memory: Myths Versus Reality*. Stanford, Calif.: A.: Stanford University Press, 2012.

Stevenson, James. *Robert F. Kennedy Campaign, 1968*. Unpublished and undated memoir, supplied by author.

Stossel, Scott. *Sarge: The Life and Times of Sargent Shriver*. Washington, D.C.: Smithsonian, 2004.

Stout, Richard T. *People: The Story of the Grass-Roots Movement That Found Eugene McCarthy—and Is Transforming Our Politics Today*. New York: Harper and Row, 1970.

Straight, Michael. *Trial by Television and Other Encounters*. Boston: Beacon, 1954.

Sullivan, Gerald, and Michael Kenney. *The Race for the Eighth*. New York: Harper and Row, 1987.

Sullivan, William C., and Bill Brown. *The Bureau: My Thirty Years in Hoover's FBI*. New York: W. W. Norton, 1979.

Summers, Anthony. *Goddess: The Secret Lives of Marilyn Monroe*. New York: Macmillan, 1985.

————. *Official and Confidential: The Secret Life of J. Edgar Hoover*. New York: G. P. Putnam's Sons, 1993.

Swanson, Gloria. *Swanson on Swanson*. New York: Random House, 1980.

Swift, Will. *The Kennedys Amidst the Gathering Storm: A Thousand Days in London, 1938–1940*. London: J.R., 2008.

Swinburne, Laurence. *RFK, the Last Knight*. New York: Pyramid, 1969.

Szulc, Tad. *Fidel: A Critical Portrait*. New York: William Morrow, 1986.

Talbot, David. *Brothers: The Hidden History of the Kennedy Years*. New York: Free, 2007.

Tanzer, Lester, ed. *The Kennedy Circle*. Washington, D.C.: Luce, 1961.

Taraborrelli, J. Randy. *Jackie, Ethel, Joan: Women of Camelot*. New York: Warner, 2000.

Taylor, Maxwell D. *Swords and Plowshares*. New York: W. W. Norton, 1972.

Thayer, Mary Van Rensselaer. *Jacqueline Bouvier Kennedy*. Garden City, N.Y.: Doubleday, 1961.

Theodoracopulos, Taki. *Princes, Playboys, and High-Class Tarts*. Princeton, N.J.: Karz-Cohl, 1984.

Theoharis, Athan G. *From the Secret Files of J. Edgar Hoover*. Chicago: Ivan R. Dee, 1991.

Thimmesch, Nick, and William O. Johnson. *Robert Kennedy at 40*. New York: W. W. Norton, 1965.

Thomas, Evan. *The Man to See: Edward Bennett William: Ultimate Insider; Legendary Trial Lawyer*. New York: Simon and Schuster, 1991.

————. *Robert Kennedy: His Life*. New York: Simon and Schuster, 2000.

————. *The Very Best Men: Four Who Dared: The Early Years of the CIA*. New York: Simon and Schuster, 1995.

Thomas, Helen. *Dateline: White House*. New York: Macmillan, 1975.

————. *Thanks for the Memories, Mr. President*. New York: Scribner, 2002.

Thomas, Hugh. *The Spanish Civil War*. New York: Harper, 1961.

Thompson, Nelson. *The Dark Side of Camelot*. Chicago: Playboy, 1976.

Thompson, Robert F., and Hortense Myers. *Robert F. Kennedy: The Brother Within*. New York: Macmillan, 1962.

Thornton, J. Mills III. *Dividing Lines: Municipal Politics and the Struggle for Civil Rights in Montgomery, Birmingham, and Selma*. Tuscaloosa: University of Alabama Press, 2002.

Touhy, John William. *When Capone's Mob Murdered Roger Touhy: The Strange Case of "Jake the Barber" and the Kidnapping That Never Happened*. Fort Lee, N.J.: Barricade Books, 2001.

Townsend, Kathleen Kennedy. *Failing America's Faithful: How Today's Churches Are Mixing God with Politics and Losing Their Way.* New York: Warner, 2007.

Trammel, Seymore. *George Wallace: The Self-Inflicted Wound.* Unpublished and undated memoir. Alabama State Archives.

Trest, Warren A. *Nobody But the People: The Life and Times of Alabama's Youngest Governor.* Montgomery: NewSouth, 2008.

Trest, Warren A., and Don Dodd. *Wings of Denial: The Alabama Air National Guard's Covert Role at the Bay of Pigs.* Montgomery: NewSouth, 2001.

Trewhitt, Henry L. *McNamara.* New York: Harper and Row, 1971.

Tuchman, Barbara W. *The Guns of August.* New York: Macmillan, 1962.

Tushnet, Mark V. *Thurgood Marshall: His Speeches, Writings, Arguments, Opinions, and Reminiscences.* Chicago: Lawrence Hill Books, 2001.

Tydings, Joseph. *Born to Starve.* New York: William Morrow, 1970.

United Press International. *Assassination: Robert F. Kennedy, 1925–1968.* New York: Cowles, 1968.

Updegrove, Mark K. *Indomitable Will: LBJ in the Presidency.* New York: Crown, 2012.

Váldes-Dapena, Jacinto. *Operation Mongoose: Prelude of a Direct Invasion on Cuba.* Havana: Editorial Capitán San Luis, 2004.

Valenti, Jack. *A Very Human President.* New York: W. W. Norton, 1975.

———. *This Time, This Place: My Life in War, the White House, and Hollywood.* New York: Crown, 2007.

vanden Heuvel, William J., and Milton Gwirtzman. *On His Own: Robert F. Kennedy, 1964–1968.* Garden City, N.Y.: Doubleday, 1970.

Van Gelder, Lawrence. *The Untold Story: Why the Kennedys Lost the Book Battle.* New York: Award, 1967.

Velie, Lester. *Desperate Bargain: Why Jimmy Hoffa Had to Die.* New York: Reader's Digest Press, 1977.

Vidal, Gore. *Palimpsest: A Memoir.* New York: Random House, 1995.

———. *Snapshots in History's Glare.* New York: Abrams, 2009.

Viorst, Milton. *Hustlers and Heroes: An American Political Panorama.* New York: Simon and Schuster, 1971.

von Hoffman, Nicholas. *Citizen Cohn: The Life and Times of Roy Cohn.* New York: Doubleday, 1988.

Waldron, Lamar, and Thom Hartmann. *Ultimate Sacrifice: John and Robert Kennedy, the Plan for a Coup in Cuba, and the Murder of JFK.* Berkeley: Counterpoint, 2005.

Walton, Richard J. *Cold War and Counterrevolution: The Foreign Policy of John F. Kennedy.* New York: Viking, 1972.

Waters, Bob. *Bobby Kennedy: Next President of the United States.* New York: G. C. London, 1965.

Watson, W. Marvin, with Sherwin Markman. *Chief of Staff: Lyndon Johnson and His Presidency.* New York: Thomas Dunne, 2004.

Watters, Pat, and Reese Cleghorn. *Climbing Jacob's Ladder: The Arrival of Negroes in Southern Politics.* New York: Harcourt, 1967.

Weatherby, W. J., and Marilyn Monroe. *Conversations with Marilyn.* London: Robson, 1976.

Weiner, Tim. *Enemies: A History of the FBI.* New York: Random House, 2012.

———. *Legacy of Ashes: The History of the CIA.* New York: Anchor, 2007.

Weis, W. Michael. *Cold Warriors and Coups D'etat: Brazilian-American Relations, 1945–1964.* Albuquerque: University of New Mexico Press, 1993.

Weiss, Murray, and Bill Hoffman. *Palm Beach Babylon: Sins, Scams and Scandals*. New York: Birch Lane Press, 1992.

Whalen, Charles, and Barbara Whalen. *The Longest Debate: A Legislative History of the 1964 Civil Rights Act*. Newport Beach, Calif.: Seven Locks, 1984.

Whalen, Richard J. *The Founding Father: The Story of Joseph P. Kennedy*. New York: New American, 1964.

White, Mark J. *The Kennedys and Cuba: The Declassified Documentary History*. Chicago: Ivan R. Dee, 1999.

White, Ray Lewis. *Gore Vidal*. New York: Twayne, 1968.

White, Theodore H. *In Search of History: A Personal Adventure*. New York: HarperCollins, 1978.

———. *The Making of the President, 1960*. New York: Atheneum, 1961.

———. *The Making of the President, 1964*. New York: Atheneum, 1965.

———. *The Making of the President, 1968*. New York: Atheneum, 1969.

Whittaker, Jim. *A Life on the Edge: Memoirs of Everest and Beyond*. Seattle: Mountaineers, 1999.

Wicker, Tom. *JFK and LBJ: The Influence of Personality upon Politics*. New York: William Morrow, 1968.

———. *On Press*. New York: Viking, 1978.

Wilkie, Curtis. *Dixie: A Personal Odyssey Through Events That Shaped the Modern South*. New York: Simon and Schuster, 2001.

Wilkins, Roger W. *A Man's Life: An Autobiography*. New York: Simon and Schuster, 1982.

Wilkins, Roy, and Tom Mathews. *Standing Fast: The Autobiography of Roy Wilkins*. New York: Da Capo, 1982.

Williams, Juan. *Eyes on the Prize: America's Civil Rights Years, 1954–1965*. New York: Penguin, 1987.

Wills, Garry. *The Kennedy Imprisonment: A Meditation on Power*. Boston: Little, Brown, 1982.

Wilson, Donald M. *The First 78 Years*. Xlibris, 2004.

Wilson, Earl. *Sinatra: An Unauthorized Biography*. New York: Macmillan, 1976.

Witcover, Jules. *85 Days: The Last Campaign of Robert Kennedy*. New York: Putnam, 1969.

———. *The Year the Dream Died: Revisiting 1968 in America*. New York: Warner, 1997.

Witker, Kristi. *How to Lose Everything in Politics (Except Massachusetts)*. New York: Mason & Lipscomb, 1974.

Wofford, Harris. *Of Kennedys & Kings: Making Sense of the Sixties*. Pittsburgh: University of Pittsburgh Press, 1992.

Wolfe, Donald H. *The Last Days of Marilyn Monroe*. New York: William Morrow, 1998.

Wyden, Peter. *Bay of Pigs: The Untold Story*. New York: Touchstone, 1979.

Young, Andrew. *An Easy Burden: The Civil Rights Movement and the Transformation of America*. Waco, Tex.: Baylor University Press, 2008.

Youngblood, Rufus W. *20 Years in the Secret Service: My Life with Five Presidents*. New York: Simon and Schuster, 1973.

NEWSPAPERS, MAGAZINES, AND JOURNALS

Acheson, Dean. "Dean Acheson's Version of Robert Kennedy's Version of the Cuban Missile Affair." *Esquire*, February 1969.

ACLU News. "Kennedy Urged to End Mail Surveillance." June 1964.

Adams, Val. "A Television Dropout." *New York Times,* October 2, 1966.

Afro-American. "New York Leaders Divide over Kennedy, Keating." October 24, 1964.

Agnew, Bruce. "Kennedy and Javits Find They're Not Quite a Team." *New York Post,* February 17, 1965.

Ajemian, Robert. "Robert Kennedy's Week to Reckon." *Life,* July 3, 1964.

Alexander, Holmes M. "Kennedys 'Won' Venezuelan Election." *New Haven Register,* January 13, 1964.

———. "RFK: How He's Building His Own Party." *Nation's Business,* July 1966.

Allen, Michael O., William Goldschlag, and Richard T. Pienciak. "Glimpse Inside the Kennedy Fortune." *New York Daily News,* February 1, 1988.

Alsop, Joseph. "The Anti-Legislative Process." *Washington Post,* October 28, 1963.

———. "Bobby!" *Washington Post,* July 1, 1966.

———. "California and Kennedy." *Washington Post,* June 8, 1964.

———. "Can Bob Kennedy Be Pressured into a Sacrificial Candidacy?" *Washington Post,* January 17, 1968.

———. "Crucial Decisions." *Washington Post,* January 8, 1964.

———. "Democratic Organization Gap." *Washington Post,* January 6, 1967.

———. "Democrats Lucky in Men Like Kennedy and Humphrey." *Washington Post,* May 31, 1968.

———. "Gaining the Objective." *Washington Post,* October 29, 1962.

———. "Hoffa: A Rewarding Subject for Close Study." *Washington Post,* June 29, 1959.

———. "The Impossible Dialogue." *Washington Post,* June 24, 1963.

———. "Kennedy and Keating." *Washington Post,* August 21, 1964.

———. "Kennedy at the Turning Point, Must Reassess His Campaign." *Washington Post,* June 3, 1968.

———. "The Khrushchev Question." *Washington Post,* January 26, 1962.

———. "Laos and the New Left." *Washington Post,* March 13, 1967.

———. "Most Excellent Among Us Fall Before Mindless Assaults." *Washington Post,* June 7, 1968.

———. "The Neo-Colonial Problem." *Washington Post,* May 29, 1963.

———. "Never Ask the End." *Washington Post,* July 15, 1960.

———. "The Nightmare." *Washington Post,* June 21, 1963.

———. "Odd Episode of Soviet Diplomacy." *Washington Post,* July 26, 1961.

———. "The Other America." *Washington Post,* June 14, 1963.

———. "The Real Intelligence Story." *New York Herald Tribune,* November 2, 1962.

———. "The Religious Issue." *Washington Post,* October 26, 1960.

———. "Robert Kennedy on the Stump Projects Image of Brother." *Washington Post,* May 15, 1968.

———. "Robert Kennedy's Future." *Washington Post,* March 9, 1964.

———. "The Roots of Horror." *Washington Post,* July 31, 1967.

———. "Since the Civil War!" *Washington Post,* July 20, 1966.

———. "The Soviet Deception Plan." *Washington Post,* November 5, 1962.

———. "Story of a Nomination." *Washington Post,* December 23, 1960.

———. "Thousands in Glens Falls." *Washington Post,* September 14, 1964.

———. "Why Legislate?" *Washington Post,* June 3, 1963.

Alsop, Stewart. "Bobby's Red Guards." *Saturday Evening Post,* May 4, 1968.

———. "A Conversation with President Kennedy." *Saturday Evening Post,* January 1, 1966.

———. "Good Bobby and Bad Bobby." *Saturday Evening Post*, June 15, 1968.

———. "Johnson Takes Over: The Untold Story." *Saturday Evening Post*, February 15, 1964.

———. "The Kennedy Hurricane." *Saturday Evening Post*, August 27, 1966.

———. "Kennedy's Magic Formula." *Saturday Evening Post*, August 13, 1960.

———. "LBJ and RFK." *Saturday Evening Post*, February 29, 1964.

———. "The Mood of America." *Saturday Evening Post*, September 22, 1962.

———. "Robert Kennedy and the Liberals." *Saturday Evening Post*, August 28, 1965.

———. "They Hate Kennedy." *Saturday Evening Post*, October 5, 1963.

———. "What Made Teddy Run?" *Saturday Evening Post*, October 27, 1962.

Alsop, Stewart, and Charles Bartlett. "In Time of Crisis." *Saturday Evening Post*, December 8, 1962.

America. "Mr. Kennedy's Crusade." Editorial. June 20, 1964.

Amsterdam Evening Recorder. "Accepts Rejection from the Democratic Party, Stratton Plans to Seek New Term in Congress." September 2, 1964.

Amsterdam News. "I'm Indebted to Kennedy." November 5, 1960.

Anatol, Karl W., and John R. Bittner. "Kennedy on King: The Rhetoric of Control." *Today's Speech*, vol. 16, 1968.

Anderson, Claudia Wilson. "Congressman Lyndon B. Johnson, Operation Texas, and Jewish Immigration." *Southern Jewish History*, vol. 15, 2012.

Anderson, Jack. "Bob Kennedy Versus Jimmy Hoffa: The Story Behind One of History's Greatest Feuds." *Parade*, February 17, 1963.

———. "The Roots of Our Vietnam Involvement." *Washington Post*, May 4, 1975.

Anderson, Pat. "Robert's Character." *Esquire*, April 1965.

Apple, R. W., Jr. "Brooklyn Crowds Engulf Kennedy." *New York Times*, September 14, 1964.

———. "Calls Campaign 'Arrogant.' " *New York Times*, October 19, 1964.

———. "4,000 at Glens Falls Welcome Kennedy at 1 A.M." *New York Times*, September 11, 1964.

———. "Group Retracts Kennedy Rebuke." *New York Times*, October 28, 1964.

———. "How Kennedy Did It: 27 Days of Hard Politicking." *New York Times*, August 26, 1964.

———. "Kennedy Appeals for Nonviolence." *New York Times*, April 5, 1968.

———. "Kennedy Decides Not to Vote Nov. 3." *New York Times*, September 5, 1964.

———. "Kennedy Disputes McCarthy on War in TV Discussion." *New York Times*, June 2, 1968.

———. "Kennedy Edge 6–5." *New York Times*, November 4, 1964.

———. "Kennedy Enlisting a Diversified Staff." *New York Times*, September 18, 1964.

———. "Kennedy Gets an Ovation; Recalls Ideals of Brother." *New York Times*, August 28, 1964.

———. "Kennedy, Keating Close Campaigns," *New York Times*, November 3, 1964.

———. "Kennedy Quits Post in Cabinet to Wage Campaign in State." *New York Times*, September 4, 1964.

———. "Kennedy Reports Gains on Keating." *New York Times*, October 29, 1964.

———. "Kennedy Says He Opposes Distant Busing of Students." *New York Times*, September 9, 1964.

———. "Kennedy's New Tactics." *New York Times*, October 14, 1964.

———. "Kennedy Steps In as Pinch Speaker." *New York Times*, November 1, 1964.

———. "The Kennedy Strategy." *New York Times*, September 21, 1964.

———. "Kennedy Swamps Stratton to Win State Nomination." *New York Times*, September 2, 1964.

———. "Kennedy to Run for the Senate from New York." *New York Times*, August 12, 1964.

———. "Mayor Endorses Race by Kennedy. *New York Times*, August 22, 1964.

———. "Power Play in Albany." *New York Times*, February 12, 1965.

———. "Rochester, Keating Home Town, Gives Kennedy Rousing Welcome." *New York Times*, September 10, 1964.

———. "7th Ave. Throng Hears Humphrey Praise Kennedy." *New York Times*, October 30, 1964.

———. "A Shadow over Albany." *New York Times*, January 8, 1965.

———. "Throngs Hail Democrat." *New York Times*, September 13, 1964.

———. "Two Managers Setting the Pace for Fast Kennedy-Keating Fight." *New York Times*, October 1, 1964.

———. " 'Unfair' Assertion Laid to Kennedy." *New York Times*, October 27, 1964.

———. "Wagner Will Nominate Kennedy for Senator Today." *New York Times*, September 1, 1964.

Archer, Eugene. "Newman to Star in 'Enemy Within.' " *New York Times*, September 23, 1961.

Armstrong, Richard. "Bobby Kennedy and the Fight for New York." *Saturday Evening Post*, November 6, 1965.

Arnold, Martin. "Chinatown Hails Kennedy on Tour." *New York Times*, October 5, 1964.

———. "During Tour He Is Replying to Attacks on American Policy and Society." *New York Times*, November 25, 1965.

———. "Kennedy Center of Primary Fight." *New York Times*, June 21, 1966.

———. "Kennedy Leaves for Yukon Peak." *New York Times*, March 22, 1965.

———. "Kennedy Mobbed in Grand Central." *New York Times*, September 5, 1964.

———. "Kennedy Puts Flag Atop Mt. Kennedy." *New York Times*, March 25, 1965.

———. "Kennedy Spends Day in Glen Cove." *New York Times*, September 12, 1964.

———. "Kennedy to the Latins: 'I Have Come to Learn.' " *New York Times*, November 28, 1965.

———. "Robert Kennedy Ends Peru Tour." *New York Times*, November 14, 1965.

———. "Robert Kennedy for President, Some Latins Say." *New York Times*, November 18, 1965.

———. "Senator Is Praised by Teammates on Homeward Trip." *New York Times*, March 26, 1965.

Ascoli, Max. "The Two USAs." *Reporter*, March 23, 1967.

Asencio, Diego C. "Low Humor in High Places." *Georgetown Journal of International Affairs*, November 1, 2001.

Atlanta Constitution. "Kennedy Opposes Push for Rights Bills Now, Wins Vandiver's Praise." May 10, 1961.

Attwood, William. "Twenty Years After Dallas." *Virginia Quarterly Review*, Autumn 1983.

Baker, Robert E. "Kennedy Greets NAACP March." *Washington Post*, June 25, 1964.

Baker, Russell. "Exchange Is Calm." *New York Times*, September 27, 1960.

———. "Kennedy Will Vie with Humphrey in Wisconsin Test." *New York Times*, January 20, 1960.

———. "Random Notes in Washington: A Look at '58 with a '32 Glass." *New York Times*, December 30, 1957.

————. "Stassen Rejects Senate Subpoena." *New York Times*, April 2, 1955.

————. "U.S. Woman Aide Testifies on Gifts." *New York Times*, May 26, 1955.

Baldwin, James. "Letter from a Region in My Mind." *New Yorker*, November 17, 1962.

Bartlett, Charles. "Two Key Winners in New York." *Washington Star*, November 5, 1964.

Bayley, Edwin R. "Dignitaries Arrive for Rites in Guard, Air Force Planes." *Milwaukee Journal*, May 7, 1957.

Beale, Betty. "Ethel Kennedy Big Campaign Helper." *The Spokesman-Review*, March 24, 1968.

————. "It Wasn't JFK's Idea—Bobby Really Wanted Cabinet Post." *Miami Herald*, December 7, 1969.

Beatty, Jerome. "Nine Kennedys and How They Grew." *Reader's Digest*, April 1939.

Becker, Bill. "Hoffa Testifies in Los Angeles; Barely Misses Robert Kennedy." *New York Times*, February 14, 1963.

Belair, Felix, Jr. "Robert Kennedy Says Sabotage Is a Major Peril to Free Nations." *New York Times*, February 29, 1964.

Bender, Marilyn. "The Robert Kennedys Dress Up to Go Skating on Thin Ice." *New York Times*, January 25, 1968.

Bendiner, Elmer. "History and Malapropaganda." *Nation*, April 17, 1967.

Benjamin, Philip. "Kennedys Donate $1.4 Million for Einstein Retarded Center." *New York Times*, March 19, 1965.

Berger, Frederick. "George C. Wallace: His Life and Legacy." *Anniston Star*, September 14, 1998.

Bergholz, Richard. "State Appears Headed Toward Close Primary." *Los Angeles Times*, June 2, 1968.

Berlau, John. "JFK Used Audits to Silence Critics." *Insight on the News*, September 16, 2003.

Bernhard, Berl, William Taylor, and Harris Wofford. "Civil Rights, Politics and the Law: Three Civil Rights Lawyers Reminisce," Woodrow Wilson Center, January 19, 2006.

Bickel, Alexander M. "The Kennedy-Javits Voting Amendment." *New Republic*, June 5, 1965.

————. "Robert F. Kennedy: The Case Against Him for Attorney General." *New Republic*, January 9, 1961.

Biddle, Francis. "Biddle Backs Kennedy." Letter to Editor. *New York Times*, August 31, 1964.

Bigart, Homer. "Keating vs. Kennedy: A Campaign Marked by Sharp Contrasts." *New York Times*, October 9, 1964.

————. "Keating vs. Kennedy: A Near-Debate." *New York Times*, October 28, 1964.

————. "Kennedy Assails Nazi-Deal Charge, Calls It 'Smear.' " *New York Times*, September 22, 1964.

————. "Kennedy Assails Surrogate Court." *New York Times*, November 30, 1966.

————. "Kennedy, Disturbed by Memory of Tragedy, Cancels Rally Here." *New York Times*, September 29, 1964.

————. "Kennedy Fulfills Some Campaign Pledges." *New York Times*, November 5, 1964.

————. "Kennedy Tames Bearish Crowd." *New York Times*, October 3, 1964.

————. "Kennedy, Told News on Plane, Sits in Silence Amid the Hubbub." *New York Times*, April 1, 1968.

————. "Kennedy Worried over Jewish Vote." *New York Times*, October 1, 1964.

————. "Negroes Are Cool to McCarthy as He Opens Indiana Campaign." *New York Times*, April 19, 1968.

————. "Shift to Kennedy by Jews Is Noted." *New York Times*, November 3, 1960.

————. "Spending an Issue in State Campaign." *New York Times*, October 11, 1966.

————. "Winner's Pledge." *New York Times*, November 10, 1960.

Binder, John J. "Organized Crime and the 1960 Presidential Election." *Public Choice*, vol. 130, March 2007.

Birmingham News. "Stars and Bars Flies as RFK, Wallace Meet." April 25, 1963.

Bishop, Jim. "Can Kennedy Afford Bob's Tactics?" *Milwaukee Sentinel*, October 27, 1960.

Blackburn, Dan. "Robert F. Kennedy—Some Personal Thoughts." Self-published, June 9, 1968.

Blanton, Thomas. "Annals of Blinksmanship." *Wilson Quarterly*, Summer 1997.

————. "The Cuban Missile Crisis Isn't What It Used to Be," *Cold War International History Project Bulletin*, Fall 2002.

Blumenthal, Ralph. "Brooklyn Negroes Harass Kennedy." *New York Times*, February 5, 1966.

————. "RFK—Rights Chiefs Share Riot Blame." *New York Post*, August 19, 1965.

Booker, James. "Evers' RFK Praise Sparks NAACP Row." *New York Amsterdam News*, October 17, 1964.

Booker, Simeon. "Atty. Gen. Kennedy Explains Position on Civil Rights." *Jet*, November 7, 1963.

————. "RFK Poverty Probe," *Jet*, May 4, 1967.

————. "RFK Retreats on Rights Bill As Negroes Scream: 'Sellout!'." *Jet*, October 31, 1963.

————. "Roy Wilkins Disagrees with Views of Robert F. Kennedy." *Jet*, November 14, 1963.

Boroson, Warren. "The Bellicose Mr. Belli." *Fact*, July 1964.

Boston Globe. "Kennedy Staff's Campaign Against Him Was Dishonest, Sen. McCarthy Says." December 24, 1968.

————. "LBJ Rules Kennedy Out as VP." July 31, 1964.

————. "R. F. Kennedy Quits." August 1, 1953.

————. "RFK Visits Miss. Negro Slums." April 12, 1967.

————. "RFK Visits Ted; Says He Looks 'Lot Better.' " June 24, 1964.

Boston Herald. "Kennedy Bids West Go Slow." September 16, 1955.

Boston Post. "World's Financial and Political Nerve Centres Rife with Rumors Kennedy to Be 1940 Presidential Candidate." January 2, 1937.

Bowes, John S. "Kennedy as Senator." Letter to Editor. *New York Times*, August 20, 1964.

Bradlee, Benjamin. " 'What's Bobby Going to Do?'—An Informal Talk with R.F.K." *Newsweek*, July 6, 1964.

Bradshaw, Jon. "Richard Goodwin: The Good, the Bad, and the Ugly." New York, August 18, 1975.

Braestrup, Peter. "Hoffa Will Press Drive on Kennedy." *New York Times*, September 23, 1960.

Branch, Taylor, and George Crile III. "The Arrest That Changed the World." *Washington Post Magazine*, October 23, 1988.

————. "The Kennedy Vendetta." *Harper's Magazine*, August 1, 1975.

Breslin, Jimmy. "Bobby's Planning a Victory Party." *Boston Globe*, August 20, 1964.

————. "A Day with RFK and McCarthy." *New York Post*, March 15, 1968.

————. "Echoes of LA, 1968 and RFK." *Newsday*, October 8, 2003.

————. "Eyewitness to a Horror Still Fresh, Columnist Jimmy Breslin Was at the Ambassador Hotel on the Night That Bobby Kennedy Was Shot." *Newsday*, November 26, 2006.

————. "'I Guess the Only Reason We've Survived Is That There Are Too Many of Us.'" *Boston Globe*, June 21, 1964.

————. "A Memory of a Kennedy Lost." *Newsday*, January 4, 1998.

————. "Nobody but Kennedy Could Have Invaded New York." *Boston Globe*, October 25, 1964.

————. "Politics Not How It Used to Be." *Milwaukee Journal Sentinel*, November 8, 2002.

————. "A Real Kennedy Handicap: Valachi Hearing Resented." *Boston Globe*, September 9, 1964.

————. "Robert Kennedy Doesn't Need Reminder." *Boston Globe*, September 28, 1964.

————. "Ted's Condition Key to RFK's Senate Bid." *Boston Globe*, August 9, 1964.

————. "They've Got to Get Daley Back." *Boston Globe*, July 9, 1972.

Brinkley, Alan. "Conspiracy . . . : David Talbot Reopens the Question of Who Killed John F. Kennedy." *New York Times*, May 20, 2007.

Broder, David S. "Campaigning Through California." *Washington Post*, October 25, 1966.

————. "Close Race Seen in Oregon Today." *Washington Post*, May 28, 1968.

————. "Indiana Not Doing for RFK What W.Va. Did for Brother." *Washington Post*, April 30, 1968.

————. "Kennedy Condemns Backlash." *Washington Post*, October 24, 1966.

————. "Kennedy Indiana Feat Raises Doubt McCarthy Can Rally." *Washington Post*, May 9, 1968.

————. "Kennedy's Vietnam Plea Spurs Popularity on Democratic Left." *New York Times*, February 21, 1966.

————. "Rival Camps Gun for RFK." *Washington Post*, April 2, 1968.

————. "Twists and Turns of New York Race." *Washington Post*, October 18, 1966.

Bryan, David Tennant. "Jack to Bobby to Jack." *Manchester Union Leader*, January 9, 1961.

Bryan, Ferald J. "Joseph McCarthy, Robert Kennedy, and the Greek Shipping Crisis: A Study of Foreign Policy Rhetoric." *Presidential Studies Quarterly 24*, Winter 1994.

Buchwald, Art. "Author at Work: A Book About Manchester Book Would End Controversy." *Washington Post*, January 29, 1967.

————. "Bobby Gets Motherly Lesson on Fiscal Responsibility." *Washington Post*, May 14, 1968.

————. "Capitol Punishment . . . : The Judge Is Nobody's Pet." *Washington Post*, May 27, 1965.

————. "The Ideal Foe: Bobby, Gene and Dick's Men Hunt Substitute for LBJ." *Washington Post*, April 14, 1968.

Buckley, William F., Jr. "Attorney General Kennedy Is Accused of Trying to Put Roy Cohn in Prison." *Los Angeles Times*, September 23, 1963.

————. "Bobby Kennedy, in Struggle for Power, Moves to Left of LBJ." *Richmond News Leader*, May 15, 1965.

————. "Bob Kennedy as Vice President? Writer Is Appalled by the Prospect." *Los Angeles Times*, June 1, 1964.

————. "Bob Kennedy's Transformation." *Los Angeles Times*, July 19, 1967.

————. "The Bugging Controversy Displays Characters . . ." *Los Angeles Times*, December 16, 1966.

————. "Dissecting Kennedy's Proposal Is Revealing." *Los Angeles Times*, March 2, 1966.

————. "An Englishman's Critique of Sen. Robert Kennedy." *Los Angeles Times*, October 24, 1966.

————. "Following Joseph Alsop." *Los Angeles Times*, January 29, 1968.

———. "The Inevitability of Bobby Kennedy." *Boston Globe*, April 8, 1966.

———. "Johnson-Kennedy Split Is Natural." *Los Angeles Times*, May 17, 1965.

———. "Kennedy Apologist Finds Going Rougher . . . Rougher . . . and . . ." *Los Angeles Times*, May 13, 1968.

———. "McCarthy May Have Helped Kennedy Plan." *Los Angeles Times*, September 30, 1962.

———. "Nixon Offers Advice—to Bob Kennedy, Yet!" *Los Angeles Times*, November 7, 1966.

———. "Oregon Wrote Kennedy's Presidential Exit Line." *Los Angeles Times*, June 3, 1968.

———. "Why Link Vietnam, Riots?" *Los Angeles Times*, August 11, 1967.

———. "Why Not Teddy?" *National Review*, October 9, 1962.

Business Week. "The Greeks, the Senator, and the Slump." April 11, 1953.

Cadden, Vivian. "The Murder of President Kennedy." *McCall's*, March 1977.

Califano, Joseph A., Jr. "A Concoction of Lies and Distortions." Letter to Editor. *Wall Street Journal*, January 28, 1992.

Capell, Frank A. "Robert F. Kennedy: Emerging American Dictator." *Herald of Freedom*, 1968.

———. "The Strange Death of Marilyn Monroe." *Herald of Freedom*, 1964.

Caplin, Mortimer M. "Kennedy Did Not Use I.R.S. as a Weapon." Letter to Editor. *New York Times*, November 14, 1997.

———. "Kennedy IRS Was Clean." Letter to Editor. *Washington Post*, January 8, 1997.

Carlson, Peter. "David A. Kennedy, 1955–1984." *People*, May 14, 1984.

Carpenter, Elizabeth. "On the Candidates." *New York Times*, April 28, 1968.

Carr, John. "With RFK in the Delta." *American Heritage*, April/May 2002.

Carroll, Maurice. "Ethel Kennedy Wins 'Horse Theft' Case After a 2-Day Trial." *New York Times*, January 11, 1967.

———. "Mrs. Robert Kennedy Is Facing Trial for Failure to Return Horse." *New York Times*, December 30, 1966.

Carroll, Ronald H., and Alan B. Tomich. "The Death of Marilyn Monroe: Report to the District Attorney of Los Angeles County." December 1982.

Carroll, Wallace. "Appointing a Relative." *New York Times*, December 17, 1960.

———. "Steel: A 72-Hour Drama with an All-Star Cast." *New York Times*, April 23, 1962.

Carter, Dan. "Bobby Says LBJ Let Fight for Rights Turn Riotous." *New York Daily News*, March 22, 1968.

Casey, Phil. Students Steal Show as Kennedy Resigns." *Washington Post*, September 4, 1964.

———. "3000 in Peaceful Rights March Here." *Washington Post*, June 15, 1963.

Chicago Daily Defender. "Ask Kennedy to Visit Ala. See How Negroes Treated." May 18, 1961.

———. "Bob Kennedy Cites Dire Need for Better Leadership in the South." June 7, 1961.

———. "Text of Wire to Kennedy." August 29, 1961.

———. "Thurgood Marshall Gets Run-Around." July 9, 1962.

Chicago Daily Tribune. "Bares Bob Kennedy's Interest in Bus Rides." June 1, 1961.

———. "Jailed Racial Integrators Refuse Meals." June 2, 1961.

———. "Kennedy Acts in Bus Riot." May 21, 1961.

———. "Robert Kennedy Backs ICC's Rule Against Bus Bias." September 24, 1961.

———. "U.S. Indicts 9 on Charge of Tax Evasion." December 22, 1961.

Chicago Sun-Times. "Will LBJ Run Again?" March 22, 1968.

Chicago Tribune. "Administration Cold Shoulders Bobby's Viet Piece Suggestion." February 21, 1966.

———. "Bobby Asks Hike in Aid to Children." April 12, 1967.

———. "Ho Chi Kennedy." Editorial. February 21, 1966.

———. "Wants Reds Kept Out of Power, Bundy Asserts." February 21, 1966.

———. "What Bobby Is." Editorial. April 20, 1968.

Childs, Marquis. "Blank Spot in Cuban Picture." *Washington Post*, March 4, 1963.

———. "Bobby and the President." *Good Housekeeping*, May 1962.

———. "A Candid Look At Bobby's Year." *Washington Post*, January 5, 1962.

———. "Democratic Rift Expected to Grow Wider." *Philadelphia Bulletin*, March 21, 1968.

———. "McCarthy Letter Contents Revealed." *Washington Post*, June 2, 1953.

Cipes, Robert M. "The Wiretap War." *New Republic*, December 24, 1966.

Clawson, Ken W. "FBI's Hoover Scores Ramsey Clark, RFK." *Washington Post*, November 17, 1970.

Clayton, James E. " 'Freedom Riders' Stir Awareness of Real Change in Southern Life." *Washington Post*, July 4, 1961.

———. "Robt. Kennedy Court Debut Set." *Boston Globe*, January 9, 1963.

———. "Robt. Kennedy 'Not a Candidate.' " *Boston Globe*, April 27, 1963.

———. "Robt. Kennedy Raps Lawyers on Rights." *Boston Globe*, September 28, 1963.

———. "Robert Kennedy's Aim in South: To Uphold Law but Take No Sides," *Washington Post*, May 27, 1961.

———. "Shun 2 States, U.S. Urging All Travelers." *Washington Post*, May 25, 1961.

Clines, Francis X. "Kennedy Buying East River Suite." *New York Times*, June 18, 1965.

Clymer, Adam. "Head of FBI Challenged for Proof." *New York Times*, December 12, 1966.

———. "Textbooks Reassess Kennedy, Putting Camelot Under Siege." *New York Times*, November 10, 2013.

———. "When Presidential Words Led to Swift Action." *New York Times*, June 8, 2013.

Coblentz, Gaston. "'Attack on Berlin Same as Attack on N.Y.' " *New York Herald Tribune*, February 23, 1962.

Cold War International History Project Bulletin, Wilson Center. "The Global Cuban Missile Crisis at 50." No. 17/18, Fall 2012.

———. "New Evidence on Cold War Crises: Russian Documents on the Korean War." No. 14/15, Winter 2003–Spring 2004.

Collman, Ashley. "Beloved Nanny Who Was a Witness to History as She Helped Raise Eleven Kennedy Children Is Laid to Rest at 105." *Daily Mail Online*, August 9, 2013.

Considine, Bob. "Joe Kennedy Sees Opportunity for Greatness." *New York Journal-American*. January 8, 1961.

Cook, Fred J. "The Hoffa Trial." *Nation*, April 27, 1964.

Cordtz, Dan. "Sen. Kennedy Defends Johnson's Policies on South American Visit." *Wall Street Journal*, November 18, 1965.

Cowan, Paul. "Wallace in Yankeeland: The Invisible Revolution." *Village Voice*, July 18, 1968.

Crawford, Kenneth. "Bobby on Vietnam." *Newsweek*, March 7, 1966.

———. "Henry A. Kennedy?" *Newsweek*, March 20, 1967.

Cuneo, Ernest. "New York State Democratic Dinner Has Deep Political Implications." *North American Newspaper Alliance*, December 14, 1967.

Daemmrich, JoAnna. "Lt. Gov. Kathleen Kennedy Townsend Talks About the Legacy of Robert F. Kennedy, Who Died 30 Years Ago Today." Baltimore *Sun*, June 6, 1998.

Dales, Douglas. "Kennedy to Seek Party Peace Here." *New York Times*, December 3, 1960.

Daniel, Clifton. "British Defend Stand on Trade with China." *New York Times*, May 24, 1953.

David, Lester. "My Father, Robert Kennedy: His Daughter Kathleen Remembers." *McCall's*, May 1988.

Davidson, Bill. "A Profile in Family Courage." *Saturday Evening Post*, December 14, 1963.

———. "What Has Tragedy Meant to Bobby Kennedy?" *Good Housekeeping*, July 1964.

Dean, Linda. "Memories with Gov. John Patterson." *Lake Martin Living*, July 2001.

Decker, Cathleen. "'92 Democratic Convention: Democrats Tap Kennedy Magic in Emotional Tribute to R.F.K." *Los Angeles Times*, July 16, 1992.

DeMichele, Matthew, and Gary Potter. "Sin City Revisited: A Case Study of the Official Sanctioning of Organized Crime in an 'Open City.'" Eastern Kentucky University.

Desmond, James. "Albany Hippodrome." *Nation*, February 22, 1965.

Detroit News. "A Lie Test for Hoffa?" May 13, 1964.

Devin, Edward. "Scene and Heard at the State House." *Boston Herald*, March 16, 1956.

Die Burger. "Senator Kennedy." Editorial. June 7, 1966.

Doar, John, and Dorothy Landsberg. "The Performance of the FBI in Investigating Violations of Federal Laws Protecting the Right to Vote—1960–1967 (1971). *Hearings Before the Select Committee to Study Governmental Operations with Respect to Intelligence Activities*. United States Senate, 94th Congress, First Session, 1975, vol. 6.

Dobbs, Michael. "The Price of a 50-Year Myth," *New York Times*, October 15, 2012.

Doherty, William. "1968 in 2008: The More Things Change . . ." *H-Net*, November 17, 2008.

Donovan, Robert J. "Golden Age of Democratic Party Coming to End." *Los Angeles Times*, January 7, 1968.

———. "GOP Senator Says Kennedy Friends Profit." *New York Herald Tribune*, March 24, 1962.

———. "Humphrey Astonished at Turn Events Have Taken for Him." *Los Angeles Times*, April 28, 1968.

———. "Indiana Primary to Put Kennedy on Hottest Spot." *Los Angeles Times*, May 5, 1968.

———. "Kennedy Declares Antiwar Campaign." *Los Angeles Times*, March 17, 1968.

———. "Kennedy Hits Trail First in Kansas City." *Los Angeles Times*, March 18, 1968.

———. "Kennedy News Chills McCarthy's Followers." *Los Angeles Times*, March 14, 1968.

———. "Nixon, Humphrey Now Likely Rivals for the Presidency." *Los Angeles Times*, May 29, 1968.

———. "O'Brien May Leave Cabinet to Aid Kennedy." *Los Angeles Times*, April 10, 1968.

———. "Withdrawal Announcement Catches Nation by Surprise." *Los Angeles Times*, April 1, 1968.

Dougherty, Richard. "Kennedy Has Little to Say After Defeat." *Los Angeles Times*, May 29, 1968.

Doyle, James S. "Bar Assn., Morrissey Conflict." *Boston Globe*, October 13, 1965.

———. "The Brothers Kennedy: A Year's End Assessment of the Two Senators." *Boston Globe*, November 28, 1965.

———. "McCarthy Can't Repeat Indiana Mistakes in Nebraska." *Boston Globe*, May 11, 1968.

———. "Morrissey Furor Mounts." *Boston Globe*, September 29, 1965.

Doyle, James S., and Martin Nolan. "U.S., State Bar Groups Fight Morrissey." *Boston Globe*, September 28, 1965.

Drew, Elizabeth. "Bobby Books." *Atlantic Monthly*, July 1969.

———. "Bush Family Values." *Nation*, March 1, 2004.

———. "A Politerary Convention." *Los Angeles Times*, August 13, 2000.

———. "Washington." *Atlantic Monthly*, April 1968.

Drummond, Roscoe. "The Headlong Pace of Robert Kennedy." *New York Herald Tribune*, February 8, 1965.

———. "See Bobby Run." *Washington Post*, August 24, 1966.

Drury, Allen. "Dio Aide Accused of Terror Moves." *New York Times*, August 7, 1957.

———. "McCarthy Rites Held in Capital." *New York Times*, May 7, 1957.

———. "Teamster Loss Put at $709,420." *New York Times*, March 23, 1957.

Dubois, Jules. "Report from Latin America." *Chicago Tribune*, May 22, 1966.

Dudar, Helen. "The Perilous Campaign." *New York Post*, June 5, 1968.

Duscha, Julius. "Big Scene for Kennedy." *Washington Post*, August 24, 1964.

Eder, Richard. "Kennedy Bids U.S. Aid Latin Change." *New York Times*, May 10, 1966.

———. "Kennedy on Alliance: 'We Can Do Better.' " *New York Times*, May 15, 1966.

Edson, Arthur. "Restive Brother of President." *Salt Lake Tribune*, April 14, 1963.

Edwards, Willard. "McCarthy Gets Agreement to Blockade Reds." *Chicago Daily Tribune*, March 29, 1953.

Egan, Charles E. "Flanders' Motion to Curb McCarthy Hit by Knowland." *New York Times*, June 13, 1954.

———. "Stassen Insists on Fair Inquiries." *New York Times*, April 3, 1955.

Egan, Leo. "Liaison Is Set Up: Nominee Tells Details of Choosing Johnson as Running Mate." *New York Times*, July 17, 1960.

Eisele, Al. "RFK Vows Return of New Frontier." *Independent Press-Telegram*, March 17, 1968.

Elliff, John T. "Aspects of Federal Civil Rights Enforcement: The Justice Department and the FBI, 1939–1964." *Perspectives in American History*, vol. 5, 1971.

Emery, Lawrence. "Congress Anti-Labor Spree in the Cards This Winter." *National Guardian*, October 28, 1957.

———. "Why the Teamsters Union Elected Jimmy Hoffa." *National Guardian*, October 14, 1957.

Evans, Rowland, and Robert Novak. " 'Freedom of Choice.'" *Washington Post*, March 25, 1964.

———. "The JFK Tribute." *Washington Post*, July 31, 1964.

———. "The Johnson-Kennedy Split." *Washington Post*, August 4, 1964.

———. "Johnson's Timing Problem." *Washington Post*, July 10, 1964.

———. "The Kennedy Win." *Washington Post*, July 1, 1966.

———. "Loss of Kennedy Leaves Blacks Wondering Where to Go in Politics." *Washington Post*, June 7, 1968.

———. "Stop Humphrey." *Washington Post*, August 6, 1964.

Fairlie, Henry. "Harvard Enclave Turns into Kennedy Power Center." *Washington Post*, January 15, 1967.

Fallaci, Oriana. "Robert Kennedy Answers Some Blunt Questions." *Look*, March 9, 1965.

Feiffer, Jules. "Bobby Twins." *Village Voice*, February 2, 1967.

Fein, Bruce. "Time to Rein in the Prosecution." *ABA Journal*, July 1994.

Feldstein, Mark. "JFK's Own Dirty Trick." *Washington Post*, January 14, 2011.

Fenton, John H. "Cabots and Lowells of Boston Society Are Less Isolated—to a Degree." *New York Times*, January 28, 1957.

———. "Senate Vacancy Stirs Bay State." *New York Times*, December 18, 1960.

———. "29 Jurists, Disputing Kennedy, Say U.S. Can Act in Mississippi." *New York Times*, July 1, 1964.

Fineman, Mark, and Dolly Mascarenas. "Bay of Pigs: The Secret Death of Pete Ray." *Los Angeles Times*, March 15, 1998.

Finney, John W. "Kennedy Sees President; Denies Bringing 'Feelers.' " *New York Times*, February 7, 1967.

———. "The New Democratic Vice-Presidential Choice: Robert Sargent Shriver Jr." *New York Times*, August 6, 1972.

Flaherty, Joe. "Bobby and the Celts: Keep It Green, Baby!" *Village Voice*, March 9, 1967.

Flannery, Harry W. "The Other Kennedy: An Interview with Bob Kennedy." *Ave Maria Catholic Home Weekly*, August 31, 1957.

Fleming, Anne Taylor. "The Kennedy Mystique." *New York Times Magazine*, June 17, 1979.

Flick, David. "Kennedys Make Rare Visit to Dallas, Say RFK Questioned 'Lone Gunman' Theory in JFK Assassination." *Dallas Morning News*, January 12, 2013.

Fontova, Humberto. "Betrayal at the Bay of Pigs: A Look Back 53 Years Later." *TheBlaze*, April 18, 2014.

Fortune. "An Interview with Sen. Kennedy on Business, Antitrust, Taxes, the Urban Crisis . . . and Lost Youth." March 1968.

Frankel, Max. "Khrushchev Letter Appears as Key in '62 Cuban Missile Crisis." *New York Times*, February 4, 1966.

———. "Otepka Accusers Placed on Leave." *New York Times*, November 10, 1963.

Franklin, Ben A. "Kennedys Spur New School Plan for Virginia Negroes as First One Fails." *New York Times*, July 21, 1963.

Free, James. "Wallace, Kennedy Talk; Neither Changes Views." *Birmingham News*, April 25, 1963.

Freedman, Monroe E. "The Professional Responsibility of the Prosecuting Attorney." *Georgetown Law Journal*, 1967.

Friedman, Andrea. "The Strange Career of Annie Lee Moss: Rethinking Race, Gender, and McCarthyism." *Journal of American History*, September 2007.

Fursenko, Aleksandr, and Timothy Naftali. "Soviet Intelligence and the Cuban Missile Crisis." *Intelligence and National Security*, 1998.

Gage, Nicholas. "Ex-Aides Say Justice Department Rejected a Sinatra Inquiry." *New York Times*, April 14, 1976.

Gallup, George. "Humphrey Surges into Lead over Kennedy with Democrats." *Washington Post*, May 15, 1968.

Garrison, Lloyd. "Africa Gets Call in Adam Deadlock." *New York Times*, June 16, 1966.

———. "Rules to Integrate Bus Transportation Urged Before I.C.C." *New York Times*, August 16, 1961.

Garrow, David J. "The FBI and Martin Luther King." *Atlantic Monthly*, July/August 2002.

Gates, Henry Louis. "Swallowing the Elephant." *New York Times*, September 19, 2004.

Gent, George. "Ambulance Aide Tells of Drive to Hospital After the Shooting." *New York Times*, June 6, 1968.

Getlein, Frank. "Kennedy's Going and Staying." *Washington Evening Star*, May 15, 1967.

Gibson, Gwen. "Kennedy Highjinks Delight GOP." *Kansas City Times*, August 28, 1962.

Gilder, George F. "Kennedy Through GOP Glasses." *The New Leader*, December 18, 1967.

Gilroy, Harry. "Robert Kennedy's Account of Missile Crisis Sold for $1-Million." *New York Times*, September 20, 1968.

Gladwin, Hill. "Woman Is Sought in Kennedy Death." *New York Times*, June 7, 1968.

Glass, Andrew J. "ADA Credits Kennedy Brothers with Perfect 1966 Liberal Scores." *Washington Post*, October 2, 1966.

———. "Angry Senators Denounce Saigon on Vote Barriers." *Washington Post*, August 12, 1967.

———. "Author Denies Breaking Faith over JFK Book." *Washington Post*, December 19, 1966.

———. "The Compulsive Candidate." *Saturday Evening Post*, April 23, 1966.

———. "German Weekly Prints Uncut Manchester Text." *Washington Post*, January 10, 1967.

———. "Governor Sees No LBJ 'Agent' On N.H. Scene." *Washington Post*, September 22, 1967.

———. "Kennedy Is Politically Less Mature Than President, Humphrey Asserts." *Washington Post*, September 27, 1966.

———. "LBJ Depicted as Fleeing Dallas in Fear of a Plot on His Own Life." *Washington Post*, January 24, 1967.

———. "Manchester's 1st Draft Depicts LBJ as 'Octopus'." *Washington Post*, July 6, 1967.

———. "McCarthy Plans to Oppose LBJ in 4 to 6 States." *Washington Post*, December 1, 1967.

———. "Mrs. Kennedy Sues to Block Book on Assassination of President." *Washington Post*, December 15, 1966.

———. "Politics Eclipses Vietnam in Johnson-Kennedy Rift." *Washington Post*, March 6, 1967.

———. "RFK Men Lean to GOP Dove for '68." *Washington Post*, October 15, 1967.

———. "RFK Says Top Figures Can't Speak in Ghettos." *Washington Post*, December 1, 1966.

———. "RFK Scores China Policy; Asks Contacts." *Washington Post*, February 9, 1967.

———. "RFK Slum Housing Plan Scored." *Washington Post*, September 15, 1967.

———. "RFK Urges Talks, Halt In Bombing." *Washington Post*, March 3, 1967.

———. "Robert Kennedy Bars Race in 1968 for Either President or the No. 2 Spot." *Washington Post*, October 6, 1966.

———. "U.S. Facing a 'Medical Crisis,' Kennedy Tells Chicago Crowds." *Washington Post*, October 16, 1966.

———. "Yorty, in Game of Hide-and-Seek, Avoids Meeting Arch Foe RFK." *Washington Post*, May 13, 1967.

Glass, Andrew J., and Leroy T. Aarons. "A Young Crew Around Young Robert." *Washington Post*, February 12, 1967.

Glass, Andrew J., and David S. Broder. "Senators Avoid the LBJ Brand in Election Bids." *Washington Post*, March 12, 1967.

Goldberg, Jay. "Reflections: The Robert F. Kennedy I Knew." *Federal Bar Council Quarterly*, March/April/May 2011.

Goldin, Harrison J. "Perspective: How One Fall Day Changed a Life." *Princeton Alumni Weekly*, November 6, 2002.

Goldman, Ari L. "Junius Scales, Communist Sent to U.S. Prison, Dies at 82." *New York Times*, August 7, 2002.

Goodwin, Richard N. "A Day in June." *McCall's*, June 1970.

———. "JFK and Che." *Cigar Aficionado*, Autumn 1996.

———. "The Night McCarthy Turned to Kennedy." *Look*, October 15, 1968.

Gould, Jack. "Behind Closed Doors." *New York Times*, October 27, 1963.

———. "TV: Too Many Cameras." *New York Times*, October 22, 1963.

Graham, Fred P. "Drew Pearson Says Robert Kennedy Ordered Wiretap on Phone of Dr. King." *New York Times*, May 25, 1968.

———. "Hoover and Kennedy Trade New Charges on F.B.I. Use of Listening Devices." *New York Times*, December 12, 1966.

———. "Hoover Asserts Robert Kennedy Aided Buggings." *New York Times*, December 11, 1966.

Greenberg, Carl. "Approval of Dr. King Wiretap Alleged: Charges by Drew Pearson Embroil Kennedy." *Los Angeles Times*, May 29, 1968.

———. "Both McCarthy, Kennedy Seek Brown Support." *Los Angeles Times*, April 2, 1968.

———. "Brother Expects Kennedy Foes to Unite in California Primary." *Los Angeles Times*, May 9, 1968.

———. "Kennedy Aide Acts to Smooth Waters Ruffled by Unruh." *Los Angeles Times*, May 1, 1968.

———. "Kennedy Primary Victory May Still Be Marred." *Los Angeles Times*, April 22, 1968.

———. "Reagan Says Nation Is Totally Out of Control." *Los Angeles Times*, May 19, 1968.

———. "Shakeup Hits Kennedy Staff in California." *Los Angeles Times*, May 30, 1968.

Greenfield, Meg. "New York: The Keating Record." *Reporter*, October 22, 1964.

Grose, Peter. "Kennedy Asserts Johnson Shifted U.S. Aim in Vietnam." *New York Times*, November 27, 1967.

Gruson, Sydney. "Cautions East Germans." *New York Times*, February 26, 1962.

Gwertzman, Bernard. "Rusk to the Hill." *Washington Sunday Star*, March 10, 1968.

Haessler, Carl. "Bobby's Campaign to 'Get' Hoffa." *National Guardian*, January 17, 1963.

Hailey, Foster. "Robert Kennedy Rebuts Critics, Calls Washington 'Pro-Business.'" *New York Times*, November 14, 1961.

Halberstam, David. "Africans Answered by Robert Kennedy on U.S. Civil Rights." *New York Times*, August 8, 1961.

———. "Alabama Bars State Police from Aiding F.B.I." *New York Times*, June 17, 1961.

———. "Bus Riders Urged to Shift Target." *New York Times*, June 20, 1961.

———. "Cites Suit on Aniline." *New York Times*, September 21, 1964.

———. "Ivory Coast Gets American Hello." *New York Times*, August 6, 1961.

———. "Kennedy Explains Refusal of Brother to Bomb Cuba." *New York Times*, October 14, 1964.

———. "Kennedy Fighting 'Ruthless' Image." *New York Times*, October 27, 1964.

———. "Kennedy Meets Foreign Press." *New York Times*, October 28, 1964.

Hamill, Pete. "In Defense of Honest Labor." *New York Times*, December 31, 1995.

———. "The Last Hours of RFK." *New York*, June 5, 1968.

———. "Two Minutes to Midnight: The Very Last Hurrah." *Village Voice*, June 13, 1968.

———. "The Woman Behind Bobby Kennedy." *Good Housekeeping*, April 1968.

Handler, M. S. "F.B.I. Augments Mississippi Force." *New York Times*, June 25, 1964.

Hangen, Welles. "Justice Douglas and U.S. Farmers Find Paths Cross on Soviet Tours."
    New York Times, August 14, 1955.
Harrington, Michael. "The South Bronx Shall Rise Again." *New York*, April 3, 1978.
Harris, Richard. "Justice." *New Yorker*, November 8, 1969.
————. "Justice II—The Transition." *New Yorker*, November 15, 1969.
Hartford Courant. "Columnist Tells Why Bob Kennedy Stayed." January 18, 1964.
————. "Manchester Takes Helm of State Kennedy Group." May 10, 1968.
Harwood, Richard. "Branigin Organization Believed Crumbling." *Washington Post*, May 5,
    1968.
————. "The Brief and Turbulent Campaign." *Washington Post*, January 29, 1969.
————. "Bugging Is an Old Federal Plague." *Washington Post*, December 18, 1966.
————. "Can 'New Politics' Retain Its Luster?" *Washington Post*, May 23, 1968.
————. "Cheers . . . Shots . . . The Hospital." *Washington Post*, June 6, 1968.
————. "Crowd Madness and Kennedy Strategy." *Washington Post*, March 28, 1968.
————. "FBI Found No Ban on 'Bugs' in '62 Order." *Washington Post*, December 16, 1966.
————. "First Week's Crowds Elate Kennedy Camp." *Washington Post*, March 24, 1968.
————. "Ghetto Moved Him Most." *Washington Post*, June 7, 1968.
————. " 'I've Lost,' Said RFK." *Washington Post*, May 29, 1968.
————. "Kennedy Declares U.S. Should Defend Israel." *Washington Post*, May 27, 1968.
————. "Kennedy Secretly a 'Dove' in Cuba Crisis, Letter Shows." *Washington Post*, Au-
    gust 29, 1987.
————. "Kennedy Still McCarthy's Prime Target." *Washington Post*, May 19, 1968.
————. "Kennedy's Words Miss Crowd Mood." *Washington Post*, April 20, 1968.
————. " 'Kiddie Corps' Is Kennedy Bulwark." *Washington Post*, May 5, 1968.
————. "McCarthy and Kennedy: Philosopher vs. Evangelist." *Washington Post*, May 26,
    1968.
————. "McCarthy Is Scornful of Arrival." *Washington Post*, March 17, 1968.
————. "Narrow Oregon Lead Alarms Kennedy Camp." *Washington Post*, May 24, 1968.
————. "Nebraska Campaign Pressed." *Washington Post*, April 21, 1968.
————. "The Old and New Kennedy Illusions." *Washington Post*, June 8, 1968.
————. "Only 'Difficult Compromise' Can End War, Kennedy Says." *Washington Post*,
    March 19, 1968.
————. "Prince of Our Disorder." *Washington Post*, September 3, 1978.
————. "RFK Attacks Johnson Plan to House Poor." *Washington Post*, March 21, 1968.
————. "RFK Banks on Indiana." *Washington Post*, April 11, 1968.
————. "RFK Barred Bugging in 1962 Memo." *Washington Post*, December 15, 1966.
————. "RFK Goes on Stump in the Rain." *Washington Post*, October 2, 1966.
————. "RFK Kids Self, Tells Stories to Cheering Crowds in West." *Washington Post*, March
    27, 1968.
————. "RFK Says Johnson Divides the Nation." *Washington Post*, March 22, 1968.
————. "RFK Troupe Invades Polish Party in Indiana." *Washington Post*, April 16, 1968.
————. "Sen. Long to Ask Airing of Bugging Controversy." *Washington Post*, December
    13, 1966.
————. "Southwest Gives RFK Quiet Welcome." *Washington Post*, March 30, 1968.
————. " 'Stop HHH' Offer Made by Kennedy." *Washington Post*, June 3, 1968.
————. "With Bobby Kennedy on That Last Campaign." *Washington Post*, June 5, 1988.
Harwood, Richard, and Haynes Johnson. "Showdown in White House: LBJ's Quiet Feud
    with Bob Kennedy." *Chicago Tribune*, November 26, 1973.

Healy, Paul F. "Bob Kennedy: Investigator in a Hurry." *Sign,* August 1957.

Healy, Robert. "BC Law School Records Don't Show Morrissey as a Student." *Boston Globe,* October 17, 1965.

Hendrix, Hal. "Backstage with Bobby." *Miami News,* July 14, 1963.

———. "'Innocents Abroad' Aid Fidel." *Miami News,* July 16, 1963.

Hentoff, Nat. "Bobby the K." *Village Voice,* September 24, 1964.

———. "Help." *Village Voice,* April 25, 1968.

———. "The Man Who Stood Up to Bobby Kennedy." *Village Voice,* January 23, 2001.

Herald of Freedom and The Metropolitan Review. "J. Edgar Hoover Versus Robert F. Kennedy." January 13, 1967.

Herbers, John. "Agony and Determination Marked Kennedy Drive." *New York Times,* June 6, 1968.

———. "Georgia Campus Cheers Kennedy." *New York Times,* May 27, 1964.

———. "Indiana Seeing a New Kennedy with Shorter Hair, Calmer Manner and Pleas for Local Rule." *New York Times,* May 3, 1968.

———. "Kennedy Campaign Evokes a Legend." *New York Times,* March 31, 1968.

———. "Kennedy Carries Criticism of Johnson into Campaign in Iowa." *New York Times,* March 11, 1968.

———. "Kennedy Credits Gains to Brother." *New York Times,* September 19, 1966.

———. "Kennedy Disputes Housing Aid Bill." *New York Times,* March 21, 1968.

———. "Kennedy Evokes the Image of '60." *New York Times,* September 25, 1966.

———. "Kennedy Is Ready to Run." *New York Times,* March 14, 1968.

———. "Kennedy Message Reaches Millions." *New York Times,* March 31, 1968.

———. "Kennedy Opens Campaign for National Democratic Candidates with Talk for Mondale in Minnesota." *New York Times,* September 18, 1966.

———. "Kennedy Pledges to Quit if Beaten in California Bid." *New York Times,* May 30, 1968.

———. "Kennedy Prods Johnson Gently on Selecting a Peace Talks Site." *New York Times,* May 2, 1968.

———. "Kennedy Seeks a Business Rapport." *New York Times,* October 1, 1967.

———. "Kennedy's Office Scene of Clutter." *New York Times,* March 15, 1968.

———. "Kennedy Starts Off Fast and Hard." *New York Times,* March 24, 1968.

———. "Kennedy Taking Campaign Risks." *New York Times,* June 2, 1968.

———. "Kennedy Uses Humor to Relax Crowds and Disarm the Hostile." *New York Times,* March 31, 1968.

———. "McCarthy Asks Equal TV Time to Rebut Statements of Johnson." *New York Times,* December 21, 1967.

———. "McCarthy Buoys Kennedy Backers." *New York Times,* November 30, 1967.

———. "New Peace Talks Urged by Kennedy." *New York Times,* May 19, 1968.

———. "President Kennedy's Vietnam Aim Debated Again." *New York Times,* November 28, 1967.

———. "Senate Democrats Lose Move to Delay Supersonic Jet Plan." *New York Times,* October 6, 1967.

———. "'Sock It To 'Em' Kennedy Slogan." *New York Times,* March 29, 1968.

Hersh, Seymour M. "Aides Say Robert Kennedy Told of C.I.A. Castro Plot." *New York Times,* March 10, 1975.

Hershberg, James G. "Anatomy of a Controversy." *Cold War International History Project Bulletin,* Spring 1995.

———. "Before 'The Missiles of October': Did Kennedy Plan a Military Strike Against Cuba?" *Diplomatic History* 14, Spring 1990.

———. "More on Bobby and the Cuban Missile Crisis." *Cold War International History Project Bulletin*, Winter 1996/97.

———. "New Evidence on the Cuban Missile Crisis." *Cold War International History Project Bulletin*, Winter 1996/97.

———. "The United States, Brazil, and the Cuban Missile Crisis, 1962." *Journal of Cold War Studies*, vol. 6, Spring 2004.

Hevesi, Dennis. "David L. Hackett, Led Efforts on Poverty and Juvenile Crime, Dies at 84." *New York Times*, April 30, 2011.

Higdon, Hal. "Indiana: A Test for Bobby Kennedy." *New York Times*, May 5, 1968.

Holmes, Alexander. "RFK: How He's Building His Own Party." *Nation's Business*, July 1966.

Hope, Paul. "Johnson and Kennedy Dispute Bid for Vietnam Policy Review." *Washington Evening Star*, March 18, 1968.

Hornaday, Ann. "Forty Years on, RFK Ad Maker Still Frames the Campaigns." *Washington Post*, May 3, 2008.

Howard, Anthony. "Old Joe: Chief of the Clan." *The Guardian*, November 19, 1969.

Howard, Lisa. "Castro's Overture." *War/Peace Report*, September 1963.

Hughes, Allen. "Kennedy Seeks Action to Save Old Met on Eve of Demolition." *New York Times*, January 8, 1967.

Human Events. "Capitol America." April 23, 1966.

———. "This Week in Washington: Bobby's Mountaineering." April 24, 1965.

Hunter, Marjorie. "G.O.P. Is Pressed to Bar Race Issue." *New York Times*, November 1, 1963.

———. "Indictment Seen as Aid to Nominee." *New York Times*, November 3, 1962.

———. "Kennedy Chides Johnson on Cities." *New York Times*, August 16, 1966.

———. "Marchers in Capital Hear Washington Will Get a Fair-Housing Law." *New York Times*, June 15, 1963.

———. "President and His Brother Give Salaries to Charity." *New York Times*, November 15, 1962.

I. F. Stone's Weekly. "While Others Dodge the Draft, Bobby Dodges the War." October 24, 1966.

———. "Why I Would Not Vote for Bobby Kennedy." October 19, 1964.

Indianapolis Star. "Kennedy Suggestion to Drop Out Gets Angry 'No' from McCarthy." May 15, 1968.

International Teamster. "Secret Memos Show Kennedy Plotted to Blacken Hoffa's Name for Prospective Jurors." August 1964.

Jacobs, Paul. "Extracurricular Activities of the McClellan Committee." *California Law Review*, vol. 51, May 1963.

James, T. F. "Flank Attack on Crime, Inc." *American Weekly*, July 8, 1962.

Janos, Leo. "The Last Days of the President." *Atlantic Monthly*, July 1973.

Jenkins, Ray. "Mr. and Mrs. Wallace Run for Governor of Alabama." *New York Times*, April 24, 1966.

Johnson, Gerald W. "Whose Waterloo?" *New Republic*, February 10, 1968.

Johnson, Haynes. "President Proposes Full Effort, Senator Wants a 'Halt Now.'" *Washington Evening Star*, March 18, 1968.

Johnston, Richard J. H. "Invective Traded in West Virginia." *New York Times*, May 1, 1960.

———. "McCarthy Buried Beside Parents." *New York Times*, May 8, 1957.

———. "R. F. Kennedy Cites Influence Proposals." *New York Times*, March 7, 1959.

Jones, David R. "Reuther Rejects Plea on Kennedy." *New York Times*, March 23, 1964.

Jourdan, Michael. "Mountain Tribute to JFK Evoked by Kennedy Trip to Yukon." *National Geographic*, August 5, 2013.

Just, Ward. "RFK Goes Overboard in High Sea." *Washington Post*, September 2, 1965.

Kaplan, Fred. "What Robert Caro Got Wrong." *Slate.com*, May 31, 2012.

Katcher, Edward. "Liberals Naming 9 to Reorganize Party." *New York Post*, November 5, 1967.

Kazin, Alfred. "The President and Other Intellectuals." *The American Scholar*, vol. 30, Autumn 1961.

Kelley, Ken. "*Penthouse* Interview: Gore Vidal." *Penthouse*, April 1975.

Kelso, John. "Chairman of Past Red Probes Became Top Targets of Smears." *Boston Post*, April 4, 1954.

———. "Robert Kennedy, Senator's Brother, Factor in Greek Ship Agreement." *Boston Sunday Post*, April 12, 1953.

———. "3 Senators Give Praise to Kennedy." *Boston Post*, August 1, 1953.

Kempton, Murray. "FBI's Hoover Stoked Paranoia." *Newsday*, April 17, 1988.

———. "Fond Memories of 'a Decent Man.'" *Newsday*, May 18, 1988.

———. "His Brother's Keeper." *New York Post*, November 10, 1960.

———. "His Catholic Conscience." *Newsday*, June 3, 1993.

———. "His Politics Come Naturally." *Newsday*, October 9, 1994.

———. "The Hosts of Unreason: Kennedy Versus Keating in New York State." *New Republic*, September 12, 1964.

———. "The Kennedy Brothers." *New York Review of Books*, January 19, 1984.

———. "A Kennedy Man Looks Back." *Newsday*, September 18, 1988.

———. "Kennedy Regnant." *New York Post*, June 30, 1966.

———. "The Message Delivered." *New York Post*, February 23, 1966.

———. "The Monument." *New York Post*, December 2, 1966.

———. "Pure Irish: Robert F. Kennedy." *New Republic*, February 15, 1964.

———. "Remembering RFK." *Newsday*, March 11, 1993.

———. "RFK—In Sorrow and Shame." *New York Post*, June 11, 1968.

———. "Running against Buckley, Lindsay Beats Beame." *New Republic*, November 13, 1965.

———. "Sen. Kennedy, Farewell." *New York Post*, March 26, 1968.

———. "Senator Kennedy—Provincial New Yorker." *New Republic*, January 2, 1965.

———. "Shouting for Help: It's About All New York Democrats Can Do." *New Republic*, September 25, 1965.

———. "Waiting for Kennedy?" *Spectator*, July 8, 1966.

———. "Why I'm for McCarthy." *New Republic*, May 25, 1968.

———. "Will Bobby Kennedy Run in New York?" *New Republic*, June 6, 1964.

———. "Wondering About Kennedy at 70." *Newsday*, May 24, 1987.

Kennedy, Dana. "Tribute to Robert F. Kennedy Planned for Convention." *Associated Press*, July 13, 1992.

Kennedy, Edward M. "Kennedy." *Life*, June 1988.

Kennedy, John F. "A Day I'll Remember." *Life*, September 13, 1960.

———. "*A Message To You From the President: Fallout Shelters.*" September 7, 1961.

Kennedy, Joseph P. "Shielding the Sheep." *Saturday Evening Post*, January 18, 1936.

Kennedy, Robert F. "Attorney General's Opinion on Wiretaps." *New York Times*, June 3, 1962.

———. "British Hated by Both Sides." *Boston Post*, June 3, 1948.

———. "British Position Hit in Palestine." *Boston Post*, June 5, 1948.

———. "Buying It Back from the Indians." *Life*, March 23, 1962.

———. "Communism Not to Get a Foothold. *Boston Post*, June 6, 1948.

———. "Crisis in Our Cities." *Critic*, October-November 1967.

———. "Hoffa's Unholy Alliance." *Look*, September 2, 1958.

———. "Jews Guard Against Red Agents in Guise of Refugees." *Boston Post*, June 6, 1948.

———. "Jews Have a Fine Fighting Force." *Boston Post*, June 4, 1948.

———. "Our Climb up Mt. Kennedy." *Life*, April 9, 1965.

———. "A Peak Worthy of the President." *National Geographic*, July 1965.

———. "Robert Kennedy Defines the Menace." *New York Times*, October 13, 1963.

———. "Robert Kennedy: On Government Injustice to Business." *Nation's Business*, June 1967.

———. "The Soviet Brand of Colonialism." *New York Times*, April 8, 1956.

———. "Sovietizing Central Asia." Letter to editor. *New York Times*, January 2, 1956.

———. "Suppose God Is Black." *Look*, August 23, 1966.

———. "Topics: 'Things Fall Apart; the Center Cannot Hold . . .'" *New York Times*, February 10, 1968.

———. "Trading with Communists." Letter to editor. *New York Times*, March 17, 1956.

———. "Trading with Soviet Russia." Letter to editor. *New York Times*, April 10, 1956.

———. "Treaty-Making and Yalta." Letter to editor. *New York Times*, February 3, 1954.

Kenworthy, E. W. "Aniline Accord Evokes Criticism." *New York Times*, March 8, 1963.

———. "Barnett Charges Kennedys Assist Red Racial Plot." *New York Times*, July 13, 1963.

———. "Goldwater Asks Senate Inquiry into U.S. Role in Cuba Invasion." *New York Times*, January 24, 1963.

———. "Kennedy Agrees with White House on Vietnam." *New York Times*, February 23, 1966.

———. "Kennedy Bids U.S. Offer Vietcong a Role in Saigon." *New York Times*, February 20, 1966.

———. "Kennedy Proposes Treaty to Check Nuclear Spread." *New York Times*, June 24, 1965.

———. "McCarthy Themes Given New Stress." *New York Times*, May 5, 1968.

———. "Test in Indiana: Kennedy and McCarthy Square Off." *New York Times*, May 5, 1968.

———. "Two Parties Shun Rights Revisions." *New York Times*, July 3, 1963.

———. "Trade Big Problem for Japan." *Boston Post*, September 9, 1951.

———. "What We Can Do to End the Agony of Vietnam." *Look*, November 28, 1967.

Kihss, Peter. "Democrat Tours Harlem." *New York Times*, August 25, 1960.

———. " 'Red-Front' Case Is Opened by U.S." *New York Times*, October 1, 1963.

———. "U.S. Finds Nothing to Support Hiss." *New York Times*, April 5, 1962.

Kiker, Douglas. "Bob Kennedy, Aides Watch Albany Row." *Atlantic Monthly*, December 19, 1961.

———. "Robert Kennedy and the What-If Game." *Atlantic Monthly*, October 1966.

Kilgallen, Dorothy. "Audience Pays So Much Attention to Cary Grant He Leaves Theater." *Daytona Beach Morning Journal*, October 13, 1962.

———. "Bulletin Reports Come Daily of Interest to New Yorkers." *Palm Beach Daily News*, January 2, 1963.

———. "Jerry Lewis and Dean Martin Might Become a Team Again." *Daytona Beach Morning Journal*, April 21, 1962.

———. "Mrs. Kennedy Can Do 'Daffy Dances.'" *Washington Post*, April 16, 1965.

———. "Suzanne Pleshette Has Found Someone Else." *Daytona Beach Morning Journal*, September 14, 1964.

———. "Title of Liz Taylor Movie Gets Changed." *Daytona Beach Morning Journal*, October 17, 1964.

———. "Waiting with Robert Kennedy." *Daytona Beach Morning Journal*, November 6, 1964.

Kilpatrick, Andrew. "Patterson Told Secret Cuban Invasion Plans to Candidate JFK." *Birmingham News*, October 24, 1982.

Kilpatrick, Carroll. "Humphrey Angered by Big Outlays." *Washington Post*, May 8, 1960.

———. "Kennedy Asks Brother, Sorensen to Help Him Out on Foreign Policy." *Washington Post*, April 27, 1961.

Kimball, Penn. "Identity and the Power Flows Freely to Him." *Life*, November 18, 1966.

King, Martin Luther, Jr. "Fumbling on the New Frontier." *Nation*, March 3, 1962.

King, Seth S. "Direct Diplomacy." *New York Times*, January 25, 1964.

Knebel, Fletcher. "Bobby Kennedy: He Hates To Be Second." *Look*, May 21, 1963.

———. "Kennedy vs. the Press." *Look*, August 28, 1962.

———. "Las Vegas: It Wins, It Worries, It Weeps." *Look*, December 27, 1967.

Knight, John S. "How Johnson Demanded (and Got) 2nd Spot." *Miami Herald*. July 15, 1960.

———. "Johnson Still a Threat? Kennedy's Forces Are Amused." *Miami Herald*, July 12, 1960.

Knowles, Clayton. "Kennedy Race Welcomed by Liberals and Wagner." *New York Times*, May 15, 1964.

———. "Kennedy Says Resident of State Would Be Preferable for Senate." *New York Times*, May 20, 1964.

———. "New Nunan Tax Case Aired; $792,094 Claim Unsettled." *New York Times*, February 29, 1952.

———. "Smear Campaign by G.O.P. Charged," *New York Times*, October 5, 1960.

Knowles, Helen J. "May It Please the Court? The Solicitor General's Not-So-'Special' Relationship," *Journal of Supreme Court History*, November 2006.

Kopkind, Andrew. "He's a Happening." *New Republic*, April 1, 1966.

———. "Waiting for Lefty." *New York Review of Books*, June 1, 1967.

Kornbluh, Peter, and Susan Lucci. "JFK and Castro." *Cigar Aficionado*, September 1999.

Kraft, Joseph. "After the Bobby Phenomenon." *Washington Post*, November 15, 1996.

———. "The Ambitions of Bobby Kennedy." *Look*, August 25, 1964.

———. "Appeal to Opposing Groups Was Key to RFK Victory." *Washington Post*, May 9, 1968.

———. "Campaign Swings Set by Humphrey." *New York Times*, September 2, 1966.

———. "Decision on the Vice Presidency." *Washington Evening Star*, July 31, 1964.

———. "Riot Squad for the New Frontier." *Harper's Magazine*, August 1963.

Kraslow, David. "Bay of Pigs Autopsy Results Closely-Guarded U.S. Secret." *Calgary Herald*, July 28, 1965.

———. "US Bay of Pigs Invasion Errors Detailed by Attorney Gen. Kennedy." [Yonkers] *Herald Statesman*, January 19, 1963.

Kraus, Albert L. "Government Eyes Banking Mergers." *New York Times*, March 5, 1961.

Krock, Arthur. "Ban on 'Unfair' Primary Is New Criterion." *New York Times*, January 15, 1960.

———. "Dave Beck Case Raises Numerous Vital Issues." *New York Times*, March 31, 1957.

———. "A Grave Racial Issue for the Attorney General." *New York Times*, August 14, 1962.

———. "'He'll Prent It' Just the Same." *New York Times*, May 26, 1966.

———. "The Kennedy Interview." *New York Times*, July 5, 1964.

———. "The Kennedy Machine." *New York Times*, July 17, 1960.

———. "The Kennedy Standards of Public Service." *New York Times*, December 22, 1960.

———. "Large Trade with China by the U.N. Members Shown." *New York Times*, July 19, 1953.

———. "Last Drippings from the Great Certified 'Leak.'" *New York Times*, December 7, 1962.

———. "A Misconceived Gesture of Brotherly Love." *New York Times*, January 25, 1963.

———. "Post-Time for the Four Horsemen." *New York Times*, September 4, 1966.

———. "Priority in the Quest for Peace." *New York Times*, June 27, 1965.

———. "Robert Kennedy's Proposal." *New York Times*, February 22, 1966.

———. "Under Watchful Eyes: Robert F. Kennedy's Integrity Will Sustain Him in His Task." *Los Angeles Times*, December 26, 1960.

———. "Unusual Accomplishment in Public Service." *New York Times*, September 18, 1959.

Kuhistory.com. "Charisma Amidst the Chaos." March 18, 1968. kuhistory.com/articles /charisma-amidst-the-chaos/

Kuhn, Clifford M. "'There's a Footnote to History!' Memory and the History of Martin Luther King's October 1960 Arrest and Its Aftermath." *Journal of American History*, September 1997.

Kuhn, Ferdinand, Jr. "Kennedy Is Active." *New York Times*, November 15, 1938.

Lahey, Edwin A. "Running for VP, Johnson Has Cake, Can Eat It, Too." *Miami Herald*, July 16, 1960.

Laing, George. "RFK's African Trip, by a Man Who Was There." *New York Daily News*, June 18, 1966.

Landsberg, Brian K. "The Kennedy Justice Department's Enforcement of Civil Rights: A View from the Trenches." (ssrn.com/abstract=1493403), October 2009.

Langguth, Jack. "Kennedy Warns of Rightist Peril." *New York Times*, June 9, 1964.

Lapides, George. "Sen. Stennis, RFK in Clash at Hearing." *Memphis Press-Scimitar*, April 10, 1967.

———. "Two Senators 'Shocked' by Mississippi Poverty." *Memphis Press-Scimitar*, April 12, 1967.

Lawrence, David. "The Crossroads." *U.S. News & World Report*, November 7, 1960.

———. "Paradoxical Bob." *Pasadena Independent Star-News*, May 26, 1968.

———. "Will Bob Kennedy Face Up to It?" *Manchester Union Leader*, January 13, 1961.

Lawrence, W. H. "Choice a Surprise," *New York Times*, July 15, 1960.

———. "Cohn Threatens to 'Get' Senator for Gibe at Schine." *New York Times*, June 12, 1954.

———. "Democrats Force Full Public Study of Talbott Affair." *New York Times*, July 24, 1955.

———. "Humphrey Given Edge by Editors." *New York Times*, April 24, 1960.

———. "Johnson Backers Urge Health Test." *New York Times*, July 5, 1960.

————. "Kennedy Bandwagon Well-Oiled." *New York Times*, June 26, 1960.

————. "Kennedy Sells His Stock to Avoid Interest Conflict." *New York Times*, January 13, 1961.

————. "Mundt Will Direct Senate Unit Study of McCarthy Fight." *New York Times*, March 17, 1954.

————. "Robert Kennedy Being Considered for Cabinet Post." *New York Times*, November 19, 1960.

————. "Roosevelt Hits Humphrey." *New York Times*, May 7, 1960.

————. "Senate to Query Secretary of Air on Business Ties." *New York Times*, July 15, 1955.

————. "Senators Seek to Determine Just What Work Schine Did." *New York Times*, May 29, 1954.

————. "State is Warned." *New York Times*, May 23, 1961.

————. "Talbott Offers to Give Up Share in New York Firm." *New York Times*, July 22, 1955.

————. "Union Aide Picked." *New York Times*, December 16, 1960.

Lehmann-Haupt, Christopher. "Bobby Business." *New York Times*, September 10, 1967.

Lelyveld, Joseph. "Kennedy a Trial for South Africa." *New York Times*, October 31, 1965.

————. "Robert Kennedy's Plan Assailed in Johannesburg." October 27, 1965.

Lembke, Daryl E. "Kennedy Hints at Withdrawal If He Loses in California Test." *Los Angeles Times*, May 30, 1968.

Lerner, Max. "On Kennedy." *New York Post*, October 28, 1960.

————. "The Victors." *New York Post*, April 16, 1962.

Levey, Stanley. "Kennedy Depicts Teamster Power." *New York Times*, March 27, 1959.

Lewis, Anthony. "Accord Pleases Robert Kennedy." New York Times, May 11, 1963.

————. "Action on Civil Rights." *New York Times*, April 30, 1961.

————. "Antitrust Policy Uses Broad Approach." *New York Times*, December 24, 1961.

————. "Civil Rights Compact." *New York Times*, October 30, 1963.

————. "Civil Rights Gains Mark Change in South." January 28, 1963.

————. "Communist Party Indicted After Failing to Register." *New York Times*, December 2, 1961.

————. "400 U.S. Marshals Sent to Alabama as Montgomery Bus Riots Hurt 20." *New York Times*, May 21, 1961.

————. "Free Legal Help For Needy Asked." *New York Times*, March 9, 1963.

————. "Group Raised 3 Million in Cash in 24 Hours to Ransom Cubans." *New York Times*, December 26, 1962.

————. "The Guns of January." *New York Times*, December 24, 1990.

————. "Help From Outside." *New York Times*, May 6, 1994.

————. "Japanese Give Robert Kennedys a Crowded and Noisy Welcome." *New York Times*, February 5, 1962.

————. "Kennedy Denies a Johnson Feud." *New York Times*, March 13, 1964.

————. "A Kennedy on the Road." *New York Times*, February 11, 1962.

————. "Kennedy Sets Pattern on Civil Rights." *New York Times*, March 12, 1961.

————. "Kennedy Sets Up Watchdog Office to Insure Justice." *New York Times*, August 11, 1964.

————. "Kennedy's Role as Attorney General." *New York Times*, September 4, 1964.

————. "Mississippi: Broader Impact of the Crisis." *New York Times*, October 7, 1962.

————. "New Curbs Sought on Police Cruelty." *New York Times*, March 21, 1962.

———. "Panel Unanimous: Theory of Conspiracy by Left or Right Is Rejected." *New York Times*, September 28, 1964.

———. "A Part of the Main." *New York Times*, May 31, 1993.

———. "Protest Over Dr. King's Arrest Was Drafted for President's Use." *New York Times*, December 15, 1960.

———. "Right And Wrong." *New York Times*, November 24, 2001.

———. "Right to Question Accusers Is Given in Passport Cases." *New York Times*, January 12, 1962.

———. "Robert F. Kennedy Argues First Case." *New York Times*, January 18, 1963.

———. "Robert Kennedy Bids Club End Band." *New York Times*, May 17, 1961.

———. "Robert Kennedy Defeats Despair." *New York Times*, January 9, 1964.

———. "Robert Kennedy Derides Leftists." *New York Times*, February 9, 1962.

———. "Robert Kennedy Helped by Snag." *New York Times*, February 18, 1962.

———. "Robert Kennedy Mocks Birch Unit." *New York Times*, April 7, 1961.

———. "Robert Kennedy Rules Out Race for Senate Seat." *New York Times*, June 24, 1964.

———. "Robert Kennedy's Boat Capsizes During Sail in Honolulu Harbor." *New York Times*, February 4, 1962.

———. "Robert Kennedy's Tour." *New York Times*, February 19, 1962.

———. "Robert Kennedy Tours Hamlets in Japan Like a Local Candidate." *New York Times*, February 8, 1962.

———. "Robert Kennedy Turns a Bar in Tokyo into a Forum." *New York Times*, February 6, 1962.

———. "Robert Kennedy Vows in Georgia to Act on Rights." *New York Times*, May 7, 1961.

———. "Robert Kennedy Wins Approval of Senate Panel." *New York Times*, January 14, 1961.

———. "7 Steel Concerns Indicted by U.S. in Antitrust Case." *New York Times*, April 3, 1963.

———. "Strategy: Negro Vote." *New York Times*, January 7, 1962.

———. "10 Years or 100." *New York Times*, January 10, 1985.

———. "Trust Consent Decrees Are Opened to the Public." *New York Times*, June 30, 1961.

———. "2 House Members Indicted by U.S. in Influence Case." *New York Times*, October 17, 1962.

———. "U.S. Sues to Force a Virginia County to Open Schools." *New York Times*, April 27, 1961.

———. "What Drives Bobby Kennedy." *New York Times*, April 7, 1963.

———. "What Might Have Been: Kennedy, 20 Years Later." *New York Times*, June 5, 1988.

———. "Wide Program Recommended to Give Equal Justice to Need." *New York Times*, March 7, 1963.

———. "A Year Without Robert Kennedy." *New York Times*, June 4, 1969.

Lewis, Ted. "Capitol Stuff." *New York Daily News*, March 4, 1966.

———. "Capitol Stuff." *New York Daily News*, April 14, 1966.

Liberty. "Will Kennedy Run for President?" May 21, 1938.

Life. "But Listen to His Canary." Editorial. October 18, 1963.

———. "A Debut into a Burgeoning Family." April 21, 1958.

———. "From Tossup in Tokyo to the Cry of the Alamo." February 23, 1962.

———. "Hold Your Nose at Bobby Kennedy's Pork." Editorial. October 18, 1963.

———. "Keating Fights the Kennedy Magic." October 9, 1964.

———. "The Two-Party System: How to Help It Survive." Editorial. October 16, 1964.

———. "Young Man with Tough Questions." July 1, 1957.

Lind, Jennifer. "When Camelot Went to Japan." *National Interest*, July/August 2013.

Linn, Edward. "The Truth About Joe Kennedy." *Saga: The Magazine for Men*, July 1961.

Lippmann, Walter. "At Stake in Split." *Boston Globe*, March 24, 1964.

———. "Blockade Proclaimed." *New York Herald Tribune*, October 25, 1962.

———. "The Bob Kennedy, Dillon Choices." *Los Angeles Times*, December 22, 1960.

———. "The Great Rift Among Democrats." *Boston Globe*, March 9, 1967.

———. "Historic Party Shift Hinges on Elections in 1968." *Los Angeles Times*, December 17, 1967.

———. "Today and Tomorrow: The Cabinet Completed." *Washington Post*, December 20, 1960.

———. "The Vice-Presidency." *New York Herald Tribune*, April 23, 1964.

Lisagor, Peter. "Portrait of a Man Emerging from Shadows." *New York Times*, July 19, 1964.

Loeb, William. "Above the Law?" *Manchester Union Leader*, April 23, 1962.

———. "Addressed to Democrats Only." *Manchester Union Leader*, January 18, 1968.

———. "The American Dictator." *Manchester Union Leader*, March 20, 1968.

———. "Dictatorship, USA." *Manchester Union Leader*, January 30, 1963.

———. "Force Is Not the Answer." *Manchester Union Leader*, June 2, 1962.

———. "Hypocrisy!" *Manchester Union Leader*, April 26, 1962.

———. "Hypocritical Hysteria." *Manchester Union Leader*, April 11, 1968.

———. "No Saints, Black or White." *Manchester Union Leader*, July 20, 1961.

———. "Poor Mr. Johnson—Poor USA!" *Manchester Union Leader*, April 2, 1968.

———. "Robert Kennedy Distorts History." *Manchester Union Leader*, April 3, 1962.

———. "Tragic and Unnecessary." *Manchester Union Leader*, June 6, 1968.

Loftus, Joseph A. "A.F.L.-C.I.O. Unit Lays Corruption to Beck's Union." *New York Times*, May 7, 1957.

———. "Beck Again Fails to Give Answers." *New York Times*, May 9, 1957.

———. "Beck Jr. Invokes the 5th 100 Times; Faces a Citation." *New York Times*, June 5, 1957.

———. "Clark and Kennedy Visit the Poor of Mississippi." *New York Times*, April 12, 1967.

———. "Crum Charges Hoffa Tried to Pack Monitors' Board." *New York Times*, July 14, 1959.

———. " 'Draft Kennedy' Unit Files in Wisconsin." *New York Times*, March 11, 1964.

———. "F.B.I. Seizes Hoffa in a Plot to Bribe Senate Staff Aide." *New York Times*, March 14, 1957.

———. "Hoffa Acquitted of Bribery Plot; Seeks Beck Post." *New York Times*, July 20, 1957.

———. "The I.C.C. Orders End of Racial Curbs on Bus Travelers." *New York Times*, September 23, 1961.

———. "Johnson Is Asked to Rush Food Aid." *New York Times*, April 30, 1967.

———. "Kennedy Assails Attack on UAW." *New York Times*, February 17, 1960.

———. "McClellan Panel Leaves Its Mark." *New York Times*, May 5, 1963.

———. "McClellan Scores Beck for 'Theft' of Union's Funds." *New York Times*, March 28, 1957.

———. "Moderates Make Gains in the South." *New York Times*, October 1, 1961.

———. "Move Is Part of the Attorney General's Cooling-Off Policy—These Are Also Expected to Leave Shortly." *New York Times*, May 26, 1961.

———. "Oregon Officials Linked to Union in 'Whitewash.'" *New York Times*, March 6, 1957.

———. "Portland Called Vice-Ridden Now." *New York Times*, March 9, 1957.

———. "Poverty Hearing Set in Mississippi." *New York Times*, April 10, 1967.

———. "Rackets Inquiry to Begin 2d Year." *New York Times*, January 8, 1958.

———. "Senators Assail Hoffa's Behavior with 48 Citations." *New York Times*, August 24, 1957.

———. "Senators Hear Beck Made Profit as Trustee of a Widow's Fund." *New York Times*, May 10, 1957.

———. "Senators Shelve Kennedy Matter." *New York Times*, March 11, 1959.

———. "Steel Rise Investigation by Grand Jury Ordered; Blough Defends Pricing." *New York Times*, April 13, 1962.

———. "Teamster Chiefs Charged with Plot to Rule Oregon." *New York Times*, March 2, 1957.

———. "Teamster Union Tied to Rackets." *New York Times*, January 6, 1957.

———. "Tips on Rackets Pour In; Senate Inquiry Broadened." *New York Times*, March 29, 1957.

———. "Union Questioned on Hiding of Data." *New York Times*, January 18, 1957.

———. "U.S. Moves for Injunction Against Police in Alabama." *New York Times*, May 25, 1961.

———. "U.S. Tells World of Rights Strife." *New York Times*, May 27, 1961.

———. "Witnesses Link Teamsters Union to Underworld." *New York Times*, February 27, 1957.

Look. "Rise of the Brothers Kennedy." August 6, 1957.

———. "Tribute to JFK." February 25, 1964.

Lopez, Steve. "The Busboy Who Cradled a Dying RFK Has Finally Stepped Out of the Past." *Los Angeles Times*, August 29, 2015.

Los Angeles Times. "Civil Rights Group Feels Dismay After Talk with Robert Kennedy." May 26, 1963.

———. "Congressmen's Phones Bugged, Expert Says." September 22, 1966.

———. "NAACP Leader Raps Kennedy on Civil Rights." July 23, 1961.

Lowell, Robert. "R.F.K. (1925–68)." *New Republic*, June 22, 1968.

Lowrey, Jim. "R. Kennedy, Others 'Hanged' at Rally." *Anniston Star*, September 6, 1961.

Lubell, Samuel. "Keating in the Lead." *New York World-Telegram*, October 8, 1964.

Lynn, Frank. "Beating the Bushes for Bobby." *Newsday*, April 16, 1968.

———. "Bobby Kennedy's Laugh-Ins." *Newsday*, May 21, 1968.

———. "He Didn't Fit into Any Niche." *Newsday*, June 11, 1968.

———. "HHH Collects 120 Delegates in Two States." *Newsday*, June 3, 1968.

———. "HHH Seen Winning Most of Michigan's Delegates." *Newsday*, May 31, 1968.

———. "Javits, RFK Votes Blur Party Lines." *Newsday*, January 9, 1968.

———. "Kennedy." *Newsday*, March 20, 1968.

———. "Kennedy Asks Fast War on City Crime." *Newsday*, January 20, 1967.

———. "Kennedy Carries Campaign to Arizona." *Newsday*, March 30, 1958.

———. "Kennedy to Run in Indiana; Gain Seen in 6 States." *Newsday*, March 28, 1958.

———. "Majority of Pennsylvania Delegates for HHH." *Newsday*, May 28, 1968.

———. "RFK." *Newsday*, March 22, 1968.

———. "RFK Carries Fight to NY 'Unity' Dinner." *Newsday*, March 23, 1968.

———. "RFK Crowds into Indiana Primary." *Newsday*, March 29, 1968.

———. "RFK Making Southern Foray." *Newsday*, March 21, 1968.

———. "RFK Praises LBJ, Asks Meeting." *Newsday*, April 1, 1968.

———. "RFK Says It: He May Run Now." *Newsday*, March 14, 1968.

———. "RFK Sees Viet Packed Curbing Reds." *Newsday*, March 26, 1968.

———. "RFK's 1st Test: 42% in Indiana Victory." *Newsday*, May 8, 1968.

———. "RFK's Road Show Loaded with Talent." *Newsday*, April 24, 1968.

———. "RFK the Favorite in Indiana Vote." *Newsday*, April 23, 1968.

———. "RFK Wins in Nebraska; Gene Fights On." *Newsday*, May 15, 1968.

———. "Studied Frenzy of RFK's Drive." *Newsday*, March 26, 1968.

———. "Up Creaky Stairs to RFK-Land, N.H." *Newsday*, February 20, 1968.

Lyons, Louis. "Kennedy Says Democracy All Done in Britain, Maybe Here." *Boston Globe*, November 10, 1940.

Lyons, Richard L. "Votes Mount for Kennedy in S. Dakota and California." *Washington Post*, June 6, 1968.

Maas, Peter. "Robert Kennedy Speaks Out." *Look*, March 28, 1961.

———. "What Will R.F.K. Do Next?" *Saturday Evening Post*, March 28, 1964.

Maechling, Charles. "Camelot, Robert Kennedy, and Counter-Insurgency: A Memoir." *Virginia Quarterly Review*, Summer 1999.

Mailer, Norman. "Superman Comes to the Supermarket." *Esquire*, November 1960.

———. "A Vote for Bobby K.—Possibility of a Hero." *Village Voice*, October 29, 1964.

Maiorana, Ronald. "Kennedy Proposes State Law Agency." *New York Times*, June 10, 1967.

Manchester Union Leader. "Bobby, the Neatnik." October 15, 1963.

———. "The Hypocrisy of the Young Uglies." May 2, 1968.

———. "Roman Orgy, 1962 Style." June 25, 1962.

Manchester, William. "William Manchester's Own Story." *Look*, April 4, 1967.

Manning, Robert. " 'Someone the President Can Talk To.' " *New York Times*, May 28, 1961.

Marion [Ohio] Star. "Sentencing Is Slated for 8 in Tax Fraud." July 31, 1962.

Martin, Harold H. "The Amazing Kennedys." *Saturday Evening Post*, September 7, 1957.

Martin, John Bartlow. "The Struggle to Get Hoffa: Part One: Kennedy Sets a Snare." *Saturday Evening Post*, June 27, 1959.

———. "The Struggle to Get Hoffa: Part Two: The Making of a Labor Boss." *Saturday Evening Post*, July 4, 1959.

———. "The Struggle to Get Hoffa: Part Three: The Labor Boss Leaves a Baffling Trail." *Saturday Evening Post*, July 11, 1959.

———. "The Struggle to Get Hoffa: Part Four: Hoffa Takes the Stand." *Saturday Evening Post*, July 18, 1959.

———. "The Struggle to Get Hoffa: Part Five: Hoffa Confounds His Enemies." *Saturday Evening Post*, July 25, 1959.

———. "The Struggle to Get Hoffa: Part Six: Revelations of the Third Hearing." *Saturday Evening Post*, August 1, 1959.

———. "The Struggle to Get Hoffa: Conclusion: How Long Will He Last?" *Saturday Evening Post*, August 8, 1959.

Mathews, Tom. "Remembering Bobby." *Newsweek*, May 9, 1988.

McCall's Magazine. "Rose Fitzgerald Kennedy." May 1961.

McCardle, Dorothy. "Race for Senate in New York Is Studied for R. F. Kennedy." *Washington Post*, May 15, 1964.

McDermott, John R. "Johnson on Ticket Only Way Out?" *Miami Herald*, July 14, 1960.

McGill, Ralph. "Behind the Headlines—'It Is Disheartening.'" *Hartford Courant*, April 28, 1967.

———. "Robt. Kennedy Gets Ovation." *Atlanta Constitution*, May 8, 1961.

McGrory, Mary. "Albosta Whodunit Has Everything but a Butler." *Miami News*, May 28, 1984.

———. "A Bewildered Man." *Miami News*, January 10, 1966.

———. "Bobby Fights Himself." *Boston Globe*, May 12, 1968.

———. "Bobby Shifts Battlefield for New Thrust at LBJ." *Boston Globe*, July 14, 1967.

———. "Bobby Takes Over." *New York Post*, November 8, 1965.

———. "Bobby Thanks Everyone—Including Fulton Fish Boys." *Boston Globe*, November 5, 1964.

———. "A Brilliant Kennedy Debut: Family, Friends Swamp Court." *Boston Globe*, January 18, 1963.

———. "Brother Tells What President Learned from Cuba: Join Chiefs Seen Friendly to Taylor." *Boston Globe*, August 6, 1961.

———. "Burke Marshall: He Did More Than Just Cry for the Negro." *Boston Globe*, December 22, 1964.

———. "Cash Customer a Pariah in California." *The Blade*, June 8, 1980.

———. "Clinton: Soul Without Steel." *Washington Post*, June 8, 1993.

———. "Closing of Vet. Hospitals Has Congress in Dilemma." *Virgin Island Daily News*, February 3, 1965.

———. "Could Robert Kennedy Be Figuring on Presidential Race in '68 Instead of Waiting Till '72?" *Boston Globe*, August 4, 1966.

———. "Disgust in McCarthy Camp: Why Didn't Bobby Wait?" *Miami News*, March 15, 1968.

———. "Harassed HHH Will Mind the Store." *Evening Independent*, October 17, 1966.

———. "Harmony Eludes Scrapping Lawmakers." *Eugene Register Guard*, May 4, 1985.

———. "Having Wonderful Time . . . Bobby." *America*, February 24, 1962.

———. "He Had to Be Explained." *Boston Globe*, June 9, 1968.

———. "A Hero or a Winner? Tough Choice for Students." *Boston Globe*, March 17, 1968.

———. "Hubert's Happy Role." *Miami News*, February 25, 1966.

———. "Inevitable Question Remains: What Will Ted Kennedy Do?" *Boston Globe*, June 11, 1968.

———. "In NYC . . . Pow! Crash! . . . Out Climbs Bobby Without a Scratch." *Boston Globe*, November 8, 1965.

———. "It Was Chilly as Senators Kennedy, Long Disagreed on Presidential Aid." *Boston Globe*, June 7, 1967.

———. "Johnson's Fever of Activity Puts Stronger Light on Speech." *Boston Globe*, March 3, 1967.

———. "A Kennedy in New York Politics." *America*, September 19, 1964.

———. "Kennedy Offered Several Positions." *Virgin Island Daily News*, August 10, 1964.

———. "Kennedy, the Reluctant Neutral." *Boston Globe*, February 5, 1968.

———. "Kennedy vs. McCarthy: A War Everyone Can Understand." *Boston Globe*, March 31, 1968.

———. "LBJ Has Reason to Be Glum." *Miami News*, August 19, 1966.

———. "Mary McGrory on Robert Kennedy's Trip Through the Deep South." *Boston Globe*, April 13, 1966.

———. "Mary McGrory Says RFK Lucky Not to Be V.P." *Boston Globe*, December 6, 1965.

———. "McCarthy Finds It Incredible." *Boston Globe*, June 6, 1968.

———. "McCarthy's Star on Rise." *Washington Evening Star*, March 10, 1968.

———. "McCarthy Taking RFK Role." *Boston Globe*, November 17, 1967.

———. "Mexican-Americans Hear Anderson's Views." *The Blade*, May 26, 1980.

———. "Murphy Creeping Up on Salinger in California." *Boston Globe*, October 5, 1964.

———. "Nearly Everyone Liked Humphrey-RFK Scene." *Boston Globe*, September 11, 1966.

———. "Picking the Second Man." *Miami News*, January 2, 1964.

———. "RFK Keeper of the Flame No More." *Boston Globe*, May 2, 1968.

———. "RFK Ponders Next Move in N.Y. Governor Hassle." *Boston Globe*, August 13, 1966.

———. "RFK to Tour Latin America." *Boston Globe*, August 27, 1965.

———. "Robert Tipped His Hand." *Miami News*, July 10, 1964.

———. "A Show of Unity." *New York Post*, September 10, 1966.

———. "Sizeups Begin: Ted Bests Bob." *Boston Globe*, January 6, 1965.

———. "Straight Talk at the Pentagon." *Palm Beach Post*, January 2, 1968.

———. "They Had Something to Say to Bobby Kennedy." *Washington Star*, August 28, 1964.

———. "Turnabout: Now It's Bobby Kennedy Calling McCarthy." *Boston Globe*, March 14, 1968.

———. "Will Bobby Join Gene?" *Boston Globe*, May 30, 1968.

McGurn, Barrett. "Rocky and Bobby in New Clash: On Aid to the NHRR." *New York Herald Tribune*, January 25, 1966.

McLuhan, Marshall. "All of the Candidates Are Asleep." *Saturday Evening Post*, August 10, 1968.

McMahon, Patrick. "Ships and Greeks—and Senator Joe McCarthy." *American Mercury*, July 1953.

Means, Marianne. "JFK Joins Drive to Help Sgt. York." *New York Journal-American*, March 22, 1961.

———. "Kennedys vs. Hoffa." *American Weekly*, March 26, 1961.

Miller, Nathan. "Poverty Hearing Results in Clash." Baltimore *Sun*, July 12, 1967.

Miller, Walter M., Jr. "Bobby and Jimmy: Round Six." *Nation*, April 7, 1962.

Millones, Peter. "Kennedy and Javits Are Shocked by Housing Migrants Upstate." *New York Times*, September 9, 1967.

Minor, F. W. "Robert Kennedy's Role in State History Told." *Times-Picayune*, June 9, 1968.

Mirtrovich, George. "Robert F. Kennedy for Our Time." *Presidio Sentinel*, March 1, 2012.

Mollenhoff, Clark. "U.S. Expels Girl Linked to Officials." *Des Moines Register*, October 26, 1963.

Morgenthau, Hans J. "On Robert Kennedy." *New York Review of Books*, August 1, 1968.

Morgenthau, Robert M. "Getting Roy Cohn." *Commentary*, January 1, 1977.

Morris, John D. "Johnson Pledges Help to Kennedy." *New York Times*, July 14, 1960.

———. "Kennedy Cabinet Sets Precedents." *New York Times*, December 18, 1960.

———. "Mundt Asks Study of Bid to Kennedy." *New York Times*, March 8, 1959.

———. "Senate Confirms Cabinet Swiftly." *New York Times*, January 22, 1961.

———. "3 Democrats Scorn Bid From McCarthy." *New York Times*, July 19, 1953.

Morris, John G. "Kennedy Claims Victory, and Then Shots Ring Out." *New York Times*, June 5, 1968.

Mountain Eagle. "Kennedy Hears of Need for Jobs During Two-Day Mountain Tour." February 15, 1968.

Moynihan, Daniel P. "The Democrats, Kennedy and the Murder of Dr. King." *Commentary,* May 1968.

Muggeridge, Malcolm. "Books." *Esquire,* November 1966.

Murphy, Charles V. "Cuba: The Record Set Straight." *Fortune,* September 1961.

Murphy, Reg. "Robert Kennedy Was Nice but Firm in Athens Speech." *Atlanta Constitution,* May 8, 1961.

Murray, David. "Branigin Charges Bobby, McCarthy Spend Huge Sums." *Chicago Sun-Times,* April 20, 1968.

———. "A Deal with Kennedy? McCarthy Spurns Idea." *Chicago Sun-Times,* April 1, 1968.

———. "Kennedy Tour Garners Two Key Plums in Indiana." *Chicago Sun-Times,* April 30, 1968.

———. "McCarthy Accepts, RFK Spurns TV Network Debate Bid." *Chicago Sun-Times,* April 18, 1968.

———. "Remove Bloodshed from the Land, Kennedy Pleads." *Chicago Sun-Times.* April 5, 1968.

———. "Sen. McCarthy Presents Himself to the Nation." *Chicago Sun-Times,* April 2, 1968.

Naftali, Timothy. "The Origins of 'Thirteen Days.'" *Miller Center Report,* Summer 1999.

Nash, George. "New York Opinion: After RFK, What?" *New York,* July 29, 1968.

Nation. "Grudge Fight." May 22, 1967.

———. "Keating for Sen." September 14, 1964.

———. "Kennedy and the Jews." November 26, 1938.

———. "The Kennedy Safari." July 4, 1966.

———. "The Swinging Senator." February 20, 1967.

Navasky, Victor S. "The Government and Martin Luther King." *Atlantic Monthly,* November 1970.

———. "The Haunting of Robert Kennedy." *New York Times,* June 2, 1968.

———. "Jack Newfield Talks About R.F.K." *New Leader,* May 26, 1969.

Newcomb, James. "Joe Buried Beside Father, Mother on Bluff Above Gently Turning Sox." *Appleton Post-Crescent,* May 7, 1957.

Newfield, Jack. "The Arrogance of Class: Humphrey Is the Enemy." *Village Voice,* May 2, 1968.

———. "A Few Rays of Hope." *Life,* March 8, 1968.

———. "Regards to Bobby." *New York Times,* April 23, 1967.

———. "A Time of Plague, a Season for Courage." *Village Voice,* December 28, 1967.

———. "What Kind of President Would Robert F. Kennedy Make?" *Boston Globe,* November 12, 1967.

Newfield, Jack, and Leticia Kent. "Runnin' Scared." *Village Voice,* December 28, 1967.

New Republic. "Kennedy and China." July 3, 1965.

———. "The Kennedy Reception." June 11, 1966.

Newsweek. "The Bobby Phenomenon." October 24, 1966.

———. "Bobby: To Be or Not to Be." January 29, 1968.

———. "The Ex-President: Bitter Aftertaste." February 3, 1969.

———. "'Freedom Riders' Force a Test." June 5, 1961.

———. "The Kennedy Caper." March 7, 1966.

———. "Kennedy Links Hoffa and Communists." December 22, 1958.

———. "Labor Rackets—a Senate Feud?" July 22, 1958.

———. "Negro in America." July 29, 1963.

———. "No. 2 Man Lyndon B. Johnson." October 31, 1960.

———. "Now West Virginia." April 18, 1960.

———. "Politics: RFK Against Himself." February 17, 1969.

———. "Robert Kennedy and New York: Decision Point." August 24, 1964.

———. "What Makes Bobby Run?" March 18, 1963.

———. "What's Bobby Going to Do?" July 6, 1964.

———. "The Young Crusader: He's Making the Spot Hot." April 1, 1957.

New Yorker. "Kennedy on Africa." July 9, 1966.

New York Herald Tribune. "Blood for North Viet: Bobby Kennedy's View." November 6, 1965.

———. "Bobby Kennedy Booed and Cheered in Chile." November 16, 1965.

———. "Bobby Kennedy in Brazil's Wilds." November 30, 1965.

———. "Surrender to the Carpetbagger." Editorial. August 22, 1964.

New York Journal American. "A Kennedy Pooch's Bow Is a Real Wow." August 3, 1962.

New York Post. "Kennedy Wife Was Lyricist's Fair Lady." August 1, 1994.

———. "Text of Bobby Kennedy's Speech to Democratic Convention." August 28, 1964.

———. "Two Men and Rev. Martin King." Editorial. October 28, 1960.

New York Times. "Acquittal Move by Hoffa Denied." July 16, 1957.

———. "ADA Is Neutral in Senate Contest." October 4, 1964.

———. "Africa Discovered." Editorial. May 28, 1966.

———. "Aftermath of the Primary." Editorial. June 30, 1966.

———. "Aide to McCarthy Resigns." August 1, 1953.

———. "Alabama Governor Hits at Attorney General." June 26, 1961.

———. "Alien Held in Threats." December 2, 1961.

———. "Allott to Oppose Robert F. Kennedy." January 15, 1961.

———. "Alter Ego of Kennedys: Stephen Edward Smith." August 26, 1964.

———. ". . . and as for the Vice-Presidency." Editorial. March 12, 1964.

———. "Another Senator Kennedy?" Editorial. May 16, 1964.

———. "Anti-Communism Won't Feed Latin Children, Kennedy Says." March 13, 1966.

———. "Anti-Crime Fight Is Pushed by U.S." February 2, 1961.

———. "Antitrust Cases Defended by U.S." September 9, 1962.

———. "Article Reports Mississippi Deal." December 18, 1962.

———. "Attorney General Alert to Black Muslim Moves." July 3, 1963.

———. "Attorney General Asked to Limit Political Activity." July 21, 1962.

———. "Attorney General Asks Pinball Law." January 17, 1962.

———. "Attorney General Cooks for 80." January 28, 1962.

———. "Attorney General Denied New Power." July 19, 1962.

———. "Attorney General Fills Post." October 3, 1961.

———. "Attorney General Scored by Faubus." May 23, 1961.

———. "Attorney General's Pleas." May 25, 1961.

———. "Attorney General Suggests Possible Oil Antitrust Move." May 18, 1963.

———. "Attorney General to Get Jewish Congress Award." October 14, 1962.

———. "Bail-Bond Revision Is Urged by Kennedy." August 5, 1964.

———. "Ban on Private Arsenal Is Proposed by Kennedy." July 12, 1967.

———. "Beck on Airliner Bound for London." February 8, 1957.

————. "Beck Visiting in the Bahamas; Plans Vacation Trip in Europe." February 6, 1957.

————. "Berlin Salutes Robert Kennedy; He Vows Support." February 23, 1962.

————. "Bi-Racial Group Cancels Bus Trip." May 16, 1961.

————. "The Birmingham News Urges Bus Riders Be 'Held in Check.'" May 23, 1961.

————. "Bufalino Files Suit." September 24, 1958.

————. "But Does New York Need Him?" Editorial. August 12, 1964.

————. "Calgary Stampede Cheers Kennedys." July 12, 1966.

————. "Civil Rights Enforcer: Robert Francis Kennedy." October 1, 1962.

————. "Clergy Gets Plea in Fight on Bias." July 22, 1961.

————. "Coalition in Vietnam." Editorial. February 22, 1963.

————. "Cohn Mail Watch Embarrasses U.S." March 2, 1964.

————. "Cohn Says He Won't Quit." June 14, 1954.

————. "Cohn Scored When Woman Denies McCarthy's Charges." March 12, 1954.

————. "Congress Urged to Act on Crime." May 18, 1961.

————. "CORE May Picket Robert Kennedy." November 15, 1963.

————. "Criticism and Retraction." October 28, 1964.

————. "Cross Is Indicted on Perjury Count." October 7, 1958.

————. "Cubans' Rights Cited by Robert Kennedy." April 21, 1961.

————. "Democratic Errors Seen by Kennedy in Campaign Here." November 6, 1965.

————. "Doctors Report Gain by Kennedy." June 23, 1964.

————. "Donovan Insists He Got Cuba Pact." December 28, 1962.

————. "Doodles by a Man Watching Inquiry." May 8, 1954.

————. "Douglas to Visit Soviet." February 28, 1955.

————. "Dr. King Released Pending His Appeal." October 28, 1960.

————. "Eavesdropping Unlimited." Editorial. December 13, 1966.

————. "8 Chinese Children to Enter the U.S." March 17, 1961.

————. "End in Sight." June 13, 1954.

————. "Enter Robert Kennedy." March 15, 1968.

————. "The Epistle to Albany." February 12, 1965.

————. "Ethel Kennedy's Brother Killed with 4 Others in Idaho Air Crash." September 25, 1966.

————. "Excerpts from Attorney General's Statement on Civil Rights Legislation." June 27, 1963.

————. "Excerpts from Bus Petition to I.C.C." May 30, 1961.

————. "Excerpts from Kennedy Speech and Texts of Rusk Statement and Johnson Letter." March 3, 1967.

————. "Excerpts from Kennedy Speech on Coast." October 24, 1966.

————. "Excerpts from Kennedy's Statement Urging Vietnam Accord." February 22, 1966.

————. "Excerpts from Robert Kennedy's Address in South Africa Assailing Apartheid." June 7, 1966.

————. "Excerpts from Statement by Kennedy." September 10, 1965.

————. "Excerpts from the Transcript of Senator Kennedy's News Conference." April 2, 1968.

————. "Fans Cheer Ride by Ethel Kennedy." October 25, 1961.

————. "'Father of Year' Named." May 27, 1960.

————. "Finnegan Gets Campaign Aide." September 22, 1956.

————. "4 Areas in South Are Sued to End Pupil Separation." January 19, 1963.

———. "4 G.O.P. Senators Score Auto Union." February 16, 1960.

———. "Four Seek to Bar Tractors for Cuba." June 18, 1961.

———. "Frank J. Parker, 75; Ex-U.S. Prosecutor." January 3, 1978.

———. "French Writer Recalls Kennedy Premonition." June 7, 1968.

———. "From the Treasury Down." Editorial. December 17, 1960.

———. "Fund Misuse Laid to Bakers Union." June 2, 1957.

———. "Goldfine Agrees to Sale of Assets." February 15, 1963.

———. "G.O.P. 'Dog Days Party' Inspired by Kennedy Pet." August 14, 1962.

———. "Grants by Kennedy Fund." August 12, 1954.

———. "Group Fights Curb on 5th Amendment." June 20, 1961.

———. "Half of U.S. Youth Called Below Par in Physical Fitness." April 25, 1962.

———. "Here Are the Reasons Why You Should Re-Elect Sen. Keating." Advertisement. November 2, 1964.

———. "High Court Voids County Unit Vote." March 19, 1963.

———. "Hiss Typewriter Revived as Issue." May 10, 1962.

———. "Hoffa and Paper Argue Phone Call." January 4, 1963.

———. "Hoffa Assails Kennedy." December 5, 1964.

———. "Hoffa Case Spurred." July 9, 1961.

———. "Hoffa Co-Defendant Declares Kennedy Aide Offered a Deal." February 19, 1964.

———. "Hoffa Is Balked on Ouster Move." September 8, 1960.

———. "Hoffa Is Berated by R. F. Kennedy." July 27, 1959.

———. "Hoffa Linked to Reds." July 12, 1959.

———. "Hoffa 'Plot' to Kill R. F. Kennedy Alleged." April 12, 1964.

———. "Hoffa's Ace in Hole Was Kennedy's Joker." March 16, 1957.

———. "Hoffa Says Remarks After Assassination Were Misconstrued." December 10, 1963.

———. "Hoffa Suing N.B.C. and Paar for Libel." May 25, 1960.

———. "Hoffa Tells Union Parley Robert Kennedy 'Is Out.'" December 2, 1963.

———. "Hoffa Union Tied to Death Threat." September 28, 1957.

———. "Hoffa View Ignored as Teamsters Here Support Kennedy." October 15, 1964.

———. "Hoffa Wins Again in U.S. Court Test." July 14, 1961.

———. "House Votes Death for Plane Hijackers in New Piracy Bill." August 22, 1961.

———. "How Johnson Informed Kennedy on 1964 Ticket: Two Versions." June 22, 1965.

———. "Indians Victims, R. F. Kennedy Says." September 14, 1963.

———. "Inquiry in Asia Asked." December 12, 1955.

———. "Inquiry Is Planned on Democratic Aide." September 1, 1961.

———. "Judge Assails U.S. in Race-Wire Case." May 26, 1962.

———. "Judge Due to Rule on Suit to Speed Up Negro Registration." March 9, 1964.

———. "Justice Department Has a Shaggy Dog: Robert Kennedy's." August 4, 1962.

———. "Justice Douglas Heads for Tour of Soviet Area." June 11, 1955.

———. "Kathleen Kennedy Is Injured in Fall as Horse Stumbles." August 30, 1965.

———. "Keating Attacks Welfare Policy." March 18, 1963.

———. "Keating Buys a TV Hour, Kennedy Refuses a Share." October 30, 1964.

———. "Keating Says He'll Debate Kennedy or Empty Chair." October 27, 1964.

———. "Keating vs. Kennedy." Editorial. October 18, 1964.

———. "Kennedy Amazed by City Park Plan." January 24, 1966.

———. "Kennedy Attacks Draft as Unfair." February 12, 1966.

———. "Kennedy Bids Nation Heed Youths on War." February 25, 1967.

———. "Kennedy Bids U.S. Invite Red China to Atom Talks." May 13, 1966.

———. "The Kennedy Blitzkrieg." August 22, 1964.

———. "Kennedy Caught in Party Row." July 31, 1966.

———. "Kennedy Clarifies Comments on War." January 30, 1967.

———. "Kennedy Denounces Apartheid as Evil." June 7, 1966.

———. "Kennedy Deplores Nation's 'Betrayal' of Indian Education." January 6, 1968.

———. "Kennedy Discusses Campaign Tactics." November 5, 1964.

———. "Kennedy Discussion with Johnson Bitter, a Time Article Says." March 14, 1967.

———. "Kennedy Draws Virginian Cheers." May 12, 1964.

———. "The Kennedy Drive on Bias." Editorial. May 8, 1961.

———. "A Kennedy Fined $40." December 17, 1960.

———. "Kennedy Gives Up Right to Massachusetts Vote." October 16, 1964.

———. "Kennedy Has a 35-Minute Audience with Pope Paul." June 19, 1966.

———. "Kennedy, in Tanzania, Asks More Investment in Africa." June 11, 1966.

———. "Kennedy Invited Back to South Africa." June 8, 1966.

———. "Kennedy in West Virginia." April 30, 1964.

———. "Kennedy Is Assailed by Editor of Stern." January 31, 1967.

———. "Kennedy Is Heckled by 2 Men at Dinner." September 11, 1966.

———. "The Kennedy-Johnson Debate." Editorial. February 27, 1966.

———. "Kennedy Jr. for Barter." January 7, 1941.

———. "Kennedy Leads 83-Mile Raft Trip." July 3, 1965.

———. "Kennedy Loses Shoe to an Admirer." April 13, 1968.

———. "Kennedy 'Meddling' Denounced by Hoffa." July 14, 1962.

———. "Kennedy Notes a Peril." July 1, 1966.

———. "Kennedy Offers a Bill for Committing Insane." August 5, 1966.

———. "Kennedy Party Ends River Trip in Idaho." July 5, 1966.

———. "Kennedy Phone Drive." November 2, 1960.

———. "Kennedy Plan to Run Reported and Denied." March 8, 1968.

———. "Kennedy Puts in Bill to Produce Jobs in the Slums." July 13, 1967.

———. "Kennedy Quits as Inquiry Aide; Confident of Reforms in Unions." September 11, 1959.

———. "Kennedy Rejects a National Race." August 26, 1965.

———. "Kennedy Says He Helped Elect 39 of 76 Nominees." November 14, 1966.

———. "Kennedys Begin Trip down Idaho Rapids." July 2, 1966.

———. "Kennedy's Boating Party Goes over Idaho Rapids." July 4, 1966.

———. "Kennedy Sees Lithuli and Finds Him 'Impressive.' " June 9, 1966.

———. "Kennedys' Friends Are Said to Profit." March 24, 1962.

———. "Kennedys Hailed on Cracow Visit." June 30, 1964.

———. "Kennedy's Nomination Drive Aided by Mixture of Amateurs, Professionals, Eggheads and Hardheads." July 14, 1960.

———. "Kennedy Son Seized for Throwing Rocks." May 3, 1968.

———. "Kennedy's Son, 12, Joins Casualties." August 31, 1965.

———. "Kennedy's Statement." December 11, 1966.

———. "Kennedy's Statement and Excerpts from News Conference." March 17, 1968.

———. "Kennedy's Statement on His Candidacy." August 26, 1964.

———. "Kennedy Swam to Ship in High Seas on Sunday." September 2, 1965.

———. "Kennedy to Act as Host at Parties for Children." December 11, 1964.

———. "Kennedy to Cut Hair; Indiana Crowd Cheers." April 11, 1968.

———. "Kennedy Unmoved by Hoffa Jailing." March 8, 1967.

———. "Kennedy Urges Political Stance." July 10, 1965.

———. "The Kennedy Victory." Editorial. November 4, 1964.

———. "Kennedy Visits Childhood Home." October 8, 1964.

———. "Kennedy Voices a Wry Regret." August 7, 1964.

———. "Kennedy Welcomes a Role in Campaign." August 3, 1964.

———. "Korth Study Urged on Robert Kennedy." October 24, 1963.

———. "Labor Inquiry Gets Secret Tape Talks." February 24, 1957.

———. "Legal Footwork in the Wilderness." August 11, 1962.

———. "Loan Case Guilt Denied by Hoffa." June 26, 1963.

———. "Louisiana Is Sued by U.S. on Voting." April 29, 1961.

———. "McCarthy Accuses Official on Ships." May 5, 1953.

———. "McCarthy Held Up Note to President." May 24, 1953.

———. "McCarthy Items Stay on Agenda." January 25, 1955.

———. "McNamara Notes 'Get-U.A.W.' Move." December 29, 1957.

———. "Metropolitan Club Welcomes a Negro." July 19, 1961.

———. "Mexican Painter Granted U.S. Visa." September 4, 1963.

———. "Miss Ethel Skakel Becomes Engaged." January 8, 1950.

———. "Moscow Perceptive on U.S. Aides' Visits." January 26, 1962.

———. "Mr. Kennedy Declares." Editorial. August 26, 1964.

———. "Mrs. John F. Kennedy Calls Times on Shooting." June 5, 1968.

———. "Negro Recommended." April 15, 1961.

———. "New Justice Aide Sworn by Harlan." August 25, 1962.

———. "New Officials Fail to Get Union Fund." September 15, 1956.

———. "New Red Trial Opposed." August 14, 1961.

———. "9 in Policy Racket Indicted on Taxes." December 22, 1961.

———. "1968 Intent Denied by Robert Kennedy." March 2, 1963.

———. "Nixon Plea Halted Letter on Vessels." May 26, 1953.

———. "Nonsense for New Yorkers." September 25, 1964.

———. "Opinion of the Week: At Home and Abroad." December 25, 1960.

———. "Patterson Not Available: Kennedy Phones Alabama in Vain." May 20, 1961.

———. "Peiping 'Exposes' Kennedy Cabinet." January 21, 1961.

———. "Peiping Widens Attack." January 31, 1962.

———. "Police Chief Says Kennedy Turned Down Security Aid." June 6, 1968.

———. "A Political Prisoner." Editorial. June 14, 1962.

———. "Pope Receives R. F. Kennedys; Gives Them a Special Blessing." February 22, 1962.

———. "President Jokes About His Brother and His University." January 22, 1961.

———. "President Seeks Action on His Fitness Program." July 25, 1961.

———. "President's Representative Hurt Helping a Girl Escape Violence." May 21, 1961.

———. "Proxmire Urges Pipeline Inquiry." May 20, 1963.

———. "Rackets Counsel Hits U.A.W. Study." September 9, 1959.

———. "Random Notes from All Over: 'This IS the Attorney General.' " June 24, 1963.

———. "Random Notes in Washington: Fall Term at Hickory Hill U." September 24, 1962.

———. "Random Notes in Washington: Schlesinger Now Half of Faculty." December 11, 1961.

———. "Receivership Urged for the Teamsters." September 22, 1958.

———. "Red Link Charged to Coast Unionist." May 25, 1961.

———. "Red Ties Denied by W. H. Taylor." December 17, 1955.

———. "Resigned Fund Posts." January 29, 1961.

———. "The Responsibility of American Intellectuals." Advertisement. May 20, 1968.

———. "Revolt in Manhattan." Editorial. May 26, 1966.

———. "R. F. Kennedy Accused." November 1, 1960.

———. "R. F. Kennedy a Scout." January 27, 1962.

———. "R. F. Kennedy Family Threatened in Call." March 16, 1959.

———. "R. F. Kennedy Finds Youth Lack Faith." November 12, 1961.

———. "R. F. Kennedy Firm on Desegregation." April 25, 1963.

———. "R. F. Kennedy Sees Donovan on Cubans." August 24, 1962.

———. "R. F. Kennedy's Part in King Case Scored." October 29, 1960.

———. "R. F. Kennedy Warm to Wiretap Change." May 23, 1962.

———. "Rightists Schedule Drive with Letters." March 22, 1962.

———. "Robert F. Kennedy Out of Party Drive." May 23, 1962.

———. "Robert Kennedy 'Adopts' 9-Year-Old Peruvian Boy." March 3, 1966.

———. "Robert Kennedy Asks I.C.C. to End Bus Segregation." May 30, 1961.

———. "Robert Kennedy Assures Vietnam." February 19, 1962.

———. "Robert Kennedy Backs Poland Aid." May 8, 1961.

———. "Robert Kennedy Bid on Reds Is Assailed." June 2, 1962.

———. "Robert Kennedy Buys Key Lincoln Document." April 4, 1964.

———. "Robert Kennedy Cautions Soviet." July 16, 1961.

———. "Robert Kennedy Chided." August 11, 1961.

———. "Robert Kennedy Chides U.S. Bar." September 30, 1962.

———. "Robert Kennedy Comments." November 3, 1966.

———. "Robert Kennedy Criticized in Asking Coast Guard Aid." March 12, 1963.

———. "Robert Kennedy for Wiretaps to Cut Politician-Gambler Link." March 30, 1962.

———. "Robert Kennedy Gives Toys to Negro Patients." December 25, 1961.

———. "Robert Kennedy Gives View." August 19, 1965.

———. "Robert Kennedy Hurts Nose." March 9, 1963.

———. "Robert Kennedy in Limelight as Senate Investigates Aide and Hoffa Foe." December 17, 1960.

———. "Robert Kennedy Is Accused of 'Fascist' Attack on Hoffa." November 27, 1962.

———. "Robert Kennedy Is Jolted as Limousine Is Rammed." January 10, 1964.

———. "Robert Kennedy Meets Gang Members Here." March 9, 1961.

———. "Robert Kennedy Names Symington's Son as Aide." May 2, 1962.

———. "Robert Kennedy Not Obeyed." June 26, 1963.

———. "Robert Kennedy Praises South on Peace in Pupil Integration." September 9, 1962.

———. "Robert Kennedy Quits Social Club." September 21, 1961.

———. "Robert Kennedy Rejects Bid for Vice-Presidency." January 29, 1964.

———. "Robert Kennedy Resumes Job After Rest in Florida." December 5, 1963.

———. "Robert Kennedy Says He Won't Read Report." September 28, 1964.

———. "Robert Kennedy Says He Won't Run in 1968." November 16, 1965.

———. "Robert Kennedy Sees Wilson." January 27, 1967.

———. "Robert Kennedy, Son of Former U.S. Envoy, Weds Ethel Skakel in St. Mary's, Greenwich." June 18, 1950.

———. "Robert Kennedys Reach Hong Kong." February 11, 1962.

———. "Robert Kennedy's Son, 14, Breaks Leg in Sun Valley." December 24, 1966.

———. "Robert Kennedy Staff Gets Gold Loyalty Pills." December 29, 1966.

———. "Robert Kennedy Target of Sit-In." March 14, 1962.

———. "Robert Kennedy to Moscow?" January 22, 1962.

———. "Robert Kennedy Urges Students to Know U.S. First." December 6, 1962.

———. "Robert Kennedy, Visiting Chile, Is Target of Abuse by Students." November 17, 1965.

———. "Robert Kennedy Warns of 'Increasing Turmoil.'" May 4, 1963.

———. "Rockefeller Seen as Target of Plot." January 30, 1963.

———. "Rockefeller's Triumph." November 13, 1966.

———. "Rogers Assailed for Delay in Rackets Perjury Cases." September 14, 1958.

———. "Rusk Supports Robert Kennedy on Recent Talk with Menshikov." August 21, 1961.

———. "A Sea Lion for Christmas." December 27, 1959.

———. "Sears, New Counsel for Inquiry, Backed McCarthy in 1952 Race." April 2, 1952.

———. "Senate Aid on Tour." July 28, 1955.

———. "Senate Investigators Call Talbott to Closed Session." July 16, 1955.

———. "Senate Unit Gets New Counsel." February 13, 1957.

———. "The Senator Is Neutral." Editorial. August 17, 1966.

———. "Senator Kennedy Hurt in Air Crash; Bayh Injured, Too." June 20, 1964.

———. "Senators Decry Anti-Crime Bill." June 27, 1961.

———. "Senators Question Talbott Two Hours." July 19, 1955.

———. "Senator's Son out of Hospital." August 29, 1965.

———. "Silent F.B.I. Man Held in Contempt." July 23, 1963.

———. "Sirhan Voices Regret at Having Killed Kennedy." June 3, 1969.

———. "Six Key Senate Races: How They Look Today." October 18, 1964.

———. "'64 Plan Is Denied by Robert Kennedy." November 21, 1963.

———. "Slow Starvation Seen in Mississippi." April 26, 1967.

———. "South Africa Bars Foreign Reporters on Kennedy's Tour." May 25, 1966.

———. "South African Denounces U.S. as Inciting Foes of Apartheid." September 11, 1963.

———. "South African Trip Begun by Kennedy; 1,000 Welcome Him." June 5, 1966.

———. "South Africa Won't Admit Kennedy Again, Paper Says." June 13, 1966.

———. "Spellman Hails Governor's Plan for New State Aid to Education." February 3, 1961.

———. "Spur Labor Bill, President Urged." August 2, 1959.

———. "Stassen Refuses Requested Data." April 7, 1955.

———. "State Department Denies Rusk Interfered in Ouster of Otepka." December 22, 1963.

———. "Stevenson vs. Keating." April 24, 1964.

———. "Still Smoke-Filled." Editorial. July 9, 1960.

———. "Suit Now $5,000,000." October 3, 1958.

———. "Sukarno Accepts Malaysian Truce." January 23, 1964.

———. "Taft Was the Politest Man in Town." July 5, 1981.

———. "Tanzanian Town Greets Kennedy." June 12, 1966.

———. "Tax Evasion Charged." May 13, 1961.

———. "Teamster Opposes Wiretap Measure." June 14, 1962.

———. "Teamster Study Is 3 Months Old." May 26, 1957.

———. "Team vs. World." Editorial. December 18, 1960.

———. "Text of Address by Attorney General Kennedy Calling on Americans to End Misinformation Abroad." April 24, 1962.

———. "Text of Edward Kennedy's Tribute to His Brother in Cathedral." June 9, 1968.

———. "The Text of Kennedy's Letter to Albany." February 11, 1965.

———. "Text of Kennedy Speech to Democratic Convention." August 28, 1964.

———. "Text of Kennedy's Speech Accepting the Democratic Nomination for Senator." September 2, 1964.

———. "Text of Kennedy Statement on Bombing in Vietnam." April 28, 1966.

———. "Text of Kennedy Statement on Talks." March 18, 1968.

———. "Text of the Attorney General's Wire to Alabamans." May 24, 1961.

———. "Text of Tribute to Joseph Kennedy by Son Robert." November 21, 1969.

———. "Texts on the Montgomery Riots." May 21, 1961.

———. "Thrifty L.B.J. and Tearful Brezhnev Are Described in Memoir by Brandt." November 8, 1978.

———. "Throng from Capitol Hill." September 3, 1955.

———. "To Seek 2nd Set Term." October 10, 1966.

———. "Tour Scored by G.O.P." February 10, 1962.

———. "Tower Terms U.S. Too Easy on Reds." March 27, 1962.

———. "Two Kennedys Urge Washington Youths to Remain in School." June 6, 1963.

———. "Two Men—So Alike yet So Different." March 17, 1968.

———. "2 Senators Back New Wiretap Law." July 5, 1963.

———. "Union Bail Eased '63 Racial Crisis." October 17, 1965.

———. "U.S. Acts to Aid Negro Farmers." March 30, 1961.

———. "U.S. Acts to Label 10 as Communists." June 1, 1962.

———. "U.S. Admonished on Colonialism." March 19, 1956.

———. "U.S. Aides Mapping Legal Move on Reds." December 22, 1961.

———. "U.S. Cites 2 Pacts to End Race Bias." July 27, 1962.

———. "U.S. Gives Aniline a Free Hand." January 25, 1962.

———. "U.S. Reds Discounted." March 25, 1962.

———. "U.S. Set to Press Red Registration." June 11, 1961.

———. "U.S. Threat Cited in '62 Cuba Crisis." April 26, 1963.

———. "Vandiver Criticizes Kennedy on Dr. King." November 1, 1960.

———. "Veteran Red Hunter Joins McCarthy Unit." June 19, 1953.

———. "Wallace Thwarts Serving of Subpoena by U.S." June 1, 1963.

———. "Washington Proceedings." September 11, 1959.

———. "Wiretap Fear Laid to Robert Kennedy." April 7, 1969.

———. "Wiretaps with Stiff Curbs Asked by Attorney General." February 2, 1962.

———. "Yorty Denounces a Kennedy Letter." December 3, 1966.

———. "Youthful Chief Counsel: Robert Francis Kennedy." March 13, 1957.

Niagara Falls Gazette. "Miller Hits Steel Probe Tactics." April 13, 1962.

Nightline. "How to Start a War: The Bizarre Tale of Operation Mongoose." December 29, 1997.

Nolan, Martin F. "Defeat of Bronx Boss Ends a Political Era." *Boston Globe,* June 4, 1964.

———. "Keating-RFK Race Like World Series." *Boston Globe,* October 12, 1964.

———. "Kennedy (D-N.Y.)." *Boston Globe,* November 28, 1965.

———. "The Kennedy Legacy." *New York Times,* November 23, 1969.

———. "The Kennedys at Home Have a Few Problems." *New Republic,* June 25, 1966.

———. "Manhattan Party Reformers Vote 'No' to Robert's Old-Line Backers." *Boston Globe*, September 2, 1964.

———. "Shuns New York City: RFK Goes Prospecting Upstate." *Boston Globe*, September 27, 1965.

———. "2 RFK Problems: Slipups and Keating." *Boston Globe*, October 10, 1964.

———. "What Are RFK's Motivations?" *Boston Globe*, July 3, 1966.

Nolan, Tom. "A Hood Made in Hollywood." *Wall Street Journal*, May 16, 2012.

O'Donnell, Kenneth. "LBJ and the Kennedys." *Life*, August 7, 1970.

O'Hara, John. "Conservatives Have More Fun." *Human Events*, July 24, 1965.

Olsen, Arthur J. "Kennedy Exhorts the Poles to Further U.S.-Soviet Friendship." *New York Times*, July 2, 1964.

———. "Kennedy Meets Polish Cardinal." *New York Times*, July 1, 1964.

———. "Kennedy Reminds Poles of U.S. Ties." *New York Times*, June 28, 1964.

———. "Kennedy's Visit Jolts Regime in Poland." *New York Times*, July 5, 1964.

———. "Robert Kennedy Says Oswald Acted on Own in Assassination." *New York Times*, June 30, 1964.

———. "Warsaw Throngs Engulf Kennedys." *New York Times*, June 29, 1964.

O'Neil, Paul. "The No. 2 Man in Washington." *Life*, January 26, 1962.

O'Neill, Thomas. "Politics and People." Baltimore *Sun*, July 1, 1966.

Opotowsky, Stan. "Bobby Stops the Show." *New York Post*, August 28, 1964.

Oshinsky, David. "In the Heart of the Heart of Conspiracy." *New York Times*, January 27, 2008.

———. "One Person Made a Difference." *New York Times*, November 7, 1993.

Osnos, Peter. "Kennedy Acclaimed on Oxford Visit." *Washington Post*, January 29, 1967.

Ottenberg, Miriam. "Behind the Rescue: A Step-by-Step Account of How Castro's Captives Were Ransomed." *Washington Star*, December 21, 1962.

———. "Justice Revised Tactics at 11th Hour." *Washington Star*, June 12, 1963.

Parton, Edward G. "An Insider's Chilling Story." *Time*, May 15, 1964.

Pearson, Drew. "Adams Case Worries R. Kennedy." *Washington Post*, April 4, 1961.

———. "The Administration: More Than a Brother." *Time*, February 16, 1962.

———. "AFL-CIO Leaders for Johnson." *Washington Post*, September 7, 1964.

———. "An Angry Call From Gov. Patterson." *Washington Post*, June 8, 1961.

———. "Attorney General Is a Cab Debater." *Washington Post*, July 7, 1961.

———. "Bobby Kennedy and Dick Tracy." *Washington Post*, October 29, 1965.

———. "Bobby Still Hankers for No. 2 Spot." *Washington Post*, July 6, 1964.

———. "Bogus Bonds Linked to Hoffa Aide." *Washington Post*, June 28, 1961.

———. "Dead Hand Blocks Appointment." *Washington Post*, July 8, 1963.

———. "Farben Wins Its 20-Year Tussle." *Washington Post*, May 25, 1964.

———. "Feighan Roasted Kennedy Abroad." *Washington Post*, April 29, 1964.

———. "GOP Campaign Charges Reviewed." *Washington Post*, October 31, 1964.

———. "Ironic Twists in Alabama Crisis." *Washington Post*, May 24, 1961.

———. "Johnson-Kennedy Feud Started in '60." *Washington Post*, March 19, 1968.

———. "Katzenbach, Aides Pro-Kennedy." *Washington Post*, February 3, 1965.

———. "Kennedy Emissary Ruled Der Stern." *Washington Post*, February 7, 1967.

———. "Kennedy Fortune Rates 12th in the Nation." *Muncie Star Press*, July 6, 1960.

———. "LBJ Aides Still Loyal to Kennedy." *Washington Post*, September 5, 1964.

———. "LBJ Passes Buck on Pardon for Boykin." *The [Fredericksburg] Free Lance-Star*, March 28, 1964.

———. "The Long-Memoried Kennedys." *Washington Post*, April 2, 1963.

———. "Looking Back at RFK." *Washington Post*, February 27, 1966.

———. "A Lot to Remember About RFK." *Washington Post*, June 8, 1968.

———. "McCarthy, Dulles Enjoy Stassen Diet." *Washington Post*, April 10, 1953.

———. "McCarthy Urged to Push Probe." *Washington Post*, April 7, 1953.

———. "New Hoffa Move Put to D.C. Judge." *Washington Post*, August 12, 1957.

———. "Nixon Figured in Hoffa Delay." *Washington Post*, January 4, 1961.

———. "'Not Grooming Anyone,' LBJ Says." *Washington Post*, August 21, 1964.

———. "RFK Aide Linked to King Fund Raising." *Washington Post*, April 26, 1967.

———. "RFK-HHH Battle Is On." *Washington Post*, November 8, 1964.

———. "Roy Cohn Faces Justice Dept. Probe." *Washington Post*, January 26, 1963.

———. "Shouting Match over Hoffa." *Washington Post*, September 17, 1964.

———. "Shriver: Kennedy Clan Loner." *Chicago Daily News*, March 28, 1968.

———. "Some Smudgepots Really Smoke." *Washington Post*, May 4, 1958.

———. "Tar Paper Diplomacy." *Washington Post*, February 16, 1964.

———. "Tourists Still Flock to Kennedy Home." *Washington Post*, January 27, 1967.

———. "2 Trials: Auschwitz and Farben." *Washington Post*, May 19, 1964.

———. "Washington Merry-Go-Round." Bell Syndicate, January 27, 1963.

Pearson, Drew, and Jack Anderson. "The Beginning of LBJ-RFK Feud." *Washington Post*, January 12, 1968.

———. "Big Business Reassured on Kennedy." *Washington Post*. May 31, 1968.

———. "Hoover-RFK Conflict Started Early." *Washington Post*, December 15, 1966.

———. "Kennedy Censorship." *Washington Post*, October 2, 1966.

———. "Kennedy Ordered King Wiretap." *Washington Post*, May 24, 1968.

———. "O'Brien Near Tears Over Resigning." *Washington Post*, April 15, 1968.

———. "Old Pros Weigh Kennedy Blitzkrieg." *Washington Post*, March 29, 1968.

———. "Peace 'Signal' Was Old Hat Here." *Washington Post*, February 11, 1967.

———. "Politics and Race." *Washington Post*, March 31, 1968.

———. "RFK Denies Initiating Baker Probe." *Washington Post*, January 22, 1968.

———. "RFK Inherits Joe Kennedy's Mantle." *Washington Post*, March 8, 1967.

———. "RFK Role in Bugging Cases Shown." *Washington Post*, May 27, 1968.

———. "Voters Must Weigh Bobby's 'Know-How.'" *Washington Post*, May 3, 1968.

———. "Whitten Blocks Food for Miss. Negroes." *Washington Post*, May 9, 1967.

———. "Wiretap Column Sparks Charges." *Washington Post*, June 4, 1968.

Pease, Harry S. "McCarthy Paid a Final Tribute." *Milwaukee Journal*, May 7, 1957.

Peeks, Edward. "After Sen. Kennedy Intervened." *Washington Afro American*, October 29, 1960.

Pegler, Westbrook. "Kennedy Clan's Builder Statesman." *New York Journal-American*, March 22, 1961.

Peluso, Dominick. "City Hall." *New York Daily News*, November 29, 1965.

Perlmutter, Emanuel. "Cohn Mail Watch Scored by Judge." *New York Times*, March 1, 1964.

———. "New Rackets Bill Submitted By U.S." *New York Times*, October 17, 1963.

———. "Robert Kennedy Cites Rise in Crime." *New York Times*, September 26, 1963.

Philadelphia Tribune. "Miss. Senators Quiz About Starving Children." July 15, 1967.

Phillips, Cabell. "Baker Inquiry Is Asked if German Woman's Ouster by the U.S. Involved Security." *New York Times*, October 29, 1963.

———. "The McClellan-Kennedy Investigating Team." *New York Times*, March 17, 1957.

———. "Naming of U.S. Judges Here Awaits End of Primary Fight." *New York Times*, August 18, 1961.

———. "Rusk Post Desired." *New York Times*, August 1, 1964.

———. "6 New Democrats Get Senate Posts." *New York Times*, January 9, 1965.

Phillips, McCandlish. "Hoffa Promises to Quash Rebels." *New York Times*, August 28, 1961.

Pittsburgh Courier. "We Must Avoid Another Little Rock." May 20, 1961.

Pomfret, John D. "Hoffa, on Trial, Pushes Public Sympathy Appeal." *New York Times*, January 24, 1964.

———. "House Fraud Case Will Receive Hearing Before Supreme Court." *New York Times*, January 26, 1965.

———. "U.S. Indicts Hoffa and Trucking Line in $1,000,000 Deal." *New York Times*, May 19, 1962.

Porter, Frank C. "20 Pct. Minimum Tax on Rich Urged by RFK." *Washington Post*, May 12, 1968.

Porter, Russell. "R. F. Kennedy Hits Greed of Public." *New York Times*, June 15, 1961.

Potter, Philip. "Closure: An R. F. Kennedy Failure." Baltimore *Sun*, November 20, 1964.

———. "Johnson Nominated as Kennedy's Running Mate on Democratic Ticket: F.D.R.-Type Framework Seen as Aim." Baltimore *Sun*, July 15, 1960.

Pou, Charles. "King Call Arranger Was George Stewart." *Atlanta Journal*, December 23, 1960.

Prettyman, Barrett. "A Day in New York with RFK." Unpublished, November 24, 1964.

Price, Don K. "A Communication." *Washington Post*, January 19, 1967.

Ralston, Lawrence. "The Senator and the Republic: Robert Kennedy and the Many Ways of Looking at South Africa." *John F. Kennedy Presidential Library and Museum, vanden Heuvel Papers.*

Rand Daily Mail. "Kennedy, Come Back." Editorial. June 9, 1966.

Ranzal, Edward. "Cohn Pleads Not Guilty in Court Where He Once Was Prosecutor." *New York Times*, September 6, 1963.

———. "Rackets Inquiry Extended to Cover Four Fields Here." *New York Times*, April 6, 1957.

Raskin, A. H. "Hoffa, Scoring Union Monitors, Complains of $1000 Daily Bill." *New York Times*, February 25, 1960.

———. "President's Aides Scored by Hoffa." *New York Times*, July 3, 1961.

Raymond, Jack. "Colonel Recants Support of McNamara on Plane." *New York Times*, March 30, 1963.

———. "McNamara Reports Gains by Vietnamese." *New York Times*, February 21, 1962.

———. "Robert Kennedy Visits McClellan in Plane Inquiry." *New York Times*, March 28, 1963.

Raymont, Henry. "Book Says Robert Kennedy and Johnson Felt a Mutual Respect." *New York Times*, March 9, 1970.

———. "Dozen New Books on Robert Kennedy Now in Preparation." *New York Times*, February 19, 1967.

———. "2 U.S. Aides Resign over Otepka Case." *New York Times*, November 19, 1963.

Redbook. "A Redbook Dialogue: Robert Kennedy and Oscar Lewis." September 1967.

Reed, Roy. "Kennedy Cheered in Ole Miss Talk by Crowd of 5,500." *New York Times*, March 19, 1966.

Reeves, Richard. "Kennedy: 2 Years After His Election." *New York Times*, November 14, 1966.

———. "Kennedy Will Aid Johnson in 1968." *New York Times*, March 18, 1967.

———. "The People Around Bobby." *New York Times Magazine*, February 12, 1967.

Reichley, James. "He's Running Himself Out of the Race." *Fortune*, March 1968.

Reid, Roy. "Report of Bitter Clash Over War Denied by Johnson and Kennedy." *New York Times*, March 15, 1967.

Reporter. "Kennedy vs. Keating." November 5, 1964.

———. "The Reporter's Notes." November 5, 1964.

———. "Superannuated Youth." June 30, 1966.

Reston, James. "Atlanta: The Kennedys—Power and Publicity." *New York Times*, March 17, 1967.

———. "Boston: Robert Kennedy's Great Gamble." *New York Times*, March 15, 1968.

———. "Censure Held Unlikely." *New York Times*, July 31, 1954.

———. "Dr. King 'Assumes' Phone Is Tapped." *New York Times*, December 15, 1966.

———. "The Final Irony of Death." *New York Times*, June 9, 1968.

———. "Harmony on Capitol Hill." *New York Times*, January 14, 1961.

———. "Johnson Declines an Offer of Kennedy Aid in Saigon." *New York Times*, June 18, 1964.

———. "The Kennedy-Hoover Controversy." *New York Times*, December 14, 1966.

———. "Kennedy's Maiden Speech." *New York Times*, June 25, 1965.

———. "Kennedy's Strategy." *New York Times*, October 2, 1962.

———. "The Latest Capital Rumor: Kennedy to Saigon." *New York Times*, June 17, 1964.

———. "The Nation and the Parties on the Racial Issue." *New York Times*, June 7, 1963.

———. "New York: Bobby Still Can't Escape From the Past." *New York Times*, September 25, 1964.

———. "New York: The Mounting Kennedy Campaign." *New York Times*, May 11, 1966.

———. "On De-Escalating the Johnson-Kennedy War." *New York Times*, March 3, 1967.

———. "Portland, Ore.: Kennedy's Western Invasion." *New York Times*, October 26, 1966.

———. "President Kennedy's Query to His Brother." *New York Times*, August 16, 1964.

———. "The Qualities of Robert Kennedy." *New York Times*, June 7, 1968.

———. "Robert Kennedy Joins C.I.A. Study." *New York Times*, April 24, 1961.

———. "Senator Robert Kennedy's Dilemma." *New York Times*, December 6, 1967.

———. " 'Tired of Chasing People'—Robert Kennedy." *New York Times*, May 6, 1964.

———. "Washington." *New York Times*, December 23, 1960.

"RFK in the Delta, Revisited." Overby Center, University of Mississippi, February 21, 2012.

Ridgeway, James. "Rebuilding the Slums." *New Republic*, January 7, 1967.

Riesel, Victor. "Robert Kennedy Turns on the Heat." *Los Angeles Times*, July 10, 1962.

Riesman, David. "McCarthy and Kennedy: Some Very Personal Reflections." *New Republic*, April 13, 1968.

Roberts, Chalmers M. "Ethel Kennedy Tells Court Why She Took Horse." *New York Times*, January 10, 1967.

———. "Exultant Family Joins Kennedy in Triumph It Helped to Forge." *New York Times*, November 10, 1960.

———. "1965 Tribute by Robert Kennedy Read at Funeral of His Father." *New York Times*, November 21, 1969.

———. "Robert Kennedy: Surmising About 'The Reservations.' " *Washington Post*, December 17, 1960.

Roberts, Sam. "The Dentist McCarthy Saw as a Threat to Security." *New York Times*, April 4, 2005.

————. "Dr. Irving Peress, Target of McCarthy Crusade, Dies at 97." *New York Times*, November 18, 2014.

Robertson, Nan. "Crisis in Capital: 2 Parties on the Same Night." *New York Times*, June 26, 1965.

Robinson, Douglas. "Kennedy Appeals for City Gun Curb." *New York Times*, August 25, 1967.

————. "Kennedy in Trouble With Italian-Americans in City About Two Issues." *New York Times*, October 13, 1964.

Robinson, Jackie. "HARYOU Muddle." *Amsterdam News*, June 27, 1964.

————. "Kennedy and Keating." *Amsterdam News*, September 19, 1964.

Robinson, Layhmond. "Kennedy Cheered with President." *New York Times*, October 16, 1964.

————. "Kennedy in Lead." *New York Times*, November 2, 1964.

————. "Nomination Seen as Bid for Unity." *New York Times*, September 2, 1964.

————. "President Greets Kennedy Warmly." *New York Times*, October 15, 1964.

————. "Robert Kennedy Consults Negroes Here About North." *New York Times*, May 25, 1963.

————. "Robert Kennedy Fails to Sway Negroes at Secret Talks Here." *New York Times*, May 26, 1963.

Rogers, Warren, and Stanley Tretick. "The Bob Kennedy We Knew." *Look*, July 9, 1968.

Rosenbaum, Ron. "Notes on a 12-Day Campaign." *Village Voice*, March 15, 1973.

Rosenthal, A. M. "His Brother's Voice." *New York Times*, February 11, 1962.

————. "Japan, Famous for Politeness, Has a Less Courteous Side, Too." *New York Times*, February 25, 1962.

————. "Leftists Heckle Robert Kennedy in Rally at University in Tokyo." *New York Times*, February 7, 1962.

————. "Robert Kennedy Debates Leftists." *New York Times*, February 10, 1962.

Ross, Irwin. "Joseph P. Kennedy: The True Story." *New York Post*, January 9–13, 1961.

Rovere, Richard H. "Letter from Washington." *New Yorker*, March 23, 1968.

Rubin, Morris H. "Robert Francis Kennedy." *Progressive*, July 1968.

Rugaber, Walter. "Kennedy Terms Primaries Vital." *New York Times*, May 22, 1968.

Rustin, Bayard. "The Meaning of the March on Washington." *Liberation*, October 1963.

Saturday Evening Post. "The Key Republican Candidates." October 24, 1964.

Savadove, Laurence D. "Father Feeney, Rebel from Church, Preaches Hate, Own Brand of Dogma to All Comers." *Harvard Crimson*, December 6, 1951.

Scaduto, Anthony. "Who Killed Marilyn Monroe?" *Oui*, October 1975.

Schanberg, Sidney H. "Kennedy Cool to Role in Constitutional Convention." *New York Times*, August 28, 1966.

Scheer, Robert. "A Political Portrait of Robert Kennedy." *Ramparts*, February 1967.

Schell, Orville. "The Strange Ordeal of Owen Lattimore." *Washington Post*, April 16, 1995.

Schlesinger, Arthur M., Jr. "Agreement at Yalta." Letter to Editor. *New York Times*, February 16, 1954.

————. "First Close Portrait of John Kennedy." *Life*, July 16, 1965.

————. "What If RFK Had Lived?" *Newsweek*, May 9, 1988.

————. "Why I Am for Kennedy." *New Republic*, May 4, 1968.

Schulberg, Budd. "RFK—Harbinger of Hope." *Playboy*, January 29, 1960.

Schumach, Murray. "Kennedy Parades to Mixed Chorus." *New York Times*, March 17, 1968.

Schworm, Peter. "Archives Shed Light on Robert Kennedy's Tenure as AG." *Boston Globe*, July 25, 2013.

Severo, Richard. "William Manchester, Whose Biographies Detailed Power in the 20th Century, Dies at 82." *New York Times*, June 2, 2004.

Shanahan, Eileen. "Revenue Service Will Remain Here." *New York Times*, January 5, 1965.

Shannon, William V. "One Man's Platform." *New York Times*, December 17, 1967.

———. "Robert Kennedy's March to Power." *Chicago Tribune*, October 8, 1967.

———. "Said Robert Kennedy, 'Maybe We're All Doomed Anyway.' " *New York Times Magazine*, March 16, 1968.

Sheehan, Neil. "Keating Reported Gaining Among Democratic and Liberal Jews." *New York Times*, October 3, 1964.

Shepard, Richard F. "Chairman Of FCC To Air His Views." *New York Times*, May 12, 1961.

Sherrill, Robert. "Court Historian of Camelot." *Inquiry*, September 18, 1978.

———. "How to Succeed on the Potomac: Be an Investigator." *New York Times*, October 8, 1967.

Shnayerson, Michael. "Bobby's Kids." *Vanity Fair*, August 1997.

Shriver, Anthony. "Kennedy's Call to King: Six Perspectives." Georgetown University, Fall 1988.

Shuster, Alvin. "U.S. Indicts Hoffa as Misusing Fund." *New York Times*, December 8, 1960.

Sibley, John. "Albany Is Split on Medicare Bill." *New York Times*, March 30, 1966.

Sidey, Hugh. "Amid Disorder in the Democratic Party He Drives to Bring About 'The Restoration.' " *Life*, November 18, 1966.

———. "A Debut into a Burgeoning Family." *Life*, April 21, 1958.

———. "The Presidency: Upstairs at the White House." *Time*, May 18, 1987.

———. "When Ike Wore His Brown Suit." *Time*, August 20, 1979.

Sikes, James R. "Kennedy Predicts Abortion Reform." *New York Times*, February 18, 1967.

Sitton, Claude. "Civil Rights Report Applauds Kennedy." *New York Times*, March 26, 1962.

———. "Conference This Week." *New York Times*, June 25, 1961.

———. "50 Hurt in Negro Rioting After Birmingham Blasts." *New York Times*, May 13, 1963.

———. "Mississippi Jury Says U.S. Marshall Touched Off Riot." *New York Times*, November 16, 1962.

———. "Robert Kennedy Unable to Budge Alabama Governor on Race Issue." *New York Times*, April 26, 1963.

Smith, Hedrick. "U.S. Again Defers Mississippi Study." *New York Times*, January 7, 1963.

Smith, J. Y. "Kennedy Sees LBJ, Denies Peace Role." *Washington Post*, February 7, 1967.

Smith, Richard Austin. "The Fifty-Million-Dollar Man." *Fortune*, November 1957.

Smith, Terence. "Bobby's Image." *Esquire*, April 1965.

———. "Bobby Won't Join 'Bosses.' " *New York Herald Tribune*, August 22, 1964.

———. "DEMOCRATS: Bobby Gets Big Boost as Angry Stratton Blasts 'Blitzkrieg.' " *New York Herald Tribune*, August 17, 1964.

———. "Father of Suspect 'Sickened' by News." *New York Times*, June 6, 1968.

Spivak, Alvin. "Covering Senator Joe McCarthy: A Former Wire Service Newsman's Recollections of Two Years on the Trail of the Controversial Wisconsin Red-Hunter." Unpublished and undated, supplied by Spivak.

Spivak, Robert G. "Kennedy's Campaign." *New York Herald Tribune*, October 4, 1964.

———. "Was RFK's Trip Necessary?" *New York Journal-American*, November 27, 1965.

Spokane Spokesman Review. "Defense Dept. Aide Resigns Under Fire." February 15, 1957.

Stahlman, James G. "A Statement of Fact." *Nashville Banner,* January 3, 1963.

Steinem, Gloria. "Link Between the New Politics and the Old." *Saturday Review,* August 2, 1969.

Stern, Laurence. "The Name Is Still Harvard University." *Washington Post,* February 5, 1967.

Stern, Sheldon M. "Beyond the Smoke and Mirrors: The Real JFK White House Cuban Missile Crisis." Essay in *The Cuban Missile Crisis: A Critical Reappraisal.* Oxford, UK: Rutledge, 2015.

———. "Errors Still Afflict the Transcripts of the Kennedy Presidential Recordings." *History News Network,* February 21, 2005.

———. "Robert Caro and the Mythical Cuban Missile Crisis." *History News Network,* June 18, 2012.

Stern, Sheldon M., and Max Holland. "Presidential Tapes and Transcripts: Crafting a New Historical Genre." *Washington Decoded,* December 21, 2005.

Stetson, Damon. "Reuther Terms Beck Borrowing Morally Wrong." *New York Times,* March 4, 1957.

Stevenson, James. "Bobby on Parade." *New York Times,* March 17, 2008.

———. "A Reporter at Large: Senator from Massachusetts." *New Yorker,* August 25, 1975.

———. "R.F.K., R.I.P., Revisited." *New York Times Magazine,* June 1, 2008.

———. "The Talk of the Town." *New Yorker,* October 23, 1965.

———. "The Talk of the Town." *New Yorker,* May 14, 1966.

———. "The Talk of the Town." *New Yorker,* July 9, 1966.

———. "The Talk of the Town." *New Yorker,* June 15, 1968.

———. "The Talk of the Town." *New Yorker,* March 15, 1969.

———. "The Talk of the Town." *New Yorker,* November 22, 1969.

———. "The Talk of the Town." *New Yorker,* June 12, 1971.

Stewart, Richard H. "Southern Negroes Starving?" *Boston Globe,* July 12, 1967.

Stolley, Richard B. "Interview with Eunice Shriver." *Life,* August 18, 1972.

Sullivan, Ronald. "Alcorn Scores 'Pressure' by Kennedy." *New York Times,* October 30, 1964.

———. "Kennedy Aide Calls Off TV Debate Negotiations." *New York Times,* October 24, 1964.

———. "Kennedy Defends Academic Liberty." *New York Times,* October 15, 1965.

———. "Kennedy Named by Liberal Party." *New York Times,* September 2, 1964.

———. "Nixon, Backing Dumont, Urges Ouster of Genovese." *New York Times,* October 25, 1965.

Summers, Anthony, and Robbyn Summers. "The Ghosts of November." *Vanity Fair,* December 1994.

Talese, Gay. "The Intellectual Vote: Salon Society Gathers at the Dakota to Sing Praises of Robert Kennedy." *New York Times,* October 15, 1964.

———. "Sorensen Argues the Case for a Friend as Suburbs Debate 'Bobby' Issue." *New York Times,* October 27, 1964.

Tanner, Henry. "Kennedy Hits the Road—in Europe." *New York Times,* February 5, 1967.

Tanzer, Jacob. "1964, My Story of Life and Death in Mississippi." *U.S. District Court of Oregon Historical Society Newsletter,* Spring 2010.

Terris, Bruce J. "Attorney General Kennedy versus Solicitor General Cox: The Formulation of the Federal Government's Position in the Reapportionment Cases." *Journal of Supreme Court History,* vol. 32, November 2007.

Tierney, Dominic. "Pearl Harbor in Reverse: Moral Analogies in the Cuban Missile Crisis." *Journal of Cold War Studies*, Summer 2007.

Time. "The Administration: Pants Too Long?" January 21, 1957.

———. "Bobby Loses Harvard." June 23, 1967.

———. "Business: Reform and Realism." July 22, 1935.

———. "The Campaign: Pride of the Clan." July 11, 1960.

———. "Candidate in Orbit." November 7, 1960.

———. "Democrats: The Shadow and the Substance." September 16, 1966.

———. "The Edge of Violence." October 5, 1962.

———. "Essay: The Lessons of the Cuban Missile Crisis." September 27, 1982.

———. "From Tossup in Tokyo to Cry of the Alamo." February 23, 1962

———. "Investigations: Star-Crossed." December 5, 1955.

———. "Kennedy's Secret Ultimatum." March 22, 1968.

———. "Little Brother Is Watching." October 10, 1960.

———. "Mississippi's Barnett: Now He's a Hero." October 5, 1962.

———. "Mr. Kennedy's Goodwill Wave in Tokyo." February 16, 1962.

———. "On Two Fronts." March 17, 1967.

———. "The Politics of Restoration." May 24, 1968.

———. "The Soft Sell." April 7, 1958.

———. "Teddy's Test." May 21, 1965.

———. "Though the Heavens Fall." October 12, 1962.

———. "Trials: The Sirhan Verdict." April 25, 1969.

———. "Trouble in Alabama." May 26, 1961.

———. "Up from South Boston: The Rise and Fall of John Fox." July 7, 1958.

Times of London. "He Stood for Justice." June 7, 1968.

Topping, Seymour. "Soviet Denounces 2 Kennedys' Trips." *New York Times*, February 26, 1962.

Townsend, Kathleen Kennedy. "The Delta in Our Home." *New York Times*, June 5, 2008.

———. "Robert F. Kennedy Advocated Ending the Ban on Travel to Cuba." *Washington Post*, April 23, 2009.

———. "Robert F. Kennedy, My Father." *New York Daily News*, May 17, 2008.

[Troy] *Times Record.* "Kennedy Wins Overwhelmingly, But Stratton Bars Unanimous Nomination." September 2, 1964.

Troyer, Thomas A. "Remembering Robert." *Rutland Herald*, June 27, 2013.

Trussell, C. P. "Action Deferred on Security Aide." *New York Times*, October 24, 1963.

———. "Crime Bill Freed for House Action." *New York Times*, August 9, 1961.

———. "House Votes Bill to Combat Crime." *New York Times*, August 24, 1961.

———. "Increase in Trade with the Reds Charged by McCarthy Group." *New York Times*, July 19, 1953.

———. "Kennedy Denounces Senate Inquiry." *New York Times*, March 4, 1965.

———. "McClellan to Bar One-Man Hearing in Hunt for Reds." *New York Times*, January 1, 1955.

———. "New 'McCarthy' Committee Changes Rules of Conduct." *New York Times*, January 19, 1955.

———. "19 Senators' Kin Found on Payroll." *New York Times*, December 1, 1959.

———. "Nixon's Aide in '52 Denies Trying to Sway Contracts." *New York Times*, May 4, 1956.

———. "100 British Vessels Cited in Red Trade." *New York Times*, May 21, 1953.

———. "Ruling Tomorrow in Security Case." *New York Times*, October 22, 1963.

———. "Sedition Act Plan Is Voted by House." *New York Times*, July 17, 1963.

———. "Ship Query Is Kept from Eisenhower." *New York Times*, May 23, 1953.

———. "Stassen Charges McCarthy Impedes Red Cargo Curbs." *New York Times*, March 31, 1953.

———. "U.S. Confirms Word British Ships Transported Red Chinese Troops." *New York Times*, May 29, 1953.

———. "U.S. Security Aide Forced Out; House Group Urges Prosecution." *New York Times*, November 21, 1961.

Tupponce, Joan. "Hickory Hill." *Virginia Living*, October 2005.

Turner, Wallace. "Justice Department, in 1961, Studied Hughes Loan to Nixon Kin." *New York Times*, January 24, 1972.

———. "Robert Kennedy Lauds F.B.I. Head." *New York Times*, August 8, 1962.

———. "Robert Kennedy's Temper Flares in Session with Labor Leaders." *Bristol (Pennsylvania) Daily Courier*, February 9, 1962.

U.S. News & World Report. "Bobby Kennedy: New Thoughts About Tackling LBJ In '68." September 11, 1967.

———. "Bobby Kennedy's Future." July 13, 1964.

———. "Growing Rift of LBJ and Kennedys." January 2, 1967.

———. "Interview with Robert F. Kennedy: A Look Behind the Russian Smile." October 21, 1955.

———. "LBJ and RFK—Now a Sharper Rift on War." *U.S. News & World Report*, March 13, 1967.

———. "A Look Inside the Johnson-Kennedy Contest." April 8, 1968.

———. "On the Campaign Trail with Robert Kennedy." November 7, 1966.

———. "RFK's New Moves to Stand Apart from LBJ." February 20, 1967.

———. "Role of Robert Kennedy: No. 2 Man in Washington." July 10, 1961.

———. "The Secret Files of J. Edgar Hoover." December 19, 1983.

———. "The Untold Story of the Warren Commission." August 17, 1992.

———. "What Party Leaders Think of Bobby Kennedy's Future." September 26, 1966.

———. "Will Bobby's Friends Trip Up LBJ In '68?" April 10, 1967.

Uviller, Richard H. "The Virtuous Prosecutor in Quest of an Ethical Standard." *Michigan Law Review*, vol. 71, May 1, 1963.

Vandenberg, Jack. "RFK Won't Run for Senate Seat." *Boston Globe*, June 24, 1964.

vanden Heuvel, William J. "Closing Doors, Opening Doors: Fifty Years After the School-Closing in Prince Edward County, Virginia." *Council of American Ambassadors*, Spring 2009.

Van Fleet, Robert. "Stratton Asks Demo Unity." *Oneonta Star*, September 2, 1964.

Vidal, Gore. "The Best Man, 1968." *Esquire*, March 1963.

———. "A Distasteful Encounter with William F. Buckley Jr." *Esquire*, September 1969.

———. "The Holy Family," *Esquire*, April 1967.

Village Voice. "Big Win in S. Village, Spectacular Elsewhere." November 19, 1964.

Viorst, Milton. "The Skeptics." *Esquire*, November 1968.

Viser, Matt. "John F. Kennedy and Robert F. Kennedy Letters to Be Auctioned." *Boston Globe*, August 30, 2014.

Wakefield, Dan. "Bob." *Esquire*, April 4, 1962.

Waldron, Martin. "Florida Primary Test for Kennedy." *New York Times*, May 22, 1966.

Walinsky, Adam. "The Crisis of Public Order." *Atlantic*, July 1, 1995.

Wallace, Robert. "The 50-Mile Walk." *Life*, February 22, 1963.

Washington Evening Star. "Kennedy Blasts Attacks on McCarthy's Loyalty." *Washington Evening Star*, March 10, 1968.

———. "Wagner Gives Kennedy 'Iffy' Senate Backing." August 11, 1964.

Washington Lawyer. "Legend in the Law: William G. Hundley." November 2001.

Washington Post. "D.C. Stadium Renamed for R. F. Kennedy." January 19, 1969.

———. "Headquarters for Kennedy Opens Today." March 18, 1968.

———. "Hoffa Claims Unions Bow to Justice Department." April 2, 1963.

———. "Keating Complaints on Campaign Backed." April 13, 1965.

———. "Kennedy Scores in Ohio." May 15, 1968.

———. "Kennedy Vs. Kennedy." March 1, 1966.

———. "LBJ 'Can't Control' Hoover." December 26, 1966.

———. "LBJ Pardons Boykin, S&L Case Figure." December 22, 1965.

———. "LBJ Reportedly Suspected CIA Link in JFK's Death." December 13, 1977.

———. "Manchester Favors RFK Bid." April 27, 1968.

———. "McCarthy Laid to Rest in Appleton." May 8, 1957.

———. "McCarthy Rites Slated for Today." May 6, 1957.

———. "Mr. Kennedy's Candidacy." Editorial. August 24, 1964.

———. "Nonpartisan Group Endorses Keating." October 22, 1964.

———. "Riders' Trial Told of Robert Kennedy's Role." June 23, 1961.

———. "Senate Chamber Rites Planned for McCarthy." May 4, 1957.

———. "Sen. McCarthy Lauded at Rites." May 7, 1957.

———. "Summary of Results in 9 Primaries." May 16, 1968.

———. "2000 File Past McCarthy's Bier." May 5, 1957.

Weaver, Warren, Jr. "Humphrey, in Coast Speech, Omits Gibes at Reagan." *New York Times*, September 27, 1966.

———. "Keating, Kennedy Meet in a Debate on Radio Program." *New York Times*, October 31, 1964.

———. "Keating Welcomes Kennedy to State; Offers a Guidebook." *New York Times*, August 26, 1964.

———. "Kennedy and Keating." *New York Times*, August 23, 1964.

———. "Kennedy: Apostle of Involvement." *New York Times*, June 7, 1969.

———. "Kennedy Courts Voters for Brown in Los Angeles." *New York Times*, October 23, 1966.

———. "Kennedy Derides Idea He Is Concentrating Now on the Presidency in 1972." *New York Times*, October 19, 1966.

———. "Kennedy (D.-N.Y.) Gets a Back Seat." *New York Times*, January 5, 1965.

———. "Kennedy: Meet the Conservative." *New York Times*, April 28, 1968.

———. "Kennedy Seeking 2 Posts in Senate." *New York Times*, December 20, 1964.

———. "Kennedy Stumps for Kennedy." *New York Times*, August 28, 1966.

———. "Mail to Kennedy Swamps Offices." *New York Times*, March 14, 1965.

———. "Nixon 'Bats' .686 for 1966 Season." *New York Times*, November 13, 1966.

———. "Senator vs. Governor." *New York Times*, February 16, 1965.

———. "Will the Real Robert Kennedy Stand Up?" *New York Times*, June 20, 1965.

Wechsler, James A. "Morning After." *New York Post*, November 3, 1965.

———. "RFK and Baldwin." *New York Post*, May 28, 1963.

———. "Robert F. Kennedy: A Case of Mistaken Identity, Part 1." *Progressive*, June 1965.

———. "Robert F. Kennedy: A Case of Mistaken Identity, Part 2." *Progressive*, July 1965.

———. "The Two-Front War: Johnson vs. Kennedy." *Progressive*, May 1967.

———. "The Victim." *New York Post*, March 9, 1965.

Wehrwein, Austin C. "Attorney General Asks Equity in Sentencing by U.S. Judges." *New York Times*, October 13, 1961.

———. "Must Go Back Home." *New York Times*, March 25, 1961.

Weigers, Mary. "Sen. Kennedy Out-Quips Star Comedians at Gala." *Washington Post*, June 3, 1968.

Weinraub, Bernard. "Kennedy Steals March on Keating in Pulaski Parade." *New York Times*, October 5, 1964.

———. "Lindsay, Javits, Kennedy in Squabble." *New York Times*, October 7, 1966.

Wexler, James A. "The Case of Junius Scales." *Progressive*, January 1962.

———. "Morning After." *New York Post*, November 3, 1965.

Whalen, Richard J. "How Joe Kennedy Made His Millions." *Life*, January 25, 1963.

Wheeler, Keith, and William Lambert. "Roy Cohn: Is He a Liar Under Oath?" *Life*, October 4, 1963.

White, Jean M. "$250 Billion Is Called 'Minimum' for Cities." *Washington Post*, August 24, 1966.

White, William S. "Kennedy Going for Broke Despite Appalling Dangers." *Washington Post*, May 15, 1968.

———. "Knowland Will Fight More China Trade." *New York Times*, February 3, 1956.

———. "Loyalty Inquiries Forecast for Schools and Colleges." *New York Times*, December 30, 1952.

———. "Schlesinger and Goodwin Demand Softer Viet Policy." *Washington Post*, October 11, 1967.

———. "Second Assault." *Washington Post*, August 23, 1966.

Whitman, Alden. "Kennedy, Financier and Diplomat, Built Fortune to Gain Real Goal, Fame for Sons." *New York Times*, November 19, 1969.

———. "Norton Will Issue Cuban-Crisis Book." *New York Times*, October 2, 1968.

Whitney, Robert F. "Robert Kennedy Says U.S. Would Use A-Bombs." *New York Times*, September 25, 1961.

Whittaker, James W. "The First Ascent." *National Geographic*, July 1965.

Whitten, Leslie H. "My Brother's Unfinished Business—RFK." *New York Journal-American*, November 22, 1964.

Wicker, Tom. "Barry, Bobby and '68." *New York Times*, October 31, 1967.

———. "Biographer's Hero." *New York Times*, September 30, 1962.

———. "Humphrey Scores Kennedy's Plan on Vietcong Role." *New York Times*, February 21, 1966.

———. "Is Bobby Inevitable?" *New York Times*, May 2, 1968.

———. "Johnson and Robert Kennedy Are Reported Ending Coolness." *New York Times*, June 25, 1964.

———. "Kennedy Asserts U.S. Cannot Win." *New York Times*, February 9, 1968.

———. "Kennedy Fears Negro Extremists Will Get Power If Moderates Fail." *New York Times*, May 15, 1963.

———. "Kennedy Has Gained Wide Approval Despite the Resistance That Has Been Shown by Congress." *New York Times*, March 18, 1962.

———. "Kennedy in Plea for Peace Talks." *New York Times*, September 25, 1966.

———. "Kennedy Refuses to Back Johnson for Renomination." *New York Times*, March 15, 1968.

———. "President Bars Kennedy, Five Others from Ticket." *New York Times*, July 31, 1964.

———. "Rights Role Hurt Kennedy Chances." *New York Times*, August 1, 1964.

———. "Robert Kennedy Is Still Boomed." *New York Times*, March 7, 1964.

———. "Robert Kennedy Turns Down Bid to Visit Moscow." *New York Times*, January 23, 1962.

———. "The Trouble with Kennedy." *New York Times*, June 4, 1968.

Wieck, Paul R. "The Indiana Trial Run." *New Republic*, May 11, 1968.

Wilkie, Curtis. "Robert Kennedy Meets Hunger in the Delta." *Clarksdale Press Register*, April 12, 1967.

Wilson, Susan N. "A Guide to Traveling with the Robert F. Kennedys," Unpublished and undated, supplied by Wilson.

Wise, David. "Bobby's Day of Destiny." *New York Herald Tribune*, August 21, 1964.

———. "How Bobby Plans to Win It." *Saturday Evening Post*, June 1, 1968.

Witcover, Jules. "Books: The Enigma of Robert F. Kennedy." *Progressive*, February 1968.

———. "The Indiana Primary in the Indianapolis Newspapers—A Report in Detail." *Columbia Journalism Review*, Summer 1986.

Witkin, Richard. "Convention Plea Lost by Kennedy." *New York Times*, May 6, 1966.

———. "Kennedy Attacks Rockefeller Stand." *New York Times*, May 7, 1966.

———. "Kennedy Considers Early Candidacy." *New York Times*, March 15, 1968.

———. "Kennedy Decides to Run." *New York Times*, March 16, 1968.

———. "Kennedy Refuses to Back McCarthy." *New York Times*, January 9, 1968.

———. "Kennedy's Problem." *New York Times*, December 2, 1965.

———. "Kennedy's Surprise." *New York Times*, May 27, 1966.

———. "Kennedy to Meet Democratic Gubernatorial Hopefuls Today." *New York Times*, April 21, 1966.

———. "Kennedy to Seek Narcotics Laws." *New York Times*, February 24, 1965.

———. "Margin Decisive." *New York Times*, June 29, 1966.

———. "Receivers Named in Defense Case." *New York Times*, June 3, 1964.

———. "Seesaw Contest." *New York Times*, November 3, 1965.

———. "2 Private Polls Find Rockefeller Trailing." *New York Times*, July 29, 1966.

Witte, Brian. "RFK's Oldest Child Discusses Legacy 40 Years Later." *Associated Press*, June 5, 2008.

Worsnop, Richard L. "Mafia Crackdown." *CQ Researcher*, March 27, 1992.

Wright, George Cable. "Hoffa Preparing to Fight Kennedy." *New York Times*, September 3, 1964.

Younger, Irving. "Memoir of a Prosecutor." *Commentary*, October 1, 1976.

FILMS AND VIDEO

ABC News. "Issues and Answers." Debate between Senators Robert Kennedy and Eugene McCarthy, June 1, 1968.

CBS. "New RFK Book Rife with Scandal." September 10, 1998.

CBS News Archives. "Keating-Kennedy Debate," October 27, 1964.

CBS News Special Report. "Senator Robert F. Kennedy, Nov. 1925–June 1968," June 6, 1968.

CBS Reports. "Robert F. Kennedy," June 20, 1967.

Drew, Robert. *Kennedy vs. Wallace.* Direct Cinema Limited, 1991.

George Wallace: Convenience or Conversion. University of Alabama Center for Public Television and Radio.

George Wallace: No Middle Ground. University of Alabama Center for Public Television and Radio.

Guthman, Edwin O., and C. Richard Allen, editors. *RFK: Selected Speeches.* Penguin-HighBridge Audio, 1993.

Kennedy, Rory. *Ethel.* HBO Documentary Films, October 18, 2012.

Kennedy at Columbia. New York Democratic State Committee, April 26, 2006.

Memory of a Man: A Tribute to Robert F. Kennedy. Archival Television Audio.

NBC News. "Meet the Press." June 23, 1963.

———. "Meet the Press." October 18, 1964.

———. "Meet the Press." March 17, 1968.

RFK: American Experience. WGBH Boston, 2004.

RFK in the Land of Apartheid: A Ripple of Hope. www.rfksafilm.org, 2010.

A Ripple of Hope. Covenant Productions, Anderson University. 2009.

Robert F. Kennedy: A Memoir. Sony Music Entertainment and Jack Newfield, June 1, 1999.

Robert Kennedy 1964 New York Senatorial Race. Guggenheim Productions.

Robert Kennedy 1968 Presidential Primary Spots. Guggenheim Productions.

Thirteen Days. New Line Productions, 2000.

Whitehead, Phillip, Geoffrey C. Ward, and Stacy Keach. "The Kennedys." *American Experience.* PBS Home Video, 2003.

INDEX

LARRY TYE has been an award-winning reporter at *The Boston Globe* and a Nieman Fellow at Harvard University. Tye now runs a Boston-based training program for medical journalists. He is the author of *The Father of Spin, Home Lands, Rising from the Rails, Satchel,* and *Superman,* and co-author, with Kitty Dukakis, of *Shock.* He lives in Massachusetts.

larrytye.com
@LarryTye